PEN

THE RIS[illegible] BRITISH N[illegible]ASTERY

Paul Kennedy was born in 1945, and educated at St. Cuthbert's Grammar School, Newcastle, the University of Newcastle (B.A.) and St. Antony's College, Oxford (D.Phil.). He was Lecturer, Reader and Professor of History at the University of East Anglia between 1970 and 1983, and is now the J. Richardson Dilworth Professor of History and Director of International Security Studies at Yale University. He has held distinguished visiting fellowships and professorships at Bonn, Princeton, Seoul, Cambridge and the LSE. Between 1966 and 1970 he worked as Sir Basil Liddell Hart's last research assistant.

Professor Kennedy has been elected a Fellow of the British Academy, the American Academy of Arts and Sciences, the American Philosophical Association, and the Royal Historical Society. He has received numerous honorary degrees from British, European and American universities. In 2000 he was awarded the CBE (Commander of the Order of the British Empire) for 'services to contemporary history'. In 2005 he delivered the Caird Lecture at the National Maritime Museum, Greenwich, on the occasion of the 200th anniversary of the Battle of Trafalgar. In 2014 he was awarded the Hattendorf Prize by the United States Naval War College for lifetime achievements in naval history.

Paul Kennedy is internationally known for his writings and commentaries on global political, economic and strategic issues. His books include *Pacific Onslaught 1941–1943* (1972); *Conquest: The Pacific War 1943–1945* (1973); *The Samoan Tangle: A Study in Anglo–German–American Relations 1878–1900* (1974); *The Rise and Fall of British Naval Mastery* (1976); *The Rise of the Anglo-German Antagonism* (1980); *Strategy and Diplomacy 1870–1940: Eight Essays* (1981); *The Rise and Fall of the Great Powers: Economic Change and Military Conflict from 1500 to 2000* (1988); *Preparing for the Twenty-First Century* (1993); *The Parliament of Man* (2006); *Engineers of Victory* (2013); many edited collections; and hundreds of articles and journals in Britain, the USA, Canada, Australia and Germany. He is a regular columnist for *The Los Angeles Times*/Tribune Media Services Syndicate.

The Rise and Fall of British Naval Mastery

Paul M. Kennedy

PENGUIN BOOKS

PENGUIN BOOKS

UK | USA | Canada | Ireland | Australia
India | New Zealand | South Africa

Penguin Books is part of the Penguin Random House group of companies
whose addresses can be found at global.penguinrandomhouse.com

Penguin
Random House
UK

First published by Allen Lane 1976
Published as a Classic Penguin 2001
Published with a new introduction 2017
001

Printed in Great Britain by Clays Ltd, St Ives plc

A CIP catalogue record for this book is available from the British Library

ISBN: 978–0–141–98382–0

www.greenpenguin.co.uk

MIX
Paper from
responsible sources
FSC www.fsc.org FSC® C018179

Penguin Random House is committed to a
sustainable future for our business, our readers
and our planet. This book is made from Forest
Stewardship Council® certified paper.

TO CATH, JIM AND JOHN (1976)

and

MATHEW, CYNTHIA AND SOPHIA (2017)

Contents

List of Maps

What Athens was in Science, Rome in power,
What Tyre appear'd in her meridean hour,
'Tis thine at once, fair Albion! to have been –
Earth's chief dictatress, ocean's lovely queen:
But Rome decay'd, and Athens strew'd the plain,
And Tyre's proud piers lie shatter'd in the main;
Like these, thy strength may sink, in ruin hurl'd,
And Britain fall, the bulwark of the world.

Byron,
'English Bards and Scottish Reviewers',
lines 999–1,006.

Introduction to the 2017 Edition

It is now a full forty years this past summer that *The Rise and Fall of British Naval Mastery* (1976) first appeared in London as an Allen Lane-Penguin hardback book.* It has also been published in various later printings, both hardback and paperback and in foreign translation, and has never been out of print. It is, after all, an extended essay upon seapower, an aspect of our global story that never disappears.

This new Foreword describes the evolution of naval affairs in the West over those four decades. It is in large part a story of further relative decline in the size and role of the Royal Navy and sister European navies, a trend that was mirrored by the shriveling of the study of naval history itself. Yet it also wonders whether, ironically, that declining trend in all matters maritime has not now come to a halt, and may be reversing itself in this second decade of the twenty-first century. And it speculates that strenuous competition among the leading naval powers of the world is going to be as much a feature of the present and future age as it was of, say, the Edwardian years. It suggests that we are at the onset of a new age of navalism.

Certainly, the maritime scene is as busy as ever it was. International commerce is growing apace, both in volume and in value, and currently over 90 percent of traded goods are carried by sea. Giant ports, from Long Beach in California to Amsterdam to Singapore, are the focal points for global trade. Commercial shipbuilding thrives, especially in Japan, Korea and mainland China. A whole host of fighting warships are being constructed – in

* Simultaneous publication in New York by Charles Scribners & Sons.

the United States, across Asia, and (even still) in parts of Europe itself – and the warships themselves are larger and more powerful than ever before. Navies are in action in many waters, whether it be in patrols against piracy off the Somali coast, launching missiles against ISIL in the Middle East, or jostling over reefs in the South China Sea. In consequence, the intellectual and political interest in what constitutes 'naval mastery' has also returned, in certain government circles, in many British and other European universities, and also in the American service academies. The themes at the core of the book – what causes nations to rise and fall, how naval powers are affected by technology and economics – are as important in the twenty-first century as they were in the seventeenth.

But the biggest reason why navies and naval power are of critical importance today is, of course, that we are at present once again witnesses to a huge shift in the global power balances, of a sort and dimension that takes place only rarely in the sweep of international affairs. This contemporary transformation, on a scale reminiscent of that shift in the strategic power balances from the Mediterranean to the Atlantic some four centuries ago, has been labelled by one acute observer as 'Easternisation'. It is a somewhat crude slogan yet one that both captures the geographic essence of this political shift and also that suggests, ironically, that the world is nowadays undergoing the reverse to what had for so long been its story and seeming destiny, namely, westernisation.[1]

Of course this trend has mostly to do with the rise, or perhaps better the return, of Asia to the centre of the world stage; as not only the most populous continent (as it always was), but also the most productive, its commercial pulse, and maybe even the planet's industrial and financial heartland. At least, most economic indicators point at present to that conclusion. Within this projection, countries such as Indonesia and India, and additionally Korea and Vietnam, will be very large economic entities. Above all, however, there looms China, already the world's second-largest economy and forecast very soon to be its largest, by the measure of total GDP (not per capita). The transformation of that vast country in so many forms of activity – its cities, its infrastructure network, its ports, its ships and aircraft, its industrial output, its overseas investments – is happening so fast that one year's statistics often seem to be out of date by the beginning of the next year.

And all this is equally true of China's maritime and overseas expansion, and of its own interest in being part of the greater historical narrative concerning 'naval mastery'. It is an idea which has seized its leadership's attention, and also a concept that makes sense at many levels, relating both to its commercial and geopolitical situation and to its delicately balanced domestic politics. For the Chinese leadership and its excited public opinion, therefore, having a very large navy to manifest its own Superpower status now seems axiomatic – as axiomatic as wielding naval power would be to various Western countries in earlier times. Allocated very large sums from the PRC's booming wealth, its naval authorities have been able to create within a relatively short period of time an extensive fleet of surface warships, nuclear and non-nuclear submarines, and a huge supporting air force. Nor is this Chinese expansion at an end. In the course of one generation, it seems fair to assert, the global naval balances have been altered, and are likely to alter still more. Naval affairs, control of the sea routes, securing fleet bases – all of this seems once more to be the order of the day.

This being the case, what is critical above all else is the position and attitude of the United States, which since 1943–4 has been the largest naval power in the world. It still remains the most powerful 'blue water' navy, thanks to its giant aircraft-carrier assets, but it is nowadays far less certain that it possesses command of the sea – or, at least, the Eastern Seas – than it did forty years ago. Neptune's trident is now in dispute. It is not surprising therefore that the story of how Britain, the world's greatest and longest-lasting maritime power, upheld its position for so long, and even in decline managed its naval strategies very well, remains of great interest to policy-makers in Washington, just as it does to the advisors on power politics in Beijing. It is also not surprising that the current Head of the U.S. Navy, Admiral Richardson (Chief of Naval Operations), has called upon all service officers both to recognize firstly that, in regard to navies, the world has once again become multi-polar; and, secondly, that it is of the greatest importance to be well versed in the writings and ideas of Thucydides, Clausewitz, Mahan, and Corbett.[2] Naval history once again counts.

The main intention in writing this book was to produce a broad historical survey of British sea power, of how it was composed, and how it manifested itself between the time of the early Tudors and the time of my research and writing in the early 1970s. There was much evidence around me that the remarkable 400-year-old story of Britain's maritime and imperial impact upon the world had reached closure. Almost two decades had passed since the Suez fiasco of 1956, and successive governments, Tory as much as Labour, had proceeded to wind up British possessions across Africa, the Gulf and the Far East as quickly as was practicable. Defence budgets overall were being hammered, naval establishments closed, warship numbers reduced, and naval personnel totals drastically cut. All this was only in part to cover the spiraling costs of the country's independent nuclear deterrent – domestic spending was a far greater competitor for government funds. I could not help but see for myself in those years the incredibly rapid shrinking, almost the collapse, of the British shipbuilding industry, including the yards on my native Tyneside. For over a century, most of the young men born in such towns as Jarrow and Wallsend had gone into the shipyards; but that age was over, and it would not happen again. The title of the pop star Sting's 2014 musical 'The Last Ship' was close to being realized. A much reduced Royal Navy still existed, of course, but British naval mastery itself was gone.

This book was not going to be a tale of sea battles and admirals. They would be referred to in the text when appropriate, but this was not their story. Something else was needed. From the 1960s historical research and writing in Britain had undergone an intellectual renaissance, driven by not one but many stimulants. Cross-Channel influences, in the form of the French 'Annales School', had led to numerous new works on History from below, the history of everyday life, cultural history, the history of attitudes, and the holistic study of regions (for example, Fernand Braudel's seminal work on the Mediterranean world of the sixteenth century).[3] A new Marxist-inspired historiography was looking at class, social structures, and the role of economic forces in driving political decisions and movements. A 'New Left' historiography among the American universities was re-interpreting the story of the United States' rise to world power. The Hamburg historian Fritz Fischer was examining anew, and controversially, Wilhelmine Germany's aims before and during the First World War. Two Cambridge historians, R. Robinson and J. A. Gallagher, were re-telling British colonial and diplomatic history through their works on the 'Official Mind' of decision-making, and on the so-called 'imperialism of free trade'. If naval history restricted itself to narratives of the War of the Austrian Succession, or to the Battle of the Dogger Bank, it would offer little by comparison.

But neither was this book going to be another study of 'British Naval Policy' along the lines of the excellent newer writings of Stephen Roskill and Arthur J. Marder, which were detailed, archivally-based analyses of Admiralty decision-making during the critical decades between 1880 and 1940.[4] That approach was obviously too dense for a book that would cover a much longer period of time, but in any case I wanted to do more than focus upon the higher decision-making of Britain's naval and political leadership, Admiralty budgets and deployments, newer weapons, and the like. The use in the title of the words 'naval mastery' implied an examination of a far bigger phenomenon, that of all the elements that contributed to a nation's exercise of an unusual degree of maritime predominance, and over an extended period of history. Not just navies and naval actions, but geopolitics, economics, logistics, statecraft, and the overall national trajectory of a country is encompassed in that term. And adding 'rise and fall' to the title implied an analysis that would cover a lengthy stretch of time.

There was another, and yet very important consideration. It seemed to me that the story of Britain's relative rise and fall as the world's greatest maritime and naval power could not be properly understood without a constant cross-reference to its relative rise and fall as the world's number one commercial, financial and industrial power. Economic strength and naval strength went hand-in-hand, as did, of course, economic decline and naval weakness. The historiography suggests that naval historians of the seventeenth and eighteenth centuries had grasped this symbiosis more readily than those of the later period, with very few exceptions.[5] In Britain at least, modern economic history in the 1970s seemed to me to have detached itself from more general (political) history; and economic historians were quite likely to be found in their own separate departments, or in departments of Economics. At the University of East Anglia library, where much of this study was researched, books on economic history were located on the third floor, while books on political history, international history, and naval policy/navies were on the second floor; the physical gap suggested intellectual distance as well. The intention of the book was therefore to make the economic dimension an integral part of the story of Britain's relative maritime 'rise and fall', without in any way this becoming a Marxist work of history. It is as a consequence of this argument that, while it doesn't overly intrude itself, the Industrial Revolution plays a central part in the background story; Britain's industrialization represented the counterpart to the *Pax Britannica*, the economic underpinning to the naval mastery. And when, near the end of the nineteenth century, its industrial-productive lead was overtaken by nations (the United States, Germany) with even greater resources of manpower, steel, electricity and other key inputs to modern national power, then of course the Royal Navy's global position was challenged. Britain spent more and more on its armed forces, yet its relative capacity to sway outcomes was less.

And this is why, so often, the adjective 'relative' (as in 'relative rise', 'relative decline') occupies such a critical part in the explanation. Even as a very young scholar, I was already interested in the study of the shifts in the long-term balances of power as an important field of historical investigation. One of the historian A.J.P.Taylor's many works, *The Struggle for Mastery in Europe 1848–1918*, had deeply intrigued me with its introductory statistical analysis on what constituted a Great Power, and by his remarks on how their relative military-economic positions shifted over those seventy years.[6] This interest of mine in the changing power–political balances of History was of course going to be investigated in much more detail in my later work *The Rise and Fall of the Great Powers*, but it also turned out to be vital to the argument of another book which I was writing during the 1970s (almost in parallel to my naval volume) on the rise of the Anglo–German antagonism between 1860 and 1914.[7]

But if economics, and economic/productive power was always relative, geography, at least as meant by geographical position (and not geopolitics) was unchanging: a country's position in regard to others, its size, its climate, its possession or lack of national resources, did not alter. Geography obviously played an integral part in Britain's maritime story, from prehistoric times onward through the Roman, Viking, Saxon and Norman eras. The Tudor story, as Chapter One of this book points out, was about the island nation developing its power and influence in both inland and more distant seas. As the continent racked itself with ferocious dynastic and religious strife throughout the sixteenth and seventeenth centuries, the advantage of being part of Europe but not in Europe could not be clearer. And as commerce developed across the Atlantic, no state was better suited to take advantage of that growth – and to interrupt the trade of others – than Great Britain itself. The pattern of the oceanic currents, the prevailing winds, the ice-free harbours (and so many of them), were of immeasurable benefit, especially in the age of fighting sail. But the geographical advantage was still there when the Kaiser's and Hitler's coal- and oil-fired navies replaced the Dutch, the Spanish and the French as newer threats. Both the British writer on geopolitics, Halford J. Mackinder, and the American novelist Alfred T. Mahan, writing separately and some years before the 1914 conflict, were insistent that the British Isles so confined and disadvantaged the German fleet that, to be fully effective, it would have to acquire 'a preponderance of naval force', which of course it never did.[8]

The Second World War showed, par excellence, the huge advantage that geographical position conferred upon Britain and its navy. Negatively, and obviously, had it been attached to the continent, it surely would have been overrun in 1940. Yet even when the borders of the Third Reich stretched from northern Norway to the Pyrenees, the Wehrmacht had no chance, given the correlation of sea and air forces which existed that summer following the Fall of France, in launching a successful invasion.* Thereafter, the favourable position of the island state and its perimeter naval and air bases (Ulster, the Shetlands, Iceland), plus its absolutely critical hold on Gibraltar, its amazing if precarious grasp on Malta, and its possession of the Suez Canal, Freetown (Sierra Leone), the West Indies, and the Cape, meant that it had enormous strength-in-depth against the great German efforts to strangle the United Kingdom's lifelines. The six-year campaign by Doenitz's navy to prevail in the Battle of the Atlantic – the longest campaign of the war, by far – saw stupendous numbers of U-boats and aircraft (and some surface warships) thrown into the fight. And only with the Allies' colossal

* Germany would have needed a massive aerial predominance over the Channel in the summer/autumn of 1940, which it didn't have; a sophisticated amphibious fleet, which it didn't have; and numerical superiority over the Royal Navy, which it certainly didn't have. Small wonder certain Wehrmacht generals found Hitler's talk of turning against the USSR by late 1940 more agreeable.

reserves of defensive force, plus superb organization, could the submarine attacks be hurled back, season after season; but the defenders also operated from, and may often have taken for granted, their remarkable geographical advantage. When, for example, very long-range planes eventually closed the critical mid-Atlantic 'air gap' after 1942, they did so from bases in Nova Scotia, Greenland, Iceland, and (slightly later) the Azores, Scotland and Ulster; and when U-boats made their surface runs into the Atlantic across the Bay of Biscay, they were pincered by Allied aircraft operating out of Gibraltar and the West Country ports.[9]

Even today, as will be noted below, when Russian surface vessels and long-range aircraft make a tentative effort at showing an Atlantic presence, geography gives NATO a formidable latent advantage. In sum, geography would always offer such an advantage, and a distinct competitive opportunity, to the peoples living on either side of what Mahan called the 'great commons' of the North Atlantic. All they had to do – and it was of course a critical condition – was to exploit that superior position by possessing a fleet, and not neglect it.

But if geography aided Britain in the fight against Nazi Germany (and, still more, against Mussolini's physically constrained Italy), it obviously could not help when, from the 1890s onwards, there steadily arose modern maritime powers outside European waters: Japan, and the United States. The geopolitical scene was altering, and with it the world order. The great fact about the international power situation after, say, 1550 had been that European countries had been able to reach out and dictate to much of the world, at least all those parts accessible to Western sea power and its cannons. The final stage of that maritime imperialism took place in the later decades of the nineteenth century, with the establishment of the Chinese treaty ports and the penetration by gunboats of the great rivers of Asia and Africa. But by then the American and Japanese were entering the scene, ending the monopoly of the European navies in Chinese waters. In the post-1919 era, only the Royal Navy among the Europeans had a significant presence in the Far East. By 1942, with Hong Kong and Singapore fallen, the British naval sway overseas was really only effective within a rough quadrilateral of Alexandria–Cape Town–West Indies–Scapa Flow. In the last year of the war, urged on by an anxious Churchill, the British eagerly reacquired Singapore and pushed a modern fleet into the Pacific, but it did not stay there for long.

By that time it was roughly a full century since Britain's economy had been at its relative zenith, and the two world wars had since taken their awful toll. Over-extended abroad, and battered at home, the nation simply had to contract, though it was an open question whether the Admiralty, overly impressed perhaps by the new nuclear age, should have slashed warship totals as much as they did. Only the far larger American Navy, boosted by the 1941–5 war as Britain once had been by the Napoleonic wars, remained as a Western presence in Asian seas. The so-called 'Vasco da Gama era' in world affairs, which the creation and continued effectiveness of the long-range, gunned sailing ship had made appear relatively easy, was now over. British naval mastery, so viewed, had been but the most successful manifestation of that lengthy episode in global history.

During the 1950s and 1960s, and for the reasons given above, the usefulness of naval power in international affairs seemed marginal, although there was an occasional quasi-imperial flourish in the deployment of warships by the dominant American navy, and then of course its very effective and demonstrative blockade of Cuban waters during the Missile Crisis of 1962. Khrushchev's order to the Russian freighter not to test the American blockade was both a recognition of the huge naval disparity between the two Superpowers, as well of course being a demonstration, again, of Russia's glaring geographical disadvantage – how could it project maritime force all the way from its home bases to the Caribbean unless it possessed carrier task groups and a fleet train akin to those of Nimitz's navy in the Pacific twenty years earlier – which of course it did not? The lesson was obvious, as was the humiliation, which was soon to cost Nikita Khrushchev his job.

So, in part goaded by the Cuban setback, and in all probability influenced by the erroneous belief that the Soviet economy was bigger than it really was while the American economy was in decline, the Politburo sanctioned a massive expansion in the nation's aerial and naval and missile forces. Whole new classes of fast-attack submarines plus ballistic-missile boats, flotillas of squadrons and destroyers, amphibious forces, and the Red Air Force's very long-range 'Bear' and 'Backfire' fleets, emerged to pose what seemed at the time to be an enormous threat to NATO's command of the North Atlantic, and even to challenge American naval mastery itself. So threatening did all this appear to Washington that during the 1980s it responded with its own fleet build-up, especially under the Reagan presidency, and for a few years analogies of the pre-1914 Anglo–German naval rivalry were a commonplace reference in the academy. And, while it was a relatively small and localized war, the Anglo–Argentine fight over the Falklands Islands in 1982, ending in Argentina's humiliating defeat, also seemed to demonstrate how important it was for countries to be able to project force out to sea, and it reversed, at least for a brief while, that long secular decline in the size of the British navy.

Then, abruptly, after 1990 the Soviet Navy collapsed, the victim of the USSR's own economic decline, which also saw the termination of the Warsaw Pact, the dissolution of the Communist Party, and the end of Russia's control over the other socialist republics. The Red Navy's submarine fleet was recalled, to be anchored in rows in the harbours at Murmansk and Petropavlovsk, their crews retired and sent home. Western visitors to Tsarist palaces along the Gulf of Riga could peer curiously at the clusters of Sverdlovsk-class heavy cruisers, rusting at their moorings off Kronstadt. Parts of the Black Sea Fleet were handed over to a now-independent Ukraine. Never before in modern times had an empire's economic and physical erosion during peacetime led so dramatically, and swiftly, to the end of its military effectiveness.

One obvious consequence of all this was that the West felt it needed to pay less attention to the significance of sea power. President Reagan's three-ocean navy, which had been built up to a total of almost 600 warships, now rapidly diminished in size. Newer vessels joined the fleet but always in smaller numbers than those they replaced, and always, like the newer aircraft, horrendously more expensive. The fleets of other NATO nations shrank even faster, and received only a few replacements. In any case, by the mid-1990s the international security items on the agenda, like Kosovo and Rwanda-Burundi, made no call upon sea power. Perhaps as a faint reflection of all this, the study of maritime affairs and naval history at colleges and universities also shriveled, especially in the United States.* Elsewhere, too, professorships originally designated as for 'imperial and naval'

* Individual naval history scholars, especially at State universities where perhaps there was a large ROTC program, still held their place; and the subject continued to be taught at the US Naval War College and the Naval Academy; but the teaching of naval and maritime affairs virtually disappeared from top institutions like the Ivy League universities.

history lost that meaning. The sea still moved around the globe at the end of the twentieth century as it always did, and vast and increasing amounts of commerce moved upon it, but the maritime dimension to world affairs seemed well and truly lost to public sight.

THE RETURN OF NAVALISM, AND OF THE IMPORTANCE OF SEA POWER

Yet it wasn't long before that situation changed yet again, and for various reasons, as noted briefly above. The first was the Gulf war of 1990–91 and the manifest display of American sea power in response to the '9/11' attacks upon its own country, and the subsequent second Gulf war in 2003. The repeated projections of American force to targets almost 6,000 miles away – first to recover Kuwait from Saddam Hussein's aggression and to destroy his divisions, then to eliminate the Taliban's chief Afghan lair and eradicate Osama bin Laden himself, and finally the second and even more decisive Iraq War, the occupation of that country, and Saddam's ignominious end – were large, long-range acts of state power that no other contemporary nation could come close to carrying out. And while General Schwarzkopf's armoured divisions could claim that they had inflicted the killer blow against Baghdad, and the U.S. Air Force would also assert its key, uncontested role, no account of America's Iraq and Afghan campaigns could deny the remarkable manifestations of naval force once again. The thunderous roar of F-15 and F-16 aircraft being catapulted off the decks of giant Nimitz-class carriers, the cascades of surface-launched and submarine-launched cruise missiles, the surreptitious landings of Navy Seals, the purposeful arrival of the huge Watson-class amphibious ships filled with hundreds of tanks and trucks… witnessing all this, might not a veteran of the Sicily and Iwo Jima landings some sixty years earlier have seen much that was familiar?

Secondly, and quite differently, there was also a large-scale and seemingly relentless rise of Asian navies throughout these years. If European nations were not investing in their fleets, the countries of East Asia and South Asia certainly were by the beginning of this century, with the vast growth of Chinese maritime power being only the most prominent sign of this new 'navalism'.

In such a change, the doubling or trebling of so many national fleets across such a large part of the globe – from Japan and South Korea to Vietnam, Australia and India – looks not dissimilar to that earlier broad historical example, the creation of numerous European navies during the sixteenth and seventeenth centuries. In some cases, these newer Asian fleets seem to be being built against neighbours, and/or in dispute of various maritime territorial boundaries. Moreover, the growing possibility of maritime conflict in East Asia and the western Pacific has in turn provoked an American strategic reaction in the form of a so-called 'pivot to the East'. A greater percentage of its fleet was deployed in these waters, and naval and air bases were either returned to their original owners (as in the Philippines) or newly created (as in northern Australia).

Thirdly, the impressive growth in the economies of Asia since the 1970s caused a large-scale expansion in sea-borne commerce, and in the number and size of the world's shipping lines. The 90 percent of all international trade that goes by sea includes most of the world's oil and LPG, coal and other ores, grain, cement, timber, electrical products, construction equipment, automobiles and a vast amount of other containerized consumer goods. These newer patterns in maritime trades could easily be disrupted, however, whether by a possible conflict in the Persian Gulf or by a further growth of piracy in the Indian Ocean. Other maritime disputes, whether concerning island groups in the South China Sea or brushes between NATO navies and Russian forces, all point to the importance of the sea, and of sea power, in international affairs.

In all these respects, then, it rather looks as if it is the declining European naval powers that may be out of step with current history. Whether one examines Europe's present naval expenditures and fleet sizes, or the actual, limited deployments of their warships, or indeed the general lack of interest shown by their publics, there is much to suggest that, far from leading a trend, the European nations are falling behind in the contemporary global rise in navalism.

While such a general comment is also true of Britain, this is not to say that the Admiralty doesn't fight for the country to keep a sizeable and all-round naval force. But just how it is to achieve that commendable aim in today's kaleidoscopic world has not proven easy. Any attempt to define Britain's naval needs has to be set within NATO's own evolving strategy, in the Baltic, the Mediterranean, and further afield. The 'special relationship' with the United States also has to be borne in mind, as do certain other international obligations and structures, such as those of the U.N. Security Council. Additionally, any assessment today would take place at a period of relatively low operational activity, with its armed forces under less strain – not necessarily the best time to measure real fighting capacity. Moreover, the Royal Navy is in a critical transition period, its newer carriers some years away from entering the fleet, and a decision on the future of its Vanguard-class submarines still deferred. Obviously, were the service to be in full possession in the near future of the carriers HMSs 'Queen Elizabeth II' and 'Prince of Wales' (at 70,000 tons the largest warships the Navy has ever had) with their special-version F-35 fighter-bombers, and each carrier group possessing modern Type 45 destroyers as their escorts; and were the heated political and technical debates in Britain over the future of the Trident-missile submarines (the four Vanguard-class boats) to be resolved in favour of a newer class of these nuclear-deterrent vessels; and, finally, were the Royal Navy to be given the full number (7) of the very advanced SSN fleet submarines, then it could probably claim to be the third most powerful navy in the world, after the United States and China.* But if financial constraints never allow for the two-carrier vision, and the same demand for economy excludes newer ballistic-missile submarines and also reduces the size of the Astute-class attack boats, then the service will indeed have lost its capacity to be a transoceanic force.

It is therefore not surprising that recent scholarly efforts to describe 'British Strategy in a Complex World' emphasize the very complexity of the global scene and caution against the rather confident tone of official documents – 'paved with good intentions' is how one author describes these statements.[10] For every work that points to Britain's still-considerable naval assets, another points to the many deficits.

This latter period of Britain's naval tale has not been a moribund one. It is after all interesting to note that the seventy years (1945–2015) between the end of the Second World War and our

* Those two large carriers giving it the edge over the navies of Russia, Japan, and France, which have no equivalents.

present time is exactly the same duration as that of the so-called *Pax Britannica* of 1815–1885. During the earlier epoch, Britain, as the imperial number one nation, carried out multiple acts of gunboat diplomacy virtually as a matter of course, though with its only example of the application of sustained maritime force being its Baltic and Black Sea operations against Russia in the Crimean War. During the first half of the later age, by contrast, Britain's navy actually campaigned on a very large scale on no less than three occasions, during the Korean War (1950–54), the Suez Crisis (1956), and finally, and under Prime Minister Margaret Thatcher's strong insistence, in the Falklands War (1982). Yet the last of those may have been Britain's final large-scale independent action abroad. During the second half of the period – a full thirty-five years – the Royal Navy has carried out no significant overseas operation, while its overall warship size has steadily and correspondingly shrunk. Its situation today has been a long time in the making.

A lot may be explained here by the simple fact that Britain, like its fellow European states, lives under what is essentially an American strategic umbrella, not just through the continuance of post-Cold War U.S. nuclear protection, but also through the Superpower's preservation of open sea-lanes, and other obvious Western interests, across much of the globe. In seeking to preserve its own political and economic needs worldwide, Washington offers global public goods to all others, including obviously Britain, which therefore can keep its naval budgets relatively modest, in fact, about one-eighth or one-tenth that of the U.S. Navy's total. Asking for much more would arouse great controversy among the electorate, but such limited defence spending in turn explains London's relatively limited military reach outside traditional NATO–European waters. The country whose warships once sailed unchecked out of Hong Kong, Singapore and Colombo has nowadays no significant role to play in East and South Asian seas. And most Britons feel only relieved at that.

Of the other European navies, only the French Marine retains the capacity to project outward force across the oceans, at least to a limited degree. This is in keeping with France's desire to show that, as a major European power and as one of the five U.N. Security Council permanent members, it can fulfill its international responsibilities; that it still retains 'hard power' at sea, along with a capacity to strike back at international terrorist networks, as well as maintaining its traditional policy of engagement in Francophone Africa. But any defence economist would be quick to point out that that budget only just reaches two percent of France's Gross National Product. Like Britain, France allocates a markedly smaller percentage of its GNP to its armed services than it did in earlier times, has significantly fewer men under arms, and possesses many fewer tanks, aircraft, and warships. While they both retain more hard power than their European NATO partners, and can operate some way from home waters, the reach of their surface warships scarcely goes beyond anti-piracy patrols off the Somali and neighbouring coastlines, and (in France's case) a brief carrier tour in the Gulf. As to the remaining smaller European navies, their very modest size, and the limited weapons-platforms at their disposal, confine them to playing a small, team-player role, always within a NATO and/or EU context. In certain cases, it is not that these European national forces lack modern firepower, but just that they are numerically so small. Thus, Germany's four brand-new and very large F125-class frigates look extremely impressive, but they replace a larger number of existing vessels, and since German defence spending seems rigidly held (around 1.2 percent of GNP), the actual result is a shrunken surface fleet.

The European Union currently possesses a total GDP as big as America's. If it also possessed a correspondingly high and unified defence budget, with a common procurement, recruitment and command structure, the contemporary world power arrangements would look very different. There would exist two giant Western democratic nations (for the EU, if possessing a common defence establishment, would clearly be so much more like a nation). Russia would find itself next to a European power–political entity with about eight times its economic heft, and America would not be the lone superpower. In naval terms, too, such an economic heavyweight could afford a very large navy, with aircraft carriers, Aegis cruisers, and the like. At present, that is merely a dream, and even further away following Britain's EU referendum (leading to a vote for 'Brexit' in June 2016). In sum: the European powers, preferring limited defence budgets and relatively small national forces, have also limited their strategic capacity to the 'near abroad', and play little or no strategic role further afield.

The most recent challenge to Europe's pacific disposition has been the forward, thrusting policies of the Russian government, with frequent displays of naval and air force might. Its submarines have been detected probing shoreline defences on the other side of the Baltic, its fighters occasionally harass NATO aircraft, and its long-range bombers have flown into the Atlantic and around the British Isles. More seriously, its cargo vessels and destroyers have unloaded heavy war materials to its naval base in Syria, where its air squadrons repeatedly intervene in the civil war in support of Moscow's assertive diplomatic stance in that country. Its takeover of the Crimea, with the Sevastapol naval base, is declared an irreversible *fait accompli*. Russia's military has been privileged within the state budget, even in a dismal economy. The liberal, accommodationist era of President Gorbachev twenty years earlier seems like a dream.

How long this assertiveness will last is an open question, for the longer story of Russian naval policy in the world has always been a fitful one that suffered from repeated overstretch. At present, there is serious evidence of the building of new surface warships, the strengthening of its large submarine flotillas (it has over 60 boats in total, including its nuclear deterrent forces), and the growing investment in a modern combat-ready air force. Yet at the same time there is much evidence of Russia's economic decrepitude. Its distorted political economy boasts a highly advanced cyber-warfare capacity, yet its only real exports are natural gas and petroleum, and arms sales. Meanwhile, among its long lists of cruisers, destroyers and frigates (approximately 35 of them) and many of its submarines, there are also many older and ineffectual vessels. Its record of warship breakdowns and accidents at sea points to very poor support systems. Most important of all, it is noteworthy that Russia spends a far higher percentage (5.4 percent) of its GDP than any of the other large Powers, although its economy is the smallest of them all, smaller indeed than Italy's.[11] In sum, Moscow asserts the importance of sea power in today's world, yet badly strains itself even to keep up. It is hardly a nation capable of altering the maritime balance of power over the longer term.

Russia remains important to American strategists for two reasons. First of all, it can use its sheer weight as a land power to put pressure upon U.S. allies and friendly states (Ukraine, the Baltic states, Turkey), reminding Washington of geographical borders that the U.S. Navy's fleets cannot protect. Secondly, and much more importantly, Russia remains one of the greatest of the nuclear powers, which includes its capacity for nuclear-force projection at sea – however unclear the extent of this may be, it is there. Nevertheless, Russia's renewed navalism will have to encounter those fundamental weaknesses that have always prevented it from being a great naval state: an extremely unfavourable geographical position that inhibits it from possessing a true 'blue water' fleet; and a persistent inability to create a flourishing and modern productive national economy. While a true revolution in Russian politics might one day make the country much more competitive economically, the geographical constraints are permanent. A sober appreciation of these two weaknesses by Moscow would be the first step in any Russian move towards a realistic grand strategy for the future.

THE RISE OF NAVIES AND NAVALISM IN ASIA

nothing more aptly reflects Russia's relatively weak naval condition than to consider by contrast what is happening from the perspective of sea power across South and East Asia. The first and most important fact is the economic vibrancy of this vast, densely populated swathe of countries. While Japan showed enormous productivity and ever-greater prosperity from the late 1950s onwards, and was joined a decade later by the 'four tigers' of South Korea, Taiwan, Hong Kong and Singapore, this pattern of economic take-off has extended to Indonesia, Vietnam, and, further west, to India itself. All of these states, large and small, border the sea or are island nations themselves, and are part of the flourishing maritime networks of this region and the links further afield. All benefit from Asia's manufacturing productivity, increasing high-tech capacity, and massive capital resources.

Ostensibly, not all of them require navies other than coastal-defence forces. But the majority have decided that they need more than that, citing uncertain relations with their next-door neighbours as well as reasons of national prestige. The result of this expansion is at present variable. India's case for a large fleet is the most plausible, and accords with that country's rise to be one of the world's economic and military Great Powers, secure if not dominant in the Indian Ocean; yet in fact its present navy looks numerically insufficient to that status and is in part obsolescent. In South Korea's case, by contrast, one observes a much smaller though immensely productive nation constructing an ultra-modern fleet of warships (with, for example, Aegis-type destroyers as big as the British heavy cruisers of the Second World War). This may not point to a single operational intent, but it does indicate Korea's purposefulness here: if navies now count in the East Asian equation of power, then Seoul will not be backward.[12] All it need do is look over its shoulder at Japan, which is currently the fourth- or fifth-largest naval power in the world. Belief in the importance of sea power by Tokyo has led to Japan's large investment in a very powerful surface navy of the most modern sort, including three helicopter-carriers and over 40 destroyers and frigates. Here is a fleet that could operate abroad, say, in the Indian Ocean, yet also be deployed to counter challenges closer to home, such as Chinese activity around the disputed and uninhabited Diaoyu (or Senkaku) Islands. Remarkably, Japan achieves all this with a total military budget that requires only around one percent of its enormous GDP, thus reassuring the still-strong pacifist domestic sentiment.[13] But it could, if it ever chose to double that percentage, have a huge conventional fleet.

In absolute terms, Asian defence spending is staggering. The continent (including here China and India) now accounts for almost half of the global market for large weapons systems – twice as much as the Middle East and four times more than Europe. Above all, and interestingly, Asian states currently have an appetite for submarines of the non-nuclear sort, and now possess more than one-half of the world's total. The Economist recently reported that:

> '... [Vietnam] has bought eight combat aircraft, four fast-attack craft, and four submarines. A further six frigates and two submarines are on order ... India has ordered six [submarines] from France, and Pakistan has bought eight from China, which is also providing two to Bangladesh. Germany is to deliver four to Singapore and five to South Korea, which has sold three of its own manufacture to Indonesia. Australia is to buy between eight and 12.'[14]

What is interesting, then, is not only the number of Asian nations purchasing warships but the remarkable number of states that can supply them; the global naval arms industry is nowadays both huge and diffuse, looking more like that prior to 1914 than to any era since then. And, each year, Asian-language translations of The Influence of Sea Power Upon History continue to sell. Mahan's influence is alive and well across the continent.

It cannot be stressed sufficiently how remarkable and distinct this Asian naval renaissance looks viewed from the long sweep of world history. On one side of the globe a host of nations in Asia and Australasia has become convinced that they must invest much more now than they ever did in a modern navy, seeing it, and sea power, as vital to secure their interests in a turbulent and unpredictable world. Yet on the other side of the globe another cluster of nations, all in Europe, does not hear this message and does not share this conviction. If a few thinkers in Paris and London still do, they have no real chance of persuading their politicians that it might be prudent for their countries to return to an age when they possessed a real naval heft, sixty or so years ago. Viewed from afar, this alteration in the tectonic geopolitical plates – Europe slipping, Asia rising – is palpable and, probably, irreversible. The global maritime weights are seeing a new Braudel-like shift, almost a lurch, from the West to the East, from the Dover Straits to the Philippine Sea. Only a few Admiralties, and even fewer Foreign Offices, have adjusted their thinking to this grand transformation.

CHINA'S NAVAL GROWTH – THE PURSUIT OF FUTURE MASTERY

Behind all this warship building and strategical reconfiguring lies one great happening: the rise of China to be, once again, a great World Power, second only (for the moment at least) to the United States. This significant change in the modern international order has occurred with unusual speed. When the first edition of this book was being written, few could possibly have thought that China would become a major naval player in world affairs by the century's end. It was hard to tell at that time if and when China would emerge from the disastrous social and economic policies that Chairman Mao was inflicting upon the country during his long dictatorship. And even when sane economic policies were implemented after 1979, and the nation responded with decades of remarkable (10 percent annualized) economic growth, it was scarcely thought that the construction of a large navy would be among China's priorities. There were new cities to be built, an entire infrastructure of roads and railways and airports to be invested in, an export-oriented drive to be orchestrated, half a billion people to be pulled out of their rural poverty, and capital and savings to be accumulated – and all this to be done while the leadership pondered over how far (if at all) to move towards an open, democratic society. When the severe crackdown at Tiananmen Square in 1989 showed that Communist Party rule would stay in place, then assuaging the population through the promise of real prosperity, via sustained and peaceful economic growth, became the leadership's top priority.

What this epic growth also did, though, was to give the PRC's leadership the option of establishing a very large navy, simply because they could now afford it, and at a relatively moderate cost. While defence spending was held at a fixed percentage of GNP (outside estimates ranged between one and two percent), a steady annual GDP growth of 10 percent from the 1970s onwards turned something like a $15 billion defence budget into $30 billion seven years later, and that into a $60 billion budget in another seven years, and so on. Even a later slowing to perhaps 5–6 percent GDP growth leads to considerable rises in defence expenditures. This has led to a military and naval establishment now much larger than any of the other second-tiered maritime nations like Britain, France and Russia. Getting a true figure on China's total defence spending is extremely difficult, but if the latest (2016) SIPRI calculation of $215 billions is roughly accurate, this amounts to a faster military spending build-up than anything which has occurred over the past half-century.[15]

This naval expansion is occurring, Chinese commentators like to point out, almost exactly six hundred years after the country once possessed a grand ocean-going navy, under the renowned Admiral Cheng Ho (Zheng He). Due to internal opposition that maritime power soon shriveled, something that is now described as a serious mistake. Ironically, Ming China abandoned overseas exploration just as the Portuguese and, shortly afterwards, Tudor England, became successful maritime powers, even facing down the might of Imperial Spain.* But this time, official sources maintain, China will have a navy sufficient for its needs as a

* The tale of the Tudor Navy's defeat in 1588 of the numerically larger Spanish Armada is one frequently shown on Chinese state TV. The implication is an obvious one.

Great Power. The waters under its jurisdiction will be defended, its trade routes will be supported, and China will play a role in supporting the international maritime order, though it will also want to fashion what exactly that order is. It is thus left to Beijing to define what its basic national needs will be, now and in the years ahead.

The expansion of the Chinese fleet, with the regular introduction of newer types of warships, aircraft, rocketry and other warfare-fighting equipment, is occurring so swiftly that any tally of its forces is soon out of date. Many of the ships are simply larger and more powerful versions of the coastal-defence warships that China has always had. But they have now been joined by a fleet of newer destroyers (19) and frigates (54) with very heavy missile capacities. Its second aircraft carrier is considerably more advanced than its first one. A prototype heavy cruiser of some 11,000 tons displacement may be compared to the American Navy's Aegis-class ships. Its amphibious fleets look larger, faster, and better equipped than those they are replacing. Some of these vessels and weapons systems are still not very advanced, and the problems of too-rapid growth are also showing themselves; and of course this is a navy that still prefers to operate usually within a relatively limited geographical space. Even so, it is formidable.

The implications of all this are now the subject of intense debate among Western policy experts. Accompanying the fleet build-up has been the erection of an extensive missile and aerial defence system all along China's coasts, with the intention of deterring any other navy (including, and especially, the United States Navy) from coming close. In so protecting its unfolding maritime capacities, many observers feel, China has not only established sea control over its immediate littoral but also perhaps for a considerable way further out, to important offshore islands and reefs. As noted below, no American captain would be happy at putting his aircraft carrier in or near the Taiwan Strait during a crisis, as if circumstances were the same as in Eisenhower's time. That change is a marked operational fact, somewhat akin to the Royal Navy's abandonment of a close blockade of the German coastline in the years before 1914, realizing that the potential costs were too high. Moving to a distant patrolling position when tactical circumstances change is a prudent step for the larger offshore navy to take, to be sure; but it is also ceding sea space, and undoubtedly represents an operational concession, in this case, on America's part.

The most discussed stage in this steady geographic expansion of China's maritime reach has been its claim to sovereignty over a significant array of small offshore islands and coral reefs that run through the South China Sea northwards, to the waters lying south of Japan (the so-called 'Nine-Dash Line'). But there are nations nearby – the Philippines, Vietnam, Indonesia – also laying their own historic claim to certain of those islands, while the United States insists on an international 'freedom of the seas' in these waters and maintains that matters of ownership should be decided by arbitration rather than occupation and force. Further north, a determined Japan, with its very competent navy, firmly asserts its claim to the Senkaku Islands. It is therefore not so easy for China to push out to the open seas militarily, even as its maritime commerce has surged and even while the country has become the greatest trade exporter and importer in the world. Yet it is precisely this – China's massive place nowadays in global production and trade – that is key. Its growth may be erratic, with occasional recessions and setbacks (as was America's in the period 1865–1917), but the overall trend is always upwards.

All this of course could be described as simply the outward, physical sign of the country's natural peaceful expansion. After all, historically China was the Middle Kingdom, at least in the Asian world, receiving tributes, trading, and having diplomatic relations in all directions. It is therefore easy for Beijing to suggest that it is becoming so again, even while also stressing that it will not do (e.g. in Africa) what the Western colonial powers did. Still, since it is now negotiating for, and constructing, naval bases along the so-called 'maritime Silk Road' from south China ports to the Persian Gulf and East Africa, that could suggest that it is also developing an option for a more sizeable military presence overseas in the future. Hence the current debate in the West: is China's outward thrust just that of one undertaken by an essentially economic giant, acting brusquely perhaps but pacifically, in pursuit of its commercial expansion, or is it also acquiring a hard, geopolitical edge to it, like so many Great-Power expansions of the past?

What is clear is that China's naval growth, accompanied by the types of weaponry with which it has chosen to equip its armed forces, has altered and is altering the strategic balances in Asia and the Western Pacific vis-a-vis every other maritime nation, including the United States. Even its lesser, asymmetric weaponry (coast-based sea-skimming missiles; quiet, diesel-engined submarines), by their very nature, constrains the American capacity to operate in the western Pacific as once it had done, and thus forces it to adjust. But what if it comes to more? What if it comes, soon, to an even larger aircraft carrier, and to long-range submarines that can operate well into the Indian Ocean? How will things look by 2025?

To a certain branch of the 'realist' school of American political scientists, a future great-power clash looks inevitable.[16] To them, China plainly seeks to expand its relative influence and power in this region, whereas the United States will not accept any relative diminution of its own position there. All the signs are arriving, therefore, for a future 'Thucydidean clash', mirroring that between a rising Athens and a resentful Sparta well over two thousand years ago – a speculation which in turn has caused East-Asian scholars (especially) to rush in, pointing to the many reasons why a conflict between the two Superpowers ought not to happen.[17]

To other scholars, China's growth has a very Wilhelminian character to it. In that previous case, the leadership of an expansionist Imperial Germany, driven forward by its massive industrial and commercial success, determined to create a large battlefleet commensurate with its new status as a world power. Yet the very creation of such a force did not occur in a vacuum, and thus Germany's 'natural' naval growth made the number one power of the time, Great Britain, increasingly nervous. So it is with Chinese naval expansion today, at least as viewed by many in the United States. Much will depend, then, on how both the status quo country and the rising nation comport themselves in the years to come. As Henry Kissinger has observed, a peacefully rising China is very different from one that is assertive and destabilizing of the existing order in East Asia; and the United States, as the status quo number one power, will reserve the right to act accordingly, as Britain did in the years after 1900.[18]

Yet two great differences exist between now and those dangerous international circumstances prior to 1914. The first is that each of today's protagonists is a nuclear power. Even if America's nuclear weapons capacities are by far the larger, China's investment in both medium-range and very long-range rocketry is now substantial, giving it something like a regional parity. Of course no-one knows what would transpire if an American–Chinese naval clash 'went nuclear' (both have tactical nuclear weaponry), which is why one might hope that this condition of mutual deterrence would prevail. And the second difference, obviously, is geographical. The Pacific Ocean is not the North Sea, where, to repeat, the swift creation of a large German fleet at Wilhelmshaven after 1900 put a new naval force only one day's steaming from England's eastern shores. The distance across the Pacific, between each side's coasts and cities, is huge, around seven thousand miles. This must, or should, allow for a lot of so-called elbow room. Here is where analogies with the Anglo–German naval race become much less useful. Still, what is very clear is that China's maritime rise has made America's leadership far more aware of the significance of sea power than it was a quarter of a century ago. As things look, the age-old story of the struggle for maritime mastery has now shifted, so far peacefully but uneasily, to waters a very long way from Cape Trafalgar.

AMERICAN NAVAL MASTERY, NOW UNDER NEW CHALLENGES

Despite China's maritime expansion, there is no doubt that at the present time the United States Navy is still in a league of its own. Its huge, nuclear-powered aircraft carriers, each with 70 or 80 modern planes and helicopters, have no equivalent in any other navies. Each carrier group has a capacity, unique in history, to strike from the sea to targets hundreds of miles inland; and any such group, while deployed on a mission, could fairly easily eliminate most surface warships that might challenge it. The carriers themselves are always supported and shielded by a cluster of cruisers, destroyers and frigates, warships that can also be deployed for many other missions. A second important strand of U.S. maritime power resides in its submarine fleet, consisting of the giant strategic-missile vessels that are part of the West's nuclear deterrent, plus a large force of fast attack submarines with their own offensive operational capacity against enemy warships. The third leg lies in the U.S. Navy's amphibious forces, with their own unique role in projecting American power into foreign waters and onto foreign shores. Altogether, the U.S. navy's budget allocation of some $161 billion in 2016 (about 30 percent of the Pentagon's total regular budget of $554 billion) is about eight times more than that of most other navies, and perhaps still three times that of China.

As impressive as the actual hardware itself is the worldwide deployment of U.S. naval forces, operating thousands of miles across the oceans from such main East Coast and West Coast fleet bases at Norfolk, San Diego and Puget Sound, as well as Pearl Harbor and other stations abroad. Comparisons with the Royal Navy's own great overseas deployments in the age of the *Pax Britannica* spring to mind, although the American squadrons in foreign waters are less likely to be based in physical harbours, and rely instead upon their fleet trains. Independent in most cases of host nations, American carrier groups can steam off the shores of the Eastern Mediterranean, or the Persian Gulf, or through the waters west of the Philippines. And global positioning systems, and an all-round intelligence and decryption capability, wrap United States fighting units in an unequalled radio-electronic environment of command and control. All this presents a portrait, for now and the foreseeable future, of a unique and well-grounded impregnability.

Where possibly, then, could there exist weaknesses in America's current naval mastery? If the patterns of the past offer any guidance here, then vulnerabilities could lie in three areas: first, in the emergence of newer military technologies, asymmetric in nature, to give a further twist to the age-old spiral of advantage and disadvantage between offensive and defensive weaponry. Secondly, in the 'overstretch' of the American armed forces geographically, in a situation in which they would be required to fight simultaneously in a number of different theatres of war, far from each other, and thus unable to summon decisive force for victory. And thirdly, in the overstretch of the United States economically in the longer term, in that its productive capacity might fall behind that of faster-growing states and thus no longer be able to provide for the armed forces to maintain its many interests and ends.

This first vulnerability is very understandable. The threat of newer, asymmetric technologies to up-end the existing military order has been one of the enduring features of the modern age. It is only a century ago that the world's navies were rushing to build the newer, Dreadnought-style class of battleship, following the example initiated by the Royal Navy when that novel, all-big-gun, turbine-driven warship appeared early in 1906. But it was just as these apparently dominant 'super'-ironclads became the measure of each rival nation's naval strength, and seemed to confirm Mahan's insistence that the core of any Navy lay in its concentrated battle-fleet, that newer, disruptive (and far cheaper) weapons systems also were being developed. The naval mine was already a danger to any warship, but the newer torpedo was even more of a threat because it could be launched from so many different platforms: from swarms of motor torpedo-boats, from the fast-evolving submarine, and, within another decade or so, from aerial torpedo-bombers. Capital ships alone soon become awfully vulnerable.

This is a historical precedent that must concern American planners even today. True, the Pacific War showed that well-defended carrier groups could beat off swarms of Japanese bombers and kamikazes, but these experiences (like the heavily contested Malta convoys fought for by the Royal Navy) also showed that the defenders must expect to take significant warship losses. No protective screen can be complete against mass aerial bombing and missile attack. If that remains true, then there are implications should American carrier groups today still plan to project a 'forward strategy' through their presence near and around the South China Sea, as well as in the Eastern Mediterranean and Persian Gulf. To at least some experts on naval warfare, and to this author, it seems highly unlikely that major U.S. vessels can operate safely in those waters any more, if indeed Chinese, Russian and Iranian missiles, airplanes, torpedo-carrying craft, and submarines are so advanced, and so many. If this is true, however, then sea power's capacity to affect land outcomes may have been short-lived, and warships may once again have to stay a long way from the shore or run the risk of severe losses. If we 'put all these dots together', then, as one American scholar points out,[19] a major rethink may be required of the U.S. Navy operationally, with its larger vessels (carriers especially) having to stay a long way from any hostile shoreline possessing a dense offensive-missile system. If so, America's future strategic reach in theatres on the other side of the globe could be very much cramped.

Then there is the risk of the dispersal of American power. Perhaps the prospect of the U.S. Navy having to fight simultaneously in three geographically distant theatres of war, and against multiple and different foes, seems a remote possibility at present. It would be a rare conjunction of bad luck, or of very inept diplomacy, that would see Washington having to rush reinforcements from the U.S. homeland to, say, the Baltics and the Korean Peninsula at the same time as it dared not move units from the Persian Gulf/Indian Ocean theatre. Yet the blunt fact is that United States planners constantly do anticipate the possibility of conflict in various and many parts of the globe: the Baltic States/Ukraine/Poland, in a scenario where Russian aggressions and miscalculations may have triggered off a NATO response; the collapse of the Syrian state, with spillover effects into Iraq, or south into Israel; the (rarely openly discussed) collapse of the Saudi state; the actions of a more hostile, even belligerent Iranian state, involving a nuclear crisis or rockets fired at Israel; the closing of the oil trade from the Persian Gulf; a war between China and any of its insular neighbours (the Philippines; Japan) over disputed islands; a Taiwan crisis; and a North Korean attack upon the South.

The point is not that America is unprepared for this: the nation's forward military deployments, alliance pledges, troop training, and weapons systems suggest that it is very well forewarned and forearmed. And policy statements by leading figures among America's top military indicate that they seem well aware that the country once again lives in a multipolar world, where both China and Russia are independently acting Great Powers. For all this, the big question remains: are American forces sufficient if the Navy had to be split up to fight in multiple wars? Currently, it possesses around 280 major warships (including its submarines and littoral warfare vessels), which is considerably fewer than the 570 or so it counted in the Reagan, i.e. later Cold War era, and forty fewer than was on its roster (318) in 2000. Perhaps it is true that, say, a Zumwalt-class destroyer is so much more powerful than the types it is replacing; but the fact is that, just as in the German or British case, a three-times-more-sophisticated ship currently entering service does not do the job of three separate fighting platforms.

Finally, there is the longer-term question of whether the American economy can continue to afford all this. Again, this is not a completely abstract matter. If the economy's relative share of total world product was considerably less than it is today, it would obviously become much harder to sustain the country's international purposes. A weakened United States, being only one of several egoistical Great Powers, might no longer be strong enough to get its own way in the world. Whether this will be a practical strategic issue for American leaders in the next decade or so is still unclear. Perhaps it is enough here simply to note the evidence accumulating that America's real long-term productivity growth is, and will probably continue to be, much slower than in its boom (1930s–1960s) decades.[20] The future economic foundations for American naval mastery may thus be less robust than they have been previously.

For the past half-century, the American global position has rested upon a curious contradiction: with only circa 4.5 percent of world population, yet an impressive 18 or so percent of world GDP, it has been willing to spend a disproportionate share of the world's total defence spending. For a long time, indeed, it was spending around 45 percent of the whole, and even now (2016) the United States spends 36–7 percent of all the world's defence expenditures. How long, the observer might wonder, can this go on, without a more proximate correlation to its actual share of world population? If the United States spent a still considerable 25 percent of total global expenditures on defence, it could hardly keep its present naval advantage. That is all at present hypothetical, and may not worry the U.S. Navy so much as sea-skimming missiles do. But in a dynamic world order, in which changes occur every so often in the long-term global power balances, and where the pace of the economic shifts seems if anything to be quickening, even American naval predominance must be seen as conditional.

FINAL THOUGHTS

The story of the rise and fall of British naval mastery was complete almost seventy years ago, by 1945, save for its government's few late-imperial ventures (Suez, the Falklands) which even when successful in the latter case in reality confirmed the larger pattern of the country's relative decline. Historically, the story had possessed a wonderful coherence and roundness, from the reign of the first Elizabeth to that of the second. In the middle of those four centuries there stood out two hundred years (say, 1715 to 1914) when that relatively small island-state had so effectively organized itself that it was the world's leading naval power and, indeed, the number one actor in almost all overseas regions outside of those of the continental U.S. and the Eurasian heartland itself. There was no equivalent in previous world history to its pre-eminence, and the only power which has come close to emulating it – the United States in present times – has largely eschewed taking the same territorial path despite possessing even greater relative economic clout.

There was also coherence throughout this narrative in the symbiosis of a country's relative economic strength and its strategic heft. When Britain's commercial and financial capacities were overtaking those of its nearest rivals, and when its industrial innovations placed it further ahead of the other nations of the world, it was easier for it to pay for a strong navy that eclipsed the rest. When the comparative productive weights shifted at last against Britain, there came in turn its imperial and maritime decline. At that stage even its advantageous geography, which had greatly aided its rise during the age of sail, could not stem its decline when the global productive weights were altering so markedly, away from itself and Europe, and towards America and then Asia.

We now live in another age to that of British and European pre-eminence, where a different nation's naval mastery – America's – is very much in evidence. This was of course very much hoped for, and much anticipated, by Mahan himself in his writings of a century ago – if the Royal Navy were no longer to rule the waves in times ahead, he insisted, then it must be done by the American fleet itself. Still, from the very beginning of his writings Mahan had always been careful to emphasize that the basic 'elements of sea power' were part of the unchanging order of things and would remain 'the same, in cause and effect, from age to age', and thus by implication regardless of individual nations.[21]

It followed, then, that if the leadership of another country, building upon vast economic resources, and encouraged by its own rising commercial and financial activities across the world, chose also to develop strong naval forces, then that in turn would lead to an alteration in the global maritime power balances, perhaps not for another generation, but surely over time. Just how such an alteration would occur in practice, that is, in an encounter between the current American strategic predominance and a rising China, and what the outcome would be, is impossible to predict. What can safely be said, however, is that navies and naval power, expressing as they do the national purposes of states and governments, will be just as important to world affairs in the future as they have been so repeatedly in the past. It is for that reason also that the story of British naval mastery will continue to be of interest in the decades ahead to more than maritime historians alone.

Paul Kennedy
New Haven, 2017

Preface

This book represents an attempt to carry out the first detailed reconsideration of the history of British sea power since that presented in A. T. Mahan's classic *The Influence of Sea Power upon History*, which was published as long ago as 1890 and has been of seminal importance to the whole study of naval history since then. In particular, the present work seeks to describe – and, more significantly, to analyse the reasons for – the rise and fall of Great Britain as the predominant maritime nation in the period from the Tudors to the present day. Because it is such an analysis, the book concerns itself to only a limited extent with the famous admirals and battles which have filled the pages of many popular works upon the Royal Navy, and even less with the finer points of tactics, ship design, gunnery, navigation and social life in the navy – at least for their own sake. The main purpose and concentration of this study has not been to place the navy itself under a microscope but to try to set it within a far wider framework of national, international, economic, political and strategical considerations without which the terms 'sea power' and 'naval mastery' cannot properly be understood. Such an aim is necessarily an ambitious one and in undertaking it I have been constantly aware of the limitations of my own knowledge and of the difficulties involved in presenting arguments in such a concentrated form. However, only the reader can fully judge how far short of its proclaimed purpose the present book falls.

Of the many arguments and conclusions which are presented in the following pages, three may be regarded as the major ones:

Firstly, that Britain's naval rise and fall has been so closely bound up with her economic rise and fall that it is impossible to understand the former without a close examination of the latter;

secondly, that sea power exerted its greatest influence upon world affairs between the early sixteenth and the later nineteenth centuries, that is, between the creation of the oceanic sailing-ship on the one hand and the industrialization of continental land-masses on the other;

and thirdly, that even within that so-called 'Columbian era' the influence of sea power had some very natural limitations which British governments needed to take account of in peacetime and in wartime. It was not by maritime methods alone, but by a judicious blending of both sea power and land power, that Britain rose to become the leading world power.

The first of these arguments can hardly be called contentious; indeed, one probably comes close to a political truism in stating that naval strength depends upon economic strength. The Royal Navy's rise in the seventeenth and eighteenth centuries was obviously connected with the Commercial Revolution and the expansion of British overseas trade in those years; the Pax Britannica was underpinned by the Industrial Revolution; and Britain's decline as a world power and a naval power in the twentieth century has equally clearly been linked to her relative economic decline. But, curiously enough, this truism has never actually been explored over the whole course of Britain's history as the leading maritime nation.

The second conclusion is also one which is not new, although many British admirals and writers in the twentieth century appear to have ignored it; already in the later nineteenth century Sir John Seeley and, after him, Sir Halford Mackinder had pointed out that the coming of industrialization and of the railway to such continent-wide states as Russia and the United States was beginning to permit land power to re-assert that dominance over sea power which it had lost when the sailing-ship had revolutionized world politics some three centuries earlier. Here again, however, a detailed examination of the classical age of sea power, and of the reasons for its growth and its decline, has been lacking. Since that period in history coincided with, and was indeed a fundamental element in, the rise and fall of Britain's world power, it seemed appropriate to scrutinize both developments in the present study.

The third argument, although of its nature less general than the previous two, is likely to prove more provoking, for it raises again that centuries-long debate between what have been termed the 'maritime' and the 'continental' schools of strategy: that is, between those who have maintained that Britain should concentrate her energies upon her navy, her colonies and her overseas trade, remaining aloof from Europe in peacetime and only carrying out peripheral raids against the enemy and offering subsidies to allies in wartime; and those who have held that under certain circumstances a continental military commitment was necessary, since their country's own security was inextricably bound up with the fate of the European balance of power, and that an isolationist policy would endanger Britain too in the long run. This debate, about the balance that should be reached between land power and sea power, between Europe and the wider world, between the army and the navy, was always a contentious one, for it had personal, emotional and domestic political aspects and repercussions which took it outside the realm of pure strategy. My own position, no doubt influenced by events in the present century, is one of support for those who, like Elizabeth I, William III, Marlborough, Chatham, Grey and others, argued the need for the British people to balance their natural wish for a 'maritime' way of life and strategy with a watchful concern for Europe and a determination to ensure that developments on that continent did not deleteriously affect their country's interests.

My attitude to this history of British naval mastery is somewhat akin to that which Seeley claimed for himself in his book *The Expansion of England* when he denied that he was writing either as a biographer or a poet or a moralist: 'I am concerned always with a single problem only, that of causation . . . that we may discover the laws by which states rise, expand or fall in this world.' Of course, this did not turn Seeley's work into 'objective' history, any more than the present study or any other history book could claim to be objective; for the historian, much as he tries, can never fully free himself from the prejudices, experiences, interests and limitations of his own age. Indeed, perhaps it is only in our contemporary, post-1945 world that such a book as this one could have been written. To place such emphasis upon the economic factor, to call into question Britain's 'natural' bias towards the overseas and maritime world, to begin to analyse with a reasonable modicum of detachment this country's 'fall' as a naval, colonial and economic Great Power, are all approaches which it would have been rare to discover in the British naval histories of earlier periods. Yet it is precisely because of Britain's changed circumstances that the older historiography needed to be reassessed and the older assumptions needed to be modified. If the present work has contributed in any way towards that process, then I shall be well satisfied.

*

Certain archival materials from the Public Record Office and the India Office Library in London, the *Bundesarchiv-Militärarchiv* in Freiburg and the *Staatsarchiv* in Vienna (which had been visited by me for quite a different purpose) provided useful evidence and quotations for this study and it seems only fitting to testify again to the helpfulness of the staff of those institutions. However, a perusal of the footnotes will reveal that my debts to the authors of printed studies are far heavier – inevitably so, in a book which attempts a broad synthesis. I should like to acknowledge here how much I have gained from a reading of the works of C. M. Cipolla, J. S. Corbett, R. Davis, J. R. Jones, C. J. Marcus, R. Pares, J. H. Parry, R. B. Wernham, J. A. Williamson, and C. Wilson for the earlier part of this book; of C. J. Bartlett, R. Higham, E. J. Hobsbawm, M. Howard, A. J. Marder and S. W. Roskill for the later part; and of C. Barnett, L. Dehio, G. S. Graham, H. J. Mackinder, E. B. Potter and C. W. Nimitz, H. R. Richmond and, of course, A. T. Mahan, for more general and continuous information, ideas and stimulation.

I should also like to take this opportunity of thanking my literary agent, Bruce Hunter, and my publishers, Allen Lane, for their part in encouraging and assisting all that follows; together with three friends, Correlli Barnett, Professor J. R. Jones and Mrs J. M. Taylor, who read through the entire manuscript, improving it immensely by their comments and eradicating many factual errors and 'infelicities of style'. For what remains I alone, of course, am responsible.

I am also very grateful to Mrs Muriel Utting, who typed the manuscript.

Finally, I should like to thank my wife, who has assisted in innumerable ways: in commenting upon passages, in eliminating spelling and stylistic slips, in compiling the bibliography and in providing information about British economic history. To her, and to our two sons, this book is dedicated.

PAUL M. KENNEDY

Norwich, October 1974

INTRODUCTION

The Elements of Sea Power

Here concludes the general discussion of the principal elements which affect, favourably or unfavourably, the growth of sea power in nations . . . The considerations and principles . . . belong to the unchangeable, or unchanging, order of things, remaining the same, in cause and effect, from age to age. They belong, as it were, to the Order of Nature, of whose stability so much is heard in our day: whereas tactics, using as its instruments the weapons made by man, shares in the change and progress of the race from generation to generation. From time to time the superstructure of tactics has to be altered or wholly torn down; but the old foundations of strategy so far remain, as though laid upon a rock.

A. T. Mahan, *The Influence of Sea Power upon History 1660–1783* (London, 1965 edn), p. 88.

It would be wise to begin a story such as this one with an exploration, however tentative and liable to later modification, of certain key phrases used frequently in the book and, in particular, of that elusive and emotive expression 'sea power'. Ever since Captain Mahan wrote his seminal books at the end of the last century, the term has become a commonplace in the language of naval men, politicians, strategists and historians: yet it remains difficult to define precisely in a few words, and even the writers who have attempted it have usually hastened to add many provisos and further comments in acknowledgement of the complexity of the topic. It is noticeable that Mahan himself did not seek to define what sea power is at the beginning of his studies, but preferred instead to show its nature by historical examples and commentary in order to prevent it remaining 'vague and unsubstantial'.[1]

Some years after Mahan, however, the English historian Sir Herbert Richmond attempted a description of sea power which may serve as our first working definition:

> Sea power is that form of national strength which enables its possessor to send his armies and commerce across those stretches of sea and ocean which lie between his country or the countries of his allies, and those territories to which he needs access in war; and to prevent his enemy from doing the same.[2]

The basically *military* part of his definition is readily comprehensible to students of history: from Rome's dominance of the Mediterranean waters in its struggle against Carthage to the Allied maritime superiority in the 1939–45 war which permitted successful amphibious operations in such disparate places as Normandy and Okinawa, one can perceive numerous examples of where a nation or group of nations has benefited enormously from this ability to project its military strength beyond the seas. Those who possess sea power, it is evident, have enjoyed a security from invasion across the oceans, a mobility and capacity to reach the enemy's shores, and a freedom to travel and trade across the seas. Such an advantageous position the naval strategists have termed 'command of the sea'.[3]

Command of the sea has never implied a total possession of oceanic waters: this is both physically impossible and strategically unnecessary. For the sea is not, like the land, of much use to man in itself. He cannot live on it, farm it, develop it, buy it or sell it. It is, instead, a medium through which he travels from one land position to another: or, in Mahan's classic description, it resembles 'a wide common, over which men may pass in all directions, but on which some well-worn paths show that controlling reasons have led them to choose certain lines of travel rather than others'.[4] If it is possible for a nation generally to preserve its traffic along these 'well-worn paths' and to deny this privilege to the enemy, then it would possess command of the sea: its trade would flourish, its links overseas would be maintained, and its troops would pass freely to desired destinations.

As soon as man had recognized the suitability of the sea as a medium through which to dispatch troops or to exchange wares, he turned his attention to constructing a weapon which would enable him to achieve and retain command of the sea – the ship of war. With a group of strongly armed, manœuvrable vessels which could drive the enemy before him, the means was at hand. Hence from the earliest days we have records of naval battles, as the combatants strove to secure the advantages of maritime predominance by destroying the enemy fleet or at least by forcing it to remain in harbour.[5] It was one of the basic tenets of the navalist orthodoxy, therefore, that in the war-fleet – later called the battle-fleet –

the kernel of sea power lay. Small-scale raiding operations or occasional attacks upon trading vessels, on the other hand, provided only a temporary and local superiority which would vanish as soon as the hostile battle-fleet arrived. A *guerre de course*, as Mahan pointed out, could not shake

> the possession of that overbearing power on the sea which drives the enemy's flag from it, or allows it to appear only as a fugitive; and which, by controlling the great common, closes the highways by which commerce moves to and from the enemy's shores.[6]

In this statement, which probably comes as close to a definition of sea power as Mahan ever attempted, the focus has shifted somewhat from the emphasis upon a nation's capacity to dispatch troops across the sea to an equal or even greater emphasis upon control of mercantile trade and routes. This difference may be explained crudely by the various stages in the development of sea power, which itself is bound to reflect more general advances in technological, economic and political development. During the first stage, when travel over any distance by water was still a novelty, the transfer of troops from one theatre to another in ships was the basic aim and definition of sea power: that Richmond, and Potter and Nimitz[7] could use it in the mid-twentieth century indicates that it has never lost that meaning. Nevertheless, the growth of western civilization led to more sophisticated aspects and aims of sea power by about the seventeenth century: trading by sea had become so widespread and developed that its furtherance and protection were recognized as being of great importance to the national good; technological advances in ship-construction, steering, navigation and gunnery led to the birth of the ship of the line – the progenitor of the modern battleship; exploration overseas, and the establishment of trading posts and colonies in America and Asia, witnessed an increasing proportion of Europe's wealth concentrated upon the sea; and as a consequence of all this nation states built and maintained standing navies.

This shift of emphasis from the short-term or tactical aim of transferring armies over water to the longer-term or grand-strategical aim of establishing permanent national strength – both in terms of regular trade and a standing war-fleet – at sea explains the variety of definitions of sea power that the reader is likely to encounter in treatises upon this subject. Indeed, certain writers of the so-called 'Blue Water' (i.e. extreme navalist) school of the late nineteenth century placed so much emphasis upon the establishment of command of the sea by the battle-fleet and the consequent damage to the enemy's commerce and war effort that they tended to allocate a very minor role to the transport of troops to overseas theatres:

the slow grinding pressures of constant blockade, it was argued, would usually be sufficient to bring an enemy to its knees. Linked in with this view was that dislike for continental warfare which was traditionally held to be more costly in British lives and money, more restrictive in Britain's operational freedom of action and, in a certain sense, 'unnatural'. Perhaps Bolingbroke best captured this isolationist attitude in his *Idea of a Patriot King* (1749) when he wrote: 'Like other amphibious animals we must come occasionally on shore: but the water is more properly our element, and in it . . . as we find our greatest security, so we exert our greatest force.'

As we shall see later, to argue thus was to adopt an exaggerated posture which ignored many basic aspects of the complex relationship between man's exploitation of land power and sea power; but it does at least illustrate the difficulty of formulating a definition of the latter solely in terms of the projection of military strength overseas. Julius Caesar or the Normans may have thought of it as such, but in the post-Renaissance world sea power has always been regarded as a more complex and far-reaching force, involving not only wartime invasion successes but also trade, colonies, economic policy and national wealth. When Halifax wrote in 1694 'Looke to your Moate. The first article of an Englishman's political creed must be, that he believeth in the sea', he was indicating that a stage had been reached where sea power had become a foremost part of the national philosophy. Little wonder, then, that all who have investigated this phenomenon have hesitated to give a brief and simple definition of sea power which is satisfying in all respects.

Moreover, if the control of sea communications through a powerful battle-fleet was for centuries regarded as the visible symbol and ultimate reality of maritime strength, it has also been recognized that that fleet's existence and effectiveness have themselves been dependent upon many other 'elements' of sea power. As E. B. Potter noted,

> The elements of sea power are by no means limited to combat craft, weapons, and trained personnel but include the shore establishment, well-sited bases, commercial shipping, and advantageous international alignments. The capacity of a nation to exercise sea power is based also upon the character and number of its population, the character of its government, the soundness of its economy, its industrial efficiency, the development of its internal communications, the quality and numbers of its harbours, the extent of its coastline, and the location of homeland, bases, and colonies with respect to sea communications.[8]

This is a lengthy list and a full analysis of all these elements is not possible here; but it is worth noting that this description, and virtually all other variants upon it that one encounters in books upon sea power, are based heavily upon Mahan's own conclusions in *The Influence of Sea Power upon History 1660–1783*. Nor was his own study new, in a strictly factual way, but it gained for its author world-wide renown because of the brilliant manner in which he had synthesized many hitherto disconnected notions into a coherent philosophy and shown that, whereas naval tactics and historical circumstances change, the underlying strategical considerations and principles 'belong to the unchangeable, or unchanging, order of things . . .'[9] Accordingly, if a nation heeded these lessons and possessed the necessary fundamental elements, it would be in a strong position to deploy its sea power successfully. Here Mahan was clearly seeking to do for the study of sea power what Clausewitz and Jomini had done for the study of land power, and his works reflect that nineteenth-century striving to discover 'laws' in society which later, less positivistic ages have rejected. Nevertheless, a brief résumé of Mahan's ideas would seem appropriate at this point.

The six principal conditions which had affected sea power Mahan listed as follows: (i) geographical position; (ii) physical conformation; (iii) extent of territory; (iv) number of population; (v) national character; and (vi) character and policy of governments.[10]

The first three, being essentially geographical, may be treated together. Mahan's reading of history taught him that a state which had neither to defend nor to extend itself by land was much more favourably placed to concentrate upon the growth of its sea power than one which was compelled to stay prepared against land neighbours; that a well-situated position, flanking important oceanic waterways, provided a further crucial advantage, as did good harbours and a seaboard which was not too great for a country's defence requirements and was not (like France's seaboard) divided; and that a sparse soil and climate was often an inducement to overseas endeavour, whereas the inhabitants of a richly endowed nation had less inclination to follow that course.

The other three elements may also be linked together, for one certainly flowed into the next so far as Mahan was concerned. By number of population he meant, not the total population, but the proportion 'following the sea', both in terms of those engaged in maritime commerce and those readily available to the navy. By the same token, national character referred to the general proclivity to exploit all these fruits which the sea offered – lucrative trade, steady employment, overseas colonies: a nation of enterprising traders and shopkeepers, ready and able to make a sufficient standing investment in maritime strength to protect its interests upon and across the oceans – this was Mahan's recipe for the successful development of sea power. Government also had a vital role to play: by fostering the country's naval and commercial potential in time of peace, and by the skilful exploitation of sea power in time of war, it could ensure that the prospects for victory – and thereby further enhancement of the country's position in the world – were bright.

Despite the somewhat questionable determinism in Mahan's analysis, most pronounced in the quasi-racialistic passage about 'national character', there is much in his work which can be accepted without question; indeed, a great deal of his treatment of the 'elements of sea power' appears to consist of truisms until it is recalled how little of what became commonplace to naval strategy was only made apparent by his writings. Nevertheless, although Mahan conceived of his underlying principles as being *generally* applicable, and although he became famous because his readership assumed that the lessons he drew from the past would be valid for the present and the future, it is worth making one basic comment at this early stage upon his entire philosophy; it was to a very great degree *inductive*, that is, it was drawn from an examination of a particular historical period and of a set of circumstances which he then presumed would be valid for the present and the future as well. Apart from brief references to naval struggles in classical times, he concentrated his major researches upon, and derived his conclusions from that series of campaigns fought between four or five west European states in the years between 1660 and 1815. Furthermore, like any other historian, he could free himself neither from the prevailing prejudices of his time nor from his background as a serving naval officer: to extol and demonstrate the wisdom of Britain's past naval policy, and to encourage the United States to emulate those successes, were motives never far from his mind.

In other words, there are in Mahan's writings certain underlying assumptions about sea power and the role of navies which he and his school took for granted but which we need *not*; and even if we did agree that his analysis is basically correct for the historical period which he examined, it may not necessarily follow that the same would always occur in a world in which immense technological, political and demographical changes were taking place at an ever-faster rate.

The first thing which Mahan and the navalists regarded as axiomatic was the superiority of the sea over the land as an 'influence' in world affairs. To do him credit, he never went so far as his more extreme followers; for instance, he did acknowledge that it would be erroneous to ignore factors other than the naval and he maintained that he had undertaken his study simply because he felt that the importance of sea power had been 'vastly underrated, if not practically lost sight of'.[11] But with statements such as the following it is not surprising that Mahan's works were largely responsible for a whole school of strategic thought being educated into accepting uncritically the idea that the sea had played *the* leading role in the advancement of civilization:

> Notwithstanding all the familiar and unfamiliar dangers of the sea, both travel and traffic by water have always been easier and cheaper than by land.
>
> . . . who can fail to see that the power which dwelt in that government [of England, during the Seven Years War], with a land narrow and poor in resources, sprang directly from the sea?
>
> The due use and control of the sea is but one link in the chain of exchange by which wealth accumulates; but it is the central link, which lays under contribution other nations for the benefit of the one holding it, and which, history seems to assert, most surely of all gathers riches.[12]

In retrospect, it is difficult to comprehend how the superiority of sea power implied in Mahan's writings can be justified by any study of the broader sweep of history; neither the Egyptian, Greek, Roman, Aztec, Chinese, Zulu, Hun, Ottoman or Holy Roman empires, to give but the more obvious examples, derived their strength basically from the sea, nor is this omission on their part at all to be wondered at. Because of the physical nature of the two elements, land and sea, by far the greater part of man's activity has been concentrated upon the former: the simple fact that most men have their feet on dry ground rather than on the heaving deck of a ship means that the land has always been more important than the sea in the development of civilization. What Mahan chose to examine was only a certain period of history – essentially, between the sixteenth and early nineteenth centuries – and a certain group of states – Spain, the Netherlands, France and especially England – which had developed colonial and maritime empires in those years. That this phenomenon occurred at such a time and in such a region was due to a concatenation of circumstances which require further examination. That is to say, leaving aside for investigation at appropriate points in this book the question of whether sea power ever played so decisive a part in the various wars as that maintained by Mahan and his followers, it is of the utmost importance to keep in mind the basic fact that they were writing about an era during which commerce and conflict at sea occupied a disproportionately large role in world affairs. Thus it would be prudent to note at the outset the historical and geographical *specificity*, and therefore to query the universality, of many of Mahan's assumptions, particularly the frequent deprecation of the role of land power by the navalist school of strategy.

Similar reservations are called for with regard to Mahan's repeated emphasis upon the importance of commerce, colonies and shipping, of which the following extract is a classic example:

> In these three things – production, with the necessity of exchanging products, shipping, whereby the exchange is carried on, and colonies, which facilitate and enlarge the operations of shipping and tend to promote it by multiplying points of safety – is to be found the key to much of history, as of the policy of nations bordering upon the sea.[13]

Here again, general principles would appear to have been drawn from a specific set of circumstances, and what applied to certain European states between 1550 and 1815 was not necessarily true of what had happened elsewhere or at another time. Colonial trade, for example, had not always been so profitable and important. Nor is it true that population and extent of territory, two of Mahan's basic elements, should be measured solely or even primarily in terms of available sailors or the length of coastline: each aspect had a far larger geopolitical contribution to make a nation's strength, as the Soviet Union today illustrates. Thirdly, while Mahan did mention 'production', he paid little real attention to this central economic factor, concentrating instead upon trade and merchants and especially shipping to such an extent that he saw them as being the sole effective foundations for naval power. That some states have possessed strong navies without a large merchant fleet, while others had the latter without the former, was ignored by him. If we are searching for universal elements of sea power in the economic sphere, an alternative and wider interpretation from a modern critic appears more suitable:

> There is perhaps a surer economic base for sea power than the mercurial fortunes of a single mode of transportation; namely the vitality of national economic life. If we examine more closely the rise and fall of the maritime states, one lesson clearly emerges: dominant sea power resides not with the nation which launches the largest merchant fleet *per se*, but with the state that buttresses the sea-faring prosperity with balanced economic growth.[14]

What all the above observations are suggesting is that the reader should not uncritically accept as gospel Mahan's exposition of the workings of sea power. As Professor Reynolds reminds us, 'Mahan is and should be regarded as a major and mortal historical figure, a man whose ideas were subject to the usual limitations of human activity.'[15] Nevertheless, it is proper that any survey of British naval history should commence with him, for his contribution to the subject was unique and his influence has been unparalleled; and the very fact that this present study will take issue with his conclusions at many points should be regarded less as a denigration than as a reflection of his importance. Mahan is, and will always remain, the point of reference and departure for any work upon 'sea power'.

Having briefly explored that crucial concept, and to a certain extent suggested modifications to any approach to its usage, we now need to explain the phrase 'naval mastery' with which this book has been titled. Sea power appears in practice to lack quantification: almost any state can claim to have or have had a certain amount of sea power. It can also exist at almost any level: a Mediterranean power of classical times, a Chinese pirate chief, or a Latin American state can be found to have possessed command of the sea for a period in their local area. By the use of the term 'naval mastery', however, there is meant here something stronger, more exclusive and wider-ranging; namely a situation in which a country has so developed its maritime strength that it is superior to any rival power, and that its predominance is or could be exerted far outside its home waters, with the result that it is extremely difficult for other, lesser states to undertake maritime operations or trade without at least its tacit consent. It does *not* necessarily imply a superiority over all other navies combined, nor does it mean that this country could not temporarily lose local command of the sea; but it does assume the possession of an overall maritime power such that small-scale defeats overseas would soon be reversed by the dispatch of naval forces sufficient to eradicate the enemy's challenge. Generally speaking, naval mastery is also taken to imply that the nation achieving it will usually be very favourably endowed with many fleet bases, a large merchant marine, considerable national wealth, etc., all of which indicates influence at a global rather than at a purely regional level. All these definitions are suggesting a measure of maritime supremacy which only a few nations have ever achieved and which has marked them off from lesser rivals. Great Britain possessed such a naval mastery in 1815, and for a period before and after that significant date; but the stages of its growth towards, and then decline from, that era of predominance occupied a far larger portion of history. Even today she possesses an amount of sea power, although she has ceded her naval mastery. For this reason, therefore, it has been necessary to extend the scope of this survey over a period of approximately four hundred years. We shall learn as much about Britain's naval mastery by studying the reasons for her rise to, and decline from, that position as we shall by concentrating solely upon the years of her primacy.

PART ONE

Rise

Thus sea power in . . . its classic age was a highly complex factor, defensive as well as offensive; economic or, more specifically, financial as much as military; achieving its greatest effects not so much by its own intrinsic strength as by its skilful exploitation of the weaknesses of its opponents. By its aid first the Portuguese, then the Dutch, and finally the British were able to wield an influence out of all proportion to their size, resources, and man power. Thanks to its unique key position Great Britain was able not merely to control the flow of overseas treasure but to manipulate on the continent of Europe the balance of half a dozen powers, each intrinsically superior to her in every other respect.

H. Rosinski,
'The Role of Sea Power in Global Warfare of the Future',
Brassey's Naval Annual (1947), p. 105.

CHAPTER ONE

The Early Years of English Sea Power (to 1603)

It was in the Elizabethan age . . . that England first assumed its modern character, and this means . . . that then first it began to direct its energies to the sea and to the New World. At this point then we mark the beginnings of the expansion, the first symptom of the rise of Greater Britain.

J. R. Seeley,
The Expansion of England (London, 1884), pp. 107–8

Even before the first stages of the development of English sea power can be traced, it is necessary to understand the broader historical and geographical circumstances in which that growth could flourish. Mankind has been engaged in various battles at sea since classical times; the exchange of wares across the waters was also a commonplace; and it could be argued that the Vikings and the Normans had already provided good examples of peoples who had exploited their maritime predominance to project their national strength overseas. Nevertheless, there are also very good reasons for considering the condition of western Europe in the fifteenth and sixteenth centuries as providing the real starting-point for our examination. At the close of the Middle Ages the prospects for this region being able to play a leading role in world affairs were not obvious. It possessed a certain coherent culture, established forms of government, trading networks, and a developed system of thought; but so too did many other regions of the globe. Economically there was little growth and it had suffered from widespread plagues, civil disorders and a general technological backwardness. Politically and militarily it was under pressure from the Ottoman Turks, both in eastern Europe and in the

Mediterranean, where Turkish land and sea power had expanded along the North African coast and threatened the Iberian and Italian peninsulas.

Against this could be set some newer and more promising developments. The population of Europe was rising and, as a consequence, so was its trade; art, thought and science were beginning to flourish in a remarkable way in the Italian states; and the secular national monarchies were emerging.[1] Of even greater importance, at least in terms of sea power and the growth of European influence in the world, were certain quite crucial advances in naval shipbuilding, navigation and weaponry. The fifteenth century, we learn, 'was a period of very rapid change and development in the design of European sea-going ships', without which the later long oceanic voyages would have been inconceivable:[2] important changes in the construction and design of the hull, masts and rigging, rudders and steering all occurred at this time and, as the size of vessels increased, so also did their reliability and complexity. Equally significant were the advances in navigational techniques, with the advent of what Professor Needham has termed the era of 'mathematical navigation'.[3] The quadrant, astrolabe, cross-staff and new tables for astronomical calculation, together with the magnetic compass, pilot-books and marine charts, not only enabled sailors to steer more accurately when land was in sight but also – and this was the great step forward – provided the navigational means for undertaking long oceanic voyages with at least some idea of relative land positions. As the frontiers of knowledge advanced, so the maps of the world assumed an increasing mathematical exactitude.[4]

Yet these technical breakthroughs only explain how the early European explorers, chiefly from Portugal and Spain, were able to travel across the world and to return again to their homelands; they do not explain why this movement occurred, nor how they, of all the civilizations on the globe, managed successfully to carve out overseas empires, defeating formidable rivals in the process. The Chinese had much earlier developed many of the above shipbuilding and navigational techniques (indeed, their vessels were often far larger); they traded frequently with Malacca and the East Indies, then into the Indian Ocean and across to Africa and Arabia; and only a decade or two before Henry the Navigator dispatched ship after ship down the African coastline, Cheng Ho, Imperial Palace Eunuch, was supervising a whole series of overseas expeditions on behalf of the Chinese Emperor.[5] In the Mediterranean, too, the Ottoman Turks had built up a formidable force of galleys which dominated that sea, and the Arabic world had traditionally been much more advanced than medieval Europe in the study of mathematics, astronomy and cartography. In retrospect, therefore, it was not inevitable that the small sailing expeditions which set forth from time to time from the Iberian peninsula should have been the advance guard of a movement which transformed world politics. Two other factors played a vital role: western European princes and merchants had the will to expand, and they had developed a superior means with which to crush any opposition. These tipped the scales decisively.

The motives for European expansion are not difficult to discover: they were a mixture of politics, economics and religious fervour.[6] Engaged in bitter if spasmodic dispute with the Turks, which the fall of Constantinople in 1453 had served to emphasize, the European powers were anxious to undermine their enemy's challenge. That Portugal and Castile, which took a leading part in this counter-attack through their respective policies in Ceuta and Granada, were also to the fore in the naval expansion was not just a simple coincidence. A sea link around Africa with the Asiatic world, thereby outflanking the Turks, could produce political and strategical successes which Christendom badly needed. At the same time it would hit at the monopoly of the spice and silk trade with Asia which the Turks (and their Venetian middlemen) operated, and thus bring rich profits to the monarchs, nobles and merchants who backed these oceanic enterprises. Indeed, it is hard to see how the maritime expansion would have continued without the support of those who quickly lost their original scepticism and perceived the economic benefits which would accrue from such developments; already naval power and commercial strength were being closely linked. Finally, the crusading zeal of Catholic Europe against the infidel Turks, which the fervour of the Counter-Reformation increased, provided religious and ideological reasons for waging a campaign against political and commercial rivals with uncompromising determination and ferocity. Neither the Portuguese and Dutch, in seeking to smash Ottoman influence and naval strength in the Indian Ocean, nor the Spaniards, in their endeavours in the New World, bothered to discriminate between Moslims and other creeds. Unlike the Chinese, who appear to have engaged in peaceful trade and to have respected indigenous religions abroad, the Europeans came to proselytize, to loot and to conquer.[7]

Europe's aggressive expansionism depended for its success, however, upon that second factor: superior naval armaments. In this sphere also Europeans, Turks and Chinese had kept roughly abreast until the fifteenth century. For example, each employed primitive iron-cast guns on land and later placed them on board ship; and each still regarded sea warfare as an extension of the practice of fighting on land. Hence the prevalent notion of closing with or ramming an enemy vessel, then storming over the sides and attempting to seize the 'castles' fore and aft.

Hence, too, the popularity of the galleys (especially in enclosed seas) and the construction of those Portuguese and Spanish carracks with their towering castles – floating fortresses, in fact. The real transformation was only rendered by the development in Europe of guns cast of alloys like gun-metal or brass, which gave a force equal to the monster iron siege guns but were of greater reliability and smaller size. Mounted on board ship, such armaments could cripple or even perhaps sink an enemy vessel, thereby dispensing with the need for the assailant to board it; such guns, in other words, were 'ship-killers' rather than 'men-killers', and they possessed a far greater range. Yet since even they required more space and greater stability than the castles could provide, they were gradually sited amidships to fire through port-holes cut into the side.

The final consequence of these changes – and the above description is a very crude summary of what was a lengthy and uneven development – was the decision to construct sailing ships specifically for fighting purposes, since the positioning amidships of large guns, their ammunition and crews took away goods-storage space.[8] Thus was born the galleon, a fighting ship which was essentially the same as the line-of-battleship in Nelson's day: a vessel which had not only powerful armaments but also the sleek lines and sail to take advantage of the wind and the manœuvrability to stand off the enemy's fleet until it had been crippled by repeated broadsides. Against such vessels both the slow, high-charged carracks and the oar-propelled, low-beamed galleys, neither of which could match this combination of firepower and speed, were shown to be all too vulnerable. Thus it took only a few of da Gama's leading ships to repulse with ease the massed Arab dhows off the Malabar coast in 1501, in what may have been the first 'stand-off' fight at sea.[9] Furthermore, as this instance reveals, the newer sailing ship had the power, the endurance, the adaptability and the seaworthiness to operate in all waters and was not – like the galley – restricted in its operational scope.

This latter fact had immense consequences for Europe's position in the world, for that superiority in naval technology which could crush the Turks could also be applied to overwhelm any other war-fleet throughout the globe. Possession by Europe of this advanced maritime power rendered all areas bordering the sea virtually helpless against its expansionism; and as the sixteenth century unfolded and the political, economic and religious rivalries of the European powers increased in bitterness and provoked the first naval arms races, the technological gap between Europe and the rest of the world widened still further. 'God, the gun and the sailing ship', as one scholar pithily noted, 'became the three pillars of western civilization'.[10] At the same time, those very national rivalries, together with the growing specialization in the construction of the fighting-ship, led to the formation of standing navies. In peacetime many of these vessels were of course laid up, but the creation of such fleets implied a recognition that national strength at sea was of lasting importance. Similarly, the significance of the sea as a means of communication was vastly enhanced by the great wealth and prestige which successful overseas expeditions brought to their patrons. And, at a more general level, the development of overseas trade and colonization contributed heavily to that 'shift' of the European centre of gravity, both economically and politically, from the Mediterranean world to the Atlantic coastline.[11] It was this appreciation of the manifold benefits accruing from maritime enterprise which led to the development of the doctrine of sea power which saw naval might and commercial advantage inextricably linked together.

The above may be summarized as follows: in the fifteenth and sixteenth centuries Europe made certain spectacular 'breakthroughs' in the fields of ship-construction and navigation which enabled its sailors to undertake long-distance oceanic voyages; at the same time advances in gunnery and the further development of the specialist fighting vessel provided the means wherewith to overwhelm the opposition of other races; while a mixture of political, prestige, religious and economic motives, particularly the latter, gave the spur to this overseas expansion. Once the Iberian fleets had demonstrated the ease of conquest over others and the financial benefits to be gained, the race was on, with Dutch, French and English adventurers joining in what soon became a scramble for loot, trading links and political advantage, which in turn necessitated the creation of more advanced warships and regular navies and led to a healthy appreciation of the gains from sea power. Through this self-generated interaction of technological innovation, economic gain and striving to achieve national power at sea, the European era of world domination had begun.

That Europe's rise to this position was based chiefly upon sea power has been obvious to all who have studied the movement. The geo-politician Sir Halford Mackinder described it thus:

> The revolution commenced by the great mariners of the Columbian generation endowed Christendom with the widest possible mobility of power, short of winged mobility . . . The broad political effect was to reverse the relations of Europe and Asia, for whereas in the Middle Ages Europe was caged between an impassable desert to south, an unknown ocean to west, and icy or forested wastes to north and north-east, and in the east and south-east was constantly threatened by the superior mobility of the horsemen and camelmen, she now emerged

> upon the world, multiplying more than thirty-fold the sea surface and coastal lands to which she had access, and wrapping her influence round the Euro-Asiatic land-power which had hitherto threatened her very existence.[12]

And what Mackinder termed 'the Columbian era' the Asian historian K. M. Panikkar differed only by calling 'the Vasco da Gama epoch', both men fundamentally agreeing that these early Iberian-based maritime ventures signified a transformation of world affairs and the beginnings of four centuries of 'authority based on the control of the seas'.[13] The fall of Constantinople may have closed Europe's gateways to the East, noted H. A. L. Fisher, but it was more than compensated for by that Portuguese expansion 'which has spread European domination through the planet and altered the economic weights and balances of the world'.[14]

But if the changes wrought by the advent of the Columbian era were to be immense, we should be careful not to exaggerate the speed with which they occurred. The trade between Venice, the Levant and Asia continued to flourish throughout the sixteenth century and to offer severe competition to the Portuguese; only in the seventeenth century was it really eclipsed.[15] And there were other reasons, apart from the oceanic discoveries and colonization, why the west European states were rising economically as the Italian city-states declined.[16] In the same way the galley remained the key fighting ship for many powers, especially in inland waters. Lepanto was mainly a battle between two fleets of galleys, which while no doubt explaining why it was less significant in naval terms than the Portuguese-Arab clashes in the Indian Ocean, does confirm that it was not until the second half of the sixteenth century that the superiority of the galleon was established.

Most important of all, it would be unwise of the historian to forget that Europe's relative advantage lay solely upon the seas; on land the balance was still tilted against her, as the steady encroachment of Turkish armies upon eastern Europe during the 'age of reconnaissance' revealed. To most European statesmen the loss of Hungary was of far greater import than the establishment of factories in the Orient, and the threat to Vienna more significant than their own challenges at Aden, Goa and Malacca; only governments bordering the Atlantic could, like their later historians, ignore this fact. And even when the western powers came to take for granted their hold over other peoples, they recognized that such domination was usually limited to the range of a warship's guns: until the invention of mobile field artillery, or even of the machine-gun, their control over foreign land was far less secure than their mastery at sea, the Spanish possessions in Latin America being the exception rather than the rule. Normally the peoples of Asia, Africa and America were immune from western influence only a few miles from the sea.

Despite these caveats, the age of western sea power had begun, trade and colonization overseas were increasing rapidly, existing European rivalries were being 'exported' to the tropics, and a growing number of states came to recognize the need to create and to maintain larger standing navies. One of these states was England, which, although smaller, far less populous and at first more backward in economic and oceanic enterprise than many of its rivals, was eventually to reap the full fruits of this Columbian revolution in world affairs.

The handicaps to England's naval development mentioned above were outweighed by a long list of more advantageous factors: indeed, it is clear that Mahan had England very much in mind when he drew up his survey of the 'general elements' favourable to sea power. Geographically she benefited immensely in being separated by the sea from her more powerful European rivals. Not only did this mean that she did not need to devote a very heavy proportion of her resources and manpower to the maintenance of a large standing army, but it also ensured that the English government's first response in times of international tension was to see that the navy was at least strong enough to ward off an invasion. This blessed position – ascribed by so many Englishmen to a divine partiality towards their race – no other European power enjoyed. The vast Empire of the Habsburgs was so disparate and faced so many continental challenges (including that of the Turks) that sea power was always regarded as being of secondary importance. Similarly, France, threatened on three sides by this Habsburg conglomeration, could not afford to indulge in oceanic activity if it was at the expense of her national security. Even the Dutch, superior though they were to the English in overseas commerce and colonization in the later sixteenth century, knew that if they lost the land struggle against the crack Spanish troops to the south they would lose everything. All that England had to fear in this respect was a challenge from the Celtic flanks which could divert her attention and resources to the north and to the west, which goes a long way to explain the great Elizabethan concern with Scotland and Ireland, and the corresponding efforts of France and Spain respectively to gain influence there. These could only be spasmodic threats if England remained strong at sea, however, and they became less likely after the conquest of Ireland and the union of the English and Scottish crowns.[17]

Other natural advantages included a wealth of good harbours, particularly along the southern English coast; flourishing coastal trades and rich off-shore fishing grounds, which encouraged seamanship generally; large sources of iron ore in the Weald, which provided the Tudors with a regular supply of good guns;[18] and wood for the construction of ships' hulls, although England never possessed the planking and spars and hemp for the masts and rigging, which made her dependent upon Baltic and other overseas supplies for almost the entire age of sail.[19] Finally, her position off the north-west coast of the continent offered her a uniquely favourable opportunity to take advantage of that shift in the European commercial and political balance which took place between the fifteenth and seventeenth centuries. For, while the Oriental trade did not overnight change from the Levant route to the Cape one, the development of Atlantic commerce was also boosted by the discovery of precious metals in the New World; and this ever-expanding flow of bullion, spices and exotic wares into the Iberian peninsula, whence it was transferred to Antwerp, stimulated the economies of all the Atlantic nations and provoked the interest of governments and private adventurers alike. Yet if the English, through their insularity, were best placed to devote their attention to the outside world, they were also in a position to intercept and frustrate the endeavours of others, be it the commercial challenge of the Hanse and Dutch merchants, or the military challenge of Spain, which relied heavily upon the sea for its link with the Low Countries. Apart from the endemic piracy for which the English were justly famous at this time, there was no move by the cautious Tudor monarchs to monopolize the growing Atlantic trade – that would have been far outside their resources and too risky a policy; but it was true that in the long term England was extremely well placed to reap the benefits of the economic changes that were transforming Europe.

All these natural advantages would have been worthless, however, had there been no disposition by the English people to exploit them. In fact, even in medieval times there had been a healthy appreciation of the role the sea could play in the national life. Not only could it be the medium through which invaders came, this alarming prospect provoking such defensive measures as the creation of naval forces by the Cinque Ports with ultimate responsibility to the monarch, but it was also the means by which the possessions in France were linked to the English throne. Furthermore, by the later Middle Ages, overseas trade, especially in wool, cloth and wine, was making England part of a wider economy and leading to the growth of such ports as Bristol and London, the development of a shipbuilding and shipping industry, and the steady increase in commercial links with the Low Countries, France, the Iberian peninsula and the Baltic. The growth of the Icelandic fishing trade was another stimulus, and especially important in providing experience of deep-sea voyages. No doubt it all seemed puny in 1500 by comparison with the Hansards' domination of the Baltic and North Sea and Venice's hold upon the Mediterranean, and even a century later it was overshadowed by the Dutch; yet in absolute terms the rise in English overseas trade was impressive. Her population expanded rapidly in this period – from about two and a quarter million in 1475 to about five million in 1640 – but it seems clear that the numbers 'following the sea', to use Mahan's phrase, grew even faster.[20]

More important still were the political attitudes which accompanied this growth. Nationalism and economic advantage have usually gone hand-in-hand, and England here provided no exception to the general rule. Even as early as the fourteenth century, merchants were urging upon, and receiving from, the Crown a discrimination in favour of native trades and against foreigners. Navigation Acts in various and ever-strengthened forms were passed by a Parliament where business interests were already of some influence, and the Hundred Years War did much to increase the chauvinism of the *parvenu* English traders against the more established foreigners whose place they wished to take over; the expulsion of the Hanseatic League from the London Steelyard by Elizabeth was neither the first nor the last of these measures. English commercial policy, it has been noted,

> carried that tinge of bellicosity which was to characterize it for centuries until the sweet reasonableness of free trade doctrines came to pervade it in the nineteenth century. International commerce was conceived of as a kind of battleground on which nations contended with one another for possession of the precious metals and for profitable employment for their merchants.[21]

It should come as no great surprise, therefore, to learn that much of the driving force behind English overseas expansion was provided by economic desires. Thus, while the early oceanic ventures in Tudor times were very desultory, because they lacked the backing of London's merchants, who remained tied to the cloth trade (and were therefore pro-Spanish), matters changed with the 1551 cloth slump, which was followed a year later by the founding by aristocrats and traders of a company to open up a north-east passage. Indeed, the uncertainties of the traditionally dominant commerce to the Low Countries were connected to a remarkable degree with the rising awareness in England of the profits that were to be made from getting into the trade in Oriental spices, American bullion and African slaves. The consequence was the founding of a whole host of chartered companies – the Turkey Company, the Venice Company, the Levant Company, the revived Eastland Company, the Muscovy Company, the Cathay Company and the East India Company – to supplement the older Merchant Adventurers; together with a variety of private expeditions, such as those of Hawkins to West Africa, all of which switched the emphasis away from the cross-Channel routes.[22] The growth of these companies in its turn augmented England's sea power, not merely by strengthening the economy but also in a more practical manner; for the large, fast and well-armed ships built, for instance, for the Levant Company to beat off Mediterranean corsairs became the real 'Royal Naval Reserve' during the Armada campaign.[23]

What is possibly of greater significance was the support which these mercantile ventures attracted from the aristocracy and the crown, with, in the latter case, Henry VII claiming in advance one fifth of any of the John Cabot's profits and Elizabeth often providing vessels for, or buying shares in, speculative maritime voyages. Modifications seem necessary to Marx and Engels's famous assertion that

> The discovery of America, the rounding of the Cape, opened up fresh ground for the rising bourgeoisie. The East-Indian and Chinese markets, the colonization of America, trade with the colonies, the increase in the means of exchange and in commodities generally, gave to commerce, to navigation, to industry, an impulse never before known, and thereby to the revolutionary element in the tottering feudal society, a rapid development.[24]

In fact, it would be truer to say that, under the Tudors at least, the monarch and older élites joined forces with the middle classes in the pursuit of overseas benefits, which satisfied the merchants' wish for profit and the government's hunger for bullion. This fusion of the desires of various social groupings might well have been 'a bellicose alliance of revengeful traders and rapacious gentry'[25] but it did provide a sense of national identity useful in a turbulent age; or, as Professor Rabb put it, the gentry's 'participation in commerce revealed a cohesiveness and flexibility in the upper levels of England's social structure that was to have a profound effect on the country's history' and to contribute to 'the rise of England to dominance among the European nations overseas'.[26] The vehicle for this 'alliance' was the joint-stock company, into which the landed gentry could place their money without needing to run it.

What is also apparent is that these ventures attracted a large number of M.P.s, particularly those coming up to Westminster for the first time; so that even the representatives of 'local' interests were drawn into support for this London-based agitation for national expansion overseas. Indeed, the steady increase in the Commons' interest in a foreign and colonial policy which reflected the country's strategical, economic and religious aims indicated how much expansionism was coming to be regarded as of real national importance. No doubt this internal consensus broke down under the early Stuarts, but it had existed for a lengthier period previously and it emerged very much strengthened by the end of the seventeenth century, when a combination of aristocrats and merchants on the one hand, and of national interest and private economic interest on the other, reflected a pattern which had been established so successfully under the Tudors. Such interlocking of interests was to ensure that the condition of the navy was, at least in theory and often in practice, more highly regarded by government, Commons and taxpayers than was the case in most continental countries.

To this economic motive was added that of religion, a fiery fuel in Counter-Reformation times, which makes it impossible to ascribe solely commercial reasons to the aggressive practical methods of the Elizabethans. Drake, for example, always had Foxe's *Book of Martyrs* as well as navigational aids on his voyages. Hakluyt, in his *Principal Voyages*, urged upon Cecil proposals whereby Elizabeth could 'increase her dominion, enrich her coffers, and reduce many Pagans to the faithful Christ', this mixture of religious and earthly motives seeming in no way incongruous to contemporaries.[27] Thus, to seize a Spanish treasure-ship was not only to become rich overnight, it was also to strike a blow against what Raleigh termed the 'ambitious and bloody pretences' of Madrid, which sought to 'devour all nations' and to subject them to the Catholic religion.[28] In addition, as Dr Andrews has pointed out, expansionism 'was one outlet for the mounting population pressure of those decades, and it may well be that this multiplication of men combined with unemployment and poverty to produce the rising tide of sea-violence which developed in the disturbed middle years of the century and reached its culmination in the last decade, when economic and social stresses were at their most severe'.[29] Directing the force of popular discontents against the foreigner was ever a useful manipulative device of governments under pressure; but the consequence was that the first impressions the Elizabethan 'sea-dogs' made upon foreigners were hardly favourable and they quickly gained an unenviable reputation for their brutality, greed and willingness to rob anyone.

Finally, although it is always difficult for an historian to write of something as vague as a national 'character' or 'mood', there was a certain undefinable element in English society at this time which is common to countries in a period of growth: a self-confidence and exuberance about the future, a bustle of activity in all walks of life, a conviction of a glowing national destiny and of being on the right side of History.[30] The flowering of English literature under Elizabeth in some ways reflects this mood, but it had many more practical manifestations. In the art of colonization, for example, the English settlers appear, at least after their early failures, to have possessed the correct combination of the qualities of initiative, endurance and will. In the development of their textile industry, in drapery, in ordnance, in naval construction, Professor Cipolla has argued, the English

> did not show much originality but an exceptional capacity for picking up profitable ideas, perfecting others' innovations, adapting their tools and their skills to new situations. In all fields they exhibited a feeling for practicality that explained itself in products which were handy to use and cheaper to produce. Their attitude and success remind us of the attitude and success of the Japanese in our own times.[31]

With the motives for overseas expansion not lacking, and with the political nation peculiarly receptive to new ideas and flexible enough to adjust to new forces in Europe's development, the growth of England's maritime strength was accorded a high priority by most Tudor governments. In the early fifteenth century the famous poem, *The Libel of English Policy*, had already revealed a strong awareness of the importance of the sea, with its advice that 'the true process of English policy is this . . . Cherish merchandise, keep the Admiralty, that we be masters of the Narrow Sea.'[32] Henry VII, by encouraging commerce and exploration, building a royal dockyard at Portsmouth and beginning another at Greenwich, and constructing first-class fighting ships, clearly revealed his general support for such nostrums, but it was left to his son, with his far greater concern for European power politics, to give the 'royal' navy its real beginnings. At Henry VIII's death in 1547 it consisted of fifty-three vessels and the king himself had played a major role in the development of the warship type through such vessels as the re-built *Great Harry*, with its lower lines and centrally-placed armaments. At the same time, he gave the navy an institutional permanence by the creation of a Navy Board with responsibility for the administration of the ships and dockyards. With some justice, Roskill calls him the 'founder of the Battle Fleet'.[33] The temporary decline under Edward VI and Mary was countered by the influence of Hawkins, who carried Henry's construction work to its logical conclusion, rebuilding older vessels to the latest galleon design and producing the superb new *Revenge* class. The nation had every reason to be grateful for his elimination of administrative inefficiency and corruption, and seamen to be grateful for these virtually unsinkable vessels, and also for his contribution to the development of the battle-fleet itself:

> The greater part of the Queen's navy was transformed from a short-range, Narrow Seas, almost a coastal-defence, force into a high-seas fleet capable of operating at long range as an ocean-going force.[34]

This transformation of the navy was effected just in time to meet the political changes in Europe and the increasing threat from Spain. It laid the basis for what has been almost universally regarded as a golden age of English naval enterprise, the high points of which were that series of great campaigns and expeditions led by Drake, Hawkins, Raleigh, Essex and others, the memorable defeat of the Armada, the valiant struggle of Grenville against overwhelming odds, the many exploratory voyages into all the oceans of the globe, the attempts to found colonies in the New World, and the compilations of Hakluyt. Since all this remains a staple part of the Tudor history courses taught in schools in Britain and throughout the Commonwealth even today, a repetition of the details need not concern us here.[35]

For this reason, alone, however, it is necessary to apply certain correctives to the traditional picture and to remind ourselves of the still limited nature of England's maritime development at this time. For the fact is that the oceanic aspect was only incidental to the great mass of the population and even to the government, which always had to take into consideration the much more important continental connections. Henry VII anticipated no revolutionary changes in England's position as a consequence of Cabot's voyages or of his own encouragement of foreign trade; both were part of his policy of steady economic consolidation, and under no circumstances did he wish to disturb relations with other European powers. His son, it is true, built up the first Royal Navy – but this was a response to the threat posed by France and no developed strategy of sea power existed in his time. Of at least equal importance seems to have been the post-1525 recognition by Henry VIII and Wolsey of the need to preserve an equilibrium between the much more powerful states of France and Spain. As Pirenne notes with approval,

> The continental policy of England, thenceforth, was fixed. It was to be pacific, mediating, favourable to a balance which should prevent any power from having a hegemony on the continent or controlling the Channel coasts. The naval security of England and the balance of

> power in Europe were the two great political principles which appeared in the reign of Henry VIII and which, pursued unwaveringly, were to create the greatness of England.[36]

Even this extract may be thought to anticipate a national strategy which was only really executed at a later date, but it does at least reveal that basic underlying connection between England's continental and naval policies, and it does acknowledge that the maritime policy of the early Tudors was concentrated upon preserving supremacy in the Channel and not upon attacking foreign convoys or challenging the colonial claims of the Iberian powers.[37]

The same can be said for the age of Elizabeth, but it is precisely because of the exploits of Drake and others that a great deal of contemporary and later attention was given to the overseas world and the grim European realities facing the Queen were obscured: it is the circumnavigation of the globe, or the Cadiz raid, rather than Elizabeth's continental diplomacy or the Netherlands campaigning, which occupy the prominent places in our national historiography. Nevertheless, Elizabeth's admirals (and their historians in the nineteenth and twentieth centuries, who did not perceive that this war was essentially defensive, not offensive) constantly criticized the Queen for failing to take full advantage of the opportunities offered her through sea power. If Her Majesty had listened to her naval advisers and not 'did all by halves and by petty invasions' which taught Spain how to defend itself, Raleigh complained, they would have been able to beat 'that great empire in pieces'.[38] Hawkins also fretted at her indecision, her anxiety about the Netherlands campaign and her unwillingness to give adequate and lasting support to his strategy of cutting the Atlantic treasure routes to Spain: 'if we might once strike them', he wrote, 'our peace were made with honour, safety and profit'.[39] As he saw it, the growth of overseas trade (particularly bullion) made economic pressure through a naval blockade of real import for the first time. Elizabeth had been criticized, too, for the failure of Drake's expedition of 1589; for not seizing bases abroad, especially the Azores; for being blind to the fact that it was the enemy's war-fleet which was the primary target, if command of the sea was to be achieved; and, of course, for her obsession with land warfare. As Richmond put it caustically,

> She chose to make her principal efforts where her enemy was strongest – on land – and, in the years from 1585 to 1603 she expended a sum of 4½ millions upon land campaigns which yielded no offensive dividend while spending approximately one million only upon the sea forces which were capable of severing Spain's life-line.[40]

What these complaints of the Queen's admirals illustrate, of course, is the 'navalist' or 'Blue Water' school of strategic thought, which was apparently also urged upon Henry VIII as early as 1511 by his councillors:

> Let us in God's name leave off our attempts against the *terra firma*. The natural situation of islands seems not to consort with conquests of that kind. England alone is a just Empire. Or, when we would enlarge ourselves, let it be that way we can, and to which it seems the eternal Providence hath destined us, which is by the sea.[41]

It is astonishing in retrospect to see how soon after the distractions of the Wars of the Roses the English came to value the navalist code of maritime supremacy, overseas expansion and isolation from Europe; indeed, the philosophy was there before the means to execute it. Nevertheless, the strictures of this school of thought upon Elizabeth were unfair and it is to the credit of recent scholars such as Professors Wernham and Mattingly that her reputation has been retrieved by reminding us that the issues facing the Queen were never as clear-cut as her admirals imagined.[42]

In the first place, Elizabeth had no inclination to break the Spanish Empire 'in pieces' – at least, not if by doing so it gave the upper hand to traditional rivals, the French, who had just humiliated England with the seizure of Calais in 1558. This disaster did not, as later historians imagined, imply England's detachment from the continent and corresponding turn to the outside world; it simply meant that the French were now uncomfortably close. Only the civil war in France and the growing Anglo-Spanish enmity forced a reassessment of the relative threats. Secondly – and of transcendent importance to the whole history of British strategy – the Queen could perceive, if Hawkins and his peers could not, the true relationship between the continental and maritime-imperial factors: that, if they abandoned their allies, turned their backs upon western Europe and allowed it to be dominated by one hostile power, then their small island would be unable to build and man a fleet sufficient to hold off in the future the accumulated strength of such an enemy. For this reason she held steadfast in her support of the Dutch, despite the many trials, costs and risks this involved, and by her defeat of Philip II's aims she entitled herself to the praise of Protestant Europe; at the same time, she had helped to preserve the European balance, putting into practice the earlier ideas of Wolsey.[43]

Thus Elizabeth always had a response to those who, like Bacon, argued that 'He that commands the Sea is at great liberty, and may take as much and as little of the Warre as he will.' 'If the nation of Spain', she remarked, 'should make a conquest of those [Low] Countries . . . in that danger ourself, our countries and people might shortly be'.[44] Even France had to be accorded the same treatment, to keep her as a check against Spain: 'Whenever the last day of France came it would also be the eve of the destruction of England.'[45] The country could survive in a world of two Leviathans, but not in a world of one. And France and Spain *were* Leviathans, whether judged in terms of land, finances and man power, compared with what Elizabethan England could muster.[46] Possessing no great silver mines and able only to wheedle spasmodic additional sums from a suspicious Commons, the Queen never had enough to pay for the Dutch and French campaigns, the Irish colonization programme and an extensive naval war at the same time. Her uncertainty and tergiversation were chiefly due to her need to achieve a balance between all these aims, and for every protest of the admirals at the lack of royal backing, there was one to match about the parsimony of her support for the Netherlands army. Moreover, when overseas expeditions were sent out, they very often failed due to the inability of their leaders to adhere to basic aims: the Lisbon venture of 1589 and the Cadiz raid of 1596 are cases in point.[47] It is true that, on occasions, the Queen appears at first to have been too cautious and penny-pinching towards the attempts to interdict the Spanish bullion flow; but she also remained deeply conscious of how vulnerable England was to invasion whenever the Royal Navy was cruising in distant waters.

Compared with Drake's 1587 attack upon Cadiz and with the resounding defeat inflicted upon the Armada in the following year, the later stages of the war with Spain were disappointing, frustrating and anti-climactic; but the reason for this appears to lie less in Richmond's claim that Elizabeth 'never understood either the capabilities or the use of the nation's sea power', than in the simple fact that England was still too weak, immature and inexperienced in the realm of naval warfare. Professor Wernham put it thus: 'it may be that the sea war launched England decisively out upon the oceans and on the pathway to empire. Yet because great oaks from little acorns grow, we should not forget that this particular acorn was comparatively little.'[48] This can be substantiated by an examination of three vital aspects of England's maritime development at this time: her naval strength *vis à vis* that of Spain; her relative success in securing overseas commerce and colonies; and the state of strategical and tactical thought and practice.

In the first instance, it is worth recalling the early predominance possessed by the Royal Navy, thanks to the administrative endeavours of Hawkins, the support of the monarch, and the superiority of the vessels designed specifically for fighting and long-range raiding. Whereas the English could field the most powerful naval force in the world by the early 1580s, Philip II had only a miscellany of ships' types: Mediterranean galleys, unsuitable for Atlantic work; high-castled carracks, which were almost as ineffective against the newer galleons; and hired armed merchantmen. This alone explains much of the early successes of the Elizabethan adventurers. However, Philip's take over of Portugal in 1580 brought him not only further territory in Europe and overseas, but also well-placed Atlantic ports and a dozen Portuguese galleons, an accretion of strength which provoked fears in northern Europe similar to those entertained by Churchill in 1940 at the possibility of Hitler seizing the French fleet. Furthermore, as soon as Philip perceived Spain's design weakness, he embarked upon a steady shipbuilding policy, exploiting materials and resources in Europe and the New World far in excess of those which Elizabeth could command. As Mattingly notes: 'English sea power in the Atlantic had usually been superior to the combined strengths of Castile and Portugal, and so continued to be, but after 1588 the margin of superiority was reduced.'[49]

By the time of the Armada, and despite Drake's preventive strike of 1587, Philip could field a first line of battle of twenty galleons and eight other large vessels, supported by a second line of forty armed merchantmen, the overall total of ships, great and small, being almost 130; and despite the vaunted qualities of the heavier English armaments, Spanish losses to the weather were far in excess of those to enemy guns. Nor did the immensity of this disaster check the challenge from Philip, who by the following year had dispatched a fleet of forty large and twenty small ships to cover the arrival of the annual treasure-fleet, while in the Biscay ports alone twenty new galleons were being constructed. In 1596 only the storms defeated his second armada, for the English fleet was in poor shape immediately after the Cadiz expedition; while a third Spanish invasion attempt, with an enormous force of 136 vessels, was likewise dispersed twelve months afterwards. Had either got through, the English would have been hard pressed to hold them, at sea or on land.

The same was true of the Spanish defence of Latin America and the bullion convoys. Once Elizabethan adventurers had exposed the weaknesses in Philip's empire in the New World and revealed their own desire to interrupt the Atlantic route, counter-measures were instituted. The real point about Grenville's glorious though hopeless fight in the *Revenge* in 1591 was that Spain had become capable of assembling a far larger force – twenty warships to Howard's six – to keep the Azores waters free of English marauders. If necessary, Philip could always hold up the sailing of the treasure-fleet for a year, yet it appeared at that time physically and logistically impossible for the Royal Navy to maintain its blockade for more than the six summer months, even had it possessed numerical superiority. In fact, more treasure reached Spain from America in the period 1588–1603 than in any other comparable time-span in her history. Plundering the West Indies region also became increasingly difficult, as Drake and Hawkins discovered to their dismay during their last voyage of 1595–6; the days of easy pickings were over, and yet England's admirals were only beginning to perceive this as their monarch lay on her deathbed. With James's coming, however, they had little chance to carry out their fresh, more concentrated and more realistic strategy.

With regard to overseas commerce and colonization, it would also be a mistake to ante-date England's rise. Gilbert's 1583 expedition, after annexing Newfoundland, ended in disaster; Raleigh's first Virginia colony was abandoned in its second year; and his second attempt was frustrated by the Armada campaign and the disappearance of the colonists.[50] All too often the colonizing ventures of Elizabeth's reign were undermined by the desire of the participants to find a silver-mine and to get rich quickly, instead of organizing themselves to found a stable agricultural and trading community. In addition, the long war with Spain both deterred colonists and investors from opening up new settlements across the Atlantic which might suddenly be overwhelmed by enemy assaults, and offered alternative opportunities for profit through the plunder of trading posts and bullion ships. As for seaborne trade, too great an emphasis had been placed upon the new oceanic commerce at the expense of the more established traffic to Europe, which, despite the crisis of the 1550s, remained by far the largest market and source of goods. 'The southward and westward enterprises . . . involved as yet only a tiny fraction of England's shipping and capital and contributed only a very small amount to the volume of England's trade.'[51] The boom in the Newcastle–London coal traffic was probably as rapid as the increase in colonial trade, but it has proved less romantic to historians. The country was still alarmingly dependent upon the export of one commodity, wool and woollen products.[52] In any case, it was apparent to all by 1600 that the Dutch rather than the English were the real inheritors of the commercial Empires of the Hansards, the Venetians and the Portuguese. Amsterdam, which replaced Antwerp as the entrepôt for Europe, possessed all the natural advantages of London, together with an enormous continental hinterland. The Dutch domination of the rich herring fields had provided the 'take-off' stimulus for maritime expansion, and their *fluyts* were superior in design as freighters if not as fighting-ships.

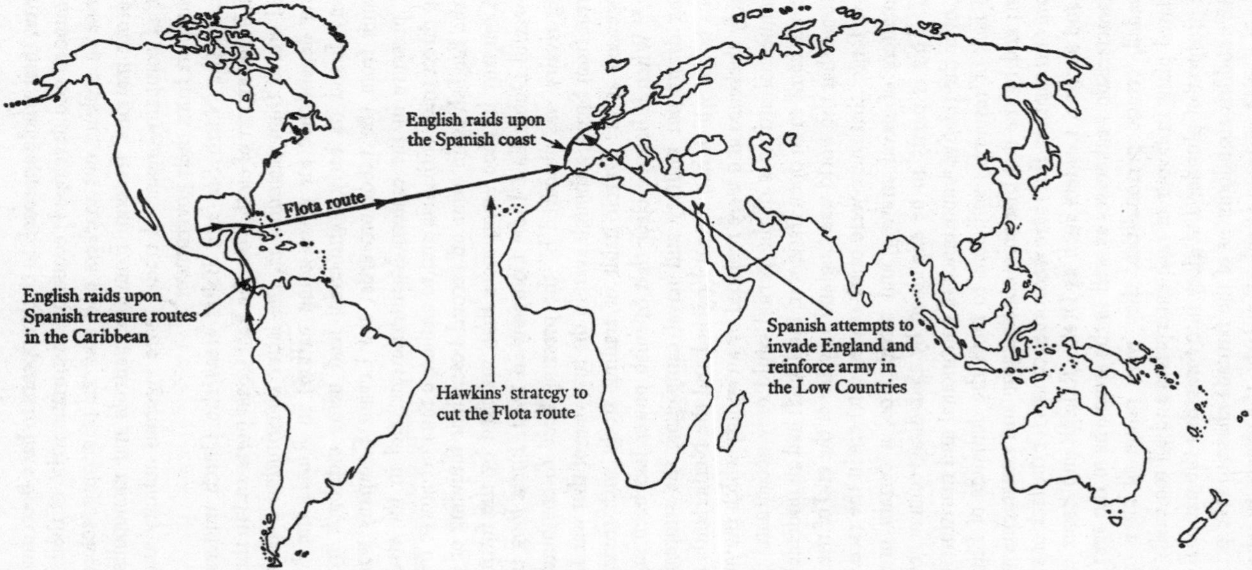

Map 1. The strategy of the Anglo-Spanish War, 1585–1603

Moreover, their whole approach to trade appears to have been much more single-minded and developed; economic historians write of their 'greater enterprise in seeking out markets and sources of supply, toleration of lesser profit margins, freedom from the controls and monopolistic tendencies of company-organized trade, more vigorous military and diplomatic support from their government'.[53]

Thus in the North Sea and Baltic areas the Dutch undersold the English in the export of cloth from the East Coast ports and in the import of naval stores from Scandinavia, the latter constituting a particularly alarming dependence for a sea-going nation; in Russia the Muscovy Company found its early commercial lead being cut back by Dutch merchants from the 1580s onwards; the Levant Company was under similar pressure in the eastern Mediterranean; and in the struggle to develop direct trade with Asia and to challenge the Portuguese monopoly there, the English again came off second-best, their founding of the East India Company in 1600 being more than matched by the formation of the powerful Dutch East India Company in 1602. For a long time this growing rivalry was obscured by the pressing need to combine against the threat from Spain, although even in the first year of that war Leicester was incensed at the Dutch habit of trading freely with their mutual enemy.[54] When it became clear that Spanish power had been sapped by the long drawn-out military and naval campaigns, the strategical and religious bonds which had drawn England and the Netherlands together inevitably slackened and were replaced by an enmity which the mercantilist commercial attitudes of the period could only accentuate. Yet if it ever was to come to an open trade war, the Dutch had an undeniable lead. To assume that the world was England's oyster at the end of the Spanish war is to forget that there were other oyster-catchers in the race.

In matters of naval strategy and tactics, too, a certain immaturity existed. This is partly to be explained by that disagreement, examined above, over the relative importance of continental and maritime policies; by the lack of resources sufficient to meet the demands of Elizabethan seamen; and by the fact that ship-construction and armaments were still in a state of transition. But there were other causes for the lack of sustained effort and success. Leaders such as Drake, Raleigh and Essex exhibited the characteristic weaknesses as well as the strengths of the age: volatile, hot-headed, erratic personalities, they were prone to alter carefully-formulated plans in favour of rash enterprises and all too easily tempted by the prospect of plunder and glory into forgetting the national strategy – Drake's sudden abandonment of the Armada chase to take prize of the *Rosario* is a good example of this. Similarly, the chance to wipe out the remainder of the Armada fleet, and with it Spanish sea power, during the 1589 Portugal expedition was ignored in favour of a rash assault upon Lisbon; the 1596 Cadiz raid also showed negligence in ignoring the main Spanish fleet in the Tagus. Indeed, the whole organization of such expeditions and the deployment of troops during them left much to be desired: logistical support was often non-existent, this necessitating the pillaging of towns, the diversion from strategical objectives, and the inevitable diseases, which were probably the cause of more failed expeditions than anything else; the element of surprise was often needlessly thrown away; and the forces used were frequently too small to hold a position permanently, yet too cumbersome to move swiftly.

On the other hand, it was scarcely surprising that there was no sustained national maritime policy, based upon a well-thought-out strategy of sea power, so long as the navy itself was not an official instrument of state. As Andrews points out,

> The royal navy was not yet distinct, in functions or in personnel, from the sea-forces of the nation as a whole, and the management and conduct of the queen's ships was the responsibility of men who had grown up in the school of oceanic trade and plunder and remained promoters and leaders of the privateering war. The very strength of these interests, reinforced as they were by London's capital and the enthusiastic initiative of gentlemen-adventurers, helped to retard the growth of a powerful state navy at a time when the resources of the Crown were extremely limited.[55]

In other words, the criticism of Richmond and others that the post-Armada strategy was the false one of *guerre de course* appears less valid than at first glance, if the resources for an alternative policy were insufficient. Since privateering was, in Andrews's phrase, 'the characteristic form of Elizabethan maritime warfare', it would be difficult to expect a deployment of England's naval forces in accordance with Mahanite principles. Moreover, it seems that the profits from these ventures came to 10 to 15 per cent of the country's imports, which boosted the capital supplies, led to a great growth in shipping and more than made up for the loss of the Iberian trade; while privateering also contributed largely to the decline of the Portuguese and Spanish merchant marines, to the ultimate benefit of the British.[56]

Yet the Elizabethans were learning by experience and at the turn of the century Essex at least, had recognized the need for a better-organized expeditionary force. More important still, they had come belatedly to recognize that to secure effective command of the sea they had to defeat or at least neutralize the main forces of the enemy, and to cut off his seaborne commerce permanently. Hence the 1603 strategy to blockade the Spanish–Portuguese coast almost throughout the year by strong squadrons, forcing Spain either to give battle or to forfeit the bullion supplies upon which she now depended like an addict upon drugs. To supplement this stranglehold, another force was to be stationed to cut off the supply of naval stores from the Baltic, this itself being a tightening of earlier measures by Elizabeth's government against neutral trading with the enemy. Foreign governments were frequently warned off, their counter-arguments ignored and the ships of their nationals seized; in 1589 Drake intercepted and captured sixty Hanse vessels off the Tagus. Already the English were rejecting the 'freedom of the seas' concept in favour of a blockading strategy favourable to the predominant naval power. And, to sustain their own shipping, protection was given against pirates and enemy privateers in the Channel, while all encouragement was offered to the growth of England's fishing fleets and merchant navy, which were recognized not only for their economic value but also as being ready sources of ships and seamen in time of war. Thus the Navigation Acts were added to by the Tudors, overseas joint-stock companies were welcomed, timber was preserved by an Act of Parliament, fishing-grounds were protected and the growing of flax and hemp (for canvas and rope) encouraged. In 1562 Elizabeth went so far as to add a third fish-eating day in the week to the calendar, the express motive for this being to restore 'the Navy of England'. It was in this widespread perception by the authorities of the role of sea power that prospects for the future lay.

The reign of the Tudors must not be regarded, therefore, as an age in which England burst forth to become a world power: there is no straight and inevitable line to be drawn between the defeat of the Armada in 1588 and the victory at Trafalgar in 1805. The early colonization attempts were failures. The Dutch overshadowed the English commercially. And in naval terms, as Professor Mattingly observes, 'nobody commanded the seas' in the Anglo–Spanish war.[57] England was still relatively backward, under-governed, immature, poor and under-populated. The peoples of Asia had been made aware of the Arabs, the Portuguese, the Spaniards and (at the turn of the century) the Dutch; they knew virtually nothing of the English. Seen from this perspective, the exploits of 'the age of Drake' begin to assume their proper, more modest proportions.

What we do perceive happening under the Tudors is the unfolding of England's *potential* to become a great maritime power. A general shift in the European balance of power had occurred, with the Atlantic and the Low Countries replacing the Mediterranean and the Lombard plain as the economic and political focal points; England was thereby placed at the centre of affairs, rather than on the periphery. She was also beginning to join in the voyages of exploration and the development of commerce overseas, utilizing, in both, her natural geographical advantages and the favourable disposition of her people. She had developed sea power in many ways, from the construction of vessels specifically for fighting to the exploitation of the strategy of land–sea cooperation; and, despite set-backs, she had gained much in tactical experience. Her government, urged on by 'navalists', had instituted various measures to protect and encourage English seamanship, shipping and overseas trade in peacetime and war-time, and had recognized the importance of trying to cripple that of her foes. A bullionist and protectionist economic policy was being actively encouraged by the government and the Commons.[58] The central axioms of the doctrine of sea power – in particular, the need to secure command of the maritime trade-routes through the superior battle-fleet – were being slowly worked out and understood.

Indeed, perhaps the danger was that this enthusiasm for the 'Blue Water' recipe of naval strength, overseas trade and colonial expansionism would cause the English to forget that their country was still a European power, and a small and insecure one at that. Elizabeth, to her lasting credit, had preserved a correct balance between maritime and continental policies and, in so doing, had helped to create a situation favourable to England's future security and growth: for the exhaustion of Spain at sea and on land had maintained that power equilibrium so necessary for the independence of the rising nation-states of western Europe. Yet her government always appreciated that the Spanish war had been not so much a victory but an avoidance of defeat, and that it was crucial for England's future, if at all possible, to avoid standing alone against one of the Leviathans. 'The surest way to avoid the burden and the strain was to keep an ever-watchful eye on the continental Powers, to see that the balance never swung too sharply towards either the one or the other, above all to keep the coast between Brest and Emden from falling under a single master.'[59] In a world where four or five countries could check each other's ambitions, England would have less cause to fear for her own security, and her natural advantages as an island nation would reveal themselves. If she had a long way to go before she dominated the world's stage, she had at least taken the first few, tentative steps from behind the wings.

CHAPTER TWO

The Stuart Navy and the Wars with the Dutch (1603–88)

In the 1620s and 1630s England had been powerless to take any action while the fate of Europe was being decided in the Thirty Years War . . . English merchants were driven out of the East and West Indies. England could not prevent Dutch and Spanish fleets fighting in her waters. North African pirates carried seamen off to slavery even in the English Channel . . .

The transformation a mere fifteen years later is astonishing . . . English strategy after the Revolution was based on a conscious use of sea power on a world scale that was new in execution if not in conception . . . Blake in the Mediterranean, Penn in the Caribbean, Goodson in the Baltic, were phenomena hitherto unknown, presaging Britain's future. English merchants were now protected in the Mediterranean and Baltic in a way which would have been quite impossible for early Stuart governments . . .

C. Hill, *God's Englishman. Oliver Cromwell and the English Revolution* (London, 1970), pp. 166–8.

That the story of the Royal Navy in the years following 1603 has generally been portrayed as one of anticlimax and deterioration should scarcely be surprising. If, as Mahan maintained, the history of sea power is largely 'a military history', then the periods of peace represent only a breathing-space, similar to the intervals taken by boxers between their rounds; and naval historians, like boxing audiences, have rarely given such periods the attention they accord to the conflict itself. The struggle with Spain, during which England had achieved world renown, was now over and the nation expected that the strains of war would be relieved by drastic reductions in the armed services. Elizabeth, that bewildering but highly effective national leader, was also gone, replaced by a scarcely known Scotsman. Her distinguished captains, Drake, Hawkins, Frobisher and Grenville were dead; the fleet was laid up and allowed to languish; corruption was rampant throughout the naval administration; the merchant fleets were at the mercy of Dunkirk pirates and Barbary corsairs; and privateering by Englishmen was forbidden by the new monarch. In such circumstances it was natural that observations were openly made, by Englishmen and foreigners alike, about this decline and that many agreed with Sir Edward Coke's nostalgic complaint that 'England never prospered so much as when she was at war with Spain'. In the words of a later historian, 'perhaps no more calamitous era in sea-operations, since the navy assumed a modern form, has found its way into the annals of our country's history'.[1] It is an unpleasant episode, to be passed over as swiftly as possible.

To the student of sea power in its broadest sense, however, James's reign is of as much interest as that of Elizabeth or of the later Stuarts, because by revealing the contrasts and the similarities with those other periods it also enables the historian to perceive more clearly the various stages of this development. On a more specific note, it helps us to see how fragile and immature English naval power was at the beginning of the seventeenth century. It only needed a monarch who lacked interest in the service or a Commons which declined to vote men into its still primitive administration – and a sharp decline was inevitable. There was no standing national concern in the existence of a large fleet, not at least if it also meant an increase in permanent taxation. That symbiosis of parliamentary support, mercantile expansion and naval strength only later developed as one of the country's chief characteristics.

Of these various elements, there is no doubt that the constant interest and encouragement of the Crown was essential for the navy's well-being, and for the creation of an overall atmosphere in which overseas commerce and colonization could flourish: the difference between Mary and Elizabeth had shown that. In this respect the coming of James I marked a definite regression. The peace settlement with Spain may have undermined much of the *raison d'être* for the maintenance at full readiness of that fleet of thirty-one warships bequeathed by Elizabeth, but not for keeping a minimum amount of naval force to protect national interests in a world which did not appear to subscribe to James's pacifist ideals. It is true that a certain number of ships were commissioned each year to serve in the Channel, but they were too few and too slow to put down the piracy that had now become endemic: no merchant vessel was safe from the Dunkirk privateers, still less from the Moors, who raided places as far apart as the Newfoundland fisheries, southern Ireland and the Thames estuary with ease and impunity. If overseas trade was to be protected, it had to be done by the merchants themselves. At the same time James appeared to have dealt a double blow by banning English privateering and refusing to issue Letters of Marque while other sovereigns kept up that policy.[2] Through his inability to obtain respect for England's claim to the 'Channel Salute', his general deference towards Spain and her colonial claims, his equally lamentable timidity against the Dutch, who openly operated in English waters against corsairs and ignored his claims to the herring fisheries, and his encouragement only of that trade which lined the Court's pocket, the King appeared to later nineteenth-century navalists to have done everything wrong.

On the other hand James might reasonably argue that much of the responsibility lay with the Commons, which declined to grant him the sums necessary for the upkeep of a large fleet: it was simply impossible for the monarch to be expected to live 'of his own' at the same time as he was also asked to maintain a *national* naval force. Yet now that the Spanish war was over, the taxpayers – and especially their parliamentary representatives – were unwilling to vote the money which they had granted Elizabeth and which even she had found quite inadequate. The dissolutions of Parliament in 1610 and 1614, with the Crown's financial problems still unsolved, aggravated the situation; and this no doubt forced James into further dependence upon the London capitalists and monopoly trading companies, who had little wish to see commerce made more open or the State assume responsibility for the protection of national (as opposed to sectional) interests. The attempts of the early Stuarts to do without the Commons, their dubious foreign policy and attitudes towards the Protestant 'cause', the conspicuous consumption and favouritism at Court, the corruption of the customs, farmers, and the sale of honours, were no doubt provocative to all those who were not benefiting from this system – the country gentry, the merchants outside London, the traders who could not get into the chartered companies and therefore demanded 'free trade' – but the latter were at the same time frequently guilty of denying to James (and later to Charles) the funds which might have gone to the creation and upkeep of that powerful fleet for which they so often pleaded.[3]

In the same way, although the King set the general tone of financial laxity and political favouritism, he can scarcely be held fully responsible for the appalling corruption in the navy itself: this must to a large degree be blamed on Nottingham's increasing senility and Mansell's financial delinquency. While the fleet decayed from year to year, with its masts and rigging rotting away and its guns rusting or sold off; while the payment and general treatment of the crews were so negligent that most seamen defected, either to merchant vessels or to the service of the Dutch or even the corsairs; and while the few warships that were built to replace those that had been sold and broken up were slow, expensive and poorly designed, these men and their satellites pocketed enormous pensions, allowances and 'travelling expenses'; in the end they had to be bought out during the reorganization of 1618. All this suggests that although the average annual naval expenditure in the first decade of James's reign was generally only half that of the 1590s, a respectable force could have been maintained had the administration been in the hands of a Hawkins or a Pepys.

The fruits of this decay of English naval power were reaped in the occasional attempts which the early Stuarts made to intervene in international politics. The clumsy and ineffectual efforts of Mansell's squadron against the corsairs at Algiers in 1620 provide a good example: after a great deal of difficulty, six King's ships were made ready but they were outnumbered by ten armed merchantmen and the financial support for the venture was chiefly provided by London – another sign of the lack of a national navy; many vessels quickly became unfit for service; and the Moors simply ignored the English admiral's efforts to check them. Even more ignominious was the Cadiz expedition of 1625, dreamt up by Charles I and Buckingham in pique at the failure of their courtship mission to Madrid, composed of over 100 ships, only nine of which were the King's (the rest were merchantmen and colliers), and staffed by a motley collection of ill-fed, poorly armed soldiers who took to the wine-cellars upon arrival in the Spanish port and could only with difficulty be persuaded to re-embark for home. Instead of the hoped-for profits, the expedition increased Charles's indebtedness, with the consequence that neither the seamen nor the soldiers were paid. In the following year, English sea power was further humiliated when Buckingham's expedition to La Rochelle, described by Penn as 'one of the most lamentable and disastrous in the annals of English history', was first checked by the stalwart French defence of the Ile de Re and then defeated with a loss of 5,000 English troops by Richelieu's powerful counter-offensive.[4] Divided leadership, poor planning, unseaworthy ships, lack of supplies, and a failure to utilize the potentialities and to recognize the limitations of amphibious warfare were the most notable characteristics of all these ventures; but in the background lay that deeper need of good naval leaders and administrators, and the ever-crippling lack of funds.

Against this picture of almost unrelieved gloom about the state of the navy can be set other considerations which indicate that English maritime expansion in the first few decades of the seventeenth century was not suffering to the extent that some writers have imagined.[5] With the union of Scotland and England under James, and the ending of the Irish campaign, the British Isles were politically and strategically united at last, and no longer provided a diversion for English policy-makers. At the same time, the continental powers were too preoccupied with each other's designs to devote their attention to England, and this tendency naturally increased with the outbreak of the Thirty Years War. Charles I might intervene in Europe but he need not fear the converse, a genuine and long-lasting European coalition against England, even though Buckingham's folly in 1627 involved the country temporarily in war with Spain and France. There were, then, no pressing dangers to the country in the period of her naval weakness, if the frequent harassment of her shipping by pirates can be ignored; and the King's penury, which compelled him to withdraw from the wars by 1620, caused the nation as a whole to disassociate itself from European affairs to a remarkable degree and to concentrate upon peaceful commerce, colonization and, of course, internal political and religious quarrels.[6] The fact that the few forces sent by James and Charles to the continent had proved incapable either of restoring the Elector Palatine to his lands or of assisting the King of Denmark – an understandable result in view of England's military weakness and of the limitations of sea power – tended to encourage this isolationism.

Yet if England was of little account in European affairs, this was certainly not the case in the outside world. James I may have conceded much to Spain after 1604, but he never gave up the right to colonization of unoccupied territories.[7] Furthermore, it is under the first Stuarts that the real beginnings of the British Empire are to be observed, fuelled by religious dissent, agricultural distress, anti-Spanish feeling and a desire for economic gain, whether through the discovery of new trade routes to the East, precious metals or fresh supplies of naval stores, or simply by a general increase in oceanic trade. The Virginia Company (1606) established a foothold in what was to be the colony of that name; Lord Baltimore's concession led to a further settlement, in Maryland, in 1634; the Pilgrim Fathers (1620) and the Massachusetts Bay Company (1628–29) founded and extended their colonies throughout New England; after 1610 settlement began in Newfoundland, and a few years later Nova Scotia was added to the list; further south the Puritans may have failed in Honduras and the repeated ventures to Guiana may have suffered the same fate, but Bermuda was taken in 1609–10, followed within a decade or two by St Kitts, Nevis, Antigua, Monserrat and Barbados. Only Charles's restoration of Quebec to France in 1632, four years after its capture by English forces, appears as a black spot in retrospect. And while the main thrust of English expansion at this time was clearly westwards, an equally significant movement eastwards was taking place under the aegis of the East India Company, which established itself at Surat (1612), Masulipatam (1611), Salasore (1633) and Madras (1639), and even into the Persian Gulf (1622). The Dutch might brutally tumble them out of the East Indies in the 1620s, but Downton's notable victory over the Portuguese off Surat in 1615 indicated that English sea power was ensuring a secure position for the company against weaker rivals. All these activities, Williamson is right to stress, represent 'an outburst of colonizing energy which renders the Elizabethan achievements insignificant in comparison'.[8] To a lesser extent, such a comment is also applicable to the growth of English overseas trade after 1603. With the returns from privateering shrinking as the Spanish counter-measures took effect, there was by then no substantial economic reason for James to continue Elizabeth's war, and many for halting it: the country was relieved of the heavy financial burdens; the colonization and trade expansion schemes planned by the chartered companies could at last be realized; and the traffic to the Iberian peninsula and the Mediterranean resumed. In consequence there was a post-war boom, for this southern commerce was the most profitable and fastest-growing of all in the early seventeenth century; the Spanish merino wool aided the 'new draperies' and the favourable trade balance with Spain boosted England's bullion stocks. In addition, the East Coast coal trade trebled in the first thirty years of the century; the Newfoundland fisheries were now attracting 500 vessels every year; and trade with America and the East, although still small, was becoming of some importance. This in turn stimulated a great growth in ship building: 'Our peace has trebled our number of ships to that of former times', wrote Sir William Monson, adding that 'Mariners are abundantly increased and wealth plentifully augmented'.[9] The stagnation of 1614–17 may have exposed England's unhealthy dependence upon woollen exports and demonstrated again the strength of Dutch economic competition after the 1609 truce with Spain, but the threat from this formidable rival receded somewhat after the United Provinces became involved in the Thirty Years War.

These facts present the historian with a major problem concerning the relationship between naval strength on the one hand, and commercial and colonial expansion on the other, for it is clearly a more complex one than may at first be imagined. Under Elizabeth the fleet had been relatively strong and active, but trade had suffered and colonization had been rendered impossible during the war; under James the latter two flourished, although they had little naval support to protect them. No doubt it would have been preferable to English merchants after 1604 to have been able to rely upon the Royal Navy to keep pirates at bay, but the evidence indicates that the activities of these raiders were not as great an obstacle to overseas trade as contemporaries imagined, and indeed the deluge of complaints about their depredations is a good measure of the commercial expansion! It also suggests that the involvement of major European states before 1609 and after 1618 in bitter land warfare, while England remained at peace, may be a more valid guide to the latter's economic resurgence and establishment of an overseas empire than the size of the navy.

Furthermore, such conclusions raise another question of great significance: did the commercial expansion of England in the seventeenth and eighteenth centuries occur because of, or in spite of, that series of wars in which she was usually successful? Navalists and Marxists (uneasy bedfellows here) have generally assumed that the former was true. But the answer is not a simple one and it will differ from one period to the next, depending especially upon the role of neutral parties who can benefit when others are at war (as the English did in 1604–9 when the Dutch were still struggling with Spain); and upon whether economic progress is to be measured in terms of absolute trade and prosperity (which usually declined in war) or in terms of relative advantage over rival powers (whose own trade might be hit more seriously still). Already, however, we have indications that an open conflict with foreign states hurts the pockets of many, even if it benefits and satisfies others, and that a survey of Britain's rise to naval mastery needs to concentrate as much upon peacetime as upon wartime developments. In this connection, it is perhaps worth noting that the intervals between wars described in Mahan's own book, *The Influence of Sea Power upon History*, are given only the most cursory treatment by him; despite the claim to be examining sea power as a whole strategy, leadership and battles are the stuff of his study, not the steady growth of trade, industry and colonies.[10]

Irrespective of this larger debate, English naval strength was never as weak after 1618 as it was under Mansell's administration as Treasurer, despite the glaring failures of the expeditions of the 1620s, which were to a large degree his legacy. Under the new Board of Commissioners the more blatant examples of corruption were eliminated, the size of the fleet was steadily increased by rebuilding and new construction, and the Chatham yard was improved. Charles I, too, sought to encourage the growth of the navy, especially in view of the rise of Dutch and French sea power, but was constantly frustrated by the lack of funds. His eventual solution, the imposition of Ship-money in 1634, produced a relatively strong force of nineteen Royal vessels and twenty-six armed merchantmen, enough to check foreign pretensions in the Channel for a while. Thus encouraged, he took the fatal step of extending the Ship-money writs to the inland counties in the following year, adding to the widespread indignation which already existed over his personal rule and which was eventually to lead to his downfall. For the moment, however, the King could be content with the increase in funds and the consequent expansion of the navy.

This is not to say that his fleet, with its poor personnel and badly-designed vessels, would really have been effective in a war against a major European sea power. Its value lay in the fact that it could tip the balance between the rival states, although this consideration too was ignored by the Dutch Admiral Tromp in 1639, when he smashed the Spanish fleet in the Downs in full view of Penington's small squadron and to an extent far more decisive than had occurred to the Armada fifty years earlier. Even this value of Charles's navy was more a result of the Habsburg need to reinforce the Low Countries, and of the equally pressing Dutch and French desire to prevent this, than of any intrinsic importance England possessed at this time. Yet if her naval strength was feeble, her military arm was almost non-existent. The Elector Palatine may have groaned in despair at each occasion his brother-in-law ordered Ship-money to be collected, recognizing that Charles had thereby elected to strengthen the navy, instead of fitting out a continental expeditionary force, but it is painful to contemplate how the ill-equipped, under-paid English troops would have fared against the formidable armies of Tilly, Wallenstein and the Cardinal-Infant on the one hand, or those of Adolphus and d'Enghien on the other.

Such speculation is superfluous, for in the same year as Tromp's victory in the Downs the revolution had broken out in Scotland which was soon to escalate into the Civil War, rendering England incapable of even the mildest intervention in European affairs. However, if the navy was ineffective on an international level it did prove its worth during that internal conflict. Not surprisingly, in view of the service's pronounced Protestantism, its links with the anti-royalist mercantile community and its maladministration under the Stuarts, the bulk of the fleet declared for Parliament, which responded by steadily improving conditions and increasing its size. The navy's role during the war hardly compares with that of the army, but Clarendon was correct in calling it 'a terrible addition of strength' to the King's enemies. By constantly reinforcing from the sea those Puritan strongholds of Hull, Plymouth and Bristol; by protecting London's overseas trade and ensuring that the parliamentary side always possessed the financial power to endure the war; and by cutting off continental support for Charles through a vigorous blockading policy, Warwick's fleet earned the gratitude of its new paymasters.[11]

Moreover, although the parliamentary support for the fleet had been motivated by self-preservation alone, the result was the re-establishment of English sea power as a factor in world affairs. Warwick's vessels not only patrolled the Channel and North Sea in search of royalist 'blockade-runners'; they also extracted from continental powers that recognition of England's primacy in the Narrow Seas. In the same way, when Rupert commenced his raiding campaign against English shipping, the response of the Commonwealth was to fit out powerful squadrons under Blake and Penn which, in addition to eradicating that threat, gave notice that this regicide government was going to be as demanding in its claims for international respect as any previous King of England had been: the Tagus was blockaded, to Portugal's immense embarrassment, until Rupert slipped out; his fleet was then followed and mauled off Cartagena, with Spain impotent to intervene; the Channel Islands and, more significantly, the Atlantic colonies were forced to acknowledge the new régime; and escorts were provided for shipping in the Mediterranean while the rights of search were enforced against all foreign vessels which were suspected of aiding the royalist cause. Furthermore, the navy's constant patrolling and frequent engagements (even if small and desultory in character), provided a wealth of experience which the service had lacked since Elizabeth's day and brought to the fore several brilliant naval commanders, especially Blake and Monck.

More significantly, the triumph of Parliament had ensured that the navy henceforward would be regarded as a 'national' force, to be provided for by the country as a whole – an abrupt change of tone by the opponents of Ship-money. Finance had always been the Achilles' Heel of the fleet, restricting all Elizabeth's ingenious efforts to utilize it fully and paralysing Charles I's capacity to restore its strength: now it was to be different. This in no way implied that the English people had suddenly become willing to pay for national defence on anything like the scale common on the continent; Parliament was entitled to, and frequently did, impose additional taxes, but the greater part of the funds for the Commonwealth navy came out of sequestered royalist lands, just as the confiscation of the monastries provided the finance for Henry VIII's naval expansion. To that extent the government was living upon its capital rather than tapping the rising wealth of its own supporters, but the results were impressive and the principle of a national fleet had been established. Wages in the navy were raised to attract fresh personnel, attention was paid to sick seamen, and pensions became more common; corruption in administration was eliminated, with capable and honest officers replacing royal favourites; additions were made to the dockyards, and logistical support to the fleet at sea was now much improved. 'Never, before or since, were the combatant branches of the Navy so well supported', noted Oppenheim approvingly.[12] The fleet itself expanded in an astonishing fashion. Between 1649 and 1651 forty-one new vessels were added to the Navy List, more than doubling its size (from thirty-nine); and between 1649 and 1660 a grand total of 207 new ships was built or acquired. Many of these were new, fast frigates, built to outspeed the Dunkirk privateers and to scout for the main battle-fleet as well as to prey upon enemy commerce.

Finally, the revolution brought into power those forces in English society which appreciated the benefits accruing from the possession of a strong navy: religious zealots who had yearned to emulate Drake's exploits and to foil the Counter-Reformation, yet who were also capable of regarding themselves as God's instrument for the chastising of fellow-Protestants; colonial enthusiasts who perceived the natural connection between maritime strength and overseas settlement; and the great mass of the merchants, who had disliked Charles's favouring of monopolistic trade companies and groaned at the lack of protection provided against privateers and pirates. All of these came to regard the navy as a vital instrument of *national* policy, revealing thereby a fusion of their religious conviction and personal prosperity with a sense of insular patriotism and a belief in the general well-being of the country which had been missing since Tudor times, if indeed it had fully existed then.

These newer ideas about trade, imperial and foreign policy – the ideological framework of what has been called 'the commercial revolution'[13] – were reflected in the famous Navigation Act of 1651, which made all overseas colonies subject to Parliament and insisted that trading with them should be the exclusive preserve of English shipping. To a very large extent the measure was motivated by short-term considerations: the country was facing a severe economic crisis, the price of corn was at its highest level that century, and shipping was suffering from the renewed competition of the Dutch following the peace of 1648 with Spain. English shipping, shipbuilding and overseas trade would thus receive a much-needed shot in the arm by this act. Furthermore, the influence of certain merchants who stood to gain from it, such as Maurice Thompson, can be detected behind its promulgation. Yet the manner of the State's response had far wider implications, which have caused it to be the object of much historical attention.[14] In the first place it took account of the 'common weal' and therefore presupposed that it was the duty of government to further the general prosperity of the country; this itself was a noticeable advance upon Charles's parasitic trading and financial practices, and marked the political emergency of the 'mercantile interest'. Instead of the Crown's restrictionist legislation, the favouring of trade monopolies and a preying upon commerce, there was to be a general alliance between government and business, with the former ensuring that the latter could flourish, and gaining in return increased customs and excise receipts, and parliamentary votes of supply, to finance its policies of trade protection.

Moreover, although the Navigation Act undoubtedly benefited such groups as the East India, Levant and Eastland companies by eliminating Dutch competition, the overall trend was towards a reduction in exclusive trading: the government would provide a legislative and power-political framework of support for trade, but individual merchants and firms would work out their own destiny. For the same reason colonies were no longer to be regarded as the preserve of certain favoured persons or chartered companies, but open to the nation as a whole. And, as a corollary, the government steadily developed a monopoly of force at sea, and the division in both composition and function of its navy and the merchant navy was made much more obvious. With one blow, or so it seemed, internal trading monopolies for overseas markets were hit, a national monopoly was established over colonial shipping and commerce, and those natural foundations of world-wide naval power, trade, shipping and shipbuilding, were fostered. In fact, neither the motives nor the effects were as clear-cut as this, and there were of course major modifications in this pattern after the Restoration; but there are still many grounds for considering that the Navigation Act, and the ideas behind it, marked the end of the Middle Ages in England as far as commercial and colonial policy was concerned. Foreigners, whether they were Dutch traders or Dunkirk privateers, were certainly made aware of the new style and aspirations of the régime in London and of the power it could deploy to defend its mercantile interests.

If we can accept that *both* schools of thought – those who stress the role of private mercantile influence, and those who see it primarily as a national and strategic design – are correct about the origins of the Navigation Act, since it neatly reconciled both public and private interests, then the same is also true of English motives with regard to the Dutch wars of 1652–74. The national and 'prestige' motives are obvious here. For decades the memory of the Amboyna massacre of 1623 had rankled among patriots. To this had been added a distrust of Dutch support for Charles

II, together with an even greater anger that the ancient English claim to primacy in the Narrow Seas had so often been flouted by disrespectful Netherlanders. England's position as a 'colonial dependency' of the United Provinces, as witnessed in the Cokayne fiasco, was resented too. In addition, the Dutch policy of 'free trade, free ships', which had so enraged English leaders during the war with Spain in Elizabeth's time, now conflicted with the Puritan efforts to search and capture shipping which might aid the royalists or France. As the two sides assembled their respective naval forces on either side of the North Sea in 1651, many could sense that a trial of strength over this basic national difference of opinion about international navigation and trading rights could no longer be avoided.

At the same time, of course, the evidence is overwhelming that many (though certainly not all) members of the mercantile community were deeply jealous of the Dutch superiority in the fields of shipping, Oriental trade, control of Baltic commerce, fisheries, and general credit and finance, and very alarmed at the recovery of the United Provinces after 1648. Some stood to gain directly from any blows to these formidable rivals; others merely resented the fact that such foreigners had achieved first place in trade, and wished to see the positions reversed. According to the mercantilist theory promulgated in books and pamphlets at this time, England's prosperity could only grow at the expense of that of her rivals, since the world's total wealth was limited; and this nostrum seemed confirmed by the manner in which Dutch and English merchants had prospered when the other was at war with a third party. If the Netherlands were to lose their near-monopoly in the Baltic, or their herring fleets were destroyed, or their fabulous East India Company was ruined, then surely England would benefit. Already the Navigation Act had caused many protests in Amsterdam. The issue, as Monck put it later, was simple: 'The Dutch have too much trade, and the English are resolved to take it from them.'[15] Following the failure of the proposed union of the two countries in 1651 on terms advantageous to the English, it was obvious that the prospects for war had further increased; if England's merchants did not actively campaign for war, they did not protest at its outbreak and they hoped to benefit from it. Motives of prestige, power and profit are hard to disentangle in any period, but they seem particularly closely connected in the seventeenth century.

This basic cause of a long-lasting rivalry over trade and primacy at sea set the style of the Anglo-Dutch wars: more than any others fought by the British in the past four centuries, they were trade wars. Invasion was not really planned or attempted by either side (except in 1673), and if a

Map 2. Naval battles of the Anglo-Dutch Wars

Names and dates of battles

1. Kentish Knock (1652)
2. Dungeness (1652)
3. Three Days Battle (1653)
4. Gabbard (1653)
5. Scheveningen (1653)
6. Lowestoft (1665)
7. Bergen (1665)
8. Four Days Battle (1666)
9. North Foreland (1666)
10. Holmes in the Wadden Zee (1666)
11. Ruyter in the Thames (1667)
12. Sole Bay (1672)
13. Schoonevald (1673)
14. Texel (1673)

threat to territorial security had been the main criterion for assessing potential foes, then both countries would have regarded France as a more likely danger. It was, instead, a quarrel about who should rule the waves and reap the commercial benefits of that privilege; as a consequence, the naval and economic aspect was the dominant one.

Although the three Dutch wars need to be treated separately, because the circumstances and results of each were so different, certain fundamental factors which remained unchanged throughout ought to be mentioned here. One glance at the map reveals the geographical disadvantages under which the Dutch laboured: like the Germans in the wars of 1914–18 and 1939–45, their exits to the world's shipping routes were flanked by the British Isles. Dutch merchantmen therefore had either to run the gauntlet of the Channel, which because of navigational hazards meant sailing close to the English coast, or to take the longer and stormier journey around Scotland, which still left them open to attack in the North Sea. Moreover, the prevailing westerly winds, which had so worried Elizabethan admirals during the Armada campaign, now stood to England's advantage: their fleets could concentrate easily before moving eastwards, whereas the Dutch always faced the problem of assembling their scattered forces and tacking out to sea in a hurry. Finally, although their superior knowledge of the coastal shoals and sandbanks off Holland allowed the Dutch to anchor in places where the English dared not follow, geography also restricted the size of their warships, many of which were really converted merchantmen in any case. Few possessed more than forty guns, because to do so would affect their draught and sailing qualities, whereas the English fleet contained many larger and more powerfully armed vessels, which was a distinct advantage in the fierce toe-to-toe battles which were to characterize these wars.

And these battles were to be so bitter and prolonged precisely because the Dutch *had* to fight at sea to survive – the basic difference between their position and that of the Germans in the twentieth century. The extent of the Dutch achievement as 'carriers of the world' is well known:

> By extraordinary enterprise and efficiency, they had managed to capture something like three quarters of the traffic in Baltic grain, between half and three quarters of the traffic in timber, and between a third and a half of that in Swedish metals. Three quarters of the salt from France and Portugal that went to the Baltic was carried in Dutch bottoms. More than half the cloth imported to the Baltic area was made or finished in Holland. The flow of colonial wares into European consumption was also to a large extent in their hands.[16]

The merchant fleet of Holland alone was estimated to employ 168,000 seamen. To this must be added the massive fishing industry, which employed thousands of boats. The whole economy of the United Provinces had been built upon its role as a trader, transporter, middleman, producer of finished goods and financier, so that if its shipping was stopped its credit in the world would collapse and it would be ruined. Englishmen such as Sir George Downing perceived this clearly, and the efforts of the navy to interdict this maritime commerce and disrupt the fisheries reveals the essentially commercial nature of the struggle. By the same token Tromp and De Ruyter, although wanting to go after their enemy, could see that success or failure depended upon the amount of protection they rendered to their merchant shipping. In other words there is a case for arguing, *contra* Mahan, that a country can be too dependent upon the sea. England, by contrast, was still basically an agricultural country, far behind her rival in terms of economic development and dependence upon overseas trade. Only in the Baltic, where the Dutch (with Danish help) could cut off her vital naval stores and enjoy an undisturbed monopoly, were the roles reversed.

The Dutch, then, were fighting for their economic lives; they had to come out, protect their trade and give battle, disregarding their enemy's occasional superiority in numbers and usual superiority in position and fire-power. They had, however, certain compensating advantages as a result of their economic dominance. Their accumulated wealth was so large that, provided their shipping was not absolutely halted, they could withstand a long war; the English government, especially after 1660, was less well-off in this respect. Moreover, because their shipping was so vast and because it was logistically and militarily impossible for the English navy (despite many efforts) to institute a close watch along the entire Dutch coastline, overseas trade, although it frequently suffered, was never cut off. Their admirals were of the highest quality, who not only took the fight to the English, but also succeeded many times in safely escorting vast merchant fleets to their destination.

On the other hand, it has been argued, the position of the United Provinces suffered from two further defects.[17] As a country with land frontiers, it could not afford to deploy all of its military resources upon the sea: the memory of the 'Eighty Years War' against Spain was too recent for that. This was hardly a factor in the first Anglo-Dutch war, however, when the Commonwealth was an international pariah and both France and Denmark generally supported the Netherlands; and even less in the second war, when France was openly in alliance with the United Provinces; but it was very important in the final tussle, when the French armies were so successful that the sluices had to be opened to protect Holland. If anything, this suggests that sea power was by itself not always decisive in the struggle between England and the Netherlands: possession of a strong continental ally could also help the English cause. A more significant weakness was the disunity on the Dutch side, which contrasted sharply with the firm control exercised by the English government and its admirals. The landward states often resented the dominance of Holland, as did of course her rival Zeeland; no less than five admiralties were responsible for their fleets; and the rivalry between supporters and opponents of the House of Orange had many deleterious results – able commanders were dismissed, even Tromp was discredited for a time by internal enemies, and it was not uncommon for a group of warships to abandon their leaders in the midst of a furious battle! Although the sheer brilliance of Tromp and De Ruyter often overcame such handicaps, it did mean that their enemy's tight, disciplined squadrons had a distinct advantage here, for it was during these wars that the Royal Navy evolved the line-of-battle formation and Fighting Instructions which were to characterize its tactics for over a century.

One final general point to be made about this struggle concerns the later debates by naval historians about battle-fleet-strategy as opposed to *guerre de course* plundering. It was with reference to the second Anglo-Dutch War that Mahan scorned 'the taking of individual ships or convoys' and praised instead

> the possession of that overbearing power on the sea which drives the enemy's flag from it, or allows it to appear only as a fugitive; and which, by controlling the great common, closes the highways by which commerce moves to and from the enemy's shores. This overbearing power can only be exercised by great navies . . .[18]

However, such a view is more a reflection of late nineteenth-century naval theory (the argument against *Jeune École* ideas) than of the reality of seventeenth-century naval warfare. It was of course true that the navy was better able to throttle hostile trade, if the enemy's main fleet had been broken, and that it was false strategy to dispatch a squadron to the Mediterranean or to lay up the fleet, if there was a danger of an attack upon the Thames. But this strategic theory assumes that it was quite feasible to 'close the highways', whereas the English navy always had great difficulty in tracing the Dutch convoys in the North Sea; and it assumes further that it was possible for a fleet to stand off an enemy port for months or even years, which, in view of bad weather, treacherous waters, limited logistics and poor seaworthiness, was not in fact the case.[19] Finally, it implies that the activities of commerce-raiders had a negligible effect; yet if, as did occur, a small Baltic convoy bringing naval stores to England was taken by the enemy, the results were considerable – in the first and third Anglo-Dutch wars, for example, the Royal Navy was gravely hamstrung by naval shortages. It was probably English privateers who put the greatest pressure for peace upon the Dutch in the first war, by capturing well over 1,000 vessels or double the size of the entire English merchant marine; just as it was the heavy English losses of over 1,500 ships in the subsequent war with Spain which allowed the neutral Dutch to regain their supremacy in maritime commerce.

At the same time it is clear that despite these *practical* difficulties, statesmen and naval leaders were beginning to realize for the first time what 'command of the sea' meant – the defeat of the enemy's main naval forces and the consequent control of maritime communications. After the Anglo-Dutch wars sea power was seen to be desirable not only to ensure 'the Defence of the Kingdom', but also because of the benefits it brought in terms of undisturbed trade, colonial acquisitions, and embarrassment to the foe. As Professor Graham suggests, it therefore became a 'new element' in the international equilibrium, causing all states which possessed a coastline to reassess the importance of a strong navy and overseas territories. After all, even governments which had little interest in trade and colonies *per se* could appreciate that they could provide new sources of wealth to finance the hideously expensive wars with which their power struggles so frequently culminated. Or, as Choiseul was to put it in the eighteenth century:

> I do not know whether they really understand in Spain that in the present state of Europe it is colonies, trade, and in consequence sea power, which must determine the balance of power upon the continent. The House of Austria, Russia, the King of Prussia are only powers of the second rank, as are all those which cannot go to war unless subsidised by the trading powers.[20]

For certain countries – France is the best example here – the result of the coming of this new element was to cause an ambivalence in national strategy for the next few centuries, for it was never clear to her leaders how much attention could be devoted to building up sea power as opposed to land power. For England, however, it pointed to the way in which she could enhance her national wealth, prestige and importance in foreign affairs – always provided that she did not totally ignore the equally important consideration that the European military balance also affected her vital interests.

The first Anglo-Dutch War (1652–4), sparked off symbolically by a clash between Blake and Tromp over the Channel salute, was the most successful for England for several reasons.[21] She was better prepared for battle, thanks to the campaign against Rupert, and the Dutch had not really worked out their convoy strategy. At first they sought to bring through the Channel the slow-moving fleets of several hundred merchantmen, against which the English could mount sustained attacks while Tromp remained bound to the convoys. After several false moves and skirmishings off places as far apart as the Shetlands and Plymouth, sixty-eight ships under Blake attacked fifty-seven under De Witt at the Kentish Knock on 28 September 1652, this battle resulting in an English victory. Elated, the English thereupon dispatched part of their fleet to relieve the Dutch blockade of their small squadron at Leghorn; but Tromp brought a huge convoy down the Channel in November, bruising Blake's inferior fleet in a clash off Dungeness, whilst the English were also routed in the Mediterranean. Stung by these defeats into improving the navy, the Council of State sent out Blake with eighty ships to stop Tromp bringing another fleet up the Channel in February 1653. In the so-called Three Days Battle the convoy was badly savaged, despite Tromp's brilliant rearguard tactics; but after the successful shepherding of further merchant fleets he was allowed to search out the English main forces whilst the convoys were diverted around Scotland. In early June his hundred sail fought for two days against Monck and Deane, and later against Blake, but the superior strength and armaments of the English fleet in this battle off the Gabbard told in the end, with the Dutch losing twenty vessels. Their coastline was blockaded then for a month until Tromp and De Witt gave battle off Scheveningen, where again the English fire-power and line discipline won the day, even though Monck's force was also badly damaged. Worst of all, Tromp himself was killed in that action. Thereafter, little of note occurred, since the English navy could not – like a victorious army – deliver the final blow; and the Dutch, their trade suffering, agreed to peace terms which was formally concluded on 5 April 1654 in the treaty of Westminster.

The war (apart from its Mediterranean aspects) and the peace settlement were very beneficial to England. While her own merchants were not greatly affected by the conflict and indeed positively gained from the damage and disruption to Dutch shipping, the traders of Amsterdam and the fishers of Holland were badly hit; the respective customs receipts of both countries illustrate the economic side of the war. In addition, the Dutch agreed to pay compensation for the Amboyna massacre, yielded in the matter of the Channel salute and acknowledged the Navigation Act.

Yet these results hardly satisfied the English mercantile 'pro-war' faction, which criticized Cromwell for his leniency. Their attitude provides an interesting comment upon the influence of 'economic factors', for the Lord Protector was clearly the tool of nobody, not even the influential London merchants. Although he genuinely wished to see England strong and prosperous, his motives were predominantly religious and patriotic, and he was quite willing to be conciliatory to the Dutch if this would free him for a crusade against Spain, particularly after the States of Holland had agreed to ban the House of Orange from the stadtholderate in May 1654. Yet it was the Spanish trade which had been so profitable for English merchants in the preceding period, and the Dutch who would benefit if an Anglo-Spanish war broke out. The economic arguments pointed in one direction; Cromwell marched in another.[22] Even when the thorny question of the right of search of Dutch shipping arose during the Anglo-Spanish war, he was willing to be reasonable, demonstrating, as Professor Wilson observes, 'that neither conflicting economic ambitions nor the problems of neutral rights need necessarily lead to war if those who held power exercised prudence and restraint'.[23]

This distinction between politico-religious and economic aspects was maintained throughout the war with Spain (1655–60). Militarily, it was very successful: Nova Scotia was overrun; an expedition sent to take Hispaniola in 1655 encountered Spanish opposition and, more seriously, the tropical disease which so often destroyed such ventures, but Jamaica was seized instead, providing a valuable future base and source of wealth in the West Indies; in 1656 a Spanish treasure-fleet carrying over £2 million was captured; in 1656–7 Blake, using the friendly base of Lisbon, maintained a relentless blockade off Cadiz, until he learnt that another treasure-fleet had landed its cargo at Santa Cruz in the Canaries, whereupon he attacked that position, silencing the batteries of the fortress and sinking the fleet; and in 1657–8 the army and the navy surrounded that nest of Spanish privateers, Dunkirk, and compelled it to surrender, although only after the major battle of the Dunes, in which the French provided the largest contingent.[24]

More significant than this were the signs of England's emergence as one of the great powers, for Cromwell brought with him that perception of his country's 'national interests' which was to be the characteristic of such later statesmen as Pitt, Canning and Palmerston, and which caused him to pay attention to all events which might affect those interests (however idiosyncratically designated). The cruise of Blake's fleet in the Mediterranean was a case in point: indemnities were received from the Duke of Tuscany and the Pope for countenancing royalist privateers,

Map 3. The growth of English naval power under the Protectorate

the Dey of Tunis's fleet was burnt as a reprisal for the raids of his corsairs, grievances at Malta, Toulon and Marseilles were redressed, the French, Dutch and Spaniards in the area were overawed, treaties with Tetuan and Tangier gave naval-base rights, and British firms trading in the Mediterranean were protected. The 1654 treaty with Portugal was another example: in return for the offer to protect that country and its possessions through the use of naval power, the English gained concessions in the trade with Brazil, Bengal and West Africa, and of course with Portugal itself, to the detriment of Dutch competitors. The seizure of Dunkirk was a check upon Spain, France and the United Provinces; Jamaica provided a spring-board to the lucrative West-Indian trade; calculations were made about the capture of Gibraltar; even commerce with China was begun under Cromwell. An interventionist policy was initiated during the Baltic struggles, with Sweden being warned off from any attempt to gain control of Norway (and thereby a monopoly of the vital naval stores), although Cromwell remained anxious to preserve Swedish power as a counter to the designs of the Danes and the Dutch. Little wonder that Clarendon declared that the Protector's greatness was but a shadow of his glory abroad. 'The governments of the 1650s', concluded Dr Hill, 'were the first in English history to have a world strategy.'[25] And judging from the petitions for assistance or offers of an alliance which flowed in from such far-away potentates as the Prince of Transylvania and the Sultan of Morocco, the world fully appreciated that fact.

In contrast the commercial and financial side of the war presents a more sobering picture. The accumulated capital from confiscated royalist property was soon spent. Taxes were imposed at an unprecedented level – an estimated annual average of over £4 million was raised during the Interregnum – but they were never enough, for the government was now spending 'four times as much as had been thought intolerable under Charles I'.[26] By the end of the 1650s the country was groaning under the twin burdens of a large standing army and a prolonged naval war; in 1660 the naval debt alone was over one million pounds and the seamen, like the soldiers, had not been paid. Trade had been badly hit by the war, for the Spanish privateers reaped a rich harvest along the Atlantic and Mediterranean routes, and perhaps as many as 1,500 ships were lost. At the same time the Dutch neatly stepped into English shoes in various markets and recovered their commercial predominance; for example, 'the Spanish wool trade and cloth market which the English had pre-empted during the Dutch War was now retaken by the Netherlands with the fish and wine trade for good measure.'[27] Shipbuilding had also been badly hit, and from the out-ports as from London itself the business community increasingly criticized the effects of the war: in 1659 the London merchants as a whole petitioned for peace, whereas four years earlier only those trading in Madrid and Malaga had done so. Yet if they grew disenchanted with the policies of Cromwell, there is little evidence that he had learnt to heed their pleas: the government's ideological aims and certain private commercial desires did not always coincide. The merchants, in warmly welcoming back the monarchy in 1660, clearly agreed.

At the Restoration, therefore, Charles II inherited a twofold legacy. The first was the existing commercial crisis and the continuing financial embarrassment of the government; the second was that set of concepts about the role of Britain in the world, the necessity for strengthening its economic and political power-base through deliberate state actions, and the recognition of a strong navy. To this he added his own views of the desirability of increasing monarchical privileges. Thus English naval, imperial and commercial policy during his reign, and that of his brother, exhibit a mixture of all three elements. Despite parliamentary grants the Crown was constantly impecunious and Charles II resorted to the early Stuart habits of granting certain monopolies and 'leaning upon' rich merchants to give loans, not to mention his negotiations for French subsidies, to gain additional funds and to reduce that dependence upon the Commons. The navy consequently suffered from a lack of finances and from the corruption and inefficiency (well described by Pepys) attendant upon the general relaxation of standards of honesty and morality; the return of 'gentlemen captains' was also much resented by the professional officers in the fleet. On the other hand both Charles and James were very eager to maintain a strong navy and to uphold the position and respect which Cromwell appeared to have won for the country. The Puritan policy of boosting England's wealth, by getting a greater share of the world's commerce and colonies and by providing a powerful fighting fleet to protect the merchant marine, was therefore cherished and improved upon by the later Stuarts 'with as much zest as they displayed in casting away the religious gospel that accompanied it'.[28]

Thus Charles flatly declined to give up the Cromwellian conquests of Jamaica and Dunkirk, although he did sell the latter to France for a handsome sum in 1662, recognizing that the costs of garrisoning it outweighed the benefits of its retention; he also refused to return Nova Scotia to France; he negotiated a marriage with Catherine of Braganza which not only assured England of her favoured position in the Portuguese trade but also brought the bases of Bombay and Tangier, the latter particularly useful for trade protection in the Mediterranean; and he agreed to the speedy passage of a Navigation Act in 1660, which by its clauses provided clear evidence of a strong, protectionist policy.

> Enumerated commodities, especially bulky goods like wine and naval stores, could be imported only in English ships or those of the country of origin, and in 1662 their import from the Netherlands was specifically prohibited. Most colonial produce was reserved for English ships, laying the basis for that spectacular growth of the entrepôt trade in sugar, tobacco and dyestuffs, and an act of 1663 compelled colonists to buy most European goods in England. All foreign-built ships were registered, and after 1663 any that were newly acquired were deemed aliens. English ships had to have preponderantly English crews.[29]

These measures were intended, of course, to hurt the Dutch, whose commercial success was seen to be the basic reason for England's economic crisis. The evidence for this widespread envy of Dutch enterprise is overwhelming, and the mercantile and shipping community appears to have had no hesitations about it; 'Make wars with Dutchmen, Peace with Spain. Then we shall have money and trade again', ran the popular verse of 1663. Charles and his court had the additional motive of wishing to strike a blow against the hated republicans, while many naval officers sought to have active employment and to obtain lasting Dutch recognition of England's claim to sovereignty of the seas. But the overwhelming motive was commercial, and in such personal advisers of the King as Downing there is revealed once again that convenient and powerful fusion of strategical and economic argument that was now carrying all before it.[30] It was no surprise that the actual conflict was triggered off by the steady escalation of trade struggles in West Africa and by the mutual reprisals of the respective naval forces. By the time Charles had actually declared war in March 1665, battles had taken place along the West African coast, the Dutch Smyrna convoy had been attacked, privateers had been let loose, and the English had captured New Amsterdam, re-naming it New York.

If the mercantile community and the national leaders were ready for war, however, the navy was not; much money was promised for it, but this came in only slowly, and the relative neglect of 1660–64 could not immediately be overcome, even though the fleet was still far superior to anything which the early Stuarts had managed to muster. Indeed, its experience, size and administration were probably high by seventeenth-century standards. The only drawback was that De Ruyter had built up an outstandingly powerful, homogeneous and well-trained battle-fleet, which was supported by the superior financial resources of the Netherlands.

Thus, although the Dutch fleet under Opdam was severely hurt by the Duke of York's fleet off Lowestoft in June 1665, the Royal Navy lacked the strength and supplies to control the seas: De Ruyter slipped home from his West Indies cruise; many convoys got through, too, and the attack upon the Dutch East Indiamen at Bergen was repulsed; and Dutch squadrons paralysed trade in the Mediterranean and blockaded Tangier. Already under the severest financial pressure, the English naval administration broke down with the onset of the Plague.

By the beginning of 1666 the French had come to the relief of their Dutch allies, causing Charles's government not only to worry about a possible invasion of the Spanish Netherlands but also to detach a squadron under Prince Rupert into the Channel. Immediately after this diversion of force, Monck's main fleet was engaged and worsted by a superior Dutch fleet in the Four Days Fight, the very name signifying the bitter and lengthy nature of these Anglo-Dutch battles. Seven weeks later, on 27 July, the two sides fought again, off the North Foreland, and this time it was the Dutch who came off worst, losing twenty vessels to England's one. Encouraged by this success, the Royal Navy blockaded the Dutch coast and a squadron under Sir Robert Holmes even penetrated the Wadden Zee and destroyed over 150 merchantmen. Yet in the following year the Dutch had sweet revenge when, with the English fleet laid up to save funds and peace negotiations already under way, De Ruyter carried out his devastating raid upon the Thames and then blockaded the south-east and south-west coastal ports until the Peace of Breda was signed in July 1667.[31]

In view of the ignominious end to the 'tradesmen's war', the peace terms for England were not harsh. The Navigation Act was slightly amended in the victor's favour, as was the definition of what constituted contraband, and the English gave up their claim to Pula Run in the Indies and surrendered Surinam. Acadia was restored to the French. Yet the English were allowed to keep Cape Coast Castle, which gave them an entrance into the lucrative slave trade, and also to retain Delaware, New Jersey and New York, thereby eliminating Dutch rivalry and consolidating the English hold in that potentially valuable region. The moderate nature of this settlement may be seen as a reflection of the basic equality in strength between English and Dutch sea power at this stage; and also of the fact that both recognized that a prolongation of the war would only cause further hardship to trade. But it has also been seen as an indication that these two medium-sized states had begun to perceive the danger posed by the France of Louis XIV, for the latter's move against the Spanish Netherlands represented a strategic threat, his encouragement of the French navy a maritime threat, his conquest of the Leeward Islands a colonial threat, and his (or rather, Colbert's) economic policy a commercial threat, to both of them. The conclusion of the Triple Alliance of England, the United Provinces and Sweden in 1668, less than one year after the Breda peace, certainly points to that interpretation.

What the war also did was to prick that bubble of chauvinistic mercantilism which had been so prevalent in the early 1660s. The heavy taxes, coinciding with the effects of the Plague and the great losses suffered in the Fire of London, were bad enough; but the decline in trade, caused by the depredations of privateers and the interruption of maritime routes, was even worse and customs receipts dropped sharply in these years. The Turkey merchants, seeking to send out a convoy of cloth to that place, were bluntly told by the Admiralty that the Dutch Mediterranean squadron would seize it. The Baltic trade was naturally affected by the war. The East Coast coal traffic was frequently raided by privateers, and then totally stopped by De Ruyter's fleet. The West African fights gave the *coup de grâce* to the struggling Company of Royal Adventurers. As Pepys sadly noted in his diary, the truth seemed to be that 'trade and war could not be supported together'.[32] Henceforward merchants and their aristocratic backers would tend to be less euphoric about the gains to be expected in wartime.

There remained exceptions to this rule, as one might expect. Downing and some anti-Dutch elements still saw the republic as the greatest rival; so, too, did Shaftesbury and other members of the Council of Trade. But the driving force came from the Court itself, where Charles and James were eager for a French alliance and a joint war against the Dutch, which would not only bring financial benefits and enhanced prestige, but also further monarchical absolutism in England. Precisely for that reason, anti-French feelings swiftly grew throughout the country, which remained of course overwhelmingly Protestant and deeply suspicious of Louis XIV's combination of autocratic power and Catholicism. From the 1670s onwards, therefore, there re-emerges a widening split between protagonists of a Protestant, 'Whig', pro-Parliament, pro-Dutch policy on the one hand, and those favouring a pro-French line, toleration at least for Catholics and a substantial increase in the King's powers and corresponding decrease in those of the Commons on the other – the whole debate being reminiscent of the pro-Dutch versus pro-Spanish dispute earlier in the century. Nor was economic rivalry missing from the later quarrel, for Colbert's protectionist policies were beginning to bite. Ironically, although the enhancement of the monarch rather than the 'common weal' was their primary aim, they were similar in form and effect to those instituted by England after 1651 and as such they were aimed chiefly against Dutch economic predominance; but the weaker English competition was hit more severely, particularly when high tariffs were imposed upon textiles. Between 1667 and 1678, in fact, the English Parliament and Colbert were waging a tariff war on behalf of their respective domestic producers. Equally alarming to English Protestants and navalists was the impressive French naval development, for by 1670 Colbert was spending nearly £1 million a year to create new bases, dockyards, naval training schools, arsenals and a fleet of warships more numerous, larger, more heavily armed and better designed than the English. The only parallel, notes Professor Jones, 'is the similar work of Tirpitz in the years before 1914' – and the reaction on this side of the Channel was similar in both cases.[33]

Ignoring the internal and external warning-signs, Charles proceeded to negotiate secretly with Louis for an anti-Dutch alliance, to wring funds from Parliament for an anti-French policy, and then to provoke the United Provinces into war in 1672 by making extravagant demands for redress of various 'grievances' and by attacking Dutch merchant shipping. With the massive naval and military forces of France now fighting with, instead of against, England, the King and his followers were confident of victory. But the course of the war was a disappointment, providing satisfaction only to later historians, who admit to the essentially selfish, unscrupulous and unwise policy of the government at this time. In an attack upon the Anglo-French fleets off Sole Bay on 28 May 1672 De Ruyter caused heavy damage to the English force and exposed the lack of real coordination between the Allied navies; and after the French armies had overrun the southern provinces and provoked the cutting of the dykes and the overthrow of the De Witts, the admiral's brilliant strategy of preserving his fleet in the treacherous shoals of the Schooneveld warded off the prospect of an English invasion, whilst at the same time ensuring that he could never be overwhelmed by superior enemy naval forces. In the final fleet action of the Third Anglo-Dutch War, De Ruyter repeated his punishing attack upon the Royal Navy, caused the permanent postponement of any invasion attempt from the sea, and again revealed the inability of the two Allied fleets to cooperate. Indeed, the apparent inaction of the French in this battle off the Texel and on other occasions, caused even James's enthusiasm for the alliance with Louis XIV to wane, while the greater part of the country displayed its open animosity towards the war and the government's leanings to a more Catholic and authoritarian policy. With the Navy Board over £1 million in debt, and the Commons refusing to vote fresh funds and demanding instead a change in the King's whole outlook, Charles was forced to give way. By the Treaty of Westminster of February 1674 he not only abandoned the war and the French alliance, but he also concluded a peace which virtually restored the *status quo ante* and served to emphasize how futile the conflict with the Dutch had been.[34]

It is not easy to reach any exact conclusions about the part played by the Anglo-Dutch wars in the growth of English sea power. They certainly heightened the public's awareness of foreign economic rivalry and increased its appreciation of a strong fleet; they stimulated many reforms in the service, from the formation of the battle-line to an improvement in supply; and they expanded England's overseas empire at the same time as they reminded other states of her importance, as a naval power at least. But, apart from the fact that it would probably have been necessary to defend the Navigation Acts by force at some point, these wars appear to have produced little direct advantage to England's traders, indeed the reverse was true except for the first war: the increased taxation and the interruption of commerce, both occasioned by wars, hit the merchant community hard and shipping was often seriously affected too by the activities of the navy's press-gangs; the summer months, the best for campaigning, were thus the worst for the shipping firms. Only if the result of this conflict had been to eliminate or drastically to reduce the Dutch commercial competition, could England be said to have benefited economically; yet the fact is that, even when Dutch overseas trade was adversely affected (as in 1652–4 and 1672–8), it very quickly recovered. As we shall see later, the repeated land struggles against France in the four decades after 1672 sapped the strength of the United Provinces far more severely than did the wars with England, not only because of the higher costs of maintaining a large field army but also because the country was forced to neglect, comparatively at any rate, its naval and overseas commercial interests. However, even in the early eighteenth century, the Netherlands was flourishing and prosperous. To suppose that England's expansion in the second half of the seventeenth century was achieved upon the carcass of the Dutch Empire is, as one historian has put it, 'to fall into the mercantilist fallacies common during the period'.[35] What is more likely is that English traders were developing markets not tapped by their rivals and that, as the total world commerce expanded, the Dutch proportion of this declined relatively, whereas the English share increased.

Whatever its relationship with the state of Dutch commerce, there is no doubt that English overseas trade expanded rapidly in the years following the Restoration and in particular after the conclusion of the Third Anglo-Dutch War.[36] And not only did it expand, but it also began to diversify, both from the excessive reliance upon woollens as an export, and from a purely European scope of operations. Neither of these trends should be exaggerated, but they are of particular importance in this study because they point to these years as being the 'take-off' stage for that fruitful interaction of colonies, shipping, trade and naval strength upon which a world empire and naval mastery was to be erected. So swiftly had this diversification occurred that by the end of the century America and Asia were providing nearly a third of all England's imports, while the re-export of these commodities to Europe, together with English exports to India and America, accounted for 40 per cent of all exports. Much of this increased trade was in new goods; tobacco, the import of which rocketed from 50,000 lbs in 1615 to 38,000,000 lbs in 1700; sugar, which after the territorial expansion into the West Indies provided a source of even greater wealth; calicoes, brought in by the now flourishing East India Company. The older traffic, such as the Newfoundland and North Sea fisheries, the cloth trade, the wine shipments, also displayed healthy signs, even if their growth was less spectacular, but the exciting prospect about the colonial trades was that their economic *potential* was far greater still and that, thanks to the Navigation Acts and a strong navy, they could be reserved solely for English exploitation. The benefits of opening up the uninviting shores of North America, and of clinging on under adversity to the trading links with India, were now beginning to show.

The consequences of this growth in overseas trade were many. The customs and excise receipts rose correspondingly, enabling Danby in 1675 to pay off debts to the seamen, for example. Shipping and shipbuilding experienced a boom, particularly in the larger vessels required for lengthy oceanic voyages or for the transport of Baltic timber, which was much in demand after the Fire of London and because of the shipbuilding boom itself; thus, between 1675 and 1680 sixteen large East Indiamen were constructed. Furthermore although the prolific captures of Dutch vessels during the three wars had given the English merchant marine many ships capable of carrying bulk cargoes, by the end of the century the domestic shipbuilding industry was at last beginning to respond to the demand for such transport. Finally, England was rapidly becoming a major *entrepôt* for colonial trade, accumulating vast profits in the process and growing ever more to appreciate the value of maritime commerce.

Predictably enough, this trade expansion did much to confirm the mercantilist attitudes first established under the Commonwealth; and it can come as no great surprise to learn that the Glorious Revolution of 1688 brought about the final demise of the older monopoly trading companies. The Merchant Adventurers, the Royal African Company, the Muscovy

Company, all in turn lost their privileges, and of the great chartered companies only the East India Company, because of its peculiar responsibilities and importance, remained intact;[37] like the Eastland Company before them, the others found that ambassadors and consuls were taking over their diplomatic role, the navy taking over their protective role, and interlopers undermining their trading role. What had been created through the Navigation Acts and naval power was an English monopoly in certain overseas areas open to the whole merchant class, and supported by an establishment which accepted this form of economic thought and was increasingly disposed 'to assess national achievement by reference to commercial performance'.[38] As such, English policy seemed to combine the commercial flair and concern of the Dutch with the respect for national power of the French – a uniquely favourable merger by all accounts. And the culminating delight to these political and economic leaders of England was that the increase in trade and shipping had a favourable 'spin-off' effect upon the navy, which was in turn better able to protect it.

For this reason, the story of the Royal Navy itself during the remaining years of the Stuarts is easily recounted.[39] Both Charles and James were passionately interested in the fleet, and Parliament was usually willing to vote adequate supplies for its upkeep. Moreover, in the person of Pepys it enjoyed the attentions of its most careful and far-seeing administrator since Hawkins. Its debt was steadily reduced, and its officers and seamen regularly paid; all officers now had to undergo some professional training; corruption was eliminated and discipline improved; a steady supply of fine warships was produced, and the dockyards and logistical services were also given the benefit of Pepys' scrutiny. Only in the period 1678–83, when the Whig agitations against 'the Popish Plot' led to the temporary retirement of both James and Pepys, was there a noticeable decline in standards; but the collapse of this movement allowed the good work to be tackled with renewed enthusiasm. By 1688 the damage had been largely repaired and the fleet was a formidable force (173 vessels including many first-rates) in European power-politics – which was just as well, for in that year William of Orange successfully engineered James's dismissal and consequently drew England into the large-scale European conflict that was just beginning to erupt in reaction to the French attempt to gain continental mastery. Decades of war against a power even more formidable than the United Provinces had been, would test every aspect of England's strength and reveal the adequacy or otherwise of the foundations upon which her navy rested.

Leaving aside for later consideration that series of Anglo-French wars, it would be appropriate at this point to summarize the chief advances in

English sea power that had occurred since the death of Elizabeth. Improvements in the *physical* sphere were, it is quite apparent, less striking than in the sixteenth century. New types of sail and rigging were developed, charts and navigational techniques were steadily bettered, and ship-construction methods became a more exact science. The size and fire-power of warships increased, but not tremendously so; after all, the first real three-decker, the *Sovereign of the Seas*, was completed as early as 1637. All these were fairly natural advances and hardly compare in their impact with the revolutionary developments in the sailing ship at the time of Vasco da Gama. Perhaps the creation of the fast frigate type, acting as a scout for the fleet or as a commerce-raider, was more significant than anything mentioned above, for by it the navy became better balanced, and new dimensions in tactics and strategy were introduced.

But the really great changes in the Royal Navy in the century between the Spanish Armada and the Glorious Revolution lay in its *functions* and *composition*. From being an assembly of vessels provided for by the monarch and certain nobles and merchants, it became a national force, paid for by regular votes of Parliament; from being an occasional and motley body, it became a standing and homogeneous fleet; from being almost without any administrative and logistical support whatsoever, it developed a structure of dockyards, provisioning, accounting, recruitment and training which, although rudimentary by modern standards, were a distinct advance; and from being a force directed by gentlemen amateurs, whose own understanding of sea power was limited and whose private interests often conflicted with those of the State, it became one which was under the control of professional seamen, guided by its Fighting Instructions and Articles of War, and directly responsible to the government as an instrument of national policy.

Because the State gained a monopoly in naval power as the seventeenth century progressed, it is also possible to detect the growing interaction of England's naval expansion with her commercial and colonial development. The latter had originally been rooted in private monopolistic ventures which had had to provide for their own defence, despite the existence of a royal charter; but now that the 'commercial revolution' had taken place and the Commons were agreeing to taxes to pay for a standing navy, it was expected that English overseas interests would be protected by that force. Thus, whereas the Tudor fleet was basically a water-borne home defence squadron, the navy under the later Stuarts saw nothing unusual in escorting convoys through the Mediterranean, or in destroying distant privateer bases: it was simply the military corollary of the Navigation Acts. In rather the same way, the role of colonial expansion, undertaken by private interests under the early Stuarts was assumed by the State itself after 1655 – through conquest in war instead of through peaceful development.

All this provides us with the recognizable outlines of the future pattern of England's growth as a world power. Flourishing overseas trade aided the economy, encouraged seamanship and shipbuilding, provided funds for the national Exchequer, and was the lifeline to the colonies; the latter offered not only outlets for English products but also supplied many raw materials, ranging from the valuable sugar, tobacco and calicoes to the crucial North American naval stores; and the navy ensured respect for England's merchants in times of peace and protected their trade and garnered further colonial acquisitions in times of war, to the country's political and economic benefit. With ever-increasing pace England was transforming itself from a backward offshore island into one of the great powers and a centre of world trade; but perceptive Englishmen had already recognized that a lasting success for this policy depended not so much upon a rejection of Europe as upon a shrewd strategy of preventing a continental balance of power from altering to the country's detriment. If the Thirty Years War, the English Revolution and the struggles with the Dutch had obscured that particular calculation, the years after 1688 were to reveal again its lasting validity.

CHAPTER THREE

The Struggle against France and Spain (1689–1756)

This general view of the wars of the eighteenth century will show you that more is meant than might at first appear by the statement that expansion is the chief character of English history in the eighteenth century. At first it seems merely to mean that the conquest of Canada, India and South Africa are greater events in intrinsic importance than such European or domestic events as Marlborough's war, or the Jacobite rebellion, or even the war with the French Revolution. It means in fact, as you will now see, that these other great events which seem to have nothing to do with the growth of Greater Britain, were really closely connected with it, and were indeed only successive moments in the great process. At first it may seem to mean that the European policy of England in that century is of less importance than its colonial policy. It really means that the European policy and the colonial policy are but different aspects of the same great national development.

J. R. Seeley, *The Expansion of England* (London, 1884), p. 36.

With the outbreak of the war with France in 1689 there begins that whole series of struggles which was to culminate only in 1815 and which produced for Britain a pattern of political and strategical problems quite distinct from that of the Anglo-Dutch wars preceding the period or of the age of Pax Britannica which followed it. Before examining that pattern or the various permutations upon it which occurred in the individual wars, it would be as well to remind ourselves of the basic political and economic developments in the country between the late seventeenth and mid eighteenth centuries; for it was upon such foundations that the increasing sea power of Britain was being built.

The most noticeable trend was the coming of 'political stability' to the main power-base of England itself, if not to Ireland and Scotland, by the second and third decades of the eighteenth century. The difference has been well described by Professor Plumb:

> In the seventeenth century men killed, tortured and executed each other for political beliefs; they sacked towns and brutalized the countryside. They were subjected to conspiracy, plot and invasion. This uncertain political world lasted until 1715, and then began rapidly to vanish. By comparison, the political structure of eighteenth-century England possesses adamantine strength and profound inertia.[1]

The succession question was settled along Protestant and parliamentary lines, and the efforts of the Stuarts to upset this were beaten off; political power gravitated chiefly towards an aristocratic Whig Cabinet, which abandoned its radicalism and now endeavoured to maintain the social and economic *status quo*; commercial interests were well represented in the councils of state, not only because successful merchants entered the ranks of the gentry whilst the great landowners partook in the profits of trade, but also because the political nation as a whole recognized that the encouragement of prosperity was synonymous with the furtherance of national power and prestige; and, finally, with the growth of government offices and the vast extension in the boundaries of patronage, the executive was generally able to control the legislature and to obtain from it the funds denied to Stuart monarchs. All this is not to say that dissensions had disappeared after 1715, for the rivalries between Tories and Whigs, and even within the Whig hierarchy itself, were fierce; but such disputes involved a struggle for control of the same apparatus of power and patronage and were chiefly about the means rather than the ends of politics. There remained 'a sense of common identity in those who wielded economic, social, and political power',[2] and all agreed upon the need to preserve and enhance Britain's position in the world. A politician like Walpole might dislike an aggressive policy and strive to keep the country at peace, but his fiscal and tariff measures give us a better clue to his general attitude to Britain's development. As Seeley noted, the country could be both commercial and warlike without the basic pattern of expansion being affected.

Equally important was the continued economic growth of Britain. The tremendous improvements in agricultural techniques and productivity in this period, together with the improved climatic conditions, are worth stressing, when it is recalled that the greater part of national wealth came from the land and that the export of cloth still dominated her foreign trade. More noticeable, perhaps, was the creation and growth of financial institutions such as the Bank of England and the Stock Exchange and the establishment of the National Debt, which not only knit the Treasury and financiers closer together, but also provided the capital for overseas ventures and for expensive wars which would have ruined earlier governments: neither the fiasco of the South Sea Bubble nor the outbreak of war, although both had their impact, could undermine the immensely strong credit system that had been developed by that time. Industry, too, showed promising signs of innovation and growth (especially in iron, instrument-making, cotton and brewing), even though it probably could have benefited from the capital that was being diverted to overseas trade and colonization. In addition, the extension of the navigable river (later canal) and turnpike road systems facilitated the steady expansion of internal trade.[3]

Yet if all these factors assisted Britain's sea power indirectly, in that they strengthened the political and economic base upon which that power was constructed, it was foreign trade and overseas expansion that more directly fostered the country's maritime growth. Here, too, steady progress was made. The almost constant state of war between 1689 and 1713, together with the collapse of the post-war boom, prevented any spectacular expansion until the mid eighteenth century – but the marvel is that there was no real decline because of such events. Britain's financial sinews could take the strain of war, her shipping could carry on despite the depredations of privateers, her traders could find alternatives to closed markets, and certain industries (iron-casting and ship building) were stimulated by armaments orders. After 1748 commerce expanded at a faster pace again and showed no signs of slackening off. The overall figures, whilst concealing short-term fluctuations, summarize this growth:[4]

	Imports (£ million)	Exports (£ million)	Shipping (000 tons)
1700	6·0	6·5	(1702) 323
1750	7·8	12·7	(1751) 421
1763	11·2	14·7	496

More detailed statistics reveal that within this general pattern significant changes were taking place: trade with Europe was growing only slowly, and in certain areas declining, but this was more than compensated for by the continuing expansion of colonial commerce, particularly in the western hemisphere. America and the West Indies, now a substantial market of two million souls, increased their exports fourfold and their imports fivefold between 1700 and 1763; Indian trade also rose substantially, if less swiftly. The benefits from this traffic meant more than the fact that colonial trade was usually the most lucrative – tobacco, sugar, silk, spices, and the disgusting commerce in slaves: much of this produce was re-exported, boosting Britain's bullion stocks and its role as a middleman, and incidentally (though not unintentionally) hitting that of the Dutch; the commerce itself was protected by the Navigation Acts and provided a monopoly for British industry and merchants; at the same time it stimulated the shipping, shipbuilding and allied industries, especially since the most powerful and expensive vessels were required for the long oceanic voyages. The prosperity of ports such as Bristol and Liverpool rested upon this new trade in sugar and slaves. Inevitably it had its political and strategical consequences, too: the more Britain devoted its energies to colonial trade, the more the nation's *élite* were concerned with overseas possessions and a strong navy.

How much this development of commerce and industry was accelerated or retarded by the frequent wars in which Britain was engaged in the late seventeenth and eighteenth centuries is not yet clear to historians. As was the case in the struggle against the Dutch, the effects of war varied from industry to industry, and from one campaign to the next. It is all too easy to find evidence of the complaints of merchants engaged in (say) the Levant trade, to observe that shipping losses in the Nine Years War (1688–97) totalled 4,000 merchant vessels, and to note that the National Debt rose from £12·8 million in 1702 to £132·1 million in 1763 due to the immense costs of successive wars. On the other hand, most of this expenditure went into the hands of contractors and industries, which further stimulated parts of the economy. By 1714 the vastly-expanded Royal Navy employed more workers than any other industry in the country, and shipbuilders, Baltic timber merchants, shipping firms, dockyard contractors and many other groups benefited from the flow of State funds.[5] In an age when defence consumed well over half of the government's expenditure, the advent of war clearly had an immense effect and may be said to have accelerated the process of industrialization. The disturbance to trade and the great losses in merchant vessels were admittedly serious, provided it is remembered that the former was usually swiftly restored in peacetime, and that most ships captured were redeemable rather than being outright losses. Moreover, there were the great gains that were made in the capture of enemy merchantmen and in the seizure of their contents – so much silver was captured in 1745, for example, that remission by bill rather than the bullion itself was required.

What the wars reveal more than anything else, however, is the sheer *strength* of the British economy. It was not bankrupted by these wars and endured them far more easily than did the other powers. Foreign trade was hurt, but in no danger of being cut off: in 1713 Britain's imports and exports combined were equal in value to those of 1701, an astonishing fact when compared with the relative figures for the beginning and end of the 1914–18 and 1939–45 wars. Merchants may have been correct in saying that they would have been even greater but for the War of the Spanish Succession, yet against this calculation of *absolute* progress must be set the more important factor of *relative* advance. In terms of world power, our guideline for assessing Britain's development in 1715 or 1763 should not be based upon a hypothetical estimate of what would have occurred without war, but upon a comparison of the country's economy, naval strength and overseas colonies with those of her main rivals, France, Spain, and the Netherlands. Only when this is done do we gain a full sense of the steady rise of British naval mastery in this period.[6]

Thus the mutually supporting elements of domestic industry, overseas trade, colonial expansion and maritime strength observable under Cromwell and the later Stuarts were also to be perceived in the decades following, their most concrete manifestation being the steady acquisition of new territories as a consequence of military victories. At the Peace of Utrecht (1713) Britain came away with Gibraltar, Minorca, Hudson's Bay, Newfoundland and Nova Scotia. The Treaty of Aix-la-Chapelle (1748) produced only a stalemate solution but after the Seven Years War, which will be treated in the next chapter, she scooped the colonial 'jackpot' of Canada, Cape Breton Island, Florida, St Vincent, Tobago, Dominica and Grenada, together with effective political control of India. Nor did it appear likely that the expansion would cease at that point, for the more these successful wars and fresh territorial acquisitions enhanced Britain's relative naval strength, the more accessible the overseas world became to her influence and domination. As Professor Wilson observes: 'There is no lack of examples of stupidity, greed, waste and ineptitude in the economic and strategic policies of this period. Yet their ultimate achievement was this naval predominance which gave effective control of the seas to Britain.'[7] Already in the sixteenth century it was perceived that Britain stood to gain greatly from the Columbian maritime revolution; but only in the eighteenth century was it clear that she was fully exploiting the potential benefits of that earlier age of discovery.

The British achievement was all the more outstanding when the formidable nature of its chief opponent, France, is appreciated. In the three Anglo-Dutch wars most of the advantages, with the exception of commercial strength, had been on the side of the English; now, this was less obviously the case. France was rich in natural resources and possessed a population over three times as large as that of the British Isles. Her government was centralized, elaborate and autocratic, intent upon directing the energies and resources of that very wealthy state to the single aim of achieving victory in war. Geographically, an Anglo-French conflict posed great problems for Britain's statesmen and admirals. France could not be cut off from her overseas trade as easily as the United Provinces; there were no natural barriers such as the English Channel, and the physical and logistical strains of maintaining a blockade of the French coastline were immense. In any case the French were far less vulnerable to such economic pressure, since they were not so dependent upon overseas trade. Conversely, the French ports of Brest, Dunkirk, St Malo and others along its Atlantic and Mediterranean coastlines, provided ideal havens for hordes of commerce-raiders. Thus the strategical roles occupied by Britain and France after the Glorious Revolution were similar to those of the Netherlands and England respectively in the Anglo-Dutch wars: in both cases the former nation had to protect its vast overseas commerce from the depredations of a power situated athwart its main shipping routes. More than ever, therefore, the Royal Navy was compelled, just as Tromp and De Ruyter had been, to seek out and destroy the naval forces of the enemy – yet the blunt fact remained that the French could dictate the course of the naval war, since Paris, not London, decided how much of the conflict would be fought at sea and in which waters it would be fought.

But if France's geographical position and invulnerability to blockade made her a more formidable opponent to Britain than the Netherlands ever was, so too did her military strength and the ambitions of her monarchs and statesmen. Unlike the Dutch, the French posed an actual invasion threat if ever they should gain command of the Narrow Seas. Moreover, French policy threatened the balance of power in western Europe, firstly by its efforts to gain control of the Low Countries, thereby heightening the invasion danger to Britain; and secondly, by its equally persistent efforts to secure influence in the Iberian peninsula, which would not only tilt the strategical balance still further against the Royal Navy and virtually close the Mediterranean to trade, but could also lead to the French taking over the colonial markets of Spain and even Portugal. An Anglo-French conflict, in other words, had continental and military ramifications as well as maritime and commercial ones. As such, it resembled the sixteenth-century struggle against Spain more than anything that had occurred in the intervening period.

It was precisely because of the similarity of these Anglo-French wars with the one against Philip II of Spain that there re-emerged after 1689 that central strategical dispute which had so divided the Elizabethans and which only the peculiar nature of the Anglo-Dutch conflict had temporarily obscured: whether Britain's policy in a European war was to become militarily involved to a large degree upon the mainland in support of allies, or whether it was better to adopt a 'maritime' or 'Blue Water' strategy of colonial conquest, commercial pressure and naval victories instead. By the end of the seventeenth century there was widespread sympathy for the latter viewpoint, particularly from the Tory side. Their cause was naturally enhanced by the staggering increases in colonial trade and shipping (although its advocates persistently ignored the fact that British commerce with Europe was still far more valuable than that with the extra-European world). Each of the wars of this period produced new proponents of this strategy, the arguments of Swift's pamphlet *The Conduct of the Allies* . . . (1711) being virtually repeated by a governor of Massachusetts, who in 1745 pleaded for the capture of Louisburg and the St Lawrence fisheries, 'all of which would be an equivalent for the expense of a French war, let the consequences of it in Europe be what they may'.[8] Against this isolationist tradition stood not only William III, who naturally sought to protect his Dutch terrorities, but also many Whig statesmen, who feared the consequences of the domination of the continent by France. As Newcastle put it in 1742,

> France will outdo us at sea when they have nothing to fear on land. I have always maintained that our marine should protect our alliances on the Continent, and so, by diverting the expense of France, enable us to maintain our superiority at sea.[9]

It was a statement which Elizabeth before him, and Sir Edward Grey after him, would have appreciated. But it was not often that the inter-connection between European policy and naval policy was recognized, or that the army and navy could be employed in conjunction, instead of separately. Usually the proponents of each school were to scorn the arguments of their rivals – to the detriment of a harmonious, balanced policy. Fortunately, the other powers committed similar errors and did not possess Britain's insular position to protect them from the consequences.

In the first of these struggles against France, the War of the League of Augsburg, or the Nine Years War, it was inevitable that much attention should be focused upon the continent. The war had actually begun in 1688, following Louis XIV's move into the Rhineland, which aroused most of the rest of Europe against him and which influenced William's decision to sail for England. This blow against the 'Divine Right' of kings and the unification of the two sea powers under William prompted the French monarch into supporting James II's Irish venture, thereby bringing England into the conflict and giving it a naval as well as a military dimension. Despite this early concentration upon the security of the British Isles, however, William and the Whigs saw to it that a large expeditionary force – in 1693, over 17,000 men, later, many more – soon took its share of the fighting in the Low Countries and also supplemented the Dutch subsidies to their Danish and German allies. Indeed, by the later stages of the war Parliament was passing annual votes to sustain an army of 80,000 men and England had become the mainstay of the anti-French alliance. Due to undistinguished generalship and to the nature of the battle zones, which lent themselves more readily to defence than offence, the land campaigns resulted in a stalemate in which both sides gradually exhausted themselves. But it is as well to remember, before we turn to the maritime side of this war, that it was the long, drawn-out bleeding of France's strength on the continent which more than anything else compelled Louis XIV to make peace in 1697.[10]

The war at sea was remarkably similar in its overall course to that on land: an early French bid for a decisive victory was beaten off, various attempts were then made on both sides to break the strategical deadlock, but the final stages were inconclusive and anticlimactic. France's ability to strike quickly at sea in 1689 lay partly in the fact that she was already at war and that her centralized administration could thus operate faster than the English Admiralty, which had become accustomed to over a decade of peace; and partly in Colbert's genius in building up her maritime power. In numerical terms the combined Anglo-Dutch navies were twice as strong; in reality, they were affected by personnel and logistical weaknesses, had many vessels requiring repair, and inevitably suffered from the problems of coordinating the actions of their fleets, whereas the French enjoyed superior initial efficiency and a single command structure. In the long term the greater resources of the English and Dutch, especially in regard to Baltic naval stores, would probably tilt the balance at sea in their favour – but this depended upon their successfully stemming the French offensive.

It was as a consequence of the early French naval superiority that James II was able to land in Ireland in March 1689 and to raise that country against the Protestant Succession, and that the Royal Navy's attempts to interdict the Jacobite supply route to France led only to the inconclusive battle in Bantry Bay. Moreover, this threat to the British Isles forced William to divide his armies between Ireland and the Netherlands and to spend the greater part of his time and energies upon home defence instead of continental affairs in the two years following – a useful example of how a flank assault by an enterprising army can divert the enemy's attention from the main theatre. Unfortunately for Louis, however, James's army was not all that enterprising; at least, it did not succeed in reducing the Protestant strongholds of Londonderry and Enniskillen; nor did the French navy, although still superior in numbers in Channel waters, maintain its initiative by seeking out the English fleet or by preventing the passage of an army of 27,000 troops which arrived in Ulster in 1690 to crush the Jacobite revolt for good.[11] On the other hand, when a French force of seventy-five warships under Tourville was attacked off Beachy Head by the Channel Fleet of half its size under a reluctant Torrington, himself prodded forward by the Queen and the Council of State into an engagement he would have preferred to avoid, the result was the loss of fifteen Dutch and English ships and a sharp reverse to Allied naval hopes. Once again, however, the French failed to exploit their advantage and by the end of 1690 and throughout 1691 the Anglo-Dutch fleets in the Channel were so strong that Tourville judged discretion to be the better part of valour.

The following year, 1692, was the most decisive in naval terms, for Louis decided to risk a surprise invasion of England with 24,000 troops, calculating that his own army and navy would be ready for the summer season before those of his enemies. Again he was doomed to disappointment, for the Allies, learning of his plan, sent out a stronger fleet to meet Tourville's vessels and inflicted a smart defeat off Barfleur and La Hougue, destroying fifteen French warships and many of the invasion barges. Since France's resources were by this time too stretched by her land campaigns in the Low Countries, the Rhineland and Italy, and since she did not possess the broad commercial and shipping strength of the sea powers to maintain and increase her fleets, Colbert's great creation declined in effectiveness, the only other sortie of note by the French fleet being the successful attack upon the Smyrna convoy in 1693. The first, defensive, phase of the war was over for the Royal Navy.

The problem remaining for England's strategists was remarkably similar to that which occurred in the war of 1914–18; how to inflict a decisive blow upon the enemy which would compel him to make peace when he would not engage in a large-scale battle at sea. To William and his Dutch advisers, the answer was clear: increase the pressure upon France's northern frontiers. Yet, although Parliament continued to vote funds for this continental commitment, no breakthrough occurred in the military stalemate in the Low Countries and there were many who murmured that the Royal Navy, now greatly increased in size, was draining the country's resources to no real effect. To the 'Blue Water' advocates, these facts were deeply perturbing. The navalists' answer, again reminiscent of 1914–18, was to maintain their battle-fleets in a state of readiness in case the Brest squadron ever came out, and in the meantime to throttle the overseas trade of France. At the very beginning of the war, in fact, William had encouraged both English and Dutch navies to combine in an assault upon French commerce, a policy which accorded well with mercantilist sentiments and received the warm support of the City of London. To increase the economic pressure, neutral nations would be encouraged to abstain from trading with France, whose ambitions had provoked the war and endangered European stability. Needless to say, the neutrals were reluctant to comply with an invitation which would have hit their pockets and a lengthy diplomatic correspondence ensued, particularly with Sweden and Denmark. But the commercial blockade was also a failure for reasons mentioned above: it was physically impossible to control the sea approaches to France, and that country was not so dependent upon overseas trade in any case. Finally, certain English merchants and many more Dutch had no scruples about trading with the enemy. No doubt William was right to seek to increase the pressure upon Louis by all the means at the Allies' disposal, but the conditions were unsuitable for doing this by sea: land warfare and diplomacy were likely to be more effective. As a consequence the 'war against French trade' came to occupy a less significant place in English strategy and in the succeeding war of 1702–13 no such attempt was made to coordinate the Allied navies and privateers.[12]

Yet if these campaigns against French shipping were ineffective, the same could not be said of the attacks upon Anglo-Dutch trade during the Nine Years War. The abandonment by Louis XIV of a battle-fleet strategy signalled that even greater effort was going to be put into commerce-raiding, which the French had indulged in from the outset of the war and in which, as mentioned above, they possessed many advantages: a favourable geographical position, a multitude of targets, an economy of effort (most privateers were individually owned and financed, thus saving Louis' exchequer), and some quite outstanding sailors, especially Jean Bart. By attacking individual vessels, or assaulting convoys with 'wolf packs', or even (as in the action against the Smyrna convoy) by sending out Tourville's fleet, the French maintained a perpetual, damaging onslaught upon Allied trade.[13]

Since it has been a fundamental principle of most naval theorists since Mahan that the strategy of commerce-raiding can never be decisive and is in fact a frittering away of a country's naval strength, this French privateering campaign is worth more than a brief mention. The motive behind Louis's decision to encourage it, apart from the obvious wish on his part to dispute the Allied command at sea without risk to his battle-fleet, was certainly not a frivolous, ill-considered one. Both sides were locked in a prolonged struggle across western Europe, and victory would go to the one which lasted out longest. France depended upon her large internal resources; the Allies, if not exclusively, then to a very considerable extent, upon the riches that accrued from the profits of English and Dutch foreign trade. If the latter were cut off, France's opponents would soon sue for peace. As Vauban, that great military expert, put it in 1695 when advocating a naval campaign which would be 'hard and inconvenient' for the Allies,

> Brest is so placed as though God had made it expressly for the purpose of the destruction of the commerce of these two nations. The most skilful policy is the shaking of the buttresses of the League by means of a subtle and widespread form of war [i.e. *guerre de course*].[14]

It was an argument similar to that used by Germany's military leaders in 1917 in favour of unrestricted submarine warfare and, since, in this case, intervention by a third party as powerful correspondingly as the United States was out of the question, there was much to be said for it. But it is in the results of the French privateering campaign that the real test lies. A staggering total of over 4,000 ships were captured or ransomed, chiefly after 1693; the attack on the Smyrna convoy dealt a tremendous blow to the Levant Company, and Mediterranean trade suffered throughout the war; and by 1697 English and Dutch merchants were eager for peace. However, by that time Louis himself was anxious to compromise, due to France's inability to keep up the costly land campaigns. Thus, if the war demonstrated the economic (and also social and political) strength of England, which was able to carry on despite these heavy losses, it also demonstrated that under certain circumstances a *guerre de course* strategy was not to be scorned. Even Mahan admitted that 'At no time has war against commerce been conducted on a larger scale and with greater results than during this period; and its operations were widest and most devastating at the very time that the great French Fleets were disappearing, ... apparently contradicting the assertion that such a warfare must be based on powerful fleets or neighbouring seaports.'[15]

If the Royal Navy was ineffective in exerting economic pressure upon France and in protecting English shipping, little was achieved in other fields of maritime operations to compensate for these failures. Many a pamphleteer had urged the need for a vigorous assault upon France's overseas territories, which would not only be a correct use of sea power but would also result in considerable economic benefit. Yet the few colonial campaigns fought during this war proved to be disappointments due chiefly to an almost complete lack of preparation and efficient organization in either North America or the West Indies, and the conflict in those regions degenerated into what one scholar has termed 'a medieval process of cross-ravaging'.[16] Until expeditions were arranged with greater care, neither financial nor strategical profit would accrue from them. The same was true of the very few ventures made in the field of what was later to be called 'combined operations'. An attempt in 1691–2 to seize Brest, stimulated by the enemy's successful invasion of Cork and Kinsale, was abandoned when the French plans to invade England became known; another was actually made in 1694, but it lacked both secrecy and strength, and the landings at Camaret Bay were easily repulsed by the French. This, too, created such a dismal precedent that no further efforts were made in this direction and, while the army concentrated thereafter upon its continental campaign, the navy opted to maintain, with little success, a purely maritime check upon French privateering ports for the rest of the war. Only in the Mediterranean was the fleet used as an effective instrument of national policy, the arrival of Admiral Russell's squadron in the Gulf of Lyons in 1694 serving the triple aim of protecting the Levant trade, dividing the Brest and Toulon fleets, and checking the French assault upon Barcelona. Indeed, so successful was this intrusion of Allied naval strength into the Mediterranean that William ordered the fleet to winter in Cadiz in order to maintain its control of that sea; but in 1696, with rumours of another French invasion attempt prevalent, the warships were recalled to the Channel and the effect of the English presence in the Mediterranean was gradually lost. When the war ended in September 1697 with the Treaty of Ryswick, which virtually restored the *status quo ante*, the stalemate on land was matched by another at sea.

Because the settlement of 1697 provided no sweeping gains for England, it is all too easy to agree with the contemporary Tory criticism that the war had been a disappointment and a waste. Yet there were many strategic benefits from the conflict. The Glorious Revolution of 1688 had been upheld. Ireland had been made secure. Louis XIV's continental ambitions had been checked, and France had been brought to a state of exhaustion. An English army had been recreated and equipped for the demands of modern warfare. Finally, although the Royal Navy had not achieved what had been hoped from it, it had regained strategical command of the sea after 1692 and it had expanded and acquired much useful experience of naval warfare, which had naturally been lacking since the Dutch wars. By 1697 the service itself had reached the enormous size of some 323 vessels, totalling over 160,000 tons, a tribute to England's productive strength. The importance of the convoy system had been made all too obvious by the privateering successes, and better protection to merchant shipping was being given a high priority; the idea of maintaining a constant blockade upon the enemy's main fleet-base was, it has been suggested, evolved during this war;[17] and the necessity of establishing a strong naval presence in the Mediterranean to counter French aims there had been recognized. All this was to prove of great value when the next round of the Anglo-French struggle began.[18]

If the period of peace between 1697 and 1702 gave British merchants a welcome opportunity to return to the more normal conditions of trade, it also offered France time for recuperation and, with the death of the childless King of Spain in 1700, provided Louis XIV with the opportunity to expand his influence in Europe and overseas by pushing the claims of his grandson to that vast inheritance. Nothing could have been more calculated to unite the various factions in English politics, Whigs and Tories, the 'continentalists' and the 'isolationists', than the series of actions undertaken by Louis in the first two years of the eighteenth century. With the country enjoying an economic 'boom', with the armed forces cut down to an exceedingly low level, and with William III still not a very popular figure in English eyes, it would have been difficult to say the least to persuade the Commons to go to war if the French king had been less provocative. But Louis's insistence that the Divine Right of Kings permitted the future merger of France and Spain, together with his recognition of James III as King of England, alarmed all who had an interest in preserving the Protestant Succession; the movement of French troops into the Spanish Netherlands scared not only the Dutch but also many Englishmen; the prospect that much of western Europe and the Mediterranean would now come under the sway of Versailles meant that the continental balance had definitely gone awry and that England's own security was involved; and the threat to English trade represented by Bourbon control of Sicily, Naples, the West Indies and much of Latin America hit another raw nerve.[19] This economic challenge aroused commercial groupings uninterested in balance-of-power politics, and their concern was heightened by the arguments of propagandists such as Defoe:

> What is England without trade? Without its Plantation trade, Turkey and Spanish trade, and where will that be when a French garrison is planted at Cuba and the French fleet brings home the plate

> from Havana? What will the Virginia colony be worth when the French have a free commerce from Quebec to Mexico behind them; what will our own northern trade be worth in time of war when the ports of Ostend and Nieuport are as full of pirates as Dunkirk and St Malo?[20]

What, indeed? It was enough to make the most pacific merchant yearn for the forcible destruction of the King of France's grand design.

The War of the Spanish Succession which followed was in many respects similar to the Nine Years War, except that this time it lasted long enough to exhaust France fully and to allow the British (as they became in 1707, with the Act of Union) to reap the benefits from what had been almost a twenty-five-year struggle against Louis XIV. In the first place, the major focus was again upon the land campaign, only now the Allies enjoyed the superb generalship of Marlborough and Eugene of Savoy, instead of that of the more mediocre William III, who had been succeeded by Anne just before the outset of the war; hence the successes of Blenheim, Ramillies and Oudenarde (Malplaquet hardly qualifies for that description), which not only revealed that Britain had an army and a strategic leader at least equal to the best in Europe but also that she was prepared to use them to the full to prevent French hegemony. On the other hand, although France was bankrupt by the end of the war and Louis would have made peace some years earlier but for the extravagance of the Allied demands, his country was not overrun and after 1710 it was increasingly aided by the Tory electoral victory in Britain and the Bourbon military successes in Spain; in other words, France at the Treaty of Utrecht resembled in certain respects the Germany of 1918 but not at all the Germany of 1945, and this meant that the European balance had not been tilted too drastically towards the Allies.[21] This, of course, was all to the good so far as the British government was concerned, since it was assured of a continental equilibrium at the same time as it had – again, like 1918 – made extensive gains in the extra-European world. The fact that the Tory settlement with France, by reversing the Whig policy of the continental commitment, had provided the first example for the legend of 'perfidious Albion' was hardly seen as a weighty counter-argument by the new administration in London, which had long felt that their country had taken too great a share of the burdens of the war.

If the conflict at sea was subordinate to that on land for the defeat of France – and the annual votes for the army and subsidies to continental allies leave us in little doubt on that account – this tendency was accentuated by the virtual disappearance of the French battle-fleet. The commerce-raiders might flourish again, but overall strategic control at sea rested firmly in British hands: the fruits of the Nine Years War, which boosted the expansion of the Royal Navy as it reduced the navies of its rivals, were now being harvested. Yet this maritime predominance, similar to that which had occurred after 1694, raised the old problem of how British sea power was to play a decisive role in the defeat of an enemy which did not seek naval mastery and was not dependent upon overseas commerce. The chief features of the previous maritime campaign – combined operations, colonial struggles, the war to protect Allied commerce, and the deployment of naval strength in the Mediterranean – not surprisingly re-occurred, and only in the latter was there a marked improvement.

Combined operations against France, certainly, were unlikely to be regarded seriously in London whilst the army was achieving great victories on the continent, and neither service possessed the equipment or the expertise to carry out a strategically useful flank attack upon the enemy's coastline. Only Nottingham for the Tories espoused this form of warfare but the few raids that were attempted – in the Channel in 1708, at the mouth of the Charente a little later – made no impression upon either the French economy or her troop dispositions. It was to be a different matter in the Mediterranean, as we shall see shortly. The establishment of a naval blockade to cut off French overseas traffic was equally ineffective, not only due to the reasons already outlined but also to the fact that the whole Spanish coastline would have required watching as well. Furthermore, the Dutch as usual insisted upon trading with the enemy, suspecting (correctly) that one reason why Britain desired to throttle France's foreign commerce was because her merchants did not have a share in it.

But if the efforts to halt French shipping in general were fruitless, perhaps a decisive blow in some specific area where the enemy was vulnerable might achieve greater results? Several opportunities offered themselves here. In 1709 the dreadful winter and the consequent famine in France persuaded the British government to order the seizure of all corn ships bound for her ports, 'to distress the enemy as much as possible'. This led to the most intensive blockading campaign hitherto mounted by the Royal Navy, but France still held out until the better harvests of the following year. Even more optimism on the British side was placed behind the scheme to cut off the Spanish *flota*, which now brought bullion from Latin America to assist the Bourbon war effort and which the French navy had helped to escort to Cadiz from 1701 onwards. Like Drake and Hawkins before them, the maritime school under Queen Anne argued that this form of institutionalized looting would be more profitable, less onerous and ultimately more effective than a military campaign in the

Low Countries. On two occasions success was achieved. In 1702 the expedition under Rooke, which had failed miserably to take Cadiz, was able to snatch victory out of defeat on its return journey by bursting into Vigo Harbour, where it sank the *flota* and also destroyed fifteen French ships of the line. And in 1708 a small squadron under Commodore Wager attacked a Spanish bullion-fleet in the West Indies, sinking or capturing treasure to the value of fourteen or fifteen million sterling. Yet, despite Sunderland's hope that this 'would prove a fatal blow to France, for I believe that this was one of their last resources for carrying on the war', it did little to shake Louis's determination.[22] One month later another *flota* had safely crossed the Atlantic but in any case France was never so dependent upon this source of finance as Swift and the Tory propagandists imagined: bullion supplies were simply a bonus to the larger and more certain forms of revenue such as the *taille* and the *gabelle*, and the belief on the British side that an easy way might be found to bring such a formidable opponent as France to her knees served to detract attention from the main theatre of war.

The colonial campaigns may similarly be classed as side-shows, although their proponents were to claim that, if one quarter of the resources which had gone into supporting Marlborough's army had been allocated to the American and West Indian fighting, things would have been different. This assertion is highly questionable. As it was, apart from the purely naval war of mutual commerce-raiding and protection, the only noticeable event was the seizure of Port Royal in Nova Scotia in 1710, in which colonial troops played the major role; but against this had to be set the failure to capture Quebec in the following year. In the West Indies inter-island raiding was endemic, but of little real import to the war. The valuable colonial gains to Britain were only to come in a later Anglo-French conflict.

Protecting British shipping from the perils of the *guerre de course* remained, as ever, the most difficult task for the Royal Navy and, as soon as the conflict broke out, French privateers revealed that they had lost none of their enterprise and aggression. Moreover, since there was no intention on the part of their government of fighting full-scale fleet battles, large numbers of royal vessels were also available to attack Allied merchantmen. Operating in groups of four or six, these frigates were fleet enough to escape the attentions of British ships of the line yet strong enough to overwhelm the few escorts provided to each convoy, while there were always sufficient privateers waiting to exploit their opportunity as soon as the British escorts were engaged. Under such daring and skilful commanders as Du Guay, Forbin and Saint-Pol, the French gained one notable success after another. The Dunkirk privateers led the way, bringing 959 prizes into port, and by 1708 the British Admiralty was even considering the closure of that base through block-ships until the impracticality of this plan was recognized.

So effective was the *guerre de course* and the outcry of the London merchants at the lack of effective naval protection that a parliamentary inquiry was begun in 1707 and the 'Cruisers and Convoys Act' passed in the next year, allotting a specific number of warships to the defence of trade. Convoys were given increased protection and cruisers were stationed off major ports and in the Western Approaches, to cover the more important shipping routes. Gradually, the situation improved: in 1710, 3,550 ships left English ports: in 1712, 4,267; in 1713, the year of peace, 5,807. However, the tighter measures around the British Isles forced the privateers to look farther afield, and colonial shipping was repeatedly harassed in the later years of the war. Moreover, it was predictable that after the Anglo-French Cessation of Arms (autumn 1712) trade was bound to increase even without the assistance of an improved escort system, the effects of which British naval historians may have over estimated. The figures of total British losses, 3,250 vessels (about one third of which were based on London) are probably reasonably accurate and the French had once again revealed the damage that could be inflicted from this form of attack.[23] What this campaign also illustrated was the enormity of the problem of trade protection facing the Royal Navy now that Britain's shipping industry had expanded so much; the service would clearly never have enough cruisers to escort all merchantmen, and even in the twentieth century (until 1930, at least) it steadfastly refused to accept any limitation upon that class of warship. A great maritime empire brought problems as well as advantages.

The most successful deployment of British sea power during the War of the Spanish Succession was in the Mediterranean.[24] This, too, was a repetition of William III's strategy, but under Marlborough it was accorded a higher priority; for, although the continental struggle remained at the centre of British interests under Queen Anne, Marlborough could perceive more clearly than many members of the Tory 'maritime' school the advantages which would follow from British domination of that sea. It would protect the Levant trade; offer assistance to Savoy; enable operations to be undertaken in Spain; and divert French forces from the north to protect their southern coastline. The Mediterranean Fleet, in a nutshell, was to be the other arm of a strategic 'pincer', which Marlborough hoped to use against France.

To a considerable degree, this strategy was successful. The abortive expedition of 1702 to seize Cadiz, compensated for only partially by the sinking of the *flota* at Vigo, was followed two years later by the overrunning of Gibraltar, at that time far less developed as a port but much more defensible from the inevitable land attacks that would follow any amphibious assault upon the enemy's coastline. Between those two occasions, in 1703, Britain concluded the famous Methuen Treaty with Portugal, which provided a foothold for the Grand Alliance in the Iberian peninsula, a valuable market for British goods, a source of gold bullion (from Brazil) and, in Lisbon, a wintering base vital for the supply of Gibraltar. After the defeat of the Franco-Spanish attempts to recapture the Rock from both land and sea, the new acquisition was secure and gave the Royal Navy an important strategic weapon with which to frustrate the merger of France's Northern and Mediterranean fleets in the future. Even in this region, however, the influence of sea power had its natural limitations. A superior Royal Navy could cover the Allied landing in Catalonia in 1705, and drive off the French coastal counter-offensive in the following year; and it could ensure the capture both of Sardinia and of Minorca with its superb anchorage of Port Mahon in 1708, thereby neutralizing the Toulon fleet, encouraging Britain's Mediterranean allies and protecting the Levant trade. But it could have little effect upon the lengthy conflict for control of central Spain; nor could it, despite the bombardment of Toulon which forced the French to scuttle their warships, ensure the capture of that base. Both required large-scale and determined armies and efficient logistical support. Neither were forthcoming. Yet, despite these failures, Britain had clearly emerged as a first-class Mediterranean power by the later stages of the war and had thus gone some way to countering the geographical disadvantages facing her in every conflict with France.

The terms of the Treaty of Utrecht, though negotiated by a Tory ministry eager to wind up the conflict, showed Britain to be the real victor of the War of the Spanish Succession.[25] Historians of empire have tended to stress its maritime and extra-European clauses: the acquisition of territory around Hudson's Bay, Nova Scotia and Newfoundland; the granting of the *Asiento*, that lucrative and awful trade in slaves to Spanish America; and the extension of British power into the Mediterranean through the conquest of Gibraltar and Minorca. But to British statesmen at the time, the continental aspects were every bit as important. The promise that France and Spain would never be united under the same crown ensured that there would be no French domination of western Europe. The allocation of the Spanish Netherlands, Naples and Sardinia to Austria, a non-maritime power, was a classic example of *divide et impera* on Britain's part, since it tied the Emperor to the defence of those key strategical points which London wished, in any case, to be kept out of Bourbon hands. Friendly relations with those British satellites, Portugal and Savoy, the latter of which received Sicily, and the acquisition of some (but not all) of the barrier fortresses by the Dutch, completed this system of checks and balances. The destruction of the privateer port of Dunkirk, and the recognition by Louis XIV of the Protestant Succession in Britain, put the icing on the cake. Mahan's claim that British demands at the peace revealed her as having become 'a sea power in the purest sense of the word, not only in fact, but also in her own consciousness',[26] should not obscure for us the importance which was also attached to the continental equilibrium.

Even more disputable is Mahan's description of the immediate importance of the naval struggle as the basic reason for Britain's victories in 1697 and 1713. It is simply not correct to write of 'the quiet, steady pressure' of sea power or of France's need for 'external activities and resources'[27] except to a very limited extent. As Professor Jones points out,

> Certainly it is true that control of the narrow seas was essential if invasion was to be prevented and trade was to continue, but both the Nine Years War and the War of the Spanish Succession showed that France could not be defeated, or even forced to concede a satisfactory peace by the use of sea power alone. French strength was essentially land-based.[28]

The real reason for the exhaustion of France was not the naval blockade but the cost of the military campaigns; and the cause of the eventual Allied success – here Mahan was on safer ground – was the economic strength of Britain, which financed much of the war effort.[29] As one scholar has put it, 'All William's tenacity or Marlborough's genius would have been of little avail had they lacked the wealth to support the armies with which they humbled the marshalls of France.'[30] This is not to decry the influence of sea power, since Britain's wealth would obviously have been lost had she herself surrendered command of the sea; but we should be careful not to over estimate the direct as opposed to the indirect, the offensive as opposed to the defensive, effects of that supremacy.

The overall result of this struggle is indisputable, however. 'At the accession of William III, England was one of the three leading sea powers; at the accession of George I, she was the leading sea power, without a rival or even a companion.'[31] For the land war, which had sapped France's strength, had also caused her to neglect Colbert's great scheme, and Allied privateers had inflicted further damage upon an already declining French merchant marine; by 1713 neither it, nor the French Royal Navy, was in any position to challenge Britain's. The same was true of the Dutch navy (though not of the mercantile marine), and for precisely the same reason: too large a proportion of national resources had had to be devoted to land warfare. It was the maintenance of an army of some 100,000 men throughout this period, and the fact that the Netherlands government was still required to keep up a large standing force thereafter, which hit Dutch sea power more than anything else.[32] Britain's insular position and social-political system, besides proving more than a match for the concentrated resources of the far more populous French state, had enabled her to maintain that fine balance between maritime and continental interests which were the prerequisite of her rise to naval mastery. Through the cherishing of her commercial and naval strength, *and* through her preservation of the European balance, she had found the recipe for her long period as the leading world power.

This intermingling of maritime and continental calculations also provides the key to an understanding of British policy in the decades following 1713, and the fact that it was a period of comparative peace should not obscure the attention London gave to promoting the country's interests by 'armed diplomacy'.[33] Anxious though British statesmen were in these years to avoid war, their policy was in many cases similar to that of Cromwell's in the 1650s: a watchful concern for all developments which might have strategical or commercial consequences for the United Kingdom. At times this involved working in close cooperation with the other obvious Great Power, France, at other times working against her, this whole century furnishing evidence for Palmerston's later claim that Britain had no eternal allies, only eternal interests. But in an age of constantly-changing alliances and *Kabinettskriege*, the other powers had little cause for complaint about Britain's unreliability.

Events in the Mediterranean and Baltic furnish the best examples of this British policy. The revival of Spanish power under Cardinal Alberoni which led to the forcible seizure of Sardinia and Sicily, his intrigues with Sweden and Russia to secure a Jacobite succession in Britain, and a farcical Spanish invasion of the Western Highlands in 1719, were checked at two levels. In July 1717 Byng's Mediterranean Fleet smashed a Spanish squadron off Cape Passaro. At the same time, an alliance was made with France and Austria, both of whom had reason to oppose Spain's actions. Whilst imperial troops were hastily sent to recover Sicily, the French army actually invaded Spain in 1719 and forced the surrender of its government – an action usually missed in British naval histories. Yet within a few years of these events the British government had ruptured relations with its former ally, Austria, when the latter backed the Ostend Company and secured for it access to Spain's overseas empire. Such a step, which might have led to the reopening of the port of Antwerp, alarmed the vociferous mercantile lobby in England; the prospect of a future imperial navy being established on the other side of the Channel worried navalists; and the general attitude of the Emperor provoked fears that the foundations for an anti-Protestant Austro-Spanish alliance were being laid. As in so many other cases in this period, it is difficult to separate the commercial aspect from the political in British diplomacy; nor, perhaps, is it all that necessary that we do so, the real point being that under statesmen such as Stanhope, Walpole and Chatham, politics and commerce, commerce and politics, were so inextricably linked as to make any division of the two artificial. So critical did Britain's relations with Spain and Austria become over these various points of dispute that an undeclared state of war existed between 1725 and 1727, during which time siege was laid to Gibraltar by Spanish forces whilst the Royal Navy sought to prevent the *flotas* from sailing. By the summer of 1727, however, Austria had abandoned its joint design and hostilities were petering out, although relations between London and Madrid were not fully restored until 1729.

In the Baltic, too, the British employed a combination of diplomacy and naval strength to secure their interests, which primarily concerned the timber trade and the preservation of a balance of power between the northern states. From 1715 to 1718 strong fleets were sent into that sea to check Sweden, which offended the British government by interrupting maritime commerce, threatening Norway and supporting the Jacobites; yet between 1719 and 1721, and again between 1725 and 1727, the Royal Navy cruised in the Baltic to support the Swedes, particularly against the rising power of Peter the Great's Russia, whose ambitions were viewed with increasing alarm in London. If anything, it was the limitations rather than the influence of sea power which the British government encountered at this time, for Norris's galleons could not prevent the frequent galley-borne assaults upon the Swedish coast by Russian troops, nor could the steady territorial expansion of the Tsar be checked unless Britain found another Great Power to act as her continental sword – but neither Austria, Prussia nor France desired to occupy that unenviable position. As a consequence, the British government could only resign itself to the steady diminution of Sweden's power and the equally steady rise of Russia's, its pessimism about the future being reflected in its encouragement of the development of American naval stores as a reinsurance against the loss of Baltic supplies.

The post-1713 period of relative peace was due not only to the influence of statesmen such as Walpole and Fleury but also to the fact that there were no serious differences between Britain and her great rival, France. By the 1730s, however, there were signs that this state of affairs was unlikely to continue for much longer: French colonial trade in North America, the West Indies and India was growing rapidly; France and Spain had drawn closer together, and the political and commercial rivalry between these two powers and Britain provoked public jealousies, which conciliatory statesmanship found difficult to overcome. The first stage of the resumption of fighting occurred between Spain and Britain in 1739, occasioned, as every schoolboy used to know, by the ignoble action of a Spanish coastguard in slicing off part of Captain Jenkins's ear. The incident was only one in a whole series of clashes which had taken place in the Caribbean since the Peace of Utrecht, the root cause being the incompatibility of the desire of British merchants to share in the lucrative trade of Latin America with the determination of the Spanish authorities to retain their control and near-monopoly there. The brief Anglo-Spanish wars in 1718 and 1727 had exposed this antipathy, as well as setting precedents for the manner in which the conflict would be fought. Nevertheless, most historians admit that 'None of these disputes was so grave as to lead inevitably to war. War was made unavoidable by the truculence and clamour of the "trading part of the nation" in England, and in particular by the intransigence of the South Sea Company',[34] which insisted upon terms for compensation which the Spanish government could hardly accept. With the Opposition exploiting these commercial grievances to whip up a public clamour for war, Walpole's ministry gave way before this storm in October 1739.[35]

But if the conflict began as a colonial and commercial one, it had quite transformed itself by the following year, when the death of the Emperor Charles VI and the succession of Maria Theresa provoked Prussia, Saxony, Bavaria and Spain, all encouraged by France, into attempting the dismemberment of Austria. This plot affected British interests not merely because of the attitude of George II – if anything, the Crown's connection with Hanover was a hindrance to the government's continental policy in these years – but more importantly because of the implications for the European balance. Austria was, in British eyes, the traditional counterweight to French hegemony and, in addition, the question of the future of the Austrian possessions in the Low Countries and Italy was always calculated to interest British statesmen. As a result, subsidies were voted for Austria, which was also informed that the 1732 promise of an army of 12,000 to defend the Pragmatic Sanction would be kept. By 1742, indeed, Walpole had been ousted and a more vigorous military commitment was undertaken, a trend which was accelerated by the open French intervention in 1744 and her attempt to overrun the Low Countries. The war of Queen Anne was being fought once again, although this time France enjoyed the support of many more allies than previously.[36]

The inevitable consequence of the addition of a European dimension to what had been originally an Anglo-Spanish conflict was the revival of the debate over the British strategy.[37] Because the great fear of France's designs in Europe outweighed the hope of colonial gain, the continentalists kept the upper hand, although the concentration upon the military side of the war was ironically helped by the French unwillingness to dispute Britain's maritime predominance. Whether the intervention in Flanders was a success or whether the money could have been better allocated elsewhere, as the critics maintained, is difficult to assess from this distance. The victory of the Anglo-Hanoverian-Austrian armies at Dettingen was cancelled out by the defeat at Fontenoy and the French gains in Flanders, and even more by the Jacobite Rebellion of 1745. Yet although the latter showed how easy it remained for the King of France to make trouble for Britain on her Celtic fringes, and provoked such panic-stricken measures as the recall of Cumberland's troops from the Low Countries, it also added one further reason – the defence of the Protestant Succession – for the continuation of the war. It was the French recognition of Britain's willingness and ability to continue fighting, despite the further victories of Marshal Saxe in Flanders in 1746–7, which prompted Louis XV to begin the peace negotiations which led to the Treaty of Aix-la-Chapelle in 1748. By that time, both the main combatants were ready to compromise, although France was the more exhausted economically and felt that she had more to lose – her colonies, in particular – if the conflict continued.

Against the French successes on land could be placed those of Britain in the maritime sphere of operations. In the West Indies itself little progress was made by either side. The surprise capture of Porto Bello by Admiral Vernon, together with Anson's epic voyage around the globe, were nullified by the disastrous result of the combined raid against Cartagena, the desultory nature of the warfare conducted between the British and French West Indian islands, and the early failure of the Royal Navy to cut the Franco-Spanish links to that region. In India another stage in the spasmodic Anglo-French duel was fought out but, although the British eventually established naval supremacy in those waters, the French captured Madras and held on firmly to their own garrisons in the Carnatic. Only in North America, where a colonial army from New England combined with a naval squadron to seize the great French base of Louisbourg, was any substantial success – strategical and commercial – achieved.[38]

At the conclusion of peace, however, Louisbourg was restored to France, which in turn surrendered both Madras and the gains in Flanders. To the New England colonists, and to advocates of maritime warfare in Britain, the return of 'the key to the St Lawrence' to their deadly enemy was a great blow, made necessary only by the foolish commitment to the Dutch and other continental allies. To such criticism two retorts were given. In the first place, the indications were that France would have joined Spain in her dispute with Britain irrespective of the Austrian Succession question arising; and the combined resources of the Bourbon powers, unhindered by continental considerations, would have meant a much harder and possibly less successful war in the extra-European field. A conflict in *both* spheres was more advantageous to Britain, since it led to an even greater strategical ambivalence and division of resources on France's part than on her own. Secondly, while Britain's colonial conquests were a major reason for France to surrender her gains in Flanders, the correct policy should have been to achieve victory overseas and on the continent *simultaneously*, for by this Britain would have preserved the balance of power and ensured that she did not have to give up colonial acquisitions to recover European losses. As Pitt perceived after 1760, since Britain was a world *and* a European power, it was futile to have the benefits of one campaign cancelled out by the losses of another – but this meant victory in both, not abandonment of one.[39]

In all other respects, the war testified to the growing maritime mastery of Britain, although this only became apparent in its later stages due to the unpreparedness of the fleet and the lack of any coherent strategy at the outset.[40] Domination of the Mediterranean was achieved quite early, for the government was well aware of the need to cover Sardinia and the Austrian territories in Italy from amphibious assault by Franco-Spanish forces; and after Admiral Mathew had scattered the enemy's combined fleet in the fiasco off Toulon in 1744 that sea became virtually a 'British lake'. Naval mastery was harder to achieve in the Atlantic, however, because of the variety of other tasks assigned to the Royal Navy. But the vital supply link to the continent was never broken and, after the defensive deployments to meet the possibility of invasion had prevented any reinforcements from France reaching the Jacobites in the rising of 1745 to 1746, the service was ready to go on to the offensive. Under Anson a strong Western Squadron was built up, its aims being to cut off French Atlantic trade and to block the dispatch of forces to North America or the West Indies which would affect the military struggle there. In May 1747 Anson's squadron badly mauled an escorted convoy under La

Jonquière which was seeking to reinforce Quebec; and in October Hawke achieved an even more decisive victory against a West Indian convoy, the overwhelming of the French escorts through the tactic of the 'general chase' being later complemented by the rounding up of many of the merchantmen by a forewarned British squadron cruising off the Leeward Islands.[41]

Thereafter, the Royal Navy was able to give almost total attention to the protection of merchant shipping, which was suffering from the inevitable depredations of a Franco-Spanish *guerre de course*, although the industry as a whole was able to withstand the strain and was actually larger at the end of the war than it was at the beginning: total losses of 3,238 ships were a much smaller proportion of her fleet than the combined enemy losses of 3,434 ships. France's overseas trade, by contrast, had shrivelled away altogether by 1748, due to the capture of her Newfoundland fisheries, the attacks of British warships and privateers and, perhaps most important of all, the rocketing cost of marine insurance.[42] And, while Professor Graham is correct in stating that 'the real strength and vigour of France lay in a *continental* self-sufficiency',[43] it does seem that Britain's naval supremacy and her threat to the French colonies inclined Paris towards a settlement in the same way that France's military predominance and her threat to the panic-stricken Dutch persuaded London to accept a peace with few tangible gains. The impressive power of the 136 British ships-of-the-line (against the thirty-one French and twenty-two Spanish) in 1747, and Saxe's capture of the great fortress of Bergen-op-Zoom in the same year, were each in their way inducements to the other side to compromise.

All contemporaries and later historians agree that the peace of Aix-la-Chapelle was a compromise. Apart from the Prussian acquisition of Silesian territory, the result was essentially a return to the *status quo ante bellum*, prompting the remark that 'Never, perhaps, did any war, after so many great events, and so large a loss of blood and treasure, end in replacing the nations engaged in it so nearly in the same position as they held at first.'[44] Furthermore, the very fact that peace had come about through a general war-weariness and a recognition on the part of the two main combatants that the other could not be induced to surrender, meant that the differences which had caused the conflict were not satisfactorily settled at Aix-la-Chapelle; the right of search by Spanish coast-guards in the Caribbean, the original spark to the war, was not even mentioned, for example. Most important of all, the Franco-British antagonism remained as deep as ever, both in the colonial world and in regard to the European balance. In addition to being a compromise, therefore, the 1748 settlement was also a truce; and while France's obvious object in any future conflict would be to gain the overseas successes to complement her expected European conquests, Britain's would be to ensure that her own anticipated maritime victories would no longer be cancelled out by continental losses. In the next round of the struggle both sides would aim for a decisive, not a partial, victory.

PART TWO

Zenith

Of the five great wars of the period, Britain was clearly on the defensive in only one. The result of this century of intermittent warfare was the greatest triumph ever achieved by any state: the virtual monopoly among European powers of overseas colonies, and the virtual monopoly of world-wide naval power.

E. J. Hobsbawm, *Industry and Empire* (Harmondsworth, Middlesex, 1969), pp. 49–50

CHAPTER FOUR

Triumph and Check (1756–93)

It will be asked why, when we have as great, if not a greater, force than we ever had, the enemy are superior to us. To this it is to be answered that England till this time was never engaged in a sea war with the House of Bourbon thoroughly united, their naval force unbroken, and having no other war or object to draw off their attention and resources. We unfortunately have an additional war on our hands which essentially drains our resources and employs a very considerable part of our army and navy: we have no one friend or ally to assist us: on the contrary all those who ought to be our allies except Portugal act against us in supplying our enemies with the means of equipping their fleets.

The Private Papers of John, Earl of Sandwich,
edited by G. R. Barnes and J. H. Owen,
4 vols. (London, 1932–8; Navy Records Society), iii, p. 170.

No period offers the historian a better opportunity of studying the rise of British naval mastery than that during which the Seven Years War and the War of Independence took place. Although at first sight nothing could appear more different than the peace settlement of 1763, where Britain gained what was probably the most decisive victory in her history as a nation-state, and that of 1783, where she suffered the only serious defeat between the Second Dutch War and the First Boer War, nevertheless the respective outcomes of both these conflicts confirm the basic principles about the application – and the limitations – of sea power. This is particularly true of that crucial relationship between 'maritime' and 'continental' warfare which we have examined earlier. Moreover, it is clear that, despite the losses suffered in the War of American Independence, the underlying growth of British maritime power had not been fundamentally affected; the navy was kept strong after 1783, foreign trade was booming and – most important of all – the country was by then well into the first stages of an industrial revolution which would enable it to outdistance all other rivals and to become the only real world power for a remarkable length of time.

Further general similarities between the wars of 1756–63 and 1776–83 also spring to mind. Both represented, like the stalemated War of the Austrian Succession, stages in that Anglo-French duel which lasted throughout the eighteenth century; they involved, in consequence, calculations about the continental balance of power and the mutual need of both rivals for European allies to divert the enemy's attention; and their origins, by coincidence, were all to be found in local struggles in the western hemisphere, which were later transferred to the other side of the Atlantic and merged into existing rivalries there. Britain's success, as noted previously, would depend upon whether she could find continental allies active enough to pin down France's resources in land wars and strong enough to avoid being taken 'hostage' whilst London was ensuring the destruction of French naval and colonial power; in the Seven Years War this aim was superbly accomplished, thanks to the leadership of Pitt and to the military brilliance of Frederick the Great. France's success, in contrast, would depend upon whether she could keep Europe at least neutral and possibly anti-British, and to a lesser extent upon whether circumstances in the overseas world would allow her to take advantage of any weakening or diversion of Britain's usual maritime superiority; in the War of American Independence this aim was also achieved, thanks to French diplomacy and to the military successes of the American rebels. Neither conflict settled this Anglo-French duel for good, but we can see in retrospect that Britain's power-political foundations were growing ever stronger in this period and that, with her statesmen reminded by the unsuccessful war of 1776–83 of the correct strategical principles, she was in a better position to endure a future struggle with her great rival.

Although previous wars had seen the Great Powers fighting both in Europe and overseas, the Seven Years War can lay a far stronger claim to the title of the first *world* war than many others before or since, because sustained and significant fighting took place in three continents and also because the two chief combatants attached a great deal of importance to their colonial campaigns:[1] far more, it may be noted, than was attached to their equivalents in the 'First World War' of 1914–18. On the British side, this healthy respect for the economic and strategical advantages accruing from the possession of overseas territories was nothing new.

On the French side, however, the war of 1739–48 had served greatly to stimulate that awareness of the extra-European dimension which had been already nourished under Fleury. France's overseas trade was growing, despite the handicap of a too-centralized State administration. In the West Indies the rivalry with Britain was resumed, accentuated both by the uncertainty over the future of the 'neutral' islands there, and by the cheaper production of sugar in the French islands, which attracted the North American colonists and in turn infuriated the West Indies 'lobby' in London and all advocates of the old colonial system.[2] In India the struggle between the two powers for predominant influence was even more open and ruthless in the years after 1748, with their respective East India companies repeatedly intervening in native affairs in the hope of gaining the advantage over their foes.[3] The most important struggle of all was taking place in North America, however, where the westward drive of the British settlers into the Ohio region clashed with the French scheme to link their Canadian territories with the Mississippi. By the mid 1750s frontier clashes had become so serious that each power was dispatching reinforcements across the Atlantic and putting its fleets upon a war footing.[4] Even without the European complications it was clear that an Anglo-French war would have been difficult to avoid. With Europe providing its own powder-barrel in the form of the Austro-Prussian rivalry and the respective attitudes of France, Russia, Britain and lesser states to that antagonism, a long drawn-out conflict, with the inevitable intermingling of continental and colonial campaigns, was virtually inevitable.[5]

The French fleet, like French trade, had revived since the Treaty of Aix-la-Chapelle, and by 1756 it consisted of nearly seventy ships of the line. Nevertheless, the Royal Navy had not been neglected and under Anson it had been built up to a strength of over a hundred ships of the line, with the same number of frigates. On both sides the actual number of warships ready for sea was considerably less, but the fact remained that Britain was always comfortably superior in naval strength to her rival and that as the war dragged on it was likely that the traditional supporting elements of sea power – a larger merchant navy, more and better naval personnel, more shipyards, a stronger economy, and control of naval stores – would swing the balance even further in her favour. Against this had to be set the usual disadvantages of needing to protect an immense merchant fleet and of the steady wear-and-tear of constant blockading, yet this too was offset by a deterioration in morale on the part of the French fleet. Quarrels among the officer corps, a chronic desertion rate, and a lack of experience at sea were no basis upon which naval victories could be built; and, with the exception of Suffren and certain kindred spirits, French fleet commanders in the eighteenth century were unwilling to act offensively. As one expert has put it, 'The more one studies French naval history, the more it becomes clear that the French problem was almost as much psychological as material.'[6] The implications were obvious: Britain's maritime superiority would ultimately lead to its control over Canada, the West Indies and India, unless false strategies threw this enormous advantage away or France succeeded in countering British gains overseas by the conquest of Hanover or Prussia.

The first stage in the war did indeed show that much was lacking in leadership and strategical insight and as a result Britain suffered a row of defeats. French squadrons, escorting reinforcements for Canada and the West Indies, managed to avoid the incomplete British blockade; the early land attacks of the British regular and colonial troops on French possessions in North America were repulsed, and a French-Indian counterstroke was soon under way; the French obtained the upper hand in the commerce warfare in the West Indies; in India, too, their native allies gained an early advantage; in Europe the obvious French preparations for a cross-Channel invasion mesmerized British attention whilst Minorca was seized (although a more vigorous defence by Byng would have made its capture a far more hazardous operation); superior French diplomacy, and the poor statesmanship of Newcastle was shown in the conclusion of the Franco-Austrian treaty, leaving London to form what appeared to be the unsatisfactory counterpoise of an Anglo-Prussian alliance; Frederick was soon fighting against great odds, and the British-financed forces under Cumberland were unable to defend Hanover and were forced into a virtual surrender at Kloster-Zeven.[7]

Of all these repulses the defeats upon the continent were the most serious, although this was not appreciated by many in Britain, where the government was harshly criticized and Byng was shot – partly as a scapegoat, partly because he had made an error and partly, as Voltaire quipped, to encourage the others. With regard to all these setbacks in the maritime and colonial sphere, it can at least be said that Anson's overriding object of gaining superiority in Channel waters had a great deal of strategical logic in it; for once this predominance had been firmly established and the French invasion threat thereby rendered hopeless, the balance would also swing in Britain's favour in the many overseas campaigns. Having a strong Western Squadron, the Admiralty correctly argued, was 'the best defence for our colonies as well as our coasts',[8] for the same patrols which kept the French fleet in port and ruined her merchant marine were also blocking any reinforcement to America and Asia and allowing British trade and expeditions to move undisturbed across the oceans. Of course, the degree of control exercised by the British blockading forces was always dependent upon the weather and upon the judgement of individual squadron commanders, and it is possible that the Admiralty's eagerness to protect trade had led it to neglect to reinforce Byng in the Mediterranean; but the years following 1757 were to demonstrate the validity of Anson's recognition that only in home waters could the maritime war be lost irrevocably, simply by failing to prevent a French invasion. Yet even this sensible 'defensive first, offensive later' strategy would be of little use if Britain's allies on the continent were eliminated by the formidable coalition of France, Austria, Russia and Sweden. Were the armies of Frederick the Great and Ferdinand of Brunswick completely defeated, then not only would Hanover be a hostage to the French, but Britain's enemies would be free to concentrate their far greater resources and populations upon a purely maritime campaign in which the Dutch, Danish and Spanish governments, always resentful of Britain's high-handed attitude towards neutral trade, might also be tempted to join.

The astounding successes achieved under the leadership of Chatham were not simply due to his power of inspiration, drive and single-minded desire for victory over France, but also to the fact that he could see the war as one strategic whole. By vigorous naval measures he would render support to the European campaign; by placing sufficient importance upon the war on the continent he would make it easier for Britain to gain victories overseas; and by the judicious balancing of the needs of both theatres he would avoid the necessity for a compromise peace such as that signed at Aix-la-Chapelle and would ensure that his country's vital interests – in Europe and overseas – were safeguarded from the designs of her foes. But perhaps even more impressive than the strategy itself was the rapidity of Pitt's conversion from his earlier 'isolationist' viewpoint to this more enlightened and mature one. Before the outbreak of war, he had railed against such 'names and sounds' as the 'balance of power, the liberty of Europe, a common cause', which were to him merely synonyms for continental entanglements; yet by 1758 he was sending, not only subsidies but a large force of troops to fight in Germany; and by the end of the war, when he was again out of office, he was roundly denouncing Bute's abandonment of Prussia and the return to a purely maritime policy, in terms scarcely less flattering than those he had used to attack Newcastle's assumption of continental obligations seven years previously.[9]

In the naval and colonial theatres Pitt built upon the strategic foundation established earlier by Anson, who was recalled as First Lord of the

Admiralty. An ever-increasing force of ships of the line and frigates tightened Britain's hold over the French Atlantic ports, with a 'close', rather than the less strenuous but also less secure 'distant', blockade being implemented by Hawke, Boscawen, Howe and the other brilliant admirals with which the navy now seemed blessed. At the same time Pitt was willing enough to curb the excesses of British privateers, lest their activities against neutral shipping brought fresh enemies into a conflict whose outcome was still uncertain. Moreover, the Royal Navy was at last strong enough to place a fleet in the Mediterranean large enough to dominate that sea and to frustrate the French attempts to sortie from Toulon: Osborne's skilful holding of Clue's squadron at Cartagena and defeat of Dusquesne's relief force in 1758 being excelled only by Boscawen's devastation of Clue's ships off Lagos in southern Portugal in the following year. The same unchallengeable maritime superiority, whilst never recognized as such by Newcastle and other nervous souls in England, rendered impossible those feverish efforts of Choiseul to dispatch invasion forces across the Channel in 1759 – although this statement should in no way detract from Hawke's quite splendid feat in the November of that year of pursuing the French fleet under Conflans into the treacherous waters of Quiberon Bay in the midst of a gale and routing the enemy there as much as was physically possible.[10] His victory, wrote Smollett, 'not only defeated the projected invasion, which had hung menacingly so long over the apprehensions of Great Britain, but it gave the finishing blow to the naval power of France.'[11]

Even before the battle at Quiberon Bay, however, the news was flooding into London of victories in overseas territories, which were now dropping like ripe fruit into British hands as a consequence of that paralysing naval mastery. In 1758 Boscawen, with a massive squadron of twenty-three ships of the line, had watched General Amherst's 11,000 troops overrun Louisbourg whilst Anson's blockade had prevented French reinforcements crossing the Atlantic; command of the Great Lakes was again assumed by British and colonial forces; and in 1759 the combined forces of General Wolfe and Admiral Saunders achieved their famous conquest of Quebec, providing a fine example of army–navy cooperation. In the same years, 1758 and 1759, expeditions were sent out to capture Senegal and Goree respectively; Guadaloupe was taken in another combined operation in 1759, and Dominica and Martinique fell in the years following; and in India, although the British and French forces were frequently exchanging the advantage, it was clear by 1760 at least that France's inability or unwillingness to commit further naval and military reinforcements to the struggle spelt her eventual defeat. No doubt many

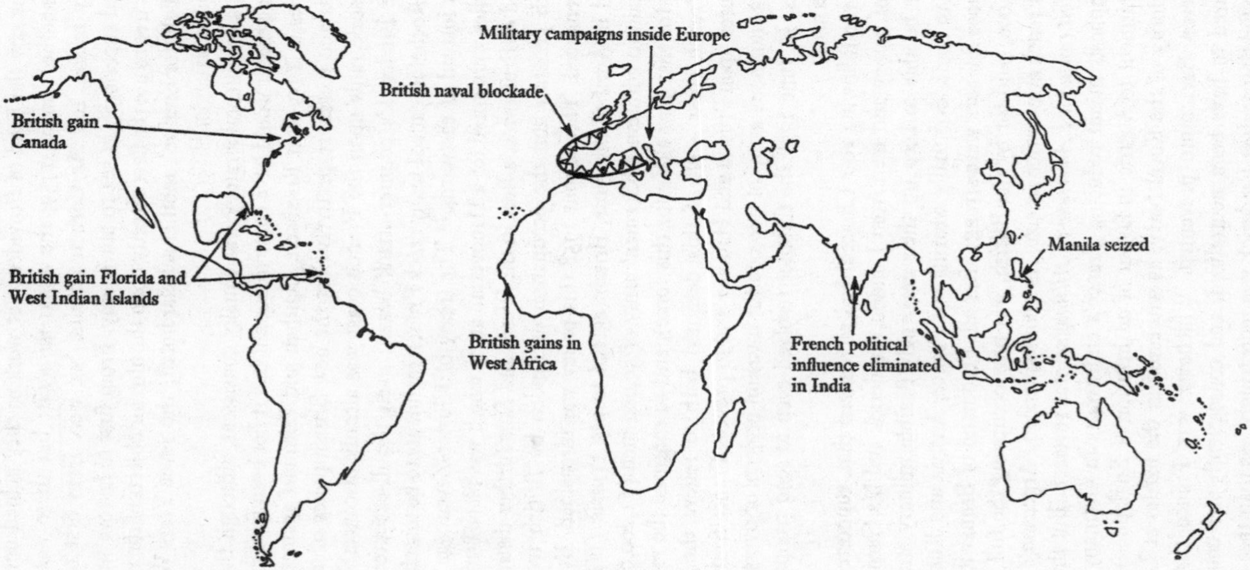

Map. 4. The world-wide nature of the Seven Years War

Britons saw the hand of Providence at work as they gained one success after another during 1759, the *annus mirabilis*; but there was a more earthly reason, too. As Corbett admits, 'we were from first to last in marked superiority at sea to our enemy. From first to last we were more or less free to use the fleet directly upon the ulterior objects of the war . . .'[12] 'As a fight for Empire', another scholar noted, 'the Seven Years War was a one-sided struggle.'[13]

Pitt's continental strategy was equally consistent, although there is no denying that it would have come to nought had it not been for Frederick's victories in 1757–8 at Rossbach, Leuthen and Zorndorf against France, Austria and Russia respectively. Yet the new British policy of launching large-scale raids upon the French coast was already disconcerting Paris before Frederick's counter-attack began; even the ill-executed assault upon Rochefort caused many crack French regiments to be marched westwards instead of eastwards.[14] The treaty of Kloster-Zeven was ignored, subsidies were voted for a Hanoverian army which was placed under Ferdinand of Brunswick, a fleet in the Weser and Ems further distracted the French generals and the occupation of Emden by British troops was countenanced. Throughout 1758 this policy was intensified. By a treaty signed in April of that year, Britain agreed to pay Prussia £660,000, to maintain in addition a 'German' army of 50,000 men (£1,200,000 being voted for that year alone for this force), and to continue the raids upon the French coast – all of this designed both to relieve the dreadful pressures upon Prussia and Hanover and to prevent France from deploying its enormous army of 300,000 for invasion projects or overseas campaigns. In June 1758 the Cabinet resolved even to send troops to fight in Germany.

By the following year Choiseul had recognized that, supported by this flow of money and men from London, Frederick and his German allies might be able to keep up their amazingly flexible military strategy for years to come, eventually wearing out France, Austria and Russia, none of whose finances were strong; after all, Ferdinand of Brunswick's army of 40,000, paid for by the British, was now occupying the full attention of a French army twice its size. As a consequence D'Argenson's policy of '*On doit conquerir l'Amerique en Allemagne*' was reversed. But this change of emphasis meant reducing France's endeavours in Germany and her commitment to Austria in favour of an invasion of England – which the superiority of the Royal Navy, as witnessed in the battles at Lagos and Quiberon Bay, quite prevented. Whichever way France turned, she appeared to have been neutralized, and consequently her contribution to the fighting against Frederick was increasingly less than that of Russia and Austria. Yet, satisfying though it was for the British to see their great rival enter into a stage of military decline, this still did not relieve Frederick, who had to undertake a great amount of desperate campaigning before the death of Elizabeth of Russia in 1762 led to the collapse of the anti-Prussian coalition and allowed the beginning of negotiations for a European peace on the basis of the *status quo ante bellum.*

With the gradual weakening of France and with Frederick becoming preoccupied with central rather than western European campaigns and territories, the British ties to Prussia were loosening;[15] after Pitt's resignation in 1761, this tendency increased. Mauduit's famous pamphlet *Considerations on the Present German War* (1760), which argued that the continental war drained Britain's resources whereas the colonial war increased them, had been well received by the isolationist faction, the Court and the general populace. Nevertheless, the alliance had lasted long enough to blunt French power and to prevent any Bourbon attempt to dominate Europe in the future, as well as safeguarding Hanover. As such, it had been well worth while for London to invest £9 to 10 million in subsidies to continental allies,[16] and to allow 18,000 of its own troops to fight inside Germany by 1761. Pitt had, as he himself put it, conquered Canada in Germany, and much else besides, because he recognized the political and strategical importance to Britain of the campaigns of Frederick and Ferdinand.[17] The only cause for regret was that the clumsy way in which relations with Prussia were handled in 1761–3 laid the ground for their future coolness towards each other.

Moreover, the British strategy and war effort had been the least painful of all, despite the murmurs of the politicians by 1761 about the cost of the struggle. Whereas Frederick could gloomily survey the devastation wrought upon his country, Britain was virtually untouched; indeed, she seemed to have flourished during the war, trade having increased in every year and shipping having risen by over 32,000 tons to well over 500,000 tons, or about one third of that of all Europe.[18] While much of this was due simply to the steady growth of overseas markets and to the early stages of an industrial 'take-off' which was going to occur in any case, it was also due to the stimulus of war orders to industry and – a very important, if negative consideration – to the Royal Navy's protection of merchant shipping. This in turn was the consequence of the British naval mastery throughout the war, as also of the sheer bulk of British trade, now being carried by over 8,000 merchant vessels, so great a number that French commerce-raiding, as Corbett noted, 'could not make a sufficient percentage impression to produce any real warlike advantage'.[19] Only in the West Indies, until the reduction of Martinique by Rodney, were losses serious. And it was, of course, from the increasing trade receipts and the growing wealth of the country that the British government could afford to finance a fleet of over 120 ships of the line (forty of which were built during the war), *and* to have over 200,000 soldiers (including German mercenaries) on British pay, *and* to subsidize Frederick. As the British ambassador to Prussia was informed, 'we must be merchants while we are soldiers, . . . our trade depends upon a proper exertion of our maritime strength; . . . trade and maritime force depend on each other, and . . . the riches which are the true resources of this country depend upon its commerce.'[20] But perhaps only Pitt could have seen how the financial, the naval, the military, the colonial and the European policies of Britain could be welded into one coherent whole.

So complete was British maritime dominance by 1761 that, even with Pitt's departure and Spain having joined France in the war, the victories continued to accumulate. The blockade was swiftly extended to the Spanish ports; Portugal was defended from invasion; Havana, the centre of Spain's trade system in the western hemisphere, was seized in 1762, together with an immense amount of booty and ships; Manila in the Philippines fell a little later, and two valuable treasure-ships were captured. The lack of any real danger at sea, together with the collapse of the anti-Prussian alliance in Europe, inclined Bute's administration further in the direction of peace. Had they sought to prolong and intensify the war, as Pitt desired, then no doubt even more swingeing terms could have been imposed upon the Bourbon powers. But the Cabinet was alarmed at the rise in the National Debt to £122 million and at the cost of a conflict that now seemed to it to be unnecessary; and it may be true that its calculation about the possibility of Britain becoming so overweening at sea that she would provoke a coalition of all other countries against herself was a shrewder perception of the preconditions for international stability than Pitt's apparent wish for the total oblivion of all her enemies.

Even after the handing back to France of Martinique, Guadeloupe, Maria Galante, St Lucia, Goree, Belle Isle and a share of the St Lawrence–Newfoundland fisheries, and to Spain of Cuba and Manila, Britain emerged from the Peace of Paris in 1763 with the greatest collection of spoils in her history. With France expelled from Canada, Nova Scotia and Cape Breton Island (and withdrawing from Louisiana on behalf of Spain), and Spain excluded from West Florida, she had virtually total control of the valuable North American continent; Minorca was restored to preserve her dominance in the Mediterranean; Senegal taken to increase her position in West Africa; Grenada, Dominica, St Vincent and Tobago acquired in the West Indies; and French political influence was eradicated in India. At the same time the continental balance of power had been upheld – and had indeed been enhanced from Britain's point of view by having its centre shifted to eastern Europe for a while[21] – while Hanover remained independent. All these gains, which laid the foundations for the British Empire of the nineteenth century, appeared the more remarkable by the fact that no other power benefited positively from the war; even Frederick had achieved only the recognition of Prussia's existing hold upon Silesia.

'The one nation that gained in this war', observed Mahan, 'was that which used the sea in peace to earn its wealth, and ruled it in war by the extent of its navy, by the number of its subjects who lived on the sea, and by its numerous bases of operations scattered over the globe.'[22] Every word of his statement is correct, and yet as a comment upon the outcome of the Seven Years War as a whole it remains incomplete. The German historian, Ludwig Dehio, put it better when he suggested that the real clue to Britain's success lay in her unique position and policy as a Janus – 'with one face turned towards the Continent to trim the balance of power and the other directed at the sea to strengthen her maritime dominance'.[23] Britain gained her greatest victory, not by a one-sided strategy, but by a recognition of the interlocking nature of developments in the Old World and the New, and of the importance of economic strength in wartime.

Within fifteen years of the Peace of Paris, however, the British Empire had sunk to its nadir, following a change of circumstances so extreme as to appear, even with the historian's benefit of hindsight, scarcely credible. Almost every factor which had helped the British during the Seven Years War was working against them or was, at the very least, only neutral during the War of American Independence. Even during that previous struggle, they had suffered some severe early defeats, yet their overall strategical position had always been favourable and indicated that victory was probable in the long run; now the odds facing Britain were so overwhelming that only the bleak years of 1940–41 compare with them.

Certain differences between the wars of 1756–63 and 1776–83 suggest themselves at once. In the first place there was no Pitt. Admittedly, even he would have had his ingenuity stretched in leading Britain to victory in the altered circumstances and his speeches of 1777–8 reveal a grave underestimation of the problems of effecting a reconciliation with the American rebels, yet the fact remains that the British leadership, both political and military, was of an unusually low standard in these decades. Neither North, nor Shelburne, nor any of their more prominent critics, could inspire the nation. 'Faction' had always played an important role in British eighteenth-century politics and it was true that earlier generations of politicians had also paid great attention to the economic interests of themselves and their class, to party machinations and rivalries, and to exploiting the patronage system; nevertheless, the post-1760 years seem to have witnessed these trends at their height. The constant interference of the monarch, the cobbling-together and then the precipitate collapse of political majorities, the manœuvrings for office, the increased incidence of mob violence, the vindictive Press and pamphleteering polemics – all against a background of rapid industrial and agricultural change – was no basis for a policy of national unity. Even the navy, which under Anson had steadfastly kept aloof from the grosser forms of patronage, was affected now by what has been termed 'recurrent discord between the Board of Admiralty and Opposition flag-officers'.[24] Some officers, such as Keppel, disapproved of the whole idea of suppressing the American revolt by force. The court-martials of Keppel and Palliser revealed the service to be split along political lines. None of the admirals, not even Kempenfelt or Rodney, seem to have displayed the intuitive leadership and daring which had characterized Hawke and Boscawen; nor was there a soldier who approached Wolfe, Ferdinand of Brunswick and Frederick the Great in their military abilities. The majority were, like the admirals, competent and reasonably intelligent, but they lacked the qualities necessary to transcend what were by any standards extremely difficult circumstances.

Because of this lack of a respected national leader and of military men of genius, British policy throughout the war never possessed a coherent strategical doctrine and effectiveness, such as that which had earlier been imposed by Marlborough or Chatham. Instead, the country's efforts were dispersed in various directions, so that it was difficult to achieve a decisive victory in any one theatre. At first all the Admiralty's attention could be concentrated upon the eastern American seaboard, but after the entry of France and Spain into the war in 1778 the gaze was shifted: 'the principal object', Howe was told, 'must now be the distressing France and defending his Majesty's possessions against hostile attempts'.[25] Yet this, too, was easier said than done. Should the fleet be concentrated in Channel waters, steadily throttling the French exits to the Atlantic, as was Anson's policy? Kempenfelt argued against the close blockade and in favour of keeping the ships ready at Torbay, on the grounds that winter gales caused great damage to his ships. In view of the fact that fifteen ships of the line were lost to 'perils of the sea' in this war compared with only one to enemy action,[26] the argument was a reasonable one when taken in isolation; but it did imply free egress for all the French squadrons which were dispatched to assist Washington, to intervene in the West Indies and to raid Indian waters. In other words the temporary saving in wear-and-tear on British warships simply transferred the problem of establishing naval control to more distant seas; and, as Mahan pointed out, 'Whatever the number of ships needed to watch those in an enemy's port, they are fewer by far than those that will be required to protect the scattered interests imperilled by the enemy's escape.'[27]

The instances of this dispersal of effort are numerous. The surrender of Cornwallis at Yorktown was the direct result of that draining of vessels from the American station, which permitted De Grasse's superior squadron to block the Chesapeake. Yet the concentration in home waters was itself often insufficient to prevent Franco-Spanish fleets from sweeping the Channel and placing England in greater danger of invasion than at any time since 1690–92. On the other hand the agitation of the King and of the West Indies merchants meant that strong forces had to be sent to that region also – even, George III wrote, 'at the risk of an invasion of this island'.[28] Three times, too, Gibraltar was relieved only by an immense effort and the dispatch of a large fleet of ships of the line. As for India, it had to remain a strategical backwater whilst Britons had their backs to the wall in so many other more vital theatres.

Of course, this ineffectual policy of living from hand to mouth leads us immediately to what has been regarded by most historians as the primary reason for Britain's defeat in this war: her lack of adequate naval force. Because she had insufficient strength to be superior everywhere and because she dared not withdraw from any of the four main theatres – the Channel, Gibraltar, the West Indies, the American seaboard – then she ended up by being too weak in every one of them. As Professor Graham notes, 'At the time [October 1781] when Rear-Admiral Graves faced superior French forces off the North American coast, and Vice-Admiral Peter Parker confronted a substantial Spanish squadron in the neighbourhood of Jamaica, a weakened and badly neglected Channel fleet was preparing desperately to defend itself against a French–Spanish fleet, nearly twice its strength.'[29] The blame for this insufficiency of naval force, for the bland disregard of the unwritten rule that the Royal Navy should be kept at least as strong as the combined French and Spanish navies, has been correctly laid at the feet of George III's peacetime administrations. The naval budget, which had been in excess of £7 million in 1762, had been reduced to £2,800,000 in 1766 and to a mere £1,500,000 in 1769, despite the warnings of Burke and Chatham and the uneasy state of international relations in those years.[30] Many of the ships of the line had been built with unseasoned timbers during the Seven Years War and had been rotting in reserve since then; not surprisingly, a large number of them, including the *Royal George*, simply foundered. Keppel is known to have complained that, of the thirty-five ships of the line allocated to the Channel fleet, only six were really in good condition. Furthermore, the problem was aggravated by the American revolt, for it was from that region that the navy's tar, masts and timbers, as well as many thousands of skilled sailors, came: now the fleet was deprived of masts and was forced to see those potential warship crews engage in a vigorous privateering campaign which led to the capture of 3,000 British merchant ships by the end of the war.[31] Add to this the inherent problems of the dockyards against which Sandwich strove with only limited success,[32] and it is all too plain to see why the Royal Navy, even after the Battle of the Saints, never approached that position of naval mastery which it had enjoyed under Anson and Pitt.

The transformation of the French and Spanish navies after 1763 was perhaps more remarkable, and certainly less predictable, than the peacetime decline of the Royal Navy. Even while Choiseul had been negotiating the terms of the Peace of Paris, he had been planning for a future challenge to Britain's colonial and maritime predominance. About eighty French ships of the line – the majority better designed, faster and larger than their British equivalents – were at hand by 1779, and they were supported by a network of dockyards, reserves of timber, a regular conscription system, an educated class of naval officers and, last but not least, the new monarch, Louis XVI. Spain, for its part, could contribute some sixty capital ships, although they were less effective in action than this total might suggest. Nevertheless, the result was that the fleets of the Royal Navy repeatedly found themselves outnumbered by their foes; to ward off the threat of invasion in 1779, for example, Kempenfelt could only institute a 'fleet in being' strategy, hovering in the west but not attempting to engage the Franco-Spanish forces in full battle. Fortunately, with the exception of Suffren, the commanders of the combined navies showed little desire to exploit their strength to the utmost. As Mahan put it, 'Neither in the greater strategic combinations, nor upon the battlefield, does there appear any serious purpose of using superior numbers to crush fractions of the enemy's fleet, to make the disparity of numbers yet greater, to put an end to the empire of the seas by the destruction of the organized force which sustained it.'[33] Only the timidity, divided counsels and differing aims of the enemy saved the British from even greater defeat.

Yet to detail the recovery of French naval power is only to provide half the picture. The more important question is surely: why was France, which had made little effort to contest Britain's maritime control in the previous three wars, now able to produce a fleet of equal and sometimes superior strength? The answer is plain from a glance at the state of international relations: for the first time in a war with Britain, French attention was not divided between a maritime and a continental campaign to which, for reasons of national security, the latter had to be given priority. Instead, the Bourbon powers could concentrate their resources upon a war at sea. The figures of the French navy budget give a clear proof of this change. In 1760 the Minister of Marine, Berryer, had complained that there was no prospect of defending the West Indies when the service was allocated only thirty million livres, of which twenty-one million were actually for the colonies, debt-repayment and other non-naval expenses: the Royal Navy, he claimed, received 150 million livres per annum! (£1 million = 18 million livres.) However, when the Minister of War, Belleisle, whose service was allocated four times as much as the navy, refused to allow any further reductions in his already-pruned estimates to help Berryer, the whole notion of challenging Britain at sea and in the colonies had to be given up.[34] By 1780, in contrast, the French naval budget totalled 169 million livres and by 1782 it had reached 200 million – a quite staggering increase in expenditure, which made the navy, for a time at least, 'the first service of the realm'.[35] Newcastle's prophecy, that 'France will outdo us at sea when they have nothing to fear on land', had been realized.

Britain's admirals, if not all her politicians, were of course aware of this need to divert France from the sea. In replying to criticisms about the loss of Minorca in 1756, the Admiralty had pointed out that 'no comparison can be made between the present war and those since the Revolution [of 1688] in every one of which there was a powerful alliance on the Continent at war with France, which employed the force and finances of that Kingdom and effectually prevented dangerous attempts on us or our colonies . . .'[36] Yet that was written at a time when the campaigns of Frederick the Great and Ferdinand of Brunswick were already beginning to absorb more and more of France's reserves, this leading to the impoverishment of the navy about which Berryer was to complain so bitterly a few years later! In the War of American Independence, however, there was no Frederick or Ferdinand, indeed there was no continental diversion at all; instead, Britain faced the consequences of an isolation from Europe which so many of her pamphleteers had professed to favour. Sandwich, the First Lord of the Admiralty, put his finger on the problem when he wrote in 1779:

It will be asked why, when we have as great, if not a greater, force than ever we had, the enemy are superior to us. To this it is to be answered that England till this time was never engaged in a sea war with the House of Bourbon thoroughly united, their naval force unbroken, and having no other war or object to draw off their attention and resources. We unfortunately have an additional war on our hands which essentially drains our resources and employs a very considerable part of our army and navy: we have no one friend or ally to assist us: on the contrary all those who ought to be our allies except Portugal act against us in supplying our enemies with the means of equipping their fleets.[37]

Just why Britain was unable to secure continental allies during the years 1776–83 is more a matter of diplomatic than of naval history.[38] Frederick, still annoyed at the Anglo-Prussian split of 1762, had no wish to become involved in a war with France as Britain's 'continental sword', particularly when his country's diplomatic position was now secure. Austria was tied too closely to France. Russia, although hardly in a position to influence a war in western Europe, appeared the most promising partner, but the British government could never bring itself to pay Catherine II's price. Hanover, which London had always assumed was a hostage to the French army, but which nevertheless might have turned Paris's eye eastwards, remained neutral in accordance with Choiseul's principle that France should not be drawn into a continental war. Amongst the smaller maritime powers, however, there existed a traditional dislike of Britain's policy towards neutral shipping in wartime – a feeling based upon that belief in 'free ships, free goods' which, cynics have observed, miraculously evaporated whenever they themselves fought on the side of the strongest naval power. During the Seven Years War, it will be recalled, even Pitt had been compelled to adopt a conciliatory line towards the protests of the Dutch, Danes, Swedes and Spaniards, out of fear that these countries might respond to the French efforts to form a maritime league against Britain. Yet the resentment of the continental states remained strong at the 'Rule of War of 1756', which forbade them to take goods to French colonies which were normally closed to them in peacetime. From the point of view of the neutrals, as Bedford had shrewdly suggested in 1761, a monopoly of all naval power 'would be at least as dangerous to the liberties of Europe as that [monopoly of land power] of Louis XIV was . . .'[39] When the British therefore sought to resume their old ways after 1778, they provoked a reaction in the form of the 'Armed Neutrality' (1780) so powerful that they were forced to give way on the point. It was one thing to declare war on the Dutch, by this time a weak naval power; but the prospect of having to face the eighty or so ships of the line of the Northern states was simply too alarming to contemplate when Franco-Spanish forces already dominated the Channel, even though this retreat meant that naval stores flowed unhindered from the Baltic to the Bourbon dockyards. By 1783, when even Portugal and the Two Sicilies had joined Russia, Sweden, Prussia, Austria and Denmark in the pact, Britain was totally isolated – 'the dominating factor', in the opinion of one scholar, for her eventual defeat in the war.[40]

The interventions of the French navy, in the Channel, off Gibraltar, in the West Indies, off Yorktown, had clearly played a considerable part in Britain's failure to win the war in America. 'Whatever the efforts made by the land forces', Washington wrote flatteringly to De Grasse, 'the Navy must have the casting vote in the present contest.'[41] Yet even had Great Britain possessed naval mastery throughout the war, could she have overcome the resistance to her rule in North America? Here, too, she was fighting a war under circumstances quite different from any she had hitherto experienced. The original British Empire had been chiefly a trading concern, with a few bases and outposts and settlements, but nothing which had required large garrisons; even when war occurred, the expeditions sent out to defend or capture the more valuable West Indies islands usually comprised fewer than 10,000 men. The colonies were essentially protected by sea power, by that ability of the Royal Navy to keep the lines of communication to the mother country secure from enemy attack; indeed, one major reason for the growth of the empire was this ability of Britain, lying on the flank of the continent, to 'isolate' the world overseas from her European rivals, a policy which broke down permanently only in the later nineteenth century, with the rise of American and Japanese navies geographically invulnerable to such a throttling process. Thus normally, the inhabitants of the early colonies recognized the need to maintain a loyalty to Britain, whose armed forces protected them from indigenous or foreign attack, and whose products and markets they depended upon. They were small, isolated, privileged communities, neither able nor willing to obtain independence.

But by the middle of the eighteenth century, the North American colonies had grown into something quite different. Their population, already over two million souls, was doubling every thirty years and, now that the French threat had been removed, their ties of loyalty to London were weakening. Nor did these colonists, many of them political and religious refugees (or their descendants), share that desire of the West Indies planters and East India Company officials to return to Britain at the end of their days – another obvious reason for loyalty. Finally, whilst the Americans certainly engaged in a busy commerce with the motherland, the fact remained that they were self-sufficient in foodstuffs and many other commodities (although they did have to import weapons). This, together with the sheer size of the country, meant that—unlike all other British colonies – the North American states were largely impervious to the workings of sea power. It was true, of course, that the Royal Navy could control the eastern seaboard and river estuaries; but farther west the rebels could act with impunity. Not all of this was appreciated by the British government, and as late as December 1774 the Secretary of State for War, Lord Barrington, was writing that 'A conquest by land is unnecessary when the country can be reduced first to distress, and then to obedience, by our Marine' – a belief that was as misguided then as were Neville Chamberlain's hopes in 1939 of bringing Nazi Germany to her knees through a naval blockade.[42] In fact, it was Britain herself which was the more embarrassed by the outbreak of hostilities in 1776, for the flow of crucial naval stores from North America very quickly dried up and affected the shipbuilding programme.

Yet if sea power alone was insufficient to crush the American rebellion, Britain's military headache was increased. It was one thing to seize an island, quite another to control a continent. The American countryside was rough, communications were poor, and many regions could not support a large army. In addition, whilst the Americans were fighting on their home ground, the British and their German mercenaries were far from home. Not only did this hamper the dispatch of reports and instructions but it created incredible problems for the primitive logistical services: 'Every biscuit, man, and bullet required by the British forces in America had to be transported across 3000 miles of ocean.'[43] Just how large an army was needed to suppress the rebellion, it is impossible to say; but by 1778 there were over 50,000 troops in North America and they were showing singularly little sign of achieving victory.[44] As Chatham had earlier pointed out, it had taken a force of that size to subdue French Canada alone, and that with American support. Part of the problem was the disparate nature of the resistance; in a European war a successful march upon the hostile capital usually resulted in a surrender, but 'Colonial society was so loosely organized that the capture of New York or Philadelphia brought no such results as the capture of Berlin or Paris . . .'[45] Conquering America produced the same problems for the British as conquering Russia did for Napoleon, and it is possible that only the presence of so many loyalists gave Britain the chance to fight at all and made her task appear less hopeless than it seems in retrospect. In fact, one military historian has recently concluded: 'It is probable that to restore British authority in America was a problem beyond the power of military means to solve, however perfectly applied.'[46]

Finally, even if the main rebel forces had been annihilated, there remained the difficulty of preserving this dominance over a resentful, populous and resourceful American people under such arduous geographical and logistical circumstances. India or Peru might be conquered and kept cowed by a few determined troops: North America never – and the effort to do this would upset Britain's traditional strategy and the balance between the services. This left the British government faced with the unpleasant alternatives of either maintaining at great cost an enormous garrison overseas, or acceding to the colonists' wishes. The ageing Chatham once again put it in a nutshell when he declared: 'You may ravage – you cannot conquer; [but even] If you conquer them, what then? You cannot make them respect you . . .'[47] In the War of American Independence the British not only encountered unprecedented military problems but also grappled for the first time with the political and constitutional consequences of the establishment overseas of large stocks of their own race, who demanded the same rights and privileges as the home-based Englishman.

Britain's difficulties in fighting a large-scale land campaign at the other end of the oceans remind one of the similar problems she encountered in the Boer War of 1899–1902 – yet in that latter conflict the Royal Navy was very strong and there was no intervention by the continental powers. In view of the parlous situation in which she found herself during the war of 1776–83, the marvel is that she held on to so much. By 1782 she had admittedly lost the war for America and many in Britain no longer wished to persist in that campaign; but she had restored her naval control in the West Indies, she had fended off Suffren's assaults in Indian waters and she had maintained her hold upon Gibraltar. By that time, too, her enemies had also grown war-weary and were willing to negotiate a more moderate peace.

At this stage, by bringing together the strategic lessons of Britain's defeat in the War of American Independence and those of her success in the Seven Years War, it is possible to perceive the conditions under which she was most likely to achieve victory over her larger and more populous French neighbour. In the first place she did not dare become too committed to a struggle for control of vast areas of land, wherever it was located, for this was beyond the capacity of her army and it deranged her whole war effort: a campaign abroad in which she could rely upon the support of her colonials or of foreign troops (e.g. Prussia) was of course a different matter. Added to this need to avoid military over-commitment was the equally pressing requirement of discovering some method of distracting her Bourbon rivals from a purely maritime war. 'The key of the situation', as Mahan observed, 'was in Europe.'[48] With British naval mastery thus underpinned by a shrewd European policy, she could eliminate French and Spanish possessions overseas, protect her own trade, and utilize this growing source of revenue to sustain her continental partners in the struggle to exhaust France in a land war; if necessary, she could also send a respectable, though limited number of her own troops to fight in Europe and to augment her subsidy policy. This was the recipe for success and recognized as such by Elizabeth I, Marlborough, Chatham and other astute strategists, often in defiance of the pleas of the isolationists. For, despite the arguments of the latter, the hard fact remains that, of the seven Anglo-French wars which took place between 1689 and 1815, the only one which Britain lost was that in which no fighting took place in Europe, and British troops became bogged down instead in an enormous colonial military campaign across 3,000 miles of water.

Although the terms of the peace settlements of 1782–4 were not harsh, they represented a check to that hitherto irresistible expansion of the British Empire in the eighteenth century. Minorca (captured by the French in 1782) and Florida were ceded to Spain, the Dutch regained Ceylon, and Senegal, St Lucia and Tobago went to France, Britain gaining the return of Dominica, St Vincent and Grenada as partial compensation. Most important of all, from London's point of view, the independence of the American colonies was formally recognized, which was not only the greatest blow ever received to imperial prestige but also appeared to have devastating economic consequences. North America had become a flourishing region, an enormous market for British goods, a source of many foodstuffs and raw materials, the builder of one third of the British merchant fleet: to lose these assets was a catastrophe in mercantilist terms. 'She was the fountain of our wealth, the nerve of our strength, the nursery and basis of our naval power', Chatham had declared in 1777.[49] And now it was all gone.

But Chatham was wrong, and for several reasons. In the first place, however useful America may have been as an overseas possession, it was clearly in the British Isles and in its people that the centre of the empire's wealth, strength and naval power lay: in the larger population, the superior communications, the more organized system of government, the more powerful army and navy, the more mature diplomacy, the more advanced economy, the greater reserves of capital and the financial expertise of the City, and the more sophisticated and developed commercial structure.

Little of this had been more than temporarily affected by the war of 1776–83, for, as one historian has reminded us, the financial exhaustion of a government in consequence of an eighteenth-century 'limited' war should not be taken too seriously, when so small a fraction of the country's wealth was collected in taxes. The frequent recoveries staged by France provide a good example here. 'When its revenue and its credit were exhausted and its fighting men could not be paid, it had to make peace; but conversely, in a relatively few years of peace it could be ready for another war of the same limited unemotional kind.'[50] And what was true of France was even more true of England, whose post-war trading 'booms' brought fresh revenues into the national exchequer. When placed in this light, the fears of a long-term British decline appear to have been vastly exaggerated.

Furthermore, at some time in the middle decades of the eighteenth century there began in Britain that 'rapid, cumulative, structural change'[51] in economic life which historians term the industrial revolution and which was to give her distinct advantages, not only in economic but also in power-political terms, over all her rivals. Just why this 'breakthrough' or 'take-off' occurred in Britain has been the subject of numerous inquiries and the topic need concern us only briefly here.[52] The political and social system, although still very much dominated by an aristocratic *élite*, was flexible, and very tolerant of economic enterprises which would boost both profits and national strength. Significant advances in agricultural techniques, together with the enclosure movement, increased food production, accelerated capital accumulation and provided the 'push' factor from the land, which the 'pull' factor of jobs in industry complemented. Internal communications, which have often been a major cause of economic retardation in other countries, were reasonably good and, with the growth of canals and the turnpike system, were improving all the time. Coal, iron-ore and other raw materials were readily available for exploitation. Finance, built up by decades of profitable commercial activities (London was at this time just beginning to take over from Amsterdam as the banking and insurance centre of the world), was at hand for new industrial developments. The population, growing at 4 to 7 per cent per decade in the period 1741–81 and then at 10 per cent per decade for the following 130 years, was relatively wealthy and able to stimulate a steadily expanding demand for food, beer, clothes, coal and industrial products. Also an astonishing concatenation of technological advances, together with the existence of a large number of engineers and craftsmen who could produce and man the new machines, led to increases in productivity far beyond the capabilities of human muscle, wind or water.

Linking in with these impressive developments within Britain itself was a post-1785 rise in overseas trade so staggering that it made the previous steady expansion of imports and exports appear negligible by comparison. The crude statistics of the time for England and Wales give us a general picture of this enormous rise:[53]

	1780	1785	1790	1795	1800
Exports (inc. re-exports)	12·5	15·1	18·8	26·3	40·8 *(figures in £ million)*
Imports	10·7	14·9	17·4	21·4	28·3

It is difficult to say whether this commercial expansion preceded or followed the beginnings of the industrial revolution in Britain. On the one hand Professor Hobsbawm has argued that the boom in the export trades provided the 'spark' which set alight the other ingredients: 'Between 1700 and 1750 home industries increased their output by 7 per cent, export industries by 76 per cent; between 1750 and 1770 (which we may regard as the runway for the industrial "take-off") by another 7 per cent and 80 per cent respectively.' This growth in foreign trade, itself a consequence of British naval dominance and the government's aggressive support of its merchants' effort to monopolize the markets of the world, was such that it made industrialization 'not only practicable for its entrepreneurs, but sometimes virtually compulsory'.[54] Yet, while it is true that Britain's eighteenth-century wars generally disadvantaged her rivals and also (as A. H. John showed) boosted her own iron, coal, shipbuilding and metal-fabricating industries, it must be assumed that British goods would not have been in such great demand had they not been so superior and cheap in the first place; neither the Americans nor the Germans, to give but two examples which reverse Hobsbawm's order of causation, were forced to buy British goods. Mantoux's compromise formula is perhaps closest to the truth: 'Sometimes the advancement of industry, by forcing trade to find new outlets, enlarges and multiplies commercial relations. Sometimes . . . fresh wants, created by the extension of a commercial market, stimulate industrial enterprise.'[55] And with such a mutually interacting process under way, Britain was advancing faster than ever to become the world's leading power.

The destination of British exports and the origin of the imports in this period give further evidence of the global nature of this expansion. The average annual values of the trade of England and Wales with the East Indies rose from £2·9 million in the years 1781–5 to £7 million in the years 1796–1800; with the West Indies, from £4·1 million to £10·2 million; with the United States, from £1·8 million to £7·4 million; with Germany, from £1·7 million to £11·5 million.[56] Yet, if these were the major trading partners, there were also many others of considerable value, inside and outside Europe. In most of these cases what was happening was the expansion of trade with already established markets: Germany or Russia, for example. The same could be said of the West and East Indies trade, with the added remark that the value of this traffic seemed to be justifying the claims of those mercantilist interest-groups which had persuaded the British government to establish political predominance there. On the other hand – and this is the second reason why Chatham's fears about the loss of the American colonies proved false – despite the establishment of direct commercial links between America and Europe for the sale of tobacco and other colonial wares, British trade with the United States after 1785 was still growing the fastest of all; the American demand for British goods apparently outweighed their dislike of their former enemies. Shelburne's slogan, that he preferred trade to dominion, was no doubt 'putting a brave rhetorical gloss on a grave imperial disaster',[57] but it did seem astonishing to contemporaries that the loss of political control had no serious economic consequences.

Yet, although this latter fact provided useful ammunition for the critics of mercantilism, it would be unwise to conclude that the British government and British traders were consciously adopting new anti-imperialist ideas and methods by the 1780s as a consequence of the American revolt. The attitude of the merchants was aggressively expansionist, and very confident in British industry's ability to hold its own if the reports of the Committee of Trade in this period are any guide.[58] Where advanced communities existed, there was no need to establish dominion; and in undeveloped societies (e.g. West Africa) the erection of coastal trading-posts seemed a much less costly and more sensible policy than the creation of colonial administrations. However, direct political control, occasioned either by local factors or by the rivalry of foreign powers, was not flinched at if it appeared to be necessary: the commercial treaties negotiated with greater and lesser states, the increasing intervention in India, the embassy of Lord Macartney to Peking, the serious consideration of the creation of a base in South Africa, the many naval exploring missions in the Pacific, the establishment of a penal settlement in Sydney, were all signs that the government was, either through a desire to protect commerce or out of strategical calculation (if those two motives could be separated), willing to take an active role in this expansionism. The actual structure – whether of a 'formal' empire along traditional lines, or of an 'informal' rule based upon commercial supremacy and occasional diplomacy – now appears less important to historians than the sheer size of the movement into North America, the Caribbean, West Africa, India, the

Orient and the Pacific, of British merchants, British goods, and British warships in increasingly large numbers.

To conclude: what was happening throughout this period, both before and after the War of American Independence, was that enormous extension of British influence which has been described by Professor Harlow as 'The Founding of the Second British Empire', and which may be regarded as the external counterpart of the industrial revolution at home and as a much more advanced stage of an expansive process which had begun under the Tudors. The zenith of British political power and economic predominance was now approaching – and with it, the zenith of British naval mastery too.

That this economic growth was also bound to augment Britain's naval potential is almost too obvious to mention. Along with the boom in foreign trade came dizzy rises in British shipping: the tonnage leaving British ports was 864,000 in 1774, 1,055,000 in 1785 and 1,924,000 in 1800; and the size of the merchant marine, which by 1773 had almost trebled from its 1702 total of quarter of a million tons, doubled again in the twenty years following.[59] New dockyards, shipworks, iron-foundries and ordnance factories proliferated; more and more men entered the shipping and shipbuilding industry; and all of this strengthened the resources upon which the Royal Navy could call in times of crisis. Furthermore, the exploratory voyages and the expansion of commerce into hitherto untouched parts of the globe were creating new areas of British influence and revealing possible harbours and trading-posts for the navy in the future: the existing fleet bases at Gibraltar, Kingston, Halifax and Bombay were soon to be joined by many others, acquired either peacefully or as the spoils of war.

In addition to the direct assistance the navy obtained from the growth of docks, shipyards, ordnance-works and seamen during the industrial revolution, there was the indirect but quite crucial support which came from the nation's expanding wealth and productivity. Due chiefly to the great cost of war, governmental expenditure was rising swiftly during the eighteenth century. Between 1755 and 1761, for example, the annual budget had been pushed from £4 million to £18 million by the Seven Years War, yet the country was able to take this in its stride, causing an astonished Adam Smith to note: 'Great Britain seems to support with ease a burden, which, half a century ago, nobody believed her capable of supporting.'[60] In part, the war costs were paid for by new taxes upon a variety of goods and by tapping the increasing flow of imports and exports; and in part, by raising loans in London and Amsterdam, where the credit of the government was always high enough to secure full subscriptions. The same factors assisted Britain's recovery after the war of 1776–83, which had caused the National Debt to soar to £231 million. The Younger Pitt's skilful fiscal and commercial policies, which led to the reform of the country's financial administration, the eradication of much smuggling, the rise in trade, and thereby in customs and excise revenues, and the establishment of a 'sinking fund' for the National Debt, immeasurably increased the City's confidence in the government.[61] How valuable an asset this strengthened credit was became clear during the following wars with France, where the enormous excess of government expenditure over revenue was covered by loans without provoking that financial collapse anticipated by Napoleon and his advisers.[62]

All that was required to complete this picture of Britain's continuing – indeed, accelerating – rise as a world power was the existence of a government which kept the navy at a strength commensurate with the nation's vital interests and obligations, and which also avoided the diplomatic isolation which had hindered her throughout the War of American Independence. In both respects the signs were favourable. Although Pitt gave first place to a policy of financial stability and retrenchment, he was always prepared to argue that the possession of a navy strong enough to deter another country from provoking hostilities was a measure of prudence and economy rather than extravagance. Consequently, he raised the peacetime establishment of the service from 15,000 to 18,000 in 1784 and added another 2,000 men in 1789; whilst thirty-three ships of the line were built between 1783 and 1790. Moreover, Pitt himself (like his father) took a great interest in the navy, even if his preoccupation with the affairs of state prevented him from exercising anything like that direct control which Chatham had obtained. In any case, the service was already in the very capable hands of Barham as Comptroller, who was – not without the inevitable difficulties – reforming and extending the dockyards, eliminating the grosser forms of corruption and inefficiency, building up stocks of naval stores, ensuring that existing warships were regularly repaired or replaced, and supervising the entire construction programme. The French navy, in contrast, deteriorated sadly after 1783.[63]

The government's diplomacy likewise revealed a refreshing change from that of Bute's or North's.[64] There was no wish on Pitt's part for an active foreign policy if that could be avoided – the domestic problems of Britain in the 1780s were enough to keep even a brilliant Prime Minister at full stretch; but he was willing to take steps with other states to prevent any deleterious shift in the continental balance of power and to check attempts to undermine Britain's interests in the extra-European field as well. Since he relied to a large extent upon the 'deterrent' of the Royal

Navy, it is perhaps not surprising that his successes were achieved in matters susceptible to the influence of sea power. The confrontation with Spain in 1790 over the British right to trade in Nootka Sound (Vancouver) was settled by the mobilization of forty of the navy's ninety-three ships of the line, and by a strengthening of colonial garrisons: facing the prospect of being expelled not only from the Pacific coast of Canada but from her colonial possessions as well, Spain gave way. On the other hand British sea power was far less decisive an element in causing Paris to hold its hand in the 1787 crisis over the influence of the pro-French party in the Netherlands than the actual invasion of Dutch territory by Prussian troops. The revival in 1788 of that Anglo-Prussian alliance which had been so successful under Chatham and Frederick was enough to make all the other powers hesitate, but it is difficult to estimate, either from the Dutch crisis, or from the Anglo-Prussian action to prevent a Danish invasion of Sweden in the following year, just how respected Britain was when acting on her own. For example, the obvious estrangement between Berlin and London by 1791 enabled Russia to expand into the Black Sea area at the expense of the Turks, without Pitt being able to do very much to prevent it.

As the reverberations from the 1789 Revolution in France began to cross that country's borders and to involve much of Europe in a struggle which would eclipse all previous general wars of the century in its bitterness and destructiveness, Britain's own position appeared comparatively strong, comfortable, attractive almost. She had steadily built herself up to be the world's greatest colonial, commercial and trading nation and even the humiliation of the war of 1776–83 had not really proved to be a check to that expansion. Her economic lead was growing more pronounced, due to the process of industrialization at home and to the success of her merchants abroad. Her internal political system was no doubt in need of reform, but it was a flexible constitution and already certain improvements were taking place; with luck, she could ride out the changing social and economic conditions without too drastic a disruption at home. Her political leadership was strong, and had a correct sense of the country's priorities in the outside world. Her diplomacy was at least improving upon that of the 1770s. Her navy was formidable, well-trained, and backed by immense resources of men, money and material. Judged from the standard of international power-politics, Britain probably possessed more advantages, and fewer disadvantages than any other nation-state at that time. In nautical terms, she was like a trim, well-built, powerful ship: which was just as well, for she was about to sail into a storm of unprecedented fury and duration.

CHAPTER FIVE

The Struggle against France Renewed (1793–1815)

Great Britain has no greater obligation to any mortal on earth than to this ruffian [Napoleon]. For through the events which he has brought about, England's greatness, prosperity, and wealth have risen high. She is the mistress of the sea and neither in this dominion nor in world-trade has she now a single rival to fear.

Comment of General von Gneisenau,
reproduced in G. J. Marcus, *A Naval History of England*,
2 vols. to date (London, 1961–71), ii, p. 501.

The two wars which Britain fought against Revolutionary and Napoleonic France are of particular interest to this survey because they represent the culminating point in the country's rise to naval mastery and encompass all the aspects of the many previous conflicts since Elizabethan times. Not only did the period 1793–1815 lead to the establishment of a virtually unchallengeable British maritime predominance in the narrow sense of the possession of a vastly superior fleet, backed by numerous dockyards and naval bases and by a massive merchant marine; but it also confirmed Britain's control in the colonial world and her lead in foreign trade; it witnessed the collapse of the French efforts to upset the continental and colonial *status quo*, and led to the stabilization of the European balance of power; and it saw further significant advances in Britain's unique industrialization process. The victory of 1815 was far harder to achieve than that of 1763 and, in crude imperialist terms of securing fresh territory, less impressive; but one only has to compare the country's international position in the few decades following the Napoleonic War with that in the years following the Seven Years War to recognize that the former struggle produced much more significant and longer-term effects than the latter. The Peace of Paris had acknowledged a British advantage that was soon to be challenged and overthrown; the Congress of Vienna admitted a maritime mastery which foreign powers, despite their various efforts, found impossible to break. A new era in international politics had begun, fundamentally different from that eighteenth-century world of swiftly changing alliances and frequent wars between the great powers, and one of its most prominent features was the 'Pax Britannica' which flowed from Britain's naval, colonial and economic lead.

It was during these struggles of 1793–1802 and 1803–15 that the long, drawn-out duel for command of the sea between the fleets of the Royal Navy and the French navy (with the latter assisted by various allied fleets) came to a climax. In terms of the battles fought by the main squadrons, the story is one of repeated British successes.[1] Howe's victory of 'The Glorious First of June' in 1794 resulted in the capture or destruction of seven French ships of the line, although admittedly the important grain convoy they were escorting escaped detection by British patrols; Jervis's squadron took on a greatly superior Spanish force off Cape St Vincent in February 1797 and captured four enemy ships in an engagement chiefly memorable for Nelson's breaking of 'the line'; in October of the same year Duncan's fleet emerged from the hard-fought battle of Camperdown with no less than eleven Dutch warships as prizes; in August 1798 Nelson smashed Napoleon's Egyptian adventure in the famous battle of the Nile, from which only two of the thirteen French ships of the line escaped; and the sinking or seizure of eighteen of the combined Franco-Spanish fleet in what was probably the most famous naval battle in history, that of Trafalgar on 21 October 1805, was so decisive that the Royal Navy's command of the sea was never seriously challenged in a fleet action for the rest of the war. When one adds to these victories the many smaller ones, the frigate actions in distant waters, and the attacks upon such harbours as Copenhagen (1801 and 1807) and Aix Roads (1809), then it is scarcely surprising that the Nelsonic period has been regarded as the high point of British naval history.

The reasons for this ability to deal devastating blows at the enemy were many, but it seems clear that numerical superiority was not usually one of them. Fleet numbers were equal at 'The Glorious First of June'; Jervis's fifteen ships of the line encountered twenty-eight Spanish off Cape St Vincent; numbers were again equal at the battle of Camperdown,

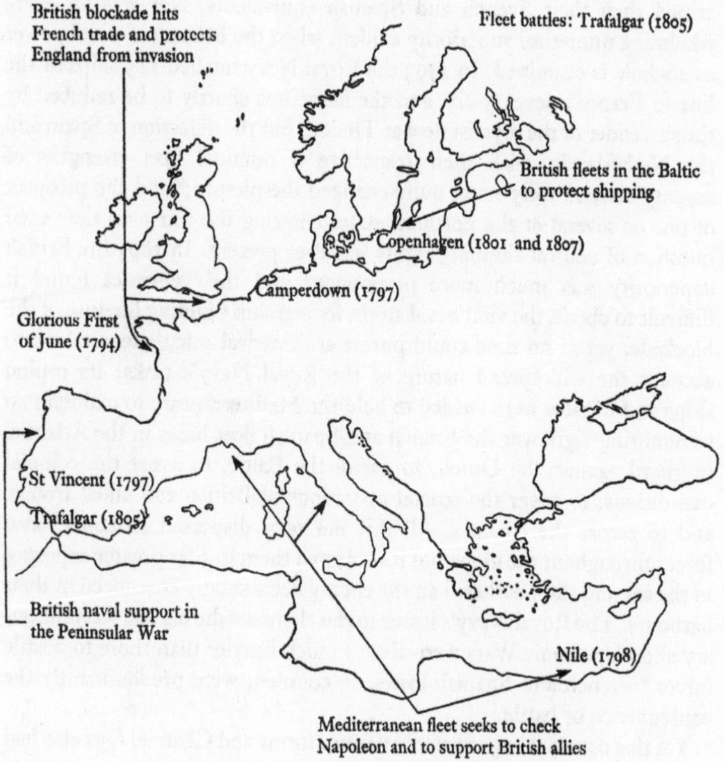

Map. 5. The strategy of the naval war in Europe, 1793–1815

although the Dutch warships were less heavily armed; at the Nile they were once more equal; and at Trafalgar twenty-seven British ships of the line fought against thirty-three of the Combined Fleet. It is worth adding here that the British vessels were usually smaller and less heavily armed than their French and Spanish equivalents. Nor was an overwhelming numerical superiority evident when the balance of naval power as a whole is examined. In 1793 the Royal Navy totalled 115 ships of the line to France's seventy-six, and the latter was shortly to be reduced by the surrender of the royalist fleet at Toulon; but the defection of Spain and the Netherlands, with their respective if nominal fleet strengths of seventy-six and forty-nine, quite changed the picture;[2] and the prospect of one or several of the northern states entering the war over the vexed question of neutral shipping rights was ever present. In 1803 the British superiority was much more pronounced and their enemies found it difficult to obtain the vital naval stores for warship building because of the blockade, yet at no time could purely arithmetical calculations take into account the widespread nature of the Royal Navy's tasks; its capital ships and frigates were needed to hold the Mediterranean, to maintain an unremitting vigil over the French and Spanish fleet bases in the Atlantic, to guard against the Dutch, to patrol the Baltic, to assist the colonial expeditions, to cover the coastal operations of British and allied troops, and to escort the convoys. All this not only dispersed Britain's naval forces throughout the globe but it subjected them to a far greater exposure to the sea and the weather than the enemy fleets snugly ensconced in their harbours. The Royal Navy's losses to the elements during the Revolutionary and Napoleonic Wars were always much heavier than those to hostile forces.[3] French and Spanish losses, in contrast, were predominantly the consequence of battle.

Yet this constant exposure to Atlantic storms and Channel fogs also had positive consequences for the service, whose seamanship was of an exceedingly high standard. Although British warships were, vessel for vessel, slower than their adversaries, the squadrons could manœuvre more swiftly and more precisely because of their greater discipline, efficiency and cohesiveness; in battle after battle British commanders were able to take advantage of 'gaps' in the enemy's line or some other tactical mistake. Another manifestation of this seamanship was the British practice of sailing into shallow, unchartered waters, relying upon pure skill to avoid navigational hazards; at the Nile and at Copenhagen (1801), for example, some of Nelson's ships of the line sailed on the *landward* of the anchored enemy vessels, throwing them into confusion by this surprise move.

This widespread willingness to take risks and to heed the Nelsonic motto that 'no captain can do very wrong if he places his ship alongside that of an enemy' was a clear sign that the formal 'line' tactics, which had gradually evolved and hardened from the Dutch wars onwards, were now breaking down completely.[4] In earlier conflicts too, of course, there had occasionally been a *mêlée* between the fleets, which provided the best opportunity for a decisive victory; but with the amended Fighting Instructions and the spirit of aggressiveness and initiative in the officer corps, close-range fighting and grappling became much more common. Annihilation of the enemy's forces was once again the main object of a battle. 'Had we taken ten sail', commented Nelson bitterly upon Hotham's cautious policy during a clash with the Toulon fleet in 1795, 'and allowed the eleventh to escape, when it had been possible to have got at her, I could never have called it well done.'[5]

A great deal of this eagerness for battle can also be attributed to the superiority of British gunnery. Particularly effective here was the carronade, an easily-manœuvrable, quick-firing gun which fired a large shot at short range and required a much smaller crew to man it;[6] from 1779 onwards more and more of these were introduced into the fleet and at the Battle of the Saints they wrought terrible damage upon the French warships. The very existence of this short-range armament offered a great incentive to British captains to close with the enemy and break through his lines, raking him from right and left in the process. In all the great battles of the Revolutionary and Napoleonic Wars – 'The Glorious First of June', Cape St Vincent, Camperdown, the Nile and Trafalgar – the carronades took a fearful toll, although the poor gunnery of the opposing French and Spanish forces may have led to their effects being exaggerated by British observers; in clashes with the Dutch and American navies the casualties were more evenly distributed. What is certain is that this weapon would not have been so effective had it not been for the constant training of the crews and for the intense interest in gunnery displayed by so many notable commanders – Broke, Douglas, Troubridge and, of course St Vincent and Nelson.

The sheer professionalism and zest and efficiency of the Royal Navy's commanders in this period stands in stark contrast to the quality of the French and Spanish leading officers. Throughout the eighteenth century the French navy had shown circumspection and prudence in battle rather than initiative, and the revolution led to the dismissal of many royalist officers and to a further deterioration in morale; ideological fervour and *élan* might create wonders in land battles, but to work a large fleet competent officers, trained crews and years of experience were required. This the French, with rare exceptions, did not possess. On the other hand it must be admitted that they were facing a remarkable galaxy of naval talent once the inadequate British officers were weeded out in the early stages of the war. If Nelson towers above them all by his unique combination of leadership, charm, tactical genius, intelligence and eagerness for victory, there were many others who also deserved respect: St Vincent, tough, thorough and intolerant of fools; Duncan, Cornwallis, Keith, Collingwood, Howe and Hood amongst the leading admirals; Troubridge, Darby, Foley, Hardy amongst a whole host of outstanding captains; Blackwood, Riou, Cochrane and other brilliant frigate commanders. Behind the officers at sea stood Barham and later St Vincent himself, directing the overall naval strategy carefully, yet always willing to support their bolder admirals – particularly in the Mediterranean – even if this involved some weakening in home waters. Moreover, it was due to the logistical and dockyard support, built up by Barham, that the enormous British fleet was sustained throughout the war. The administrative difficulties remained formidable: the supply of naval stores was always a critical problem, especially during the time of the Continental System; the dockyards were still too slow in refitting and repairing warships; and the navy could never secure enough sailors, thanks to conditions of service so primitive and brutal that in 1797 they provoked serious mutinies. Nevertheless, the overall achievement of the Admiralty in the face of such problems was remarkable.

Parallel to, and dependent upon, the Anglo-French duel for command of the sea went their struggle for overseas bases and colonies; here, too, the culminating point in a century-long race was reached, with Britain emerging in 1815 with a position so strengthened that she appeared to be the only real colonial power in the world.

That the fighting against France in what was originally and essentially a European war should have spread so swiftly to the tropics was a result of many factors, most of them predictable. In the first place Pitt, Dundas, Castlereagh and other British ministers were to a great extent advocates of a 'maritime' strategy. As Dundas argued in 1801:

> From our insular position, from our limited population not admitting of extensive continental operations, and from the importance depending in so material a degree upon the extent of our commerce and navigation, it is obvious that, be the causes of the war what they may, the primary object of our attention ought to be, by what means we can most effectually increase those resources on which depends our naval superiority, and at the same time diminish or appropriate to ourselves those which might enable the enemy to contend with us in this respect.

> . . . It is therefore as much the duty of those entrusted with the conduct of a British war to cut off the colonial resources of our enemy as it would be that of a general of a great army to destroy or intercept the magazines of his opponent.[7]

By so doing, it was felt, Britain would contribute more to the defeat of France than by the dispatch of military forces to fight on the continent. This was a return to the strategy of non-involvement, a rejection of the main lesson of all previous eighteenth-century Anglo-French wars; and it is not surprising to see that it had to be abandoned after years of peripheral and overseas operations revealed that Napoleon could only really be defeated on land. But the consequence of this attitude was that colonies occupied a high place in British policy throughout the wars.

There were, naturally enough, other motives present to reinforce this inclination. The Admiralty was eager to secure naval harbours across the globe, partly to gain advantageous positions alongside the major trade routes but chiefly to eliminate enemy bases from which commerce-raiders might operate: the second occupation of the Cape of Good Hope provides a good example of this strategical motivation.[8] More powerful still, perhaps, was the economic factor. The West Indies, which provided four fifths of the income from Britain's overseas investments and which were now the concern of Lancashire cotton manufacturers as well as sugar planters, shippers and financiers, were deemed to be so important that London had no hesitation in sending numerous expeditions to that unhealthy region – causing, in the words of one historian, '100,000 casualties while contributing nothing to the main course of the war'.[9] Furthermore, since the war with France, Spain and the Netherlands automatically affected British trade with the continent, there arose a desperate need as Dundas put it, 'to provide new and beneficial markets, as a substitute for those in which there is a temporary interruption'. With the introduction of the Continental System, this search became ever more pronounced.

As always, the course of the colonial struggles between Britain and her European rivals was ultimately decided by sea power; the Royal Navy's ability to contain the hostile fleets within European waters and to punish them severely whenever they emerged from port determined the fate of the various overseas possessions in the Americas, Africa, the Indian Ocean and the East Indies. In 1793 Tobago, part of San Domingo, Pondicherry and St Pierre and Miquelon were taken; in 1794 the important West Indian islands of Martinique, Guadeloupe, St Lucia, the Saints, Maria Galante and Deseada; in 1795 the vital eastern territories of Ceylon,

Malacca and the Cape of Good Hope; in 1796 Dutch possessions in the East and West Indies; in 1797 Trinidad was taken and the French colony at Madagascar destroyed; in 1798 Minorca was captured and Napoleon's strike at Egypt blunted; in 1799 Surinam fell into British hands; in 1800 Goree, Curaçao and Malta; in 1801 Danish and Swedish islands in the West Indies were overrun; and in India the brothers Wellesley smashed pro-French native princes and greatly extended the British hold upon the sub-continent. All of these territories, with the exception of Ceylon, Trinidad and parts of India, which were retained as British possessions, and Malta, which was 'neutralized', were handed back to their former owners at the Treaty of Amiens in 1802. When that precarious peace broke down in the following year, the British simply repeated their colonial conquests, aided by a still greater naval superiority. St Pierre and Miquelon, St Lucia, Tobago and Dutch Guiana were taken before Trafalgar, and further advances were made in India; the Cape fell in 1806; Curaçao and the Danish West Indies in 1807; several of the Moluccas in 1808; Senegal and Martinique in 1809; Guadeloupe, Mauritius, Amboyna and Banda in 1811; Java in 1811. 'There were no spectacular victories or dramatic feats of arms, but quietly the overseas empires of France and Holland disappeared into Britain's grasp.'[10] By 1814, as Napoleon himself admitted, the British were strong enough to retain all these captured territories at the conclusion of peace, had they so desired it.

That same British naval mastery which disposed of the enemy's fleet challenges and invasion attempts (apart from a few sporadic French raids upon Ireland), and permitted the swift overrunning of hostile colonies, also forced the weaker navies to revert to the strategy of *guerre de course*. In this respect, too, the wars of 1793–1802 and 1803–15 witnessed the culmination of another major aspect of the Anglo-French naval rivalry since 1689 – the contest between a main battle-fleet strategy and commerce-raiding as a means to defeat the enemy. To the navalist historians of the later nineteenth century, the outcome of this conflict was never in question. The French, wrote Mahan, had hoped to bankrupt England by commerce-raiding alone: 'what they obtained was the demoralization of their navy, the loss of the control of the sea and of their own external commerce, finally Napoleon's Continental System and the fall of the Empire.'[11] Insofar as the maritime supremacy of the British allowed them to frustrate invasion attempts, to send expeditionary armies to the continent and to protect their own and seize enemy colonies, this preference for battle-fleet operations was entirely justified; but it should in no way lead to any sweeping dismissal of the possible effects of a well-organized *guerre de course*. During the Revolutionary and Napoleonic Wars, in fact, the attack upon British seaborne trade was more successful than any since the War of the Spanish Succession. As in that previous conflict, the run-down of the French main fleets and of the merchant marine freed thousands of Frenchmen for privateering, which remained the only occupation left at sea – and a highly profitable one at that. In addition, raiding squadrons of perhaps four or six naval vessels were sent to scour the trade routes and, when other countries fell into the French orbit, British shipping was subjected to attacks from most of the nations of Europe. The majority of these assaults took place in the Channel, Bay of Biscay, North Sea, Baltic and Mediterranean, but the larger and more powerful privateers joined the raiding squadrons in commerce-destroying operations all over the globe. From such bases at Martinique, Guadeloupe and Mauritius the valuable West and East Indies trade was under frequent attack. Finally, two additional factors made this campaign more formidable than ever before. The French, although deficient in fleet commanders, had at this time many daring raiders, Blanckmann, Leveille, Lemême, Surcouf, Dutertre, Hamelin, Bouvet, who exploited every opportunity to disrupt trade; and the overseas commerce of Great Britain was now so enormous that a vast array of targets lay open to their attacks. London, which carried on more than half the commerce of the country, recorded entries and departures averaging between 13,000 and 14,000 each year.[12] To safeguard all these ships all of the time was clearly beyond the bounds of possibility.

Almost 11,000 British merchant vessels, if we are to believe contemporary lists, were captured by the enemy in the years 1793–1815; and, although Mahan has calculated that even this figure represented only 2½ per cent of both the total numbers of ships and tonnage involved, the absolute losses were nevertheless quite unprecedented. Marine insurance rates rose dramatically, complaints poured into the Admiralty from shipping and trading firms, and the Press criticized the laxness of the navy's counter-measures. In 1810, after Napoleon had struck against British commerce in the Baltic and the total shipping losses reached the highest ever – 619 – for one year, the Committee of Lloyds was formally censured by its members. When taken in consideration with the effects of the Continental System itself, the French campaign to disrupt British seaborne trade had severe economic consequences and should not be lightly dismissed.

Prodded on by an agitated mercantile lobby, and itself only too aware of the importance of giving adequate protection to overseas trade, the Admiralty instituted a whole series of measures designed to neutralize the *guerre de course*. Patrols were deployed in focal areas such as the Soundings and the lower North Sea, and frigates were dispatched to watch enemy ports. 'Q-ships', armed vessels disguised as peaceful merchantmen, operated along the English coast, hoping to surprise the many privateers which sailed in those waters. Expeditionary forces were sent out to eliminate enemy naval bases overseas, from which the attacks upon the rich colonial trades were mounted. No great speed attended this strategy, however, for it was not until 1810 that Mauritius, that nest of daring commerce-raiders, was taken; with its fall, and with the occupation of Java in the following year, the *guerre de course* in Eastern waters petered out.[13] But the most effective measure of all was the institution of a world-wide convoy system, which the Admiralty worked out in conjunction with Lloyd's and which the two bodies, by reference to the Convoy Acts of 1793, 1798 and 1803, imposed upon the mass of reluctant shipowners. In so doing, the navy and the insurers gave protection to the important overseas trade routes and undoubtedly reduced the rate of shipping losses. Only the large ships of the East India and Hudson's Bay companies and certain other specialized vessels were exempted from the obligation to collect in port for a convoy; then, when the escort arrived, vast fleets would set off and proceed under naval direction to their destination. Often 200, and occasionally as many as 500 merchantmen would be assembled at a south coast harbour such as Portsmouth and escorted out of the 'danger zone' by ships of the line and frigates. Extraordinary steps were undertaken for special circumstances; to protect merchant vessels sailing through the Belt from Danish attacks in 1808, for example, the Admiralty stationed ships of the line at each end and at intervals along the way.[14] Through a combination of all these measures, the British were able to beat off the continuous assault upon their commerce and thereby to safeguard the prosperity upon which their entire war effort depended. But perhaps the most astonishing thing about this whole struggle was the way in which the clear strategical lesson about the use of convoys was disregarded by later Admiralties, with consequences which nearly proved disastrous for Britain in 1917!

In this epic and drawn-out contest, in which, to use Mahan's words, 'France and Great Britain swayed back and forth in deadly grapple over the vast arena', the ancient dispute between sea power and land power re-emerged in heightened form. Napoleon was, after all, the personification of the latter element, conquering nations and dominating the continent in a way which Philip of Spain and Louis XIV had never done; and in Nelson we have what Mahan in his biography called 'the embodiment of sea power'.[15] Once again, the British faced the problem of how to defeat a country which was not greatly susceptible to the workings of sea power but which possessed the potential – under Napoleon's genius and drive, at least – to conquer Europe and to threaten the security of the British Isles.

It was true that Britain was not now so diplomatically isolated as it had been during the War of American Independence; but the repeated efforts to cobble together coalitions against France were frustrated time and again by Napoleon's military achievements.[16] Even the First Coalition, which ranged virtually all the states of western and central Europe against the disorganized French revolutionaries, had begun to crumble by 1795 and with the defeat of Austria two years later Britain was, apart from her link with Portugal, isolated. The failure of Napoleon's stroke against Egypt permitted British diplomacy to tempt Austria and Russia into the War of the Second Coalition, yet the abstention of Prussia, the withdrawal of Russia and the defeat of Austria again revealed the fragility of this alliance.[17] Instead of Britain finding allies to contain the French on land, the latter had browbeaten the Dutch and Spanish governments into cooperating against the Royal Navy at sea and the League of Armed Neutrality had been recreated; even Portugal had been eliminated as an ally by 1801. By the Peace of Amiens in 1802 both sides acknowledged that a strategical stalemate existed similar to that at the end of the War of the Austrian Succession: Britain dominated the seas and the colonial world, France, the European continent, and neither could get at the other. When war broke out again in 1803 the British remained alone for two years until the Third Coalition, with Austria and Russia, was formed; but in the period 1805–7 Napoleon knocked out Austria, Prussia and Russia in turn, and with the establishment of the Continental System practically the whole of Europe was united against Britain, which was forced to concentrate upon peripheral operations in Spain, the Baltic and the Mediterranean. Only with the failure of Napoleon's attack upon Russia in 1812 was it possible to build up a coalition determined and united enough to overcome France's military power finally.

Britain's problem, as Professor Brunn has pointed out, was that it required a combination of herself and the three great military powers of Austria, Prussia and Russia to defeat a regenerated France; yet each of these states was at times prepared to abandon the coalition and to ally with Napoleon, either out of fear or of greed.[18] Only Britain was consistently anti-French but without this combined 'continental sword' she could do little. While this explains why it took the British so many years, despite the most intense diplomatic efforts, before their arch-enemy was defeated, it also illustrates the limited influence of sea power in a struggle for control of the entire continent. After all, the post-Trafalgar years, when the predominance of the Royal Navy had reached an unprecedented level, were also the years during which Napoleon enjoyed the most unchallenged mastery in Europe. The whale and the elephant, to use Potter and Nimitz's phrase, were finding it difficult to grapple with each other;[19] and if this strategical discrepancy ensured the security of the British Isles, Egypt and the colonies, it did not help London in its basic war aim of restoring the *status quo* of 1789.

The task was further compounded by London's poor diplomacy in the early part of the struggle and by the reluctance of the British government to become involved in military operations on the continent in the manner of Marlborough or the Elder Pitt – which European allies always regarded as the necessary proof that Britain was serious and would not desert them. She was willing, as we have seen, to engage the fleets of France and her satellites and to drive them from the seas; she was willing to undertake costly expeditions across the globe against enemy colonies, although it was difficult to persuade the Austrians or the Prussians that such actions were for the common good; she was willing to exclude French commerce from the oceans by a vigorous blockading policy, so that by 1800 France's trade with Asia, Africa and America was less than $356,000;[20] she was willing, as the actions against Denmark showed, to disregard international law in her determination to reduce France's influence in Europe; she was willing to offer continuous naval support in the Baltic and Mediterranean to allied armies involved in coastal operations; she was willing to pour out ever-increasing sums in subsidies to her allies, so that by 1815 the total financial support amounted to a colossal £65 million;[21] and, finally, she was willing to dispatch her own soldiers upon 'hit-and-run' raids along the shores of French-dominated Europe.

By these latter measures especially, it could be argued, the British revealed that they were not oblivious of the need to engage or divert French military strength. In 1795 they captured Corsica and held it for a year. In 1799 an Anglo-Russian naval and military force operated at the Texel but soon withdrew. In 1800 an expedition sent to Ferroll was quickly re-embarked. In the same year Malta was seized, two years after the capture of Minorca. In 1807 Stralsund was occupied in an effort to help the Swedes and an army was landed near Copenhagen to support the operation to capture the Danish fleet. In 1809 the largest raid of all took place, when 40,000 troops were made ready for the strike against the Dutch. However, whilst these widely dispersed peripheral assaults demonstrated the strategical benefits accruing to the power which possessed command of the sea, few of the attacks had any influence upon the European balance of power; indeed, many were undertaken for purely naval purposes. Corsica and Minorca were seized to mask the naval base at Toulon; Malta to cover the eastern Mediterranean; Stralsund to protect the supply of naval stores. Yet in 1800, whilst the Cabinet wavered over the relative advantages of raiding Brest, Cadiz or Ferroll with the 80,000 men at its disposal, their Austrian ally was being beaten at Marengo, a closely-fought battle in which a British contribution might well have been decisive.[22] Similarly, the massive investment in men and resources for the ill-fated Walcheren expedition, precisely at a time when the Spanish campaign was getting under way, has appeared inexplicable to most historians of the Napoleonic War; and, as in so many other 'conjunct' operations of this period, the British troops never stayed long enough to produce a major diversion of the enemy's armed strength. Much of the decisive continental fighting in the years 1793–1815 took place in areas which were remote from the sea and therefore less sensitive to British flanking assaults; but this inability to influence events significantly was simply furthered by the transitory nature of these amphibious raids.

The campaign in the Spanish peninsula proved to be the brilliant exception to this rule and, as such, has always been regarded as 'the classical example of one of the great strategical advantages conferred by sea power'.[23] However, while the Royal Navy's mastery gave logistical support and an added mobility to the British army, it is doubtful if even this campaign would have succeeded had it not been for the cautious genius of Wellington; the crucial fact that the Portuguese and Spanish populations were by now bitterly anti-French; and Napoleon's concentration upon matters elsewhere in Europe, notably in Germany and Russia. Whatever the weight assigned to these individual elements, it remains true that their combination produced the first *lasting* check to Napoleon's ambitions, amply justifying the British government's decision to continue the Peninsular War after 1809 despite the opposition to it at home. The campaign occupied much of the French army – at one time, some 370,000 French troops were trying to hold down Spain – and eventually cost the death of 40,000 of them; it breached the Continental System by boosting British trade not only with Spain and Portugal but also with their colonies; and it provided an example of resistance to the rest of Europe.

In the larger strategical history of the war, however, the peninsular campaign probably occupies a position similar to that which the North African fighting assumed in 1940–43 – a drain upon the enemy's resources and a booster for Allied morale, but not the theatre in which the decisive military blow was dealt to the foe. In both wars, it is worth arguing, that blow was delivered in eastern Europe, where Napoleon, like Hitler, over-reached himself and then had to suffer the consequences. 'Of the 430,000 men who had marched into Russia [in 1812] perhaps 50,000 found their way back and 100,000 remained as prisoners; but over 100,000 had died in battles and skirmishes, and nearly twice as many had perished of disease, cold, and famine.'[24] After that disaster all of Napoleon's discontented satellites, Austria, Prussia, and Sweden threw off the French yoke and joined in the battle. Although they were hampered by indecision and the lack of an outstanding military commander, their sheer numbers overwhelmed Napoleon's forces, which were also suffering from a lack of cannon, wagons and other forms of military *materiel.* In the fighting which culminated in the 'Battle of the Nations' at Leipzig in 1813, the French lost nearly 200,000 troops and an exhausted remnant of 40,000 was all that reached the Rhineland by the end of that year. It was this loss of virtually two entire armies which bled French military might and ensured that, even when Napoleon attempted the gambler's last throw on the field of Waterloo in 1815, his resources were simply too weak to conquer the armies of Wellington and Blücher.

As we shall see, it can reasonably be argued that the British support for Russia, Austria and Prussia in the form of almost unlimited subsidies and munitions in the years 1812–14 had played a large part in the victories in eastern Europe; and that it was the Royal Navy's protection of commerce which had permitted Britain to afford assistance of such dimensions to her continental allies. Nevertheless, it is a long step from that statement to the claim that 'it was our all-but complete sea-control, challenging Napoleon's equally complete land-control, which not only saved us but, in the end, defeated him'.[25] In actual fact, these two elements often tended to cancel each other out. 'The Glorious First of June' and the early colonial conquests were balanced by the defection of Prussia, Spain and the Netherlands, and the Royal Navy's withdrawal from the Mediterranean; the battles of Cape St Vincent and Camperdown by the conquest of northern Italy and the capitulation of Austria; the Nile campaign and the formation of the Second Coalition by the withdrawal of Russia and the further defeat of Austria at Marengo and Hohenlinden; Trafalgar, it will be remembered, took place between the battles of Ulm and Austerlitz, provoking that arch-navalist, Admiral Fisher, into emphasizing a century later: 'Trafalgar did not stop Austerlitz! And Pitt said, notwithstanding Trafalgar: "Roll up the map of Europe", and he died of a broken heart!';[26] the fate of Britain's allies in Italy, whom Collingwood laboured for years to help, was likewise 'decided on the battlefields of central Europe';[27] and while the Royal Navy rendered temporary assistance to Sweden in 1808–9, it could not prevent the overrunning of Finland nor frustrate the combined Franco-Russian pressure which compelled the Swedes to adhere to the Continental System. Britain's naval mastery preserved her independence and gained her fresh colonies overseas; but that was only one aspect of a struggle which encompassed land power as well as sea power. Only the patriotic bias of British naval historians makes it necessary to point out the truism that a war for the military domination of Europe had to be fought, logically enough, inside Europe and by armies. To defeat Napoleon, 'maritime' methods had to be supplemented by 'continental' ones.

Near the close of Britain's struggle with Napoleon one further aspect of previous wars manifested itself – the North American dimension. For the bitter Anglo-French conflict, into which other European states were dragged, often willy-nilly, also had repercussions upon relations with the United States, which by the beginning of the nineteenth century had become a major trading nation. America's shipping and overseas trade, like that of Denmark, had taken advantage of its country's neutrality and expanded swiftly, but they inevitably suffered from the British Orders in Council and the various French prohibitory decrees. Of the two pressures the British, due to the Royal Navy's blockade, was the more effective; and American annoyance at this interference was compounded by the British policy of searching their vessels for British seamen – an indication both of London's desperate need to man its enormous navy and of the continued lack of a satisfactory system of recruitment. Although the British government was eventually to rescind the Orders, it was too late to prevent an American declaration of war.[28]

In the North American struggle of 1756–63 the British had won because of their numerical superiority in that continent and because the French had been too distracted by European wars to challenge the Royal Navy's control of sea communications. In the renewed conflict of 1776–83 the British had lost because they had attempted to subdue a vast continent with inadequate manpower and logistical support and because the French and Spaniards were free from European entanglements and able to exploit London's colonial embarrassments. In this third and final round the result was a draw, because these various determinants were mixed and tended to cancel each other out.[29] The French navy was in no position to interfere in North America, indeed, there was no cooperation at all between Paris and Washington in this war although they were both facing a common enemy; instead of the European situation assisting the French, Napoleon was engaged in a deadly struggle in Russia and Germany, which occupied all his attention, and the other European powers had no desire to embarrass the British – Russia even attempted to mediate between London and Washington in order to bring their duel to a halt. It must be admitted that the continental war distracted British attention as well – troops were withdrawn from Spain to fight in Canada yet Wellington's campaign had to go on – but the fact remains that the international situation in 1812 was much more favourable to Britain than it had been in 1776. Opposed only by an enterprising but inferior American navy, the Royal Navy could swiftly achieve maritime control along the eastern seaboard and carry British expeditionary forces to their selected destinations. In the local naval war on the Great Lakes, and in the defence of trade from American privateers, the service was far less successful – a sign, perhaps, that Britain's earlier naval victories had been too easily won over inefficient and demoralized French and Spanish fleets and that since Trafalgar a certain complacency had grown up. 'Command of the sea' by main fleets remained a British monopoly, however.

At the same time, Britain still faced that basic military problem of 1776 to 1783; how was she to conquer an enemy so enormous in size as the United States without engaging in a vast military campaign which it would be beyond her logistical and manpower capacities to sustain? After all, British politicians could hardly go on emphasizing their country's 'limited population not admitting of extensive continental operations'[30] in Europe without seeing that the same applied to warfare in America: a successful war in either continent inevitably involved very large armies. It was true that London could count upon the support of the Canadian loyalists, but this was clearly no equivalent to the help rendered by the Austrian, Russian or Prussian armies in the wars against France; in fact, it simply extended the strategical dilemma by making it necessary to defend the lengthy American–Canadian border as well. Possibly the best solution for the British was to seize coastal points and systematically to reduce the wealth of the United States until the latter was willing to surrender, for since the Americans' foreign trade and shipping had expanded so rapidly after 1783 they had become more susceptible than France to assaults upon these bases of their prosperity, and there were many merchants and planters who disliked the whole idea of fighting Britain in any case. Nevertheless, although this was the course the British adopted, it was by its very nature a lengthy campaign, with no prospect of a sudden and decisive victory, and there were also circles in Britain who disliked a conflict with the country which had been their best customer and had many cultural links with themselves. While the United States was suffering the most by 1814, the conclusion of peace was the most appropriate expression of the stalemate which existed between land power and sea power and of the mutual realization that the war would benefit neither of them. The argument over maritime rights was simply shelved, not settled.

Set in the context of the Napoleonic War, the Anglo-American dispute appears to be more of a local quarrel, a strategical diversion, than anything else. In the wider story of Britain's rise to naval mastery, its lessons have more significance. The war of 1812–14 provides another confirmation of the importance of the interaction between the European and North American theatres in Britain's imperial and maritime expansion during the eighteenth century; it thereby underscores Chatham's belief that only by having a due regard for the military equilibrium in both continents could Great Britain, an island and predominantly naval state located between the two, ensure that her vital interests were safeguarded. Furthermore, it also confirmed the limitations of British sea power, even at a time when the Royal Navy was without a serious rival, in a conflict with a continent-wide power such as the United States. It is not surprising to learn that later British statesmen took due note of this fact and, although fully prepared to defend Canada against American aggression, were privately aware of the military difficulties of such a task and were therefore always anxious to preserve good relations with the United States if at all possible.[31]

The Revolutionary and Napoleonic Wars were, finally, a test of whether the British economy was strong enough to endure the incredible strains of prolonged and costly military and naval campaigns without collapsing. As Professor Mathias has aptly remarked, 'One of the few constancies in history is that the scale of commitment on military spending has always risen',[32] and the eighteenth-century wars proved to be no exception to this rule. The cost of all the previous struggles paled into insignificance compared with these two, however. In 1793 the British government spent £4·8 million upon the army and £2·4 million upon the navy out of a total expenditure of £19·6 million; but by 1815 total outgoings had risen to £112·9 million, out of which £49·6 million went to the army and £22·8 million to the navy – a tenfold increase in defence expenditures.[33] The overall cost of the war to Britain was a staggering £1,657 million. Few Britons could believe that such sums could be paid out year after year without a drastic weakening of the economy, an expectation which Napoleon shared, though with a great deal more eagerness.

For Britain to emerge triumphant three conditions would have to be fulfilled: her industry, agriculture and commerce would need to grow sufficiently quickly to permit the government to tap this rising wealth through a variety of taxes without, however, killing off the sources of such prosperity or provoking internal opposition; the government would also have to be able to preserve its financial credit in order to raise funds from financiers; and the country would need to maintain and indeed to expand its foreign trade in order to pay its way in the world, a task which was made especially difficult by the imposition of the Continental System in 1806. Moreover, all this had to be done more successfully than in the far larger and more populous continental *bloc* which the French dominated. As it happened, the three conditions were fulfilled, but it was, to use Wellington's words about Waterloo, 'a close-run thing'. The unrest in industry and agriculture, the Bank of England's decision not to honour its commitments in gold in 1797, the widespread relief at the Peace of Amiens, and the strain caused by the Continental System and the simultaneous American economic pressures, were all indications of the way in which the country was being stretched to its limits.

Yet, if Britain was being stretched, she rose to the challenge; once again, war was to reveal itself as a catalyst and accelerator of economic change even though its effects could also be disruptive. In respect of the first of the above three conditions, the expansion of the country's productivity and hence its wealth, all the signs are that, despite spasmodic short-term checks, such growth did take place. Agriculture benefited from the war, because many European products, particularly grain, were cut off and English landowners rushed in to fill the gap. Industry's rise was much more spectacular, for the years 1793–1815 revealed beyond any shadow of doubt that a real revolution in technology and output was under way. The steam-engine was being used in a variety of ways, and many further technological advances were made. A whole network of canals – the Grand Junction, the Basingstoke, the Kennet and Avon, the Caledonian, the Mersey-Humber link-up – was built to improve internal communications; new turnpikes and iron rail-tracks supplemented them. Pig-iron output soared from 68,000 tons in 1788 to 125,000 tons in 1796 to 244,000 tons in 1806. Cotton, the fastest-growing industry of all, was a catalyst or 'multiplier' in itself, demanding ever more machinery, steam-power, coal and labour. In 1793 cotton exports had totalled £1·65 million; by 1815 they had risen to £22·55 million, becoming Britain's greatest export by far. The steel, machine-tools, armaments, woollen and silk industries were also expanding, although at a more modest pace. The shipyards, too, were busy catering for the Royal Navy's orders, even if civilian demand slackened off. The population was rising rapidly, fuelling the demand for foodstuffs, clothing and household goods, and already the hastily built industrial townships of central and northern England were beginning to change the landscape. Banking and insurance companies naturally encouraged, and shared in the profits from, this boom.

So, too, did the British government under Pitt and his successors, whose fiscal and taxation policies contrived to stimulate and to partake in the benefits of the country's increasing prosperity; there was, after all, no other way to pay for the spiralling costs of the war. Customs and excise receipts automatically grew with the expansion in foreign trade, from a total of £13·57 million in 1793 to £44·89 million in 1815; land taxes rose less spectacularly, from £2·95 million to £9·50 million in the same period; whilst income and property tax, first introduced in 1799, was bringing in £14·62 million by the final year of the Napoleonic War.[34] To contemporaries this taxable strength of the British was astonishing; 'between 1806 and 1816 a population of less than fourteen million people paid nearly £142,000,000 in income taxes alone'.[35] Upon this solid base of a growing national prosperity, which could be tapped, the tenfold rise in defence spending had good prospects of being sustained.

Yet even this colossal effort could not bridge the gap between the government's revenue and its expenditure; in the crucial year of 1813, for example, taxes could only produce £73 million of the £111 million which were spent. The difference had to come from loans, but here the government possessed yet another trump card. Because of Pitt's stabilization of the economy of the country after 1783 the government's credit was high; and because of the very flexible and superior financial facilities of the country, public borrowing was already a long-established and successful expedient, particularly in wartime. As soon as war broke out, Pitt adopted a policy of heavy long-term borrowing, to which the public eagerly responded. Even the 'suspension of cash payments' in 1797, it is worth noting, did not check this willingness, and the alarm was soon over. 'In practice', an economic historian notes, 'the Bank of England had so secured itself in the public confidence that its now unbacked money was just as acceptable as it had been when gold could be got for it at a fixed price . . . The banking and mercantile community in London and the provinces, with virtual unanimity, pronounced its readiness to carry on business as normal with a pure paper currency.'[36] – which was just as well, for the government had to raise over £440 million by loan in the years 1793–1815, this representing between one quarter and one third of its total expenditure.[37] As a consequence, the National Debt soared from £299 million in 1793 to an enormous £834 million in 1815, without any visible sign of the country going bankrupt or of the lenders doubting the government's ability to repay in the future. French credit, despite Napoleon's brilliant military successes, the greater population and natural wealth of France, and the more concrete securities offered by its government, was never able to match this performance. Britain had gained greatly in the eighteenth century by having made clever alliances, comments P. G. M. Dickson; 'More important even than alliances, however, was the system of public borrowing . . . which enabled England to spend on war out of all proportion to its tax revenue, and thus to throw into the struggle with France and its allies the decisive margin in ships and men without which the resources previously committed might have been committed in vain.'[38]

Both the growing industrialization and the continuing high credit of the government depended upon a third factor: the expansion of foreign trade, particularly exports, which allowed Britain to pay her way in the world. Since the American war of 1776–83 commerce had been booming, but there was always the danger that the conflict with France would disrupt this process; after all, the greater part of Britain's trade was still with Europe. At first, such fears turned out to be groundless. War stimulated various trades, such as the British armaments industry, whose products were now highly valued in Europe. More important still, a great deal of British overseas trade was scarcely affected by the European struggle: commerce with the United States, for example, continued to soar, as did that with Asia and the West Indies, although how much of this was stimulated by the desperate need to discover and exploit new fields of commerce, because of troubles in Europe, is an open question; and when Britain overran enemy colonies, she automatically gained fresh markets for her own goods. Conversely, French, Dutch and Spanish industries were hit, not only by the loss of protected colonial markets but also by the Royal Navy's blockade in European waters. Naval power, together with commercial flexibility, enabled the British to switch the flow of their products from one part to another: when the French increased their hold upon the Mediterranean, British trade with northern Europe suddenly multiplied, and vice versa. Ultimately, the British were prepared to relax the Navigation Laws, electing to protect their commerce and industry even at the temporary expense of their traditionally protectionist shipping policy. Despite the domestic stresses, therefore, the economy remained sound. As one contemporary writer boasted in 1799:

> We can most incontrovertibly prove that, under the pressure of new burdens, and during the continuance of the eventful contest in which we are engaged, the revenue, the manufactures, and the commerce of the country, have flourished beyond the example of all former times. The war, which has crushed the industry, and annihilated the trade and shipping of her rival, has given energy and extent to those of Great Britain.[39]

The country's two major economic assets in any trade war were obvious to all observers: she was, thanks to her industrialization, producing finished goods of a quality and cheapness and variety which had no equal in the world; and she possessed, because of her extensive empire and her naval mastery, a near-monopoly in colonial produce. Whatever the decrees emanating from Napoleon, the European nations found it impossible to get along without British manufacturers on the one hand or tobacco, tea, coffee, sugar, spices and other tropical goods on the other. Nevertheless, the establishment of the Continental System in 1806 did involve the most determined and systematic attempt ever to prevent this flow of British exports and re-exports; it was the logical consequence of the Franco-Spanish defeat at Trafalgar, the recognition that unless Britain's economic strength was undermined, Napoleon would never be able to force her to her knees.[40] After he had bludgeoned Austria, Prussia and Russia into acquiescence, the prospects for Britain looked gloomy. Virtually the whole of Europe was ordered to boycott British goods. Worse still, the increasing friction with the United States affected trade with that valuable market and customer as well. Together, this combined pressure spelt a mortal danger for British industry.

The chief reason why such a disaster did not occur was that the Continental System was not applied long or consistently enough to take full effect. By 1808 the economic situation in Britain was very serious, but the revolution in Spain blew a hole in the Napoleonic system and the products of Lancashire and the Midlands poured into the peninsula. In the Baltic, Sweden, too, provided an exception until she broke under the Franco-Russian pressure. Then British industry suffered again – until the Russian rebellion against Napoleon and the decisive campaigning of 1812 destroyed for ever the French attempt to 'isolate' the continent. Since Anglo-American relations had deteriorated to the point of war by then, Britain had once again been relieved just in time. Even before that date, however, the difficulties of carrying out Napoleon's decrees had revealed themselves. Few non-Frenchmen in Europe wished to deprive themselves of British or colonial produce; they therefore contrived in all manner of ways to obtain the forbidden goods. Forged documents disguised the real place of origin of such imports. Smuggling was rife, particularly where officialdom was prone to look the other way; and when the French hold upon a certain region was tightened, trade was switched to another channel. Goods destined for Germany were landed in places as distant as Archangel and Salonika. Britain herself encouraged this flouting of the regulations whenever possible. Ports and countries dependent upon or friendly to London, such as Malta, Gibraltar, Sicily, Heligoland and Sweden, became vast depots for British manufactures.

The Navigation Acts were again relaxed to permit neutrals to carry these goods. Significantly enough, even the French themselves worked against the system. Commerce with the overseas world was permitted in France and the Netherlands under certain conditions, and this provided the opportunity for much evasion. 'Deals' across the Channel were arranged, during which sugar and coffee was exchanged for brandy and wine. The export of farm produce, a measure favoured by Napoleon, clashed with the strategy of interdicting trade with Britain. Even some of the boots and uniforms for the Grand Army were ordered in England! In the same way the New England ports, abetted by the British and Canadians, continued to trade with the enemy during the war of 1812–14.

Finally, the British were able, because of their near-monopoly of trade and maritime power outside Europe and the United States, to export more and more of their goods to this overseas world. Even before the outbreak of war this branch of foreign commerce had been growing rapidly, but the need to find new markets, together with the increasing domestic production of cotton cloth, household goods and metal wares, led to a real boom. Trade with the British West Indies rose from £6·9 million in 1793 to £14·7 million in 1814; with the foreign West Indies and Latin America, both newly opened during the war, rising from virtually nothing to £10·5 million.[41] Asia, Africa and British North America were also growing in importance. The enormous expansion of the London dockyard system – where the West India, Brunswick, London, East India and Commercial Docks were opened between 1802 and 1813 – was a reflection of this development in Britain's overseas, and particularly her *entrepôt*, trade. All provided useful crutches when British commerce was suffering in its traditional operating areas.

Nevertheless, the commercial warfare of the French and the Americans brought the country closer to an economic crisis in 1808 and 1811–12, than at any time in the two decades of war. The latter slump was particularly severe. Vast stocks of manufactures piled up outside their factories. The London docks were filled to overflowing with colonial produce. The supply of naval stores dropped off alarmingly, despite the British exploitation of the forests of the Empire as a substitute. Bankruptcies of firms rapidly increased. Unemployment and the rising cost of bread produced a spate of riots. The gap between the government's revenue and expenditure was widening alarmingly. Napoleon's overrunning of the Baltic saw hundreds of British vessels captured in that sea. An adverse trade balance caused the pound to depreciate. Economists such as Ricardo pleaded for peace. This was the physical reality behind the trade figures, which tell the story of that post-1810 slump in another form:[42]

Computed or Declared Values of U.K. Overseas Trade (£ million)

	Imports	Exports	Re-exports
1796	39·6	30·1	8·5
1800	62·3	37·7	14·7
1810	88·5	48·4	12·5
1812	56·0	41·7	9·1
1814	80·8	45·5	24·8

Without the Continental System and the American 'non-intercourse' policy it is clear that British foreign trade would have expanded continuously throughout this period, so great was the demand for British and Imperial produce. As it was, even during the worst years, a considerable amount of these goods found their way to their customers and as soon as Napoleon abandoned his efforts to strangulate trade it rapidly recovered; exports to northern Europe, which dropped from £13·6 million in 1809 to £5·4 million in 1812, bounded to £22·9 million in 1814.

By 1813–14 Britain could be seen to have withstood the test, not only in this economic struggle but in all other spheres. Her funds and munitions were pouring into eastern Europe to assist the uprisings against French hegemony. Wellington's army had recovered Spain and entered southern France, Canada was being held and the blockade along the eastern seaboard of the United States intensified, the attacks upon British seaborne trade were petering out, and the enemies' colonial empires had been overrun. There was still the reduction of Napoleon's final bid for power to come, and the North American war had to be resolved; but the end was in sight, and British statesmen could begin to appreciate that their country would come through its greatest challenge to date with its national power and its position in the world consolidated and even enhanced.

At this stage, it may be possible to bring together the various strands which, interacting with each other, explain the eventual victory of Britain in 1815. Her insular position, complemented by her naval mastery, provided that basic security from a Napoleonic invasion which no other European country possessed; her stable yet relatively flexible political and social system enabled her people to endure the strains of war, without serious domestic upheaval; her rapidly-expanding industrialization and foreign trade allowed the government to tap fresh sources of wealth; her sophisticated financial system offered insurance to the merchant shipper, capital for industry, and loans to the State; this economic and credit strength in turn supported a colossal navy and a quite considerable army; that navy, by smashing all enemy attempts to dispute command of the sea, not only reduced still further the chances of an invasion of England, but it permitted the capture of hostile colonies, the elimination of the foes' overseas trade, the protection of British commerce, and the sustenance of allies on the continent; that army, benefiting from the command of the sea, could be dispatched to seize hostile colonies and naval bases or to operate on the peripheries of Europe, in conjunction with allies and to the embarrassment of the enemy.

This symbiosis of British power was impressive to contemporaries and remains so to present-day historians; yet it is doubtful whether it alone could have succeeded in overthrowing Napoleon and enforcing a return to the *status quo ante bellum*. In a war with a great continental military state the Royal Navy, despite its offensive strategy, necessarily fulfilled a mainly *negative* role. The essential task was to defend Britain, her trade, and her wealth. The enemy's overseas colonies and commerce would naturally be eliminated wherever possible, but this alone could not bring France to defeat. Even the Peninsular campaign, valuable though it was, was not likely by itself to undermine Napoleon's hegemony over Europe: only the forcible uprising of the conquered peoples, and the driving of the French armies from the chief battle areas, would do that. Until then, Britain must hang on, playing a strategically passive role, but ever willing to exploit an opportunity and to assist a friend, and providing all the time an example of resistance to anti-French forces.

Why Napoleon failed was due to a combination of external *and* internal causes, of British pressure from without and rebellion from within. 'Viewed in historical perspective', Professor Brunn has argued, French expansionism 'contradicted a dominant political trend that had been shaping European society since the later Middle Ages, the trend towards a system of individual sovereign territorial states . . . [Napoleon's efforts] ran counter to the emotions and aspirations of the leading European nations.'[43] In this sense, perhaps the breakdown of the French rule was inevitable; there certainly was plenty of evidence that the effect of this rule was to awaken nationalist feelings in conquered territories, rather than to invoke notions of a European unity under a Napoleonic dynasty. After the disaster to the Grand Army in Russia, the artificial and temporary nature of this unity revealed itself and Bonaparte's grandiose design collapsed.

In this process, too, the British had played their part: for the widespread dislike throughout Europe of French domination and military plundering had been intensified by the institution of the Continental System, which dislocated the economy and was nothing other than a deliberate attempt to prevent Europeans from obtaining the British manufactures and colonial produce they desired. The Spanish and Russian resistance to Napoleon was to a considerable degree caused by a resentment at this economic deprivation. In the trade war of 1806–12 one side had to crack eventually. Britain, for reasons outlined above, had avoided that fate; and the struggle had not only devastated the French economy, but it also helped to provoke the internal European resistance which was necessary to unseat Napoleon. Secondly, the British had to be ready to utilize that rebellion even more effectively than they had done with the Spanish revolt, and here again their economic strength was vital. As Professor Sherwig puts it, 'Britain had never been able to give her allies the will to fight France, but by 1813 the great powers had found that essential requirement within themselves. What they now required of Britain was what she could send them: the money and the arms needed to transform that will into victory over the common enemy.'[44] In 1814 over £10 million was spent in subsidies, and Castlereagh was expecting that in return Austria, Prussia and Russia would each keep 150,000 men in the field against Napoleon. Only with such a massive military effort would the European balance of power be restored.

In conclusion, the Revolutionary and Napoleonic Wars represented the greatest test which Britain hitherto had had to encounter in its rise to naval mastery, and they confirmed once again the essential prerequisites for such a successful development: a healthy economy, a sophisticated financial system, commercial expertise and initiative, political stability, and a strong navy. The latter, it appeared, was unlikely to flourish if the other elements were not also prominent; defence meant more than armaments. Yet the conflict with France also confirmed the limitations of sea power, the necessity of watching carefully the European equilibrium, the desirability of having strong military allies in wartime, the need to blend a 'maritime' strategy with a 'continental' one. In all respects, then, the lessons of these wars had been useful ones. If they were to be well remembered by British statesmen and their public, and if the foundations upon which this successful policy had been based were not undermined, the likelihood was that this naval mastery would also continue in the future.

CHAPTER SIX

Pax Britannica (1815–59)

England is mistress of the seas, not by virtue of any arrogant or aggressive pretensions, but by virtue of her history, of her geographical situation, of her economic antecedents and conditions, of her Imperial position and expansion. These conditions have given the dominion of the seas to her, not by any prescriptive right, but by a normal and almost natural process of evolution; and, so long as they subsist and she is true to herself, they will retain it for her.

The Times, 3 February 1902.

If there was any period in history when Britannia could have been said to have ruled the waves, then it was in the sixty or so years following the final defeat of Napoleon. Here was an epoch, Professor Lloyd has noted, where 'British sea power exercised a wider influence than has ever been seen in the history of maritime empires'.[1] So unchallenged, so immense, did this influence appear, that people spoke then and later of a 'Pax Britannica', finding the only noteworthy equivalent in history to be the centuries-long domination of the civilized world by imperial Rome. Now it was the turn of the island people of north-west Europe to impose their rule on the world, the 'peace of Britain'. The very phrase gives a twofold impression, of a long period of tranquillity efficiently and firmly supervised by the Royal Navy, and of an overwhelmingly powerful nation upon which all others were to a varying extent dependent.

Neither impression is fully correct, but both contained a sufficient portion of the truth to secure a widespread acceptance of this overall portrait. A century or more later, when it has become evident that Britain's position as the world's greatest power has matched that of Rome neither in time nor in thoroughness, it may be possible to examine this phenomenon in a more balanced light. In particular, the claims of nineteenth-century poets, historians and politicians that their unrivalled sway of the earth's destinies was in some way natural and inevitable, can now be subjected to more critical scrutiny. When this is done, it becomes clear that the age of the Pax Britannica was only pre-ordained in the sense that a number of those vital factors, both positive and negative, which make up a nation's position in the world had combined together in the first three quarters of the nineteenth century – to the great advantage of Britain.

What were those factors? The positive ones deserve examination first, if only to check the notion that this British domination in world affairs was merely an illusion of the time, a myth of history. In the years considered in this chapter and the first half of the next, it would be fair to say that Great Britain was the only really industrialized nation in the world; that her predominance in commerce, transport, insurance and finance was great, and in most cases increasing; that she possessed the most extensive colonial empire ever seen, yet one which was to multiply in size during the century; and that, despite occasional scares, her naval strength and potential was virtually unchallengeable. What was more, she managed to maintain this dominance, this peace of Britain, at a cost to the nation of £1 or less per annum per head of population in defence expenditure – equivalent to somewhere between 2 and 3 per cent of the national income. Rarely has such a position in the world been purchased so cheaply.

This special place of Great Britain in the nineteenth century was rooted in her industrial revolution, and in the fact that her main European rivals had been crushed by 1815 through a long series of wars. While the French, Dutch and Spaniards had seen their economies weakened, their colonial empires reduced and their naval power eradicated in these contests, the British had – apart from the exceptional circumstances of 1776–1783 – gone from strength to strength. 'The result of this century of intermittent warfare was the greatest triumph ever achieved by any state: the virtual monopoly among European powers of overseas colonies, and the virtual monopoly of world-wide naval power.'[2] This whole movement provided a beautiful example of alternating cause and effect in Britain's rise to world predominance. The navy's decisive victories in the eighteenth century had given its merchants the lion's share in maritime trade, which itself had stimulated the industrial revolution; yet this in turn was to provide the foundations for the country's continuing and increasing growth, making it into a new sort of state – the only real world power at that time. Industrialization not only furthered the British ascendancy in commerce and finance and shipping, it also underpinned its own naval supremacy with a previously unheard-of economic potential.

Moreover, this was only the beginning: the years 1815–70 saw the full flowering of Britain's predominance in the fields of industry, commerce, finance and shipping.[3] Through the industrial revolution, the island people has been transformed from 'a nation of shopkeepers' into 'the workshop of the world'. Neither *cliché* was accurate, yet both summed up what appeared to observers of different ages to be Britain's most noticeable characteristic. The latter comment can certainly be understood in the middle of the nineteenth century, when she produced about two thirds of the world's coal, about half its iron, five sevenths of its steel, two fifths of its hardware and about half its commercial cotton cloth. After 1815, British trade with the tropical world increased rapidly, even though Europe was not ignored: Latin America, the Levant, Africa, the Far East and Australasia were drawn into a world economy centred chiefly upon London, which already possessed established links with North America, India and the West Indies. International trade boomed, particularly between 1840 and 1870, and Britain benefited from this in many ways apart from the purely industrial. In fact, she was later in the century to assume a far more imposing lead as an investor, banker, insurer and shipper than as a producer of goods. The spread of industrialization to Europe and North America, and the opening up of new markets and sources of raw materials in the tropics, were in the main financed from London. Britain's return on overseas investment of £10½ million in 1847 had risen to £80 million by 1887; by 1875 she had over £1,000 million invested abroad, with the interest therefrom being continually re-pumped into old or new areas of investment. Her lead in shipping was enormous, for she had fully replaced the Dutch as the carriers of the world, gaining yet another important source of earnings. After shaking off an American challenge in the first half of the century by switching from sail to steam – one further advantage of her early industrialization – she had by 1890 more registered tonnage than the rest of the world put together. And by being able to export coal, and thus earn revenue, on the outward journey as well, British vessels had a distinct advantage over foreign rivals. This great fleet was all insured in London, where Lloyd's had achieved a unique position. The City had become the centre of international finance in all its aspects: loans, private and governmental, were floated there, currencies exchanged there, insurance arranged there, commodities bought and sold there, shipping chartered there; and every one of these services increased the centralizing tendency by the establishment of branch offices and agencies abroad, from Valparaiso to Shanghai, from

San Francisco to Singapore. Finally, as can readily be imagined, Britain's lead in one field (e.g. insurance) sustained and reinforced her lead in another (e.g. shipping), and usually in a reciprocal fashion.[4]

Perhaps even more spectacular was the British adoption of a revolutionary system of commercial interchange – free trade – and the success they had in persuading many other nations to copy this, at least to a certain extent. The Mercantilist doctrine of fostering wealth through monopoly and state power, which had been the ideological driving force behind so much of Britain's expansion in the previous two centuries, had been thrown overboard by the followers of Adam Smith, Ricardo and their school. To some, this reversal of policy, precisely at the point when Britain had the power to enforce a crushing mercantilist victory, seemed incredible. To the Free Traders it was purely commonsense. Britain depended upon a growing world trade – the more, the better. Furthermore, with her great industrial lead, her large merchant marine, her financial expertise, she above all was uniquely suited to benefit from the greater exchange of commodities; whereas a rigorous mercantilist attitude would merely force other states to build up their own industries the more quickly behind tariff walls, thus hitting international commerce. Now that Napoleon had been defeated, this philosophy could come into its own. Hence the reduction of customs duties, the abolition of the Corn Law, the repeal of the Navigation Acts and the far more casual attitude towards colonial possessions. Later, Cobden and Bright were to argue that free trade was the panacea for all ills: it brought prosperity to all, it ensured international goodwill, it prevented war. Non-Britons were less convinced, though, suspecting that mercantilism had only been cast aside when it was discovered to have no further advantage for Britain. As a German economist put it in 1840, 'It is a very common clever device that when anyone has attained the summit of greatness [i.e. industrialization], he kicks away the ladder.'[5] To them, free trade was simply a measure to preserve Britain's economic dominance. Nevertheless, many states of western Europe, including France, paid partial heed to Cobden's teaching and world trade boomed; in the 1850s alone it rose by 80 per cent. Not unnaturally, many firms, individuals and states benefited from this trend; most of all, the British did.

Since this one side of the strategic and economic triangle of 'trade, colonies and the navy' had thus undergone a complete transformation, in outward form at least, the other two were bound to be affected – and so indeed they were. The general attitude in Britain to the possession of colonies and the general role in overseas affairs of the Royal Navy – always an instrument of national policy – both changed. Yet once again it was rather an alteration in style than in substance: that is, the transformation of imperial and naval policy after 1815 only occurred because – like free trade – it suited the development of the country as a whole. The substance, Britain's 'eternal interests', as Palmerston liked to call it, remained the same: prosperity, progress and peace, always provided that the latter could be secured with honour. All that was happening was that they could now be achieved more advantageously by newer policies.

The corollary in the imperial field to the revolutions in British industry and economic theory was the decline of interest in a large colonial empire. Yet the 'anti-imperialism' which historians have claimed in the period 1815–70 can only be described as such in regard to public attitudes towards *formal* control of overseas territories. The latter made little sense, the Free Traders argued, in an age when the markets and raw materials of the world were to be opened to all; and when the costs of their administration and defence were, to use Disraeli's words, simply 'millstones' around the necks of the British taxpayer. Employing a host of profit-and-loss calculations well suited to the utilitarian mind, they were able to convince others that it would be more beneficial to the country as a whole if the areas of overseas settlement were not deliberately increased and were encouraged to look after themselves; after all, trade with the United States had multiplied many times since 1783. It was not loss and retrenchment and withdrawal from the world's stage that people such as Huskisson, Wakefield and Grey offered, but the untold profits, influence and prestige that would accrue when a complete global market was open to exploitation by their own uniquely favoured nation: 'The whole world lies before you', urged Wakefield time and again. And what moved these men was not that the possession of overseas colonies was felt to be morally wrong, but that it was both expensive and superfluous.

Behind all this was the growing need of the booming factories, particularly textile, which were producing far more than the domestic market and old empire could ever consume. British merchants therefore, turned towards opening up and developing 'a whole series of new, unsophisticated, non-Empire countries – south-east Asia, Brazil and Argentina, the west coast of Africa, Australia and the west coast of Central and South America'.[6] Hence the steady rise of a policy, or rather an attitude, which has been described as 'the imperialism of free trade'.[7] Formal empire was not popular – though there are remarkably few examples in the nineteenth century of the British government withdrawing from colonial territories – and instead the informal influence of the trader, the financier, the consul, the missionary and the naval officer was preferred. The carrot of commercial profits, which trade with Britain would bring on the one hand, and the occasional stick of a Royal Navy cruiser or gunboat on the other, were considerable inducements to the West African chiefdoms, the newly independent republics of Latin America, the sultanates of the Mohammedan world and the decaying kingdoms of the Orient. With regard to the United States and the 'white' settlement colonies, where like societies and stable governments prevailed, the stick was unnecessary and politically senseless; in other regions it had to be shown and used, for British prosperity was becoming heavily dependent upon the maintenance and development of foreign commerce. It is perhaps an adequate comment upon the shortsightedness of merely looking at the areas painted red on the map to remind oneself that almost 70 per cent of British emigration (1812–1914), over 60 per cent of British exports (1800 to 1900) and over 80 per cent of British capital (1815–80) went to regions outside the formal empire.[8]

Nevertheless, it would be a mistake to ignore the significance of the latter, for it was upon the possession of a world-wide chain of strategic bases that British sea power in the tropics depended and from which the necessary influence was exerted. Compared with the British Empire at its full extent, in the late nineteenth or early twentieth centuries, these territories of 1815 appear rather small and insubstantial: Newfoundland, parts of Canada, parts of India, New South Wales, and a string of islands and coastal settlements. The last group cannot be so easily dismissed, however. At a time when overseas territory was so easy to acquire, when land communications were poor and when international commerce was growing so rapidly, advantageously placed bases were of great value to the power that owned them. That string of islands and settlements, more closely examined, contained most of the choicest strategic ports along the sea-lanes of the world; to use Admiral Fisher's later phrase, they were the 'keys' which locked up the globe. The clear-headed thinking of the British government in this matter was reflected in its acquisitions during the struggle against France which were confirmed at the Vienna settlements of 1814–15. Heligoland, Malta and the Ionian Islands strengthened Britain's grip upon the North Sea and Mediterranean, and incidentally provided her with additional bases from which to institute a future continental blockade. More important still were those spoils of victory acquired along the increasingly vital routes to India and the Orient: in the Atlantic, Gambia, Sierra Leone and Ascension; in the south, Cape Town, perhaps the most important strategical position in the world in the age of sea power; in the Indian Ocean, Mauritius, the Seychelles and Ceylon; and further east, Malacca. In the West Indies, St Lucia and Tobago, plus Guiana, were also picked up. As Professor Graham comments, 'Great

Britain now possessed a convenient base in every ocean of the world'[9] – apart, that is, from the Pacific Ocean.

Nor was this the end of the British annexations; even in the 'anti-imperialist' decades following 1815 certain other choice acquisitions were made. As one authority has put it,

> Among the projects for territorial expansion with a view to commerce, which constantly beset them in the nineteenth century, British governments found least objectionable, those for island entrepôts, designed for commercial centres under British control amid wide and populous areas. When these strategically located places with good harbours and defensible positions were also useful as naval stations, the resistance by a government disinclined to take on additional expense and territorial responsibilities was less.[10]

Thus in 1819 Singapore, controlling the main entrance into the China Sea from the west, was taken over; in 1833, the bleak Falkland Islands which overlooked the route around Cape Horn; in 1839 Aden, guarding the southern entrance into the Red Sea; in 1841 Hong Kong, soon to become a great trading port. Further bases, Lagos, Fiji, Cyprus, Alexandria, Mombasa, Zanzibar and Wei-hai-wei, were acquired later in the century, though possibly none were so important as the earlier ones. In all cases, though, the supremacy of the Royal Navy and the expansion of British commerce made the acquisition of these strategic points both easy and desirable, while their very possession reinforced this supremacy and furthered the opportunities for economic growth; once again, the mutually-supporting triangle of trade, colonies and navy had worked to Britain's benefit.

Most of these bases were carefully selected for overwhelmingly maritime reasons, even the later ones: Cyprus and Wei-hai-wei were taken to check Russia, for example, while Lagos and Zanzibar were used for the squadrons respectively patrolling the West and East African coasts. There was, in all this, little sign of what has been called 'reluctant imperialism', nor was there any significant 'absence of mind' in their acquisition. As such, the bases stood in contrast to the other, more 'continental'-style extensions of Crown territory in the half century or so after Waterloo: large parts of India, Canada to the west of the Great Lakes, the vast hinterland behind Cape Town, the unexplored regions of Australia and New Zealand. Here the land hunger of white settlers, and the military need to stabilize 'crumbling' frontiers, provided the chief impulses to expansion, the growth of British trade a far smaller one and the strategic requirements of the Admiralty none at all. In terms of size, trade and population, India and the future white dominions were to provide the brightest and most noticeable gems in the imperial diadem; in terms of actual maritime power, they had little to offer and were in fact strategical liabilities since (with the exception of Australia and New Zealand) they could not be defended by the Royal Navy alone. In the early nineteenth century, however, this was not an acute problem outside North America.

The third and final side of the Pax Britannica was the navy itself. Its size in 1815, following its great growth in the prolonged war against Napoleon, was enormous: 214 ships of the line and 792 cruisers of all types.[11] Many of these vessels were ineffective, it should be added, and even the British found it impossible to maintain much over a hundred ships of the line in service at any one time. In any case, there was no need to keep up such a large navy now that the French challenge had been defeated. Instead, there was the inevitable pressure from the Treasury and the political nation at large for drastic economies. The Admiralty thereupon proposed to maintain in peacetime approximately a hundred ships of the line and 160 cruisers, a force which would provide adequate security against any two other naval powers. Although most of the fleet, including eighty-six of those ships of the line, would be laid up in ordinary, it was recognized very quickly that even this scheme was too optimistic. Too many vessels were old and useless, despite the scrapping or selling of over 550 warships in the years 1814–20; and the hard-pressed naval dockyards were unable to maintain a replacement programme to keep the navy at full strength. The number of ships of the line fit for service without repairs fell from about eighty in 1817 to sixty-eight in 1828, and further to fifty-eight in 1835. In smaller classes the decline was even more noticeable.[12]

Although naval circles were eloquent in opposing this reduction, their arguments made little headway, and with fair reason. As the most recent authority upon this period has noted,

> Britain's battlefleet was finding its true level, not an abstract one based on hypothetical needs, but one determined by the fleets of rival powers. This was only natural, and the important point would seem to be that the Admiralty had set their sights sufficiently high at the outset to counter the political tendency to the other extreme.[13]

In point of fact Britain's naval rivals in these years were in no state to present any threat which would necessitate a much larger shipbuilding programme and standing fleet. The Spanish and Dutch navies, those age-old rivals, were now permanently shattered, and the Danish and Swedish ones were little better. The Russian navy seemed large on paper but geography and maladministration combined to make its strength of forty ships of the line purely nominal. The United States, which had taken the lessons of the War of 1812 to heart, was planning to expand its fleet, but the total proposed was still not large. France thus remained in possession of the world's second largest navy – about fifty ships of the line – but the greater part was unfit for service and it was not until the mid century that a potential threat arose from that direction. Although there was occasional worry about the size and design of newer American and French vessels, Britain's numerical and general strategical supremacy remained.

This, then, was the three-sided equation which the Pax Britannica represented. An adequate, not to say overwhelming, world naval force which utilized a whole host of bases and protected an ever-growing global trade; an expanding formal empire which offered harbour facilities for the navy and focal centres of power, together with a far larger informal empire, both of which provided essential raw materials and markets for the British economy; and an industrial revolution which poured out its products into the rest of the world, drew large overseas territories into its commercial and financial orbit, encouraged an enormous merchant marine, and provided the material strength to support its great fleets. It was an outstandingly strong framework for national and world power, and one which would remain effective, provided that no one side of it was so weakened that the whole edifice collapsed.

Yet only the positive face of this picture has been described so far, and it would be as well to examine briefly its negative aspect even though much of it has already emerged by inference. Put bluntly, Britain enjoyed effortless naval supremacy in the years following 1815 not only because every one of the other powers found it impossible to build and man the same number of warships, had an insufficient merchant marine to back it up in time of war, lacked adequate overseas bases and possessed an industrial strength that was infantile by comparison, but also because they made little effort, either individually or collectively, to mount any sort of prolonged challenge to this mastery. Circumstances had given the British manifold advantages which they were not slow to seize; yet to a certain extent their world-wide maritime predominance existed by default. Their rivals simply did not wish to spend the time and energy necessary to curb it.

One reason for this was that Britain's activities in the post-Napoleonic decades were not a great danger to the other nations. Since, as Eyre Crowe noted in his famous memorandum of 1907, every nation accessible by sea lay open to the Royal Navy,

> It would therefore be but natural that the power of a State supreme at sea should inspire universal jealousy and fear, and be ever exposed to the danger of being overwhelmed by a combination of the world. Against such a combination no single nation could in the long run stand, least of all a small island kingdom not possessed of the military strength of a people trained to arms, and dependent for its food on overseas commerce. This danger can in practice only be averted . . . on condition that the national policy of the insular and naval State is so directed as to harmonize with the general desires and ideals common to all mankind, and more particularly that it is closely identified with the primary and vital interests of a majority, or as many as possible, of the other nations.[14]

This, indeed, the British managed to achieve, and it may be that here free trade had one of its greatest successes. Cobden certainly argued that the commercial policy he so consistently advocated would lead to the 'harmonization' of mankind's general desires and ideals, and it is hard to dispute this. The obvious British desires for world peace after 1815, the handing back of the greater part of the East and West Indies to the Netherlands and France respectively, the abandonment of protectionist tariffs in the British Empire, the suppression of piracy and the policing of the seas, for all these actions the smaller naval and trading nations could be grateful. Moreover, few of them were so heavily dependent upon overseas commerce that they could feel that the Royal Navy threatened their national prosperity; and many of the increases in this direction which did occur as the nineteenth century developed were either in the formal empire which the British had so obligingly opened to all or in the informal empire, the trade of which the Royal Navy so often protected with its gunboats. Even a bitter and suspicious United States recognized the great advantages in trading with Britain and in the maritime muscle of the Royal Navy which turned the Monroe Doctrine from an optimistic proclamation into a political reality. No doubt every country would have preferred to exercise naval mastery itself; but since this was not possible, it seemed better that Britain rather than any other rival should do so. Occasionally, of course, the flaunting of this supremacy in the efforts to abolish the slave trade or in the policy in Latin America in the 1820s or in the Mediterranean in the 1830s caused annoyance to one or more powers, but never at any time did it appear that Britain would become a threat to 'the primary and vital interests of a majority . . . of the other nations'.

If these other powers had no positive incentive for carrying out a large-scale and vigorous naval policy against Britain, they had many negative reasons also for not doing so. In the first half of the nineteenth century in particular, the European nations were too busy with internal affairs, where their basically conservative governments were struggling to prevent the social and political upheavals which followed the spreading of the ideas of the French Revolution. The picture has been aptly summarized by David Thomson:

> One of the reasons for international peace after 1815 was the endemic civil war that produced the great outbreaks of insurrection in 1830 and 1848, as well as a host of intermediate revolts. National cohesion was not yet strong enough to override sectional interests and the conflicts of political principle: human energies were devoted more to seeking an overhaul of internal political and social systems than to pursuing the nationalist causes of war against foreign states. Governments, conscious of revolutionary threats at home, received no encouragement to engage in battle with other states. Peace was popular not only with governments aware of their own fragility, and not only because exhausted people welcomed a respite from war, but also because enemies at home seemed more immediate and more menacing than enemies abroad, and civil war absorbed belligerent spirits, later to be diverted into the cause of militant nationalism.'[15]

Thus if the post-1815 period in international affairs was one 'conducive to the success of the foreign policy of a power which was prepared to exploit its naval power',[16] it would be a great error to suppose that it was British naval supremacy alone which had brought it about; the disinclination of the European nations for war was of equal significance.

These domestic factors were especially true of France, Britain's main naval rival, and only later were her leaders to think of external diversions as a means to escape from internal problems; but it was also the case in Spain, Portugal, Austria and Turkey. The Tsarist *régime*, beset by similar problems, was only too aware of the backwardness of its still expanding country to think of opposing British naval mastery seriously. The peoples of Italy and Germany were just beginning their gropings towards national unity, which were to absorb their energies until the second half of the century. Outside Europe the picture was similar: Japan was still feudal and inward-looking, and the United States was concerned with its westward expansion and, later, its ruinous civil war. Naturally, Britain too suffered from similar domestic tensions, especially in the years 1815–32; but its more flexible constitution which allowed for the steady extension of political power to the middle classes, and its growing prosperity which by the mid century had removed some of the more obvious causes of social unrest, combined to prevent the occurrence of an 1848 revolution there. The main domestic obstacle to an adequate fleet was nothing more than the continuous demand for governmental retrenchment, especially in years of economic difficulty; yet even such radical critics of armaments as Richard Cobden and Joseph Hume were willing to admit that the country's naval supremacy must be preserved, while the actual cost of maintaining the fleets was one which the economy could support without too much difficulty.

Furthermore, if Britain's former rivals retained some of their overseas territories after 1815, these no longer posed a threat to British commercial interests as they had done in the eighteenth century. Portugal was virtually a British *protégé*. Spain still possessed a nominal empire in Latin America but she was unable to enforce her control there without the support of the British government, which openly sympathized with the nationalist movements, and she was soon forced to acknowledge the latter's independence. The Dutch, too, kept many of their overseas territories at the Congress of Vienna since this was strongly favoured by Castlereagh, who considered it to be much more important to restore the Netherlands as an independent and defensible state in Europe than to hold on to additional colonies which posed no danger to British interests – another indication that at this time the continental equilibrium still played a major role in London's foreign policy calculations.[17] Even France, although too strong a state ever to be dependent upon another great power, was being so closely watched by her former enemies and was so absorbed in domestic political matters that she had little time and energy to devote to colonization or to the building of a large navy; and overseas bases without sea power, as Richmond once put it, were like sentry-boxes without sentries.

In addition, while the prolonged struggle between 1793 and 1815 had on the whole led to the development of Britain's industry and national wealth, the same had not been true of her European rivals.[18] The increased taxes, the conscription of artisans and farm labourers for armed service, the political uncertainties and social upheavals, the changes in national and customs barriers, and the destruction wrought by invading armies or by indigenous 'scorched earth' tactics would have had severe enough effects in any case; but, combined with the British maritime blockade and with the 'self-blockade' of the continent imposed by the French, which together dealt a drastic blow to international trade, the economies of most of the European states were grievously hit. The great seaports, and their environs, Bordeaux, Nantes, Marseilles, Amsterdam,

Copenhagen, Hamburg, Barcelona, Trieste, witnessed the total shutdown or at least a very considerable reduction in their hitherto flourishing foreign commerce as soon as their countries were at war with Britain. As the war dragged on their condition deteriorated; ships accumulated in their harbours, warehouses were closed down, industries which had 'finished off' such colonial produce as raw sugar, tobacco and cotton decayed, populations decreased and grass grew in the streets. When the Continental System and the Orders in Council were imposed, the deathblow was given to many industries and regions which were already declining. Industrial output in Marseilles in 1813 was a quarter of that in 1789; Amsterdam's eighty sugar refineries in 1796 fell to three in 1813; cotton-printing in Hamburg and Nantes was virtually wiped out; the linen industries of France, the Low Countries and Germany were reduced by as much as two thirds in the worst affected areas. Seaboard districts went into 'a lasting deindustrialization or pastoralization'.[19] It is true that certain industries, such as cotton, benefited from the Continental System to the extent that they now gained protection from the superior and cheaper British goods; but this was offset by the shortage and high price of raw cotton, and by the slowing-down of the introduction from England of new techniques and skilled workers. The technological gap widened, while British cotton output certainly increased more than that of the continent. The woollen, silk, chemical and certain metal industries of Europe also grew, yet the evidence suggests that this expansion would have been greater had it not been for the war.

There were, then, two major consequences for the continental economies of the 1793 to 1815 struggle relevant to this study. In the first place, their 'Atlantic' sectors suffered so severely that there was no real recovery of overseas trade and markets after the war. Even before the French Revolution British goods had been infiltrating the protected French and Spanish colonial markets, but now 'war conditions greatly helped the British to engross overseas markets and made it impossible for continental industries to adapt fast enough to resist English competition and to regain a foothold in those markets after the peace'.[20] Secondly, the industrialization process in Europe, which in the 1780s had not been all that far behind Britain's, suffered a severe setback in relative terms and, in some cases, in absolute terms as well: in other words, the gap between Europe and Britain had decisively widened. In the two vital areas of colonial trade and industrial development, therefore, the war had had a beneficial effect upon Britain's relative world position, whatever the local and short-term difficulties it may have caused on the domestic front. Against this was to be set a disadvantage which only manifested itself in later decades: being jealous of Britain's economic supremacy and eager to imitate her industrial advances, the European states retained their protectionist tariffs long after 1815. The efforts of British diplomacy to 'liberalize' trade met with considerable reserve and cynicism on the continent and had only a moderate success despite Cobden's preaching.[21] By the 1840s, in fact, British goods were already being ousted from Europe by the products of native industries carefully nurtured in a protectionist 'hothouse'; and at that point it was all too easy for British merchants to withdraw from these more competitive markets and to turn instead to that enormous overseas market which the victory of 1815 had laid at their feet.

This, however, is to anticipate a phenomenon which was much more evident in the second rather than in the first half of the nineteenth century. In the earlier period it was the economic retardation of the continent compared with Britain which was its most obvious characteristic. Moreover, even when the other powers began to industrialize, this implied no direct political challenge to the British, since it compelled European statesmen to take an even greater interest in domestic developments. This transformation of their hitherto fairly stable way of life placed additional strains upon the political order and social fabric of Europe; the great rise in population, the end of feudalism and the drift from the land, the growth of the middle classes and the challenge to the predominance of the landed aristocracy, the large-scale urbanization and 'massification' of the proletariat with the attendant growth in class consciousness, posed grave problems which engaged all European leaders from Metternich to Bismarck and beyond. The result was that the nations of Europe were too involved in the stages of economic 'take-off' to have a deep interest in overseas territories until the great crisis of industrial overproduction in the 1870s. In any case, in the early stages of their industrialization these countries were heavily dependent upon British engineers, British machinery, British expertise and British capital, all of which was willingly provided after the repeal of the various laws which forbade many such exports; and undue hostility to or war with Britain could bring these developments to a halt.

Two further points upon the state of the world, and especially European politics in the early nineteenth century, are worth making. With the defeat of France, there existed no obvious threat to the balance of power, quite apart from the fact that few if any countries sought territorial increases by means of force at this time. With Austria and Prussia holding the centre, and France and Russia the wings, Europe was to be in a state of political equilibrium until 1866 or so. While this naturally led to intense diplomatic manœuvres by each government to secure the most favourable position, the chief consequence for British policy was that London did not need to fear the agglomeration of so much power by any one state that it felt required to adopt its traditional habit of opposing such a development. Secondly, there was also no threat to Britain's own spheres of influence from any overwhelmingly strong coalition of powers: a factor due not merely to the British government's clever and unselfish exertion of its naval and commercial strength, nor to the prevailing concern of other governments with internal problems, but also to the preoccupation of virtually all European statesmen with purely continental power-politics. It was the moves of their neighbours, not the usually discreet workings of British sea power, which interested them. In such a situation, the Admiralty's two-power standard was entirely theoretical until the mid century. In short, Europe did not concern itself with the outside world, Britain did not interfere on the continent except in peripheral (mainly Mediterranean) matters. This was the power-political framework in which the Pax Britannica operated.

Britain's period of world supremacy rested upon positive and negative foundations, therefore; but in what specific ways did she exercise her naval mastery within this general structure? Put at its briefest, the Royal Navy carried out the roles which reflected the long period of peace after 1815, the growth of British trade overseas and the accumulation of fresh colonies; it became the protector of maritime commerce, the defender of British interests in regions where organized government appeared to be lacking, a 'policeman' to a certain extent, but also a surveyor and a guide. And never at any time did it lose its role as the major instrument of the government's foreign policy. Indeed, there were to be occasions under Palmerston when the Clausewitzian dictum that warfare was merely the continuation of foreign policy in a more extended form was clearly in evidence.

One of the British contributions in this period was their encouragement of the idea of the openness of the seas – a reflection of the liberal free trade mentality which was gaining strength in the nation at large. This notion was given substance by a number of measures, such as the repeal of the Navigation Acts in 1849, a step of revolutionary daring in view of the great benefits to Britain's merchant marine which had accrued from them in the past. It is true that the British themselves stood to gain most from this newer policy, but a growth in international trade, contacts and goodwill was also to be anticipated from its adoption throughout the world. Another remarkable example of the anti-mercantilist attitude of the British government had been the renunciation in 1805 – the year of Trafalgar – of the centuries-old claim to the Channel Salute.

This told the world in unequivocal terms that no stretch of salt water – not even that peculiarly personal one which divides Shakespeare Cliff from Gris-Nez – was *our* sea. Like every other stretch it was 'free sea'. Again, both then and since, whenever the knotty question of territorial waters arose, Britain has invariably stood for narrowing them to the minimum.[22]

Even more effective in encouraging the idea of the seas being open to all was the herculean task of charting the oceans which the Admiralty took upon itself after 1815. Slowly, painstakingly, a fleet of survey vessels measured coastlines and sounded depths all over the world. The labour was to continue for many decades, and the results were to be seen in the growing number of superb charts which were then sold at a minimal price to mariners of any nation in the belief that trade would benefit and accidental wreckings diminish – again a reversal of the earlier selfish policy of keeping secret all cartographical knowledge. At the time, of course, Britain benefited most from the charting of the oceans, yet Sir Geoffrey Callender was surely correct in suggesting that the Royal Navy's survey ships had left behind a worthy memorial of their toils.[23]

There were other obstacles to the freeing of the seas for trade than the legal fetters and attitudes of the mercantilist era, however. To make the oceans safe for all vessels, the Royal Navy was also required to take the leading part in the suppression of piracy, which still flourished outside Europe despite earlier efforts to eradicate it. With a long period of peace, and higher stakes in the form of international commerce, the impetus to root out this ancient practice was now far greater. The campaign began in earnest, somewhat to the surprise of the British government, with the bombardment of that lair of the Barbary corsairs, Algiers, by Lord Exmouth's squadron (supported by Dutch warships) in 1816. After five hours of shelling, the Dey capitulated and agreed to the British terms, a not uncommon occurrence for foreign potentates located near the sea in the nineteenth century; but neither this nor the equally vigorous action in 1824 brought about the complete destruction of piracy in the area, which had to await the occupation of Algiers by the French in 1830. In the eastern Mediterranean and Aegean, too, Admiral Codrington's frigates were diverted to a similar activity following the battle of Navarino; and at the same time the Caribbean was finally cleared of a menace which had been British and Dutch in origin three centuries earlier. Slowly, piracy in those regions closer to home declined, but it continued to flourish in the Orient, especially in the Dutch East Indies and in Chinese waters. In fact, the Royal Navy was still engaged in this work in the twentieth century, although the activities of pirates were by then more of a nuisance than a grave threat to trade: China provided the scene of many furious battles, the most notable being the campaign in the autumn of 1849 by Captain Dalrymple Hay's squadron against the war-lord Shap-ng-tsai whose forces were shattered by the loss of fifty-eight junks and 1,700 lives while no Britons at all were killed.[24] With British merchants and their members of Parliament pressing for action to protect their vessels, here once again was a case of the main benefactor being the crusader himself; yet the fact that the general benefits of this campaign fell to all nations was never grudged.

It is also hard to perceive signs of deliberate hypocrisy and self-interest in an even greater activity of the Royal Navy at this time – the suppression of the African slave trade. Here was a traffic in which British ships had secured the lion's share and upon which the ports of Bristol, Liverpool and Glasgow directly, and the Lancashire cotton industry indirectly, benefited; but despite all its commercial attractions, and despite the fact that few other countries showed any inclination to abandon the practice, the pressure from Wilberforce and his followers eventually succeeded in persuading the British government to forbid the slave trade in 1807 and slavery itself in most British dominions in 1833.[25] This same evangelical force was responsible for pushing the Royal Navy into what the latter regarded as its most unrewarding, tedious, unhealthy and strenuous task, for although Castlereagh had persuaded the powers to make the trade illegal at the Congress of Vienna, there was no international agreement for implementing this decision. The main burden therefore fell upon the British squadrons which toiled for the next fifty years to eliminate the slavers. Diseases in the legendary Bight of Benin – where 'one comes out for forty goes in!' – led to the death of over one quarter of the entire West African Squadron in 1829, but this problem paled beside that of actual enforcement against the vessels of other powers. With Spain, Portugal and Brazil, menacing diplomatic pressure was used to secure the right of search; with more powerful nations such as France and the United States, unlimited patience and tact was required. It is to the credit of Foreign Secretaries like Palmerston and Russell that these efforts at wiping out the traffic were maintained in the face of international opposition, Admiralty reluctance and the growing indifference of the British public by the mid nineteenth century.

The navy's efforts can hardly be deemed a success, despite the growth of the West African Squadron to thirty-two warships by 1847. This itself is as much a comment upon the obstructionism of other governments and the cunning of the slavers as upon the effectiveness of British sea power.

The number of slaves exported from Africa to America annually is estimated to have risen from around 80,000 in 1800 to 135,000 by 1830, and the real decline to this nefarious commerce came only after Lincoln's decision in 1861 to grant the right to search ships flying the American flag. This, combined with Palmerston's tough attitude towards Brazil somewhat earlier, the annexation of Lagos and the treaties with native chieftains, and the Royal Navy's introduction of fast steam-vessels, dealt it the death-blow. The export of slaves in the opposite direction, towards Arabia and Asia, still occupied the attentions of the Cape and East Indies Squadrons until the forceful proceedings against the Sultan of Zanzibar in 1873. Even so, some anti-slavery patrols were needed in the Persian Gulf until after the First World War, while the Australia Squadron was preoccupied with suppressing 'blackbirding' in Pacific waters until the turn of the century. In all these regions the cooperation of other authorities, be it the United States government or the Sultan of Zanzibar, or the seizure of slavery centres such as Lagos, were the really effective measures, and the Royal Navy probably only succeeded in freeing about one tenth of the slaves carried overseas from Africa during the nineteenth century. Without these patrols, however, international agreements to suppress the trade would have had no teeth and the world would have readily ignored the problem; the work of the warships, Professor Lloyd reminds us, does deserve the recognition of all.[26]

Retrospectively, and perhaps too cynically, one could point out a further benefit to the British from their crusade, apart from this lightening of conscience: that, without it ever having been intended by the original abolitionists, the continuous presence of the Royal Navy's warships off African and other coasts immeasurably strengthened Britain's influence in those regions, added several useful naval bases to the Empire and confirmed the impressions of European and native observers that an 'informal rule' actually existed. It was scarcely surprising that foreigners suspected the motives behind Palmerston's interest in the eradication of the slave trade. After all, in the constant use of naval vessels to enforce London's will and in the forceful actions against native potentates, the occasional seizure of a strategic point and the bullying of weaker powers, he was employing all the methods associated with that practice for which he has become most famous – gunboat diplomacy.

The expression itself is a misleadingly narrow one, if by it one understands simply the employment of shallow-draught gun-vessels to police the trade of the Yangtse Valley, or to overcome the slave-trading King of Dahomey. Since that type of warship, only really developed after the Crimean War, perfectly suited the mid Victorian political philosophy by being cheap to build and maintain, and since its fire-power and shallow draught were ideal for the expansion of western influence up rivers in the tropics, it is easy to see how its name was taken up to symbolize this British habit. Yet the term would be better defined in a more general manner as 'the use of warships in peacetime to further a nation's diplomatic and political aims'.[27] The occasional punitive measures by gunboats in support of British interests in Africa and China were far less important than the existence of the main battle-fleets in waters of international interest. As far as the Foreign Office was concerned, the former were minor irritations which should always be kept to a minimum and never allowed to get out of hand; the latter, however, were recognized as being an essential prop to British diplomacy and a reminder to other powers of the need to accord due weight to London's opinion. A fleet of warships, to use Nelson's quip, were always the best negotiators.

It does not lie within the scope of this study to describe the many occasions upon which British warships were used to underpin the government's foreign policy in the nineteenth century.[28] What is worth attempting, though, is an analysis of the various degrees of effectiveness of this instrument of national policy upon those different occasions. The result, not surprisingly, is yet another pointer to the efficacy and the limitations of sea power itself.

Since it is always the successes of a nation in the fields of war and diplomacy which are most readily remembered in its history books, the achievements of the British government and navy in the decades after 1815 need be only briefly recalled here. There was the famous policy of preventing the European powers from interfering in the revolutions of Latin America, the steady strengthening of the fleets in Atlantic waters being a more potent warning than President Monroe's message of 1823; the smashing of the Turkish fleet at Navarino in 1827 by Codrington's squadron, assisted by French and Russian forces, which contributed to the later independence of Greece; the further actions against Mehemet Ali in 1840, where Palmerston's success in isolating France diplomatically allowed the Mediterranean Fleet to capture Beirut and Acre, and to frustrate the Egyptian efforts to secure Syria, without fear of graver complications; the constant support of the Portuguese monarchy against internal and external dangers; the two wars and many smaller clashes with the Chinese, whereby the latter were forced to give in to the British demands for commercial intercourse with full security for western merchants; near the end of this period, the gestures of protection for Garibaldi's crossing of the Straits of Messina in 1860; and, last but certainly not least, the notorious Don Pacifico case a decade earlier, where Palmerston's bullying of the Greek government and flamboyant speeches enraged both Queen Victoria and the English radicals, yet delighted the public at large.

Was there not, then, a 'Pax Britannica'? The Foreign Secretary's defence of those very actions in 1850 indicated that he saw a distinct comparison with the former empire of the Caesars: 'as the Roman, in days of old, held himself free from indignity, when he could say *Civis Romanus sum*, so also a British subject, in whatever land he may be, shall feel confident that the watchful eye and strong arm of England will protect him against injustice and wrong.'[29] Palmerston's tone was similarly self-confident on other occasions. The French were bluntly told in 1840 that Britain was ready for war 'and that Mehemet Ali will just be chucked into the Nile';[30] the slave-trading Arabs of the East African coast were warned that it was in vain 'to endeavour to resist the consummation of that which is written in the book of fate: that they ought to bow to superior power . . .'[31] Most governments heeded this advice and all admitted the wide-ranging power of the Royal Navy. Bolivar testified that 'Only England, mistress of the seas, can protect us against the united force of European reaction'; Mehemet Ali admitted that 'With the English for my friends I can do anything: without their friendship I can do nothing'; Garibaldi called himself 'the Benjamin of these lords of the Ocean'.[32]

It is worth noting a connection between all the above actions, however: they occurred in regions distinctly favourable to the application of sea power. Latin America could only be approached from Europe by sea; the Greeks could be freed, and then bullied, from the sea; Mehemet Ali could be checked, the Sultan of Zanzibar overawed, the Queen of Portugal supported, the Chinese viceroys threatened, from the sea. Yet there were other events in these years which give one cause to wonder how extensive this British dominance really was. The post-1815 policy of monarchical reaction under Metternich's guidance needed to take little account of British opinion. Ignoring London's protests, the Austrian armies crushed all resistance in Piedmont in 1823; two years later, in defiance of Castlereagh's famous State Paper of 5 May 1820, the French moved into Spain, abolished the liberal constitution and restored to King Ferdinand his former powers. Canning might well have boasted that he had brought in the new world to balance the forces of the old; but this was simply a reaction to his failure in Spain, where the British government recognized that they could do little unless they undertook extensive military operations, which had become politically impossible. And if France and Austria could not be checked from overland aggression by naval pressure, how on earth could Russia? Turkey might be sensitive to maritime force but it was even more so to the threat from the north, as the events of 1832–3 revealed. Military power in eastern Europe, and not naval power in the west, settled the fate of Polish liberties in 1830, as they did incidentally about one century later. Similarly, the Royal Navy's blockade of the Dutch harbours in 1832–3 was quite ineffective in preserving Belgian neutrality and the British government was forced to rely upon the French army, an unreliable weapon in London's eyes at the best of times, to effect its aims in the Low Countries. Nor could the United States be cowed by naval actions alone, as had been shown in previous Anglo-American struggles, and as the nineteenth century developed so too did the prospect that Canada might be overrun by its already formidable southern neighbour. Even in the colonial arena certain breaches occurred in the system of British naval predominance; the French managed to seize Algiers in 1830, although they were later warned against attempting a similar action in Tunis.

The plain fact of the matter was that even in the age of the Pax Britannica sea power still had many limitations, particularly that imposed by geography, and the statesmen of Britain were well aware of them; they were also aware that the relatively inexpensive use of maritime pressure could not be supplemented by any great military commitment, except in cases of dire need. The true success of British foreign policy in this period lay precisely in the recognition of these limitations. Possessing the gift of knowing where the fleet might be exploited and where not, Foreign Secretaries such as Canning and Palmerston added much to their country's and to their own reputations, which to a great extent obscured the fact that British sea power after 1815 was not as all-embracing as has generally been believed. Skilful though these statesmen were, they were also fortunate 'in that so many of the great questions of this period were susceptible to naval pressure, and they were aided by the naval weakness of Britain's rivals'.[33] But it was not impossible that both of these preconditions might be missing in future international crises; in fact, the latter one was to disappear in the 1840s, if only for a while.

As a result of the many fresh responsibilities assumed by the British government, the normal distribution of the Royal Navy underwent a drastic transformation after 1815. Instead of consisting chiefly of fleets of ships of the line concentrated in home waters, the Baltic and the Mediterranean, it now had its energies and man power diverted into a variety of miscellaneous tasks and areas. The change is best summarized in the following table:[34]

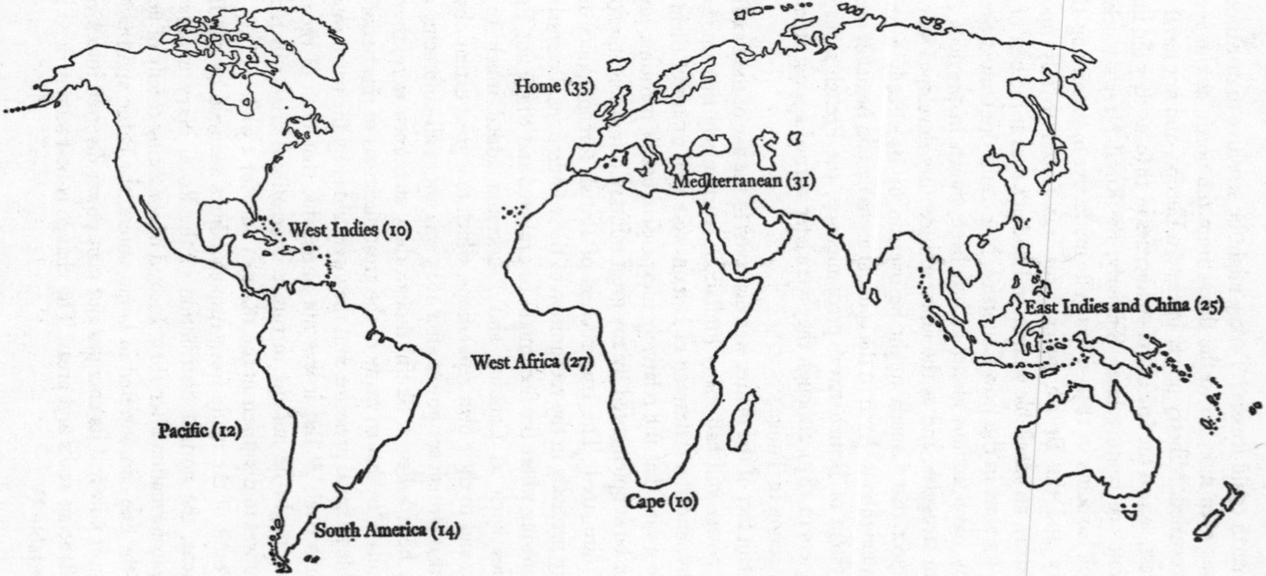

Map 6. Distribution of British warships in commission in 1848
(Warship numbers follow name of station)

Year	Number of British warships on foreign stations
1792	54
1817	63
1836	104
1848	129

In the final year listed, for example, thirty-one warships were deployed in the Mediterranean to maintain British interests and to counter the efforts of rivals there; twenty-five were needed on the East Indies and China Station, one for each of the newly-opened treaty ports and the rest to suppress the endemic piracy; twenty-seven toiled against the slavers off the west coast of Africa, aided by ten at the Cape and a further ten in the West Indies; fourteen were protecting commercial interests along the south-east coast of South America; and twelve patrolled the vast stretches of the Pacific. In contrast, only thirty-five were active in home waters, twelve of them being stationed in Ireland to check political disturbances. In an age of continuous pressure from the Treasury and the taxpayer for economy, the steady growth of the Royal Navy's strength in foreign waters appears at first sight to be a miraculous achievement.

A closer glance would force one to a different conclusion, however. What had happened was that the whole nature of the navy as an organized fighting force had been altered: pressed to economize on the one hand, and to incur fresh responsibilities all over the globe on the other, the Admiralty had no alternative but to dilute repeatedly the strength of its home fleets. The increased estimates, the numbers of seamen borne and the ships in commission, it has been pointed out, 'could give a very misleading impression of the actual battle worthiness of the Navy . . .'[35] The more frigates and gunboats that received a commission, the fewer the ships of the line that could be manned and maintained. Even the Royal Navy was inadequate to satisfy all the demands made upon it, as Grey and Palmerston found out in 1832–3, when, with most of their larger warships either blockading the Dutch coast or anchored in the Tagus, they simply could not field the force necessary in Mediterranean waters to support the Sultan of Turkey from the dangers posed by Egypt and Russia.

The consequences of this weakening of the fighting power of the Royal Navy were only fully seen in the years 1844–6 and 1852–3, when the growth of the French marine produced the first two of that whole series of nineteenth-century invasion scares.[36] By this time, too, the introduction of steam power into warships was having effects: France's decision to build a number of these vessels seemed to have made obsolete the greater part of the Royal Navy, and many agreed with Wellington's opinion that steam had finally bridged the English Channel. Spurred on by an alarmed public, the government poured money into local defence projects, such as coastal fortifications and a militia. Even the eloquent advocates of retrenchment could not overcome this tide of fear, which the national Press only inflamed. To follow the public debate, and still more the private calculations of the Cabinet ministers, is to obtain a healthy reminder that British naval supremacy was not all that unchallenged throughout this period.

Nevertheless, it would also be a mistake to make too much of these mid century scares. The government's reaction was similar to, if more emphatic than, those during previous, smaller alarms: the apparent threat which had been posed by the very large American first-rates was answered by the Admiralty's decision in 1826 to construct or rebuild ten ships of the line; and the growing Russian strength under Tsar Nicholas I had provoked the government into obtaining an increase of 5,000 seamen from the Commons in 1836. In the same way, the total naval estimates in 1847 exceeded £8 million for the first time since 1816 and there were 45,000 men in the service, almost double that of the years 1817–20. What was more, once the age of the steamship arrived, Britain's industrial strength enabled her to regain any temporary lead which the French may have obtained in the design of individual vessels. The ability to build more and faster than anyone else, the virtual monopoly of the best stoking coals, and the immense financial resources of the nation – it was upon these very firm foundations that Britain's maritime mastery rested for the remainder of the century, together with the sheer experience and professionalism of the crews compared with those of less well-exercised navies. Bestirred out of their relative complacency by the challenge from France, the British reasserted their naval predominance and marched away from their rivals once again. In its way the threat posed by the policies of Napoleon III had provided a welcome stimulus to the Royal Navy. As the naval historian of this period concludes, 'In 1853–4 the British fleet probably enjoyed a greater measure of superiority over the French, Russian and American fleets than at any other time since the accession of Victoria.'[37]

The same might be said about the effects of the great French scare of 1859, although this is not to imply that the widespread nervousness of that time was totally unjustified. Napoleon III was too unstable, in the opinion of most Englishmen, to permit his pacific assurances to be accepted on trust. The facts of the matter pointed in another direction. France's policy in Italy was under great suspicion; the fortification of

Cherbourg was even more alarming; her colonial policy, from the Mediterranean and Red Sea to the Pacific, from Indo-China to Latin America, appeared to have as its one unifying theme a desire to challenge British influence. Worst of all, the French fleet had been greatly expanded after the Crimean War, whereas the Royal Navy had declined in strength: 'In 1859 the total British fleet was 95 sail of the line to 51 French, and 96 frigates to 97 French, but many of the British capital ships were obsolete.'[38] Moreover, the French had laid down the first sea-going ironclad warship, the *Gloire*, in 1858 and seemed to have taken a decisive lead in naval construction. To this should be added that widespread unease, noted earlier, about technological advances such as the steamship, the railway and the electric telegraph: the general conclusion was that the offence had taken an advantage over the defence. 'Lack of information led to doubts that predominant sea-power would still suffice to prevent invasion, and the obviously changed conditions of war on land and sea led to conjecture and anxiety regarding Great Britain's inviolability from overseas attack.'[39]

This nervousness even affected the Admiralty, although its wish to benefit from the scare also cannot be excluded. In 1859 the First Lord openly admitted in the House of Lords that the Royal Navy was not 'in a proper and adequate state for the defence of our coasts'.[40] The reaction of Parliament and public to this and other gloomy prophecies was not wholly satisfying from a navalist point of view, however. Disregarding the traditional doctrine of command of the sea, the government invested heavily in a series of coastal fortifications – which even had defences on the landward side! – to protect the major ports; while with great enthusiasm burgers and country dwellers enrolled in the much-expanded militia. The exact military worth of these measures is hard to assess but they appeared reassuring enough to convince the frugal mid Victorians to invest £11 million in the forts alone. This tendency towards 'brick and mortar' defences died hard; as Taylor notes, it is a curious fact 'that Great Britain spent more on her army than on her navy until almost the close of the nineteenth century'.[41]

Nevertheless, Palmerston's administration did not forget the navy. The *Gloire*, with its corselet of iron above the water-line, was answered by the *Warrior*, with an iron hull and a belt of iron armour; and a large programme of ironclad warship construction was commenced, much to Gladstone's distress. After 1864 the situation eased for a number of reasons: British ironclads, though still numerically inferior to the French, were far superior in fighting power; Napoleon had lost interest in maintaining the naval challenge, if only because he needed to concentrate upon the rising danger in the east; and Britain's industrial strength in an age of rapidly advancing technology, together with her vast supplies of coal and her widespread network of coaling stations, could not be approached by France. Economy-minded Chancellors of the Exchequer were able to reduce naval expenditure steadily, checked more by the multifarious calls upon the Royal Navy in the tropics than by any fear of a European challenger.[42]

If these French threats temporarily disturbed British complacency about their naval supremacy, the Crimean War performed a similar function. With strong British and French fleets in the Black Sea and Baltic, of course, the Russians did not dare to offer themselves in a fleet battle; but the local operations revealed many defects in British warship design, armaments, logistics, recruitment and training of officers and seamen and the general management of the fleets, all of which were improved as a consequence. The exposure of such weaknesses was predictable after a long period of peace, but to a British public reared upon memories of the Nile and Trafalgar the navy's role during the Crimean War appeared most disappointing and inglorious. *Punch* captured this mood with its bitter riddle: 'What is the difference between the fleet in the Baltic and the fleet in the Black Sea?' 'The fleet in the Baltic was expected to do everything and it did nothing; the fleet in the Black Sea was expected to do nothing and it did it.' In retrospect, this must be seen more as a reflection of the exaggerated notions of sea power prevalent at the time and later than as a fair assessment of the navy's performance. British maritime supremacy could not produce successes in this war for a number of reasons. With the Russian fleet permanently in harbour, a great sea battle was impossible. The only opposition offered to the Anglo-French squadrons was by the fortresses, yet even here a naïve optimism prevailed in Britain, founded upon the misleading precedents of the bombardments of Algiers and Acre: Cronstadt and Sebastopol proved tougher nuts to crack. Thirdly, there was the traditional policy of the blockade, which Clarendon and others felt 'may take two or three years or more, but is certain in the end'.[43] This was Utopian in the case of Russia, which produced a surplus of food and raw materials; she, perhaps more than any other great power, was invulnerable to naval pressure. To effect real damage, therefore, the war against her had to be undertaken by land; but this gave the leadership of the campaigns to France, exposed the mid Victorian army to stresses for which it was totally unprepared and reduced the navy's role mainly to one of protecting the supply lines across the Black Sea.

At the conclusion of the peace British naval mastery received a far heavier blow, at least in theory. By the Declaration of Paris of 1856, Britain abandoned her traditional right to prevent the carriage of contraband goods in neutral bottoms in time of war. This was an incredible gesture by the world's strongest sea power in favour of the continental states' view that the nationality of any merchant vessel should cover its cargo: at one stroke the weapon of the blockade had been neutered. Of course, there were reasons for the move, none of which appeared very convincing sixty years later and some doubts were expressed even a short while afterwards. The British government felt that it would be unwise to defy world opinion upon this heated issue, and hoped in any case to have secured an adequate *quid pro quo* by the agreement to abolish privateering. Above all, the British acceptance of these clauses symbolized a high point in the power and influence of the Manchester School, and in the idea of 'the freedom of the seas'. Aware that Britain, more than any other power, benefited from the removal of obstacles to world trade and that the British merchant marine would be most affected if belligerents were allowed to seize neutral vessels, and believing that she if not all nations were entering upon a period of universal peace, the government had few qualms about this part of the treaty. Disregarded in the revival of confidence in *laissez-faire* was the importance of the weapon of total blockade by a predominantly naval power against rivals who were susceptible to this form of economic pressure – possibly because of the failure of this strategy against Russia. Only when the confidence and international goodwill disappeared was there the prospect of the older tradition reasserting itself again.

CHAPTER SEVEN

Mahan versus Mackinder (1859–97)

It is an interesting commentary on human affairs that Mahan's exposition of the influence of sea power on the course of European and American expansion should have occurred at the very time when new instruments of the Industrial Revolution were beginning to erode principles and theories upon which his doctrines were based.

G. S. Graham, *The Politics of Naval Supremacy* (Cambridge, 1965), p. 124.

The year 1859 is an unsuitable dividing-line for a traditional survey of British naval history in the nineteenth century, for the power-political framework in which the Pax Britannica operated was not undergoing any revolutionary change which would make this time an historical watershed in the usual sense. Nevertheless, it is necessary at this point to undertake an analysis of certain long-term developments, the origins of which were rooted in the second half of the nineteenth century and the consequences of which were to be of far-reaching significance. Between Queen Victoria's inspection of the 250 craft assembled before her at the end of the Crimean War and the great Spithead review to celebrate her Diamond Jubilee in 1897, the effectiveness of sea power itself, and the predominance of British naval mastery in particular, was being slowly but surely undermined.

Since these trends were to escape the attention of some navalists until well into the twentieth century, it is scarcely surprising that they were not detected by most observers at the time. Glad to be freed from the taxation burdens of the Crimean War and to forget the inglorious way in which it had been fought, the mid Victorians relapsed into a state of complacency about their navy and their world politics, which, despite occasional challenges from the French, remained unshattered for a further few decades. An unease at the overall situation led to an additional three ironclads being laid down in 1867 but the Franco-Prussian War gave a further boost to the Royal Navy's position. The German navy was non-existent; the French fleet, powerless to affect the result of the conflict, sank into decay afterwards as all the European powers concentrated their energies upon land armaments. The United States remained preoccupied with its civil war and reconstruction, but was in any case gradually losing some of its intense anglophobia. Hence the pleasant situation occurred in which Britain's naval superiority rose while her expenditure on the fleet fell or was at least kept steady. Even the 'jingo' outburst in the Eastern Crisis of 1877–8 had little lasting effect, the country relapsing into its old state of indifference soon afterwards.

This era of inexpensive maritime supremacy came to a sudden end in 1884. Even before then, the French had been engaged for several years upon a large shipbuilding programme, unnoticed by a British public which retained an unjustified confidence in its navy's invincibility; in fact, the two fleets were almost equal in numbers of first-class battleships. The revelations of naval weakness by W. T. Stead, editor of the *Pall Mall Gazette*, fell like a bomb upon a public already uneasy at the commercial and colonial threats to Britain's world interests, and the clamour became so great that the battered Gladstone government was in that year alone forced to spend an extra £3·1 million upon warships and £2·4 million upon naval ordnance and coaling stations. Momentarily the unrest was calmed but it rose to a new height in 1888 after Salisbury's Conservative administration had relaxed its efforts. Unfortunately, the foreign scene did not allow any such return to the casual indifference of former days. Ever since the British government's decision to occupy Egypt in 1882, the French had been persistently hostile all over the globe, especially in Africa, and their own fleet programme remained large. At the same time, Russia, which had almost been on the brink of war with Britain in 1885 over Afghanistan and was now threatening to upset the political balance in the Balkans, was building up its fleet and becoming more receptive to an *entente* with France. The prospect of a Franco-Russian naval alliance, which would pincer the under-strength Mediterranean Fleet and cut that vital line of communication in time of war, was too grim to be dismissed with soothing phrases and half-measures. In March 1889 the government proclaimed its intention to maintain a two-power standard by introducing the Naval Defence Act into Parliament – under which £21·5 million was to be spent upon new construction, including ten battleships. Yet even this was insufficient to eradicate the Achilles' Heel of the Mediterranean and four years later the Press and public, now totally unable to relapse into their former apathy, recommended the agitation. The result of this heated political debate was that in the following spring the laying-down of seven battleships and many smaller vessels was announced, only a few days after the final retirement of Gladstone on this very issue. There could be no more appropriate symbol of the changed conditions and attitudes since the mid Victorian period than the defeat of this constant opponent of swollen naval armaments.[1]

Although the British were to remain anxious about the Franco-Russian naval challenge until the events of 1905, it seems in retrospect that they probably overestimated the danger from this direction, forgetting the weaknesses of their rivals and seeing only those in their own fleet. The French navy, impressive on paper, suffered from constant political interference and strategical controversy, and its ineffectiveness was fully revealed during the confrontation at Fashoda in 1898, where the obvious superiority of the Royal Navy provided Salisbury with one of his strongest trumps.[2] The Russian navy was in an even worse state, its fleets lacking homogeneity in speed and size, and its sailors, confined much of the year to land, lacking the necessary gunnery practice and even the elementary navigational skills to take on their British counterparts; its pathetic performance in the war against Japan in 1904–5 showed how overrated it had been. Even if the two powers had fought jointly against Britain, the situation would have been far brighter than that painted by the Navy League and other agitators at home: the 'enemy' had virtually no experience of combined fleet operations; language and signalling difficulties were great; and neither dared to concentrate more resources upon their navies whilst the attitudes of Austria, Italy and especially Germany were so problematical. Britain's strategical weakness in the Mediterranean was admittedly grave but the threat there could be neutralized in the last resort by withdrawing the fleet to Gibraltar, strengthening the newly acquired base at Alexandria and sending all merchant shipping round the Cape instead. In the final analysis the Franco-Russian challenges were probably a good thing for the Royal Navy, forcing it to make radical improvements in its fighting strength and efficiency and to hasten the end of its practice of employing so many ships and men upon that variety of miscellaneous tasks which had characterized the previous decades.

For these were the activities into which the greater part of Britain's naval energies had been redirected ever since the end of the Crimean

War. The old responsibilities remained and were added to by new ones to make an impressive list of duties: the African slave trade patrols, debt-collecting expeditions in Latin America, the campaigns against piracy in the Red Sea and East Indies, enforcing British claims in Malaya and Burma, the protection of missionaries and traders all over the globe, and the steady charting of coasts and seas. In 1861 sixty-six warships and almost 8,000 men were deployed on the China and East Indies Station, even though the Second China War had been concluded; to which should be added forty more vessels in the Mediterranean, twenty-three on the North America and West Indies Station, fifteen each on the Pacific and the West African Stations, eleven at the Cape, nine off the south-east coast of South America and nine also in Australian waters.[3] With some right the Admiralty called out against the pressures from merchants, missionaries, Colonial and Foreign Offices, the First Lord complaining:

> from Vancouver's isle to the river Plate, from the West Indies to China the Admiralty is called upon by Secretaries of State to send ships . . . The undeniable fact is that we are doing or endeavouring to do much more than our force is sufficient for. It is fortunate that the world is not larger, for there is no other limit to the service of the fleets.[4]

The same, incidentally, was true of the British army in this period, which, apart from its standing commitments to the defence of India and the major colonies, was involved in a whole host of what Bismarck once derisively called 'gentleman's wars' – against the Ashanti, the Zulu, the Burmas, the Boers, the Egyptians, the Afghans and the Dervishes.[5] Here again was an armed service diluted and broken up into small contingents all over the globe so that its effective fighting power was much reduced. Considerable withdrawals of military and naval forces deployed overseas were made, under Gladstone's prodding, by Cardwell and Childers in the period 1868–74 but this did not transform the basic picture: both services remained chiefly specialists in colonial warfare. Most of the naval officers who were later to transform and lead the Royal Navy had their first baptism of fire and early experiences in these minor colonial engagements: Fisher in the Second China War of 1859, Beresford in the bombardment of Alexandria in 1882, Jellicoe at Alexandria and in the relief of the Peking legations in 1900, Beatty in the Nile campaign of 1896–7 and again in the Boxer uprising, Sturdee during the Samoan civil war of 1899. The marvel was that their minds and habits were not so moulded by this somewhat artificial and esoteric form of naval warfare that they were unable to react effectively to more serious threats.

In many other ways, too, the pre-Crimean position of the British

Empire seemed to continue unaltered in the decades following. While the European powers were fully preoccupied with the diplomatic and military struggles which accompanied the unifications of Italy and Germany, they became even less interested in those parts of the world to which Whitehall attached great importance; only the French, as ever, kept up their game of upsetting British consuls and traders in the tropics but until 1882 this was always checked in the final resort by a *Quai D'Orsay* more anxious about European affairs.[6] More important still, after the death of Palmerston successive British governments became increasingly inclined to adopt a policy of non-intervention in Europe, establishing that tradition which was later in the century to be given the proud though misleading name of 'splendid isolation'. In the late 1860s, however, this policy was anything but splendid. It had chiefly been induced by an awareness that Britain did not possess the armed forces necessary to intervene on the continent with any prospect of success: Palmerston's ignominious defeat at the hands of Bismarck over Schleswig-Holstein in 1864 was yet another of those very necessary reminders that sea power alone often possessed but a limited effectiveness in European politics.

At the same time the Empire continued to expand, steadily, inexorably, in all directions. The annexations of the 1850s and 1860s, listed earlier, were soon to be eclipsed by later acquisitions; for in the final three decades of the nineteenth century, Britain laid claim to Cyprus, Egypt, the Sudan, Somaliland, Kenya, Uganda, Rhodesia, Nyasaland, Zanzibar, Bechuanaland, the Transvaal, Orange Free State, most of present-day Ghana and Nigeria, Papua, North Borneo, Upper Burma, several Malayan states, Wei-hai-wei, the southern Solomons, the Gilbert, Ellice, Tongan, Fijian and many smaller groups in the Pacific Ocean. Even when the situation later changed and other nations joined in a frenetic scramble for overseas colonies, the British, aided by their established position in the tropics, appeared to come out the best: 'between 1871 and 1900 Britain added four and a quarter million square miles and sixty-six million people to her Empire'.[7] Furthermore, in many aspects of economic life the British predominance remained unshaken, despite the 'great depression' of 1875–95. The £1,000 million invested abroad in 1875 had risen to £4,000 million by 1913, bringing in around £200 million annually as interest to cover the growing gap in visible trade. In shipping, too, Britain possessed more merchant vessels than all other nations together at the turn of the century and was still the carrier of the world, again a useful aid to the balance of payments. Insurance and banking maintained London's grip upon the global financial market as well.[8]

Not only did the picture seem reassuring in those respects, but navalists inside Britain at the close of the nineteenth century could also feel relieved that politicians and the public as a whole had at last developed a regard for their navy and learned to appreciate its close link with their commercial expansion and rise to world empire: before 1880, as Professor Marder had noted, 'the subject of naval defence was almost foreign to English thought'.[9] That this situation changed so rapidly was not only due to the Press agitation at the Franco-Russian danger but also to the publicizing activities of a host of naval strategists and historians.[10] Of these, by far the most famous was the American naval captain, A. T. Mahan, whose study *The Influence of Sea Power upon History 1660–1783*, published in 1890, won international acclaim and 'appeared to reveal immutable rules concerning the role of navies in international affairs that could be neglected only at a nation's peril'.[11] Written to stimulate American interest in a larger fleet, this widely-read and oft-quoted book became the bible of navalists everywhere, particularly in Britain, where its author was fêted and revered.

Mahan's notion about the role of sea power in history have been sufficiently examined earlier in this study and require no further elaboration here.[12] Whether or not one agrees with his interpretation that great power rivalries between 1660 and 1815 had their outcome decided chiefly by maritime campaigns is less important at this stage than an understanding of the strategical and political implications *for the future* which emerged from his writings, or were in some cases read into his publications by his enthusiastic but one-sided followers. From these works one gained an impression that large battlefleets, and a concentration of force, decided control of the oceans, whereas a *guerre de course* strategy was always ineffectual; that the blockade was a very effective weapon which would sooner or later bring an enemy to its knees; that the possession of select bases on islands or continental peripheries was more valuable than control of large land masses; that overseas colonies were vital for a nation's prosperity and that colonial trade was the most treasured commerce of all; that 'travel and traffic by water have always been easier and cheaper than by land'; that an island nation, resting secure upon its naval might, could with impunity ignore the struggles of land powers and adopt if necessary an isolationist policy; and that the rise of a country to world greatness without sea power was almost unthinkable. Taken together, they formed the basic tenets of the pre-1914 navalist philosophy, much of which endured well past that particular epoch; it centred upon the belief that sea power had been more influential than land power in the past and would always continue to be so. Finally, Mahan, whilst urging the need for a strong American fleet, fully expected and firmly hoped that Britain's naval predominance would remain unassailed in the future.

Whatever reservations one may have upon Mahan's analysis of the past, it is clear that his interpretation and ideas were most significant, throwing a new light upon the course of European history; no scholar since his day could write about the rise of the British Empire without acknowledgement to the role of sea power. What was true of the past was not necessarily so of the future, however, yet at the time it was as an 'evangelist of sea power' rather than as a naval historian pure and simple that he was regarded; journalists, admirals and statesmen hung upon his predictions and accepted his teachings as a virtually complete doctrine of power-politics. In point of fact, Mahan's mind was too rooted in the past to be much of a success in this field of prophecy. As one of his biographers has explained,

> In activity and by disposition Mahan largely looked to the past; he gained his lessons from a study of the past and used the past for analogies. There can be no doubt that Mahan was so absorbed with the past that he often failed to appreciate future trends in naval warfare. He was not sufficiently alive to the fact that history frequently does not repeat itself and that the shape of things to come may not always follow the pattern of the past.[13]

Ironically enough, it was only a year before Mahan published his plainest appeal through the guise of history to the American people, *Sea Power in Relation to the War of 1812* (1905), that a much more perceptive prophecy of future world politics was being elaborated. On 25 January 1904, the famous geopolitician Halford Mackinder read a paper to the Royal Geographical Society entitled 'The Geographical Pivot of History'.[14] In it he suggested that the Columbian epoch – that period of four centuries of overseas exploration and conquest by the European powers – was coming to an end, and another, far different one was about to begin. With very little of the world left to conquer, 'every explosion of social forces' would take place in a much more enclosed environment and would no longer be dissipated into unknown regions; efficiency and internal development would replace expansionism as the main aim of modern states; and for the first time in history there would be 'a correlation between the larger geographical and the larger historical generalizations', that is, size and numbers would be more accurately reflected in the sphere of international developments. This being the case, Mackinder continued, it was important to consider what the future would bring to the great strategical 'pivot area' of the world – central Russia. That vast region, once the source of the many invading armies which had for centuries poured into Europe and the Near East, had been outflanked, neutralized and much reduced in importance by the mariners of the Columbian era, who had opened most of the rest of the world to western influence. For 400 years the world's trade had developed on the sea, its population had on the whole lived near to the sea, political and military changes had been influenced by sea power. Now, with industrialization, with railways, with investment, with new agricultural and mining techniques, central Asia was poised to regain its previous importance:

> The spaces within the Russian Empire and Mongolia are so vast, and their potentialities in population, wheat, cotton, fuel and metals so incalculably great, that it is inevitable that a vast economic world, more or less apart, will there develop inaccessible to oceanic commerce.[15]

Mackinder's stress upon the importance of the 'heartland', later taken up with enthusiasm by Haushofer and the Nazi geopoliticians, and somewhat discredited as a consequence, is probably too simple, one-sided and deterministic to be accepted in its entirety today; but the broad outlines of his argument were prescient and compel the closest attention. Certainly, his audience at the Royal Geographical Society was impressed by this unusually wide-ranging paper. One of them, Leo Amery, ventured to go further and, while not laying stress so specifically upon central Asia, elaborated one aspect of Mackinder's message in even clearer power-political terms:

> Sea power alone, if it is not based on great industry, and has not a great population behind it, is too weak for offence to really maintain itself in the world struggle . . . both the sea and the railway are going in the future . . . to be supplemented by the air as a means of locomotion, and when we come to that . . . *the successful powers will be those who have the greatest industrial base. It will not matter whether they are in the centre of a continent or on an island; those people who have the industrial power and the power of invention and of science will be able to defeat all others.*[16]

These predictions, of the rise of certain super-powers with massive populations and industrial and technological strength, were not new to political thinking – as early as 1835 de Tocqueville had forecast the inevitable rise of the United States and Russia – but they were now being expressed in a much more definite form. Some twenty years before Mackinder, for example, Sir John Seeley had pointed to the immense developments which 'steam and electricity' were bringing to those two great continental states, against whose consolidated resources and man-power the widely scattered British Empire would find it impossible to compete unless drastic changes occurred in its own structure. 'Russia and the United States will surpass in power the states now called great as much as the great country-states of the sixteenth century surpassed Florence.'[17] Yet if Seeley still placed hopes upon the transformation of the Empire into a much more organic unit, Mackinder could not be so sanguine. Britain would continue to maintain its strategical and maritime advantages *vis-à-vis* Europe, but these would count for little against the rising super-powers. Already in his book *Britain and the British Seas*, published in 1902, Mackinder had insisted:

> In the presence of vast Powers, broad-based upon the resources of half continents, Britain could not again become mistress of the seas. Much depends on the maintenance of a lead won under earlier conditions. Should the sources of wealth and vigour upon which the navy was founded run dry, the imperial security of Britain will be lost. From the early history of Britain herself it is evident that mere insularity gives no indefeasible title to marine sovereignty.[18]

Nevertheless, although the course of the past seventy years has only served to reveal the correctness of his forebodings, these views had only limited support in Britain in the late nineteenth and early twentieth centuries. There might be an awareness that all was not well in the colonial and industrial world, but most politicians and newspapers continued to believe in their country's ability to rule the waves and therefore to maintain its place in the international system; and the fears that were expressed concerned more immediate dangers rather than the longer-term premonitions of Seeley or Mackinder. This complacency was indirectly reinforced by the intellectual superiority of the advocates of the 'Blue Water' or navalist school over their 'Brick and Mortar' or army rivals, a victory which not only led to the reversal of the mid-nineteenth century policy of raising a militia and building fortifications against possible invasion but also to an almost absolute belief in the effectiveness of sea power.[19]

If it were possible to express the newer and rather isolated views described above with the utmost simplicity, one might say that a decline in Britain's relative world position was being hinted at, if not openly forecast, because of two closely-linked developments:

1. Britain's naval power, rooted in her economic strength, would no longer remain supreme, since other nations with greater resources

and manpower were rapidly overhauling her previous industrial lead, and

2. sea power itself was waning in relation to land power.

The first of these developments was undoubtedly true and in it, clearly, lies the root of Britain's long-term decline. Although she was maintaining her predominance in the world of finance and international services as mentioned above, her position as an *industrial* power of the first order – indeed, in a class of her own – shrank rapidly in the final three decades of the nineteenth century as other nations overtook her in many basic fields of industry and technology, which are after all the foundations of modern military strength. It might at first seem odd that 'As her industry sagged, her finance triumphed, her services as shipper, trader and intermediary in the world's system of payments became more indispensable.'[20] But it was not. As we shall see, both were part of a similar movement which occurred when British industry felt real competition for the first time. Instead of meeting the latter it was avoided; and as a result she lost, somewhere in these years, her formerly unquestioned place as the workshop of the world.

In a certain sense this had always been quite probable, for Britain's economic domination of the world after 1815 had rested upon a unique concatenation of very favourable circumstances. It was not to be expected that she would remain eternally either the only or even the greatest industrialized nation; when others, with larger populations and more resources, took the same path, a relative decline was inevitable. In some ways she herself made decisive contributions to this process, both by building railways in the foreign countries which were to enable their industries and especially agriculture to rival Britain's, and by establishing and developing those foreign industries with repeated financial injections. Moreover, none of these rivals were to feel any compunction about imposing protectionist tariffs upon imports, especially when the depression of 1875–96 brought a slowing-down in the momentum of the world's trade and industrial production. British statesmen, whether Liberals or Tories, held on to free trade as an article of faith, an expression of their basic philosophy; but there were practical grounds for this, too. Britain was simply too dependent upon international trade to prejudice that commerce, whereas neither the United States, Russia, France or Germany exported so great a proportion of their manufactures nor were they so heavily dependent upon imported foodstuffs. The results were inevitable: whilst British industrial goods faced tariffs as high as 57 per cent (Dingley Tariff) into the United States, American wheat, cheaply grown and cheaply transported, crushed the life out of British agriculture. More alarming still, foreign *manufactured* wares were imported into Britain in ever-increasing proportions.

This latter development was an indication that Britain's industrial decline in this period is not simply to be described as an unavoidable and natural process; it was also caused by complacency and inefficiency.[21] Otherwise, there would have been no reason why British goods could not have held their own against their chief rivals, Germany and the United States in the home market, or in neutral ones. In fact, they were badly hit in both, and this was due in the main to the unwillingness of British manufacturers to keep ahead or at least abreast of their competitors. New machinery, new techniques, rationalization of resources, these all took time and energy and money, and did not appear very attractive when one could still make adequate profits from traditional methods. Very little was being invested in the modernization of British industry compared with the many millions which were flowing out to benefit foreign governments, railways, mines and industries. *Laissez-faire* seemed to produce, with some notable exceptions, a casualness of approach, and there was little attempt at grouping together the scattered and usually small-scale British firms into large trusts and cartels, as the Germans and Americans did. Public school education – described by one critic as being 'actively anti-intellectual, anti-scientific, games-dominated' in its effects[22] – and the élitist and classics-dominated universities were more adept at producing pro-consuls of empire than scientists, technologists, engineers and business managers. Germany and the United States, in contrast, possessed not only many more universities but also infinitely more graduates with a scientific education.

Perhaps this all might have changed, had the pressure upon Britain been really severe, had the shock-waves from the depression and these new challenges been more traumatic. Unfortunately, they were not and in any case the British were able to employ two extremely convenient assets to cushion any blows and to keep life comfortable: their 'formal' and 'informal' empires, and their enormous earnings from invisibles. The former provided ready receptacles for British goods when other areas became too competitive or unattractive; for example, Australia, India, Brazil and Argentina took the cotton, railways, steel and machinery that could not get into the American and European markets. In the same way, whilst British capital exports to the latter dropped from 52 per cent in the 1860s to 25 per cent in the few years before 1914, those to the Empire rose from 36 per cent to 46 per cent, and those to Latin America from 10·5 per cent to 22 per cent. Britain escaped from the great depression 'not by modernizing her economy, but by exploiting the remaining possibilities of her traditional position'.[23] Nor was there any of the now-familiar balance-of-payments problems for the economy, thanks to the immense rise in invisible earnings. In terms of actual goods exchanged, the gap had been widening alarmingly since the mid century – a sign both of this lack of competitiveness in industrial products and of the increasing dependence upon imported foodstuffs – but it was always handsomely covered by the income from services and investments. Although this was in the short term better than actually having a payments crisis, it was hardly a satisfying position for a nation that was also a world power, subjected to international challenges and crises.

> For good or ill the root of success for the new industrial state was the efficiency of its productive machine. If that failed disastrously, in an industrialized world, then national disaster would undoubtedly follow. Did the cushion of income from foreign investment, which was masking certain industrial problems and hiding the absence of new export sectors by increasing *rentier*-status in the world, encourage the breeding of *rentier* attitudes? Was Britain becoming another Holland of the eighteenth century, moving from industry and trade towards finance? The point was that the springs of wealth from financial income were less secure, less resilient, more subject to disturbance under the stress of political insecurity abroad or the shock of war than the solid indigenous strength of an efficient system of production and trade.[24]

Mention of the 'shock of war' prompts the final remark that healthy industries not only provide the weapons necessary for victory but also produce continuous fresh wealth, assuming (fairly reasonably) that their products can be sold; whereas investments, if ever once liquidated to purchase abroad the sinews of battle lacking at home, cannot be recovered and this must quickly lead to a balance-of-payments crisis afterwards.

There were, of course, many exceptions to this overall trend; there were entrepreneurs and firms with drive and imagination. The successful men behind Boots the Chemist, Rington's Tea, and Pear's Soap were chiefly involved with domestic custom, however, and it must be agreed that they were not 'developing technologies which were to prove strategic in terms of the major growth industries of the twentieth century'.[25] More important still, they were not trades which would contribute much to the military and maritime strength of an empire at war. With these latter, and far more vital types of industry, the picture was bleaker. Coal production and exports rose rapidly in this period, but only because of a vast increase in labour and not because of new techniques and machinery. In any case

Germany's total production by the first decade of the twentieth century had drawn close to Britain's, while that of the United States was more than equal to both. Oil, still in its infancy as an industry, was chiefly produced in Russia and the United States. British iron production steadily increased, but once again due simply to expansion of labour and capacity. The story of the steel industry, an even more vital one, epitomizes much that was wrong with British industry at this time. Although 'every major innovation in the manufacture of steel came from Britain or was developed in Britain',[26] its capitalists were simply too reluctant to invest in new plant. By the early 1890s both Germany and the United States had overtaken her and were drawing away; 'In the United States Andrew Carnegie was producing more steel than the whole of England put together when he sold out in 1901 to J. P. Morgan's colossal organization, the United States Steel Corporation.'[27] Textiles, Britain's greatest export of all in the nineteenth century, were already beginning to decline, even though cushioned by their tropical markets; again, a failure to modernize, to get rid of the old mule-spinning techniques, was a major cause. In machine-tools, a field in which Britain had been supreme for decades, the collapse was even faster. And what of the new, vitally important industries of the twentieth century – electrics and chemicals? In both, British pioneers had made many of the first advances; in both, Germany and the United States were to be much more successful in production and sales. The automobile, where the British were not pioneers, was chiefly in the hands of the French, the Americans and the Germans. The production of optical equipment, small arms, glass, shoes, agricultural machinery and many other items were also, in the main, the work of foreigners. Quite often, a British firm, competing successfully, turned out upon closer inspection to be either a subsidiary of a foreign company or one in which the owner-managers were recent immigrants (e.g. Brunner-Mond, the core of the later Imperial Chemical Industries).

One might summarize the above by saying that, whilst failing to seize the opportunity to develop important new industries, Britain was also neglecting to re-equip her traditional ones, relying instead upon a comfortable but unspectacular increase in her usual exports (cloth, coal, iron) to less competitive markets and a vast increase in invisible earnings to conceal these omissions. Industrial production, which had been growing at about 4 per cent p.a. in the years 1820–40 and at about 3 per cent p.a. between 1840 and 1870, became steadily more sluggish: between 1875 and 1894 it grew at just over 1½ per cent p.a., far less than Britain's main rivals. 'In 1870, the United Kingdom contained 31·8 per cent of the world's manufacturing capacity, as compared with 13·2 per cent in

Germany and 23·3 per cent in the United States. By 1906–10, Britain's relative share had dropped to 14·7 per cent, while Germany now held 15·9 per cent and the United States 35·3 per cent.'[28] British exports, which had expanded at 5 per cent p.a. in volume between 1840 and 1870, dropped to a rate of growth of only 2 per cent p.a. in the years 1870–90, and to 1 per cent p.a. in the decade following.[29] The consequence, naturally enough, was that Britain's share of world trade shrank, even though her overseas commerce rose in absolute terms:[30]

Percentages of World Trade

	1860	1870	1880	1889	1898	(1911–13)
Britain	25·2	24·9	23·2	18·1	17·1	(14·1)
Germany	8·8	9·7	9·7	10·4	11·8	
France	11·2	10·4	11·2	9·3	8·4	
USA	9·1	7·5	10·1	9·0	10·3	

If economics are any guide to politics – and since Marx most people will admit that they are – the Pax Britannica was beginning to rest upon shaky foundations. That 'outstandingly strong framework for national and world power' mentioned in the preceding chapter was now sagging a little. Britain's unique industrial and commercial lead, upon which Pitt, Canning and Palmerston had been able to find the ultimate support for their foreign and naval policies, was gone. To spend further time explaining or regretting the fact in this narrative would be superfluous. Even the cataloguing above of the failures of British industry, although these were certainly of significance in explaining the speed of this collapse, might appear somewhat unnecessary, when one considers the inevitability of the trend which resulted in Britain being able to produce only one quarter of the steel of the United States by 1913; after all, as Professor Mathias reminds us, 'When half a continent starts to develop then it can produce more than a small island.'[31] What is now necessary is to examine the political and strategical consequences of Britain's industrial decline. This itself can only be done in the next, and later, chapters but some very general observations could appropriately be made at this point.

Before this is done, however, it is worth briefly looking at one solution which many British statesmen of the period 1880–1914 believed might help them to arrest this relative decline – Imperial Federation, the welding together of the disparate parts of the Empire into an organic customs and military unit. In his book, *The Expansion of England*, Seeley had advocated the fusion of the white dominions with the motherland into a sort of

'Greater Britain', which would then be able to join Russia and the United States in the first rank'.[32] Viewed strategically, this was a dubious proposition from the start: the white population of the Empire totalled only fifty-two million in 1900, smaller than that of Germany, let alone those of Russia and the United States, and instead of being concentrated in one mass unit it was scattered across the globe. In any case, whatever the long-term futures of such states as Canada and Australia might be, their populations and industries were then too small to provide much more than marginal assistance in any conflict with a great power. Nevertheless, prominent politicians such as Joseph Chamberlain and Alfred Milner took up the cause of imperial federation with great cry, and received a sympathetic response from many strategists and politicians in Britain for this concept. Some favoured it because they welcomed the help or moral support of the dominions; others because they genuinely thought it would make a vital difference. Oppenheim wrote in 1902 that 'Historically the doom of Great Britain would seem to be certain but for the new factor introduced by the existence of powerful and patriotic colonies . . .'[33] The famous warship designer, Sir William White, deeply impressed by his visit to the United States in 1904, where he saw fourteen battleships and thirteen armoured cruisers being simultaneously built in American yards, declared: 'Unaided by our colonies we cannot long hold the sceptre of the seas in the teeth of American competition.'[34] Yet, while attempts were made for almost half a century after the first Colonial Conference of 1887 to realize this aim of federation, the movement met with the unyielding opposition of the dominions, especially Canada and later South Africa (and later still, Eire). Having only recently secured constitutional and financial independence from Westminster, they had no wish to surrender it again. Measures of partial cooperation in the military and naval fields were to be instituted: a Greater Britain was not. Nor was the majority of the British people prepared to abandon the policy of free trade for the sake of the Empire's greater unity, and this resistance proved to be an even more formidable stumbling-block.

That this steady decline in Britain's relative economic strength, and the parallel failure to turn the idea of imperial federation into something effective, did not immediately have severe consequences for the country's world-wide naval power, that in fact many experts and all the public held that the Royal Navy was in a more unchallengeable position in 1914 than at any other time in the previous century, should not surprise us. What we are trying to analyse here is a very long-term development, the first signs of which were already appearing by the end of the nineteenth century, although the overall trend was not to be fully recognized until decades later; only the prescient few could perceive a future decline in naval terms as well, therefore. In the first place, as we have seen, the economic crisis was masked and avoided by the favourable balance of trade, by the cushion of invisibles. In the second place the British shipbuilding industry itself was not hit by the challenges of foreigners, probably because its products at that time were individually constructed; as Hobsbawm puts it, ships 'were no more mechanized than palaces' in production.[35] At this stage the industry was in its hey-day, boosted along by civil orders and by the increasing warship demands of the British and other governments. Thirdly, the Royal Navy naturally still benefited from its control of the many overseas bases, of the superb cable communications system, of the near-monopoly of good steaming coals, and from the ultimate support which it and the giant merchant marine gave to each other. In strategical terms these were of immense value, as her naval rivals fully recognized. Fourthly, there was the constant negative factor, which these rivals could not share, that Britain did not need, or at least did not appear to need, a large and expensive standing army which would necessarily bite into the money available for the navy. Finally, as we shall see in the following chapter, the Foreign Office after 1900 responded in a remarkable swift and perceptive fashion to what it recognized to be the ineluctable flow of events. By giving way on the peripheries, by alliances or *ententes* with former rivals, it allowed the navy to concentrate again to control the waters of vital interest and to check the chief danger. For all these reasons, a decline in Britain's naval position *was* hard to recognize; in numbers of warships alone, Britannia seemed to be ruling the waves as effectively in 1900 and 1914 as she had done in 1820 and 1870.

Nevertheless, Palmerston would have noticed the differences immediately, had he returned to survey the world scene about the turn of the century. The major change was that the spread of industrialization, besides hitting Britain's supremacy in that field, had enabled all other modern powers to build a navy of their own; not merely France, but also Russia, Austria-Hungary, and more importantly, the United States, Germany and Japan, now had this capacity. And not only *could* they build a navy, but they all *were* actively doing so; for in the last decade of the nineteenth century every sea-going nation, and not just Britain, took to heart Mahan's teachings about the influence and importance of sea power. The great powers were so entranced by his doctrines, and the application thereof for their own ends, that the age has been described by Professor Langer as one of the 'new navalism'. Even if none of these countries would or could attempt to build a fleet equal to the Royal Navy, the culminative effect of this orgy of warship-building was the same: Britannia could not hold them all off. A surrender of local naval mastery in certain regions was bound to follow.

In the second place the long-term financial tendency was also serious in view of the rapid technological changes in warship armour, weapons and propulsion in this period. As the size of vessels steadily rose because of military and technical reasons, so their cost increased too – but at a far greater pace, a phenomenon of which we are well aware today, but which in Victorian Britain was regarded as inexplicable. A ninety-gun warship of the mid century cost almost half as much again if it was fitted with a screw propellor (£151,000 as against £108,000); but by the end of the century the tendency had become much more alarming, particularly after the introduction of turbines and larger guns, as the following figures show:[38]

Class of battleship	*Year of estimate or laying-down*	*Average cost*
Majestic	1893–5	£1 million
Duncan	1899	£1 "
Lord Nelson	1904–5	£1·5 "
Dreadnought	1905–6	£1·79 "
King George	1910–11	£1·95 "
Queen Elizabeth	1912–13	£2·5 "

Little space has been devoted in this survey to the nineteenth-century changes in warship construction, which within a half-century turned the ship of the line which Nelson and even Blake would have recognized into something akin to the ironclad of modern times. This is because, although there were many tactical consequences of this development, the strategical ones were far fewer: the greatest, seen in very broad terms, was the benefit Britain received, due to her advanced industrialization, of being able to build faster, and therefore to react quicker, to innovations in design. By the end of the century, however, the staggering rise in warship prices had made the picture much graver. In the near-crisis year of 1847, naval costs totalled £8 million, but the annual expenditure in the early and mid Victorian periods was usually less than that. A half-century later, the estimates were spiralling at an unprecedented rate for peacetime:

Year	Naval estimates (£ million)
1883	11
1896	18·7
1903	34·5
1910	40·4

This greatly accentuated the pressures upon the Royal Navy for, although other, less wealthy countries suffered from the same development, the British felt that they could never compromise on this issue: whatever the cost, they *had* to stay supreme. Yet this bald assertion, however natural it appeared to British politicians and admirals at the time, faced two enormous obstacles which were in the future to ensure that it became no political absolute. Firstly, the government, slowly abandoning the principles of *laissez-faire* and responding to the demands of a mass democracy for social and economic improvements in the country at large, was aware that other ministries were seeking a greater share of the budget; and, though expenditures soared all round, compromises had to be made by each side. Gladstone's resignation in 1894 had not symbolized the end of an age-old quarrel over resources after all, merely the temporary victory of the Liberal Imperialists. Preference was also to be given to defence expenditures under the Unionist cabinet which followed, but the Liberal administration of 1905–14, elected upon a reformist platform and aware of rising social expectations and tensions, found this dilemma much more acute. The whole problem of whether a democracy is willing in peacetime to meet the calls of those who urge military readiness in case of war was beginning to be argued and worked out. The second obstacle to the above-mentioned absolute lay simply in the fact that no country's resources were inexhaustible. The higher the cost of armaments rose, the greater would be the number of countries that would ultimately be forced to abandon the race, at least on a great-power scale. The question was, would Britain herself be able to stay the pace – or would it be possible only for those continental states of enormous resources, of which Mackinder had written?

It would be a long time before the answer to that question was clear; but even at the turn of the century it was obvious that the spread of industrialization was altering the world's international balance in many ways. Nations long dormant, though potentially powerful because of their populations and resources, had been galvanized by the Unbound Prometheus – the impact of technology and organization – and these revolutions were already having important strategical consequences. In the western hemisphere the United States was assuming a more and more dominating position, its economic activities and political influence permeating the Caribbean and Latin America. In the same way Japan was pulling ahead of its neighbours in the Far East and extending its control there. The newly united German Empire, boosted by an amazingly swift industrial and commercial expansion, was steadily changing the old balance of power in Europe. Finally, industrialization was not only allowing Russia to take the first real steps to develop its immense resources, but strategic railway construction was giving it a means of direct military pressure upon China and India. All of these changes implied at least a consequent diminution of Britain's influence in the areas concerned, and some a distinct restriction upon her hitherto almost unchallenged predominance and freedom of action. The same was true for the other great political development of the later nineteenth century – the colonial expansion of the great powers. A demand for fresh markets and sources of raw materials, a rise in nationalism and changes in the balance of power, a yellow Press catering for the first time to a mass readership, internal challenges to the political *status quo*, the spread of Darwinistic notions – perhaps all consequences or associates of the industrial revolution – had pushed these countries into a frantic search for overseas possessions. Hitherto, the British had usually had to contend with the spasmodic challenges of the French. Now many more nations entered the fray, with the result that Britain's comfortable and extensive 'informal empire' in Africa and Asia virtually disappeared: it either had to be made formal or it was annexed by others. The whole experience was most unpleasant for British statesmen. No doubt they secured a larger share of colonial real-estate in this scramble than anyone else – with their head-start, this was scarcely surprising – but once again their position had relatively declined; informal control of most of the tropics was exchanged for formal control of one quarter of it. Strategical supremacy was also affected by the acquisition by foreign powers of important bases along the world's shipping routes, for instance, Bizerta, Dakar, Diego Suarez, Manila and Hawaii.

These changes bewildered many Britons, even though their feelings were often concealed by a display of national pride and bravado which mid Victorians would have considered as both unnecessary and distasteful, Palmerston always excepted. The British public of the 1880s and 1890s would have been more upset still had the second aspect of Mackinder's thesis been known to them: that the sea power was itself waning in relation to land power. This, too, was a very long-term trend, measurable only over decades, whose consequences were to be fully perceived only in the next century; but once again it is worth while to examine briefly its general characteristics.

Perhaps the real villain of the piece was the railway, ironically a British invention, and one which had greatly benefited the British economy and people. Nevertheless, the transformation it wrought upon such areas as central Europe, the 'Heartland' of Russia and the mid-west of the United States was far more decisive; the industrialization of those regions, despite the assertions of certain economists in recent years, was scarcely feasible without the railway. The transport of goods, which had for centuries been cheaper and faster by water, now became easier by land, a tendency which was to increase with the introduction of motorized transport in the twentieth century. And not only was industry stimulated, but commerce, which had long been difficult, now flourished under the new conditions; the opening of the Mont Cenis (1871) and St Gotthard (1882) tunnels greatly increased the northward flow of Mediterranean fruits and vegetables, for instance. The Columbian epoch of which Mackinder spoke, when most trade and populations had remained close to the sea, was slowly ending as continental countries were freed from this physical constriction. With the improvement of land communications, a nation without much seaboard, but with a large population and extensive territories, could now exploit its resources, and the peculiar advantages of small, predominantly naval–commercial countries such as Holland and Britain were gradually being lost.

People, too, could be transported across land much faster, a fact which not only affected shipping companies (especially those going around Cape Horn) but also had direct military implications. The body which appears to have appreciated this first was the Prussian General Staff, whose efficient planners turned railway time-tabling into a work of art. In 1866 it had been able to put 400,000 into the field in a very short time for the campaign against Austria; and 'it mastered the problems of mass organization and movement so brilliantly that in 1870 1,183,000 men passed through the barracks into the army in eighteen days, and 462,000 were transported to the French frontier in the same time.'[37] The traditional British strategy against one power or a coalition dominating Europe, of dispatching expeditions to the peripheries, be it the Low Countries or the Portuguese or Italian coast, would now be a much more risky proposition if the enemy could swiftly rush a far greater force to the threatened point by rail, instead of having to rely upon road communications and forced marches. Conversely, a land power could be freed from its dependence upon the sea in certain circumstances – the most notable example of this being the advantages which Russia acquired by the construction of the trans-Siberian railway. The latter, so argued the Russian finance minister Witte in a memorandum to the Tsar in 1892, 'would not only bring about the opening of Siberia, but would revolutionize world trade, supersede the Suez Canal as the leading route to China, enable Russia to flood the Chinese market with textiles and metal goods, and secure political control of northern China'.[38] These hopes were soon to be blunted by the war with Japan, the result of which reassured navalists everywhere; but in retrospect it is possible to see the Russian defeat as being due more to unreadiness and inefficiency than to the workings of sea power. By 1945 at least the boot was on the other foot and no Japanese navy could have helped much to hold Manchuria. Even as it was, the Russian expansion by land at the turn of the century was quite impressive, Mackinder later noting in one of his perceptive comparisons:

> It was an unprecedented thing in the year 1900 that Britain should maintain a quarter of a million men in her war with the Boers at a distance of six thousand miles over the ocean; but it was as remarkable a feat for Russia to place an army of more than a quarter of a million men against the Japanese in Manchuria in 1904 at a distance of four thousand miles by rail.[39]

More worrying still to the British was the threat which Russian railway construction offered to their control of India. For centuries this important possession had been only accessible to a great power by sea, but by 1900 it appeared to be in deadly danger from the approaching Orenburg-Tashkent railway, to which the British simply had no answer. Only a large army, not the Royal Navy, could hold India from the north-west. Truly, the defence of an empire susceptible in so many places to attack from land was a desperate problem for a country that was basically a sea power, as *The Naval and Military Record* pointed out in 1901 in a leader which is worth quoting at some length:

> There has never been room for doubt that certain limitations must hamper the expansion of a naval Power. The familiar truth has been somewhat obscured by the writings of Captain Mahan, which may easily be misread by Englishmen who are naturally proud of their Navy and of their expanding Empire. It may be doubted, however, if Captain Mahan ever intended to suggest that an extensive Empire, scattered over all parts of the globe, can be held for many centuries by sea power alone. The defence of India, as we recently pointed out, is based upon sea power, but it also involves the maintenance of 300,000 troops, and makes a considerable drain upon the limited supply of military recruits under our voluntary system of service. The Canadian frontier, again, could hardly be held with security in the event of war against the United States. Our conquests in South Africa may oblige us to maintain a permanent garrison of 50,000 troops, and at present it is not very clear how that army is to be raised under the voluntary system ... Singapore, for example, is a valuable naval base, but it cannot be held by the Navy alone. The port requires a large garrison.

> Thus, the limitations of sea power begin to be felt when territorial expansion can no longer be safeguarded exclusively by the guns of the fleet, backed by minor garrisons.[40]

There were other changes, too, which had taken place or were still in process in the nineteenth century, which might cause one to wonder if Mahan's strategical analysis of Britain's previous naval wars would be of much relevance in the future. Particularly significant here was the alteration in the effectiveness of the blockade, whose effects, even if exaggerated by navalist historians, had usually been considerable. The newer world powers, the United States and Germany, and the old enemy, Russia, having less of their national wealth bound up in overseas trade, were far less susceptible to defeat by naval pressure alone than ever Spain, the Netherlands or even France had been. To seize the Spanish *flota* or to interrupt the Dutch trade with the Indies had been to deal the enemy's economy a very severe blow indeed; but now it was different, as was emphasized in a very interesting lecture given at the United Services Institute by an Inner Temple barrister, one Douglas Owen, in 1905. As he explained, the trade which British privateers of the seventeenth and eighteenth centuries had harassed was that between ports which then belonged to her rivals – Ceylon, Mauritius, Cape Colony, Guinea, Dominica, Trinidad, St Vincent, St Lucia, Demarara, Grenada, French Canada. Since those times they had all become British. In the second place, colonial trade as a whole had declined in importance; the gold and silver from Latin America, the spices from the East Indies, the rum and tobacco and sugar from the West Indies, had no modern equivalents – except perhaps the carriage of raw materials and foodstuffs to the British Isles itself. In other words the best targets were now nearly all British. Thirdly, the coming of the railway had reduced the effectiveness of the blockade and the possibility of paralysing the enemy's trade:

> Since those times, railways have been introduced and so developed as to link together city, town, and port, whilst inland waterways have on the Continent been created and developed to an extent of which most Englishmen have no conception. Even if it were possible for us to close absolutely our adversary's ports, his trade would go on with little interruption ... Today France can supply herself through Belgium; Germany, through Holland and Belgium; Holland, through Belgium and Germany; Russia, through Germany and the Low Countries ... The days of coastal blockade, in the case of European States, with any thought of starving out the enemy, or with any idea of making prizes of his coastal traffic, have gone for ever.[41]

As the final sentence indicates, this paper was written under the belief that the clauses of the Declaration of Paris of 1856 concerning the inviolability of neutral vessels would be observed in future wars; and that the enemy would simply proceed to lay up all his ships and to rely upon neutral carriers. Most people accepted that this would be so, and it was such a consideration which had caused Salisbury in 1871 to protest that that particular treaty had made the fleet 'almost valueless' for anything other than preventing invasion. Even if Britain was in the future to reject this agreement, however, Owen's analysis still possessed a certain validity: the European powers could obtain supplies more easily from neutral neighbours under modern conditions of transport than they ever could have in the past. And it was laughable to think of trying to starve out Russia or the United States.

What was more – and this one can see increasingly in the twentieth century – the new inventions of the mine, the torpedo, the submarine and long-range coastal ordnance were making the operational problems of a blockade even more difficult than hitherto. Nor was it easy to perceive how modern warships, dependent as they were upon coal, could maintain a watch upon an enemy's harbour for more than a couple of days. As early as 1893, the First Lord, Spencer, had thought 'an effective blockade with steam power will be extremely difficult, if not impossible', and *The Times* said the same publicly in 1895. Most interesting of all, Mahan had also voiced his doubts about it in a well-known article published in 1896.[42] While it was to be a number of years before these developments caused an official alteration in Britain's traditional policy of the close blockade, even by the end of the century it was evident that the matter was regarded with uncertainty and unease in some quarters. Furthermore, although at first the new inventions seemed only to restrict the freedom of action of battleships operating near hostile coasts, it was later recognized that there was no inherent reason why the mine and the torpedo could not be employed on the high seas also. Escorts for the battle-fleet could no doubt be provided as a counter-measure; yet the more these monstrously expensive capital ships (so vulnerable despite all their armour to one blow from such weapons) depended upon the protection of smaller warships, the more their very existence was called into question. Some far-sighted strategists quickly drew their own conclusions: Admiral Sir Percy Scott, who transformed gunnery standards in the Royal Navy, caused a minor *furore* by a letter to *The Times* of June 1914, in which he prophesied that submarines and aircraft would make the battleships worthless and pleaded instead for a naval policy based upon a large air force, a great fleet of submarines and many cruisers (for trade protection).[43]

His critics protested that the case was not proven and that Mahan's principles would continue to be valid. To see the victory of such heretical theories at this time of the great power and efficiency of the British battle-fleet would have been too bitter a pill to swallow; but behind these protests might one not also detect the deeper fear that the supremacy of the submarine, torpedo-boat and aeroplane on the naval battlefield would presage the fall of Britain's own maritime mastery? A battle-fleet, after all, could only be built by a limited number of states and took many years to create, giving the British time to take counter-measures; but any reasonably ambitious country could afford aircraft and submarines, thus assuring to itself at least local naval dominance.

If industrialization, changing forms of transport and innovations in technology, had made Britain's traditional weapon of the blockade a much less useful one, these same processes had also caused her to be much more vulnerable to hostile naval pressures upon her own lines of communication with the outside world. The vast rise in her population, which had multiplied sixfold between 1750 and 1913, together with the industrialization of the country, had led to an enormous increase in the demand for foodstuffs and raw materials; rising prosperity accelerated this trend; the free-trade system did even more so, turning Britain into the centre of world trade, dependent as no other country was for its prosperity upon the import and export of commodities; and the coming of the steamship and refrigeration permitted foreign farmers to take advantage of the lack of tariffs and to flood the British market with their own products. The transformation was dramatic; as late as the 1830s over 90 per cent of the food consumed was also grown in Britain, but by 1913 55 per cent of the grain and 40 per cent of the meat consumed was imported. In raw materials the dependence upon imports was even more marked: seven eighths of these supplies came from abroad by 1913, including all of the cotton, four fifths of the wool, most of the non-phosphoric iron ore and almost all non-ferrous metals.[44] By 1869, just as this development got under way, Malmesbury was stating nervously: 'We cannot grow or supply half the food we want for our increased population.'[45] The protection of the thousands of merchant ships carrying this immense commerce was seen to be a far more crucial task for the Royal Navy in any future conflict than it had been in the past. As Admiral Fisher put it in characteristically blunt fashion: 'It's not *invasion* we have to fear if our Navy's beaten, *it's starvation*.' From an economic point of view, Britain was more susceptible to blockade than any other power on earth.

There was one further consequence of the industrialization of the western world which caused Britain's position as a power to be relatively reduced: the organization and deployment of mass armies, following the Prussian model. Well before the nineteenth century, it is true, there had been occasions when large bodies of soldiers had been assembled for battle; but more often than not they had only been effective inside their own country, or for a short period of time, their assembly and deployment had taken ages, their uniforms were raggle-taggle, their weaponry assorted and their logistics primitive. The industrial revolution, with its accompanying rise in population, not only permitted still larger armies to be recruited but also provided the financial and material strength for them to be clothed, armed and fed for a very long time. In other words, as Ivan S. Bloch intuitively suggested in his book *Modern Weapons and Modern War*, future conflicts between the great powers were going to be endurance tests where the defensive would have the upper hand:

> instead of a war fought out to the bitter end in a series of decisive battles, we shall have as a substitute a long period of continually increasing strain upon the resources of the combatants. The war, instead of being a hand-to-hand contest in which the combatants measure their physical and moral superiority, will become a kind of stalemate, in which neither army being able to get at the other, both armies will be maintained in opposition to each other, threatening each other, but never able to deliver a final and decisive attack.[46]

Despite the fact that the new railways now enabled generals to transfer troops at great speed right across a country, industrialization was paradoxically likely to see future wars turn out to be long drawn-out affairs of mass armies. All this made the small professional army which Britain possessed a nonentity. Previously, the landing of 30,000 or so troops at a chosen point in Europe was either very effective in itself or was at least of considerable assistance to an ally. Now, with an army which was smaller than Switzerland's, and which was to a large extent locked up overseas, Britain's ability to influence continental affairs through military pressure was negligible. If the British were to land their army on the German coast, Bismarck is reported to have quipped, he would call out the local police force and have it arrested!

This sharp decline in Britain's military effectiveness did not escape observers inside the country. In 1869 Colonel Walker, well positioned as British military attaché at Berlin, shrewdly observed:

> that we should ever again play the part of earlier days in great Continental wars is impossible, the magnitude of the disciplined and

> expensive forces of other nations, whose armies are supplied by conscription . . . precluded us from a participation in the numerical contest for supremacy.[47]

By the turn of the century, General Maurice too could sadly report that 'It appears that despite the historic past of the British Army on the Continent the general impression among foreign officers is that literally we have no army at all.'

To reverse this decline, however, would have meant the introduction of some form of national conscription on the continental model, an undertaking which seemed to politicians and public alike not only expensive and unpopular but one which contravened basic political principles and traditions. A combination of genuine belief, political tactics and a regard for economy ensured that the existing ideas of what Liddell Hart later termed 'the British way of warfare' – naval actions and blockade, seizure of colonies, peripheral attacks on the continent – were to be preferred in any future conflict with a European enemy. And since this approximately coincided with a period in history (roughly 1879 to 1905) when a balance of power existed upon the continent, the need to reconsider this traditional policy was small. But what if that balance should ever be upset by the rise of one nation or a coalition which, besides appearing unfriendly in outlook towards Britain, threatened to dominate Europe and against which the military strength of the opposition was simply too weak? Colonial actions, blockade, small-scale landings, would be irrelevant here, yet to stand aside would probably be to permit the whole continent to fall into the hands of an unfriendly power, the most dangerous event in the world to all British statesmen aware of their country's history and traditions. Although this contingency still seemed unlikely at the turn of the century, several British writers were pointing already to certain developments which made it less remote. The whole argument about a military commitment to Europe, upon the size of that commitment, and upon the consequences for Britain's entire defence and foreign policy, lay just around the corner; and upon its outcome depended much of the future of the Royal Navy itself.

PART THREE

Fall

... it is very doubtful whether our 'traditional' strategy is workable any longer. In the past it really depended on the balance of power, more and more precarious from 1870 onwards, and on geographical advantages which modern technical developments have lessened. After 1890 Britain was no longer the only naval power, and moreover the whole scope of naval warfare had diminished. With the abandonment of sail navies became less mobile, the inland seas were inaccessible after the invention of the marine mine, and blockade lost part of its power owing to the science of substitutes and the mechanization of agriculture. After the rise of modern Germany it was hardly possible for us to dispense with European alliances, and one of the things allies are apt to insist on is that you do your fair share of the fighting. Money subsidies have no meaning when war involves the total effort of every belligerent nation.

The Collected Essays, Journalism and Letters of George Orwell, 4 vols. (Harmondsworth, Middlesex, 1970), ii, p. 284, from a review of Liddell Hart's *The British Way in Warfare*.

CHAPTER EIGHT

The End of Pax Britannica (1897–1914)

> Because of that formidable and threatening Armada across the North Sea, we have almost abandoned the waters of the Outer Oceans. We are in the position of Imperial Rome when the Barbarians were thundering at the frontiers. The ominous word has gone forth. We have called home the legions . . .
>
> *The Standard*, 29 May 1912.

On 26 June 1897 the most powerful naval force the world had ever seen was assembled in Spithead to celebrate the Diamond Jubilee of Queen Victoria. Over 165 British warships, including twenty-one first-class battleships and fifty-four cruisers, demonstrated the immense size and fighting strength of the Royal Navy. Foreign observers were very impressed by it all, and few were inclined to dispute the proud boast of *The Times* that

> The Fleet . . . is certainly the most formidable force in all its elements and qualities that has ever been brought together, and such as no combination of other powers can rival. It is at once the most powerful and far-reaching weapon which the world has ever seen.[1]

This weapon, readers also knew, was complemented by, and in turn offered protection to, the world's greatest merchant marine, for Britain was still the leading trading nation and derived most of her national wealth necessary to finance the Royal Navy's building programmes from overseas commerce and investment. In addition, by her possession of an enormous colonial empire, Britain enjoyed the strategical benefits of the most important collection of naval bases throughout the world: 'Five strategic keys lock up the globe!', gloated Admiral Fisher, and they (Dover, Gibraltar, the Cape, Alexandria, Singapore) were all in British hands.[2] Moreover, that empire and those bases were being rapidly linked together by an intricate imperial cable communications network, which even further enhanced British strategic domination of the world's sea-ways; in 1900 the French government enviously noted that 'England owes her influence in the world perhaps more to her cable communications than to her navy. She controls the news, and makes it serve her policy and commerce in a marvellous manner.'[3]

In other respects, too, the average Briton could feel confident in his fleet. The Unionist government, with Goschen as First Lord, had always been generous with the annual estimates, and as a result the navy was more modern and better equipped as a peacetime force in 1897 than had ever been the case since 1815. The navy seemed, moreover, to be wisely distributed to meet the various threats to Britain's world-wide interests. Pride of place was given to the Mediterranean Fleet, where ten (later twelve or fourteen) first-class battleships based on Malta posed a solid check to the Franco-Russian squadrons. In addition, it could be reinforced in time of crisis by the eight first-class battleships of the Channel Fleet, which operated between Gibraltar and the south coast of England. This second force could also render assistance to the eleven second-class battleships of the Reserve Fleet, which protected Britain's North Sea coastline. In the Far East, too, it was deemed necessary to deploy three battleships and many other vessels to ensure that London's voice was listened to with respect. Certain other stations (Cape, American) were also important enough to justify a battleship in the squadron, and there were many smaller vessels scattered elsewhere. The world-wide display of British naval power was likely to continue into the future, for the 1898–9 estimates (introduced a few months before the Spithead review) totalled almost £22 million and included provision for four new battleships.

Nor was this simply a façade of power, ready to collapse like a pack of cards at the first real test of strength, as the French army was to do in 1940. The numerical, material and strategical superiority of the Royal Navy was a cold, hard reality, as the French nation found to its dismay at the end of 1898 when faced with a Britain ready to go to war over the Upper Nile. Observing France's humiliating diplomatic retreat, many saw this as being due to the Royal Navy's dominance and would have agreed with Kaiser Wilhelm's perceptive comment: 'The poor French . . . They have not read their Mahan!'[4] One year later the navy also ensured the safety of communications to South Africa during the struggle

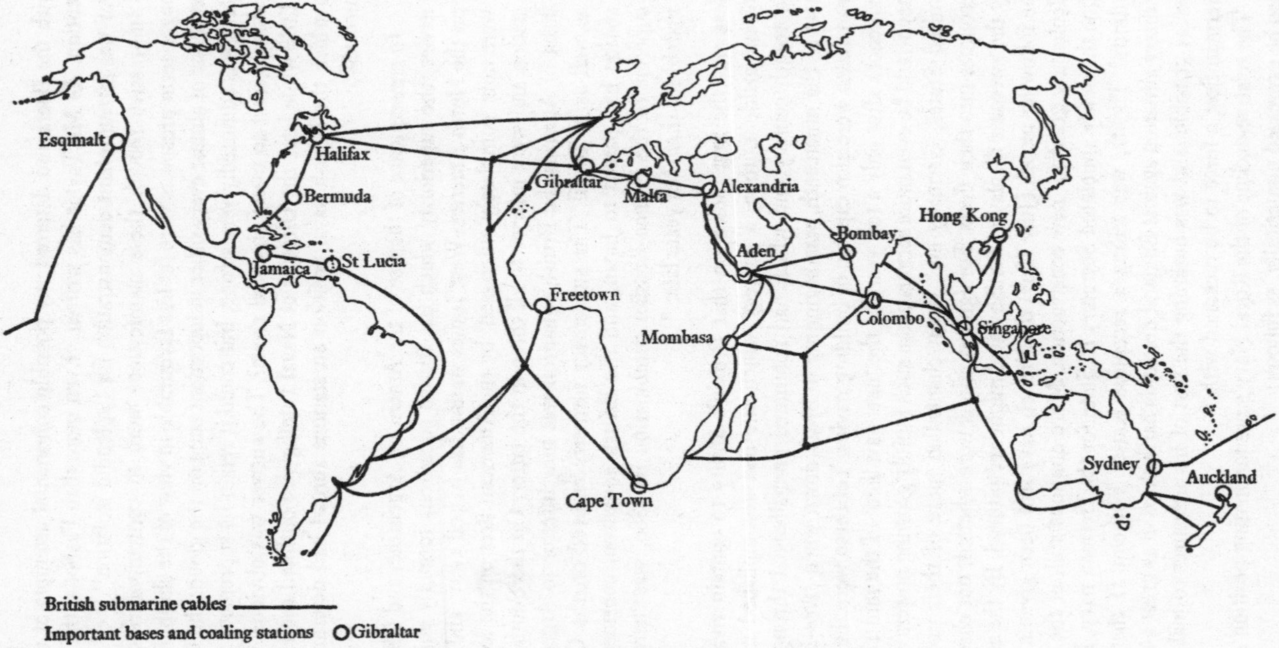

Map 7. Naval bases and submarine cables of the Empire, *c.* 1900

with the Boers and deterred any possible continental attempts at intervention. As Mr Taylor has written, 'Even more than Fashoda, the Boer war was a triumphant demonstration for "splendid isolation".'[5]

Impressive though these manifestions were to contemporaries, the longer-term prospects were far less favourable in view of the shipbuilding exertions of almost every other independent state on the globe: the Royal Navy was admittedly very strong, but could it retain its supremacy in all waters against so many potential rivals? The answer was obvious. Only a little while later the Director of Naval Intelligence outlined the extent to which the British naval position on stations abroad had deteriorated since 1889:

> In consequence of the rise of the American, Argentine, and Chilean navies, the superiority which the British squadrons formerly enjoyed on the North America–West Indies station has passed away, and they were now 'completely outclassed' by the American fleet on the former station and were inferior to all three in the latter. On the South-East coast of America the British squadron was now inferior to Argentina as well as to Brazil. The supremacy formerly enjoyed on the China station had passed to Japan, and the British squadron, considerably superior to the Franco-Russian combination in 1889, was 'hardly a match' for them ten years later.[6]

Here was the first indication that Britain's ability to contain rival sea powers inside Europe, a strategy which she had accomplished in the eighteenth century and which had continued unchallenged throughout most of the nineteenth, was beginning to break down when *extra*-European states were also capable of building navies. Yet these were the consequences after only a few years of the 'new navalism' of the mid 1890s; they would be even more serious when such rapidly growing powers as the United States, Germany and Japan channelled more of their national resources into their fleets. Foreign ambitions were whetted, not checked, by the awesome display of British naval might at Spithead. By the end of the following month (July 1897) the French navy had been given a supplementary grant for new construction. More ominous still, at the same time the newly appointed Secretary of State for the German navy, Rear-Admiral Tirpitz, was telling a receptive Kaiser Wilhelm II that 'the military situation against England demands battleships in as great a number as possible' and was outlining the first of his measures to make the German fleet a force to be reckoned with.[7]

The relative decline of the Royal Navy's predominating position could also be expressed numerically, as follows:

Country	Battleships in 1883	Battleships in 1897 (plus those building)
Britain	38	62
France	19	36
Germany	11	12
Russia	3	18
Italy	7	12
USA	0	11
Japan	0	7

In other words in 1883 the number of British battleships almost equalled the total of all the other powers combined (thirty-eight to forty); by 1897 this comfortable ratio had shrivelled away (sixty-two to ninety-six). There are, moreover, grounds for believing that the actual totals were worse than those presented here.[8] At a time of splendid isolation this was not an attractive picture.

In retrospect the historian can perceive that the Diamond Jubilee celebrations of 1897 did not denote the zenith of Britain's power, but constituted rather the defiant swan-song of a nation becoming less and less complacent about the increasing threats to its world-wide interests. The real apogee of British might had occurred somewhere in the middle of the century; now it was a time, as many politicians and certain other perceptive persons realized, for strenuous efforts and decisive actions to meet the challenges of the coming century when Britain could no longer rely upon those advantages which Palmerston had taken for granted. The alternatives which lay open to them were all full of obstacles and dangers. Imperial Federation, the rallying cry of the arch-imperialists, was clearly impracticable in military terms, even allowing for the objections of the Dominions. The simplistic remedy of increasing the defence budget until Britain's navy and army were capable of satisfying all the demands which were placed upon them was financially impossible; and the coming of the Boer War, with the subsequent exposures of the military unpreparedness and inadequacy of generalship, meant that the navy was once again likely to take a back seat to the army in the estimates. The policy of throwing Britain into one of the European alliance *blocs*, though it appealed to Joseph Chamberlain, contained grave disadvantages and was opposed by many, including the Prime Minister, Salisbury.

In view of the obstacles to such extreme solutions, what remained was the less dramatic policy of rationalization in all spheres of defence and foreign policy, of a greater coordination between ministries, and of a gradual reduction in commitments in the less vital regions of the globe. Attempts would be made to garner more financial help from the Dominions, and to find new sources of revenue at home; improvements in the armed forces would be effected, for fighting power could be raised by more means than simply increasing taxes; if necessary local *ententes* would be arranged with foreign powers, so as to allow Britain to concentrate elsewhere; and the diplomats would endeavour to reach amicable solutions of pressing problems with certain other nations, thereby reducing the number of potential foes. The strategical over-extension and dilution of naval forces, reminiscent of the pre-Crimean period but now much riskier since the challenges were more numerous and persistent, had been partially altered by the rise of the Franco-Russian alliance, and the policy of concentration would continue at a faster pace. Yet the habit of believing that an independent Britain could look after herself in all corners of the world died hard, and many found it difficult to adjust to the great changes which took place in British defence and foreign policy between 1897 and 1914. For in those years, it would be no exaggeration to say, both the Pax Britannica and the concomitant foreign policy of 'splendid isolation' were brought to an end with incredible swiftness.

It would be a truism to state that naval and strategical factors played a decisive part in this transformation of Britain's world role. Galvanized in particular by the shocks of the Boer War, ministers such as Balfour, Selborne and Lansdowne pressed ahead with urgency to rationalize their policy. Already at the beginning of 1901, the First Lord, Selborne, challenged the traditional policy of a Two Power Standard which was numerically calculated and which was to operate against *all* comers, thereby suggesting that in his view the friendship of certain powers had to be taken for granted in the future:

> I propose therefore to consider our position almost exclusively from its relative strength to that of France and Russia combined and from that point of view it seems to me that what we should aim at is, not a numerical equality, but a strength drawn partly from numbers (and partly from superior organization).

This principle, as Monger notes, was 'a significant step away from isolation . . . She (Britain) was no longer to depend entirely on her own strength but was to rely on the forbearance of other Powers.'[9] Cutting her naval coat according to her financial cloth had now become inevitable, but this still left many painful decisions as to the regions and interests which would no longer justify full attention and limitless sacrifices.

There were some areas, certainly, where a withdrawal seemed to be both unavoidable and desirable. The growth of American power by the turn of the century, for example, was making the British position in the western hemisphere increasingly untenable. The problem of the defence of Canada had always been an insoluble one, despite the persistent attention given to it by strategic experts in Whitehall for almost a century.[10] Here a large navy was of slight value, as the Permanent Under-Secretary at the India Office, Godley, privately admitted to Curzon in 1899:

> I will confess to you that there are two Powers, and two only, of whom I am afraid, *viz.* the United States and Russia, for the simple reason that they have or (in the case of Russia) must soon have better military access to an important part of our dominions, than we have ourselves. It is to be regretted that Canada and India are not islands, but we must recognize the fact, and must modify our diplomacy accordingly.[11]

Added to this military reason for withdrawal were several others. Any conflict between Britain and the United States would be financially disastrous to both sides. On the political and emotional front, the mutual suspicion and antagonism was slowly being replaced by a pride in the racial and cultural similarities of the two Anglo-Saxon powers; many Britons saw in the United States a future ally in troubled times ahead, and many Americans substituted for their earlier Anglophobia an (admittedly temporary) appreciation of Britain's imperial problems.[12] Finally, there was the naval aspect. In 1898 the United States possessed only six modern battleships, but the war with Spain sparked off widespread enthusiasm for naval expansion; by 1905 she had twelve modern battleships and was building another twelve. Only if Britain was free to send the greater part of her navy across the Atlantic could she be reasonably certain of a naval victory which might offset the invasion of Canada; yet with the diplomatic scene so threatening, it was precisely this precondition which could not be fulfilled. Even during the Venezuelan confrontation of 1895, when the United States possessed only three first-class battleships, it proved impossible to strengthen the British squadrons in American waters; the European situation was simply too critical. Nor had it improved by the turn of the century, when the Admiralty gloomily noted:

> Centuries of triumphant conflict with her European rivals have left Great Britain the double legacy of a world-wide Empire and of a jealousy (of which we had a sad glimpse during the South African war) which would render it hazardous indeed for us to denude our home waters of the battle squadrons which stand between our own land and foreign invasion.[13]

The logical alternative for Britain was to withdraw gracefully, avoiding a war which it was unlikely to win, and gaining in return (so it was hoped), the lasting friendship of a powerful nation. This was exactly the policy of the new foreign secretary, Lansdowne, over the tricky question of permitting the Americans to build and fortify alone an isthmian canal contrary to the Clayton–Bulwer treaty of 1850. When the Admiralty pointed out that to give way here would be detrimental to Britain's naval interests, Lansdowne skilfully turned this reasoning upside down by employing their further argument that supremacy at sea would ultimately decide the control of the canal, which really made the question of its ownership superfluous; and since Britain was no longer able to compete in battleship strength in the Caribbean, it was wisest not to provoke American antagonism. In actual fact the Admiralty was not opposed to the Foreign Office's point of view, for it was also basically pro-American and saw the need to divest itself of this embarrassing strategical inheritance. As Dr Bourne points out, 'the appeasement of the United States at the end of the nineteenth century was the natural, if belated, conclusion of a policy which Great Britain had long since adopted in the interest of her security.'[14] But that she should have done so at this time was an indication of how much London felt itself to be on the defensive by the beginning of the new century.

This retreat over the canal question, Alaskan boundary and elsewhere, in the face of American expansion, was not resented in Britain, at least after Salisbury's departure; in fact, naval leaders such as Selborne, Fisher, and Lee shrank from the task of fully preparing a war plan against the United States, so horrible and unbelievable did this prospect appear to them. Yet this equanimity was not so obvious in the Far East, where the British government was under heavy pressure to protect the country's commercial and political interests in the face of the threatening actions of France, Germany and especially Russia. China presented a classic example of a region where decades of British commercial and 'informal' political predominance were rapidly crumbling away, and where London felt too weak to oppose the advances of other powers without the assistance of a major ally. Not only were they helpless to preserve Chinese sovereignty from the overland advances of the Russians from Siberia and the French from Indo-China, but the naval balance of power was also alarming. By the end of 1901, Selborne informed the Cabinet, Britain would have four first-class battleships and sixteen cruisers in Chinese waters compared to a combined Franco-Russian strength of seven first-class and two second-class battleships, plus twenty cruisers: the consequences for Britain's Oriental interests in a war with the Dual Alliance were obvious, even to those who favoured a concentration in waters nearer home. For this reason the Admiralty advocated a naval alliance with Japan, presenting arguments which are worth reproducing at some length, since they so clearly encapsulate the strategical considerations behind an abandonment of 'splendid isolation' and in favour of a certain reliance upon the support of another power:

> It is true that victory in European waters would scarcely be dimmed by even serious disasters in the Far East, but its value, though not obliterated, would be impaired to a dangerous degree if British naval power in the Far East were crushed out of existence. We could afford to lose a certain number of merchantmen, or even to see a weaker squadron of battleships blockaded for a time in Hong Kong; but we could not afford to see our Chinese trade disappear, or to see Hong Kong and Singapore fall, particularly not at a moment when a military struggle with Russia might be in progress on the confines of India . . .
>
> For us the odds of nine battleships to four would be too great, and we should have eventually to add to our battleships on the China Station. The effect of this would be twofold. It would leave us with little or nothing more than a bare equality of strength in the Channel and Mediterranean, and a bare equality at the heart of the Empire is a dangerous risk. It would strain our naval system greatly and would add to our expenditure on the manning of the Navy . . . The case would bear a different aspect were we assured the alliance of Japan.
>
> Great Britain and Japan together would next year be able to show eleven battleships against the French and Russian nine, as well as a preponderance of cruisers.
>
> Great Britain would be under no necessity of adding to the number of battleships on the China Station, and at last would be in a position to contemplate the possibility of shortly establishing a small margin of superiority in reserve at home; the number of our cruisers could be reduced on that station, and increased on other stations where badly required; our Far Eastern trade and possessions would be secure.[15]

Equally alarmed at the prospect of a Franco-Russian domination of the Far East, the Japanese were eager to enter such an alliance. With its signing on 30 January 1902, the British felt that they could breathe more easily in the Orient. Yet even they underestimated at the time the advantages which were to accrue to them from this decisive step.

While the Anglo-Japanese alliance has been generally regarded as marking the end of 'splendid isolation', it is important to note that its applicability was restricted to the Far East only, and that it actually confirmed isolation from Europe by making it less necessary to seek the support of Berlin over the China crisis. It would therefore be false to see the alliance as the start of a deliberate and long-term policy to involve Britain more in European affairs, offering large-scale support to France, and thinking only of the German challenge; that was a later development. Both the withdrawal from the western hemisphere and the reduction in Britain's naval commitment in the Far East had been greatly affected by local factors, and by a general recognition that the Royal Navy could not hope to keep pace with the shipbuilding efforts of the rest of the world combined. Nor was much publicity given to these moves, again a contrast with later redistribution measures. As Clarke, the Secretary to the newly formed Committee of Imperial Defence, noted to Balfour,

> What it is best not to say is that we believe that the idea of opposing the navy of the U.S. in the Caribbean and the North Atlantic close to its bases must be abandoned. This has naturally altered some of the strategic aspects of this part of the world. In years not far distant we shall be quite unable to oppose the navy of Japan in its own waters. It is best to recognize facts but not always to proclaim them from the house-top.[16]

Yet if these reductions in Britain's overseas commitments had an inherent logic of their own, there is no doubt that by 1903 or so British planners and the public were beginning to develop at least a suspicion about Germany's great naval expansion, which also necessitated a redeployment of the Royal Navy. Maritime predominance in the western hemisphere and Far East would be impossible to maintain in the future in any case, but even the attempts to do so appeared mistaken, if there was a need to concentrate against a newer challenger much nearer home. After all, Britain's Oriental trade, important though it was, hardly compared with her own national security. Germany's naval expansion arose from the same root causes as those of the United States and Japan – rapid industrialization, and a consequent interest in overseas markets, colonies, and international power-politics. What made it more alarming to British eyes was its particular form, direction and association with Berlin's foreign policy, which since the fall of Bismarck had assumed a much more restless and aggressive character. Kaiser Wilhelm's great ambition, fired by his reading of Mahan and by his intimate knowledge of the Royal Navy (of which he was an honorary Admiral of the Fleet), was to create as large a navy as possible, which would assure to Germany her rightful 'place in the sun' in the coming century. Although not anti-British in origin, it soon became so because of the basic political and geographical situation – Britain controlled Germany's routes to the outside world and regarded her unstable *Weltpolitik* with suspicion – and because of the strategy adopted after 1897 by Tirpitz. In his opinion Germany could only achieve her 'world political freedom' if she created a homogeneous force of battleships stationed in the North Sea, which would be able not only to defend the German coasts but also to threaten the overall maritime superiority of the most powerful navy existing; in other words, it would be a power-political lever, since the British, unable to concentrate their many battle squadrons in home waters, owing to pressing commitments elsewhere, would recognize the significance of his 'risk fleet' and become more amenable to German aspirations. Thus, whilst the German Foreign Ministry strove to keep Anglo-German relations smooth during the 'danger zone', the battle-fleet would quietly be made so strong that 'England will have lost every inclination to attack us and as a result concede to Your Majesty such a measure of naval mastery and enable Your Majesty to carry out a great overseas policy'. By the First Navy Law of 1898 a fleet strength of nineteen battleships was envisaged; by the Second Law of 1900 this was doubled to thirty-eight; but Tirpitz's final total was even greater than that.[17] Although it was to be a number of years before Britain's political leaders decided that Germany really did pose the most serious threat to their security, the Admiralty had been carefully assessing the Kaiser's naval programme for some time. Already in 1897 there was disquiet at the way in which the First Navy Law would spur on France and Russia to renewed efforts, but by the turn of the century this was replaced by the greater fear that Germany would hold the balance between Britain and the Dual Alliance – which was indeed one of Tirpitz's aims. By 1902 even the sceptical Selborne was forced to tell the Cabinet: 'I am convinced that the great new German navy is being carefully built up from the point of view of a war with us . . .'[18] The financial implications of this were enormous, for it meant that the First Lord's 1901 statement that it would be sufficient to build against the Franco-Russian combination alone was no longer valid: a *Three* Power Standard, such as the navalist Press demanded, was the logical answer but this would strain the whole budget. The naval and political situation thus seemed more desperate than ever, although certain members of the Foreign Office and the public were beginning to argue that the only alternative left was a *rapprochement* with France, and perhaps even with Russia also.

It was in this gloomy atmosphere; of disappointment at the army's poor role in the Boer War, of suspicion at the rising German navy and at the continued challenge of France and Russia, and of despair at the horrendous rises in military and naval expenditure, that the entire defence system was given a thorough and much-needed overhaul. The Committee of Imperial Defence (C.I.D.) was established as an advisory body to the Prime Minister to coordinate strategic matters, and quickly became far more effective and influential than the older Colonial Defence Committee. The army was thoroughly revamped, with a War Office now established on the collective lines of the Admiralty Board, a General Staff set up, and a whole host of reforms to achieve greater efficiency as a fighting force enacted. In addition, troops were withdrawn gradually from the West Indies, Bermuda, Crete and Canada, while the garrisons in South Africa and the Mediterranean were reduced in number. The navy, enjoying the nation's firm favour at this time, was not under such heavy public pressure to change itself; yet its transformation in the years 1904–7 was almost as radical, for no section of the Senior Service was to escape the 'shake-up' forced upon it by the promotion to First Sea Lord in October 1904 of that brilliant, ruthless, demonic man, Sir John Fisher.[19]

Many of his reforms require only brief mention here, since they are incidental to the main theme of this book: dockyards, pay, officer entry and training, service conditions, gunnery, and general efficiency were all improved under Fisher's drive, though it is worth noting that certain reforms had been under way in the preceding years too. It was Fisher's unique style that added greatly to the impression that a virtual revolution was taking place at the Admiralty.

The other, and major, aspects of Fisher's reforms deserve much more attention, for they implied that the Admiralty at least had fully acknowledged that the age of Pax Britannica had passed away. Even before then, as we have seen, naval predominance on some overseas stations had been quietly ceded to foreign powers, while in March 1903 the government announced that a new naval base was to be established in the Firth of Forth; somewhat later (spring 1904) the Home Fleet was increased in size and efficiency, both measures being recognized by all as counters to the rising German navy. Yet none of these steps approached the single-mindedness and ruthlessness with which Fisher was to tackle the strategical reorganization of the whole navy.

For Fisher, efficiency, fire-power, speed, economy and a concentration of force were the key yardsticks with which to measure the fighting capacity of a navy. From this point of view nothing was more preposterous than the maintenance of vast numbers of slow, obsolescent small cruisers and gunboats all over the globe, wasting money and especially men. In time of war, he argued, 'An enemy cruiser would lap them up like an armadillo let loose on an ant-hill!' Nor, apart from their deployment on the rivers of China and West Africa, were the gunboats of much military worth; they were 'merely a symbol of the power of a nation, not a concrete embodiment of it'. Occasional visits by more powerful vessels would secure the same end just as well, if not better. The same was true of the many older vessels, maintained at great expense in the Dockyard Reserve for some future war – a 'miser's hoard of useless junk', Fisher called them. Although his own more drastic scrapping solution was toned down by a special committee, 154 ships were struck off the effective list in a manner which their destroyer proudly described as 'Napoleonic in its audacity and Cromwellian in its thoroughness'. Cruisers, sloops, gunboats and gunvessels, which had earned the respect of African chiefs, the dislike of Oriental potentates and the hatred of pirates and slavers everywhere in the post-Crimean decades, had their long years of service brought to an end.

The driving reason behind this ruthless act, apart from Fisher's distaste for inefficiency, was the need to build up the Royal Navy's strength in home waters: 'the peace distribution of the fleet should also be its best strategical distribution for war' and Nelson's adage that 'The battle ground should be the drill ground' were two of his more frequent aphorisms and they contrasted sharply with the previous role of the navy as the world's policeman. The famous Australia, China and East Indies stations were therefore to be amalgamated into the Eastern Fleet, based on Singapore, in time of war, while the South Atlantic, North America and West Africa stations were taken over forthwith by a much expanded Cape Station; the Pacific Station was simply abandoned, and the number of vessels based upon the two new centres of concentration was greatly reduced. More important still, Fisher radically switched the weight of Britain's battleship fleets from overseas stations into home waters; this may be best expressed by statistics showing the strengths of the various fleets both before and after Fisher's redistribution measures of 1904–5:

Before	*Home*	*Channel*	*Mediterranean*	*China*
	8	8	12	5
After	*Channel*	*Atlantic*	*Mediterranean*	*China*
	17	8	8	–

The Mediterranean Fleet could not be reduced any further in view of the Franco-Russian threat but, as Professor Marder notes, 'England, instead of looking, as she had looked in the wars of the eighteenth century, to the south and west, now began to look to the east and north.'[20] A strategical revolution was under way. Moreover, preference in the more modern types of battleships was henceforward to be given to the Channel and

Atlantic commands, and there were to be regular manœuvres between these fleets. It is also worth remarking that the attached cruiser squadrons for these battle-fleets were often formed out of ships withdrawn from disbanded overseas stations, and that the Japanese victories over Russia in the Far East allowed five battleships to be transferred to the Channel Fleet – the greatest benefit to date, in naval terms, of the Anglo-Japanese Alliance (which the British then hastily revised and renewed). In addition, the crews from the scrapped warships were redeployed, either in the active squadrons or used in Fisher's famous nucleus-crew system, which meant that reserve ships could be mobilized much more efficiently.

Fisher's approach is best typified by the great warship creations for which he is most famous, the all-big-gun *Dreadnought*, which made all other battleships obsolete with its strength, speed and fire-power; and the battle-cruiser *Invincible*, an even faster vessel, though with two fewer main guns and far less armoured protection. The astonishing thing about all these improvements was that the naval estimates were actually *reduced*, thereby proving Fisher's point that large sums and numerous warships were not necessarily an indication of fighting power. After jumping sharply from £27·5 million in 1900 to £36·8 million in 1904, the estimates were reduced in the following year by £3·5 million. Nevertheless, this particular aspect of the reforms should be seen for what it was – the cutting away of unnecessary expenditure. Naval costs in general continued their relentless upward trend, accelerated by the larger and more complex types of warships. Fisher's root-and-branch measures, combined with some skilful British diplomacy at this time, were to give Britain a breathing-space; but the recognition that she could no longer afford to build a navy to take on all others had already been made.

Fisher's reforms, as he had always forecast, provoked bitter dissension inside and outside the navy. Some criticisms, such as the fact that he had denuded the fleet of many small ships needed in time of war, had some validity; others, such as the allegation that he had thrown away Britain's decisive battleship lead and given Tirpitz the chance to catch up, were quite false, as has recently been shown.[21] Of central importance, however, although it was at first conducted at an official and confidential level until the long-term trend became obvious to the public, was the debate upon the 'recall of the legions'. The Admiralty might have made up its mind by the time of the first Moroccan crisis that the only real danger lay in Germany; but many others felt that the running-down of the overseas squadrons to the benefit of the North Sea was detrimental to Britain's world interests.

Among these critics were the Foreign and Colonial Offices. They complained repeatedly in 1906 and 1907 that earthquakes, revolutions and other troubles had recently occurred overseas, without the navy being present to assist, and urged the need for an adequate 'Imperial police . . . as a safeguard against civil disturbances . . . in the various portions of the Colonial Empire'. Indeed, the manner of the Foreign Office's notes became quite stiff:

> If the number of ships is to be reduced to such an extent that the navy will be unable to give the foreign policy of this country such support in the future as the Foreign Office have felt entitled to expect, and have received in the past, the only possible conclusion will be that the exigencies of British world-wide policy and interests, in the present and immediate future, are being sacrificed to a scheme of concentration for defensive purposes against an attack which is not likely to be made for some years to come.[22]

The Admiralty's private reaction to such criticisms was, predictably enough, one of anger: 'if everybody had everything that was desirable, the Navy Estimates would be a hundred millions!', snorted Fisher to the King. While the specific Foreign Office charges of neglect were contested in a lengthy memorandum which won Cabinet approval, the *general* defence of this concentration policy had already been publicly stated in the Cawdor Memorandum of 1905 for all interested parties (including, one suspects, the Germans) to see:

> The periods of European rest as well as the stable grouping of international interests during the latter part of the last century, had assigned certain degrees of relative importance to our various squadrons . . . So much has this been the case that today people are apt to look on a definite number of ships on any given station as a fixed quantity rather than a strategic exigency.
>
> This idea must be entirely dispelled. Squadrons of varying strength are strategically required in certain waters; but the kaleidoscopic nature of international relations, as well as the variations or new developments in Seapower, not only forbids any permanent allocation of numbers, but in fact points the necessity for periodic redistribution of ships between our Fleets to meet the political requirements of the moment.[23]

In other words, the Admiralty was suggesting, no deployment of the fleet should ever be taken for granted: what was suitable in the 1860s, when Europe was in balance and there existed only the spasmodic French naval threat, was not so after 1900, when the international situation had radically altered. Nevertheless, we can see that behind this logical justification of the new scrapping and redistribution measures lay a deeper and longer-term trend which probably even they did not fully perceive. The post-1900 withdrawal bore no real resemblance to that during the French invasion scares of the mid nineteenth century. This time the redistribution had an air of permanence, and the scrapping policy confirmed this. As two students of this period have noted, 'The gunboat's decline was the logical result of the rising challenge to Britain's status as a world power.'[24]

Despite the obvious necessity for their changes, Fisher and his successors were continually subjected to the criticism that they had abandoned the rest of the globe in their obsession with the German menace. Quite often the protests came from *within* the service and were more emphatically rejected; the complaint of the Commander-in-Chief at the Cape that he had insufficient warships to deal with German vessels on his station in wartime drew the obvious retort from Battenberg, the Director of Naval Intelligence:

> If our position in Africa relative to that of Germany is to be measured by the respective naval forces of the 2 countries in African waters, our squadron should be still further very greatly reduced, as the German squadron is almost a negligible quantity. As a matter of fact it is chiefly the concentration of German seapower in European waters that forces upon us the necessity of acting in a similar fashion.[25]

More formidable critics were soon to appear, however – the Dominions, from whom Britain was attempting to secure increased contributions to the costs of imperial naval defence. Responding to Chamberlain's portrayal at the 1902 Colonial Conference of 'the weary Titan staggering under the too-vast orb of its fate', Australia and New Zealand had increased their payments; more important still, they accepted the Mahanite philosophy of 'one sea and one fleet', and Australia abandoned to the Admiralty its previous say in the movements of auxiliary forces on the Australia Station. Within a few years, though, Dominion nationalism and a growing fear of Japan led to an agitation for local navies, which culminated in the Imperial Defence Conference of 1909. Much against its will, the Admiralty accepted the notion of an Australian force and conceded that 'in defining the conditions under which the naval forces of the Empire should be developed, other considerations than those of strategy alone must be taken into account . . .'[26] Because of the ever-growing German navy, however, the Admiralty soon ignored these promises, despite the frequent complaints of Canberra, Wellington and Ottawa. The argument was never a severe one, but it was a clear indication that the Dominions regarded Britain's promise and capacity to defend them as steadily less satisfactory.

This divergence of view was again evident in the debate over the renewal of the Anglo-Japanese alliance in 1911. London's early euphoria at the results of that arrangement – the defeat of Russia, the ending of the Far Eastern crisis, and the withdrawal of the battleship squadron – was changing to an unease at Japan's future ambitions. After the defeat of Russia and the Anglo-Russian *entente* of 1907, Britain's focus of interest was shifting from the defence of India to the defence of her Pacific empire. The Dominions themselves were far more hostile to Japan, feeling exposed to the 'Yellow Peril'. Moreover, the Americans held the terms of the alliance as revised in 1905 (a *casus belli* if a signatory was attacked by only one other power) to be a distinct threat to themselves, try as the British did to convince Washington that they would never fight against the United States. Despite all these points, however, the alliance was still vital to a British government ever more concerned to have her Far Eastern position protected, whilst concentrating upon Germany's threat to the naval and military balance in Europe; as Grey put it, 'the relation between the Japanese alliance and naval strategy is an intimate one'. With her fleet of eleven battleships and thirty cruisers, Japan dominated the Far East, thereby protecting her ally's interests; but if the alliance was terminated Japan would probably adopt a more aggressive policy and Britain, Grey argued,

> would have to keep – if we are to secure the sea communications between the Far East and Europe, and between the Far East and Australia and New Zealand – a separate fleet in Chinese waters which would be at least equal to a two-Power standard in those waters . . . In the interests of strategy, in the interests of naval expenditure and in the interests of stability, it is essential that the Japanese Alliance should be extended.[27]

To create a two-power fleet in the Far East was impossible, for it would give Germany naval supremacy in the North Sea; nor could the friendship of Japan be allowed to change into enmity. With such arguments the Dominions were persuaded into agreeing to the early renewal of the alliance in 1911. But the whole debate had revealed some ominous signs: of Britain's dependence upon Japan, of the uncertain and negative aspects of the alliance, and of the Royal Navy's inability to protect imperial interests in the Far East and Pacific without losing naval control in European waters. All these were portents of what was to occur two and three decades later in the Orient.

The decision to withdraw from the western hemisphere, the Far East and other distant seas, and the consequent dependence upon the navies of Japan and America in those regions were, though taken reluctantly, always regarded in Whitehall as both sensible and necessary; there was, after all, a grim inevitability in the rise of those two foreign powers, which the British government had long admitted in private. This was not the case with the Mediterranean, however, where British naval might had predominated for centuries, where vital political interests (defence of Egypt, friendship with Italy, independence of Turkey) existed, and through which one of Britain's major trade routes ran. To such sober considerations had been added an intense emotionalism, based upon the prestige factor, the memory of Nelson and a pride in Britain's rise to maritime supremacy. As the influential Viscount Esher was to put it: 'Britain either is or is not one of the Great Powers of the World. Her position in this respect depends solely upon sea-command and sea-command in the Mediterranean.'[28] The vast majority of the 'political' nation agreed that it would be calamitous to allow foreign powers to close 'the windpipe of the Empire'.

It was precisely because the Mediterranean was so highly regarded that the Franco-Russian threat in the 1880s and 1890s had been taken so seriously and that so much political controversy surrounded the debates upon the strength of the fleet.[29] Even then there had been advocates of a 'scuttle' policy, who argued that the Mediterranean would be an uncertain route in wartime, that the vessels at Malta were in grave danger of being pincered by the two enemy navies, and that the logical strategy would be to strengthen Britain's hold at Egypt and Gibraltar, thereby turning those waters into a 'dead sea'; but the government's preference had always been to increase the estimates and to strengthen the fleet at Malta. Yet the situation had become so grave by the mid 1890s that London privately decided that it could no longer assume the responsibility of defending Constantinople and the Straits from a Russian assault: instead, a tighter grip was placed upon Egypt. This tacit abandonment of the traditions of Palmerston and Disraeli, it is worth noting, was based upon the twin argument that British naval power had relatively declined since the mid century, not only *vis-à-vis* the navies of her rivals but also *vis-à-vis* land-based defences. The Admiralty itself, supported by the majority of the Cabinet, had absolutely refused to send the Mediterranean Fleet to Constantinople during the Armenian crisis of 1895, while it could be cut off in the rear by the French; and the Turks had not only cooled to their earlier friendship for Britain, but also had shown a preference for fortifying the Dardanelles whilst neglecting the defences of the Bosphorus, which threw doubt upon their determination to resist the Russians and also gravely prejudiced any British attempt to force the Straits. The latter, warned the Commander-in-Chief, Mediterranean Fleet, as early as 1890, 'would in all probability end in disaster', for warships were less suited than hitherto to engage well-armed forts, a belief the events of 1915 were to justify. This timidity of the Admiralty throughout the 1890s shocked Salisbury, who once sarcastically remarked that their ships must be made of porcelain; but he was realistic enough to agree to the abandonment of Constantinople and to concentrate instead upon Egypt.

Even this revolutionary turn in British foreign and defence policy did not solve the problem: the French and Russian fleets continued to grow, forcing the Admiralty to expand too. After the turn of the century there were often as many as fourteen first-class battleships based on Malta, yet even they were outnumbered and would require support from the Channel Fleet in any crisis. The great change came, as we have seen, in Fisher's reorganization of 1904–5, by which time it had become necessary to take precautionary measures against the German threat. But these steps could not have been taken had not Russia's naval and military strength been eclipsed, and had not Anglo-French relations undergone a remarkable transformation which culminated in their colonial treaty and political *entente*. Had these two powers continued both to increase their navies and to display hostility to Britain, the Admiralty's predicament would have been enormous. Skilful diplomacy, aided by fortuitous circumstances, did more than anything else to solve Britain's strategic dilemma in this period.

As the Anglo-French *entente* steadily flourished in the years following the first Moroccan crisis, and as the Germans continued to increase their battle-fleet, the Admiralty inclined more and more to the idea of withdrawing further vessels from the Mediterranean. Already in late 1906 the fleet there had been reduced again, from eight battleships to six, and the recall of the remainder was postulated in various war plans which were drafted between 1908 and 1911; but since the political implications of such a step were so numerous and grave, one of them being a virtual dependence upon France, this proposal was always combatted fiercely. Even Fisher and the anti-German members of the Foreign Office opposed the notion. What changed this traditional policy was, firstly, the advent of Churchill as First Lord in 1911; more importantly, Tirpitz's supplementary Naval Law of 1912; and finally, the growing strength of the Austro-Hungarian and Italian navies.[80]

Churchill's contribution was his single-minded and fluent advocacy of the need to concentrate against the chief danger, Germany: 'if we win the big battle in the decisive theatre we can put everything straight afterwards' was his line. The German fleet increase offered more food for thought to those unimpressed by Churchill's enthusiasms. Not only did Tirpitz plan the construction of three additional battleships, but he proposed to raise the number of warships in the *active* German fleet from seventeen battleships and four battle-cruisers to twenty-five battleships and eight battle-cruisers. Even to keep pace with the new construction the Admiralty would have to ask for another £3 million for extra warships and personnel, but the prospect of thirty-three German capital ships ready for action just across the North Sea posed a more intractable problem, for the Royal Navy normally maintained only twenty-two capital ships in full commission in home waters – including the six at Gibraltar! Finally, the Austro-Hungarian navy was actively creating a fleet of four Dreadnought-style battleships, while Italy had four such launched and another two under construction; they also possessed nine and eight pre-Dreadnoughts respectively. Against these the six pre-Dreadnoughts at Malta would be decidedly inferior.

The naval crisis of 1912 posed one of the most agonizing dilemmas of all for Britain's statesmen and strategists, symbolizing perhaps more than anything else the way in which the nation's position had declined. Four equally unpleasant courses were open to them:

> to reduce the margin in the North Sea – which naval advisers stated would imperil the country; to abandon the Mediterranean – which would be very injurious; to build a new fleet for the Mediterranean – which would cost £15 to 20 million and could not be ready before 1916; or to make an arrangement with France and leave enough ships in the Mediterranean to give an undoubted superiority.[31]

To cut the North Sea forces was obviously impossible: 'it would be very foolish to lose England in safeguarding Egypt', Churchill argued, and he threatened later to rouse the country on this issue. Nor could a solution be found in building ten extra battleships, although the Admiralty and most navalists favoured it as the only way to preserve Britain's security *and* free hand: the staggering costs would see the Cabinet split in half, the ships would not be ready in time, and it seemed most unlikely that the necessary personnel could be found. To withdraw from the Mediterranean without any provision for Britain's great interests there would equally cause enormous public controversy. The Foreign Office deplored the idea: it would send a wavering Italy back into the Austro-German camp, unsettle Spain, drive Turkey into Germany's arms, and gravely affect Britain's hold upon Egypt. The War Office, too, was alarmed, pointing out that their garrisons at Malta, Cyprus and Egypt were in no position to look after themselves, if maritime supremacy was lost. Moreover, the shock waves of any withdrawal would carry through the Middle East to India: the whole Empire might be endangered. From another angle the Radical–Liberals, who on principle opposed all armaments increases and military alliances, insisted that the danger from Germany was not all that great and that any agreements with France should be avoided, but Churchill pointed to the rising Austro-Hungarian and Italian navies: British influence in the Mediterranean was declining in any case, no matter what Germany did.

Little by little, the choices were whittled down to a naval agreement with the French; such a combination would avoid an enormous rise in naval expenditure, maintain Britain's lead in the North Sea, and preserve her commercial and imperial interests in the Mediterranean and Near East. It would also be a logical extension of the political friendship which had grown up between the two countries since 1904–5, and as such it was advocated by the Foreign Office, the General Staff and those politicians who saw the greatest threat of all in Germany's ability to overrun France and to dominate western and central Europe. Of course, Paris would welcome such a move to strengthen the *entente*; in addition, the French marine had been concentrating its strength in the Mediterranean to the detriment of its Channel and Atlantic station, and was therefore particularly well disposed towards an agreement respecting mutual naval deployments. The British army had already begun staff talks with the French, but the navy, under Fisher's influence, was always more aloof, although the beginnings of discussions were under way; now circumstances would compel it to be far less reserved. 'A definite naval arrangement should be made with France without delay', emphasized Churchill; the army agreed that 'a reliable and effective arrangement with France is . . . essential to the general situation'; and Nicolson, the Foreign Office Permanent Under-Secretary, held this to be 'the cheapest, simplest and safest solution'.

The idea of an agreement provoked fierce opposition, and not only from the Radicals; the Conservative Press railed against the withdrawal from the Mediterranean, McKenna (a former First Lord) argued that 'our colonies and our trade will depend not on British power, but on French goodwill', and Esher urged the King that 'Any attempt to rely upon "Alliances", or the Naval Forces of friendly Powers, is bound to prove illusory.' Furthermore, the French were likely to demand a more definite British commitment to assist militarily against Germany as their price for cooperation, a thought which horrified Radicals and navalists alike. Nevertheless, Nicolson's comment was correct: it *was* the cheapest, safest and simplest solution, at least in the short term – and speed was of the highest importance to the Admiralty, which insisted that a quick solution be found. Already, in March 1912, Churchill had announced a reorganization of the fleets which included the withdrawal of the Atlantic Fleet to home waters, and of the Mediterranean Fleet to Gibraltar. Following meetings of the Cabinet and C.I.D. this was modified in July to the compromise:

> There must always be provided a reasonable margin of superior strength ready and available in Home waters. This is our first requirement. Subject to this we ought to maintain, available for Mediterranean purposes and based on a Malta port, a battle fleet equal to a one-power Mediterranean standard, excluding France.[32]

The jubilation of Esher, McKenna and others at having forced Churchill to keep a battle-fleet in the Mediterranean strong enough to deal with Austria-Hungary was short-lived, however, since the Admiralty quickly interpreted this decision in a manner best suited to itself, stationing only a few battle-cruisers at Malta. More important, the British and French governments agreed to allow the resumption of the talks about naval cooperation which had taken place rather tentatively in the previous year. These negotiations were ultra-delicate, for neither Churchill nor Grey was anxious to assume any binding commitment to France, even though they recognized the threat Germany posed to her; but Paris also had a strong hand to play by offering to protect British interests in the Mediterranean and, in any case (as Poincaré remarked), a Convention which did not provide assistance to each signatory in time of need was 'superfluous'. The result was yet another compromise, whereby, whilst insisting that consultation between staff experts did not constitute any binding political commitment, Grey accepted in November 1912 that in a future crisis both governments should consult together over the possibility of joint measures, taking the contingency plans into account. Consequently, both Admiralties soon arrived at specific agreements covering the disposition of forces and command questions, the essence being that, apart from the small battle-cruiser force at Malta, the British abandoned naval control in the central and western Mediterranean, whilst assuming responsibility for both sides of the Channel.

As 1914 was to show, it was the latter aspect which was the more important; for however much the British might deny a legal obligation to protect France, they had assumed a *moral* one to defend her northern coastline against German attack. Like so many compromises, the agreement was unsatisfactory to both sides. In 1912, however, the question of the withdrawal from the Mediterranean was probably of greater concern in London, simply because of what it implied: the decline of Britain's world position. We should let Esher, the most constant critic of this arrangement, have his gloomy last word here:

> It means an alliance with France under the cover of 'conversations', and conscription . . . Adieu to the sea command of Great Britain until after the next war. Perhaps then, for ever. Rome had to call in the foreigner to help her when the time of her decadence approached. I shall, like Candide, cultivate my garden.[33]

It is easy to sympathize with Esher's point of view. Within a few years, or so it seemed, Britain had withdrawn from one position after another, and there appeared little prospect of the situation being restored in the future; steadily, inexorably, the islanders were having to retrace their steps and to rely upon others. Yet Esher's own solution of vast increases in naval expenditure, was clearly out of touch with the reality of domestic politics, where Britain was suffering from a host of troubles – strikes, suffragettes, constitutional crisis, Ireland – which required urgent attention. Since the armament expenditure *per capita* in Britain since 1900 had been in excess of that of any other great power, swingeing increases in taxation for defence purposes could have possibly provoked further disturbances and the collapse of the Liberal government, followed in turn by a right-wing reaction and then by some form of revolution.[34] And even if the government had been united and willing enough to run this risk, it was uncertain whether the country would have had the financial and industrial might to stay ahead of the rising young world powers indefinitely. Even Fisher, arch-navalist though he was, was willing to admit that 'we cannot have everything or be strong everywhere'.[35]

Nevertheless, while a steady withdrawal can be seen to be inevitable because of world-wide developments, there is no doubt that one particular factor, the German menace, greatly accelerated the trend; only that could have seen the British pull out of the Mediterranean so swiftly. In a sense, therefore, Tirpitz must take joint honours with Fisher as being the man who had contributed most to the ending of Pax Britannica. From about 1902 onwards Germany became the focal point of British foreign and defence policy, a magnet, drawing the scattered far-away squadrons back into the North Sea, whence they had emerged centuries earlier to dominate the world's oceans. This Anglo-German naval race, described by Professor Marder as 'the Ariadne's thread' of British naval policy in these years, was characterized by one escalation of building programme after another, one scare after another, one round of failed negotiations after

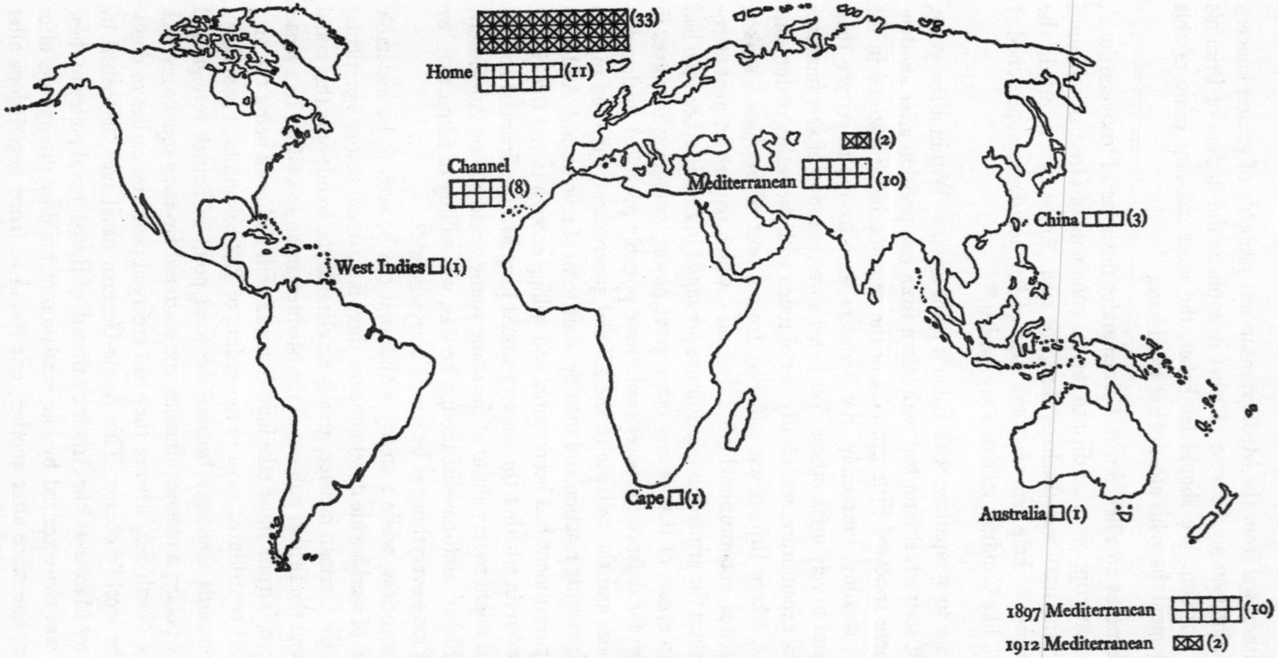

Map 8. Distribution of British capital ships in commission in 1897 and 1912
(Capital ship numbers follow name of station)

another, reaching a stage so serious that (ironically enough) the French began to worry that they would be dragged into a European war on Britain's account. The obsession with the German threat led ultimately to another reversal of traditional policy – the abandonment of the Two-Power Standard. This decision had originally been taken in private by the Admiralty in 1909, when it was recognized that to build against both Germany and the United States (as the two next largest) was financially impossible and made little sense in terms of foreign policy; but by 1912, following the failure of the Haldane Mission, Churchill was brutally frank in stating to Parliament that Britain was building against one nation only – Germany. His admission that the Admiralty intended to preserve a 60 per cent superiority in capital ships drew applause from most of the country but did nothing to check the German programme.[36] By the autumn of 1914 the British battle-fleet totalled thirty-one modern capital ships (with another sixteen building) and thirty-nine pre-Dreadnoughts. It was a force of unequalled size and strength, yet virtually all these vessels were being prepared for the expected Armageddon in the North Sea: the rest of the world hardly mattered, in naval terms at least. Tirpitz's calculation that Britain would not dare to abandon her many overseas interests to concentrate in the North Sea had thus proved to be quite mistaken – but few of the statesmen in London felt cause to rejoice over it.

Yet this reduction in Britain's world-wide naval role was perhaps not as serious in its consequences as the far greater revolution in her defence policy after 1905 – the virtual abandonment of that strategical isolation from the continent which had become so entrenched since 1815 that it was widely regarded as both natural and eternal. Because of a new and unexpected challenge to the European equilibrium, however, the old eighteenth-century debate between the 'maritime' and 'continental' schools of strategy now broke out again. And the result, according to a more modern adherent of the former school, was that by 1914 the British government had made the navy 'a subsidiary weapon, and grasped the glittering sword of Continental manufacture' by assuming an ever-greater commitment to engage in a military campaign in Europe.[37]

It was not the case, of course, that Whitehall deliberately planned such an astonishing change in its now traditional policy – in fact, most statesmen and their advisers loathed the prospect of being embroiled in a continental conflict – but circumstances gradually whittled down Britain's freedom of action until it appeared almost inevitable that an expeditionary force should be dispatched across the Channel. The root of the problem, which the British had not needed to face for over a century, was that they could not make their homeland secure by naval measures alone: the balance of power in Europe was also important. Yet that balance, in equilibrium since the fall of Napoleon was collapsing again as a united and powerful Germany assumed the preponderance to which her enormous industrial strength and population entitled her;[38] and this was accentuated by the sudden collapse of Russian military might in 1905. The age-old lesson had to be painfully learnt again:

> basically our security remains involved with that of our continental neighbours: for the dominance of the European land-mass by an alien and hostile power would make almost impossible the maintenance of our national independence, to say nothing of our capacity to maintain a defensive system to protect any extra-European interests we may retain.[39]

To contemporaries the German army was judged to be so superior to the French in numbers, efficiency, logistical support and morale that the result of any war between the two was hardly in question; and the indications were that Berlin might not be satisfied with overrunning France alone, but might conquer Belgium and the Netherlands on the way. Even as early as 1875 the British government had shown alarm at the possibility of a further German strike at France, and rumours of a war which might also involve Belgium's neutrality arose again in the 1880s. The Franco-Russian alliance, and the interest of the European powers in overseas affairs, then stabilized the situation for a further fifteen years; but after the first Moroccan crisis this prospect could no longer be ignored. Moreover, Germany was no longer friendly but antagonistic to Britain, no longer in the steady hands of Bismarck but controlled by the impulsive and immature Kaiser Wilhelm II, and no longer absorbed by Europe but quite clearly determined to be a world power and to create an enormous fleet to challenge the British. In view of Germany's great strength, her aggressiveness was deeply disturbing to Whitehall. As Sir Eyre Crowe of the Foreign Office put it: 'The building of the German fleet is but one of the symptoms of the disease. It is the political ambitions of the German Government and nation which are the source of the mischief.' And Esher predicted: 'within measurable distance there looms a titanic struggle between Germany and Europe for mastery. The years 1793–1815 will be repeated, only Germany, not France, will be trying for European domination.' All these fears were only confirmed by the constant efforts of the German Foreign Ministry to persuade Britain to declare itself neutral in any future Franco-German war – which was indignantly seen in London as giving a *carte blanche* for aggression.

The first reaction of the British to the German threat had chiefly been a naval one; few could contest Grey's simple statement that 'If the German Fleet ever becomes superior to ours, the German Army can conquer this country', accepting thereby the need for naval increases to prevent such an event. But was this response going to be sufficient? What would happen if Germany overran the whole of western Europe or (a likely possibility if Britain ignored the European situation) turned France and the Low Countries into political appendages? The answers were chilling to any Briton who pondered upon them: firstly, such an agglomeration of industrial strength would probably enable Germany to outbuild the British, whatever the efforts of the latter; and secondly, instead of being restricted to the North Sea, the High Seas Fleet could be based upon the harbours of Brest and Cherbourg, while German torpedo-boats closed the Channel – the Mediterranean, of course, would have to be abandoned in the face of the Franco–Italo–Austrian forces. Slowly, reluctantly, men began to realize that Britain's naval position and the balance of power in Europe were inextricably linked, though Radicals and imperialists continued to deny this.[40] Grey made the connection clear in his important statement of 1912 to the C.I.D.:

> if a European conflict, not of our making, arose, in which it was quite clear that the struggle was one for supremacy in Europe, in fact, that you got back to a situation something like that in the old Napoleonic days, then . . . our concern in seeing that there did not arise a supremacy in Europe which entailed a combination that would deprive us of the command of the sea would be such that we might have to take part in that European war. That is why the naval position underlies our European policy . . .[41]

On reading Grey's argument, one cannot help being reminded of the year 1940, when Britain was indeed alone to face a continent dominated by Berlin, and the threat of German control of the French fleet.

But how was Britain to 'take part in that European war' when she lacked any worthwhile military force? For almost a century after Waterloo the country had preferred to maintain minimal numbers of troops: in 1897, for example, the Regular Army totalled some 212,000 men which had to be deployed on a variety of duties, and the lack of any form of conscription prevented it from being rapidly expanded. There were some reserves, it was true, together with a miscellaneous assortment of Militia, Yeomanry and Volunteers, but the whole system revealed an amateurish approach and a traditional distrust of militarism which contrasted sharply with continental practice, where governments could swiftly field well-trained and well-equipped armies of millions; even Switzerland had a larger army than Britain.[42] Yet, paradoxically, the British army budget was very high, chiefly due to voluntary recruitment. For a European and world power with so many interests to defend, these forces seemed totally inadequate to foreigners. The Kaiser, proud commander of many army corps, could only shake his head in disgust in 1900:

> The present calamitous war with the tiny Transvaal clearly shows that the simple one-sided cherishing of naval forces is insufficient for a country with such great colonial possessions. The shabbily treated army, which reveals itself now as being little different from that in the late eighteenth and early nineteenth centuries, is totally unsuited for that greater power position on land which is occasionally necessary for the defence of widespread colonial territories.[43]

The strategic justification for this weakness was, of course, that the British government had no wish to be considered a great military power, and especially a European military power. According to the Stanhope Memorandum of 1891 the duties of the army had been defined in descending order as: the defence of the United Kingdom; the defence of India; and the defence of other colonies, which involved holding in preparation two army corps for overseas operations. There was no thought of intervention in Europe, the memo specifying that 'it will be distinctly understood that the probability of the employment of an Army Corps in the field in any European war is sufficiently improbable to make it the primary duty of the military authorities to organize our forces efficiently for the defence of this country'.[44] Even for these smaller tasks, Britain's armed forces were inadequate by themselves: the tropical colonies were protected by sea power, and their garrisons employed more for internal 'pacification'; Canada, as we have seen, was indefensible against the only power which might threaten it; the defence of India against Russian assault was a problem which dominated British planners and statesmen for decades – it virtually obsessed a balanced mind like Balfour's – simply because her forces there were too few; and home defence involved the army in a prolonged inter-service squabble over the navy's capability to defeat an invasion force.

The Boer War of 1899–1902 and the diplomatic revolution of 1904–7 brought all this to an end. The war itself led to the most drastic and thorough-going reforms the army had experienced, at the end of which it might still have been small, but it was at least becoming more professional. (Moreover, conscription was being urged by Roberts, Milner and others.) At the same time the navy emerged victor in the invasion debate, which had the effect of freeing the army for operations elsewhere, something that the General Staff warmly welcomed. At first the army thought only in imperial terms, of possessing a larger expeditionary force to send out to India; but the defeat of Russia by Japan and the beginnings of the Anglo-Russian conversations for an *entente* in Asia threw this policy in doubt also. In addition, some army planners had been considering since 1903 what they might do in the event of a war with Germany, envisaging at that stage amphibious operations along the enemy's coast. The first Moroccan crisis and the threat of a German attack upon France decisively changed these plans which had been vague, ineffective and dependent upon close naval support. Now it was becoming clear that the only effective military way of aiding France would be to send an army across the Channel, the only trouble being that the existing expeditionary force was not likely to be of much assistance. Even the Chancellor of the Exchequer, Austen Chamberlain, could see that:

> England can no longer give a European ally money, or find soldiers on the continent. A continental ally wants help in men, and that help at once. If we had 250,000 men or 300,000 men fully trained and able to move at short notice, an open alliance with us would be an absolute protection and a sure guarantee of peace . . . But France might well hesitate to proclaim, as it were offensively, a solidarity with us, and bring upon herself a war, in which assuming that we supported her, we could not effectively restore the balance in point of numbers, already weighed down by an excess of 200,000 men on the German side.[45]

His concluding remark brings us back to an earlier point: if France, already dismayed at the collapse of her Russian ally, could not rely upon substantial British military support, then she might in despair become a political satellite of Germany. This very possibility gave Grey and the Foreign Office constant nightmares in later years; only if Britain supported France would she herself escape isolation and forestall a calamitous future combination against her. But in all these calculations the Royal Navy would be bound to play only a subsidiary role, for to rely upon the traditional naval strategy would not only be too late to save France, but it might also provoke Paris to be suspicious of 'perfidious Albion'.

The crisis period of late 1905 to early 1906 must be regarded as one of the most decisive in British history, therefore. Grey's steady diplomatic support for France and especially his warning to Germany of January 3 1906, that British opinion might make it impossible to stay out of a Franco-German war, marked a real revolution in foreign policy: indeed, this event lays far greater claim to being regarded as the end of 'splendid isolation' than does the signing of the Anglo-Japanese alliance. Coinciding with this warning, moreover, was the decision taken by part of the Cabinet to allow the continuance of those unofficial talks begun a month earlier between British and French military experts over the ways in which London could offer assistance in time of war. It was stressed then, and was repeatedly emphasized later, that these technical discussions carried with them no political obligation: yet it was also true that, in creating a French attitude of looking to Britain, they had established a subtler form of obligation, a moral one. And, as might be expected, the military experts soon arrived at the conclusion that the only useful form of British help in wartime would be the dispatch of an expeditionary army to fight alongside their ally. Even if the extent of Britain's commitment was still debatable, the strategical possibilities open to her were being swiftly narrowed down.

And what of the navy? It is one of the most astonishing aspects of this whole affair that the so-called *Senior* Service, which only a short time earlier had enjoyed a clear ascendancy over the discredited army, both lost its superior position and had its isolationist policy increasingly circumscribed after 1906.[46] One cannot avoid the conclusion that this was to a large extent the fault of Fisher and his successors: energetic and far-sighted though the First Sea Lord was in so many ways, he was no great strategist and had crushed all moves to create an effective naval staff. The Admiralty was simply too vague over this crucial issue – Fisher going so far as to say that no one would know his war plans until *Der Tag* itself – to convince others that it was serious, and it chose to ignore the C.I.D., whose very task it was to attempt to coordinate divergent policies; Fisher also declined to enter into serious talks with the French naval authorities. By so doing he lost both status and credibility. Even when the Admiralty made noises about joint operations, their proposals were impracticable: witness their various schemes to land and hold the German coast or offshore islands with an expeditionary force, blithely disregarding navigational hazards, logistical problems, and the recent advances in mines and submarines, not to mention the fact that the small forces involved would probably be wiped out without them having any effect whatsoever upon the main theatre.[47] The cold facts of the situation pointed to the need to maintain the independence of France and the Low Countries – but that also implied that the navy's chief role would be to preserve intact communications across the Channel, a bitter pill for this proud service to swallow. Thus, while the military talks proceeded and ineluctably assumed a greater significance, the navy held aloof, supported by all those in the government who abhorred any idea of a continental commitment: Radicals, navalists, traditionalists, economy-minded politicians, etc. The political balance was stacked high against the army, for it had only the support of the Germanophobes in the Foreign Office and certain Conservative newspapers; but the strategic logic was with the General Staff.

The decisive battle was fought and won by the army at the time of the second Moroccan crisis. Even three years earlier, in October 1908, a sub-committee of the C.I.D. had examined the various schemes of both services and concluded that:

> in the initial stages of a war between France and Germany, in which the British Government decided to support France, the plan to which preference is given by the General Staff is a valuable one, and the General Staff should accordingly work out all the necessary details.[48]

Needless to say, the General Staff went to work with a will, while the Admiralty retired in a huff and obstructed all efforts at joint planning for the transport of the expeditionary force to the continent. The result was that at the famous C.I.D. meeting of 23 August 1911, General Sir Henry Wilson was able to convince his listeners of the good sense of the army's plan, while Admiral Wilson (Fisher's successor) appeared to offer dangerous and ill-thought-out schemes. No firm conclusions were arrived at by the C.I.D., yet in another way everything was settled. It was as a direct result of the Admiralty's poor performance that the young Winston Churchill was installed in McKenna's place as First Lord – to restore the Cabinet's confidence in the navy's ability to act decisively in times of crisis, and, more importantly, to bring it into line with general strategical policy. For, as Hankey, the omni-competent Secretary to the C.I.D., noted afterwards,

> From that time onwards there was never any doubt what would be the Grand Strategy in the event of our being drawn into a continental war in support of France. Unquestionably the Expeditionary Force, or the greater part of it, would have been sent to France as it actually was in 1914.[49]

This is not to say that the opponents of the 'balance-of-power' theory ceased their strivings – in fact, Grey's foreign policy came under the heaviest pressure ever in the following year – but that the overall strategy itself, *if Britain intervened*, had been decided upon. The argument in the years 1912–14 focused upon *whether* France should be supported, not *how* it should be supported, which is a very important distinction. No doubt the radicals and the arch-navalists and imperialists, who for differing reasons opposed a continental entanglement, would have striven with even greater energy against the C.I.D.'s decision and its grave implications, had they known of it: but they did not. Their own arguments against participation in a European war, of morality and of Britain's traditional policy, were overwhelmed in 1914 by equally cogent counter-arguments: the morality of defending 'poor little Belgium' against 'Prussian militarism', the need to honour the moral obligation to France (at last openly admitted by Grey to exist), and the importance, understood by every British statesman since Elizabethan times, of preventing a powerful hostile state from gaining control of the Low Countries. Critics at the time and afterwards may have detected in Britain's ultimatum to Germany of 4 August 1914 an abandonment of their country's traditional policy; but one feels that those Britons who had faced the challenges of Philip of Spain, Louis XIV and Napoleon in preceding centuries would have given their full approval. Francis Bacon's fine reasoning, 'He that commands the Sea is at great liberty, and may take as much and as little of the Warre as he will', was judged in 1914 to be inadequate.

While it is hardly necessary to remind the reader that Britain's decision to oppose Germany *on land* was regarded then and later as a disastrous one, flouting the benefits that usually accrued from the traditional sea-based, economic strategy, it would also be false to assume that Grey, Haldane and their camp enjoyed that benefit of hindsight which has allowed historians to claim that:

> The new war policy, introduced in 1905, could be implemented only at enormous cost, bleeding the nation white, destroying its wealth, severely endangering its political and economic influence throughout the world, and finally transforming its social structure almost completely.[50]

Clearly no statesman of any of the warring nations would have provoked or entered this conflict, if he had known of such dire consequences. In fact, Grey, sharing beliefs common at the time, stated in his great Commons speech of 3 August 1914, that 'if we are engaged in war, we shall suffer but little more than we shall suffer even if we stand aside'. A small expeditionary force, not a large army with its attendant evil of conscription, was the extent of the Liberal government's commitment. Only Henry Wilson in those pre-war years appears to have appreciated the enormity of the growing concern with Europe: in 1910, when commenting upon the lack of interest British officers displayed in the topography of Belgium, he suggested that 'most of them may be buried there before they are much older'.[51] Yet even this prediction, sobering though it was, does not seem to have halted his own efforts. His mind was set, and he converted others to his point of view in the years following. There was no other way. As Kitchener was to put it in 1915: 'Unfortunately we have to make war as we must and not as we should like to.'

Between the Spithead Review of 1897 and the declaration of war upon Germany in 1914, Britain's foreign, naval and military policies had undergone enormous changes, all of which formed part of an even greater development: the steady decline of her world-wide predominance and the ending of the age of Pax Britannica, consequent upon the loss of her early economic lead and the industrialization of the other powers. Connected with this, too, was the relative decline of sea-power *vis-à-vis* land-power as the 'Columbian era' drew to a close. Yet, if the underlying reasons are known, there is no denying that the pace of this withdrawal into the North Sea was remarkably swift. At first, this was due to what one might call local pressure, the inability to oppose rising naval powers in their home waters, when there were so many other important British interests elsewhere; but after the turn of the century the compelling need was to neutralize the new threat arising near to Britain's own waters, to look at one's moat. It would be a somewhat futile intellectual exercise to analyse the 'pull' and 'push' factors any further: both were part of the same broad trend. So, too, in a more indirect way, was the gradual military commitment to France, for the alternatives to this strategy were postulated upon assumptions which had been quite overtaken by events. The only question remaining was, would this widespread and bloody continental conflict, if fought to a victorious conclusion, enable the British to return afterwards to their former habits and policies, secure in the knowledge that the great threat from Germany had been beaten off; or would it, as a few percipient commentators suspected, so embroil and exhaust them that they would in the future keep their world-wide Empire, with its bases and trade and raw materials, chiefly upon the sufferance or temporary weakness of others?

CHAPTER NINE

Stalemate and Strain (1914–18)

Because the world position of Britain was in a sense more of a *tour de force* than that of her rivals, because it depended on so unique a set of circumstances and the deployment of so wide a range of skills, the effect of the First World War upon Britain was perhaps the greatest, though it took longest to show itself. Britain in 1914, by all the rules of politics, took the right decisions; but this did not and perhaps could not do more than postpone the dissolution of Britain's empire and the end of her world position . . .

Max Beloff, *Imperial Sunset*,
vol. 1, *Britain's Liberal Empire 1897–1921* (London, 1969), p. 180.

If there is one image which the First World War has bequeathed to posterity, it is that of trench warfare – of millions of men engaged for years in a futile struggle through the mud to achieve niggling gains at immense cost, bleeding white the populations and resources of the combatant nations in the process. It was, contrary to the expectations of 1914, a war in which mobility was replaced by stalemate, in which the defence was normally superior to the attack, and in which the sheer number of men, machines and munitions was the ultimate deciding factor. Yet, if the effects of this prolonged conflict were deemed to be disastrous for the continental powers, they were even more so for Britain. The former, after all, had had little choice in the matter, once the war was begun; bordered as they all were by powerful neighbours, they knew that a full-scale European war would mean immense strain and suffering, even if the most pessimistic pre-war observer did not anticipate the full horrors that were to come. But for Britain, so it was argued by many at the time and afterwards, the war was especially cruel and damaging. Her people were prepared neither for the shock of total war, nor for the mobilization of the economy by the State, the conscription of millions of men for military service, and the dreadful losses on the western front. And why indeed should they have been? Britain, thanks to her insular position, *was* free to avoid the futile stalemated bloodbath of Flanders and to adopt her traditional economic, peripheral, maritime-based strategy.

The political and especially the military arguments against this assumption that Britain had a totally free hand, and that she could enjoy full national security irrespective of what happened in Europe, have been examined already in the previous chapter and require no extensive repetition here: in plain terms, she could not run the risk of a German domination of west-central Europe, with all its possible consequences. Nevertheless, the critics were correct in pointing out that a large-scale military commitment to Europe was a great break with the nineteenth-century traditions of strategy, irrespective of the fact that this change had been implicit since the political *entente* with the French of 1904–5. In a sense, therefore, the meeting of the War Council on 5 August 1914, to decide upon British war strategy, was as important as the government's decision a few days earlier to support France and Belgium against German aggression; for it was at this meeting that the political leaders and their strategic experts overwhelmingly voted for the dispatch of the Expeditionary Force to the continent, a decision the full Cabinet endorsed on the following day.[1] In both cases the fact that the army was organized almost solely for this particular end was a crucial consideration. As Professor Williamson has concluded,

> The staff talks, which had bestowed the ability to intervene upon the Asquith Cabinet, also dictated the contours of that intervention. In August 1914 the British government, no less than its French and German counterparts, was committed to a "plan".[2]

Once this step had been taken, of course, it was almost impossible to reverse it. A continental commitment, as the critics had always warned, was quick to take roots and even quicker to escalate: defending France and Belgium with five or six divisions made less sense, in terms of strict military logic, than the mobilization and dispatch of fifteen or twenty-five or more divisions, at which stage the prospects of victory and a way out of the stalemate temptingly beckoned. After the Battle of Ypres this large-scale build-up developed in earnest. Implicit in such army expansion, however, was the necessity for compulsory national service. At first the Cabinet baulked at this drastic abandonment of one of the most sacred

Liberal principles and preferred to rely instead upon voluntary recruitment, which was a great if somewhat disorganized success. In January 1916, however, this flood of recruits had dried up and military service was introduced for all unmarried men between the ages of eighteen and forty-one. Yet by the end of that year, following the half million British casualties suffered in the bloody maw of the Somme, the generals were demanding a further 940,000 men for future campaigns and the raising of the upper age limit to sixty. These developments, coupled with Lloyd George's accession to the Premiership on 7 December were dramatic enough in themselves but they may be said to have symbolized something far greater: the introduction of organized total war, government controls, a belief in the 'knock-out' blow as opposed to a more economic and selective offensive strategy, and the collapse of those liberal concepts of individual and State action which had been so much a part of the self-confident age of Palmerston and 'Pax Britannica'.[3]

As the nation's habits became more 'continental', so the role and importance of the navy was bound to decrease relatively. This, too, had been anticipated in the pre-war years, but the onset of the European conflict confirmed the trend. The Admiralty under Churchill knew its place. On 31 July 1914 the First (Grand) Fleet assumed its battle stations at Scapa Flow and other Scottish bases. At the War Council meeting of 5 August, the navy put forward no proposals for amphibious assaults upon Germany, nor did it object to the dispatch of the Expeditionary Force. No doubt the admirals, like virtually everyone else except Henry Wilson, had little idea of the way in which Britain's military contribution on the western front would escalate; but they had already admitted that the primacy of combating German aggression was in the army's hands.

Nevertheless, the navy was still confident that it would contribute decisively to the defeat of Germany. In the first place it expected to meet and overwhelm the High Seas Fleet in some second and even greater Trafalgar – that Armageddon in the North Sea for which Fisher and his successors had been training the service for a full decade; it also planned to carry out commerce warfare and to exert an ever-increasing pressure upon the enemy through the time-honoured policy of the blockade; and, finally, there were still a few who followed Fisher in advocating amphibious operations along the German North Sea or Baltic coastlines in order to divert the enemy's troops from the main theatre. In all these aims the Admiralty was to be disappointed. The blockade policy had some partial success: the other two were complete miscalculations.

It is easy in retrospect to understand why the decisive surface battle in the North Sea never took place. Britain's geographical position *vis-à-vis*

Germany was of great importance here; this was, without doubt, Britain's 'number one naval asset'[4] and one which is clear from a glance at the map. Twelve years earlier Mahan had pointed out the lesson for the German navy:

> For all communities east of the Straits of Dover it remains true that in war commerce is paralysed and all the resultant consequences of impaired national strength entailed, unless decisive control of the North Sea is established. That effected, there is security for commerce by the northern passage; but this alone is mere defence. Offence, exerted anywhere on the globe, requires a surplusage of force, over that required to hold the North Sea, sufficient to extend and maintain itself west of the British Islands . . . This is Germany's initial disadvantage of position, to be overcome only by adequate superiority of numbers . . .[5]

The importance of the geographical setting for an understanding of the Admiralty's policy in the two world wars which Britain waged against Germany in this century cannot be exaggerated. The situation would have been completely different if the war had been against France or Spain, where a wide blockade strategy was far more difficult and where the many risks attendant upon a close blockade would have had to have been run instead. In 1914–18 and again in 1939–40, however, Britain could luxuriate in this great geographical advantage *vis-à-vis* Germany. As a consequence, it is worth suggesting, the extent of Britain's naval decline was partly concealed during the first half of the twentieth century. Few saw how great a role geography played in the checking of the German challenge.

For, to Berlin's regret, that 'surplusage of force' could never be established, especially since the lion's share of Germany's defence budget went to the army. At the beginning of the First World War the British Admiralty stationed twenty-one dreadnoughts, eight pre-dreadnoughts and four battle-cruisers at Scapa Flow to hold the northern exit, and nineteen pre-dreadnoughts at Portland to hold the southern one: the High Seas Fleet, in contrast, could only field thirteen dreadnoughts, sixteen pre-dreadnoughts and five battle-cruisers. A *sortie* into the Atlantic via the northern route, logistically near-impossible and strategically dubious in any case, would almost certainly lead to a battle against overwhelming odds. Yet even a thrust down the Channel would encounter heavy opposition and most probably lead to the High Seas Fleet being cut off from behind by the Grand Fleet. Geographically, logistically and numerically, Germany's position was decidedly inferior – and as the war developed the numerical imbalance tilted even further in Britain's direction.[6]

The obvious conclusion to be drawn from this situation, as Professor Marder has noted, was 'that Britain's principal strategical aims at sea, offensive and defensive, could be met by keeping the two holes to the north and south blocked'.[7] She could, if she so wished, simply stand on the defensive, exerting pressure upon Germany's economy through the time-honoured expedient of the blockade, protecting her own overseas trade by these locks upon the North Sea exits and allowing the Dominions to overrun the German colonies and to send reinforcements to Europe. If the High Seas Fleet chose to engage in battle, it would be heavily outnumbered and speedily overwhelmed; but if it did not come out, the victory was Britain's anyway. A stalemate in the North Sea was the most secure strategy imaginable for Britain, since she simply could not lose the surface naval war by it.

Neither the British public, led by the Press to expect great deeds from the navy, nor the service itself, which had for years been preparing for *Der Tag*, were prepared to accept such a tame policy, however. Just why the latter was so convinced that the High Seas Fleet would emerge willingly to give battle now appears quite puzzling. The numerical odds against Germany were well known, as was the Kaiser's great fear of his precious warships being destroyed. In addition to the opposition of the 'All-Highest' to a reckless strategy, there was the pressure from German statesmen to retain the fleet intact as a political bargaining counter. Only if the Royal Navy was foolish enough to rush into the Heligoland Bight, where it could first of all be engaged by submarines and torpedo-boats, and had to steam through unknown minefields, was it likely that Germany's naval leaders would consider a full-scale battle; otherwise, the High Seas Fleet had to live in the hope of surprising and sinking a part of the Grand Fleet.

Given this German insistence that they would only fight a full fleet battle 'under favourable circumstances',[8] the onus for provoking such an engagement clearly lay on British shoulders. But what chance was there that the Admiralty would permit the Grand Fleet to steam recklessly into the enemy's coastal waters? No doubt the officers and crews were itching for action, but there were other factors at work which pointed in the direction of caution. The new developments of the mine, the torpedo and the submarine, mentioned in an earlier chapter, had had a decisive effect upon Britain's traditional strategy of the close blockade by 1914. Though Admiral Wilson might talk of a strict surveillance of, or even of attacks upon, enemy bases, his successors perceived the stupidity of such an attitude under the altered circumstances. Steam-driven warships required frequent withdrawals for coaling, during which time the Germans might strike; swiftly-laid minefields could decimate an unsuspecting battle-fleet; long-range coastal ordnance could do severe damage to even the strongest warships; and submarines and torpedo-boats, operating in waters they knew intimately, could pick off the larger blockading craft until a balance of forces was achieved (which was precisely the German strategy). As the Royal Navy could see, it would itself be on the defensive as soon as it assumed a close blockading position. Hence the interim decision of 1908 to keep the battle-fleet not less than 170 miles away from the German coast, relying upon cruisers for reconnaissance; and the later (1912), fairly inevitable, acknowledgement that the distant blockade would be enough to retain command of the sea, whilst a method was devised of tempting the High Seas Fleet into giving battle. Geography again played a role by offering the Royal Navy a very favourable opportunity of retreating from what had become an untenable position, without abandoning any strategical advantages.

The result, of course, was that a strategic stalemate existed in the North Sea: each side would only risk a fleet action on terms of its own choosing, which naturally disadvantaged the enemy – and caused him to decline an engagement. Only upon a few occasions during the whole course of the First World War was this mutual insistence upon 'safety first' to be abandoned – and then usually by the Germans, who had everything to lose and nothing to gain by a maritime stalemate.

The greatest effect upon the British side had been wrought by the advent of the submarine. It is true that the possibilities of this new weapon had not gone unrecognized in the pre-war years: indeed, even before he had created the *Dreadnought*, Fisher had warned of the 'immense impending revolution which the submarines will effect as offensive weapons of war'. Balfour had appealed to the effectiveness of submarine defences when seeking to bring the invasion debate to a close in 1905, and this same consideration had led to the abandonment of the early Admiralty plans for amphibious operations along the German coast. Yet, with the exception of Sir Percy Scott and a few naval radicals, few in either the British or German navies saw the submarine as anything more than an undersea coastal defence vessel: only the launching of the longer-range ones in the immediate pre-war years transformed the situation. In July 1914 General French gloomily concluded that the English Channel would lose its maritime character as a defence line due to the advent of submarines and aircraft, which could not be so easily checked.[9] To navalists this was rank heresy, yet as soon as war broke out they too began to fear for the safety of their battleships, and Jellicoe, the able Commander-in-Chief of the Grand Fleet, became so concerned at the lack of adequate protection at his bases that in the early months of the war he went so far as to base his dreadnoughts on Loch Ewe; this was admittedly out of range of existing enemy submarines, but also so far distant from the southern North Sea that the High Seas Fleet could have disrupted the cross-Channel line of communications had Berlin known of this. Such fears on the British side were only confirmed by the easy sinking of the armoured cruisers *Cressy*, *Hogue* and *Aboukir* on 22 September 1914 by one U-boat. A whole host of escorting destroyers became the *conditio sine qua non* for a Grand Fleet sweep into the North Sea; and even then Jellicoe remained jittery. Small wonder that Admiral Wilson had earlier declared that this new weapon was 'underhand, unfair, and Damned unEnglish!' But it was Balfour who drew the obvious conclusion, when he wrote that the North Sea was 'neither commanded by the British Fleet nor by the German Fleet, it is the joint occupation by (*sic*) the submarines of both countries . . .'[10] Already the vast pre-war expenditure upon the battle-fleets was made to look absurd, as was the Mahanite insistence upon the primacy of the capital ship and the decisive naval battle.

While the British grew more wary of stationing valuable warships in the North Sea out of fear of the U-boats, the Germans did the same out of a fear of being overwhelmed by superior surface forces. On 28 August 1914 Beatty's battle-cruisers penetrated into the Heligoland Bight to cover lighter forces which had got into trouble; the sinking there of three German cruisers and one destroyer at no loss to themselves, which was received with euphoria in Britain, provoked the Kaiser to order even tighter restrictions upon the use of his fleet. Worse still was to follow for Wilhelm on 24 January 1915, when Beatty's force put to flight Hipper's battle-cruisers at the Dogger Bank, sinking the *Blücher* in the process. In both cases glaring faults had been revealed in British warships, organization and leadership, but much of this was ignored or only slowly made good in the general jubilation. For the Germans, however, these were devastating blows to morale, confirming the Kaiser's worst fears and discrediting the navy in the public's eyes. Admiral von Ingenohl, criticized for not having supported Hipper with the battle-fleet, was replaced as Commander-in-Chief High Seas Fleet, by Admiral von Pohl, who was in fact even less adventurous. In an age when technical innovations were restricting the movement of the battle-fleets and where numbers were apparently of greater importance than boldness and strategic imagination, it is clear that even Nelson might have been cramped; but it still remains to be said that the German naval leadership during the twelve months after the Dogger Bank battle was limp and ineffective. Five small sorties into the North Sea were made by Pohl's ships that year but as none of them went far past Borkum or Heligoland there was no chance of a conflict with the Grand Fleet.

This trend against a bold strategy on both sides was merely brought to a head by the Battle of Jutland in the following year. The story of this most famous – and only real full-scale – fleet encounter of the First World War is well known. Under the bolder leadership of Admiral Scheer, the High Seas Fleet sortied on 31 May 1916, and met up with Beatty's battle-cruisers, punishing them heavily before Jellicoe's main fleet arrived to turn the tables. After forcing the British battle-fleet to turn away, by the desperate expedient of a massed torpedo attack by his smaller vessels, Scheer then eluded his powerful foe and returned home by a circuitous route to receive a rapturous reception from a grateful nation. In terms of men and major warships lost (6,097 men, three battle-cruisers and three armoured cruisers of the Grand Fleet; 2,551 men, one pre-dreadnought and one battle-cruiser of the High Seas Fleet), the German navy felt entitled to claim a major victory. In retrospect it can be seen that this boast, based as it was upon purely material considerations, was both misleading and irrelevant. The German aim throughout these years had been to reduce the crushing superiority of the Grand Fleet so as to have a chance to gain command of the sea: yet within twelve hours of returning to harbour Jellicoe could report twenty-six dreadnoughts and six battle-cruisers ready for action. Scheer, greatly chastened by his narrow escape and with four dreadnoughts and all his battle-cruisers badly damaged, was numerically in a far weaker position than beforehand. The North Sea stalemate was again confirmed, and the whole situation was aptly summed up by a New York newspaper, which announced: 'The German Fleet has assaulted its jailor but it is still in jail.'[11] It is one of the ironies of naval history that Scheer's final report upon the Jutland battle plainly advised the Kaiser that Germany could not win the surface war in the North Sea against Britain:

> there can be no doubt that even the successful outcome of a Fleet action in this war will not force England to make peace. The disadvantages of our military-geographical position in relation to that of the British Isles, and the enemy's great material superiority, cannot be compensated by our Fleet to the extent where we shall be able to overcome the blockade or the British Isles itself . . .[12]

Yet even if this was more widely recognized on the British side of the North Sea, the Royal Navy too had much to think about. Apart from the heavy and quite unexpected battle-cruiser losses, and the escape of

Scheer's ships from the avenging hands of the whole Grand Fleet, both of which caused widespread gloom and controversy, there was also a growing unease in official circles in the following months at the way in which the vulnerability of the battleships had once again been demonstrated. Jellicoe's famous 'turn-away' order when the German destroyer flotillas attacked to save Scheer's battleships was the great symbol of this weakness, as Vice-Admiral Hoffmann percipiently noted in a private letter about the battle a few days later:

> The result incidentally strengthens my conviction that the days of super-dreadnoughts are numbered. It is senseless to build 30,000-ton ships which cannot defend themselves against a torpedo shot.[13]

In this connection, therefore, the lesser-known sweep of both fleets on 19 August 1916, was probably more significant than Jutland itself, even though no contact was made between the major surface units. The whole operation turned Jellicoe's great unease about the menace posed by the U-boats to his battleships into a virtual obsession. His flagship *Iron Duke* had been narrowly missed by a torpedo as it steamed ahead of the fleet to pick him up off the Firth; the cruiser *Nottingham* was sunk near the Farne Islands, an event which caused him to order an about-turn for the whole fleet for almost two hours; and as his disappointed force returned northwards after learning of Scheer's retreat it was subjected to repeated alarms and attacks, one of which led to the sinking of the cruiser *Falmouth*. For Jellicoe this sweep proved to be the last straw. Backed up by Beatty, he insisted that the Grand Fleet must avoid going farther south than latitude 55° 30′ North (the Farne Islands) and farther east than longitude 4° East unless it had sufficient destroyers: only if 'the need were very pressing' should this rule be broken. In effect, Jellicoe was proposing to abandon most of the North Sea to the German forces, should they wish to occupy it; and he was also admitting that the Grand Fleet could not guarantee the east coast harbours against Scheer's 'tip-and-run' raids, a decision which, if publicly known, would have greatly alarmed the British people. Unable to meet the Commander-in-Chief's demands for destroyers because of their requirements elsewhere, the Admiralty was forced to agree to this proposal on 13 September 1916. Five weeks later, on 18 October, this remarkable policy of deliberate abstention was carried out when the Grand Fleet remained at Scapa while Scheer made a short sortie into the North Sea. Flouting the traditions of the service, the Royal Navy played 'safety first'.

While Jellicoe chose not to move the Grand Fleet into the North Sea without sufficient destroyers, Scheer for his part always maintained that

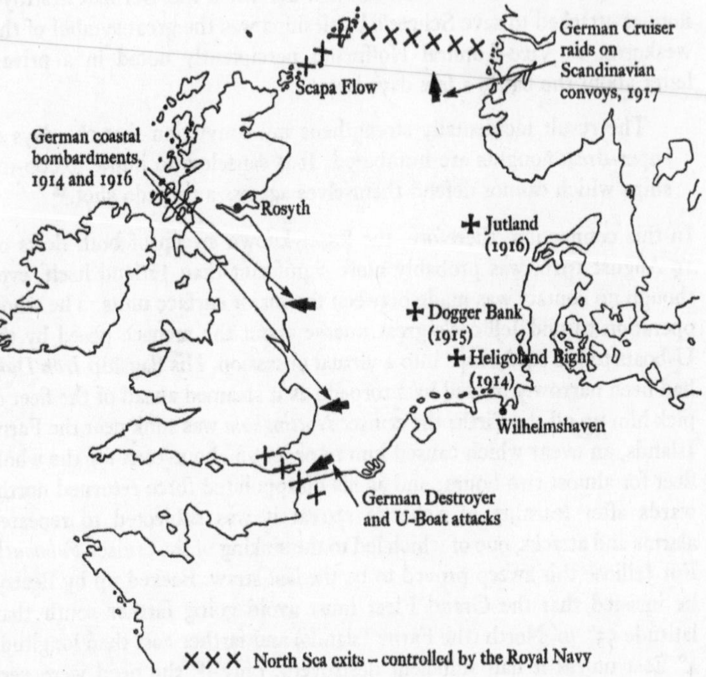

Map 9. The strategic situation in the North Sea, 1914–1918

the High Seas Fleet dared not venture forth without sufficient submarines, which served the vital dual purpose of spotting and crippling the superior enemy battle-fleet. When the U-boats were taken away from him once again after the 19 August sweep for the blockade of Britain's commerce, Scheer refused to move. The naval war in the North Sea, as far as the battle-fleets were concerned, came to a virtual standstill in the autumn of 1916. Seen in this light the operation of 19 August could be rated as one of the most decisive in the history of the entire war.

Thus it was that the submarine had developed from being regarded as being purely a coastal defence vessel into the greatest threat to Britain's naval mastery – and not only as an attacker of battleships but, more importantly, as an almost perfect commerce raider. For by 1917 the very supplies from overseas, upon which Britain's life-blood and fighting strength depended, were being sunk so swiftly that Jellicoe was prophesying defeat by the end of the year, and Beatty was admitting, 'The Navy is losing the war as fast as the Army is winning it.' Unable to win the maritime struggle with the High Seas Fleet, the Germans had turned to the only weapon left to them. By an ironic turn of events, the U-boat was fulfilling the desperate assertion in 1912 of Admiral von Heeringen that, 'If the English have really adopted a wide blockade, then the role of our beautiful High Seas Fleet could be a very sad one. Our U-boats will have to do the job then!'[14]

A detailed investigation of the great Atlantic struggle between the German submarines and the Allied merchantmen and their escorts is hardly required here;[15] but a few important points need to be made. There is no doubt but that this new weapon almost brought the British Empire to its knees: only the belated decision to re-institute the old convoy system saved its seaborne trade, but by the end of the war almost eight million tons of merchant shipping had been lost to these underwater predators. No surface vessel was safe unless protected by destroyers – yet British yards could never produce sufficient of these escorts to keep the Admiralty happy, nor could they replace all the shipping losses: only the gigantic economic strength of the United States could do that. Worse still, Britain's naval mastery in the future would never again be so secure as in the pre-submarine era. As the critics had forecast, this weapon was to be eagerly seized upon by lesser naval powers as a way to strike at British maritime superiority, without incurring the costs of an enormous battleship construction programme. Submarines could be built swiftly, as Germany had shown with the massive expansion of its U-boat fleet between 1916 and 1917. The end of the battleship was in sight when it was no longer able to command the seas without a bevy of escorts, and when it came to be regarded by both British and German admiralties as a drain upon their precious supplies of destroyers and submarines, which were so desperately needed for the vital struggle elsewhere.

In the North Sea, as we have seen, the submarine brought surface engagements by capital ships to a virtual halt. Both sides diverted their smaller vessels to the Channel area, where a whole series of exciting though indecisive 'dog-fights' took place, and to the Atlantic, where the most crucial battle of all was being fought. Symbolic of this changed attitude was Scheer's admission that 'during the further progress of the submarine war (upon which, in my view, our whole naval policy will sooner or later be compelled to concentrate) the fleet will have to devote itself to the single task of bringing the submarines safely in and out of harbour'. The pre-war roles of the battleship as the major weapon, and the U-boat as the subsidiary one, had thus been neatly reversed. Throughout 1917, this stalemate between the fleets continued, the sole prospects for action appearing to lie in the British efforts to mine the exits from enemy U-boat bases, and the German efforts to sweep them clear again; but although a brief engagement – in fact, the last big-ship encounter of the war – took place on 17 November 1917, the results were inconclusive.

Moreover, under Beatty the Grand Fleet's strategy became more cautious than ever before: a fleet action was longed for, of course, but only under such conditions that a sensible enemy would always decline. A variety of proposals for offensive actions against the German coasts were put forward by officers frustrated at this inaction, but they were all turned down as being too reckless. By the beginning of 1918, in fact, Beatty had persuaded the Admiralty and War Cabinet to agree that 'the correct strategy of the Grand Fleet is no longer to endeavour to bring the enemy to action at any cost, but rather to contain him in his bases until the situation becomes favourable to us'.[16] Here the Commander-in-Chief was simply confirming his predecessor's strategy in a more open way, and as a cold-blooded assessment of the situation it was no doubt correct to advocate that a passive policy offered the least risk; but it was an enormous departure from the offensive traditions of the Royal Navy. Nor was there any prospect by the final year of the war that Scheer would risk a full fleet action with the odds so heavily stacked against him (thirty-four British dreadnoughts and nine battle-cruisers to his own nineteen dreadnoughts and five battle-cruisers). After one daring last cruise up to the Norwegian coast on 22–5 April, the High Seas Fleet languished in harbour, producing thereby the resentment and boredom which culminated in the sailors' revolution of October 1918.

The German naval mutinies, and the final surrender of the High Seas

Fleet on 21 November 1918, were in their way tributes to the success of British naval strategy and to the overwhelming strength of the Royal Navy; but the whole service shared the First Sea Lord's 'feeling of incompleteness' that the war had come to an end without the opportunity to re-fight the battle of Jutland. If this return match had been staged on open seas, there was little doubt that the Grand Fleet would have emerged the victor. On the other hand, it is worth recalling that the British strategy, admirably logical though it had been, was also so cautiously formulated that it left little opportunity for such a fleet action unless the Germans accepted unsuitable conditions: in the post-Jutland period it would be true to say that Scheer was more willing than Beatty or Jellicoe to take risks. As a result, the naval war of 1914–18 was regarded by the British nation both at the time and later as a great disappointment, an anticlimax – which certainly did the navy's reputation and influence no good.

This alarming drop in its prestige was seen most clearly in the reactions of the Allied political and military leaders during the armistice negotiations to the navy's demand for a surrender of the entire German fleet. The French, the Americans, and even the War Cabinet, regarded this as unjustified, excessive and likely to provoke the continuation of the war. For them it had been the land campaign which had had overriding priority, which had cost them so much, and which had eventually forced the enemy to surrender. They would certainly demand, Foch declared, that Germany hand over her U-boats, for these had proved most dangerous to the Allied cause; but they hardly felt that it was necessary to run the risk of prolonging the war by demanding the cession of the High Seas Fleet, which had been so inactive in any case, simply to satisfy the *amour propre* of the Sea Lords. Internment in a neutral port was all that was agreed to, and it was only the inability of the Allies to find a willing neutral which led to the eventual ordering of the High Seas Fleet to Scapa Flow.[17] But it was an interesting commentary upon the course of the war as a whole that the Admiralty's wishes should have received so lukewarm a reception at the moment of victory. Compared with the army's continuous and bloody struggle, the contribution of the fleet appeared as inglorious and subsidiary; and, furthermore, the much-vaunted battleship had been severely cramped in its usefulness by the small, cheap submarine. Things had not gone at all as the navalists had expected and their earlier fears of declining influence had only been confirmed, and increased, by the blast of total war.

Naturally enough, the naval lobby had tried throughout the war to regain its primacy in defence strategy and to steer the nation back to 'the British way of warfare'. This time, however, the policies which had been implemented in the wars of the eighteenth and nineteenth centuries proved to be less successful and effective against Germany – just as the pre-war critics had foretold. There is little doubt that the traditional methods would have been enthusiastically supported by the vast majority of the public and politicians in Britain, had they offered any prospect of success and a viable alternative to the slaughter on the western front; but, one by one, the cheap maritime-based, peripheral ways of defeating an enemy were discovered to be inadequate when dealing with a continental *bloc* as strong and as self-sufficient as the Central Powers.

Germany's overseas colonies were of course quickly overrun by the Allies. South African forces took South-West Africa, British and French troops occupied Togoland and the Cameroons, New Zealand took Samoa, Australia took New Guinea and Nauru, Japan overran Kiaochow and the central Pacific dependencies, and only in East Africa did Lettow-Vorbeck succeed in offering resistance beyond 1915. However, these operations could not be compared in importance with the Anglo-French struggles in earlier wars for India, the West Indies and Canada. The German colonial empire, although 1,000,000 square miles in extent by 1914, housed only 21,000 Germans, took only 3·8 per cent of Germany's foreign investment and contributed to only 0·5 per cent of Germany's foreign trade. Losing such possessions was hardly a mortal blow to Berlin, therefore, especially when it is recalled that they provided few raw materials for German industry and that they had had to be heavily subsidized by the *Reich*, possibly to the tune of £100 millions by 1914.[18] In strategic terms they were considered irrelevant by the German government: Tirpitz had always argued that the challenge to Britain's world position had to be mounted in the North Sea and that, if the Germans were successful there, they would be able to recoup all the territorial losses he anticipated in the extra-European field. For this reason the German navy was neither enthusiastic about the possession of colonies nor willing to accept much responsibility for their defence. South-West Africa, Samoa and the rest were simply the first few unimportant pawns in a great and complex world struggle.

Equally insignificant, in terms of the total war effort, was the effect of the British destruction of the few German surface commerce-raiders. Here, too, geography had compelled Tirpitz deliberately to eschew any large-scale naval commitment overseas, and the vessels which were on foreign stations were to 'show the flag' – and were openly regarded in Berlin as hostages to fortune in the event of war. Their fate was confidently predicted by Churchill on the eve of war, and for the very same reasons:

> Enemy cruisers cannot live in the oceans for any length of time. They cannot coal at sea with any certainty. They cannot make many prizes without much steaming; and in these days of W/T their whereabouts will be constantly reported. If British cruisers of superior speed are hunting them, they cannot do much harm before they are brought to action.[19]

In the event this confidence proved amply justified. Of the ten German surface commerce-raiders operating in the early months of the war, only a few, notably the *Emden* and the *Karlsruhe*, achieved worthwhile successes; but even they were soon silenced, and the total of British vessels sunk by such raiders throughout the war (442,000 tons) was not a significant blow. Moreover, by such measures as the State War Risks Insurance Scheme, the British government ensured that there would be no widespread panic as a result of enemy raiding activities. The only tangible threat emerged in the form of Spee's East Asian Squadron; but after its victory at Coronel it was quickly wiped out by Sturdee's battle-cruisers at the Falklands. These battles, it has been pointed out, were the last ones of the war between surface ships by gunfire alone: 'Thereafter, torpedoes, mines, submarines, and, to some extent, aircraft introduced complications unknown to Sturdee and Spee.'[20] The greatest change, of course, was the development of the U-boat as the commerce-raider *par excellence* – which was a predictable step once the German navy had no other obvious means of hitting its enemy, the political opposition inside Germany had been overcome, and the necessary numbers of U-boats had been made ready. As soon as this campaign began in earnest, however, the Admiralty's pre-war preparations for the defence of seaborne trade were shown to be quite out-of-date.

The other great weapon in the Royal Navy's armoury was the blockade. This, too, was now encrusted with tradition. Whilst Napoleon's armies had ranged all over Europe, so Mahan had taught, 'there went on unceasingly that noiseless pressure upon the vitals of France, that compulsion whose silence, when once noted, becomes to the observer the most striking and awful mark of Sea Power'. Before the war the Admiralty firmly believed that this strategy would be deadly in its effects: did they not control the enemy's sea routes to the outside world, and did not Germany, like all modern industrialized nations, depend so heavily upon this traffic that its interruption would have the most disastrous consequences for its entire war industry? All this was true, but it was offset by many other factors, and it was a mistake to equate her position with that of an island state like Britain or Japan. Approximately 19 per cent of her national income derived from exports, but of these only 20 per cent were extra-European; and only 10 per cent of Germany's national wealth was in overseas investment (cf. 27 per cent of Britain's), the returns from which contributed to only 2 per cent of her national income.[21] Theoretically, then, the loss of about 6 per cent or perhaps 8 per cent of her national income was not a disaster. This would be swiftly altered if certain essential raw materials could not be obtained, but the Central Powers already possessed or soon took over vast resources (e.g. Rumanian wheat and oil), and could also secure supplies via neutral neighbours. They had the technology, in addition, to create many *ersatz* goods. In the long term, naturally enough, the consequences of the Allied blockade were very serious, but it was not until late in the war that German soldiers were affected by it. And it is worth suggesting that the civilian sufferings from the blockade would have been far fewer had not the great military campaigns swallowed up such astronomical amounts of foodstuffs, industrial products, and especially the men who were needed to farm the land. Indeed the blockade was, in the opinion of one British official historian, 'a small thing' in comparison with the neglect of agriculture in causing the 'hunger' in Germany.[22]

Moreover, as Sir Herbert Richmond has wisely observed, the nineteenth-century improvements in land communications had greatly assisted the Central Powers and limited the implementation of an effective blockade *by Britain alone*; as a result,

> It was only owing to the fact that the land frontiers of the enemies were sealed by the armies, and that every nation of importance was either actively assisting with her navies at sea, or passively by withholding trade, that the eventual degree of isolation was procured which contributed to the victory.

This statement from one of the most perceptive naval historians of our century is certainly more moderate in its claims for the effectiveness of the blockade than many made before or afterwards, and leads us straight to the weak point of the navalists' arguments – that this weapon, unless it be used against an island state heavily dependent upon overseas trade, is bound to be only a subsidiary one. Only when it is used in conjunction with a land blockade, and as an additional means of pressure against the constant assaults of armies, was its long-term and formidable influence upon an enemy such as Germany to be felt. For not only did the bloody wars of attrition on the western and eastern fronts sap the manpower, economy and morale of the Central Powers at a far higher rate than the maritime blockade ever did, but the latter could easily be neutralized by a German military victory in either theatre:

> The collapse of Russia, which burst the barriers in the East, broke this blockade, and then the supplies drawn from the Ukraine preserved Austria and relieved Germany. If the Western barrier could also have been broken, whatever might have happened to the armies, a vast territory would have fallen into German hands on which they could have lived and continued to hold out and defy the oceanic blockade. But it would have done still more; it would have aided to a high degree the German offensive at sea.[23]

It was a similar fear, this time of a successful enemy push into the Balkans and Middle East, making Germany 'practically independent of maritime blockade and . . . able completely to outstrip the rest of Europe in the reconstruction of their economic and military resources', which caused the dispatch of British troops into the Caucasus and towards the Caspian Sea in 1918.[24] Berlin, Britain's strategists could see, was in danger of dominating the 'Heartland'. The truth of the matter, as Richmond further observed,[25] was that sea power and land power were interdependent, that both were necessary to check the enemy challenge, and that the isolationists' hope of avoiding a continental commitment and relying upon maritime pressure alone would have led to the German domination of the European land-mass and beyond. Furthermore, while nothing was 'more misleading or objectionable than the attribution of success to one or the other separately' (Richmond), it was also true that in the First World War Britain was obliged *nolens volens* to commit an ever-increasing share of her resources to the land struggle, thereby giving that theatre an unprecedented military and political predominance.

The only solution remaining was for the navalists to argue for joint operations, to use the army, in Grey's phrase, as 'a projectile to be fired by the navy'. In the pre-war years, as we have seen, Fisher and Wilson had argued for a large variety of amphibious schemes, all of which had foundered upon the opposition of the General Staff and the scepticism of the Cabinet. This dispute, as everyone could see, was as much political as strategic, for, by arguing in favour of combined operations against the German coast, the Admiralty hoped to have the major say in the conduct of the war and to prevent too great a proportion of Britain's resources being diverted into a large-scale continental war. No doubt the traditional-minded British politicians shared the navy's fears, but the War Office emerged supreme from this tussle, because it could present the more convincing strategic case. The battle-fleet would run all sorts of risks if it operated for a prolonged period close to the enemy's coasts, but these paled in comparison with the dangers the expeditionary force would encounter. As General Nicholson had put it in 1914, 'The truth was that this class of operation possibly had some value a century ago, when land communications were indifferent, but now, when they were excellent, they were doomed to failure. Wherever we threatened to land, the Germans could concentrate superior force . . .'[26]

Yet if the army had gained the decisive first victory in this inter-service dispute, the continental strategy was not to go unchallenged during the war itself. Indeed, the more the casualty figures on the western front rose, the more longingly the Cabinet looked towards the alternative, sea-based strategy; once again, political factors became enmeshed in the military considerations, as traditionalists like Esher appealed for a return to what he considered to be the policy of Pitt:

> When the army of Sir John French was committed to war on the Continent there was no irrevocable breach of this great principle, but, as time went on, and reinforcement after reinforcement was sent to France, absorbing all the available military reserves of the country, its amphibious power was gradually sapped, and has, at the present time, practically been destroyed . . . It is as true to-day as it was then [the Seven Years War], that our military power, used amphibiously in combination with the Fleet, can produce results all out of proportion to the numerical strength of our Army . . . the moment has come.[27]

The Allied strike against the Dardanelles in 1915 seemed to provide that 'moment' to emulate Pitt and to 'produce results all out of proportion' to the forces used – which is no doubt why it attracted a Cabinet looking for a cheaper way to win the war. By seizing Constantinople, so it was argued, the Allies could relieve Russia and Serbia, Turkey would be knocked out of the war, other Balkan states would be favourably impressed, and Britain's position in the Middle East would be strengthened. Unfortunately for this quite ingenious scheme, the forceful Churchill managed to convince the Cabinet that it could be done even more cheaply than that – by the navy alone. The result, almost inevitably, was disaster, a confirmation of all that the experts had predicted would happen when warships attempted to force their way past strongly-held land defences. While Turkish gunnery sank the French battleship *Bouvet* and seriously damaged two others, the minefields took the British battleships *Irresistible* and *Ocean* as their victims and sent the battle-cruiser *Inflexible* limping away to Malta. Had the naval forces pressed ahead undeterred by these heavy losses, it is possible that they might have forced their way past the weakened Turkish defences, despite the costs this would have involved; but the first encounter had been so disheartening that it was decided to wait for an expeditionary force to arrive before recommencing the assault – and by that time the Turks had immeasurably strengthened their defences and the Allied troops which landed were virtually confined to the beachheads until their evacuation at the end of 1915. With casualties for this campaign exceeding 250,000 men, the operation was seen as a complete defeat and Churchill paid for it with his office. But far more than one man's career had suffered: it also spelt the defeat of the 'Easterners'' strategy of overrunning the enemy by peripheral, sea-based operations. The disasters at Gallipoli simply reinforced the views of those who insisted that any diversion of troops from the western front weakened the Allied war effort.

This did not fully stop the efforts to find a 'back-door' route to Berlin, however. In fact, part of Fisher's own hesitating attitude towards the Dardanelles operation was due to his wish to deploy the ships and the men elsewhere – on the Pomeranian coast! Admiral Wilson, for his part, preferred an assault upon Heligoland, while their political chief, Churchill, predictably enough, was in favour of virtually any daring stroke. Later on in the war there were again to be proposals for a large-scale intervention in the Baltic to keep Russia in the war, or at least to forestall a German seizure of its fleet. All such ideas fell down in the face of the enormous practical disadvantages, even on the naval side alone. As the Deputy Chief of Naval Staff reported:

> Any attempt to enter the Baltic in force was ruled out by the undoubted presence of minefields whose positions were unknown, by the distance which disabled ships would find themselves from our bases, and by the strategical advantages possessed by the enemy in the existence of the Kiel Canal, which enabled him to move his Battle Fleet at will in a comparatively short time, through the Canal, to the North Sea or the Baltic. A project for attacking one or other of the German naval bases was considered impracticable for similar reasons and on account of their heavy coast defences.[28]

In addition, there still remained that even greater obstacle, which the navy had never been able to overcome: the army positively refused to have anything to do with amphibious operations which would not only weaken the major land-onslaught upon Germany, but which also threatened to throw away many fine units. An assault upon such well-defended places as Borkum or Heligoland alone would have been extremely costly, and the mind recoils at the fate which would have befallen an expeditionary force landed on the Pomeranian coast, even had the fleet managed to break into the Baltic. Whilst the French political and military leaders saw such diversions as a virtual betrayal, British generals regarded them as a nonsense: together with the disastrous precedent set at Gallipoli, they could also point to the inglorious contribution of the Anglo-French expeditionary force at Salonika, where the 300,000 troops sent to assist Serbia were bottled up, not by German, but by Bulgarian and Turkish troops until September 1918.

Only in one region, in fact, were the Easterners to have their success – the Middle East. Here the imperialists were able to come into their own, forgetting the sordid mess of the western front and pressing, as Amery did, for measures

> which will enable that Southern British World which runs from Cape Town through Cairo, Baghdad and Calcutta to Sydney and Wellington to go about its peaceful business without constant fear of German aggression.[29]

The Middle East was indeed the one area where Britain herself was on the offensive, not only seeking to frustrate any German thrust to India, but also quite positively desirous of 'rounding off' her control of that semicircle around the Indian Ocean and of gaining the strategically valuable oilfields. Here, it must be said, she was supremely successful, encountering perhaps more difficulties in the political talks with the French and the Arabs than in the military campaigns, once the early losses in Mesopotamia had been recouped; and it was understandable that Paris frequently suspected that London had resumed its traditional eighteenth-century strategy of plucking the ripest overseas fruits, whilst her European allies concentrated on the life-and-death struggle on the continent. Mesopotamia and Palestine were in their way the modern equivalents of Canada and Louisiana, of Bengal and the Cape. In terms of naval strategy, such gains could only be applauded: they strengthened the British hold upon Egypt and the Suez Canal, they sheltered the Indian Ocean from any northern challenger, and they made safe the oilfields. But the 'sideshows' of which Lloyd George was so proud were, as the Westerners duly pointed out, an expensive business: by early 1918, just before Ludendorff's final great offensive, there were over 750,000 Empire troops (including twelve British divisions) serving in the Middle East and Salonika.[30] Moreover, in no way could the campaigns of Maude, Allenby and Lawrence be described as combined or amphibious: they were essentially land affairs, with the navy's role a very minor one indeed. Once again, it found little opportunity to increase its stature, and was forced to stand in the army's shadow.

The world conflict of 1914–18 proved in the main to be no cheap and swift maritime-based campaign, but a hard and bloody war of attrition by mass armies in which sea power appeared to be a subsidiary factor. It is perfectly true, of course, that had the U-boats won the Battle of the Atlantic, the war as a whole would have been lost by the Allies; and in both world wars the security of the sea routes to Britain was clearly London's *first* aim, without which little else could be done. Yet two major points counted against the navy here. In the first place, this aim was essentially a negative one. The Senior Service could lose the war, but it could not win it: that had to be done by the army, which garnered all the credit thereby. In the second place this war against the U-boats was a continuous series of small-scale actions which were hardly capable of exciting a public which had expected glorious fleet battles and did not understand that these were not necessary to achieve that basic negative aim. In this respect, it would be no exaggeration to state that the course of the First World War substantially discredited that mighty host of great grey battleships, swinging on their anchors in the distant harbour of Scapa.

In addition to these fairly obvious aspects of the decline in the effectiveness of British sea power, there were two further, and equally serious developments: the financial and industrial losses Britain suffered during the war, and her increasing dependence upon the goodwill of other naval powers whilst she concentrated her fleets in European waters.

The exact balance-sheet of Britain's industrial and financial losses during the First World War is still a matter for debate;[31] but what is clear is that instead of boosting the country to the front rank of the world's military–naval and commercial–industrial powers as the Napoleonic conflict had done, it caused grievous strain. It is true that it had stimulated a whole host of newer industries and led to a great deal of rationalization in industry – chiefly under the government's prodding; and that it also proved to be the catalyst for widespread social changes. But these were not fully appreciated at the time, or, if they were noticed, they seemed hardly to compare with the negative aspects of the war and did not check the *psychological* sense of loss which one writer has suggested may have been the greatest effect of all.[32]

About 745,000 Britons (9 per cent of the male population under forty-five) were killed in the war and a further 1,600,000 injured, many very seriously: this loss to the nation's potential productivity and economic strength is impossible to calculate, but it must have been considerable.

Admittedly, the French and Germans suffered greater casualties, but a more significant yardstick for our purposes would be the still rising American nation, which presented a more formidable challenge. Britain suffered few material losses in a direct sense, except in merchant shipping, of which seven and three quarter million tons was sunk (representing 38 per cent of British tonnage in 1914). Since the Admiralty's warship construction programme had priority, these sinkings could only be fully replaced from American yards, although Japan, Holland and Scandinavia also enlarged their share at Britain's expense: her proportion of the world's launchings fell from 58·7 per cent in 1909–14 to 35 per cent in 1920 before a recovery was staged (though mainly in the older type of vessels). British exports were also lost, in a direct sense to Central Europe, and in an indirect sense through the concentration of her industries upon war production: either the United States and Japan filled the gap she left, or the less developed countries established their own infant industries and became fresh competitors. Moreover, if the war necessitated the creation of new industries in Britain, it also gave an artificial stimulation to those older, declining ones (iron and steel, coal, engineering, and perhaps agriculture), which then collapsed the faster when the conflict was over and the government-inspired capital investment was withdrawn.

Financially, the changes were even more serious. The sheer costs of modern warfare were quite staggering: by 1915 it was costing £3 million every day, and by 1917 this had risen to £7 million per day, thanks to the great military effort. The naval expenditure of £51½ million in 1914 increased dramatically and even in the armistice budget of 1919–20 it totalled £160 million but, and here we have a significant confirmation of the predominance of the land war, army expenditure for those same periods was £29 million and £405 million respectively. Although taxes were substantially increased to meet the thirteen-fold rise in total annual expenditure by the end of the war, revenue could only provide 36 per cent of this amount and, as a consequence, large-scale borrowing became necessary, the National Debt rising alarmingly from £650 million to £7,435 million in that period. Fortunately, Britain was cushioned by her enormous capital reserves and also by the invisibles trade which covered the widening trade gap; and her borrowings of £1,365 million from foreign creditors (mainly the United States) was less than her loans of £1,741 million to her weaker allies. However, she did poorly out of the post-war settlement of these various international debts, and her financial position was greatly weakened *vis-à-vis* the United States, from whom Britain had been obliged to purchase a large variety of vital products, partly through the sale of dollar securities. As the United States replaced Britain in many world markets and took over as the greatest creditor nation, therefore, the pound steadily weakened in value against the dollar and Britain's trade balance with dollar countries worsened. As for that cushion of invisibles, those services depended upon a high level of international trade and prosperity: if this was affected by any financial collapse which the war might cause, Britain's basic weaknesses would stand exposed. Her industrial predominance had long since gone, but it was hard to admit that her financial supremacy was also slipping away.

The same was true with regard to Britain's increasing dependence upon foreign navies on overseas stations. Here, too, was a continuation of a pre-war trend which has been described earlier; but now that she was engaged in actual fighting, the dependence was much more real than when she was simply instituting a precautionary concentration of force against the rising German navy. Even in the Mediterranean, it has been pointed out, it was the Italian decision to remain neutral in 1914 which assured the Allies of naval superiority and her later entry into the war which greatly reinforced this: had she been hostile, the Franco-British position would have been gravely threatened and the Mediterranean route jeopardized.[33] In 1912 London had reluctantly acknowledged the need for French assistance to keep open the 'windpipe of the Empire'; now it was dependent, perhaps temporarily but possibly for a longer period, upon an even weaker and less reliable ally.

More ominous still, because less controllable and reversible, was the dependence upon Japan. Here, too, the war accentuated a pre-1914 trend: 'greater British involvement in Europe and growing Japanese power in the Far East and Pacific'.[34] By entering the war at its onset Japan had done Britain a great favour in liquidating the strong German position in China, but all the signs were that Tokyo, whose appetite was clearly not satisfied with Tsingtao and the central Pacific islands, would prove to be an embarrassing partner, if not a potential threat, in the future. Her traders challenged the British for Asian markets, and her 'Twenty-One Demands' of 1915 threatened Britain's great interests in China; she was often suspected of spreading seditious ideas in India; the very existence of the Anglo-Japanese alliance, besides making London appear as an accomplice to Tokyo's manifest ambitions, provoked the rising suspicion and animosity of the United States, where domestic political factors outweighed all the efforts of successive British governments to persuade American statesmen that this agreement could not operate against them; and it complicated Whitehall's relations not only with Canada, who disliked it out of regard for the United States, but also with Australia and

New Zealand, who appreciated its strategical value yet feared Japan's future expansion into the Pacific.[35]

Yet if these factors were causing the British to regard the alliance with diminishing fervour, hard strategic facts forced the Cabinet to swallow its distaste, Grey even arguing that they must willingly allow Japan to expand somewhere in Asia to prevent her turning against the Allies. The major motive was thus a negative one, fuelled by rumours that Tokyo was possibly not averse to a bargain with Berlin and made more alarming by the awareness of the British Empire's almost total dependence upon Japan for naval security east of Suez: not only had the Japanese navy chased Spee's squadron out of Far Eastern waters and taken over control of the Pacific, but by 1916 it was also patrolling in the Indian Ocean at Britain's request and a little later in the war it dispatched a dozen destroyers for anti-submarine work in the Mediterranean! From time to time the Admiralty also attempted to buy warships (particularly battle-cruisers) from the Japanese, but these requests were always politely declined with the excuse that this was politically impossible and that Japan needed them to protect her own considerable interests – remarks which gave the British 'further cause for uneasiness over Japan's post-war intentions in the Far East'.[36] Of course, the Admiralty and all British officials in the Orient held that this dependence signified only a temporary eclipse of their influence, which would have to be recovered after the war, but we have seen previously that Britain's withdrawal from there began long before 1914 itself. For the Cabinet and the C.I.D., at least, as one scholar has recently shown, the real problem was to evolve 'a diplomacy and strategy to underpin the permanent decline of British power in this region'.[37] In this sense, the war had only acted as an accelerator rather than as a catalyst; and the more Britain poured her resources into the European struggle, the weaker relatively her Far Eastern position became. Even if victory was finally achieved over Germany, this area promised to be full of problems in the future.

More alarming still by the closing stages of the war was the attitude of the United States.[38] American feelings towards Britain had somewhat cooled since the turn-of-the-century *rapprochement*, which was in any case confined to the East Coast establishment. It was true that German actions and ambitions were regarded with far greater suspicion in Washington, and that there was a sincere hope that the Allies would win the war, considerations which eventually compelled America's entry in 1917; but there was also a dislike of 'old-world' politics and secret diplomacy, and President Wilson regarded the west European democracies as being tainted with many of the characteristics which disfigured Wilhelmine

Germany and from which they would have to be cleansed through following the true example and leadership provided by his superior wisdom. To him the most deplorable aspect, in naval terms, was the British practice of the blockade, which contradicted the American neutralist tradition of 'the freedom of the seas'. Cynics were later to point out that this cliché had been raised to the level of a sacred principle when the United States Navy was weak, but was quickly forgotten about when it became the world's strongest. During the years 1914–17, however, Wilson's indignation was so great that the British Cabinet compelled a reluctant Admiralty to modify its strict blockading policy. Skilfully exploiting all these incidents, as well as the now traditional American phobia about a future two-ocean war, the 'big navy' circles in the United States persuaded Congress and the President to accept the idea of a 'navy second to none' – an aim which even Tirpitz, though he privately hoped for it, had never publicly outlined. Given the vast industrial resources of the United States, this ambition was clearly realizable: already by the end of the war the United States Navy had sixteen dreadnoughts and a multitude of smaller warships in commission (this being equal to the combined navies of France, Italy and Japan), and the Navy Department was asking Congress for an eventual force of thirty-nine dreadnoughts and twelve battle-cruisers. Such a fleet, Professor Marder notes, 'dwarfed even the Grand Fleet in its prime', particularly as all these vessels were modern whereas the majority of the British capital ships had been built before the war. And while Professor Schilling has argued that the real objective of this enormous programme was 'to force Great Britain to support the league-of-nations project and then to collaborate in a general reduction of armaments on the basis of naval equality with the United States', it is clear that Anglophobes like Admiral Benson were out to get the decisive *superiority* that this total implied.[39]

Here was the greatest naval challenge to the Royal Navy's mastery yet seen – and launched at the worst possible time, when Britain was heavily in debt to the United States, physically and psychologically exhausted by the war, and desperate to reduce her enormous defence expenditures. To emerge from the most destructive war in history with the prospect of a ruinous naval race – and all its financial and domestic consequences – looming ahead simply appalled British politicians and admirals, yet this seemed very probable unless an agreement could be reached with the touchy and suspicious Americans. The portents for such a deal were not encouraging. Lloyd George and Wilson had quarrelled over the 'freedom of the seas' concept when formulating the Allied reply to the German demand for an armistice, and could only agree to reserve this point for the Peace

Conference itself. In private talks held in London and throughout 'the naval battle of Paris', the Prime Minister also threatened to oppose the creation of the League of Nations and to lay claim to the greater part of the surrendered German battlefleet if the Americans would not reduce their expansion. The scuttling of the High Seas Fleet at Scapa removed one of these cards, and even before then Lloyd George had declared that he was satisfied with American promises to abandon or substantially modify the additional programme of 1918, rather than the basic 1916 'second to none' plan. Although the Cabinet as a whole also professed its satisfaction with this compromise, it was apparent to all involved that only a truce rather than a lasting settlement had been reached, and that it was impossible to persuade the United States to acknowledge British maritime supremacy. Equally obvious was the underlying reason for Lloyd George's conciliation:

> What Britain needed to compete successfully with the United States Navy was a throbbing economy capable of undertaking new ships comparable to the dreadnoughts and battle-cruisers already authorized by Congress and far more. This Lloyd George did not have . . . In 1919 British statesmen and naval men fought to retain acknowledged first place for the Royal Navy, but they failed because the exhausted island kingdom was unable to match the great resources of continental United States. By 1919, in short, the trident was passing peacefully from Britain to the United States.[40]

The British Empire emerged successfully from the First World War with its enemies defeated, its territory enhanced, and its army and navy stronger than ever before; yet its real position was 'quite different in fact from what it appeared to be outwardly'.[41] 'Victory in the true sense', Liddell Hart has pointed out, 'surely implies that one is better off after the war than if one had not made war. Victory in this sense, is only possible if the result is quickly gained or the effort economically proportioned to the national resources.'[42] By this definition, it is clear that there had been no real victory for Britain: she had suffered grievous losses in manpower and shipping, strained her industrial and fiscal system, declined further in world commerce, lost her hitherto unchallenged financial predominance and – as a result of all this – was now in no position to maintain maritime supremacy against the United States: naval equality, and that on the basis of an uneasy truce, was all that could be hoped for.

Yet if her traditional commercial–financial and naval leadership was disappearing, the writing was on the wall for the Empire itself, the third side of that power framework which had evolved in the two preceding centuries. Had not Sir Robert Borden of Canada declared in 1912 that 'When Great Britain no longer assumes sole responsibility for defence upon the high seas, she can no longer undertake to assume sole responsibility for, and sole control of foreign policy' for the Empire? Imperial Federation, always a dream rather than a reality, was now fast fading away in the light of Britain's military and economic decline. Australia and New Zealand still relied, though with increasing pessimism, upon the Royal Navy, but Canada and South Africa preferred to resume a more distant policy, their prejudices, if anything, confirmed by the war.

On the other hand, it simply was *not* true that this could all have been avoided by a 'wise economy of force', by the traditional British strategy of commercial pressure and peripheral attack.[43] To have shrunk from a large-scale continental commitment would have been to accede to a German domination of Europe – and to a later, far more serious, threat to Britain's security. Faced with a choice between two evils, London had naturally elected that which appeared to be the lesser. Probably this selection was correct, but the consequences of it were now to be faced. A prolonged modern war, with its attendant costs, could be afforded only by the richest, most populous industrialized states: those with smaller populations and fewer resources, like Britain, were faced instead with the danger of ruin. 'History', Mahan had asserted, 'has conclusively demonstrated the inability of a state with even a single continental frontier to compete in naval development with one that is insular, although of smaller population and resources.'[44] By the twentieth century, with the rise of super-powers rich enough to support both a large army and a navy, this was no longer true. Mackinder, as it turned out, had proved to be far more prescient; but this was no consolation to a proud people, faced openly for the first time with the prospect of decline.

CHAPTER TEN

The Years of Decay (1919-39)

What was required for the success of this [British] political style was a margin of security, a surplus of means over needs, a reserve of time to allow for adjustment to the more barbaric realities of the day, a balance out of which errors and misjudgements caused by good-natured trust in human reasonableness could be compensated. The circumstances of the day unhappily made no allowance for this. Strain was continuous, resources consistently less than needs, the balance of world forces at most times precarious and at some times decisively unfavourable.

F. S. Northedge, *The Troubled Giant* (London, 1966), p. 622.

That British naval policy, and in particular the total framework of British naval strength, cannot be satisfactorily understood without frequent reference to the nation's economic situation, has been a major theme of this book so far. The point is, after all, a fairly obvious one: the interconnections between her commercial expansion and her rise to maritime supremacy, and between her industrial revolution and the Pax Britannica, are historical facts which few would contradict. But what was true of Britain's naval position between the sixteenth and the nineteenth centuries remained valid for the twentieth also, only this time the economic factor was to be more exposed, more dominant, and much more deleterious in its consequences. In the heyday of British naval mastery, trade and industry on the one hand, and the navy on the other, had mutually assisted each other: now an ailing economy, linked with an unprecedented public demand for defence cuts, was dragging down a service that had just been built up to be the most powerful maritime force the world had ever seen.

It would have been foolish, of course, for any admiral to have expected that the Royal Navy's strength in 1919 – 438,000 men and fifty-eight capital ships, 103 cruisers, twelve aircraft-carriers, 456 destroyers and 122 submarines[1] – would be maintained at anything like that level in the period following. Indeed, with the German threat eliminated and the relationship with Japan and the United States unsettled rather than dangerous, it was hardly likely that even the pre-war standards of strength and readiness would be preserved. As had happened in the post-1815 era, the Royal Navy was inevitably bound to be run down. Nevertheless, there were some quite vital differences in the respective naval retrenchment programmes which followed Waterloo and Versailles. In the first place, the 'axe' wielded by Geddes and others was applied with a ruthlessness from which even Gladstone might have shrunk. Secondly, never at any time in the nineteenth century had there been a prospect of Great Britain accepting naval *parity* with another power, nor to her agreeing to the limitation of her fleet by international treaty. And finally, Britain's economic power – and therefore her naval potential – had been growing rapidly in the decades after 1815, even if the fleet's active strength decreased; in the post-1919 period this was no longer the case. The traditional Victorian economy, as Hobsbawm pithily puts it, 'crashed into ruins between the two world wars'; it not only ceased to grow, it actually contracted for a while.[2] The weary Titan was showing his age.

Even in the early 1920s, at least as soon as the artificial post-war boom was over, the British economy was showing signs of stress, with a high rate of unemployment and a poor performance in exports.[3] Both tendencies increased after 1925 when the Gold Standard was restored at too high a level for British productivity to match, but the real crash came with the world-wide slump in 1929. All those already declining traditional industries, which had formed the basis of the country's early economic lead and which still were responsible for so much of her exports, simply withered away. Textile production, which provided over 40 per cent of British exports, was cut by two thirds; coal, which provided 10 per cent of the exports, dropped by one fifth; shipbuilding was so badly hit that in 1933 production fell to 7 per cent of its pre-war figure and 62 per cent of its workforce was unemployed; steel production fell 45 per cent in three years (1929–32), pig-iron by 53 per cent in the same period. Moreover, in all these cases it was the *export* trade that had disappeared, due to foreign competition, tariffs and international financial uncertainties; domestic consumption remained relatively high, but this was no help to the balance of payments. It is true that the inter-war years also saw the development of many new industries – automobiles, electrical goods, glass, chemicals, rubber, plastics, etc. – but almost all of these, by coincidence or design, tended to concentrate upon the now protected domestic market rather than to try their hand against foreign competitors. Before 1914 one quarter of Britain's total production went to export; by 1939 only one eighth followed that pattern, and this was further affected by the fact that 'the largest category of British exports was in commodities expanding least in world trade'.[4] Hence, although *overall* industrial production in Britain did rise in the inter-war period, thanks to the recovery staged in the mid and late 1930s, the amount of exports fell from a notional 100 in 1927 to sixty-six in 1932 and was still only eighty-eight in 1937. And Britain's share of world trade continued its downward trend, from 14·15 per cent in 1913 to 10·75 per cent in 1929 to 9·8 per cent in 1937.

This decline in the export industries was not a new problem for Britain. As we have seen, there was already a steadily growing *visible* trade gap from the 1870s onwards. But this was always handsomely covered by the vast invisible earnings from shipping, insurance, and overseas investments. Now it was different: not only did exports decrease *absolutely* instead of relatively, but the world economic crisis ravaged the service industries which the City of London provided, because they totally relied upon a high level of international trade and prosperity. After 1929 world trade in manufactures fell by a third, in primary products by over a half. With millions of tons of shipping laid up, earnings from that source plummeted from £143 million in 1924 to £68 million in 1933; and even after the slump Britain never fully recovered her share of the world's carrying trade. By 1938 her proportion of the world's merchant shipping had fallen to 26 per cent (from a 1914 figure of 41 per cent), due chiefly to the competition of heavily subsidized foreign lines. Earnings from commissions and financial services were also halved, from about £80 million (1913) to £40 million (1934–8). Most important of all, earnings from overseas investments, which were only just recovering from the effects of the war, fell from £250 million in 1929 to £150 million in 1932. With a total annual loss in invisibles of some £250 million, Britain's most important 'cushion' fell away. After the large balance of payments' deficit in both visibles and invisibles of £104 million in 1933, Britain started to live on her capital. Even ageing pensioners hesitate to take that drastic step, lest they outlive their spending power; for a Great Power the position was even more serious.

However, the full extent of this problem was still concealed by a remarkable change in the terms of trade which made imports of raw materials and foodstuffs considerably cheaper. And there also remained, after the historic decision of 1932 to abandon Free Trade and to institute Imperial Preference, the vast formal Empire, together with certain specially dependent small powers who would accept British manufactures – if only because Britain took their primary products. This, together with the turn to the domestic market, offered an easier way out than the drastic restructuring and modernization of industry and attitudes that the country so badly needed. Even so, there was no one in Britain in the inter-war years who was unaware that there was an economic 'problem'. What was not so widely recognized was the effect of all this upon her potential as a first-class naval power.

In retrospect the very savage cuts in defence expenditure might be strongly questioned, not only on political and strategical grounds but also on economic ones. As the late 1930s in Britain (and still more in Germany and the United States) were to show, heavy investment in armaments both reduced unemployment and stimulated new industries and techniques. In the 1920s, however, politicians and economists – a few radicals like Keynes excepted – held firm to a mainly *laissez-faire* policy, which was most clearly seen in the hasty dismantling of many of the government controls and offices which the First World War had forced upon industry. For them the Gladstonian ideal of a balanced budget was still to be striven for and the need had now become much more urgent as a result of the war, with its large-scale public borrowing and the eleven-fold rise in the National Debt. The annual interest payments on this account rose to 40 per cent of the total budget 'and as prices fell in the early 1920s, the real burden of this debt . . . became distinctly heavier'.[5] The classical answer to this problem was simple – to pare governmental expenditure to the bone. Nothing would escape the keen scrutiny of the Treasury, whose eagerness was increased by the way in which the dislocation in public finances was continuing, inevitably enough, well past the actual armistice itself.

The armed services would provide no exception here: indeed, they were clearly the Number One target for public and politicians alike. This is partly explained by the simple fact that they had consumed so great a proportion of public expenditure during the war itself; and partly by the bleak economic prospects facing the country. But there was more to it than that. Other factors were at work. Democracy and socialism were on the march and at last making their presence fully felt. The sixth and final topic in Mahan's list of the formative 'elements' in sea power was a wise government, which understood the importance of maritime strength and the ways it could be used.[6] On the whole the Royal Navy had been blessed with such governments, although its ascendency in peacetime had occasionally been dangerously low. Even Cobden and Gladstone, whilst attacking burgeoning arms expenditure, had not denied the need for Britain to retain sea mastery. But while their sense of politics had been middle-class, liberal, ethical and utilitarian in character, it was being slowly succeeded by somewhat different forces: a working class which, enfranchised by the Reform Acts of 1867, 1884, and 1918, was steadily organizing itself in both economic (trade unions) and political (Labour Party) terms. To them, and to many of the lower-middle classes, widespread social and economic reforms were the order of the day. The political battles which had shaken the Liberal Party in 1892–5 and 1905–14 – in effect, between guns or butter – were to be refought, this time without the Liberal Imperialists at home and the Franco-Russian or German dangers abroad.

The inevitable outcome did not imply actual rule by the proletariat itself, even though the years 1919–39 saw two Labour governments in office and the collapse of the Liberal Party: for the Labour leaders were too moderate and unsure of themselves to think of creating full state socialism, and the Conservative leaders were shrewd enough to recognize that they could still offer an attractive electoral alternative. Nevertheless, the 1920s mark the real *end* of that long era in which Britain's policies were decided by a select group of aristocrats, country squires and men of commerce, who argued without much concern for the views of the masses about 'the national interest' and who usually displayed a wish to preserve that interest energetically, if need be by armed force; and the real *beginning* of the period when the attitude of the majority of the population in regard to improved social services – pensions, insurance, health, education, etc. – was to be the most influential factor of all in the success and failure of governments. To stay in power the Conservatives simply had to respond to these demands, and this meant a distinct change in the traditional government priority towards the armed forces. A political and social *élite*, comfortably off in economic terms too, had the leisure and the interest to pay attention to Britain's role in the world; but a democracy, as Mackinder observed in 1919, 'refuses to think strategically unless and until compelled to do so for purposes of defence'.[7]

The result of this development was predictable: whereas social service payments in 1913–14 had totalled £41½ million, they had reached £234 million in 1921–2 and £272½ million in the crisis year of 1933–4.[8] Sandwiched between the crushing burden of the National Debt repayments and the ever-increasing cost of civil expenditures, the defence forces were under an unprecedented pressure to economize. Just before the war (1913–14), government expenditure had totalled £197 million, of which £50 million went to the navy and £35 million went to the army; but by 1932, whilst the figures for those two services were almost exactly the same as in 1913 despite the vast rise in costs, government expenditure totalled £859 million. Put in another form, the Royal Navy had been allocated 25 per cent of total government expenditure before the war; by the time of the slump, it could only get 6 per cent.[9] That was a measure of its decline in the politicians' regard.

Moreover, there was one further reason why the public's attitude towards the armed forces was particularly antagonistic in these years: the psychological scars which the First World War had inflicted upon the entire nation. With almost unanimous fervour and emotion, the British people revolted against the idea of war and all that the contemporary sources of wisdom – politicians, historians, publicists – claimed could cause it: arms races, secret diplomacy, military *ententes*, imperialism. The anti-war sentiments of such bodies as the Union of Democratic Control had been largely ineffective during the conflict itself. Now, reinforced by the spreading of Marxist views about the nature of 'capitalist imperialism' and more particularly by the broad realization of what the war had cost and how little had been gained by it, they were accepted by public opinion in general. Even the middle classes, though they were worried at the idea of a Labour government, were in full agreement with that picture of war as being horrid and senseless which was portrayed in the literature of the time: Blunden's *Undertones of War*, Graves' *Goodbye to all That*, Owen's *Poems*, etc.[10] The demand was universal: 'No More War'.

Against these sentiments of the public, and the alacritous response of the politicians to them, the generals and admirals could do little. The cease-fire of November 1918 *had* to mean the end of all fighting, whatever Henry Wilson's protests; the campaign against the Bolsheviks *had* to be swiftly run down; the war in Ireland *had* to be abandoned. As for Britain's enormous overseas interests and commitments, they too should not involve the country in either war or heavy defence expenditure. After all, the common refrain went, there was no need to worry about such interests: had there not just been 'a war to end all wars'? Now everything would be taken care of by the newly formed League of Nations, which would prevent all aggression. In such circumstances, why go on insisting that the country's ailing economy should be further burdened by heavy armaments? To do so only revealed a regrettable tendency towards old-fashioned power-politics.

To labour this point any further would be superfluous. The politicians of the inter-war years have become the most abused in recent British history, because of the disastrous consequences of their hasty and too extreme run-down of the armed services, and their failure to confront the public with the unpleasant facts of world politics. Yet it is all too easy *in retrospect* to say that war can never be outlawed by moral suasion, or even sanctions; that a League of Nations lacking so many of the Great Powers was bound to fail; and that to maintain such slender forces to defend the entire British Empire was a scandal, or sheer self-delusion. The fact remains that those statesmen neither enjoyed the benefit of hindsight, nor did they believe that there was any viable alternative to the course which they took. Their task, after all, was to stay in power – if only to prevent the situation worsening. As Stanley Baldwin, then Chancellor of the Exchequer, gloomily warned in 1923, expenditure had to be slashed still more, otherwise

> the inevitable result will be the stabilization of taxation at something very near to its present level (5/- in £1), the consequence of which may easily be the substitution for the present Government of one whose regard for the defence Services is not particularly marked.[11]

To this logic there seemed no ready answer.

As it turned out, despite its apparently unimpressive wartime performance, the navy emerged from this economy drive rather better than did the army – but this was just another reflection of the national revulsion against the four years of mass slaughter in the trenches. That intervention in Flanders, it was widely maintained, had been a catastrophic mistake, an aberration, a foolish rejection of the older and wiser methods by which the nation had waged war. Thenceforward, any steps which could lead to the repetition of such an error were to be avoided. Thus the army returned to the size and functions of Victoria's time – an imperial police force once again – and a military commitment to Eastern Europe or even to France was steadfastly eluded. But the navy, at least, could not be committed to the continent and there was still a sufficiently strong feeling that the Empire's bases and routes needed *some* protection. In imperialists such as Milner, Curzon, Amery, Smuts and Churchill, these thoughts came to the fore very naturally.

Nevertheless, the cutback in naval strength was very severe. In August 1919 the armed services were given the order – now infamous but actually quite prophetic – to draft their estimates 'on the assumption that the British Empire would not be engaged in any great war during the next ten years . . .' On such an assumption, of course, quite drastic cuts could be made, and so they were, under the constant prodding of the Treasury. The actual naval allocations for the period 1918–23 were as follows:[12]

1918–19	£356 million
1919–20	£188 million
1920–21	£112 million
1921	£80 million
1922	£56 million
1923	£52 million

The speed of this decline caught the Admiralty genuinely by surprise. Throughout the war they had been aware of the great responsibility of maintaining command of the sea and, as we have also seen, they were latterly becoming increasingly anxious about the rise of the United States Navy. Thus, although by June 1919 they had cancelled many construction contracts, they had also formulated a scheme for a generous post-war navy of thirty-three battleships, eight battle-cruisers, sixty cruisers and 352 destroyers, with annual estimates totalling £171 million. The scuttling of the German fleet at Scapa Flow, the tacit 'truce' in the Anglo-American naval rivalry, and the introduction of the Ten Year Rule combined to torpedo these hopes. Consequently, the Cabinet directed the Admiralty to bring the 1920–21 estimates down to a *maximum* of £60 million. This demand proved impossible to fulfil, but by March 1920 reduced estimates of £84½ million were asked for by the First Lord and were granted without much comment, in a rare fit of Treasury and public generosity or forgetfulness. Already the manpower, warship strength and real purchasing power of the annual vote of the Royal Navy was less than in the immediate pre-war years. At the same time – and this was the most alarming point of all, in their Lordships' opinion – there were no modern (post-Jutland) capital ships under construction apart from the battle-cruiser *Hood*, whereas the Americans would within a few years have twelve and the Japanese eight.

The prospect of possessing only the third most powerful fleet in the world galvanized Beatty and his fellows into demanding the laying-down in the next two years of eight large battleships, which, together with new or converted aircraft-carriers, would cost £84 million. So obvious was the Admiralty's case on strategical terms that the prospects of its being generally accepted were good; in fact, the Board had only agreed to the previous directives under the strongest protest that they were thereby ceding naval mastery outside European waters. This declaration was clearly sinking in. But then the Fates, or so it seemed to Britain's navalists, struck another cruel blow: President Harding, under pressure from his own economy-minded circles, invited the powers to a conference in Washington on naval disarmament and Far Eastern affairs.

A blow-by-blow account of the Washington Conference and its preliminaries need not concern us here.[13] Its main conclusions – and their consequences in naval terms to Britain – were, however, of the utmost importance. In the first place there were those provisions regarding capital ships: all building programmes would be stopped (with exceptions for only a few ships) and also certain older vessels would be scrapped so that the British and American navies would possess only 525,000 tons of capital ships, Japan 315,000 tons, and France and Italy 175,000 tons; there would be a ten-year 'naval holiday' as regards replacements; and there would be strict limitations upon their size and age. A similar sort of arrangement was reached respecting aircraft-carriers, but no agreement could be achieved upon smaller surface vessels or submarines. At the same time, the Anglo-Japanese Alliance, the main target of the Americans, was dissolved, although this was partially concealed by a Four-Power (Britain: the United States: Japan: France) Treaty to respect each other's possessions in the Pacific and Far East; added to which were clauses forbidding fortifications by the powers in that area, with only a few exceptions such as Singapore and Pearl Harbor.

These provisions, chiefly American in origin but accepted very readily by the British government, aroused the most angry protests from the Admiralty, which were, however, overruled. To those imbued with the country's maritime traditions, two points especially stuck in the gullet: for the first time for centuries the Royal Navy had declared itself content with mere parity rather than naval mastery; and it had agreed to have its strength bound by international treaty rather than based upon a consideration of its own defence needs. No less an authority on world power-politics than Adolf Hitler recognized in *Mein Kampf* that the Conference implied that at some time in the future the refrain 'Britannia rules the waves!' would be replaced by 'the seas of the Union'.[14] Then there was the fact that, apart from the *Hood* and the two new 'treaty' battleships *Nelson* and *Rodney*, there would actually be a gap of fifteen years in the capital ship construction programme. Not only was this deleterious in technical, training and morale terms, but it was also harmful to the shipbuilding industry; already, Beatty warned, skilled craftsmen were having to leave the yards, and in ten years' time it would be impossible to build swiftly all those vessels due then for replacement. Moreover, whilst the capital ship was limited in numbers and size and age, the submarine – the bane of the Royal Navy during the war – escaped from all limitations, including those regarding its use, owing to the ferocious opposition of the French.

In the Far East, too, the consequences for Britain seemed ominous. In 1919, following the defeat by the Dominions of the Admiralty's final attempt to create a single Imperial Navy, Jellicoe had been sent out to the Pacific and Far East to report upon future naval strategy in those regions. Of his various recommendations, the most important was the establishment of a large Far Eastern Fleet, centred upon a new base at Singapore and composed of eight battleships, eight battle-cruisers, four carriers, ten cruisers and forty-three destroyers – of which the maintenance costs alone (divided between Britain and the Dominions, with Britain paying 71 per cent) would total £20 million p.a. No doubt this scheme would hardly have been acceptable in its full form in any case – the Dominions were aghast at the size of the (actually, rather small) contributions demanded of them, and in Britain opinion was hardening against the armed forces and the Admiralty refused to approve it – but it was totally emasculated by the Washington Conference proposals. The Royal Navy was thenceforward to have only twenty capital ships, of which many would be in reserve and the rest needed to form the Atlantic and Mediterranean Fleets. For the Singapore base there remained nothing. Moreover, while it is true that Jellicoe's plan was too optimistic and that imperial security in the Pacific and Far East had long ceased to depend upon Britain's naval strength there, it had at least been protected by the friendship with Japan for the past two decades. In the future, as Professor Beloff notes, 'Instead of the Anglo-Japanese alliance, based upon a nice calculation of mutual interests and relative capacities, Britain was to enter into a new system whose functioning would principally depend upon the incalculable shifts and whims of the American democracy.'[15] Given that power's isolationism and its often quite open anglophobic and anti-imperialist mood, this was hardly an encouraging development.

Why, then, did the British government accept it so readily? Partly because of the Canadian and South African pressure at the 1921 Imperial Conference for the elimination of any serious Anglo-American differences. Partly because the Cabinet was more optimistic about foreign affairs: admirals and generals by training assume the worst, but politicians must hope for the best, and they could perceive that Britain and the United States had no directly conflicting interests. Partly because they were feeling more acutely what Michael Howard has nicely described as 'the heavy and ominous breathing of a parsimonious and pacific electorate'.[16] Partly, too, because the economic situation had worsened rapidly: the immediate post-war boom had broken, the unemployment level had risen above two million, and the Treasury demanded that savings of £175 million p.a. must be found in the ordinary Supply Services (i.e. those departments requiring a parliamentary grant). The newly formed Geddes Committee, investigating the armed forces' expenditure, was pressing strongly for the full adoption of the practice of the Treasury, announcing what funds were available and leaving the services to work things out as best they could – a complete reversal of the latter's practice of specifying what funds were needed for Britain and the Empire's defence.[17] In view of this the navy would scarcely have been much larger, even had there not been that Far Eastern dilemma which the Washington Conference resolved.

But the overriding reason, of course, was the haunting fear of an Anglo-American naval race, the costs of which were incalculable. The budget would, especially in the existing circumstances, suffer far greater strains from this than it had from the pre-1914 race against Germany. The public, if required to carry crushing taxation burdens and to see the expected spending upon the social services heavily curtailed, would respond angrily. Just how angrily no one wished to predict, but an electoral defeat would be the least of the possible domestic evils. And in any case, if the Americans were really serious about a 'navy second to none', Britain could not hope to compete with them indefinitely. To engage in open rivalry, as Lloyd George warned, was conceivably a decision greater than that taken in August 1914: 'We should be up against the greatest resources in the world.'[18] The eventual financial collapse of the country, hastened by the American demand for the return of war loans, would be a blessing compared with the alternative course – war with the United States itself, a war which Britain could not possibly win. The prospect, the whole Cabinet agreed, was 'ghastly', 'horrible', 'unthinkable'. Against it, Washington temptingly held out the offer of a naval limitations treaty, set within an attractive though admittedly vague framework of international goodwill and cooperation in the Pacific and Far East. In view of all this, it is not surprising that the British were willing in the last resort to abandon the Japanese alliance and to clutch at the establishment by treaty of naval parity with the United States. This would, after all, serve to disguise Britain's actual weakness. It is only when one considers the sheer bad-tempered fury of the American 'Big Navy' men at the Conference's decisions that one is forced to admit the weight of the argument behind the British Cabinet's choice. According to one calculation, the United States Navy would have possessed a total displacement of 1,118,650 tons compared with Britain's 884,110 tons, had their full building programme been implemented.[19]

The Washington Conference, together with the great domestic need for economies in public spending, established the financial – and, to that extent, the strategical – limits for the inter-war navy. Luckily, the efforts of such restrictions were not too deleterious in the 1920s because of the favourable state of international relations, which appeared to justify the assumptions behind the Ten Year Rule. In the Far East the Japanese were quiet, and far more attention was paid to the anti-foreign campaign of the Nationalists in China. Italy, too, apart from a flurry of muscle-flexing over the Corfu affair in 1923, offered no threat to peace. The German fleet, thanks to the Scapa Flow scuttling and the Versailles Treaty limitations, was no longer a problem, and the Admiralty could at last turn their attention away from the North Sea for a while. The operations against Russia had been abandoned in 1920 and the Communist leadership was preoccupied with internal problems. The Middle East seemed quiet after the Treaty of Lausanne with Turkey in 1923. France was maintaining an extremely rigid attitude towards the defeated Germany, which affected both international trade and financial co-operation, and, as a consequence, British feelings towards Paris. But this age-old enmity appeared to be settled finally with the Locarno Treaty of 1925, guaranteeing the inviolability of the Rhine boundary. The German entry into the League of Nations, the continuing talks on disarmament and reparations, and that whole orgy of treaty-making known as the Pact of Paris (1928), whereby most powers voluntarily renounced war as an instrument of policy, augured well for the future.[20]

It was perhaps another indication of this state of relative tranquillity that the only serious political dispute in the naval arena was the continuation of the Anglo-American rivalry, this time with regard to cruisers.[21] The British preferred, if there were to be any limitations upon this class of vessel at all, to have a larger number (seventy) of mainly light cruisers for trade protection; American strategy dictated that they build fewer (fifty) cruisers, mainly of a heavier sort. At the London Naval Conference of 1930 the British position was abandoned by the Labour government, whose overriding regard was for economy. This particular treaty, from which both the French and Italian governments withdrew their ratification, can be seen as the high point in Britain's policy of naval disarmament, even though the estimates were to sink further in the slump years of 1931–2. The Royal Navy's cruiser and destroyer programmes, which had already suffered heavily from economic pressures in the 1920s, were now very strictly controlled by treaty, despite the continued failure to get any agreement upon submarine numbers; the 'holiday' in battleship construction was extended for another five years, and the number of British and American capital ships reduced to fifteen; the construction of the Singapore base, proposed by Jellicoe in 1919 and half-heartedly begun in the early 1920s, had again been discontinued; and the Ten Year Rule was, owing to the Treasury's insistence, now on a daily moving basis. Against all these developments the Admiralty could only protest in vain and after Beatty's departure it offered no effective opposition to the politicians. It did, however, give a general warning to the public, and partly reassured itself of its own policies, by stressing that

> In the preparation of these Estimates the continued placidity of the general Naval situation has been constantly in our minds, and many important services have either been deferred entirely or are being provided at a leisurely rate *which the expectation of a long period of peace alone warrants.*[22]

In such a situation the navy was actually able to resume its pre-war dispositions. An Atlantic Fleet, consisting initially of fourteen capital ships and then quickly reduced to six, was maintained in home waters. Reversing their controversial 1912 realignment, the Admiralty also created a Mediterranean Fleet of six battleships; both main forces were supported by cruiser, destroyer and submarine squadrons. In a further return to the age of Pax Britannica, cruiser squadrons were allocated to each of the West Indies, North America, South America, Cape, East Indies and China stations; but once again economic factors soon led to the South American squadron being withdrawn, and to some others being reduced in numbers. Nevertheless, it was difficult, apart from the obvious signs in weapon and ship design, to detect much of a difference between the naval policy of the 1920s and that of the mid nineteenth century. 'Showing the flag' again became a major function of the fleets, and it would hardly be an exaggeration to state that the most exciting occurrence in the life of the great battle-cruiser *Hood* in these years was that orgy of festivities which accompanied the world tour in 1923–4.[23] More serious encounters occasionally befell the squadron in Chinese waters in the 1920s, but the defence of western interests by naval force in that region could not be considered a novel activity by any means.

That these few years of 'placidity' were to be virtually the last the armed services enjoyed, has made the British government, and its economic and strategic advisers, easy targets for retrospective criticism. It would, however, have taken a prophet of rare sagacity and insight to have foreseen that the international situation would change so swiftly, and that so many *simultaneous* threats to the British Empire would occur precisely at a time when its defences were weakest and when the public's attention was riveted upon the domestic scene. Probably the government's greatest failure was that it was unlucky, which is always fatal in politics.

On the other hand there is no doubt that it failed to see how hard it would be for a democratic government swiftly to change gear, if ever it should be necessary to increase the unpopular defence spending, and that it ignored until the very last moment the possibility that its own pacifistic inclinations might not be shared by others. Even at the time it was well known that other powers were not disarming to anything like the degree Britain had done. In the Far East, despite the Singapore base scheme and the plan to send out a fleet within sixty days, Whitehall was simply gambling upon the hope that Japan would not be aggressive. In Europe the desire to avoid any unpleasantness or commitments was even more deliberate. In 1919 Mackinder had returned to his main theme with a plea for the Allied victors to create and actively to support East European 'buffer' states, in order to prevent Germany from again seeking to dominate the continent: 'The test of the League', he warned, 'will be in the Heartland of the Continent.'[24] Whilst Hitler and Nazi geopoliticians such as Haushofer were taking up Mackinder's ideas with enthusiasm, the British disregarded them and remained cool to the notion of a continental commitment of any sort. The Polish Corridor, Austen Chamberlain rashly claimed during the Locarno negotiations of 1925, was not worth the bones of a British Grenadier – an historical allusion which ultimately turned out to be as false as that original prophecy by Bismarck from which he had clearly borrowed.[25] For, despite the border rectifications and reparations clauses of Versailles, Germany had been left nearly intact; and even the implementation of that treaty, as A. J. P. Taylor notes, depended basically upon German goodwill.[26] Its central position, its large population and its immense industrial resources would, if ever utilized by expansionist politicians, once again tend towards the domination of Europe. Against such a development, an isolationist, Empire-centred, pacifistic foreign policy by London would be a simple recipe for disaster, particularly when the new advances in tank construction and strategy were to make land forces more mobile and harder-hitting than ever before.

But if German military power still posed a threat to Britain's traditional maritime-based policy, it was a latent one. A far greater challenge, however, had been growing rapidly at this time and convincing many observers that national strength based upon maritime action alone was swiftly coming to an end: the age of the aircraft, and of air power, had arrived.

It is difficult to pinpoint exactly when air power first began to encroach effectively upon the two established theatres of war, but even in the early days of man-made flight it was recognized that aircraft would be able, through acts of reconnaissance and attack, to influence military and naval operations to an immense degree. Amery, commenting (as we saw in chapter 7) on Mackinder's ideas in 1904, predicted that air power would one day be an important addition to a nation's armoury, requiring large-scale industrial resources. Fisher, too, with his uncanny insight, expected that warfare would be revolutionized by this new development. Nevertheless, it was not until well into the First World War itself that the extent of the challenge was realized. As with the land forces, the first use by the navy of aircraft – and, until their demise, airships – apart from home defence, was for reconnaissance purposes, the near-constant enemy shadowing of the British fleet at Jutland being an uncomfortable reminder of how backward the Admiralty was in this regard. By the end of the war steps had been taken to procure better aircraft, to construct a force of aircraft-carriers and to institute offensive operations; but the progress made was not very dramatic and many senior naval officers considered aircraft as either useless or, at the most, of secondary importance compared with a capital ship. It surely could not be that these still frail and unreliable flying machines could pose a threat to a battle-fleet.[27]

Yet by 1919 the challenge had been mounted and the navy was to find itself affected in a number of ways. In the first place, the amalgamation of the Royal Naval Air Service and the Royal Flying Corps into the R.A.F. in April 1918 meant that there was now a *third* independent armed service competing for funds from the defence budget. Nor was the R.A.F. an inexpensive institution: by the end of the war, thanks chiefly to the expansion of air forces along the Western Front, it comprised over 20,000 aircraft and 290,000 personnel, and was costing £1 million per day to maintain. Traditionalist admirals and generals expected that the R.A.F. would be dismantled into its previous constituent parts after the armistice, but they received an unpleasant shock when the government agreed to its continuation as a separate service. Closely allied to this decision, of course, was the claim of the air enthusiasts that their new weapons would render most previous forms of warfare redundant. In the words of a special sub-committee of the Imperial War Cabinet in 1917,

> The day may not be far off when aerial operations with their devastation of enemy lands and the destruction of industrial and populous centres on a vast scale may become the principal operations of war, to which the older forms of military and naval operations may become secondary and subordinate.[28]

Such a theory of air power – of an independent strategic force striking deep into a combatant's homeland – was accepted by Britain's political leaders, already impressed by the public anxiety at the Zeppelin raids, worried at the costs of enormous land campaigns and often ignorant of the less spectacular workings of sea power. There was also the novel possibility that an air deterrent might be a cheaper, and certainly a politically more attractive way of preventing future aggression in Europe; instead of an expeditionary force, one would have bombers, which were not required to be stationed outside Britain in such a fixed and almost irrevocable manner.

An equally serious challenge to the navy came from the claims of the air power lobby that bombers had rendered big warships obsolete. Admiral Percy Scott renewed his pre-war criticism of the capital ship, asserting that submarines and aircraft together had made Mahan's concept of control of the oceans by battle-fleets quite irrelevant. Rear-Admiral Hall called the battleship 'a fraud' and forecast that

> By the time they [the *Nelson* and *Rodney*] are completed the inevitable development of air warfare will have left them entirely out of the picture . . . The attack of the future will be by clouds of planes at dusk, early dawn or moonlight on the ships before they go to sea.[29]

Such opinions were naturally reinforced by those of Trenchard, Groves and other R.A.F. enthusiasts, who claimed that air power had become 'the predominating factor in all types of warfare' and that 'victory cannot but incline to that belligerent able first to achieve and later maintain its supremacy in the air'.[30] Against this Beatty and the more traditional admirals reacted strongly, insisting that command of the sea was still in the hands of the battle-fleet, which existing aircraft would not be able to destroy under realistic conditions of battle (in contrast to the artificial 'trials' currently being held in fine weather against virtually stationary warships). At the time this was probably a correct statement of fact; but whether it would be true in decades following was less certain. All that this bitter open quarrel did was to make the Admiralty less receptive (compared with Japan and the U.S.A.) to the development of an effective Fleet Air Arm than it might otherwise have been. As for the politicians, the battleship construction 'holiday', accepted at the Washington Conference and renewed at the London one, provided a convenient excuse for postponing a final decision and thus saving money. As Lloyd George put it, 'We cannot exclude from our minds the possibility that in ten years' time the march of science in aviation, in submarines, torpedoes, shells and explosives may render it impossible to construct an inexpugnable capital unit . . .'[31] The longer one waited, however, the less likely the Admiralty would be to win its case.

The final consequence of the growth of air power was that, no matter how great a navy Britain possessed, she was no longer fully free from attack by a foreign state: the 'wooden walls' of the island nation had at last been breached. The Royal Navy's claim to primacy in the defence of the British Isles had now been overtaken by events, and the doctrines of the 'Blue Water' school suffered a defeat similar to that which they had inflicted upon the 'Brick-and-Mortar' school twenty years earlier. Frequent aerial bombing attacks from continental bases, it was gloomily forecast by a C.I.D. sub-committee in 1922, would produce so much damage and demoralization that the public would insist upon an armistice; and only an adequate *aerial* defence could counter such a danger. Driven on by a temporary suspicion of France, the Cabinet agreed to the creation of a Metropolitan Air Force, but few then perceived the deeper implications of this military revolution – that the defence of *any* region from which bombing raids upon Britain could be launched had now become essential to national security. In other words, as Baldwin was to express it in 1934, their frontier had moved from Dover to the Rhine.[32] Here was a further and very substantial reinforcement of the traditional strategic need to preserve the independence of the Low Countries and to keep northern France from occupation by a hostile power. Yet it was to be many years before this fact dawned upon the politicians, who were striving to 'isolate' Britain once again from political or military commitments to the continent.

The 'age of Locarno', of international peace and goodwill, which had made much of the above debate about Britain's defence policy seem academic, came to an abrupt end in September 1931: Japanese troops began their conquest of Manchuria, which within two years they had turned into a puppet state. To this the British government, despite its repeated acknowledgements to the principles of the League, offered only a limp and half-hearted policy of protest. The reasons for this attitude were many: the United States appeared unwilling to offer anything more than verbal condemnation, and few other powers had either the strength or the will to take sterner action; the economic crisis – which had just brought about the collapse of MacDonald's second Labour government, and led to the first serious mutiny in the Royal Navy since 1797 – absorbed all attention, and the public would have strongly opposed extensive military or naval commitments over such a distant matter as Manchuria; there was at the time much sympathy for the Japanese case; and last but not least, British power in the Far East had been completely neutered by the Washington Conference and the economy drives of the 1920s.[33] The construction of the Singapore base, as we have seen, had again been discontinued; nor was there any battle-fleet to occupy it had it been ready for use. Only a few months earlier, in April 1931, the Admiralty had reported that their naval strength 'in certain circumstances is definitely below that required to keep our sea communications open in the event of our being drawn into war'. The circumstances referred to were plainly spelt out by the additional statement that capital ships could not be sent to the Far East without jeopardizing British security *vis-à-vis* a European power. In addition, the number of destroyers (120) was well below that required for escort and anti-submarine duties, and the fifty cruisers were completely inadequate to protect imperial trade routes.[34] Small wonder that London preferred to forget the Manchurian episode.

Yet the lesson from Japan's action was clear: aggression and extreme nationalism were still at large in the world, and the League of Nations did not seem to be the hoped-for instrument for checking them. At the same time the disarmament discussions were breaking down without result, and the German problem – how to prevent that powerful state from inevitably dominating its neighbours – was raising its head again. By the beginning of 1933 it was clear that European politics had become much more critical with Hitler's advent to power. Both in the Far East and in Central Europe there existed great states with unfulfilled ambitions and bitter memories. In addition, there was the isolationism of the United States; the steady disintegration of any sense of imperial defence, thanks to the efforts of Canada, South Africa and the Irish Free State; the existence of another ambitious and unscrupulous dictator in Italy; and there was left as a possible ally only France, now ever more fearful of a violation of her 'security' and ever more rigid towards any sensible compromise with Germany. It was not an encouraging state of foreign affairs that faced the newly created National Government as it looked around in the early 1930s; even those Cabinet members most absorbed with domestic affairs and suspicious of the military mind would acknowledge that. It was clearly time to re-examine some of the assumptions upon which British defence and foreign policy had been based for the past decade.

From 1932 onwards this process of reassessment got under way.[35] The resumption of work upon the Singapore base was ordered. The Ten Year Rule was abandoned. A Defence Requirements Sub-Committee of the C.I.D. was established to recommend a programme for repairing the worst deficiencies in British and imperial defence. In their reports, and in many other papers submitted by the three services, a full picture was steadily built up of an alarming lack of armed force to protect what was still the largest conglomeration of political and economic interests and commitments in the world. Although the navy was not the worst affected, its position was grim. 'After the London Treaty [it] was left not only with unmodernized battleships, but also with 600,000 tons of destroyers unreplaced, with 40,000 tons of submarines unbuilt, with little reserve ammunition and stores, and with almost no defended bases. By the thirties Britain was below the one-power standard.'[36] In point of fact, there was not one adequately defended base throughout the entire Empire. Yet the maintenance of naval supremacy and the consequent protection this afforded to all British territories against invasion from the sea was still accepted as the basis of the total system of Imperial Defence. The gap between theory and actuality was now enormous. The British Empire, like Spain in 1898, Russia in 1904, and France in 1940, had lost its muscle: its existence depended upon the now-dubious assumption that no one would find this out. The only way of avoiding the fates which befell those other powers was to eliminate the weaknesses as swiftly as possible. This, however, was easier said than done.

In the first place, that assortment of political and financial obstacles which had proved so effective in whittling away Britain's defence forces could not be easily overcome. The Labour and Liberal parties opposed the idea of rearmament and still continued to favour the collective security system of the League of Nations, though never satisfactorily explaining how this was to work if the peace-loving countries lacked armed strength. The Conservative party, the natural supporter of adequate defence forces, was compromised by being part of the National Government and was overwhelmed by the belief, which such events as the East Fulham by-election tended to confirm, that the public was implacably hostile to further expenditure upon armaments. Of its leaders, Baldwin stressed the need to heal domestic divisions by avoiding controversy, whilst Neville Chamberlain laid the accent upon reducing commitments to a level consistent with Britain's capabilities. Then there were the voices who argued that Hitler represented no real threat and that he would quickly become friendly if his grievances were rectified. Most important of all, there was an economy which had reached an all-time low, and an unemployment rate which had reached an all-time high. An improvement here – which meant a tighter-than-ever control on public spending – was the overriding priority of the government, and the Treasury insisted that 'today's financial and economic risks are far the most serious and urgent that the country has to face'. Thus, although the Cabinet abandoned the Ten Year Rule in 1932, it somewhat contrarily added that 'this must not be taken to justify an expanding expenditure by the Defence Services without regard to the very serious financial and economic situation which still obtains'.[37] The hamstrings of 11, Downing Street were still there.

Secondly, the main accent which the National Government placed in the defence field was upon air strength, not naval power. And, as the Chancellor, Neville Chamberlain, put it, with the development of large-scale air defences, 'we certainly can't afford at the same time to re-build our battle-fleet'. The grounds for this – a tacit admission that the navy's claim to be the Senior Service had now been rejected – are not difficult to discover. In the first place, a battleship would cost about £11 million to construct. Secondly, a large naval construction programme implied a break with the Washington and London treaties, thereby embarrassing Anglo-American public relations once again. Moreover, it also implied support for the Admiralty's wish to establish a strong naval presence at Singapore and this – apart from a continental military commitment – was the most unpopular policy of all. In regard to the Far East, so it would appear, virtually everyone was an appeaser; had they not been, the navy would have had priority before the R.A.F. Most important of all, by the mid 1930s the public had become aware of the alleged German superiority in the air and was openly fearful of the consequences should war break out. Although this strengthened the arguments of those who sought to appease Hitler, the Cabinet could not accept the risk of leaving Britain's cities and industries defenceless to air attack and they actually *increased* the size of the allocation which the R.A.F. had originally asked for. And the more information they obtained about Germany's air strength the more they accelerated and enlarged their own aircraft construction schedules. Finally, there remained that tempting thought that a large air force was a gesture towards maintaining European peace, without actually committing British manpower and provoking domestic controversy. As a result the R.A.F. rose from being the third service to being the first in the 1930s, as the individual defence allocations show:[38]

	Army	Navy	R.A.F.
1933	37·5	53·5	16·7 (£ million)
1934	39·6	56·5	17·6
1935	44·6	64·8	27·4
1936	54·8	81·0	50·1
1937	77·8	101·9	82·2
1938	122·3	127·2	133·8
1939 (before war)	88·2	97·9	105·7

A third fact in restricting the navy's expansion was more alarming still: when the Royal Navy began its plans for new ships which the war clouds looming on the horizon dictated and which even the Treasury found it impossible to resist fully, it was discovered that Britain no longer possessed the productive strength to satisfy these urgent orders.[39] The long lean years of virtually no construction, the lack of incentive for technological innovation, the unwillingness to invest capital in what had been regarded as unprofitable fields and, above all, that steady, cancerous decay of the country's industrial sinews, were now showing their fruit. The drastic reduction in the shipbuilding industry – in 1914 it was building 111 warships, in 1924 only twenty-five – was the chief cause of delays in the Admiralty's rearmament schemes. Skilled labour had drifted away. Old plant remained. Designs were out-of-date. Far fewer foreign orders, the ending of the state guarantees for shipbuilding loans, and the explicit favouring of the Royal Yards had led to the winding-up of many firms in the private sector, but it was only from here that the main expansion could come. The supply and fitting industries, from the gunnery firms like Vickers to companies which produced small technical instruments, had also slumped into a state of virtual non-activity or gone out of business. The dependency upon foreign supplies grew the more modern a product was; while steel was in such short supply that some of the new carriers and cruisers had to have Czechoslovak armour. Expansion was providing as many problems as contraction and brought home Fisher's warning of 1902 that 'You cannot build ships in a hurry with a Supplementary Estimate.' In fact, there was so much leeway to make up and such a decrease in construction facilities that until 1939 the Admiralty could do little more than supervise the replacement of vessels to bring its standard up to what it should have been in 1932, even under the naval treaties.

In the nineteenth century, even in the pre-1914 period, Britain had been able to build warships faster and more efficiently than any other power, because of her great lead in this industry. Now this was no longer the case: a battleship took four to five years to design and build, whereas the Americans could do the same in three and a quarter years. And any attempts by the Admiralty to accelerate or increase production simply meant that the construction of other warships or of merchant vessels was further delayed. Nor were the British warships the largest, the fastest and the best armed, as they had been under that arch-materialist, Fisher, before 1914. The new *King George V*-class battleships, following treaty guidelines and encountering production problems which prevented any changeover, were given 14-inch guns; whereas the German, French and Italian vessels had 15-inch, the Americans 16-inch, and the Japanese *Yamato*-class 18·1-inch guns. Furthermore, both in the new construction and in the modernization programmes, insufficient anti-submarine equipment was provided in the smaller vessels, whilst the anti-aircraft defences on all warships indicated that the extent of the danger posed by this new means of warfare had not been fully recognized, particularly in respect of torpedo-bombers.

The latter fact was confirmed by the comparative neglect of the Fleet Air Arm in the inter-war years.[40] This was partly due to the sheer pressure for economies and the need to maintain intact the traditional but still vital surface-fleet squadrons and yards; but it was also due in a large degree to inter-service jealousies with the R.A.F. (which only gave up its control in 1937) and to a continuation of the Admiralty's suspicion of air power into a period when this was no longer justified and was, indeed, positively dangerous. The aircraft used were always slower and less effective than their land-based contemporaries, until American carrier aircraft were purchased during the war; one might add that the dependence of the Fleet Air Arm upon American help in 1939–45 was a measure of its neglect in the inter-war period. The construction of aircraft-carriers, too, had stalled: the only *designed* fleet carrier in 1939 was the *Ark Royal*, in addition to which there were four converted warships (*Eagle, Courageous, Glorious* and *Furious*) and the small *Hermes*. But perhaps the greatest failure was in the field of strategy: there was little development in the organization of a fast carrier force, which would itself have an *offensive* capacity, reaching out to cripple the enemy fleet or securing command of the air (and *ergo*, the sea) in a certain region. While the Americans and Japanese developed larger naval air forces, they also adopted new techniques for the use of this weapon. At the outbreak of war, however, the Admiralty still favoured using carriers singly, on anti-submarine patrols or in operations with battle-cruisers to detect surface raiders. Like the French tanks in 1940, the crucial weakness was in the actual concentration and deployment, and instead of being the chief weapon they were still regarded as auxiliaries.

While these gaps in Britain's power were being steadily discovered – and it was not until 1936–7 that the warship construction programme really got under way – the government's strategic planning had to be modified in order to bring its foreign policy more into line with its existing armed strength. The result was that policy known as 'appeasement.' That it also had other origins, in the optimistic self-delusion, misjudgement, and sense of guilt at the Versailles Treaty and in fear of the pacifism of domestic opinion, which characterized Britain's leaders in the inter-war years, would not be disputed;[41] but it is abundantly clear that strategic weakness played a very large role indeed, particularly with the defence advisers, who were less affected than politicians by the domestic mood.

The great fear of the Admiralty, for instance, was that the basic strategy which they had adopted after 1922 was no longer capable of fulfilment. This was a modified Two Power Standard (with the United States Navy now naturally excluded) postulating a situation in which Britain might need to send a fleet to the Far East to counter Japanese aggression, whilst leaving a sufficiently strong force in European waters to check the next strongest naval power there. With the rise of Hitler, and the Japanese seizure of Manchuria, this possibility appeared much more likely. Unfortunately, as we have seen, the Royal Navy's *effective* strength precluded the implementation of this strategy, and the 'main fleet to Singapore' plan grew ever more remote. Indeed, the haste with which the Admiralty pressed the proposed Anglo-German naval treaty of 1935 upon the government was clearly dictated by the desire to regain this Two Power Standard. It might well be, as the critics observed, that this agreement broke the 'Stresa Front' against Germany and permitted the latter to triple the naval force it possessed under the Versailles Treaty; but the notion that Berlin would agree to a fleet of only 35 per cent of the size of the Royal Navy (45 per cent in submarines) seemed at first to suggest that the defence of Far Eastern interests was more realizable now. In the event, the Germans felt that they had obtained the main benefits, since they saw the naval treaty as an instrument for securing undisturbed progress for a number of years until they were ready to repudiate the limits imposed by it; while the steady expansion of the German navy even to these levels began to mesmerize the Admiralty, to the eventual detriment of deployments elsewhere. Churchill was not totally in error when he prophesied that the consequence of this treaty would be that 'The British Fleet . . . will be largely anchored in the North Sea.'[42]

No sooner was this agreement signed, however, than the strategical assumptions upon which much of it was based were shattered by another event: the Italian war upon Abyssinia, and Mussolini's growing adhesion to the Axis powers. Hitherto, Italy's friendship, if not support, had always been taken for granted in London. Now, because of the aggression in Abyssinia and the British government's need to support the principles of the League, the two nations drifted swiftly apart and the prospect of open war between them seemed probable, if Britain persisted in pushing for a policy of effective sanctions. In the end, discretion seemed the better part of valour and Whitehall sought to gloss over the affair, although unable to conceal the fact that the League had been discredited once again as an instrument of world peace-keeping. Nevertheless, this faintheartedness, as Professor Marder has shown, 'was founded on compelling considerations of strategy and fleet efficiency'.[43] Although the

Royal Navy was superior to the Italian fleet alone and the Abyssinian campaign could be throttled by the closure of the Suez Canal, there were many other factors that gave the Admiralty cause for caution. The prospect of Italian air attack in narrow waters, especially when the anti-aircraft guns at Malta, Egypt and Aden were so few and had only sufficient ammunition for twenty-five minutes' firing at the most, became so worrying that the Mediterranean Fleet was withdrawn from Malta to Alexandria (the first real acknowledgement by their Lordships that air power had arrived?). Yet to send aerial reinforcements to the area would denude the British Isles in the face of the German threat. Oil sanctions might upset the Americans; and the French did not wish to drive Italy into the German camp. Most important of all, as the First Lord, Monsell, put it: 'We could not afford to overlook Japan.' British involvement – or worse, warship losses – in the Mediterranean would leave China and the whole of South-East Asia open to Japanese expansion.

Once again, therefore, the Cabinet had to be reminded that Britain's interests were *world-wide*, but that she lacked the armed strength to protect them adequately. The personnel problem of the Royal Navy was so great that after the deployment of extra warships in the Mediterranean there were only three ships remaining in home waters capable of engaging the new German pocket battleships – and nothing left over to face the far more formidable Japanese navy. And to cap it all, Hitler took advantage of London's predicament to move into the Rhineland, as Laval had always suspected he would.[44] Britain, whilst bickering with the French, was in the awful situation of being opposed by three hostile, volatile aggressor-states, each of which was only waiting to see the western democracies engaged elsewhere before striking again.

The first consequence of this new development was to turn the Chiefs of Staff into ardent appeasers – of a strategic, rather than a moral kind. For them the overriding priority was to repair all those weaknesses in Britain's imperial defence system which they had pointed to – in vain – for the previous fifteen years; and the political logic of this situation was clear, as they stated in December 1937:

> we cannot foresee the time when our defence forces will be strong enough to safeguard our trade, territory and vital interests against Germany, Italy and Japan at the same time . . . We cannot exaggerate the importance from the point of view of Imperial Defence of any political or international action which could be taken to reduce the number of our potential enemies and to gain the support of potential allies.[45]

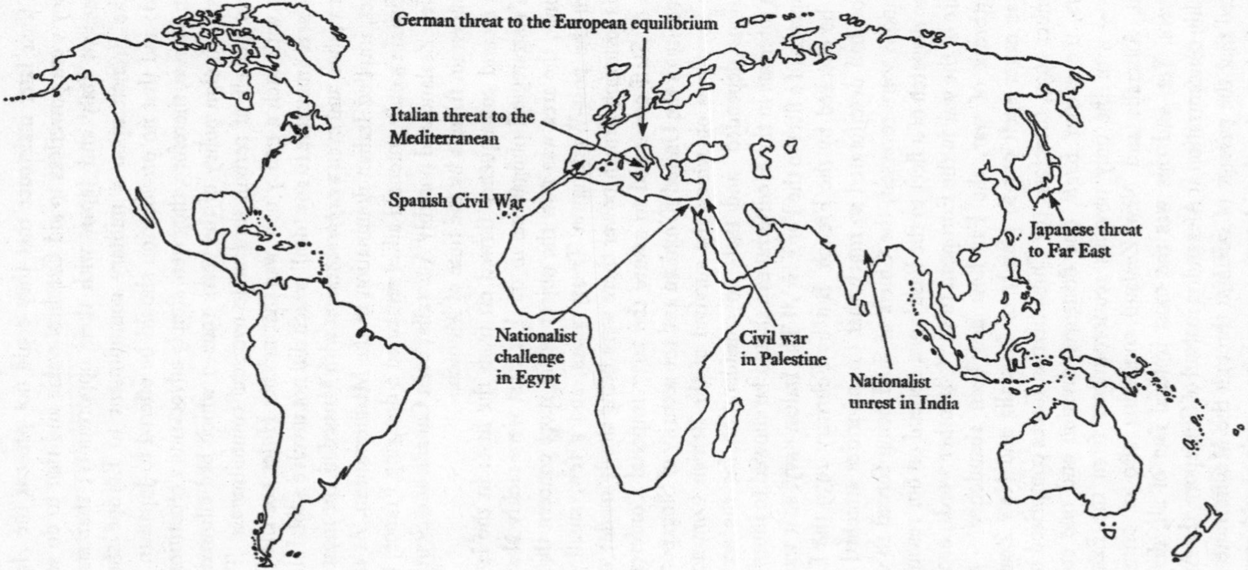

Map 10. The world-wide nature of British defence problems in the 1930s

Hence their later insistence that they could not prevent the *Anschluss*; that they were powerless to aid Czechoslovakia and that to do so would only present Italy and Japan with their opportunity; that staff talks with the French upon a military commitment to Europe should be avoided; and that no provocation should be offered to Japan in the Far East. In a sense, therefore, they were simply advocating a repetition of that successful foreign policy of the years 1902–7 which had allowed Britain to divest herself of certain untenable overseas commitments. The only trouble with such a policy now was that neither Hitler nor the Japanese leaders were amenable to any 'deal' which did not involve a total surrender to their wishes, and even a *rapprochement* with Mussolini, the most hopeful prospect, implied Italian domination in the Mediterranean. At the same time, Britain's only potential allies remained a decaying France, together with New Zealand and possibly Australia; even Canada and South Africa were uncertain friends by the time of Munich.

The second consequence flowed on from the first: in the late 1930s Britain's strategical obligations in the Far East were tacitly abandoned. Of course, the area was now the object of far more concern than it had been in the post-Washington Treaty years, and a few, small gestures towards restoring British power there were being slowly made; while the Chiefs of Staff continued to assure the 1937 Imperial Conference that 'the security of the United Kingdom and the security of Singapore would be the keystones on which the survival of the British Commonwealth of Nations depended' and that 'no consideration for the security of British interests in the Mediterranean should be allowed to interfere with the dispatch of a fleet to the Far East'.[46] The Italian navy, so it was hoped, would be checked by the French. But by February 1939 the European situation had deteriorated so much that the priorities attached to these two regions were reversed, the Chiefs of Staff being forced to conclude that the dispatch of a fleet to the East 'must depend on our resources and the state of the war in the European theatre'. In other words, even before the outbreak of war, the Far East had been abandoned – although this was never spelt out so plainly to Australia and New Zealand. In September 1939, therefore, the China Station forces comprised only four cruisers, the carrier *Eagle*, one destroyer division and one submarine flotilla – with the only obvious reinforcements from the East Indies Station, Australia and New Zealand consisting also of cruisers and destroyers. Yet, and this was the most ironical fact of all, despite the battleship concentration at Alexandria instead of Singapore, the Admiralty accepted that the passage of *warships* through the Mediterranean 'could *occasionally* be undertaken' but that merchant vessels would have to take the far longer route around the Cape. The Mediterranean theatre might have been given priority – but it was in no way secure.[47]

The third consequence of this horrifying concatenation of threats to Britain's world interests – and in particular, of the German danger as manifested in Hitler's actions in 1938 – was that the economic objections to rearmament were overcome, although the Treasury and Neville Chamberlain fought a bitter rearguard action. Income tax was progressively raised from 4s. 6d. in the pound in 1934 to 7s. 6d. in 1939, and in 1937 a £400 million rearmament loan was launched, to be doubled in value in spring 1939. But, apart from the fact that the R.A.F. continued to be given priority in defence terms, the Royal Navy suffered in another way: the 'go-ahead' simply came too late to be effective. As late as mid 1938 the Cabinet, in deciding that the financial factor must still be respected, turned down the Admiralty's construction plans for an effective Two Power Standard; only in August 1939 was this objection fully overcome. By that time, however, the concern to create a fleet of twenty battleships, capable of taking on both Japan and a European enemy at the same time had been overshadowed by the more pressing problem of fighting a war against Germany alone, when Britain had a superiority in capital ships but was desperately short of escort vessels to counter the U-boat threat. As a result, between 1939 and 1941 top priority was given to the small ship programme and the longer-term construction projects were continually postponed.[48] If command of the sea was still to be defined in terms of main battle-fleets – or even carrier squadrons – Britain was steadily losing that control.

At the outbreak of war, in fact, the effective naval strength of the British Empire was only twelve battleships and battle-cruisers, six aircraft-carriers, fifty-eight cruisers, a hundred destroyers and 101 smaller escorts, and thirty-eight submarines. Although they would soon be joined by some re-fitted vessels, a large proportion of the Royal Navy was, as Beatty had forecast in 1922, obsolescent: 'It was stated (1935) that by 1942 seven battleships, twenty-four cruisers, eighty-three destroyers, two aircraft carriers, not to mention a host of smaller ships, would be well over age and would need replacing . . .'[49] There were, in addition, the new warships authorized from 1936 onwards: five *King George V*-class battleships (with four 16-inch battleships coming later); six fleet carriers; twenty-one cruisers; thirty fleet, and twenty *Hunt*-class destroyers. But the major units would not be ready until 1940 or 1941 at the earliest. On the face of it, it was ample to check the German surface fleet, which consisted of two battle-cruisers, three pocket battleships, one heavy and five light cruisers and seventeen destroyers; but this, it may be noted, was only due to the fact that war came once again five years too soon for the German navy. It was already constructing the two giant *Bismarck*-class battleships, an aircraft-carrier and scores of U-boats, but the famous 'Z-Plan' of 1938 contemplated for the mid 1940s a force of thirteen battleships, four carriers, thirty-three cruisers and 250 U-boats, all of modern design. Against such a fleet the Royal Navy, even with its projected increases, would hardly be adequate.

Moreover, there was a growing Italian navy which consisted of (1940 figures) six battleships, seven heavy and twelve light cruisers, sixty-one fleet destroyers and 105 submarines – against which the French fleet of five battleships and battle-cruisers, one carrier, fifteen cruisers, seventy-five destroyers and fifty-nine submarines was not a sufficient counterweight: this necessitating, as mentioned before, the basing of a considerable part of the British battle-fleet at Alexandria. Yet all this, with its clear implication that Britain's naval forces were stretched in European and Atlantic waters alone, did not take into account the greatest naval threat of all – Japan. Her energetic shipbuilding policy had produced a front-line fleet of ten battleships, ten aircraft-carriers, eighteen heavy and eighteen light cruisers, 113 destroyers and sixty-three submarines, with such massive reinforcements as the mammoth *Yamato*-class battleships on the way, by the outbreak of war in the Far East in 1941.[50] The *entire* Royal Navy would have had an enormously difficult task in taking on the Japanese alone. In this connection, it is worth while glancing at the American construction programmes for their planned 'Two Ocean Navy' – a direct equivalent of the Two Power Standard. Under the Vinson Naval Expansion Act of May 1938 a total of $1,156,546,000 was granted to give the United States Navy an under-age fleet of eighteen battleships, eight carriers, forty-five cruisers, 150 destroyers and fifty-six submarines, together with a fleet air arm of 3,000 aircraft; to this could be added many over-age warships which were still useful. Yet by the following summer fresh warships were ordered, and soon afterwards eight 16-inch battleships were under construction, with these appropriations being steadily increased the nearer war came to the United States.[51]

Furthermore, by 1939 sea power was clearly dependent upon air power; but when one compared the air strengths of Britain and her enemies or potential enemies, the picture was even bleaker. At the outbreak of war the German air strength (excluding transport aircraft) of 3,609 planes was numerically far superior to the British figure of 1,660, many of which 'were not up to modern standards', and remained superior when the French total of 1,735 planes, the vast majority of which were in a pathetic condition, was added to it. And, to quote the official historian once again,

'Figures apart, events soon showed that effectively the Luftwaffe was substantially stronger than the British and French air forces put together.'[52] To this had necessarily to be added the threats from an Italian air force of approximately 1,200 aircraft (1939), and from the Japanese strength of 1,865 first-line planes (1939), the greater part of which was the well-trained and (against warships) deadly Naval Air Force. (By late 1938, it is again worth noting, the Americans were planning for a force of 10,000 planes in the near future with an ultimate first-line figure of 20,000 – which was later raised to 50,000.)

Britain's naval position at the outset of war might thus be summarized as follows: an adequate superiority – in alliance with France – over the surface units of the Germany navy, and of the Italian too if she came into the fight: but her position in the Far East was totally exposed; she was extremely weak in anti-submarine and escort craft, despite the First World War lesson that dependence upon overseas supply was her real Achilles' Heel; and, even with French aid, she was much inferior in air strength against Germany alone. Only if one judged naval strength by the old-fashioned 'Blue Water' School method of tallying battleships, *and* forgot about the Japanese danger, could the position be said to be satisfactory; but it was now the middle of the twentieth century, not 1895 or 1815.

In any case, even if the Royal Navy had been at the strength that the Admiralty desired for it, the basic problem remained: how could naval power alone defeat an enemy such as Nazi Germany? The First World War had given the answer already: it couldn't. The inter-war years had then provided further revealing examples: the reoccupation of the Rhineland, the 'rape' of Austria, the acquisition of the Sudetenland and the final occupation of the Czech rump state. In all four cases the threat of gunboat diplomacy alone would have been about as effective as Palmerston's bluster at the time of the Schleswig-Holstein crisis. Professor Northedge is surely correct in his observation that 'perhaps the most noticeable weakness of British naval power in this period was not so much its actual magnitude as compared with that of rivals, as its irrelevance to the task of correcting the strains in the political balance as it then existed.'[53] Only the possession of a powerful air force together with a strong continental military commitment, supporting a French hard-line policy, could have prevented the expansion of Germany; but such a policy was morally and politically unacceptable to the British government and public in the 1930s until after Munich. 'Never again' was the word of the day, with its grim warning that the 1914 taste of mass warfare on land had been more than enough for the nation. Here, too, Chamberlain captured the general mood when he wrote in 1936: 'I cannot believe that the next war, if it ever comes, will be like the last one, and I believe that our resources will be more profitably employed in the air, and on the sea, than in building up great armies' – a view, incidentally, which he was to repeat as late as 1940.[54] As in 1797 the British government hoped to offer subsidies and a fleet to its allies instead of an army. Hence the continuation of restrictions upon army expansion, when the R.A.F. and even the navy was permitted large increases in expenditure; and the 1937 definition that 'the defence of any territories of any allies we may have in war' was the last of the four objectives of Britain's armed forces. In 1938 the Chiefs of Staff were cool to the idea of cooperation in military matters with the French, simply because they had 'nothing to offer', if the request for a continental commitment arose – as it inevitably would.

Yet by February of the following year the whole Cabinet was forced swiftly to abandon its 'stay clear' policy out of fear – a fear (provoked by a flood of reports) that France would submit to Hitler's domination of the continent if not effectively supported in the field, a fear that Germany would gobble up all of Europe, the dull, persistent fear of Elizabeth I and William III and Pitt and Grey that Britain herself would be overwhelmed eventually, if she did not intervene across the Channel.[55]

The measures taken in the spring of 1939 were certainly impressive in view of the government's previous policy: the granting of territorial guarantees to Poland, Turkey, Greece and Yugoslavia; military conversations with the French and preparations for the dispatch of a Field Force of six divisions; the doubling of the Territorial Army from thirteen to twenty-six divisions; and the introduction of a limited form of national conscription, the first time that this had ever taken place in peacetime. But they were hardly decisive as a *military* check to Germany, now freed from the restraining force of thirty-four Czech divisions from the previous year and from any threat from Russia after the Molotov-Ribbentrop Pact. Hitler could deploy ninety-six divisions against an obsolete Polish army and against fifty-four French divisions, some of which were needed to keep an eye on Italy's seventy divisions. And in the Far East Japan commanded forty-one divisions in 1939 and was expanding her army very quickly. The British Expeditionary Force, in other words, even when added to by certain Territorial Army divisions, was more of a political gesture, a moral reassurance to the French, than anything else. On land Britain was a pygmy. Nor did the Cabinet see any need to revise their figures once the war was begun. It was proving difficult enough to equip the projected thirty-two divisions, even though this would not be one fifth of the *Wehrmacht*'s numbers. And comfort was only to be found in the fact that it would be a lengthy conflict in which the Allies would show themselves to possess the superior staying power. By using the traditional economic weapon of the naval blockade, by steadily augmenting the world-wide resources of the British and French Empires, and by dealing with Italy first if that power dared to engage in war, the strategic experts hoped to find the best method of achieving eventual victory without too excessive a cost.[56]

The fallacy of placing many hopes upon the blockade was an obvious one in view of Germany's position, as the previous war had shown and as the existing power-political situation suggested:

> Compared to her neighbours in September 1939 Germany's strength was very great ... The basis of German production had recently increased as a result of a long period of territorial expansion; the steel and oil of Austria, the steel and armaments of Czechoslovakia, the coalfield of the Saar, all had been considerable accretions of strength. In 1938 greater Germany produced 22,000,000 tons of steel, one-quarter as much again as the United Kingdom and France. Her coal resources in the Saar, Silesia, and the Ruhr, were much greater than those of France and the United Kingdom. Her machine-tool industry was the strongest in Europe . . .[57]

And what she didn't control she could secure from near-by neutrals – or take by further expansion. But this particular British fallacy, great though it was, paled in comparison with its corollary – that the Allies, and especially Britain, were *in the long run* financially and industrially the stronger, provided that, as in 1914, they were given sufficient time to turn their industry upon a war footing and to liquidate some of their accumulated reserves of capital. Confidence in this, 'the fourth arm of defence' as Inskip had called it, was the most misplaced confidence of all.

For the final irony of British defence policy in the inter-war years was that the Treasury, cursed by the 're-armers' at the time and almost universally scorned in historical literature since, was in fact perfectly correct in its Cassandra-like forebodings of the consequences of this large-scale spending upon the armed forces. These great increases in government expenditure, these enormous loans, did cause inflation; the many orders abroad for machine-tools, steel, aircraft, instruments, much of which a weakened British industry could no longer produce itself, drastically raised the amount of imports; yet the steady transition of the economy from a peacetime to a wartime basis meant that the proportion of goods devoted to exports was falling rapidly; nor did the general level of international trade and finance in an increasingly protectionist world give any hope that Britain's earnings from 'invisibles' would cover the yawning trade gap. It was, of course, true that the Treasury's draconian policies after 1919 had exaggerated the doctrines of normal trade and a balanced budget to the detriment of every other consideration; and that, for a modest increase in defence expenditure not only would the services have had fewer deficiencies when war came but unemployment would have been cut and unused resources exploited. But by 1939, with defence allocations spiralling upwards at a rate which (it was estimated) would lead to a deficit on trade of £400 million in the first year of war alone, these criticisms of 11, Downing Street, were no longer valid. In the April of 1939 – in the midst of a whole host of political and diplomatic actions which showed that Britain was once again going to take a hand on the continent and that she was expanding all three services at an enormous pace in the expectation of a gigantic and long drawn-out struggle with Germany – the Treasury coldly pointed out that 'If we were under the impression that we were as well able as in 1914 to conduct a long war, we were burying our heads in the sand.'[58]

In other words the policy which the Chiefs of Staff and the Cabinet had accepted as the only possible one for Britain, given the existing circumstances – the policy of a long war, with the premium on stamina – was also the one which the Treasury found most calamitous. When the conflict came, exports, re-exports and invisibles would rapidly shrink whilst the demand for imports would surge forward. Yet even before that final agonized decision to go to war, Britain was swiftly becoming bankrupt; and the harder she increased her armaments production, and the more determinedly she waged war, the quicker the final financial collapse would be. It was a grim prospect for a nation that had once been called 'the workshop of the world' and whose industrial and financial strength had been her chief weapon in the struggle against Napoleon. Now, instead of her economy being a supporting 'fourth arm' of defence, it was likely to be her Achilles' Heel.

CHAPTER ELEVEN

The Illusory Victory (1939–45)

The successful termination of the war against our present enemies will find a world profoundly changed in respect of relative national military strengths, a change more comparable indeed with that occasioned by the fall of Rome than with any other change occurring during the succeeding fifteen hundred years ... After the defeat of Japan, the United States and the Soviet Union will be the only military powers of the first magnitude. This is due in each case to a combination of geographical position and extent, and vast munitioning potential ... Both in an absolute sense and relative to the United States and Russia, the British Empire will emerge from the war having lost ground both economically and militarily.

U.S. Military Staff predictions for the post-war world, cited in M. Matloff, *Strategic Planning for Coalition Warfare 1943–1944* (Washington, D.C., 1959), pp. 523–4.

In terms of actions fought and battles won the performance of the Royal Navy in the Second World War was incomparably better than in the first.[1] In part, this was due to the fact that many lessons were learned from that earlier struggle, especially the freeing of individual initiative; officers such as Pound, Harwood, Tovey, Cunningham and Fraser had observed the stultifying effects of the Admiralty's obsession at that time with the maintenance of its numerical superiority *vis-à-vis* the High Seas Fleet and of a too rigid adherence to line-of-battle tactics, and sought to avoid a repetition of that policy when they later secured Fleet Commands.[2] Moreover, they had from the outset a First Lord who encouraged them to think and act offensively, and who did not cease to do so after he had assumed the office of Prime Minister.[3] Most important of all, that overwhelming superiority in ships and men, which had permitted the Royal Navy to adopt a predominantly passive strategy between 1914 and 1918 and to reap the benefits therefrom, no longer existed: the inter-war economy measures, and the inability of Britain's weakened finances and industries to do more than repair the most basic fleet deficiencies in the few years of rearmament, left the service and the country in what was probably its most parlous position since 1778. Stretched and strained throughout the globe, the British were fighting for their lives. Under such dire circumstances it was scarcely surprising that they displayed an ingenuity and a ruthlessness which more comfortable situations rarely bring forth.

In the early months of the war, however, the naval situation looked somewhat similar to that of 1914. With Italy and Japan still neutral, the Anglo-French fleets held a decisive superiority over Raeder's embryo navy, and all the indications were that the basic strategical problem would once again be that of devising a method of persuading the enemy's smaller surface fleet to give battle. With a sense that history was repeating itself, the Royal Navy's main fleet was concentrated at Scapa, blockade patrols were instituted and the Expeditionary Force was carefully shepherded to France. Nor was this feeling lacking in stations overseas, where Germany's few commerce raiders were being searched for by numerous task forces. The defeat of the *Graf Spee* in December 1939 called forth, both because of the name of the ship and of the region in which it sank, vivid memories of Sturdee's success at the Falklands.

In the early summer of 1940 this illusion of similarity was totally shattered. By the successful invasions of Denmark and Norway Germany not only upset the Allies' own calculations but also broke through that North Sea 'gate' which had been such a hindrance to the High Seas Fleet in the First World War: now the Atlantic itself was open to the German navy, just as Wegener and other strategists had foretold and encouraged in the inter-war years.[4] Worse was to follow as the *Wehrmacht* unleashed its strength in the west, overrunning Belgium and the Netherlands, crushing the French and sending the British force reeling back to the Channel coast, where only a miracle of improvisation enabled it to be embarked for home. At Dunkirk, as in Norwegian and Cretan waters, the navy suffered heavy losses from aerial assault, but in strategical terms the picture was far more serious. The Low Countries, whose position as 'a pistol pointed at England' had caused British governments for almost four centuries to strive to keep independent, were now in the hands of the mightiest ruler Europe had seen since the days of Napoleon; so, too, were the French Atlantic ports, which meant that Hitler had broken out of the North Sea at its southern end also; an invasion of England was now distinctly possible; the considerable French Navy, instead of being a form of assistance, was at best neutral and indeed in great danger of falling into enemy hands; and Mussolini, with a jackal's sense of occasion, had just thrown in his equally strong navy on Hitler's side, these two latter events meaning an enormous change in the naval balance against Britain (of fifteen capital ships, thirty-seven cruisers, nearly 200 destroyers and torpedo-craft and 200 submarines), the virtual closure of the Mediterranean and a serious threat to Egypt. At the same time, the U-boat menace was unfolding with the same vigour and the same grim results as it had done in 1914 to 1918 and was threatening to cut the vital flow of imports to Britain; while the Nazi assault upon the Soviet Union in June 1941 and Churchill's response to it meant that the navy assumed an additional – and extremely arduous – convoy escort obligation. Meanwhile the Japanese threat in the Far East continued to grow.

Despite a strategic situation which made the Chiefs of Staff's gloomy pre-war premonitions pale by comparison, British naval forces astonishingly held their own. 'Force H' was established at Gibraltar and the Italian challenge was effectively neutralized; the prospect of the French fleet falling into German hands was forestalled, in part at least, by the attack upon the ships at Oran and Dakar, actions so ruthless that only those against the Danish fleet in 1801 and 1807 are at all comparable to them; the U-boat and aerial attacks upon British merchantmen were never allowed to disrupt totally the maritime routes to Malta, to Russia or to the British Isles; and the occasional forays of the German surface fleet, such as the epic cruise of the *Bismarck*, were also contained – although with great loss and often with the Fates clearly on Britannia's side. Even that most dreaded of all events, a Japanese onslaught upon the exposed British position in the Far East, was not an unmitigated disaster. Though the *Prince of Wales* and *Repulse* were sunk, the A.B.D.A. forces scattered, the port of Hong Kong, the great base at Singapore, and the valuable colonies of Malaya, Borneo and Burma lost, and Somerville's fleet chased away from Trincomalee, the United States had at last been brought into the war, providing not only naval support but also vast financial and industrial resources. In the longer term there was good reason for Churchill to sleep 'the sleep of the saved and the thankful' when he learnt of the news about the attack upon Pearl Harbor.[5]

Yet not even the American entry into the war prevented the naval struggle from being as critical in 1942 and 1943 as it had been a year earlier, especially in the battle of the Atlantic, which was once again the most important of all: if Britain lost this one, she had lost herself. Nevertheless, despite Allied merchant ship losses of almost eight million tons in 1942 alone, the lines of communication were kept open. And in the same year Anglo-American naval forces themselves carried the offensive to the enemy by escorting invasion troops to North Africa; later they provided cover for the assaults upon Sicily, southern Italy and eventually France itself. In the Pacific war the United States Navy did most of the fighting but by 1945 a British Pacific Fleet was also active there and preparing to take part in the invasion of Japan. By May of that year, despite the loss of 451 warships of all categories in the war to date, the Royal Navy had expanded to the enormous size of 1,065 warships, 2,907 minor war vessels and 5,477 landing craft, manned by 863,500 personnel. Once again, although suffering in the early stages of the conflict from the consequences of the country's previous neglect and parsimony, the service had fought the good fight and emerged victorious at the end of it all. The heart of oak remained undefeated. The glorious traditions were further enhanced. And, with the collapse of the German, Italian and Japanese empires, Britain's naval position had been fully recovered and even consolidated.

But had it? And is the above synopsis of the course of the naval war, an admittedly brief account, but typical of many with the accent heavily upon the ships and the men and the battles, at all adequate for our survey of that much more elusive element, British sea power? Clearly not: for a 'naval history of the war' in that simple sense, may help us to know what happened, but that is about all. Once again we must make our approach broader – and deeper – than the traditional one and scrutinize again the factors which lie behind naval mastery. As soon as we do that, the picture looks much bleaker. Far from having emerged in a strengthened position at the close of the Second World War, British sea power had been grievously – mortally may not be too strong a word – stricken by it. Those trends which we detected as early as the nineteenth century had just received their greatest confirmation.

Essentially all that the navy had done – and could do – in strategical terms was to keep open the sea routes to Britain from the outside world, just as it had done in the First World War. This was a quite vital function; in Churchill's words it was the 'foundation' upon which victory was based; yet basically it remained a negative, defensive contribution. Even here, however, the struggle was much more in the balance than it had been during the earlier conflict: the Mediterranean and Far Eastern routes were interrupted, the Arctic route had to be suspended occasionally, and the Atlantic losses were far heavier than in 1914–18 despite the early adoption of the convoy system. It is also clear that Britain only survived the U-boat onslaughts because of weapons and countermeasures which had little to do with the traditional ways with which she had maintained command of the sea: the introduction of American-built very-long-range Liberators to close the Atlantic 'gap'; escort-carriers, again American-built in most cases; the strategic bombing campaign, which caused delays to the German submarine construction programme; and the launching of sufficient merchant vessels to keep pace with the sinkings, an activity where the United States equalled and then surpassed its staggering First World War production performance. The development of new methods of detecting submarines, the exhausting labours of convoy duty, and the grim fights with the enemy were overwhelmingly an affair of the Royal Navy; but it is doubtful whether they would have sufficed without the assistance of these non-British, non-naval factors.

The most important of the new elements, predictably enough, was air-power, indicated perhaps by the fact that whereas 246 German U-boats were sunk by Allied surface craft, 288 were sunk by Allied aircraft (excluding bombing raids).[6] The Second World War saw the full arrival and exploitation of this revolutionary weapon and the fulfilment of the prophecies of Douhet, Mitchell, Trenchard and the others that aircraft were vital to achieve dominance over land and sea theatres. As such, this did not invalidate Mahan's doctrine that command of the sea meant control of those 'broad highways', the lines of communication between homeland and overseas ports; but it did spell the end of the navy's claim to a monopoly role in preserving such sea mastery. And the Admiralty's established belief that a fleet of battleships provided the ultimate force to control the ocean seaways was made to look more old-fashioned than ever – and very erroneous and dangerous.

It is astonishing to discover just how much military and naval experts such as Churchill, Ironside, Pound and Phillips underestimated the threat from the air to surface vessels at the outset of war. In the Norwegian campaign, for example, there was no hesitation in sending 'a squadron into Trondheim with no reconnaissance, and with the certainty that they would be bombed'.[7] The aerial attacks upon the Home Fleet soon forced a reconsideration of this attitude – and, with it, the eventual withdrawal from central and northern Norway.

Although the Fleet Air Arm bombers based upon the Orkneys achieved a remarkable feat in destroying the cruiser *Königsberg*, the first major warship to be sunk from the air, this could hardly compare with the way in which the navy's activities as a whole had been neutralized by the

Luftwaffe. Traditionally, sea-borne landings had incurred the risk of swift enemy counter-attacks from land; now they had to ward off the danger from the air as well. The official British historian of this campaign could only conclude that 'It was the threat from German air power, effective against smaller ships in the narrow waters of the Leads and fjords, which prevented our naval superiority from exercising its accustomed influence on the operations . . .'[8]

The lesson was repeated at Dunkirk, where an armada of small ships succeeded brilliantly in its strategical aim, but at a heavy cost in destroyers and other warships. Off Crete, where the *Luftwaffe* again enjoyed aerial superiority, the navy operated in a maelstrom of bombing attacks, which sank three cruisers and six destroyers and badly damaged two battleships, one carrier, six cruisers and seven destroyers – the greater part of the Mediterranean Fleet. But the most disastrous manifestation of what well-trained aircrews could do to the Royal Navy's warships came in the first few months of the war in the Far East. On 8 December 1941 the new battleship *Prince of Wales* and the battle-cruiser *Repulse* were attacked by Japanese aircraft and, despite their violent manœuvrings and intense anti-aircraft fire, were torn apart and sunk by bombs and torpedoes within a couple of hours. It is with a tragic sense of irony that one notes that the British Admiral on that day was none other than Tom Phillips, who had been one of the most scornful of all about the dangers posed by aircraft. And in early April 1942 a Japanese carrier force attacked Ceylon and southern India, forced Somerville's Eastern Fleet to withdraw to Africa, and punished whatever ships they could still find in the area – notably the small carrier *Hermes* and the cruisers *Cornwall* and *Dorsetshire*. The latter ship, shattered by nine direct bomb hits, disappeared within eight minutes of first being attacked. Beatty, had he lived to see the sight, would scarcely have believed his eyes.

It is, in fact, difficult to discover many naval encounters of the Second World War whose results were not decidedly influenced by the use of aircraft: the battles of the River Plate, the Barents Sea and the North Cape in the Royal Navy's war against Germany may be instanced, and in the Pacific the American–Japanese engagements known as the Second Naval Battle of Guadalcanal and the Battle of the Surigao Strait. Otherwise, the role of air power was of enormous significance, both tactically and strategically, to the Royal Navy: the success of the Atlantic, Mediterranean and Arctic convoys was dependent upon it; the Italian fleet at Taranto was gravely crippled by it; the long-standing threat posed by the *Tirpitz* was eliminated by it; even the sinking of the *Bismarck* had hung upon the efforts of a few, frail Swordfish torpedo-bombers. And as newer and more effective aircraft, air-sights and bombs were developed during the war the danger to warships became greater.

The Admiralty was swift enough, of course, to recognize the significance of this trend after the first few disastrous campaigns, and to utilize their own carriers to the utmost. As Captain Roskill has noted,

> Rarely can the flexibility of maritime power have been more convincingly demonstrated than by *Ark Royal*'s accomplishment in flying Hurricanes to Malta from a position well inside the Mediterranean on 21 May [1941] and crippling the *Bismarck* with her torpedo-bombers 500 miles to the west of Brest six days later.[9]

The only question is whether this still may be claimed as a demonstration of 'maritime power' or whether in fact it was a new hybrid form of power, part air, part sea, which the Admiralty could never fully control when actions took place within range of land-based aircraft and which it could only exploit by abandoning its traditional weapons and claims. At any rate by 1942 their Lordships had become so conscious of the importance of the carrier that they decided to have between fifty-five and sixty-two of them.[10] In view of Britain's cramped shipbuilding facilities, however, it proved impossible to do more than to complete the *Illustrious*-class fleet carriers and to build six light fleet carriers by the end of the war.

It was in the Pacific war that the rise of the carrier and the consequent decline of the battleship was most apparent – in part because the devastation wrought upon their battle-fleet on the 'day of infamy' forced the Americans to rely solely upon their carriers in the first part of this struggle. Then the battles of the Coral Sea and Midway confirmed the lesson of Pearl Harbor itself. As a result powerful carrier task forces were created and became the spearhead of Nimitz's advance across the Central Pacific – isolating the enemy's island groups, crushing his land- or sea-based air strength, devastating his naval bases (Truk) and mauling his fleet wherever it ventured to give battle, much as in the struggles of the Philippine Sea and Leyte Gulf. By the later stages of the war, Mitscher's force of sixteen or more carriers could launch over 1,000 modern aircraft against enemy targets, whereas the battleships were reduced to the role of pre-invasion bombardment vessels. It was quite symbolic, therefore, that the largest battleship ever built, the 72,000-ton *Yamato*, was to be overwhelmed by bombs and torpedoes from American carrier planes alone, during its 'suicide run' to Okinawa. Like the *Tirpitz*, she had never fired her massive main armament against enemy battleships. 'When she went down', Morison wrote, 'five centuries of naval warfare ended.' It was not purely a coincidence that those five centuries marked the period of the rise and fall of British naval mastery. The old was giving way to the new in more ways than one.

Yet if the Second World War demonstrated that command of the sea was dependent upon a prior command of the air, it also failed to confirm the superiority and effectiveness of maritime power in its more ancient relationship – with continental land power. In the American campaign against the widely dispersed Japanese Empire, of course, the outcome was different; but the British seemed never to have understood the basic geographical contrast between their two main enemies. Thus it was that the strategical role played by the Royal Navy against Germany was a mere repetition of that in the years 1914–18: holding the line. The fact that it was much more difficult and called for more frequent displays of heroism to accomplish this task, because the odds were greater, the convoy routes more dangerous and attacks from the air more common, should not obscure this basic point. In all other respects, too, the navy's tasks – and accomplishments – were to be repeated. There was no need to overrun enemy-held colonies (except those of Italy), but even if Germany had possessed overseas territories it is doubtful whether their capture by the British would have had any profound effect upon the war. Nevertheless there remained the more important naval weapons of the blockade and the landing of troops, either for peripheral raids or for larger-scale strategical purposes. Yet in neither case was the part played by the navy as decisive as one might have imagined.

In view of the experience of the First World War, of Germany's dominant military and economic position in Europe by 1939, and of the fact that she was bordered by neutrals, it is difficult to understand how British leaders could have been so confident of the effects of a naval blockade, even in the long term. Before the outbreak of war, as we saw in an earlier chapter, the Chiefs of Staff had declared their faith in this weapon; and the swift overrunning of Poland did nothing to check their opinion that it was economic pressure 'upon which we mainly rely for the ultimate defeat of Germany'.[11] The American Neutrality Acts, which had the political effect of making the 'freedom of the seas' dispute an irrelevancy, were adjudged to be an additional advantage. As a consequence, Whitehall possessed a quite unjustified optimism about the struggle with Germany, the sole result of which was to make it disinclined to end the period of the Phoney War. 'What we ought to do is just to throw back the peace offers and continue the blockade', noted Chamberlain, 'I do not believe that holocausts are required.' 'The Allies are bound to win in the end . . .'[12] Despite the commitment of the Expeditionary Force to France, there lingered that traditional fear of trench warfare on a massive scale; which, together with the exaggerated notion of the effects of the 'Hunger Blockade' upon Germany in 1918–19, combined to persuade the British that it would not be necessary to oppose the enemy's vast armies until his resources and morale were crumbling.

The flaw in this calculation was a massive one: London's estimate of the enemy's military strength contrasted sharply with its estimate of his economic power, even though those two elements had been so closely fused together that they were virtually indistinguishable. The many Russian and American charges of British tergiversation and reluctance to open a Second Front were undeniably true, yet London's attitude is easy to understand. To oppose a much enlarged *Wehrmacht* in complete control of the continent with a far smaller British Empire force was, even apart from the problems of air command and logistical support, a suicidal gesture, and Churchill was correct in resisting the pressure from his allies for a premature invasion. But it was precisely because Germany was in such a dominant position and controlled the destinies and economies of the greater part of Europe that the British should have been wary of any hopes of Nazi rule collapsing due to maritime pressure alone. Mahanite methods were ineffectual against a power which had adopted a Mackinder-ite expansion programme.

On the face of it, the British experts reckoned, Germany was very susceptible to blockading pressure: like any modern industrialized state, she traded extensively with the outside world and her war economy was dependent upon some absolutely vital raw materials.[13] Over 66 per cent of her ores for steel production came from abroad, as did 25 per cent of her zinc, 50 per cent of her lead, 70 per cent of her copper, 90 per cent of her tin, 95 per cent of her nickel, 99 per cent of her bauxite, 66 per cent of her oil, 80 per cent of her rubber and even 10 to 20 per cent of her foodstuffs. She was also heavily dependent upon imports of cotton, wool, mercury, mica, sulphur and manganese. Presented with these facts, it may not be surprising to learn that 'both Government and country regarded the blockade as Britain's chief offensive weapon, and looked to it for decisive, or at any rate dramatic, results'.[14] Yet this presumption could only be justified if Germany was an island; if the German leaders had been unable to take precautionary measures; if they could not secure supplies, either from friendly neutrals or conquered territories; and if her armed forces were so heavily engaged in battle that her stocks were being run down and her productivity insufficient. However, none of these provisos was to be true until the later stages of the war, when reliance upon the blockade had been abandoned for more direct measures in any case.

From the outset of his policy of aggression, Hitler had realized the dangers that might come about from the cutting off of overseas supplies and he strove, through the Four-Year-Plan and other measures, to combat the effects of a possible blockade. His aim, widely proclaimed, was economic autarky, an absolute freedom from dependence upon other states – and as such a direct contrast to the liberal concepts of international economic interdependence which influenced British attitudes. Such a target was to be achieved in part by the creation of substitutes, despite the higher costs involved: synthetic wool (from a wood base), rubber (from buna) and motor and aviation fuel (through hydrogenation) were the main products here. On similar grounds, low-grade iron ores which hitherto had been considered unusable were now exploited, and domestic foodstuffs production was intensified. Secondly, there was a ready flow of materials from pro-Axis and neutral states: ores from Sweden; oil, foodstuffs and copper from Rumania, Russia and Yugoslavia; molybdenum from Norway; nickel and chrome from the Balkans; wolfram from Spain and Portugal; bauxite from Italy and Hungary. Only by a decisive blow in Scandinavia to cut the flow of Swedish iron ore to Germany could great damage be done to the Nazi economy by the Royal Navy – which goes far to justify the Allies' Norwegian policy and at least part of the way to explain Churchill's reckless scheme for operations in the Baltic.[15] The threat from German air-power quashed this latter project, however, as it did the whole Norwegian venture.

Finally, there was conquest: the looting of Europe to enrich the Thousand-Year-Reich and to create a completely autarkic economy. Once again, Hitler was quite clear about his plans. Russia, the Heartland, he enthused, would be the key: 'We shall be the most self-supporting State, in every respect, including cotton, in the world . . .'[16] But on the way to this great aim many other countries could be pillaged. The victories in the west in 1940, for example, were not simply the military one of defeating enemy armies or the strategical one of gaining access to the Atlantic; there was also the acquisition of the Lorraine–Luxembourg–Minette iron ore deposits; the stockpiles of various important metals in Belgium; more oil reserves in France than the *Wehrmacht* had used in the Polish, Norwegian and French campaigns together; and the opening of a land route to the tungsten and ores and wolfram of Spain and Portugal and the bauxite of North Africa. Similarly, the seizure of Norway secured the supply of molybdenum and nickel, the over-running of Yugoslavia and Greece provided bauxite and other metals, and the virtual takeover of Rumania greatly eased the oil situation. As agents of this new *Herrenvolk*, the occupation forces and offices had no scruples about intensive exploitation of captured resources; the 'contributions' from these territories to Germany's national income rose from 8 per cent in the early years of the war to 20 per cent by 1942.

Nor was it true, until after 1942 at least, that the actual operations of war were draining the Nazi economy: until the battles of Moscow and Stalingrad the Germans were leisurely waging war, enjoying both the guns *and* butter that a *Blitzkrieg* strategy allowed. As a result British war production, far behind in the pre-war years, caught Germany up and by 1942 Britain was actually spending half as much again on munitions, giving her a 60 per cent superiority in aircraft and small arms production and a 33 per cent superiority in tank output. In that year, however, with the defeats on the Eastern Front and the entry of the United States combining to convince the Nazi leadership of the need to organize for a long struggle, German production shot ahead again. Under Speer's leadership, the vast German labour force of 41·2 million (cf. Britain's 22·6 million; both 1943) and enormous industrial potential of half a continent was made much more efficient. The aircraft production figures alone tell the story better than words:[17]

	1940	1941	1942	1943	1944
Germany	10,825	10,775	15,550	25,000	40,000
Britain	15,050	20,100	23,670	26,200	26,500

In the same way, German tank production increased from 6,200 in 1942 to 19,000 in 1944, artillery pieces rose from 23,000 to 71,000 in the same period, and the British superiority in small arms production of 60 per cent had changed to a German one of 100 per cent by 1944. On the eve of the Normandy invasion, ironically enough, Germany was better stocked in most types of military equipment than ever before – making the strategy of wearing down her resistance by blockade appear quite absurd.

Yet if British war production was being outpaced by a reorganized German industry this provided little consolation in Berlin when Russian and American output was growing even faster. In the years 1942–4, Germany's annual production averages of 26,000 aircraft and 12,000 tanks and self-propelled guns were far behind the Russian averages of 40,000 and 30,000 respectively.[18] American war production was simply phenomenal: in 1941 it was only 75 per cent of Germany's, but by the following year it was already 2½ times as great and still in its early stages. Whereas the Americans had built only 2,100 aircraft in 1939, this had risen to 48,000 in 1942, 86,000 in 1943 and to a staggering 96,300 in 1944. In fact, in the five years 1940–45 the United States produced 297,000 aircraft, 86,000 tanks, 17,400,000 small arms, 64,500 landing vessels and 5,200 larger ships (of nearly fifty-three million tons).[19] In terms of military potential, therefore, the Americans were in a virtually unchallengeable position, with Russia second, Germany third and Britain only a modest fourth.

Nevertheless, if the 1939 beliefs in the effectiveness of a blockade and in the long-term British economic superiority over Germany were illusions, it remains true that the Nazi industrial machine collapsed into ruins between 1944 and 1945. The first cause of this was obvious: the losses in men and materials in the prolonged fighting against the Allies, particularly on the Eastern Front, were now far in excess of Germany's resources. Furthermore, as the *Wehrmacht* was forced to surrender territory, so correspondingly did Speer lose vital supplies of raw materials – a trend which was further aggravated by the increasing unwillingness of neutrals to provide help to a failing empire. Rivalries within the Nazi hierarchy, and the diversion of workers from production into fighting in October 1944, were equally deleterious in their effects. Most important of all, however, was the strategic bombing campaign, which after a disappointing first few years had by 1944 achieved the strength and the accuracy which its prophets had forecast for it two decades earlier. In February of that year the assaults upon the German aircraft industry caused structural damage in 75 per cent of all air-frame component and assembly plants. Later in the year the bombers switched to oil production, causing such a crisis that German tanks, aircraft and warships were frequently unable to operate in crucial campaigns due to the lack of this commodity; and in early 1945 they struck at the German transport system with devastating effect, isolating the coalfields from industry. 'The development of the long-range bomber', Milward writes, 'provided a means of economic warfare infinitely more effective than the traditional blockade.' It was far more positive and specific, and the fact that 'many of the calculations on which the naval blockade had been based had been nullified by Germany's extension of her territorial area of control' made no difference to it. 'It effected a virtual revolution in economic warfare.'[20] Yet if Allied statesmen could rejoice at the achievements of this new weapon and encourage its use – and Britain is estimated to have devoted 50 to 60 per cent of her entire war production to the R.A.F. – this simply served to illustrate the decline in the importance of the naval blockade and of sea power itself. The best that could be said about the traditional policy was that to abandon it might have eased the economic pressure upon the enemy. Nevertheless the system of contraband control and preemptive buying at source was more effective than naval measures, and the official historian of this topic has concluded that 'At no stage of the war was Germany decisively weakened by shortages due to the blockade alone.' Her Achilles' Heel was struck 'by the bomber and not by the blockade'.[21] Only Japan and Britain herself, both being island states heavily dependent upon sea-borne trade, proved economically susceptible to enemy naval pressure in the Second World War, although in both cases it was the submarine and not surface warships which provided the danger.

In almost the same way the navy's importance in amphibious operations was also overtaken by air and land power. Crete and Norway showed that such steps could only be taken when command of the air had been secured; Dieppe and Greece showed that small-scale interventions would always be punished by superior enemy forces, able to rush swiftly to the point of attack. All signified, as the British Chiefs could see, that an invasion of western Europe would have to be a massive one and that they would have to wait upon the Americans. Yet the success of Overlord, when it came, was heavily dependent upon Allied air superiority, which had been steadily won in the preceding two years. British and American bombers devastated the enemy's communications system before the invasion started; their fighters protected the massive convoys and the bridgehead from aerial interference; and their bombers were again at work in the period after D-Day, checking the enemy's counter-attack and forcing him to travel at night. By comparison, the navy's role was far less significant; their supporting gunfire was certainly of use to the invading troops, 'but the decisive factor was the paralysing effect of the Allied air forces . . .'[22] In any case, despite the undeniable success of the Overlord operation, the real stuffing was knocked out of the German Army on its Eastern Front, where it suffered over four-fifths of its casualties and where Soviet military casualties were greater than those of *all* combatants in the First World War. Compared with this struggle for Mackinder's Heartland, the British-led campaigns in North Africa and Italy were mere sideshows in the Churchill–Lloyd George tradition of avoiding the slaughter of frontal confrontations. Yet if the Second World War did anything – apart from illustrating the overall decline in the effectiveness of warships alone – it was to break the myth of the efficacy of the 'British way of warfare' against a power which straddled half a continent. In the two German wars they had earnestly sought for an indirect approach:

> But the historical truth is that there *was* no shorter way, until the possession and use of the atomic bomb by one side created it . . . What the past has shown is that armies of millions, equipped by modern technology, cannot be defeated quickly, and that war economies show almost

> incredible capacity for survival even under the most intense duress, as Germany proved in 1944 and 1945. It requires the fullest, sustained pressure on both the military and economic fronts to achieve "victory" . . .[23]

The greatest flaw in the British over-estimation of the effects of their sea power lay in the associated calculation that, whilst the blockade was steadily sapping the enemy's strength, the superior economic resources of the Empire would be assembled to provide the eventual retribution; that, just as Britain's combined maritime and financial pressure had caused the collapse of the Dutch and French challenges in the seventeenth and eighteenth centuries, so too it would undermine the German threat in the twentieth. Yet this assumption, accepted by almost everyone from armchair strategists to the Chiefs of Staff, was based upon the fallacy that Britain's productive strength, her control of raw materials and especially her financial resources, were as well equipped to withstand war now as they had been in the era of her rise to economic supremacy in the western world – which clearly was no longer the case. Contrary to expectations, it was she who experienced shortages of raw materials, caused partly by the Japanese conquest of Far Eastern sources of rubber, tin, sisal, hemp, tungsten and hardwood; and partly by the successful German 'counter-blockade' of the U-boats. Moreover, as we have seen above, Britain could not match the munitions' production of her enemy, once Speer had re-organized the German armaments industry; nor could she, even with substantial Commonwealth reinforcements, hope to field an army strong enough to challenge the *Wehrmacht* on the continent. In May 1942, as the rapid rise in munitions output was beginning to reach that plateau dictated by the size of Britain's population, the Minister of Labour warned Churchill that further demands upon manpower for the armed forces must be met mainly by diverting workers from industry, and thereby reducing production.[24] To keep up the war effort, to achieve the proclaimed aim of 'victory at all costs', they were forced more and more to rely upon the United States: she alone had the industrial capacity and the manpower to ensure the defeat of Germany in the West.

In the second quarter of 1942 American military output caught up with the British; by the end of 1943, her production of aircraft was double, her launchings of merchant vessels six times, that of Britain; and by 1944 her overall armaments' production was six times as large.[25] The full potential of her continent-wide resources, her great population, her more modern industry, was at last being realized – to produce a super-power which was as far ahead of Britain as the latter had been of the declining and smaller states of Spain, Portugal and the Netherlands centuries earlier. The figures for total arms expenditures alone go a long way towards explaining the eventual outcome of the Second World War in Europe:[26]

	1941	1943
USA	4·5	37·5 ($ billion)
Britain	6·5	11·1
Russia	8·5	13·9
Germany	6·0	13·8

Moreover, whilst American munitions' output outclassed that of all other combatants, this in no way strained its finances: 63 per cent of the German GNP was devoted to military expenditure by 1943 and the British figure was not far short of that, yet America's level was never more than 43 per cent.[27] With less effort, with far fewer sacrifices, she was winning the war; and the British soldier's frequent complaints about the profligacy of his better-fed, better-paid and better-equipped American counterpart were simply indirect manifestations of this overwhelming material and financial superiority.

It would therefore be no exaggeration to argue that Churchill's greatest contribution to the British war strategy was to recognize from the beginning that American support was absolutely essential, and to strive with all his charm and all his wiles to secure that assistance in a form best suited to the interests of the British Empire. Nevertheless, there is something pathetic as well as touching about his reaction to the news of the Japanese attack upon Pearl Harbor:

> So we had won after all! Yes, after Dunkirk; after the fall of France; after the horrible episode of Oran; after the threat of invasion, when, apart from the Air and the Navy, we were an almost unarmed people; after the deadly struggle of the U-boat – the Battle of the Atlantic, gained by a hand's breadth; after seventeen months of lonely fighting and nineteen months of my responsibility in dire stress, we had won the war. England would live; Britain would live; the Commonwealth of Nations and the Empire would live.[28]

Yes, Britain and her Empire would live and their history 'would not come to an end'; but it would only be because a rising young power had been dragged into the war and compelled by circumstance to prop up her hard-pressed and sagging partner.

The chief consequence of this disparity in strength was that Britain became dependent upon American aid to an ever-increasing degree – somewhat akin to those continental states of the eighteenth century for whose upkeep she herself had provided subsidies in her better days. Even before the outbreak of war she was importing a vast amount of American machine-tools to rebuild her own armaments industry, together with an increasing number of aircraft; but by the summer of 1940, when the collapse of France brought the prospect of invasion closer than at any time since 1805 and when Churchill had taken office on a 'fight to the death' policy, the orders to the United States were multiplied, regardless of cost. Between April and July of that year the steel requirement of £12·6 million for 1940 was raised to £100 million for 1941. In August 1940 the Ministry of Supply ordered 3,000 cruiser tanks in the United States; in September it asked for 1,600 heavy anti-aircraft guns, one million rifles, 1,800 field guns and 1,250 anti-tank guns. But this was only a beginning: if a fifty-five-division army was to be created, if an enormous strategic bomber force was to batter Germany's cities every day, if the navy was to be given an effective two-power standard and merchant ship losses were to be replaced, the flow of munitions from the United States had to be increased still further.

Britain herself was making heroic sacrifices, of course, stretching the energies of her workers and the capacity of her industries to abnormal levels – but it was not enough. Indeed, she severely overstrained herself and was forced to see production decline in the final part of the war; while her aircraft output levelled off, the number of tanks she produced fell from 8,600 in 1942 to 4,600 in 1944, and artillery pieces completed fell from 43,000 to 16,000 in the same period. The dependence upon American supply rose correspondingly: in 1941 10 per cent of the Empire's munitions came from that source, but it had risen to 27 per cent in 1943 and to 28·7 per cent in 1944. More specifically, the United States supplied 47 per cent of the Empire's total consumption of tanks, 21 per cent of small arms, 38 per cent of the landing craft and ships, 18 per cent of the combat and 60 per cent of the transport aircraft. Yet as Hancock and Gowing note,

> To the British inquirer, perhaps the most impressive demonstration of American strength is the fact that the aid which so decisively reinforced the war effort of his own people was only a subsidiary element in the American war effort.[29]

In the peak year of 1944, for instance, the aircraft sent to Britain amounted to only 13·5 per cent of total American output, the ships 6·7 per cent, the vital food imports 5 per cent, ordnance and ammunition 8·8 per cent and only in vehicles and their equipment was the British share in any way considerable – 29·4 per cent. In the two years 1943–4, when lend-lease reached its maximum volume, 'deliveries of all types of military equipment amounted to approximately 11½ per cent of American output'.[30] Finally, there were ominous indications – from new naval construction and the B–29 Superfortress, for example – of American *qualitative* as well as quantitative superiority.[31]

The financial consequences of this victory 'at all costs' programme and the increasing reliance upon the United States were disastrous for Britain; her position as an independent great power was shattered. In the spring of 1939, as we noticed in the previous chapter, the Treasury was full of forebodings: 'The position had radically changed for the worse compared with 1914 . . . we had not the same resources for purchasing supplies from abroad . . . We were already experiencing anxiety as to payment for stores from abroad for which dollars are required.'[32] With an estimated adverse trade balance of £400 million on 1940 alone and total gold and dollar reserves of £700 million, it was doubtful if Britain could wage war for more than two years. That was its opinion in February 1940; by August, with the pace of war accelerating, the Chancellor was forced to warn the Cabinet that the nation's gold and dollar reserves would be exhausted by Xmas.[33] The root of the problem, so it appeared to Britain's leaders, lay in the fact that they had to pay 'cash and carry' for all these American munitions in compliance with the Neutrality Acts – and the more Britain ordered, the swifter she would become bankrupt. By the end of 1940 the orders totalled $10,000 million, which was far in excess of her First World War debts and quite outside her capacity to pay. Only emergency shipments of gold, and borrowing from Canada and the Belgian government, helped to keep her solvent by 1941, when her gold and dollar reserves dipped to a mere $12 million. In March of that year, however, Roosevelt had succumbed to Churchill's pleadings and to his own fears of a Nazi victory, and he persuaded Congress to pass the famous Lend-Lease Act.

At the time, and in many later accounts of this measure, it was seen as a magnanimous gesture, 'a most unsordid act'. Lately, it has been subjected to more critical assessments, and not merely from British historians. In the first place, its main aim genuinely was 'to promote the defense of the United States' as its title suggested: for the fall of the British Isles implied for the United States what the fall of France and the Low Countries had implied for Britain. Hence, too, an American anxiety over the future of the Royal Navy no less great than the Admiralty's concern for the French fleet. In the second place, even if the United States was lending its

Anglo-Saxon neighbour a financial 'hosepipe', it required considerable compensation for this gesture to appease its own domestic critics. Like any bank manager, it felt it necessary to dictate conditions before proferring benefits upon a needy customer. Britain's gold and dollar reserves were rigorously controlled in order to prevent them from rising above the level thought desirable in Washington – even though a similar scrutiny was not exercised over other powers receiving lend-lease. No lend-lease goods could go into exports, nor could similar *British-made* products be sent to overseas markets lest this provoke resentment in United States commercial circles. Not surprisingly British exports, already hit by the war, tumbled from a notional 100 in 1938 to twenty-nine in 1943. The consequences of this were clear. 'In a war allegedly governed by the concept of the pooling of resources among Allies', the official historians note, 'the British had taken upon themselves a sacrifice so disproportionate as to jeopardize their economic survival as a nation.'[34] 'She sacrificed her postwar future for the sake of the world', observed A. J. P. Taylor, recalling Keynes's admission that 'We threw good housekeeping to the winds.'[35] The decline in exports, Correlli Barnett has noted in a less homely metaphor, 'testified . . . to the degree to which, like a patient on a heart-lung machine, she was now dependent for life itself on the United States'.[36]

But these conditions, it has been suggested, were only the short-term requirements of the United States Treasury: the longer-term demands were more alarming still. Pushed on by a desire to increase their control of the raw materials of the world, and by a determination to see the breaking-up of those trading blocs which had hampered American exporting drives in the 1930s, Washington's political and business leaders sought an end to the Sterling Bloc and to the imperial preference system established at Ottawa in 1932; strove to ensure that British industries and traders – whose strength they greatly exaggerated – would not recover the markets they had been forced to surrender to their American rivals after 1939; and worked for an end to the European colonial Empires and a full freedom for their own firms to secure the oil of the Middle East, the rubber and tin of Malaya, and the markets of India and the colonies – at the same time ensuring that American raw materials, tariffs and spheres of influence (especially Latin America) would not be tampered with by the allies from whom she was demanding so much. Hence the constant insistence, in the Atlantic Charter, the 1942 Lend-Lease Agreement and elsewhere, upon 'access to the trade and raw materials of the world'; the frequent collisions with London over control of the oilfields of the Gulf States, Saudi Arabia and Iran; the efforts to control the size of the sterling balances by reducing lend-lease supplies; and the plan for an American-dominated International Banking Fund. So alarming did the American policy appear that the British government always strove to write into any agreements 'escape clauses that would permit them to save the sterling bloc as their major postwar crutch should that prove necessary'. Nevertheless, being in such a weakened position London could not always defend itself: by December 1943 Britain's sterling liabilities were seven times its gold and dollar holdings, which were only one-eighteenth of the American gold reserves and one third of France's gold and dollar reserves. It was long suspected that the United States had never really recognized the British Empire as a unit in any sense of a sovereign state, even if no open opposition had been showing. But now lend-lease, notes the chronicler of this unequal relationship, was rendering the British economy 'ill-equipped to resist American objectives at the end of the war'.[37]

Indeed, even the briefest survey of Britain's economic position in 1945 would illustrate just how disastrous the conflict had been for her. Only in terms of casualties could it be said to have been an improvement upon the First World War[38] – and that because of the determination to avoid mass assaults until the enemy's resistance had been sapped by the Russian army and the bombing campaign. Her losses in merchant ships totalled 11,455,906 tons, bringing the size of the fleet down to 70 per cent of its 1939 figure despite frantic rebuilding efforts (whereas the American merchant marine was now greater than all of Europe's together). Bombing had caused extensive damage to housing and industrial property, and the strain of six years of war had worn out much of Britain's plant and led to a heavy depreciation of capital equipment – which together destroyed some 10 per cent of her pre-war national wealth at home and left her in a poor position to recapture her world markets. Lend-lease conditions and the single-minded determination to prosecute the war regardless of the financial consequences had led to the collapse of her export trade, which declined in value from £471 million in 1938 to £258 million in 1945. During the same period, imports rose from £858 million to £1,299 million, overseas debts increased nearly fivefold, to £3,355 million, and capital assets to the tune of £1,299 million were liquidated, thereby halving the net overseas income from this source and making it even more difficult to achieve a balance of payments. She had probably lost about one quarter (£7,300 million) of her pre-war wealth and was now in the unenviable position of being the world's largest debtor nation.

In the later stages of the war the British government was planning a gradual transition from a wartime to a peacetime economy, through the reorganization of industry and the revival of export trades, so that the country would again be able to pay its way in the world; but the defeat of Japan in three (instead of the estimated eighteen) months after the German collapse, together with Truman's decision to cut off lend-lease, destroyed these hopes and left Britain terribly weak and dependent upon securing further American support. With Keynes dispatched to Washington to negotiate a fresh loan, the American demands for discussions about imperial preference and the Sterling Bloc could no longer be put off.[39] Against all these disadvantages could be set the immense social changes brought about by the war and the creation or development of newer industries which had potential for peacetime purposes (electronics, aircraft, chemicals, cars); but in terms of power politics – and more directly, in terms of a capacity to maintain a first-class navy – the prolonged struggle had had a shattering effect upon Great Britain.

The war had also stimulated the creation and use of a quite novel military device – the atomic bomb. That one such weapon could cause damage equal to a 1,000-bomber raid, and that the development of even more terrifying bombs was possible in the future, appeared to render all traditional forms of warfare obsolete. Land power was as irrelevant as sea power in any situation where these might be used, and it seemed to behove all states who wished to remain independent Great Powers to develop such weapons and, if possible, adequate defences against them. Yet here again, despite her major contribution to such a project in its early stages, Britain soon found herself being left behind. Since the United States was proceeding so swiftly with its own research upon the A-bomb, warned Sir John Anderson in 1942, 'the pioneer work done in this country is a dwindling asset and unless we capitalize it quickly we shall be rapidly outstripped'. But how could the British go ahead with their gaseous diffusion and heavy-water plants when, irrespective of the high financial costs, it would be almost impossible to secure the necessary labour, steel and electricity? Stretched to her limits industrially, she could only rely upon the promised magnanimity of the United States to keep her abreast of this development and to maintain some sort of say in its use against an enemy – a means of control which as the war progressed became ever more uncertain. By 1945 British 'consent' had become a formality, and Whitehall was soon forced to recognize that if it wanted this weapon it would have to develop it itself.[40]

The consequences of the war to the Empire, or rather to the notion of imperial unity, were also disastrous. Of course, both the concept and the actual system were ailing in the inter-war years in any case, furnishing greater liabilities than they did assets to Britain from the strictly strategical point of view; and it may be that the main consequence of this façade of imperial unity was to cause the Americans to over-estimate its strength and the extent to which it might challenge their economic plans in the post-war world. By 1945, however, even the façade had been ripped away. It is true that the Dominions and the Colonies (with the predictable exception of Eire) gave generously of their financial, material and human resources to combat the Axis threat to western democracy; but politically the war served to loosen the ties between Westminster and overseas in many ways. The unrest in India, leading to the promise of self-government as soon as the world conflict was over, was a good example of this. So, too, was the Japanese seizure of Burma. Indeed, the quick collapse of the British Empire in the Orient – Hong Kong, Borneo, Burma, Malaya and the great base at Singapore – dealt a psychological blow which was probably more damaging in the long run than the losses of men, munitions and such raw materials as rubber, tin and oil. As has been pointed out elsewhere,

> Singapore in particular had been a symbol, admittedly a false one, of the military and naval might of the Empire. When it fell, so too did much of the mystique and glamour of that institution. The reoccupation in 1945 after three years of Japanese rule could not restore the old colonial empires in the East along the previous lines, for their prestige could never be recovered. Percival's surrender to an Asian power on 15 February 1942 meant not just the end of a campaign: it meant the end of an age.[41]

Nor were the Dominions slow to recognize the reality of the world situation. Eire, too bitter to forget the past, had remained neutral, and South Africa had only entered the conflict after a cabinet crisis; but even the more loyal members of the Commonwealth found it prudent to reinsure with the rising star of the United States, when it was apparent that Britain no longer possessed the strength to protect them. In August 1940 Canada entered into unilateral arrangements with its southern neighbour for hemisphere defence. Australia's Prime Minister, Curtin, had warned in 1941 that she was looking to America, 'free from any pangs as to traditional links or kinship with the United Kingdom'; and when Singapore fell, his sense of urgency increased. Even New Zealand demanded 'direct and continuous access to the power which . . . is solely responsible to the conduct of naval operations in that part of the world which includes New Zealand'.[42] Not surprisingly, it was the American and not the British Chiefs of Staff who were given operational responsibility in Australasia from early 1942 onwards. In view of the military situation in the Pacific this was no doubt the correct decision; but it is easy to envisage the shocked reaction of Victorian statesmen to the idea that their antipodean colonies would be under the control of an American general (MacArthur) within two generations of their passing.

If the political picture in distant waters looked bleak to British statesmen, it was scarcely more promising nearer home. By 1944 it seemed clear that the enormous superiority of the Americans in men and materials would soon bring them victory over a rapidly weakening Germany; but the steady rise in suspicions between Russia and the West led Churchill and others to the conclusion that the tyranny of the Nazi Gauleiter over Central and Eastern Europe was about to be replaced by that of the Soviet Commissar. The 'big battalions', to use Stalin's phrase, had decided who would control the Heartland, and the Red Army was now steadily advancing into Poland, Hungary and the Balkans – a development which the British had as little power to prevent as they had had in defending the Polish Corridor in 1939. Until the United States could be persuaded to recognize the possible danger and to support the liberties of Europe in both economic and military terms, there was little that Churchill could do, except to try to arrange a 'deal' with Stalin in the hope of defining the limits of Russian expansion.[43] As the most exhausting war in her history was drawing to its close, therefore, Britain was as far away as ever from preserving that continental balance of power which was so congenial to her world interests and for which she had entered the struggle against Germany in the first place.

With the United States dominating the overseas world and Soviet Russia likely to dominate Europe, the age of the super-powers, predicted many decades earlier by de Tocqueville, Seeley and others, had at last arrived – and the British Empire was not among their number. Instead she was swiftly declining to the ranks of the second-class powers. The contrasts with the United States – and with Britain's own growth in an earlier age through the catalyst of war – were glaring enough to provoke the official historians to point them out at the end of their study of the British war economy:

> Despite all the contrasts of technology and of economic magnitude between the wars of the Napoleonic Age and those of the twentieth century, there are some striking parallels between the situation of the United Kingdom in the earlier age and the situation of the United States in the later one. Each of these two countries, in its own fortunate time, was able to use the expansion of its exports as an instrument of war; each found itself, at the conclusion of war, in some degree compensated for its efforts and sacrifices by an immense enhancement of

> its comparative economic strength among the nations. But the United Kingdom in the twentieth century found itself in quite the opposite situation. The nation's struggle after the Second World War to overcome the consequences of an effort which had so heavily overtaxed its economic strength was bound to be a long one.[44]

Even at the height of the war the United States Military Staff could confidently predict that the profoundly changing world would soon see America and Russia as 'the only military powers of the first magnitude' a fact they attributed in each case to a Mackinder-like 'combination of geographical position and extent, and vast munitioning potential'. At the same time, there was little likelihood that either could emerge supreme since 'the relative strength and geographical position of these two powers preclude the military defeat of one . . . by the other'. To which prediction they offered the further statement that 'Both in an absolute sense and relative to the United States and Russia, the British Empire will emerge from the war having lost ground both economically and militarily.'[45] All great conflicts in the past had witnessed the rise and fall of empires: now it was the turn of two new states to achieve prominence, and of a third to withdraw from the centre of the international stage which she had dominated for so long.

In view of the deleterious consequences of the Second World War to British power, it may well be queried whether she should have fought so regardless of cost – or even fought at all.[46] Since it is difficult to perceive what she gained from the war, should not the title of this chapter have been re-phrased 'The Pyrrhic Victory'? So sweeping a judgement appears upon reflection to exaggerate the case, however: Britain may have suffered grievously in the struggle, but from what is known of Hitler's unpredictable nature and of the plans for the disposal of her population if ever a German invasion had been successful, such British losses were distinctly better than the risk or the actuality of Nazi control. Moreover, they had, for all their blundering, fought well – perhaps better than they had ever done previously – and against heavy odds. The Royal Navy in particular had improved upon its performance in the First World War and it would be churlish to deny to the service the praise it rightly deserved.

Nevertheless, valour was not enough. In terms of naval *power*, and all that that expression implies, there had been a quite noticeable decline, symbolized in part by the fact that the Royal Navy's budget and personnel were now lower than those of the other two services. The industry, trade and finances upon which Britain's real maritime strength rested had been sharply eroded. Air power had chased the battle-fleet from the ocean and posed a threat to every surface warship. Land power had shown itself in most cases impervious to the pressures exerted by naval forces alone. The atomic bomb challenged the relevance of all orthodox weaponry in a Great Power clash. Yet in 1945 much of this was still unclear. It was easy for many Britons, under the circumstances of victory and with an inadequate knowledge of the effects of the war (especially in its economic aspect), to assume that their country was still one of the world's great military and naval states: indeed, all the outward signs pointed to such a conclusion. The true state of its decline, and of the more general decay of the effectiveness of sea power, remained concealed for a few years more. Thus, for Britain the glorious victory in the Second World War was an illusion, not only because her gains were purely negative ones and her losses were considerable, but also because it was not generally recognized by her people that it had caused the collapse of her independent national power. And, as far as the future is concerned, an illusory victory is conceivably even worse than an open defeat.

CHAPTER TWELVE

The End of the Road: British Sea Power in the Post-war World

If the sea power related closely to balanced economic growth in the sixteenth, seventeenth and eighteenth centuries, the age of commercial capitalism, then the proposition would hold *a fortiori* for the twentieth century, the age of industrial capitalism . . . We need only compare the procurement lists of the Royal Navy today with a century ago to appreciate the point.

J. J. Clarke, 'Merchant Navy and the Navy: A Note on the Mahan Hypothesis', *Royal United Services Institution Journal*, cxii, no. 646 (May 1967), p. 163.

The decline in Britain's position as a world power and the consequent reduction of her naval strength throughout the globe began, as we have seen, a little before the Diamond Jubilee year of 1897. But, thanks to the two world wars, the pace of this withdrawal in the twentieth century was never a steady one. Although strategical disengagement from many overseas commitments together with the threat from the German fleet saw the greater part of the Royal Navy already concentrated in the North Sea by 1914, the First World War itself resulted in an extension of the British Empire. That this fresh expansion was simply too great for Britain's real strength to manage, and ran in contradiction to its steadily deteriorating *potential* as a Great Power, was tacitly acknowledged by the Washington treaties of the 1920s and by the Chiefs of Staff and the Treasury in the 1930s, when both warned of the consequences of fighting a prolonged modern war against one or more of the dictatorships.

Nevertheless the exigencies of war again forced the British into a world-wide struggle which left them in 1945 in possession of many territories overseas and enormous armed forces to defend them. Once more, however, this imposing appearance was not justified by the realities of power, for Britain had severely overstrained herself in the effort to survive. As a consequence, the post-1945 period witnessed the final and greatest contraction of all. Those long-term trends detected earlier – the relative weakening of the British economy, the rise of the super-powers, the disintegration of the European empires, the decline of sea power in its classical form *vis-à-vis* land and air power, the growing public demand for increased domestic rather than foreign expenditure – now combined finally to overwhelm a British naval mastery that had long been in question.[1]

To British politicians and military leaders in 1945, however, the inevitability of a swift withdrawal was not so apparent as it has become thirty years later.[2] In the first place, there still lingered that habit of regarding Britain as one of the 'Big Three', or at least as possessing a particularly important place in Europe, Asia and Africa – an attitude of mind not challenged by much of the British Press and in some way reinforced by the fact that fellow second-grade powers such as France, Germany and Japan had been devastated or at least severely hit by the war. Secondly, the coming of the Cold War and the real or imaginary threat from Communism throughout the globe, together with guilt feelings about the 'Appeasement' of the 1930s, combined to prevent any swift running-down of British defence forces on the lines of the post-1815 and post-1919 retrenchments.[3] In addition, the Second World War had been the catalyst for a widespread outburst of nationalistic agitation in the colonial world, which prompted the diversion of British troops, fresh from their wartime victories against modern powers, into a variety of 'peace-keeping' roles in the tropics against indigenous revolutionaries: the terrorism in Palestine and the Hindu–Muslim rivalry in India were only the greatest of these problems but there were many others, in Egypt, Burma, Malaya and elsewhere. The sheer fact of victory had also added to the number of troops stationed overseas. Apart from the considerable garrisons in Germany, Italy and Austria, there were forces in Greece, the greater part of North Africa, Iraq, East Africa, Indo-China, Siam and the Dutch East Indies. In view of all this it was scarcely surprising that a swift retreat from Britain's overseas responsibilities was not widely envisaged in the aftermath of VE Day.

Nevertheless while certain realities pressed the British to stay others pressed them to go. Choosing which of these to respond to was a particularly difficult task, and it is only fair to point out that much of the confusion and untidiness attached to British defence policy in the twenty years following the war was caused by the complexities of the political, strategic and technological problems that arose: no solution was simple or could be taken without grave risks. The world, and Britain's position in it, had been greatly changed, but the dust had not subsided enough for statesmen to see clearly how much of the earlier structure remained. Reluctantly, and often very slowly, the extent of the transformation – and the greater strength of the pressures to go – were realized; but sometimes the British government failed to recall Salisbury's adage that nothing was more disastrous in a changing scene than clinging to the carcasses of past policies. Step by step the British retreated – or rather stumbled – back to their island base, whence they had emerged some two or more centuries earlier to dominate a great part of the globe and its oceans.

Of all the various stages in this withdrawal, there is little doubt that the most decisive occurred in 1947, when the British government fulfilled long-standing pledges and pulled out of the Indian sub-continent. It would be erroneous, however, to see this act as being motivated solely by the Labour Party's well-known opposition to imperialism. Attlee and his colleagues shared the Tories' fear of the consequences of a premature withdrawal, yet they were moved by other practical considerations, too: as Dalton, the Chancellor of the Exchequer, put it, 'If you are in a place where you are not wanted and where you have not got the force to squash those who don't want you, the only thing is to get out.'[4] It was about the same time that Bevin also announced the British government's intention to abandon Palestine and declined to renew the commitments to support Greece and Turkey. Whether the withdrawal from India was a virtue or a necessity, however, one thing was clear: the British Empire, of which India had for almost two centuries been the centre-piece, was coming to an end. The retreat from India, cherished by Victorian statesmen as 'the grand base of British power in the East',[5] and the consequent loss of the Indian Army, undermined both the *raison d'être* and the manpower for those many British posts elsewhere, which had been acquired to protect the lines of communication to that most precious possession. Had not Curzon declared in 1907:

> When India has gone and the great Colonies have gone, do you suppose that we can stop there? Your ports and coaling stations, your fortresses and dockyards, your Crown Colonies and protectorates will go too. For either they will be unnecessary as the toll-gates and

> barbicans of an empire that has vanished, or they will be taken by an enemy more powerful than yourselves.[6]

It is therefore astonishing to learn that 'no reappraisal [of British defence policy] ever took place' following the abandonment of the Indian subcontinent.[7] Once again, traditional patterns of thought, an inadequate decision-making process and a concentration upon issues elsewhere, prevented any fundamental alteration in attitudes or policies – with deleterious consequences for the future. Because there were no considered long-term assessments of Britain's place in the world, of the processes of decolonization, and of the changing global military balance, her forces were compelled to fight a whole series of *ad hoc* 'brush-fire' wars and to be mobilized for various confrontations in the tropics: Malaya, Kenya, Suez, Kuweit, North Borneo, Cyprus, Aden, the Trucial States, East Africa, the Falkland Islands, British Honduras, Mauritius, the sheer number and geographical disparity of such places being yet another reflection of the overstretched imperial structure that the British had erected in happier days. Some of these actions were small and are now almost forgotten about; others were far larger and even today evoke memories of pain or pride. Some were judged to be very successful at the time, a tribute to the mobility and still appreciable strength of Britain's defence forces – against natives; others were humiliating failures. But even the successful encounters were often followed by events which negated their meaning: revolutionary leaders were recognized as heads of state; agreements were made with once hostile nations, which turned them overnight into friends; and the overall effect of such British interventions was more to act as a delaying force, to create 'stability' for a certain length of time, than to herald a return to the days of gunboat diplomacy. They were the death spasms of a sinking empire – frequent and large-scale at first, but slowly ebbing away as the patient's strength became exhausted and his muscles atrophied. One might detect the last shudder in Harold Wilson's announcement of 16 January 1968 that British forces would be withdrawn from the Far East and the Persian Gulf by 1971, for the marginal amendments made by the succeeding Conservative administration could hardly be said to have revived the corpse.

The steady process of imperial disintegration meant that one aspect of Mahan's now anachronistic three-sided recipe for sea power – colonies, which facilitate and protect shipping – had completely collapsed. This, too, was simply the culmination of an already well-developed movement; the Second World War, as we have seen in the previous chapter, had merely exposed to open view the strategical disunity of the Empire. With the granting of freedom to India, however, the whole notion of 'imperial' defence came to an end: the Empire might be transformed into the Commonwealth, but the successor body could in no way retain even the patched-up political cohesion of the inter-war years. India under Nehru and Mrs Gandhi became neutralist, frowning upon the presence of *all* Great Powers in the Indian Ocean; regarded the United Nations as a much more meaningful forum for international debates; and even went to war against another Commonwealth member, Pakistan. Development aid and cultural interchanges became the sole remnants of that dream of federation pursued by Seeley, Chamberlain and the rest. That Australia and New Zealand could sign the ANZUS Treaty with the United States in 1951 without much regard to the feelings of hurt and irritation this provoked in Britain indicated the extent to which the myth had been shattered by the hard realities of world politics.[8] The very idea that such a widely dispersed group of territories as the British Empire could be moulded into an organic defence unit was only worth contemplating in an age when Britain was financially strong and uninvolved in Europe, when the dependencies valued the links with Whitehall above all others, and when sea power was predominant. By 1945 none of these preconditions applied.

What was more, if the other members of the Commonwealth preferred to concentrate upon their regional political, economic and strategical needs, so too did the British – although here again the decision-making *élite* in London was torn between various aims, best symbolized by Churchill's and Eden's optimistic claim that their country lay conveniently within three circles, represented by the Commonwealth, the United States and Europe. Of these, there was no doubt that the latter was the least popular: links with the former Empire had sunk too deeply into the Englishman's consciousness to be rejected easily, despite the rebuffs administered by Dominion leaders; the so-called 'special relationship' with the United States, forged by the war and possibly increased by the dependence upon Washington afterwards, was something else to bemuse those Britons who did not perceive that it was less valued on the other side of the Atlantic; but Europe had been a hotbed of trouble throughout the century, an encumbrance to foreign policy and to all the efforts to preserve Britain's freedom of action in world affairs. It was the two interventions in Europe – with their deleterious consequences – which had bled British power white; and with the continent now devastated by the war, with large Communist parties in France and Italy, and with Germany still distrusted, was it not advisable for Britain to maintain her distance politically from that area?[9]

Yet however attractive these arguments – and the resentment against the Common Market still reveals signs of this attitude – it simply flew in the face of geography, of the British experience since the turn of the century, and especially of the political and military situation in 1945. 'Splendid isolation', too, could only be maintained at a time when a continental balance of power existed and British sea power was supreme; when both were undermined, Britain's stance had to change. The desperate but futile attempts to avoid 'the continental commitment' (Howard) in the inter-war years pointed a lesson which had become more and more apparent as land power and air power gained in influence. What was more, the Allied military campaigns into the heart of Europe had presented the British leaders with a virtual *fait accompli*: it was clearly going to take some time before the European economy and communications were restored, famine averted and Nazism eradicated, all of which prevented an early withdrawal. Most important of all, the British, American and French garrisons in Germany, Italy and Austria were now contiguous to Red Army divisions, under the command of a dictator who seemed to show no signs of respecting the ideals of liberal democracy for which the West had fought the war, and many signs – inside and outside Europe – of wishing to extend Communist influence further. With the Foreign Office concentrating upon checking Russian aims by persuading the United States to remain in Europe, by aiding the recovery of France, and by seeking to rebuild a shattered continent, it was obviously impossible for Britain to wash her hands of an extensive commitment herself.

This basic fact the army, perhaps naturally, was the first to point out. In 1946 Montgomery urged the creation of 'a strong western bloc' and the promise by Britain 'to fight on the mainland of Europe, alongside our allies'.[10] It was no more possible to tolerate western and central Europe falling into the hands of Russia now than it had been to have it fall into German hands in 1914 or 1939; and the advent of long-range rockets simply reinforced Baldwin's point about Britain's frontier being on the Rhine. Equally natural was the Admiralty's fight against this line of reasoning, and the implications for the priorities in the country's defence budget. The debates of 1906–14 and 1920–39 were being fought out again, but this time the historical precedents could merge with the logic of the existing power balance to overwhelm the navy's appeal to 'the British way of warfare'. The long struggle to stay uncommitted had ended: the defence of Europe had become the first priority, and the tensions during the *coup* in Czechoslovakia and the Berlin airlift increased this trend. The signing of the NATO Treaty in 1949 – the most comprehensive military obligation ever undertaken by Britain, and one which reflected above all else the country's strategic identity with western Europe and strategic dependence upon the United States – was the formal confirmation of this priority. By comparison, the CENTO and SEATO pacts were insignificant affairs, gestures rather than real commitments against Communism, and never taken very seriously by Whitehall subsequently.

As if the Admiralty had not received a crushing enough blow to its hopes and prestige by the identification of a land war – or a nuclear one – as the most likely contingency for Britain's defence forces to anticipate, it encountered a fundamental challenge to its autonomy by the post-1945 series of decisions (especially those of 1946, 1963 and 1967) to integrate all three armed services into a Ministry of Defence.[11] There were, of course, certain precedents for this move, as the activities of the C.I.D. and the Minister for the Coordination of Defence in the 1930s had revealed. The pressing need to allocate Britain's declining resources in a manner best suited to give her a *balanced* defence force was the major reason for the new measure, but there were also good strategical ones too. The traditional dichotomy, according to which the army interested itself in the defence of India and the navy in the maintenance of the imperial seaways, had lingered long into the twentieth century and had indeed been accentuated by the bitter quarrels about a continental commitment. A few more percipient writers, like Julian Corbett, had endeavoured to show how much the army and the navy had complemented each other in Britain's past wars, and how either one acting in isolation possessed a greatly reduced role and effectiveness.[12] But it had taken the Second World War, and particularly such operations as the D Day landings, to illustrate once again the need for the services to have a joint strategy in which each would cooperate to achieve their overall aim. The existence of aircraft carriers, the creation of airborne divisions, and the development of amphibious techniques all suggested that the operational roles of the services now overlapped.[13] Nevertheless, if there were cogent grounds for this integration, it did mean that the Board of the Admiralty's special claims to decision-making were ended, and it did imply that the navy could no longer regard itself as the 'Senior' service.

On the other hand a cursory glance at the defence estimates since the war would seem to indicate that in the financial sphere the reverse was true – that the navy's share of the 'cake' was steadily rising. In view of the additional fact that it had been accustomed to receive around £55 million per annum in the 1930s, there would appear to be little cause for concern. Both absolutely and relatively the admirals could be thought to have done well:[14]

Defence Expenditures (£ million) and Percentages of the Services

	Army	Navy	R.A.F.	Other*
1946–7	717 (43·4%)	266·9 (16·1%)	255·5 (15·5%)	414 (25%)
1956–7	498·9 (32·1%)	342·6 (22·5%)	471·5 (30·9%)	212·1 (13·9%)
1966–7	573·3 (27·1%)	586·4 (27·7%)	514·0 (24·3%)	441·1 (20·9%)
1968–9	591·4 (26·5%)	674·7 (30·2%)	562·3 (25·2%)	403·6 (18·4%)

* Central defence expenditures; and expenditures for defence items by other ministries (e.g. Aviation, Technology, Atomic Energy Authority, Public Building and Works).

Upon closer examination, however, these figures are less impressive. Wartime and post-war inflation, especially in military hardware and in wages, has eaten away any real gains from the substantial absolute increase in naval expenditure since the pre-1939 period. Moreover, it is a commonplace in the history of British defence policy for the navy's percentage to rise in peacetime as the large armies were disbanded – which suggests that there is almost an inverse ratio between the importance attached to the army and the navy in peacetime and that attached to both in wartime. In this case the navy's increased share in the post-war years reflects more the even swifter decline in the army and the R.A.F. than an actual improvement in its own position. The so-called 'Sandys White Paper' of 1957, composed in the aftermath of the Suez fiasco and with a firm belief in a massive nuclear deterrent, ran down the large standing army which conscription had produced.[15] In regard to the R.A.F. the hopes and then repeated collapses of its plans to establish an effective strategic bombing/missile system – Blue Streak, the Avro 730 bomber, Skybolt, TSR–2, F–111 – account for the rise and subsequent reduction in its proportion of the defence estimates. Measuring the navy's role and effectiveness by a financial yardstick is likely to be deceptive in the confused post-1945 years, therefore.

A far more meaningful examination of the place of the Royal Navy in British defence strategy today can be achieved by looking at the various obligations and war contingencies which, according to the government's defence papers,[16] the armed forces of the country are designed to meet.

The first of these is the most dreaded of all – nuclear warfare. Here the development of the Hydrogen bomb, of the inter-continental ballistic missile, and of the Russian military and technological capacity has rendered a small, densely populated area like the British Isles extremely vulnerable. In the 1930s it was feared that the bomber had done the same, until the invention of radar and the creation of the Hurricane and Spitfire fighters;

but now it seems unlikely that there will be any defence at all for Britain against the horde of fast-travelling missiles with multiple warheads which Russia is able to deploy: about ten Hydrogen bombs would be enough to reduce the country to cinders, and the Soviet defence forces are estimated to have well over 2,000 delivery vehicles at the present time. The obvious conclusions from this were drawn by Whitehall as early as that White Paper of 1957.

> It must be frankly recognised that there is at present no means of providing adequate protection for the people of this country against the consequences of an attack with nuclear weapons . . . the only existing safeguard against major aggression is the power to threaten retaliation with nuclear weapons.[17]

There was a fearful logic in all this: as Churchill was to put it, safety had to be based upon terror, and survival to rely upon a mutual fear of annihilation. So much has the nuclear deterrent neutralized the ability of either East or West to attack its foe without risk that a virtual strategical stalemate has been established, broken only by the occasional disagreement, which has caused the world to sweat profusely at the possible outcome; and it may be that a more permanent *détente* can be arranged in the future.

Yet such an East–West agreement between the nuclear states would depend almost exclusively upon the two super-powers Russia and the U.S.A.: Britain's role, as has so often been the case since 1945, would be marginal and limited. Its efforts to create an independent nuclear deterrent following the McMahon Act and the American refusal to share information about the bomb have been so well chronicled that it would be superfluous to describe them here.[18] It is a story of continual disappointments and checks, of cancelled projects and changed decisions, and of an ever-increasing gap between the means and the end; and it now appears probable that the more single-minded French policy will produce better results.[19] Nevertheless, both European powers are mere midgets compared with the Big Two, as the latest estimates of nuclear delivery vehicles indicate:[20]

	USA	Russia	Britain	France
Intercontinental ballistic missiles	1,054	1,527	–	–
Intermediate ballistic missiles	–	600	–	18
Submarine-based ballistic missiles	656	628	64	32
Long-range bombers	443	140	–	–
Medium-range bombers	74	800	56	58

Indeed, the obsolescence of the V-bombers and the abandonment of the many attempts to build a successor to it that would be both financially and technologically viable would have led to Britain's dropping out of this 'nuclear club' apart from the Polaris submarines. With such vessels, each possessing the capability of firing from under the sea sixteen missiles with nuclear warheads at enemy targets, it would seem that Britain's position in the table – and the Royal Navy's claim to a certain distinction – could be justified. Yet here again first assumptions are soon undermined by harsher realities. Polaris is, of course, an American weapon and was only made available to the British by the special Nassau agreement of 1962; and the comparatively low capital and maintenance costs of this system – without which, one suspects, Whitehall would have abandoned the nuclear deterrent there and then – were 'palpably dependent on American goodwill and assistance'.[21] In the advanced technological world of the 1960s and 1970s Britain relies upon American rocketry as much as Turkey and certain Latin American states relied upon Britain for dreadnoughts in the pre-1914 period. Furthermore, doubts have been expressed about whether the force of four Polaris submarines is sufficient to have one vessel on station all the time,[22] but there are no signs that the number will be increased. Finally, the impressive recent development of the Russian anti-ballistic missile system has indicated that the Polaris missile will soon need to be replaced by the superior MIRV-type Poseidon – again, an American weapon – if it is to avoid becoming obsolete.[23]

The second military contingency for which the British armed forces must prepare is the defence of the land frontier of western Europe – the continental commitment at last fully accepted by the stationing of 55,000 troops and eleven R.A.F. squadrons in Germany. Compared with the far larger contributions from the United States, West Germany and other European NATO countries, the British offering is useful rather than decisive, and even a doubling or quadrupling of this commitment would make little impact upon the present imbalance between NATO and the Warsaw Pact powers, with the latter enjoying a great superiority in tactical aircraft, tanks and troops.[24] The Soviet deployment of 300,000 troops into Czechoslovakia in 1968 was a grim confirmation of Russia's capabilities in the crucial central European zone; in the northern zone Russia possesses an even greater superiority over Norwegian forces; and the numerical lead of NATO in the Southern Command area masks many weaknesses in the Mediterranean states. In any case, since European defence involves primarily a commitment of land and air forces, the Royal Navy's role is minimal (Polaris – and nuclear warfare – always excepted).

Only in the guarding of the maritime flanks of Europe do the British occupy a more prominent position.

Since the sea is indivisible, it is probably better that any assessment of Britain's position in that respect is merged into an examination of its ability to defend its own maritime communications in general, for in both instances Whitehall and its allies face a Soviet naval challenge of gigantic and still-growing proportions.[25] In the past two decades the Russians have added to their great land and air power the newer dimension of sea power, and this to an extent which is still generally underestimated in the West. As the editor of *Jane's* put it recently,

> The plot on the map of the world of the appearances and movements of Soviet warships, represented by red dots, has been likened to a rash of measles but, unlike the spots of the latter which quickly disappear, the red dots are there to stay, for the USSR has learned from the century of Pax Britannica, and the quarter century of American naval predominance which followed, that sea power is national power, international power and deterrent power up to nuclear deterrent power.[26]

The present Russian Navy consists of ninety-five nuclear-powered submarines, 313 diesel submarines, one carrier, two helicopter-carriers, twelve guided-missile and fifteen gun cruisers, thirty-two guided-missile and sixty-six gun destroyers, 130 frigates, 258 escorts and numerous smaller craft. Only the United States Navy, with its fifteen large attack carriers and many other surface vessels, is superior to it, although the steady decline in the size of that force, its tendency to prefer a few enormously expensive new warships to a myriad of smaller ones, and the domestic political mood in America following the Vietnam war, have caused many observers to wonder if this lead will be maintained in the face of the steady and apparently irreversible Soviet naval growth.

What is unquestioned, at least, is that the Royal Navy alone would be in no position to check the Russian fleet. From a 1945 strength of fifteen battleships and battle-cruisers, seven fleet, four light fleet and forty-one escort carriers, sixty-two cruisers, 131 submarines, 108 fleet destroyers, and 383 escort destroyers and frigates, it has deteriorated to a total of one carrier, two helicopter-carriers, four Polaris, eight other nuclear-powered and twenty-three diesel submarines, two assault ships, two cruisers, ten destroyers and sixty-four frigates; and there is every prospect of a further decrease in the future. Even in a struggle between surface fleets it could not match the Russians, but the greatest weakness lies in the size of its anti-submarine forces. Britain's dependence upon overseas trade, that Achilles' Heel of the two world wars, is just as great today, although her ability to protect herself has shrunk alarmingly. In 1939 this country could field 201 destroyers and frigates against forty-nine German U-boats, and still came close to defeat; at present it possesses seventy-four such vessels to face over 400 Russian submarines.[27] Add to this the vulnerability to missiles, bombs and torpedoes of all surface vessels, whether merchant or naval, or what Paul Cohen has referred to as 'the erosion of surface naval power',[28] and the position becomes even grimmer for the West. Small wonder that *détente* is favoured on strategical as well as financial and political grounds: a war with Russia, whether nuclear or conventional, would be disastrous.

Outside the NATO area the naval situation is far more serious, for the Russian fleet is repeating in distant seas the successes it has gained in the Mediterranean, where its warships shadow and strive to neutralize the predominance of the United States Sixth Fleet and its foreign policy has secured political influence and naval bases in certain Arab states. In the Indian Ocean especially, the activities of the new Russian Navy have created concern[29] – the more so because they occur precisely at a time when that region has become almost a power vacuum. With the Royal Navy already mainly withdrawn from an East of Suez role and with the United States aching to abandon that position as the world's policeman which it took up so readily after 1945, Russian naval forces go eagerly outwards, apparently unhindered by cost, obsolescence or domestic political considerations. Whilst the dependence of the industrialized West upon raw materials and overseas trade grows inexorably, and their merchant fleets are now larger than ever, the capacity to defend the seaways – the first and only real definition of 'command of the sea' – has diminished. At the same time the traditional weapon of the naval blockade, even if it could be implemented in the face of Russia's aircraft, submarines and surface vessels, would have little or no effect upon the economy and fighting capacity of that country.

The fourth strategical objective of Britain's armed forces is the defence of her territories, interests and obligations outside Europe. In the early years of the Cold War, with Communist threats apparent throughout Asia and the Middle East, this occupied almost as high a priority with the Service chiefs as it had done, say, in 1902 or 1936; and innovations were made in the services to ensure that so-called 'brush-fire' wars could be dealt with. Commando carriers, the development of amphibious and airborne units, the teaching of jungle-warfare techniques, all implied that the role of a policeman would continue to be of importance. Kuwait, East Africa and Malaysia appeared to have more relevance than Suez. In recent years, however, this attitude has altered.[30] Apart from a few odd islands, the Empire is no more; military interventions overseas would be widely resented in this country, and even more so abroad; Britain's finances could not stand the strains of a major crisis; and it is doubtful if Whitehall possessed the military muscle-power, let alone the political will, to achieve such an aim. The balance of world power and changes in public opinion are altering too swiftly and decisively to turn the clock back. Only a few years after leaving the Gulf states to look after themselves, for example, Britain was temporarily crippled by their oil embargoes. Nor are the measures attendant upon the ANZUK treaty in South-east Asia likely to reverse this trend: even that navalist organ *Jane's Fighting Ships* has admitted that it would be useless now to maintain 'a worthwhile Fleet in the Far East'.[31]

Thus, in all four war contingencies in which Britain is thought likely to be involved it is obvious that its defence requirements far exceed its strength, particularly in the naval field. A nuclear war would be a calamity for Britain, nor can its deterrent be regarded as effective as that of other powers: naval forces cannot hold western Europe; neither, in view of the present size of the Russian fleet, could they adequately defend NATO's maritime flanks and the world-wide lines of communication; and their role and capability in overseas theatres is being pared down rapidly. As *Jane's* admitted,

> The stark truth is that the Royal Navy has fallen below the safety level required to protect the home islands, to guard the ocean trade routes for the world-deployed mercantile marine . . ., to protect the vast commerical and financial interests overseas, and to meet the NATO, ANZUK and other treaty commitments.[32]

It should come as no surprise to learn of the solution put forward by that annual to repair these weaknesses: increase the amount of expenditure upon defence, currently equal to around 5 per cent of Britain's Gross National Product, to a proportion comparable with that of Russia and the United States (8 per cent). Or, as another naval authority has expressed it,

> the major problem . . . is to provide sufficient forces to enable Britain to meet her obligations which, if she is to retain any semblance of her former greatness, she must do. The nation needs to be made conscious of its heritage and its dependence on sea power for its daily bread and butter.[33]

Such voices have, of course, been heard many times before in the history of British defence policy: they are the present-day voices of Beatty, Chatfield and their predecessors, a long line of admirals and generals who sought, usually in vain, to convince their political leaders of the magnitude of the potential dangers their country faced, and of the pressing need for more ships and more men. Alternatively they are the voices of an entrenched minority, isolated from those domestic pressures which force politicians into a natural compromise, disapproving of the sums being diverted to the nation's social and economic requirements, and too prone to suspicions of other powers and to exaggeration of the threats they pose. Between these two extreme beliefs in preparing for everything and preparing for nothing, a sensible middle way has to be sought, for Britain's rulers can neither pin their hopes upon the assumption that they will never be involved in wars or confrontations in the future nor can they provide for armaments to super-power level. With its relative military strength and role in world affairs shrinking away, and with a too narrow population and industrial base to allow it to provide its own security independently, it must join with its allies to create a common defence; it must, because of its peculiar vulnerability both to military and economic pressures, be the first to encourage an East–West *détente* and a peaceful solution to the world's problems; and it must recognize that the age of gunboat diplomacy is over and that negotiation rather than force should be used to protect its overseas interests. It was not the previous policy of Britain, even in its prime, to presume that the rest of the world was hostile and full of malevolent intent, against which it needed to be armed to the teeth; nor should it be now.

Nevertheless, in an unpredictable and ever-changing world in which nation states remain as disposed as ever to protect their 'vital interests' by force, it is equally clear that Britain requires a certain minimal level of armed strength: she cannot make up the difference between her peacetime and wartime requirements overnight. And by all the criteria for measuring ends and means, it is also clear that its defence forces are at the present time quite inadequate unless it is to rely almost entirely upon NATO's nuclear deterrent, which is not only an extremely risky policy but one which is inappropriate in many circumstances.

Yet the cruellest part of this dilemma is that the navalists' appeals for a somewhat higher share of governmental spending are no real solution. Apart from the domestic political difficulties of such a step at the moment, any foreseeable increases would be negligible in their strategical effects. Would another *Polaris*-type submarine and a couple of through-deck cruisers, together costing a cool £200 million, much alter Britain's capability to fulfil the obligations listed above? A much greater, and longer-term, construction programme would be far more logical. But what many of those who nod their heads at this proposition tend to ignore, and what most of the retired rear-admirals who write letters to *The Times* or *Telegraph* or present papers to the R.U.S.I. along such lines all too frequently skate over *is the simple fact that Britain is too poor to afford any such programme*. Even in the inter-war period Chatfield had privately admitted that 'We literally have not got the income to keep up a first-class Navy.'[34] Now it must be admitted that a good second-class navy is also outside the nation's capacity. For maritime strength depends, as it always did, upon commercial and industrial strength: if the latter is declining relatively, the former is bound to follow. As Britain's naval rise was rooted in its economic advancement, so too its naval collapse is rooted in its steady loss of economic primacy. We have come full circle.

To explore this truth of Britain's poor economic performance and its implications for its power position in the post-1945 world in greater detail, as we shall do shortly, is not to imply that this country could have retained in any conceivable way its nineteenth-century predominance. Mackinder was fully correct in arguing that the industrialization of other states with greater populations, area and sources of raw materials would lead to a fundamental shift in the global power-balance and to a relative decline on Britain's part: to this extent the ability to finance the world's greatest navy was also bound to be affected. Nor does such an exploration undermine the further major contention of this book that sea power as Mahan and his disciples saw it - sea power based upon the primacy both of national dependence upon oceanic trade and of the largest surface warships to control such commerce – has been overtaken by the development of industrialized land empires and by a host of newer weapons. Those two trends would have ensured the fall of British naval mastery in any case. What follows, therefore, is admittedly of less universal significance: it is to seek to understand why Britain is not likely to possess even a second-rate navy in the future, and why something more fundamental than a simple addition to the defence estimates is required to reverse this decline.

It is all too easy to appreciate how the Second World War affected Britain's economic strength: the decay of export industries, the loss of overseas markets, the wearing-out of so many machines and the devastation through bombing to plant and property, the loss of invisible earnings and the vast increase in the nation's debts have been described elsewhere.[35] It was this grim financial picture which provoked Keynes's well-known report to the Cabinet at the end of the European war that Britain was facing 'a financial Dunkirk' and that without American aid the trade deficit would be so large that she would be 'virtually bankrupt and the economic basis for the hopes of the public non-existent'.[36] The virtual cancellation of the Lend-Lease obligations and the long-term American loan of $3,750 million at the end of 1945 proved welcome aids, therefore, but the attached condition that Whitehall should soon arrange free convertibility of sterling revealed that the United States still harboured its wartime financial aims and its overestimation of British economic strength; indeed, one scholar has argued that Washington put its 'junior partner' in an impossible position by weakening Britain's capacity to remain in such places as the Middle East yet still wanting her stabilizing presence there.[37] The economic crisis which occurred in 1947, when convertibility was permitted, indicated how unfavourably Britain's chances were regarded in the international financial market. Even the massive devaluation of the pound which followed the next crisis in 1949 provided only temporary relief, for the Korean War – where defence expenditure jumped to 9·9 per cent of G.N.P. – had its inevitable effect upon export trades and commodity prices. To this posture of Cold War preparedness could be added the burden upon the balance of payments of the high military expenditure overseas, which reached £140 million in 1952 and £215 million in 1960 (whereas total governmental expenditure abroad in 1938 had been £16 million). Here again, it appeared that the over-extension of Britain's strength caused by the wartime victory and maintained as a result of the international tensions after it, severely hindered the creation of a balanced economy.

This conclusion is, however, only part of the story, for the war was less a catalyst upon Britain's position than an additional burden upon an economy already exhibiting to an increasing degree those trends of the later nineteenth century which were examined earlier: a widespread refusal to recognize that the traditional attitudes and methods of management and trade unions required modification; an inability to exploit new ideas and techniques adequately; shoddy workmanship and poor salesmanship; a distaste for science, technology and commerce in education and public life; a depressingly low rate of investment; poor labour relations; and a propensity for the nation to spend more than it was earning. It is only after appreciating the importance of these longer-term traits that one should add the more recent reasons of overseas military expenditure; the decrease in that 'cushion' of invisible earnings, followed by the further loss of imperial markets; and the change in the terms of trade, and in particular the hefty rises in the price of such a vital raw material as oil, to Britain's detriment. For if the British were burdened by economic problems in 1945, their situation could hardly be compared with that of the Japanese, Germans and other peoples whose commerce and industry had been almost eradicated. No amount of pointing to the effects of the war upon Britain can explain away the fact that nations hit far more severely have flourished economically since, while she has not. Almost every figure relating to manufacturing productivity in the post-war period – whether national rates of growth, rises in output per man-hour, capital formation and investment, and exports – has shown Britain to be at or near the bottom of the table of industrialized powers. Her share of the world's export of manufactures, for example, slumped from 29·3 per cent in 1948 to 12·9 per cent in 1966.[38]

This reminds us once again that we are examining the *relative* success of economies; in absolute terms the years since the war have witnessed widespread and very great advances in the wealth of the British people, while it is also true that many industries are efficient and that the country is exporting proportionately more today than at any time in the past century. Nevertheless, it is little comfort to learn that the British are becoming, in relative terms, the 'peasants of Europe'. Not only is that position unenviable in itself, but its implications for the country's military potential are grim. Finally, some pundits, such as the economic editor of *The Times*, have argued gloomily that the slow growth and cyclical 'stop-go' course of the economy in the past twenty-five years actually represents a golden age, for

> the evidence is that each cycle is more difficult to sustain than the last, that the periods of "go" get shorter, that the peak rate of inflation gets higher, that the nadir of the balance of payments gets deeper and that the peak and average levels of unemployment get higher. Government policies yaw in a progressively narrower and more frantic zig-zag between the converging limits of "stop" and "go".[39]

Intertwined with, and possibly as fundamental as, this poor economic performance were certain psychological changes. The first, that general turning-away from a desire to play an imperial and Great Power role – perhaps best symbolized by Attlee's replacement of Churchill as Prime Minister in 1945 and the subsequent social innovations of the Labour Government – is a readily identifiable one. It is worth noting, however, that this movement is deeper than the parallel retraction of Britain's military commitments, for the transfer of loyalties by the 'official mind' from the Empire to Europe has not been followed by the nation at large: entry into the Common Market is more an issue of contention than of agreement. Dean Acheson's pointed remark that 'Great Britain has lost an Empire and has yet to find a role' still applies, therefore, and it will continue to do so until the present introspective mood is replaced by something less self-pitying and xenophobic. Foreign and military affairs of any sort are inevitably of less interest to the public than domestic political and social matters, but this is particularly so when the management of the economy has become so contentious an issue. In such a situation it is hardly surprising that internal quarrels have increased and that the country appears divided: the middle classes have lost that remarkable self-confidence which took them to the ends of the earth, and remain troubled and uncertain; the working classes display either a widespread apathy or, in the case of well-organized trade unions, a militancy not seen since the 1920s; the political system itself provokes cynicism and disillusionment; religion has declined without being replaced by any fresh 'opium' (which Marx, contrary to common belief, recognized that a people needs); excessive nostalgia, or neophilia, is evident. With this general malaise affecting the economic aspect, and the latter simultaneously acting upon the public's mood, it is often difficult to separate cause from effect. Such manifestations are not, of course, unique to Britain; but they seem more deeply rooted here, so much so that Europeans can refer with pity or alarm to 'the English sickness'.

These symptoms of relative economic decline, national introversion and domestic political dissensions are easily recognizable to scholars of world history: they represent fairly common characteristics of an empire in decline. In this respect it is interesting to note those shared economic and psychological developments detected by Carlo Cipolla in his summary of the decline of the Roman, Byzantine, Arab, Spanish, Italian, Ottoman, Dutch and Chinese Empires:

> Whenever we look at declining empires, we notice that their economies are generally faltering. The economic difficulties of declining empires show striking resemblances. All empires seem eventually to develop an intractable resistance to the change needed for the required growth of production. Then neither the needed enterprise, nor the needed type of investment, nor the needed technological change is forthcoming. Why? What we have to admit is that what appears *ex post* as an obsolete behaviour pattern was, at an earlier stage in the life of an empire, a successful way of doing things, of which the members of the empire were proud ... To change our way of working and doing business implies a more general change of customs, attitudes, motivations and sets of values which represent our cultural heritage ... If the necessary change does not take place and economic difficulties are allowed to grow, then a cumulative process is bound to be set into motion that makes things progressively worse. Decline enters then in its final, dramatic stage.

> When needs outstrip production capability, a number of tensions are bound to appear in society. Inflation, excessive taxation, difficulties in the balance of payments are just a small sample of the whole series of possible tensions. The public sector presses heavily over and against the private sector in order to squeeze out the largest possible share of resources. Consumption competes with investment and vice versa. Within the private sector, the conflict among social groups becomes more bitter because each group tries to avoid as much as possible the necessary economic sacrifices. As the struggle grows in bitterness, cooperation among people and social groups fades away, a sense of alienation from the commonwealth develops, and with it group and class selfishness.[40]

Further comment upon these historical precedents would be superfluous.

The post-war years have also seen an acceleration of governmental expenditure upon social and economic needs, with the amount allocated to defence falling proportionately – another sign, perhaps, of national introvertedness, although an inevitable development in a democratic society where the normal man is preoccupied with more immediate concerns than foreign policies. Gone for ever are the days of Fisher, when, in 1905, £36·8 million could be spent upon the navy and £29·2 million upon the army, whereas only £28 million was devoted to the government's civilian services of all kinds.[41] Even in the inter-war years the balance had shifted dramatically, and since the Korean War and Suez crisis defence expenditure has continued to decrease relatively, as the following table overleaf shows.[42]

Only another national emergency, it seems clear, would reverse this trend. In an age of *détente* especially, it is difficult to make out a case for large defence expenditure when there are so many domestic needs which appear more pressing than the country's external requirements. This Mahan himself had forecast, rather gloomily, when he wrote:

> Whether a democratic government will have the foresight, the keen sensitiveness to national position and credit, the willingness to ensure its prosperity by adequate outpouring of money in times of peace, all which are necessary for military preparations, is yet an open question. Popular governments are not generally favourable to military expenditure, however necessary, and there are signs that England tends to drop behind.[43]

Another long-term tendency which is having serious effects upon British military strength is the sheer costliness of modern armaments. This, too,

Public Expenditure upon Defence and Other Selected Services, 1962–72 (£ million)

	1962	1963	1964	1965	1966	1967	1968	1969	1970	1971	1972
Defence	1,840	1,892	1,990	2,105	2,207	2,412	2,443	2,294	2,466	2,768	3,097
Transport and communication	465	470	509	602	644	745	886	768	916	1,017	1,016
Other industry and trade	735	757	905	1,015	1,215	1,744	1,901	1,869	1,888	2,197	2,117
Housing and environmental services	969	1,067	1,355	1,559	1,642	1,874	1,966	2,050	2,288	2,428	2,770
Education	1,173	1,282	1,417	1,585	1,768	1,970	2,182	2,346	2,640	3,020	3,508
National health	971	1,035	1,130	1,275	1,401	1,552	1,688	1,767	2,018	2,292	2,644
Social Security Benefits	1,744	1,988	2,099	2,408	2,577	2,900	3,340	3,571	3,923	4,307	5,119
Total Public Expenditure	11,013	11,666	12,759	14,143	15,314	17,528	19,138	19,810	21,825	24,266	27,144

is not a phenomenon unique to Britain, but it would be true to say that a country financially weak and with great inflationary and balance-of-payments problems is less well-equipped to deal with it than others. The *Dreadnought*, the first British nuclear-powered submarine, cost over £18 million; a few years later the *Polaris*-type boats, such as the *Resolution*, cost £40 million but that was without the missile system. With the latter the cost soared to £52–5 million per vessel and it would no doubt have been far higher but for American assistance. The aircraft carrier *Eagle*, which cost £15¾ million when new, was refitted in the early 1960s for £31 million. The Type 42 guided-missile destroyers cost £17 million each, and the Type 82 *Bristol* costs £27 million; with each new model the increase in price is steeper. It is perfectly true that these vessels are far more advanced and pack a far greater punch than their equivalents of 1914–18 or 1939–45, but it is equally true that an increasing amount of money has to be concentrated upon a smaller number of warships although Britain's merchant fleet and oceanic lines of communication have not shrunk but increased in size. The building of major warships is now financially impossible without vast resources: the American nuclear-powered guided-missile cruiser *Long Beach* cost $332 million, the latest nuclear-powered attack cruiser is estimated to cost $1 billion, and tentative figures for the *Trident*-type submarine (with a complex very-long-range missile system to replace existing boats) have produced a similar estimate – $1 billion for one submarine![44]

Furthermore, since the ending of national conscription in Britain the services have had to compete with the rates of pay offered by industry, with the result that the proportion of the defence budget devoted to equipment is much reduced: in 1972, for example, £1,567 million (57·9 per cent) of British defence expenditure was allocated to pay, allowances and maintenance, with only £624 million (24·9 per cent) to 'Procurement' and £307 million (5·9 per cent) to research and development.[45] In the future the share which equipment can expect to secure will probably drop further.

The consequences of all these financial pressures upon Britain's ability to maintain adequate defence forces and her previous role in the world are twofold. In the first place there are those many instances of where she was forced to retreat from overseas territories because the cost was too great, or compelled to abandon new weapons due to their rising prices and to general budgetary considerations:[46] the 'large army' policy of national conscription was scrapped chiefly because of the costs (although the result of voluntary recruitment, as mentioned above, has not been to reduce this figure); the burden upon the balance of payments of such events as the Indonesian confrontation led to demands for a withdrawal from that part of the world; weapon systems such as the TSR–2 were cancelled due to their costs escalating beyond the country's capacity to pay for them; the 1966 Defence White Paper came out against the construction of new carriers because of the Treasury's insistence that the defence budget should not exceed £2,000 million; the *Eagle*, despite its refit in the early 1960s, required another modernization to remain on terms with the *Ark Royal* and when this was found to be too expensive she was paid off, with the Fleet Air Arm thereby 'ceasing to exist';[47] after the construction costs of the Type 82 destroyer were seen to total £27 million, the plan to build another three was abandoned; the same may occur to the proposed through-deck cruisers after the news that they could each cost £65 million. The best-known example of all is probably that series of decisions made by the Labour government in 1967–8 as a result of the grave economic crisis: the abandonment of the 'East of Suez' policy with its expensive bases in the Persian Gulf and Far East, the cancellation of the F–111 aircraft, the reduction in the personnel of the armed forces and the earlier phasing-out of the carriers, were body-blows from which the services have not recovered.

The second consequence concerns Britain's *relative* ability to afford adequate defence forces. Other countries, too, experience inflation, the hideous rise in the costs of new weapons, and domestic pressures for improved social services; but if their industrial and financial strength is increasing far more swiftly than Britain's, they will find it easier to pay for both civil *and* military requirements. Sharing the cake, in other words, is less contentious an exercise when the cake is always growing in size. The following figures are therefore the most significant of all in our attempt to comprehend Britain's recent decline:[48]

Gross National Product of the Powers ($ billion)

	USA	Japan	West Germany	France	Britain	USSR
1952	350	16	32	29	44	113
1957	444	28	51	43	62	156
1962	560	59	89	74	81	229
1967	794	120	124	116	110	314
1972	1,152	317	229	224	128	439

From being in third position in 1952 Britain is now sixth and falling further behind every year, with obvious military and political results. To provide defence forces equivalent to those of West Germany, France and other comparable second-class powers, she has to devote a larger proportion of her G.N.P. to military expenditure: like Austria–Hungary before 1914, she must struggle to maintain her place. For example, the Federal German Republic's defence budget in 1972 of $7,668 million equalled only 2·9 per cent of G.N.P., whereas Britain's smaller total of $6,968 represented 4·6 per cent of G.N.P. French defence spending, which equalled 3·1 per cent of G.N.P. despite being only slightly less in absolute terms than Britain's, will rise steadily with that country's economic growth, so that she will not only possess more ballistic-missile submarines than Britain but is also likely to have the world's third most powerful navy before much longer.[49] Japan, which spent a mere 0·9 per cent of G.N.P. upon defence in 1972, would possess a colossal navy, if ever it raised this proportion to Britain's level. All this leaves Whitehall in the uncomfortable dilemma of either slashing expenditure upon defence forces, which are already inadequate to carry out their professed tasks, or of facing the political and economic consequences of devoting far more upon armaments than other industrial states of a comparable size and population.

Nor is it likely, according to those economic forecasters who peer into the mists of the future, that such a gloomy trend will alter. It is not too difficult for the historian to point out how often similar sorts of predictions have proved wrong in the past, due to unforeseen political developments; thus, Hermann Kahn's belief that Japan's G.N.P. could exceed that of the U.S.A. by the end of this century may have received a fatal blow from the present world oil crisis. It is less easy to ignore his point that the list of twelve 'qualitative–quantitative' reasons for this growth to continue still apply *in reverse* to Great Britain.[50] The terms of trade, too, seem destined to worsen in the future. Perhaps the 'oil miracle' in the North Sea may effect a transformation; perhaps, although it is less likely, the consequences of joining the Common Market will also bring great benefits. Most of the signs, however, indicate that a fundamental alteration in Britain's growth rate, and wealth, and defence capacity, probably requires an equally basic change in attitudes and assumptions.

But this is moving away from the tangible facts of politics and economics into the intangibles of mass psychology; and from the established data of the past and the present into the unpredictable realm of the future. In both cases the historian has either to abandon his discipline or to cease writing. I prefer the latter. For whatever the future holds for the British, it is clear that the period in which they strove for, and achieved, naval mastery has finally come to a close. Maritime warfare along the traditional lines, and Britain's position in the world, have been irrevocably transformed in this past hundred years. Whether she is in the future to remain under the American 'umbrella' or to merge with European allies in an integrated defence unit, whether she will settle the relationship between the various services and arrive at a satisfactory solution respecting the use of conventional and nuclear weapons, all questions which are anxiously debated today,[51] shrink into their proper perspective when compared with the larger movement we have traced of the rise and fall of Britain as an independent world naval power. Since she is no longer the latter, this story can safely be brought to its conclusion.

Epilogue

Writing of the decline of Spain in the middle of the eighteenth century, the British historian Campbell observed,

> That extensive monarchy is exhausted at heart, her resources lie at a great distance, and whatever power commands the sea, may command the wealth and commerce of Spain. The dominions from which she draws her resources, lying at an immense distance from the capital and from one another, make it more necessary for her than for any other State to temporize, until she can inspire with activity all parts of her enormous but disjointed empire.[1]

At that point in time Great Britain had just emerged with enhanced prestige and territory from the Seven Years War, in the course of which Spain's already decaying position in the world had been further eroded. Few Britons then would have spared a thought for the nation they had vanquished yet again; all minds were turned to the future, which seemed to promise for their own country a period of unequalled dominance at the centre of the world's stage.

Some two centuries after the decline of Spain, however, it was Britain's turn to follow suit. And, whilst making all allowance for the differences in circumstance between these two events, one cannot help being struck by the applicability of the above quotation to the position of the British Empire in, say, the 1930s. Britain's economic decay had left her close to being 'exhausted at heart' and, if she did not rely so heavily as Spain had done upon the wealth of her colonies, yet a very large proportion of her markets, sources of raw materials and investments lay overseas and were extremely susceptible to the many foreign threats to imperial lines of communication. The British Empire itself, just like Spain, provided a classic example of what Liddell Hart once called 'strategical over-extension': the possession by a state of numerous defence burdens and obligations, without the corresponding capacity to sustain them. In such a situation the disintegration of that Empire, through internal disruption or external attack or a combination of both, was only a matter of time. Thus, the rapid dissolution of the greater part of the Spanish Empire in the early nineteenth century was but the consummation of a fate that could be predicted long beforehand. So, too, was it to be with Britain, whose world-wide Empire contracted even more swiftly in the post-1945 years, leaving only the original rump to govern itself and to adjust to the loss of its industrial, colonial and naval mastery.

It is interesting to recall, when looking at Britain's present status as a naval power, those six general preconditions for success which Mahan singled out in the first part of his work *The Influence of Sea Power upon History*.[2] Her 'geographical position' (no. 1) is now much less favourable than in former centuries, for air power has eliminated that advantage she possessed as an island and she is no longer self-sufficient in foodstuffs and other essential materials; in addition, the rise of new and powerful nations outside Europe has undermined her earlier capacity to contain rival navies within European waters. As for her 'physical conformation' and 'extent of territory' (nos. 2 and 3), we have witnessed in this century the fulfilment of Mackinder's prophecy that vast continental states with enormous natural resources would overtake the small, peripheral, sea-trading nations. The 'number of population' condition (no. 4) merely confirms this transformation and even if the British people still have a proportionately greater total 'following the sea', this is a slight consideration when the basis for naval strength lies more in a country's advanced technology and financial sinews than in the ability to recruit seamen.

It is difficult to take the next factor, 'national character' (no. 5) all that seriously, if by it is meant some quasi-Darwinistic commentary upon the merits of various human races; for history suggests that, at a given time and under certain conditions, any nation may be able to tread prominently across the world's stage. On the other hand, if by it there is meant that cluster of more ascertainable considerations, such as commercial aptitude, national efficiency and productivity, and a widespread interest in maritime affairs, then Mahan's point becomes very apposite to contemporary Britain, which is somewhat lacking in all these respects. The same would be true of 'character of the government' (no. 6): the days when a small group of aristocrats and 'trading gentry' and West India merchants directed the nation towards the pursuit of colonial and naval mastery, or even the days when the announcement of an additional German naval law could excite the country, are long gone. The Soviet naval build-up occupies only the attention of a few strategic experts and Conservative back-benchers; the fact that France will soon have – for the first time since 1779 – a larger navy than Britain will pass generally unnoticed. In this introspective age, when domestic, social and economic problems dominate the headlines, it would be considered anachronistic to dwell too much upon the condition of British sea power. By all of Mahan's criteria for judging successful maritime states, therefore, this country would fail to qualify.

To approve or to regret these changes in Britain's place in the world, and in the public attitudes which have accompanied them, would be irrelevant to the present analysis: the fact is that they have taken place and that the historian must acknowledge them. Anyone with even a slight knowledge of the past will be aware that no country which reached the pinnacle of world power has kept that place for ever. As an official report written as long ago as 1727 put it, 'Command of the sea has frequently passed from one nation to another, and though Great Britain has continued longer in possession of the superiority than perhaps any other nation ever did, yet all human affairs are subject to great vicissitudes.'[8] It is a fitting epitaph to our story, and at the same time a reminder of how long the British managed to play a role in world affairs out of all proportion to their numbers and size of territory. In this undeniable fact may lie some small consolation for those who have regretted Britain's abandonment of that role and have argued that an empire based upon sea power was usually more beneficial and less heavy-handed than those based upon land power.

It will be for the historian of the far-distant future to undertake a more detached examination of the period of Britain's naval mastery and to see how her dominion is to be compared with the empires which preceded hers and those which have followed. Nevertheless, this should not prevent us from already seeking to make fruitful comparisons and to understand better the reasons why certain nations rise and fall. In so doing, we not only illuminate the past, but we help to make more comprehensible the present state of world politics. Here, surely, is ample justification for the further study of what that writer in 1727 termed those 'great vicissitudes', to which all human affairs are subject.

References

Introduction to the 2017 Edition

1. G. Rachman, *Easternisation: War and Peace in the Asian Century* (London, 2016); and compare with the intriguing older work, T. von Laue, *The World Revolution of Westernization: the Twentieth Century in Global Perspective* (Oxford, 1987), passim.

2. Statements by the CNO, Admiral John M. Richardson, in his report 'A Design for Maintaining Maritime Supremacy', http://www.navy.mil/cno/docs/cno_stg.pdf, a very bracing document, with many references to the need for History to inform policy.

3. F. Braudel, *The Mediterranean and the Mediterranean World in the Age of Philip II*, 2 vols. (London, 1972, 1973), passim.

4. S. W. Roskill, *British Naval Policy Between the Wars*, 2 vols. (London, 1968, 1972); A. J. Marder, *The Anatomy of British Sea Power: British Naval Policy 1880–1905*, (New York, 1940); idem., *From the Dreadnaught to Scapa Flow*, 5 vols. (Oxford, 1961–1970).

5. One such an exception being Professor Jon Sumida's *In Defence of Naval Supremacy: Financial Limitation, Technological Innovation, and British Naval Policy, 1889–1914* (London, 1993), which argued convincingly that it was the spiraling naval estimates that drove post-1900 British governments to adopt newer naval technologies, newer ships' types and newer forms of taxation. N. Lambert, *Planning Armageddon: British Economic Warfare and the First World War* (Cambridge, Mass, 2012), re-captures some of this economic dimension to British naval strategy by showing Admiralty thinking (not all of it very realistic) for waging economic warfare against Germany if and when war came.

6. A. J. P. Taylor, *The Struggle for Mastery in Europe 1848–1918* (Oxford, 1954), Introduction.

7. The dates of the author's works here show the sequence: *British Naval Mastery* [started 1973, published 1976); *Anglo-German Antagonism* (started 1972, published 1980); *The Rise and Fall of the Great Powers* (started 1981, published 1988), with the late 1970s/early 1980s also seeing my journal articles like 'Why Did the British Empire Last So Long?', and 'The Tradition of Appeasement in British Foreign Policy', and 'The First World War and the International Power Balances'. Long-term trends, and the measure (and importance) of relative power, are the topics that re-appear, again and again. Relative naval power is thus one aspect of this.

8. A. J. Mackinder's in *Britain and the British Seas* (London/New York, 1902); Mahan's brilliant piece 'Some Considerations on the Location of Navies', reprinted in his collection of essays, A. T. Mahan, *Retrospect and Prospect: Studies in International Relations, Naval and Political* (Boston, 1902).

9. For this story, see my *Engineers of Victory: The Problem Solvers Who Turned the Tide In the Second World War* (London/New York, 2013), chapter one.

10. J. Devanny, 'Co-ordinating UK Foreign and Security Policy: The National Security Council', Royal United Services Institute (RUSI) Journal, vol.160, no.6 (December 2015), pp. 4–11. See also the other contributions in that issue, which is entitled 'UK Strategy in the 21st Century: Paved with Good Intentions'. There's a very sensible [19-page] survey of the RN, with a history and bibliography, in https://en.wikipedia.org/wiki/Royal_Navy, accessed 24 August 2016. And, for the longer story, see E. Grove, *From Vanguard to Trident: British Naval Policy Since 1945* (USNI Press, Annapolis, 1987), passim.

11. Stockholm International Peace Research Institute [hereafter SIPRI], Military Expenditure Database 2015, http://milexdata.sipri.org, for the GDPs of the pertinent countries in that year.

12. *Jane's World Navies 2016–17*, Republic of Korea, https://Janes.iha.com/JANES/Display/1322709 (Accessed 1 June 2016).

13. For these statistics, see again the 2015 Military Expenditure Database of SIPRI; and also the informative article, Kyle Mizokuma, 'The Five Most-Powerful Navies on the Planet', *The National Interest*, 6 June 2014, also nationalinterst-org/the-five-most-powerful-navies-the-planet-106107, pp. 1–3.

14. 'Taking Arms', the Economist, 27 February 2016, p. 34. The Australian contract [it was for 12 submarines] was finally awarded to a French company, which beat off strong Japanese and German competition.

15. The SIPRI total for China's defence budget includes more categories and departments of state expenditure than the other chief source for defence spending, the International Institute for Strategic Studies (IISS), *The Military Balance*, London, 2016, which gives a total of $146bn for 2016.

16. J. J. Mearsheimer, *The Tragedy of Great Power Politics* (New York, N.Y., 2001), passim.

17. G. Allison, 'The Thucydides Trap: Are the U.S. and China Headed for War?', *Atlantic Monthly* (September 2015). For an anxious rebuttal, see for example the South Korean journal *Global Asia*, Volume 10, no. 4, Winter 2015, passim but especially pp. 60–64, and the more forthright T. J.Pempel, 'Thucydides (Clap) Trap', idem., pp. 88–93.

18. H. Kissinger, *On China* (New York, 2011), uses a historical discourse about the famous Eyre Crowe Memorandum of 1907 [on Anglo-German relations back then], Epilogue, pp. 514–27, to indicate the conditionality of the U.S. tolerance of China's continuing growth.

19. R. C. Rubel, 'Connecting the Dots: Capital Ships, The Littoral, Command of the Sea, and the World Order', *Naval War College Review*, vol. 69, no. 4 (Autumn, 2015), pp. 46–62.

20. As argued by Richard Gordon, *The Rise and Fall of the American Economy* (Princeton U.P., Princeton, 2016).

21. A. T. Mahan, *The Influence of Sea Power Upon History, 1660–1783* (orig. Boston, 1890), p. 88.

Introduction: The Elements of Sea Power

1. A. T. Mahan, *The Influence of Sea Power upon History 1660–1783* (London, 1965 edn), p. iii.

2. H. W. Richmond, *Statesmen and Sea Power* (Oxford, 1946), p. ix.

3. On this, see B. Brodie, *A Guide to Naval Strategy* (New York, Washington and London, 1965 edn), Chapter IV, 'Command of the Sea'.

4. Mahan, *The Influence of Sea Power upon History*, p. 25.

5. J. Mordal, *25 Centuries of Sea Warfare* (London, 1970 edn), pp. 3–46; E. B. Potter and C. W. Nimitz (eds.), *Sea Power: A Naval History* (New Jersey, 1960), pp. 1–15.

6. Mahan, *The Influence of Sea Power upon History*, p. 138.

7. Potter and Nimitz, *Sea Power: A Naval History*, p. vii.

8. ibid.

9. Mahan, *The Influence of Sea Power upon History*, p. 88.

10. ibid., pp. 25–89. See also W. E. Livezey, *Mahan on Sea Power* (Norman, Oklahoma, 1947), Chapter III.

11. Mahan, *The Influence of Sea Power upon History*, pp. 90–91.

12. ibid., pp. 25, 65 and 225–6.

13. ibid., p. 28.

14. J. J. Clarke, 'Merchant Marine and the Navy: A Note on the Mahan Hypothesis', *Royal United Services Institution Journal*, cxii, no. 646 (May 1967), p. 163. In this article Clarke gives many examples to disprove Mahan's argument that a fighting navy always springs naturally out of commerce and shipping.

15. C. G. Reynolds, 'Sea Power in the Twentieth Century', *Royal United Services Institution Journal*, cxi, no. 642 (May 1966), p. 135; Livezey, *passim*.

Chapter One: The Early Years of English Sea Power (to 1603)

1. See generally, *The New Cambridge Modern History*, i, *The Renaissance*, edited by G. R. Potter (Cambridge, 1961); J. Pirenne, *The Tides of History*, ii, *From the Expansion of Islam to the Treaties of Westphalia* (London, 1963 edn), pp. 213 ff.

2. J. H. Parry, *The Age of Reconnaissance* (London, 1963), p. 54 and *passim*; C. M. Cipolla, *Guns and Sail in the Early Phase of European Expansion* (London, 1965).

3. J. Needham, *Science and Civilization in China*, 5 vols. to date (Cambridge, 1954–71), iv, part 3, *Civil Engineering and Nautics*, p. 554.

4. Parry, *The Age of Reconnaissance*, pp. 83–114; J. A. Williamson, *The Ocean in English History* (Oxford, 1941), pp. 1–27.

5. Needham, iv, part 3, *Civil Engineering and Nautics*, pp. 379–587.

6. Parry, *The Age of Reconnaissance*, pp. 19–37; Cipolla, *Guns and Sail in the Early Phase of European Expansion, passim*; Needham, iv, part 3, *Civil Engineering and Nautics*, pp. 508–35.

7. However, Needham also suggests that other reasons why the Chinese did not emulate western Europe in the creation of a maritime-based empire were the internal opposition and the strength of conservative Confucian doctrines, both of which led to a considerable decline in Chinese naval power in the fifteenth and sixteenth centuries; Needham, *Civil Engineering and Nautics*, pp. 524–8.

8. On the development of naval armaments, see again Parry, *The Age of Reconnaissance*, pp. 114–24; Cipolla, *Guns and Sail in the Early Phase of European Expansion*, *passim*; P. Padfield, *Guns at Sea* (London, 1973), pp. 9–70.

9. Padfield, *Guns at Sea*, pp. 25–7.

10. Padfield, *Guns at Sea*, p. 9.

11. R. Davis, *The Rise of the Atlantic Economies* (London, 1973), *passim*, but especially pp. 73–87; Pirenne, *The Tides of History*, ii, pp. 357 ff.

12. H. J. Mackinder, 'The Geographical Pivot of History', *Geographical Journal*, xxiii, no. 4 (April 1904), pp. 432–3.

13. K. M. Panikkar, *Asia and Western Dominance. A Survey of the Vasco da Gama Epoch of Asian History 1498–1945* (London, 1959 edn), p. 13.

14. H. A. L. Fisher, *A History of Europe*, 2 vols. (London, 1960 edn), i, p. 430.

15. Parry, *The Age of Reconnaissance*, p. 48.

16. C. T. Smith, *An Historical Geography of Western Europe before 1800* (London, 1967), pp. 403 ff.

17. A. L. Rowse, *The Expansion of Elizabethan England* (London, 1955), chapters I–IV, XI.

18. Cipolla, *Guns and Sail in the Early Phase of European Expansion*, pp. 36–41.

19. On this, see R. G. Albion, *Forests and Sea Power, The Timber Problem of the Royal Navy 1652–1862* (Hamden, Conn., 1965 edn).

20. D. Howarth, *Sovereign of the Seas. The Story of British Sea Power* (London, 1974), pp. 11–63; C. J. Marcus, *A Naval History of England*, 2 vols. to date (London, 1961–71), i, pp. 1–20; B. Murphy, *A History of the British Economy 1086–1970* (London, 1973), pp. 51–9, 83–98.

21. B. Murphy, *A History of the British Economy*, p. 89.

22. On this, see J. A. Williamson, *A Short History of British Expansion*, 2 vols. (London, 1945 edn), i, pp. 81–124; Williamson, *Maritime Expansion 1485–1558* (Oxford, 1913); W. Oakeshott, *Founded upon the Seas* (Cambridge, 1942).

23. R. B. Wernham, *Before the Armada. The Growth of English Foreign Policy 1485–1558* (Cambridge, 1964), p. 349.

24. K. Marx and F. Engels, 'Manifesto of the Communist Party', in *The Essential Left* (London, 1960 edn), pp. 15–16.

25. K. R. Andrews, *Elizabethan Privateering. English Privateering during Spanish War 1585–1603* (Cambridge, 1964), p. 18.

26. T. K. Rabb, *Enterprise and Empire. Merchant and Gentry Investment in the Expansion of England, 1575–1630* (Cambridge, Mass., 1967), p. 13.

27. L. B. Wright, *Religion and Empire. The Alliance between Piety and Commerce in English Expansion 1558–1625* (New York, 1965 edn).

28. *The Cambridge History of the British Empire*, i, edited by J. H. Rose, A. P. Newton and E. A. Benians (Cambridge, 1929), p. 111.

29. K. R. Andrews, *Drake's Voyages* (London, 1970 edn), p. 209.

30. This impression comes over very strongly in the books of Dr A. L. Rowse: see especially *The Expansion of Elizabethan England* and *The England of Elizabeth* (London, 1951).

31. Cipolla, *Guns and Sail in the Early Phase of European Expansion*, p. 87.

32. Williamson, *A Short History*, i, pp. 28–9.

33. S. W. Roskill, *The Strategy of Sea Power* (London, 1962), p. 24.

34. Wernham, *Before the Armada*, p. 343.

35. See Oakeshott, *Founded upon the Seas*, *passim*, and J. A. Williamson, *The Age of Drake* (London, 1938), for general surveys.

36. Pirenne, *The Tides of History*, ii, p. 429.

37. Wernham's study, *Before the Armada*, reveals not so much that there was a fixed balance-of-power policy by the early Tudors but that they became increasingly aware that they were living in a world of stronger powers, between which they must steer cautiously; L. Dehio, *The Precarious Balance* (London, 1963), p. 39, suggests that Wolsey and Henry VIII were both thinking of such a policy but often lacked the means or the will to see it carried out.

38. Quoted in R. B. Wernham, 'Elizabethan War Aims and Strategy', in *Elizabethan Government and Society*, edited by S. T. Bindoff, J. Hurstfield and C. H. Williams (London, 1961), p. 340.

39. Richmond, *Statesmen and Sea Power*, p. 9.

40. ibid., p. 24. (Corbett called the Queen 'the first little Englander'.)

41. *The Cambridge History of the British Empire*, i, p. 95.

42. See Wernham, 'Elizabethan War Aims and Strategy', *passim*; Roskill, *Strategy of Sea Power*, pp. 30–32; G. Mattingly, *The Defeat of the Spanish Armada* (Harmondsworth, Middlesex, 1959 edn).

43. Apart from Wernham, praise for Elizabeth's Netherlands policy has come from Rowse, *Expansion*, pp. 413–14; and Dehio, *The Precarious Balance*, pp. 50, 54–7. The reservations of C. Wilson, *Queen Elizabeth and the Revolt of the Netherlands* (London, 1970) are that she did not intervene enough, rather than that she should not have intervened at all.

44. Quoted in Richmond, *Statesmen and Sea Power*, p. 7.

45. ibid., pp. 17–18.

46. Wernham, *Before the Armada*, p. 12, gives details of early Tudor England's population and finances compared with those of Spain and France; and some later financial figures in 'Elizabethan War Aims and Strategy', pp. 355–7.

47. ibid., pp. 362–6; C. Barnett, *Britain and her Army, 1509–1970: A Military, Political and Social Survey* (London, 1970), pp. 50–2.

48. Wernham, 'Elizabethan War Aims and Strategy', p. 367; cf. Richmond, *Statesmen and Sea Power*, p. 24.

49. Mattingly, *The Defeat of the Spanish Armada*, p. 414.

50. See Williamson, *A Short History*, pp. 125–33.

51. Wernham, *Before the Armada*, p. 286; R. Davis, *English Overseas Trade 1500–1700* (London, 1973), pp. 32 ff.

52. L. Stone, 'Elizabethan Foreign Trade', *Economic History Review*, 2nd series, ii (1949–50), pp. 37–9. Stone in general provides a sobering, almost pessimistic, re-assessment of Elizabethan foreign trade here.

53. Murphy, *A History of the British Economy*; C. T. Smith, *An Historical Geography of Western Europe*, pp. 428–61.

54. Richmond, *Statesmen and Sea Power*, pp. 13–14.

55. Andrews, *Drake's Voyages*, p. 211.

56. ibid., pp. 128, 226–31.

57. Mattingly, *The Defeat of the Spanish Armada*, p. 414.

58. On this, see E. Schulin, *Handelsstaat England. Das Politische Interesse der Nation am Aussenhandel vom 16. bis ins frühe 18. Jahrhundert* (Wiesbaden, 1969), pp. 9–60.

59. Wernham, *Before the Armada*, p. 408.

Chapter Two: The Stuart Navy and the Wars with the Dutch (1603–88)

1. C. D. Penn, *The Navy under the Early Stuarts and its Influence on English History* (London, 1970 edn), p. iii. See also Marcus, *A Naval History of England*, 1, pp. 123–8; H. W. Richmond, *The Navy as an Instrument of Policy 1558–1727* (Cambridge, 1953), chapter III; M. Oppenheim, *A History of the Administration of the Royal Navy . . . 1509–1660* (Hamden, Conn., 1961 edn), pp. 184–215.

2. M. Lewis, *The History of the British Navy* (Harmondsworth, Middlesex, 1957), pp. 72–3.

3. C. Hill, *Reformation to Industrial Revolution* (Harmondsworth, Middlesex, 1969), pp. 72–108; R. Ashton, 'Revenue Farming under the Early Stuarts', *Economic History Review*, 2nd series, viii, no. 3 (April 1956), pp. 310–22; Ashton, 'The Parliamentary Agitation for Free Trade in the Opening Year of the Reign of James I', *Past and Present*, no. 38 (December 1967), pp. 40–55.

4. Penn, *The Navy under the Early Stuarts*, p. 174; chapters IV, VI and VII provide the basic account of these three expeditions.

5. For example, by G. Callender, *The Naval Side of British History* (London, 1924), chapter VI.

6. See J. R. Jones, *Britain and Europe in the Seventeenth Century* (London, 1966), pp. 14–25, for a brief account of early Stuart foreign policy.

7. D. B. Quinn, 'James I and the Beginnings of Empire in America', *The Journal of Imperial and Commonwealth History*, ii, no. 2 (January 1974), pp. 135–52.

8. Williamson, *A Short History of British Expansion*, i, p. 156. The early Stuart expansion is covered in ibid., pp. 153–230; and A. D. Innes, *The Maritime and Colonial Expansion of England under the Stuarts* (London, 1931), pp. 41–193.

9. B. Tunstall, *The Realities of Naval History* (London, 1936), p. 51. See also, J. R. Jones, *Britain and Europe in the Seventeenth Century*, p. 15; and R. Davis, *The Rise of the English Shipping Industry in the Seventeenth and Eighteenth Centuries* (Newton Abbot, 1972 edn), pp. 7–11.

10. See, for example, pp. 139–44 or 173–8 or 281–5 of Mahan's *The Influence of Sea Power upon History*.

11. Penn, *The Navy under the Early Stuarts*, pp. 265–97; J. R. Powell, *The Navy in the English Civil War* (London, 1962).

12. Oppenheim, *A History of the Administration of the Royal Navy*, p. 306.

13. On this, see C. Hill, *Reformation to Industrial Revolution*, pp. 155–68; and especially Schulin, *Handelsstaat England*, pp. 107–74.

14. Schulin, *Handelsstaat England*, pp. 137–51; J. E. Farnall, 'The Navigation Act of 1651, the First Dutch War, and the London Mercantile Community', *Economic History Review*, 2nd series, xvi, no. 3 (April 1964), pp. 439–54; C. Wilson, *Profit and Power. A Study of England and the Dutch Wars* (London, 1957), pp. 54–8; R. K. W. Hinton, *The Eastland Trade and the Common Weal in the Seventeenth Century* (Cambridge, 1959), pp. 84–94; L. A. Harper, *The English Navigation Laws* (New York, 1964 edn), *passim*; B. Martin, 'Aussenhandel und Aussenpolitik Englands unter Cromwell', *Historische Zeitschrift*, 218, no. 3 (June 1974), pp. 571–92.

15. M. Lewis, *The History of the British Navy*, p. 89; and see generally, Wilson, *Profit and Power*; Farnall, 'The Navigation Act of 1651', pp. 449–52.

16. Wilson, *Profit and Power*, p. 41.

17. In Marcus, *A Naval History of England*, i, p. 140.

18. Mahan, *Influence of Sea Power upon History*, p. 138.

19. Richmond, *The Navy as an Instrument of Policy*, pp. 118, 147, 152 and 178.

20. Quoted in H. Rosinski, 'The Role of Sea Power in Global Warfare of the Future', *Brassey's Naval Annual* (1947), p. 103. See also, G. S. Graham, *Empire of the North Atlantic* (Toronto, 1950), pp. 19, 50; Graham; *Tides of Empire* (Montreal and London, 1972), pp. 25–6.

21. The following is based chiefly upon Mahan, *Influence of Sea Power upon History*, pp. 95–126; Wilson, *Profit and Power*, pp. 61–77; Marcus, *A Naval History of England*, i, pp. 138–47.

22. J. R. Jones, *Britain and Europe in the Seventeenth Century*, p. 55; Farnall, 'The Navigation Act of 1651', pp. 452–4; C. Hill, *God's Englishman. Oliver Cromwell and the English Revolution* (London, 1970), pp. 156–7.

23. Wilson, *Profit and Power*, p. 81.

24. Richmond, *The Navy as an Instrument of Policy*, pp. 127–39.

25. ibid. See also, Hill, *God's Englishman*, pp. 166–8; Hill, *The Century of Revolution 1603–1714* (London, 1961), pp. 156–60.

26. Hill, *The Century of Revolution 1603–1714*, pp. 160–61.

27. Farnall, 'The Navigation Act of 1651', pp. 453–4.

28. Williamson, *A Short History*, i, pp. 255–6.

29. J. R. Jones, *Britain and Europe in the Seventeenth Century*, p. 56. See also Harper, *The English Navigation Laws*, pp. 52–8.

30. See Wilson, *Profit and Power*, pp. 93–126, for the details mentioned in this paragraph.

31. ibid., pp. 127–42; Richmond, *The Navy as an Instrument of Policy*, pp. 140–67.

32. Wilson, *Profit and Power*, p. 131; K. G. Davies, *The Royal African Company* (London, 1957), pp. 42–4.

33. J. R. Jones, *Britain and Europe in the Seventeenth Century*, pp. 70–74.

34. Marcus, *A Naval History of England*, i, pp. 163–73; Richmond, *The Navy as an Instrument of Policy*, pp. 168–92; Mahan, *Influence of Sea Power upon History*, pp. 139–58.

35. J. R. Jones, *Britain and Europe in the Seventeenth Century*, pp. 65–6: C. Wilson 'The Economic Decline of the Netherlands', *Economic History Review*, ix, no. 2 (May 1939); P. Geyl, *The Netherlands in the Seventeenth Century*, 2 vols. (London, 1966–4), ii, pp. 147 ff.; C. R. Boxer, *The Dutch Seaborne Empire 1600–1800* (London, 1965), pp. 104–12, 268–94.

36. What follows is based upon Marcus, *A Naval History of England*, i, pp. 184–7; Williamson, *A Short History*, i, pp. 304–37; Innes, *The Maritime and Colonial Expansion of England under the Stuarts*, pp. 223–366; Hill, *Reformation to Industrial Revolution*, pp. 155–64; R. Davis, 'English Foreign Trade, 1600–1700', *Economic History Review*, 2nd series, vii, no. 2 (December 1954); Davis, *English Shipping Industry*, pp. 14–21. Because of the nature of the historical data upon the growth of English overseas trade in the later seventeenth century, it has been necessary to transgress the chronological limits of this chapter.

37. In any case the company's shares could be purchased on the stock exchange. The Levant Company had considerably declined in importance, due to French competition; and the newly founded Hudson's Bay Company was still in its infancy. The Eastland Company lost its exclusive rights as early as 1673 because of the government's wish to increase the import of naval stores.

38. Murphy, *A History of the British Economy 1086–1870*, p. 300.
39. See briefly, Marcus, *A Naval History of England*, i, pp. 173–92.

Chapter Three: The Struggle against France and Spain (1689–1756)

1. J. H. Plumb, *The Growth of Political Stability in England 1675–1725* (London, 1967), p. xviii and *passim*.
2. ibid.
3. Hill, *Reformation to Industrial Revolution*, pp. 213–59; C. Wilson, *England's Apprenticeship 1603–1763* (London, 1965), pp. 141–336; A. H. John, 'Aspects of English Economic Growth in the First Half of the Eighteenth Century', *Economica*, xxviii (May 1961), pp. 176–90. The growth of English financial strength is well covered in P. G. M. Dickson, *The Financial Revolution in England. A Study in the Development of Public Credit 1688–1756* (London, 1967).
4. Wilson, *England's Apprenticeship*, pp. 264–8; Davis, *English Shipping Industry*, pp. 26–7; Davis, 'English Foreign Trade, 1700–1774', *Economic History Review*, 2nd series, xv, no. 2 (December 1962), pp. 285–303; D. A. Farnie, 'The Commercial Empire of the Atlantic, 1607–1783', ibid., pp. 205–18.
5. Plumb, *The Growth of Political Stability in England*, pp. 119–20.
6. This paragraph is based upon Wilson, *England's Apprenticeship*, chapter 13; Hill, *Reformation to Industrial Revolution*, pp. 226–53; A. H. John, 'War and the English Economy 1700–1763', *Economic History Review*, 2nd series, vii, no. 3 (April 1955), pp. 329–44; T. S. Ashton, *Economic Fluctuations in England 1700–1800* (Oxford, 1959), pp. 64–83.
7. Wilson, *England's Apprenticeship*, p. 285. The overseas rivalries of the eighteenth century are covered in J. H. Parry, *Trade and Dominion. The European Oversea Empires in the Eighteenth Century* (London, 1971); G. Williams, *The Expansion of Europe in the Eighteenth Century* (London, 1966); Graham, *Empire of the North Atlantic*, pp. 83–236.
8. Richmond, *Statesmen and Sea Power*, pp. 61–2, 121; also, Schulin, *Handelsstaat England*, pp. 289 ff.
9. Richmond, *Statesmen and Sea Power*, p. 117; and see generally, R. Pares, 'American versus Continental Warfare, 1739–63', *English Historical Review*, li, no. CCIII (July 1936), pp. 429–65.
10. J. B. Wolf, *Toward a European Balance of Power 1620–1715* (Chicago, 1970), pp. 106–19, 143–50.
11. E. B. Powley, *The Naval Side of King William's War* (London, 1972), *passim*.
12. Richmond, *Statesmen and Sea Power*, pp. 63–6; and especially, G. N. Clarke, *The Dutch Alliance and the War against French Trade 1688–1697* (New York, 1971 edn); Clarke, 'The character of the Nine Years War, 1688–97', *Cambridge Historical Journal*, xi, no. 2 (1954), pp. 168–82.
13. Marcus, *A Naval History of England*, i, pp. 206–8.
14. Quoted in Richmond, *Statesmen and Sea Power*, p. 76; see also J. R. Jones, *Britain and Europe in the Seventeenth Century*, pp. 90–93.
15. Mahan, *The Influence of Sea Power upon History*, p. 193.
16. Richmond, *The Navy as an Instrument of Policy*, pp. 265–74.
17. A. N. Ryan, 'William III and the Brest Fleet in the Nine Years War', in R. Hatton and J. S. Bromley (eds.), *William III and Louis XIV. Essays 1680–1720 by and for Mark A. Thomson* (Liverpool, 1968), pp. 49–67.

18. See, in great detail, J. Ehrman, *The Navy in the War of William III, 1689–1697* (Cambridge, 1953), *passim*.

19. Wolf, *Toward a European Balance of Power*, pp. 127–55.

20. Cited in Richmond, *The Navy as an Instrument of Policy*, p. 279. See also Schulin, *Handelsstaat England*, p. 289; G. N. Clarke, 'War Trade and Trade War, 1701–1713', *Economic History Review*, i, no. 2 (January 1928), p. 262; Parry, *Trade and Dominion*, pp. 92–8.

21. Wolf, *Toward a European Balance of Power*, pp. 192–6.

22. Richmond, *The Navy as an Instrument of Policy*, pp. 290–91, 341–2.

23. J. S. Bromley, 'The French Privateering War, 1702–1713', in H. E. Bell and R. S. Ollard (eds.), *Historical Essays 1600–1750, presented to David Ogg* (London, 1963), pp. 203–31; Marcus, *A Naval History of England*, i, pp. 238–42; J. H. Owen, *War at Sea under Queen Anne 1702–1708* (Cambridge, 1938), pp. 55–70, 101–28, 193–243.

24. Owen, *War at Sea under Queen Anne*, pp. 71–100, 129–92; Richmond, *The Navy as an Instrument of Policy*, pp. 276 ff.

25. The latest studies of this topic are B. W. Hill, 'Oxford, Bolingbroke and the Peace of Utrecht', *Historical Journal*, xvi, no. 2 (1973), pp. 241–63; and A. D. MacLachlan, 'The Road to Peace 1710–1713', in G. Holmes (ed.), *Britain after the Glorious Revolution* (London, 1969), pp. 197–215.

26. Mahan, *The Influence of Sea Power upon History*, p. 217.

27. ibid., pp. 191, 200, 209.

28. J. R. Jones, *Britain and Europe in the Seventeenth Century*, p. 90.

29. Mahan, *The Influence of Sea Power upon History*, pp. 222–9.

30. J. B. Wolf, *The Emergence of the Great Powers 1685–1715* (New York, 1950), pp. 187–8.

31. Ehrman, *The Navy in the War of William III*, p xv.

32. P. Geyl, *The Netherlands in the Seventeenth Century*, ii, pp. 311 ff.

33. British policy after the Peace of Utrecht is covered in Richmond, *The Navy as an Instrument of Policy*, pp. 363–97; J. O. Lindsay, 'International Relations', *New Cambridge Modern History*, vii, *The Old Régime 1713–63*, edited by J. O. Lindsay (Cambridge, 1957), pp. 191–205; D. B. Horn, *Great Britain and Europe in the Eighteenth Century* (Oxford, 1967), *passim*.

34. J. H. Parry, 'The Caribbean', *New Cambridge Modern History*, vii, p. 518.

35. R. Pares, *War and Trade in the West Indies 1739–1763* (London, 1963 edn), pp. 1 ff; Parry, *Trade and Dominion*, pp. 107–10.

36. The best brief account of the War of the Austrian Succession is probably that by M.A. Thomson in the *New Cambridge Modern History*, vii, pp. 416–39.

37. Richmond, *Statesmen and Sea Power*, pp. 113–23; Richmond, *National Policy and Naval Strength and Other Essays* (London, 1928), pp. 144–60; and especially, R. Pares, 'American versus Continental Warfare, 1739–63'.

38. These events are covered briefly in Marcus, *A Naval History of England*, i, pp. 252–67.

39. Pares, 'American versus Continental Warfare, 1739–63', pp. 461–2.

40. The most thorough account is by Richmond, *The Navy in the War of 1739–1748*, 3 vols. (Cambridge, 1920), but there are shorter surveys in Richmond, *Statesmen and Sea Power*, pp. 113–23; Marcus, *A Naval History of England*, i, pp. 250–77; and Mahan, *The Influence of Sea Power upon History*, pp. 254–80.

41. These two battles are briefly described in J. Creswell's *British Admirals of the Eighteenth Century. Tactics in Battle* (London, 1972), chapter 5, which is the most recent survey of the old controversy concerning 'general chase' as opposed to the strict 'line of battle' tactics.

42. C. E. Fayle, 'Economic Pressure in the War of 1739–48', *Journal of the Royal United Services Institute*, 68 (1923), pp. 434–6.

43. Graham, *Empire of the North Atlantic*, p. 141 (my italics).

44. Quoted in Mahan, *The Influence of Sea Power upon History*, p. 278.

Chapter Four: Triumph and Check (1756–93)

1. Basic studies of British policy during the Seven Years War are: J. S. Corbett, *England in the Seven Years War. A Study in Combined Strategy*, 2 vols. (London, 1918); L. H. Gipson, *The British Empire before the American Revolution*, 14 vols. (New York, 1936–68) iv–viii; O. A. Sherrard, *Lord Chatham. Pitt and the Seven Years War* (London, 1955); B. Williams, *Life of William Pitt*, 2 vols. (London, 1915); R. Savory, *His Britannic Majesty's Army in Germany during the Seven Years War* (Oxford, 1966).

2. Pares, *War and Trade in the West Indies*, pp. 184 ff; Gipson, *The British Empire before the American Revolution*, v, pp. 207–30.

3. V. Purcell, 'Asia', *New Cambridge Modern History*, vii, pp. 558 ff.

4. Gipson, *The British Empire before the American Revolution*, iv–v, *passim*; Graham, *Empire of the North Atlantic*, pp. 143 ff; P. Louis-René Higonnet, 'The Origins of the Seven Years War', *Journal of Modern History*, 40, no. 1 (March 1968), pp. 51–90.

5. For the European background to the outbreak of the Seven Years War, see D. B. Horn, 'The Diplomatic Revolution', *New Cambridge Modern History*, vii, pp. 440–64; *Cambridge History of the British Empire*, i, pp. 460 ff.

6. Graham, *Empire of the North Atlantic*, p. 148.

7. Gipson, *The British Empire before the American Revolution*, vi, *passim*; Marcus, *A Naval History of England*, i, pp. 278–86; Mahan, *The Influence of Sea Power upon History*, pp. 284–93; Corbett, *England in the Seven Years War*, i, pp. 63–179.

8. Quoted in Richmond, *Statesmen and Sea Power*, p. 127.

9. Pares, 'American versus Continental Warfare 1739–63', pp. 436, 448, 459–65; Williams, *Life of William Pitt*, i, pp. 302–6, 354–8; ii, pp. 67–8, 130–39; Corbett, *England in the Seven Years War*, i, pp. 76–7, 240–43, 285–6; ii, pp. 363–4 and *passim*. Corbett's portrayal of this growing 'maturity' of Pitt's thought is not helped by his own strategical predilections, for although he was a critic of the 'battle-fleet only' ideas of his time and argued instead for the value of combined operations, he nevertheless held that maritime and colonial interests were always the most important to Britain and this caused him to put forward conclusions about Pitt's policy which are assertion and conjecture (e.g. vol. i, p. 191) rather than fact. However, it remains a most useful book and one that is much more even-handed about the respective merits of sea power and land power than many other naval histories.

10. C. J. Marcus, *Quiberon Bay* (London, 1960); Creswell, *British Admirals of the Eighteenth Century*, pp. 104–19.

11. Quoted in Marcus, *A Naval History of England*, i, p. 325.

12. Corbett, *England in the Seven Years War*, i, p. 8.

13. Graham, *Empire of the North Atlantic*, p. 154.

14. Corbett, *England in the Seven Years War*, i, pp. 227–8, 244–5.

15. E. Robson, 'The Seven Years War', *New Cambridge Modern History*, vii, pp. 479 ff; *Cambridge History of the British Empire*, i, pp. 485 ff; Sir Richard Lodge, *Great Britain and Prussia in the Eighteenth Century* (New York, 1972 reprint), pp. 107–38; M. Schlenke, *England und das Friderizianische Preussen 1740–1763* (Freiburg and Munich, 1963), pp. 249 ff.

16. I take this figure from B. Tunstall, *William Pitt, Earl of Chatham* (London, 1938), p. 492; but see also, in much more detail, C. W. Eldon, *England's Subsidy Policy towards the Continent during the Seven Years War* (Philadelphia, 1938), especially pp. 161–2.

17. cf. Corbett, *England in the Seven Years War*, i, pp. 190–91, where a different interpretation is attempted (and my remarks in note 9 above).

18. Marcus, *A Naval History of England*, i, pp. 334–5; Mahan, *The Influence of Sea Power upon History*, pp. 317–20. Agriculture was more severely affected, according to H. Wellenreuther, 'Land, Gesellschaft und Wirtschaft in England während des siebenjährigen Krieges', *Historische Zeitschrift*, 218, no. 3 (June 1974), pp. 593–634.

19. Corbett, *England in the Seven Years War*, ii, p. 375; *Cambridge History of the British Empire*, i, pp. 535–7.

20. Corbett, *England in the Seven Years War*, i, p. 189.

21. Robson, 'The Seven Years War', *New Cambridge Modern History*, vii, pp. 485–6.

22. Mahan, *The Influence of Sea Power upon History*, p. 329.

23. Dehio, *The Precarious Balance*, p. 118.

24. Marcus, *A Naval History of England*, i, p. 414.

25. Richmond, *Statesmen and Sea Power*, p. 150.

26. Figures from ibid., p. 157.

27. Quoted in Graham, *Empire of the North Atlantic*, p. 147; and see also, Mahan, *The Influence of Sea Power upon History*, pp. 522–35.

28. Quoted in Richmond, *Statesmen and Sea Power*, p. 151.

29. Graham, *Tides of Empire*, p. 37.

30. Tunstall, *William Pitt, Earl of Chatham*, p. 492; Richmond, *Statesmen and Sea Power*, pp. 140–42.

31. Marcus, *A Naval History of England*, i, pp. 416–18; Albion, *Forests and Sea Power*, pp. 281–315. (I am conscious of not having devoted much space in this survey to the 'timber problem' of the Royal Navy in the eighteenth century, but this is an enormous and complex matter, involving not only the wood planking and masts but also hemp, tar and other naval supplies. Albion is still the standard source on this topic.)

32. R. J. B. Knight, 'The Administration of the Royal Dockyards in England, 1770–1790', *Bulletin of the Institute of Historical Research*, xlv, no. 111 (May 1972), pp. 148–50; Knight, 'The Home Dockyards and the American War of Independence', paper read to the fourteenth Conference of the International Commission for Maritime History, Greenwich, 12 July 1974.

33. Mahan, *The Influence of Sea Power upon History*, p. 538; and see also, A. Temple Patterson, *The Other Armada. The Franco-Spanish Attempt to Invade Britain in 1779* (Manchester, 1960).

34. Pares, 'American versus Continental Warfare, 1739–1763', pp. 451–3.

35. Graham, *Empire of the North Atlantic*, p. 201; Marcus, *A Naval History of England*, i, pp. 421–2.

36. Quoted in Richmond, *Statesmen and Sea Power*, p. 131.

37. ibid., p. 151; and Graham, *Empire of the North Atlantic*, pp. 215–16.

38. For the following, see Lodge, *Great Britain and Prussia in the Eighteenth Century*, pp. 139–59; M. S. Anderson, 'European Diplomatic Relations, 1763–1790', *New Cambridge Modern History*, viii, *The American and French Revolutions 1763–93*, edited by A. Goodwin (Cambridge, 1965), pp. 252 ff; J. F. Ramsay, *Anglo-French Relations, 1763–1770* (Berkeley, 1939); Dehio, *The Precarious Balance*, pp. 120–22.

39. Williams, *Life of Pitt*, ii, p. 85. See also Marcus, *A Naval History of England*, i, pp. 336–9, 430–31; *Cambridge History of the British Empire*, i, pp. 549–59.

40. Graham, *Tides of Empire*, p. 38.

41. Quoted in Richmond, *Statesmen and Sea Power*, p. 156.

42. G. S. Graham, 'Considerations on the War of American Independence', *Bulletin of the Institute of Historical Research*, xxii (1949), p. 23. For Neville Chamberlain's attitude, see below, pp. 296, 306.

43. D. Syrett, *Shipping and the American War 1775–83* (London, 1970), p. 243. See also N. Baker, *Government and Contractors. The British Treasury and War Supplies 1775–1783* (London, 1971).

44. Figures from pp. 524–5 of P. Mackesy, *The War for America 1775–1783* (London, 1964), which is the best military study of the war.

45. E. E. Curtis, *The Organization of the British Army in the American Revolution* (Menston, Yorkshire, 1972 reprint), p. 149.

46. Barnett, *Britain and Her Army*, p. 225.

47. Quoted in Williams, *Life of Pitt*, ii, p. 317.

48. Mahan, *The Influence of Sea Power upon History*, p. 525.

49. Quoted in Marcus, *A Naval History of England*, i, p. 416.

50. Parry, *Trade and Dominion*, pp. 130–31.

51. P. Mathias, *The First Industrial Nation. An Economic History of Britain 1700–1914* (London, 1969,) p. 3.

52. I have used, *inter alia*, Mathias, *The First Industrial Nation*, pp. 1–227; E. J. Hobsbawm, *Industry and Empire* (Harmondsworth, Middlesex, 1969), pp. 23–55; P. Mantoux, *The Industrial Revolution in the Eighteenth Century* (London, 1964 edn), *passim*; D. S. Landes, *The Unbound Prometheus. Technological Change and Industrial Development in Western Europe from 1750 to the Present* (Cambridge, 1969), pp. 41–123; Murphy, *A History of the British Economy 1086–1970*, pp. 317–513; Davis, *The Rise of the Atlantic Economies*, pp. 288–316.

53. Figures from E. B. Schumpeter, *English Overseas Trade Statistics 1697–1808* (Oxford, 1960), tables I and IV.

54. Hobsbawm, *Industry and Empire*, pp. 48–9. Further evidence for the boom in colonial trade is to be found in Davis, 'English Foreign Trade, 1700–1774', pp. 285–303.

55. Mantoux, *The Industrial Revolution in the Eighteenth Century*, p. 91; and, for the role of wars in stimulating sections of industry, see John, 'War and the English Economy, 1700–1763', pp. 329–44.

56. Figures from Schumpeter, *English Overseas Trade Statistics 1697–1808*, tables V and VI. Once again, the statistics are crude and often distorted by war (e.g. Germany, 1796–1800), but they are offered as a general indication of the extent of the expansion.

57. R. Hyam, 'British Imperial Expansion in the Late Eighteenth Century', *Historical Journal*, x, no. 1 (1967), p. 14.

58. See, for example, V. T. Harlow, *The Founding of the Second British Empire, 1763–1793*, 2 vols. (London, 1952–64), i. p. 593, and *passim*. Also important here are

Parry, *Trade and Dominion*, pp. 154–79, 242–290; J. Ehrman, *The Younger Pitt. The Years of Acclaim* (London, 1969), pp. 329–466; and especially, J. Blow Williams, *British Commercial Policy and Trade Expansion 1750–1850* (Oxford, 1972), *passim.*

59. Figures from Mantoux, *The Industrial Revolution in the Eighteenth Century*, p. 100; Marcus, *A Naval History of England*, i, pp. 399–400.

60. Quoted in Williams, *Life of Pitt*, ii, p. 56.

61. The best brief account of this financial transformation is in Ehrman, *The Younger Pitt*, pp. 239–81.

62. See G. Brunn, *Europe and the French Imperium 1799–1814* (New York and London, 1938), pp. 101–2.

63. Ehrman, *The Younger Pitt*, pp. 313–17; Marcus, *A Naval History of England*, i, pp. 460–62; M. Lewis, 'Navies', *New Cambridge Modern History*, viii, p. 186.

64. For the following, see Horn, *Great Britain and Europe in the Eighteenth Century*, pp. 64–8, 164–74, 222–30; Ehrman, *The Younger Pitt*, pp. 516–74; Anderson, 'European Diplomatic Relations, 1763–1790', *New Cambridge Modern History*, viii, pp. 272 ff; Lodge, *Great Britain and Prussia in the Eighteenth Century*, pp. 165 ff; Richmond, *Statesmen and Sea Power*, pp. 158–69.

Chapter Five: The Struggle against France Renewed (1793–1815)

1. For general accounts of the naval war, see Mahan, *The Influence of Sea Power upon the French Revolution and Empire*, 2 vols. (London, 1892); Marcus, *A Naval History of England*, ii, *passim;* Richmond, *Statesmen and Sea Power*, pp. 170–257; Potter and Nimitz, *Sea Power*, pp. 108–224.

2. Figures from Richmond, *Statesmen and Sea Power*, pp. 170–72.

3. See the figures in ibid., p. 351.

4. On this, see again J. Creswell, *British Admirals of the Eighteenth Century, passim.*

5. Quoted in Potter and Nimitz, *Sea Power*, p. 119.

6. Padfield, *Guns at Sea*, pp. 105–10.

7. Quoted in Richmond, *Statesmen and Sea Power*, pp. 338–9.

8. L. C. F. Turner, 'The Cape of Good Hope and the Anglo-French Conflict, 1797–1806', *Historical Studies. Australia and New Zealand*, 9, no. 36 (May 1961), pp. 368–78; Graham, *Tides of Empire*, pp. 48–56.

9. C. E. Carrington, *The British Overseas*, part i (Cambridge, 1968 edn), p. 239.

10. Williams, *The Expansion of Europe in the Eighteenth Century*, p. 281.

11. Mahan, *The Influence of Sea Power upon the French Revolution and Empire*, i, pp. 202–3; see also ii, pp. 206–18.

12. For the war on trade in general, see ibid., ii, pp. 199–351; and Marcus, *A Naval History of England*, ii, pp. 102–23, 361–405.

13. C. N. Parkinson, *War in the Eastern Seas 1793–1815* (London, 1954), pp. 397 ff.

14. A. N. Ryan, 'The Defence of British Trade with the Baltic, 1808–1813', *English Historical Review*, lxxiv, no. ccxcii (July 1959), p. 457.

15. Mahan, *The Life of Nelson. The Embodiment of the Sea Power of Great Britain*, 2 vols. (London, 1897).

16. For the following, see G. Brunn, 'The Balance of Power during the Wars, 1793–1814', *New Cambridge Modern History*, ix, *War and Peace in an Age of Upheaval 1793–1830*, edited by C. W. Crawley (Cambridge, 1965), pp. 250–74; Brunn, *Europe and the French Imperium 1799–1814*, pp. 36–61, 109–33, 157–209; J. M. Sherwig,

Guineas and Gunpowder. British Foreign Aid in the Wars with France, 1793–1815 (Cambridge, Mass., 1969).

17. A. B. Rodgers, *The War of the Second Coalition 1798 to 1801. A Strategic Commentary* (Oxford, 1964).

18. Brunn, 'The Balance of Power during the Wars, 1793–1814', pp. 257–8.

19. Potter and Nimitz, *Sea Power*, p. 111.

20 Mahan, *The Influence of Sea Power upon the French Revolution and Empire*, ii, pp. 218–20.

21. Sherwig, *Guineas and Gunpowder, British Foreign Aid in the Wars with France*, pp. 345, 365–8; K. F. Hellenier, *The Imperial Loans. A Study in Financial and Diplomatic History* (Oxford, 1965); J. H. Clapham, 'Loans and Subsidies in Time of War, 1793–1914', *The Economic Journal*, xxvii (1917).

22. Richmond, *Statesmen and Sea Power*, pp. 205–6. (This is not to imply that all the blame for the lack of closer Anglo-Austrian cooperation should be placed upon London; see ibid.)

23. ibid., p. 238. On the military campaign itself, see J. Weller, *Wellington in the Peninsula* (London, 1962); M. Glover, *The Peninsular War 1807–1814* (London, 1974).

24. Brunn, *Europe and the French Imperium 1799–1814*, p. 189. See also Barnett, *Britain and Her Army*, pp. 267–8, and Graham, *The Politics of Naval Supremacy*, p. 7, for further comments and comparisons between the Peninsular War and the other campaigns against Napoleon.

25. Lewis, *A History of the British Navy*, p. 207. Also, Roskill, *The Strategy of Sea Power*, pp. 87–8.

26. A. J. Marder (ed.), *Fear God and Dread Nought. The Correspondence of Admiral of the Fleet Lord Fisher of Kilverstone*, 3 vols. (London, 1952–9), iii, p. 439.

27. Marcus, *A Naval History of England*, ii, p. 299; and especially, P. Mackesy, *The War in the Mediterranean 1803–10* (London, 1957).

28. B. Perkins, *Prologue to War. England and the United States 1805–1812* (Berkeley and Los Angeles, 1961); R. Horsman, *The Causes of the War of 1812* (Philadelphia, 1961).

29. On the Anglo-American war of 1812–14, see A. T. Mahan, *Sea Power in its Relation to the War of 1812*, 2 vols. (London, 1905); T. Roosevelt, *The Naval War of 1812* (New York, 1968 reprint); R. Horsman, *The War of 1812* (London, 1969); Graham, *Empire of the North Atlantic*, pp. 237–61; Marcus, *A Naval History of England*, ii, pp. 452–84; Potter and Nimitz, *Sea Power*, pp. 207–24.

30. Richmond, *Statesmen and Sea Power*, p. 339; and see note 7 above.

31. K. Bourne, *Britain and the Balance of Power in North America 1815–1908* (London, 1967).

32. Mathias, *First Industrial Nation*, p. 44.

33. B. R. Mitchell and P. Deane, *Abstract of British Historical Statistics* (Cambridge, 1967 edn), pp. 288–96.

34. Figures from N. J. Silberling, 'Financial and Monetary Policy of Great Britain during the Napoleonic Wars', *Quarterly Journal of Economics*, xxxviii (1923–4), pp. 214–33; E. B. Schumpeter, 'English Prices and Public Finance, 1660–1822', *Revue of Economic Statistics*, xx (1938), pp. 21–37.

35. Sherwig, *Guineas and Gunpowder. British Foreign Aid in the Wars with France*, p. 352; and, in more detail, A. Hope-Jones, *Income Tax in the Napoleonic Wars* (Cambridge, 1939).

36. Murphy, *A History of the British Economy 1086–1970*, p. 490.

37. Schumpeter, 'English Prices and Public Finance, 1660–1822', p. 27; Silberling, 'Financial and Monetary Policy of Great Britain during the Napoleonic Wars', pp. 217–18 (but see Schumpeter's comments upon his statistics); Dickson, *The Financial Revolution in England*, p. 10.

38. Dickson, *The Financial Revolution in England*, p. 9. See also, E. L. Hargreaves, *The National Debt* (London, 1966 reprint), pp. 108–34; and A. Cunningham, *British Credit in the Last Napoleonic War* (Cambridge, 1910).

39. Quoted in Marcus, *A Naval History of England*, ii, p. 209.

40. The following section is based upon ibid., pp. 295–330, 406–25; Mahan, *The Influence of Sea Power upon the French Revolution and Empire*, ii, pp. 272–357; E. F. Heckscher, *The Continental System. An Economic Interpretation* (Oxford, 1922); and especially, F. Crouzet, *L'Économie Britannique et le Blocus Continental (1806–1813)*, 2 vols. (Paris, 1958); Crouzet, 'Wars, Blockade, and Economic Change in Europe, 1792–1815', *Journal of Economic History*, 24, no. 4 (1964), pp. 567–88; Williams, *British Commercial Policy and Trade Expansion 1750–1850*, pp. 346 ff.

41. Figures from B. R. Mitchell and P. Deane, *Abstract of British Historical Statistics*, p. 311. More generally, see C. N. Parkinson (ed.), *The Trade Winds. A Study of British Overseas Trade during the French Wars 1793–1815* (London, 1948).

42. B. R. Mitchell and P. Deane, *Abstract of British Historical Statistics*, p. 282.

43. G. Brunn, 'The Balance of Power during the Wars, 1793–1814', p. 274.

44. Sherwig, *Guineas and Gunpowder. British Foreign Aid in the Wars with France*, p. 352.

Chapter Six: Pax Britannica (1815–59)

1. C. Lloyd, *The Nation and the Navy. A History of Naval Life and Policy* (London, 1961), p. 223.

2. Hobsbawm, *Industry and Empire*, pp. 48–54.

3. See generally, C. J. Bartlett (ed.), *Britain Pre-eminent. Studies of British World Influence in the Nineteenth Century* (London, 1969); A. H. Imlah, *Economic Elements in the 'Pax Britannica'* (Cambridge, Mass., 1958).

4. Hobsbawm, *Industry and Empire*, pp. 134–53; Mathias, *First Industrial Nation*, pp. 290–334; S. G. E. Lythe, 'Britain, the Financial Capital of the World', in Bartlett (ed.), *Britain Pre-eminent*; J. D. Chambers, *The Workshop of the World. British Economic History from 1820 to 1880* (2nd edn, Oxford, 1968), pp. 60–100.

5. Quoted by K. Fielden, 'The Rise and Fall of Free Trade', in Bartlett (ed.), *Britain Pre-eminent*, p. 85.

6. Mathias, *First Industrial Nation*, p. 295.

7. J. Gallagher and R. Robinson, 'The Imperialism of Free Trade', *Economic History Review*, 2nd series, vi, no. 1 (August 1953), pp. 1–15; B. Semmel, 'The "Philosophical Radicals" and Colonization', *Journal of Economic History*, 21 (1961), pp. 513–525; B. Semmel, *The Rise of Free Trade Imperialism* (Oxford, 1970).

8. Gallagher and Robinson, 'The Imperialism of Free Trade', p. 5.

9. Graham, *Empire of the North Atlantic*, p. 264.

10. Williams, *British Commercial Policy and Trade Expansion 1750–1850*, p. 78.

11. C. J. Bartlett, *Great Britain and Sea Power 1815–1853* (Oxford, 1963), p. 22. (This excellent book is essential reading for any student of nineteenth-century British naval history.)

12. ibid., pp. 23–7.

13. ibid.

14. Quoted in Graham, *Empire of the North Atlantic*, p. 263.

15. D. Thomson, *Europe since Napoleon* (Harmondsworth, Middlesex, 1966), p. 111.

16. Bartlett, *Great Britain and Sea Power*, p. 57.

17. C. K. Webster, *The Foreign Policy of Castlereagh*, 2 vols. (London, 1963 edn), i, pp. 297–305; ii, pp. 47 ff.

18. The following is based upon Crouzet, 'Wars, Blockade, and Economic Change in Europe, 1792–1815', *passim*; Heckscher, *The Continental System*, pp. 257 ff.

19. Crouzet, 'Wars, Blockade, and Economic Change in Europe', p. 573.

20. ibid

21. See especially, Williams, *British Commercial Policy and Trade Expansion 1750–1850*, pp. 176 ff.

22. Lewis, *The History of the British Navy*, p. 215.

23. Callender, *The Naval Side of British History*, pp. 232–233.

24. G. Fox, *British Admirals and Chinese Pirates, 1832–1869* (London, 1940), *passim.*

25. The contention of E. Williams, *Capitalism and Slavery* (Chapel Hill, 1944), that the abandonment of slavery was due to changing economic circumstances has not found acceptance among professional historians: see R. T. Anstey, 'Capitalism and Slavery: A Critique', *Economic History Review*, 2nd series, xxi, no. 2 (August 1968), pp. 307–20.

26. C. Lloyd, *The Navy and the Slave Trade* (London, 1969 reprint), p. 274. See also the briefer accounts in Bartlett, *Great Britain and Sea Power*, pp. 267–70; and A. Preston and J. Major, *Send a Gunboat! A Study of the Gunboat and its Role in British Policy 1854–1904* (London, 1967), pp. 115–31.

27. ibid., p. 3.

28. For such a narrative, see Sir Laird W. Clowes, *The Royal Navy. A History*, 7 vols. (London, 1887–1903), vi–vii, which cover the years 1816–1900. Specific regional examples are provided by G. S. Graham, *Britain in the Indian Ocean. A Study of Maritime Enterprise 1810–1850* (Oxford, 1967); B. Gough, *The Royal Navy and the North-West Coast of America 1810–1914* (Vancouver, 1971); J. Bach, 'The Royal Navy in the Pacific Islands', *Journal of Pacific History*, iii (1968), pp. 3–20; G. S. Graham and R. A. Humphreys (eds.), *The Navy and South America 1807–1832* (Navy Records Society, London, 1962).

29. Quoted in Lloyd, *The Nation and the Navy*, p. 225.

30. Richmond, *Statesmen and Sea Power*, p. 264.

31. Lloyd, *The Navy and the Slave Trade*, p. 235.

32. Bartlett, *Great Britain and Sea Power*, pp. 68, 95; Lewis, *The History of the British Navy*, p. 221.

33. Bartlett, *Great Britain and Sea Power*, p. 101.

34. ibid., pp. 55, 260, Appendix II.

35. ibid., p. 2.

36. On these scares in general, see I. F. Clarke, *Voices Prophesying War 1793–1984* (London, 1970 edn); H. R. Moon, *The Invasion of the United Kingdom: Public Controversy and Official Planning 1888–1918*, 2 vols. (Ph.D. thesis, London, 1968), *passim*, and especially pp. 1–18.

37. Bartlett, *Great Britain and Sea Power*, p. 333.

38. Graham, *Empire of the North Atlantic*, p. 275; Richmond, *Statesmen and Sea Power*, pp. 267–9.

39. Moon, *The Invasion of the United Kingdom*, pp. 6–7.

40. ibid., pp. 8 ff.

41. A. J. P. Taylor, *The Struggle for Mastery in Europe, 1848–1918* (Oxford, 1954), p. xxvii.

42. C. J. Bartlett, 'The Mid-Victorian Reappraisal of Naval Policy', in K. Bourne and D. C. Watt (eds.), *Studies in International History* (London, 1967), pp. 189–208; and R. Millman, *British Foreign Policy and the Coming of the Franco-Prussian War* (Oxford, 1965), pp. 148–58. These two short surveys provide the only modern accounts of naval policy in the period between 1853, where Bartlett's *Great Britain and Sea Power* ends, and 1880, where A. J. Marder's *The Anatomy of Sea Power: A History of British Naval Policy in the Pre-Dreadnought Era 1880–1905* (Hamden, Conn., edn 1964), commences; a thorough investigation of these years still remains to be written.

43. Richmond, *Statesmen and Sea Power*, p. 265.

Chapter Seven: Mahan versus Mackinder (1859–97)

1. On the scares of 1884–94, see the definitive treatment in Marder, *Anatomy*, pp. 119–205.

2. ibid., pp. 321–40; C. Andrew, *Théophile Delcassé and the Making of the Entente Cordiale* (London, 1968), pp. 91–118.

3. Bartlett, 'The Mid-Victorian Reappraisal', p. 208.

4. ibid., pp. 101–2; Preston and Major, *Send a Gunboat!*, pp. 32 ff.

5. B. Bond (ed.), *Victorian Military Campaigns* (London, 1967).

6. H. Brunschwig, 'Anglophobia and French African Policy', in P. Gifford and W. R. Louis (eds.), *France and Britain in Africa: Imperial Rivalry and Colonial Rule* (New Haven and London, 1971).

7. Thomson, *Europe since Napoleon*, p. 498.

8. Hobsbawm, *Industry and Empire*, pp. 134–52; Mathias, *First Industrial Nation*, pp. 303–34.

9. Marder, *Anatomy*, p. 44.

10. ibid., pp. 44–61; D. M. Schurman, *The Education of a Navy: The Development of British Naval Strategic Thought 1867–1914* (London, 1965), *passim*.

11. ibid., p. 61; and M. T. Sprout, 'Mahan: Evangelist of Sea Power', in E. M. Earle (ed.), *Makers of Modern Strategy* (Princeton, 1952).

12. See especially pp. 1–9 above.

13. Livezey, *Mahan on Sea Power*, p. 274.

14. Mackinder, 'The Geographical Pivot of History', *passim*. Livezey, *Mahan on Sea Power*, pp. 286–92, and Graham, *Politics of Naval Supremacy*, pp. 29–30, point out the significance of Mackinder's theories for an understanding of the development of sea power in this past hundred years.

15. Mackinder, 'Geographical Pivot of History', p. 433.

16. ibid., p. 441 (my stress).

17. J. R. Seeley, *The Expansion of England* (London, 1884), p. 301.

18. H. J. Mackinder, *Britain and the British Seas* (Oxford, 1925 edn), p. 358.

19. Moon, *The Invasion of the United Kingdom*, pp. 67–246.

20. Hobsbawm, *Industry and Empire*, p. 151.

21. The conclusions which follow are based upon Hobsbawm, *Industry and Empire*,

pp. 134–53, 172–85; Mathias, *First Industrial Nation*, pp. 243–53, 306–34, 345–426; C. Barnett, *The Collapse of British Power* (London and New York, 1972), pp. 71–120; D. H. Aldcroft (ed.), *The Development of British Industry and Foreign Competition 1875–1914* (London, 1968); J. Saville (ed.), *Studies in the British Economy, 1870–1914*, 17, no. 1 (1965), *The Yorkshire Bulletin of Economic and Social Research*; R. S. Sayers, *A History of Economic Change in England 1880–1939* (London, 1967); Landes, *The Unbound Prometheus*, pp. 326–58.

22. Hobsbawm, *Industry and Empire*, p. 169. See also Mathias, *First Industrial Nation*, pp. 421–4.

23. Hobsbawm, *Industry and Empire*, p. 151.

24. Mathias, *First Industrial Nation*, pp. 332–3.

25. ibid., p. 405.

26. Hobsbawm, *Industry and Empire*, p. 181.

27. G. Barraclough, *An Introduction to Contemporary History* (Harmondsworth, Middlesex, 1967), p. 51.

28. D. C. M. Platt, 'Economic Factors in British Policy during the "New Imperialism" ', *Past and Present*, no. 39 (1968), p. 137.

29. Mathias, *First Industrial Nation*, pp. 399–400.

30. The 1860–98 figures are to be found in the Bundesarchiv-Militärarchiv, Freiburg, F 7590, vol. 1, in an undated memorandum by Admiral Hollweg which seeks to refute the British view that Germany had provoked the naval race. The 1911–13 figures, added in parenthesis for Britain alone, come from W. Ashworth, *An Economic History of England, 1870–1939* (London, 1972 edn), p. 147. See also S. B. Saul, *Studies in British Overseas Trade 1870–1914* (Liverpool, 1960), *passim*.

31. Mathias, *First Industrial Nation*, p. 255.

32. Quoted in Barraclough, *An Introduction to Contemporary History*, p. 100. More detailed analysis of the Imperial Federation movement can be found in N. Mansergh, *The Commonwealth Experience* (London, 1969), pp. 120–56; D. C. Gordon, *The Dominion Partnership in Imperial Defence, 1870–1914* (Baltimore, 1965); M. Beloff, *Imperial Sunset*, i, *Britain's Liberal Empire, 1897–1921* (London, 1969).

33. Richmond, *Statesmen and Sea Power*, p. 276.

34. *The Naval and Military Record* (London), 5 January 1905.

35. Hobsbawm, *Industry and Empire*, p. 179.

36. *Jane's Fighting Ships 1914*. The figures for the mid century warship costs are taken from Bartlett, *Great Britain and Sea Power*, p. 290 footnote.

37. Barnett, *Britain and Her Army*, pp. 295, 303.

38. Quoted in Barraclough, *An Introduction to Contemporary History*, p. 61.

39. H. J. Mackinder, *Democratic Ideals and Reality* (New York, 1962 edn), p. 115.

40. *The Naval and Military Record* (London), 26 December 1901.

41. D. Owen, 'Capture at Sea: Modern Conditions and the Ancient Prize Laws', given at the United Services Institute on 6 April 1905, *printed for private use*. A copy of this interesting paper came into the hands of the German naval attaché, a frequent visitor to the Institute, and is to be found in the Bundesarchiv-Militärarchiv, Freiburg, F 5145, *II.Jap.11b*, vol. 2, Coerper to Reichsmarineamt, no. 246 of 7 April 1905. See also Richmond, *Statesmen and Sea Power*, p. 284.

42. Livezey, *Mahan on Sea Power*, pp. 280–81. See also P. M. Kennedy, 'Maritime Strategieprobleme der deutsch-englischen Flottenrivalität', in H. Schottelius and

W. Deist (eds.), *Marine und Marinepolitik im kaiserlichen Deutschland 1871–1914* (Düsseldorf, 1972), p. 198.

43. Bundesarchiv-Militärarchiv, Freiburg, F 7224, PG 69125, Müller (German Naval Attaché, London) to Reichsmarineamt, no. 501 of 9 June 1914, enclosing *The Times* of 5 June 1914; A. J. Marder, *From the Dreadnought to Scapa Flow*, 5 vols. (London, 1961–70), i, p. 333.

44. Mathias, *First Industrial Nation*, pp. 244, 249, 253; Hobsbawm, *Industry and Empire*, p. 97.

45. Cited in Millman, *British Foreign Policy and the Coming of the Franco-Prussian War*, p. 149. This was an exaggerated statement at that time, of course, but it soon turned out to be a very shrewd forecast.

46. Cited in Clarke, *Voices Prophesying War 1763–1984*, p. 134.

47. Millman, *British Foreign Policy and the Coming of the Franco-Prussian War*, p. 146.

Chapter Eight: The End of Pax Britannica (1897–1914)

1. *The Times*, 25 June 1897.

2. 'Another proof', he added, 'that we belong to the ten lost tribes of Israel!' Quoted in Marder, *Dreadnought to Scapa Flow*, i, p. 41.

3. P. M. Kennedy, 'Imperial Cable Communications and Strategy, 1870–1914', *English Historical Review*, lxxxvi, no. CCCXLI (October 1971), p. 448.

4. J. Lepsius *et al.* (eds.), *Die Grosse Politik der europäischen Kabinette*, 40 vols. (Berlin, 1922–7), xiv, part 2, no. 3927.

5. Taylor, *Struggle for Mastery in Europe*, p. 387.

6. Marder, *Anatomy*, p. 351.

7. J. Steinberg, *Yesterday's Deterrent: Tirpitz and the Birth of the German Battle Fleet* (London, 1965), pp. 208–21. See also V. R. Berghahn, *Der Tirpitz-Plan* (Düsseldorf, 1972), *passim*, for the most detailed account of German naval aims.

8. The figures come from 'Die Seeinteressen des Deutschen Reiches', a memorandum laid before the Reichstag on 30 December 1897 in an effort to convince the deputies that the German navy needed to be increased. Although it was simply stated that these totals were all of battleships over 5,000 tons, the Imperial Navy Office had a habit of allotting to Britain's number many vessels which the Admiralty in London held to be unseaworthy. According to *Brassey's Naval Annual* (1898), eighteen of these British ships would be third-class battleships, and the battleship totals for her rivals were considerably higher.

9. G. W. Monger, *The End of Isolation: British Foreign Policy 1900–1907* (London, 1963), pp. 11–12.

10. Bourne, *Britain and the Balance of Power in North America 1815–1908*, *passim.*

11. India Office Library, Curzon Papers, vol. 144, Godley to Curzon, 10 November, 1899.

12. The Anglo-American 'rapprochement' has been covered in a host of studies; for a recent survey of the literature, see B. Perkins, *The Great Rapprochement: England and the United States 1895–1914* (London, 1969). The most important studies of the strategical aspects are: Bourne, *Britain and the Balance of Power in North America*, pp. 313–401; Marder, *Anatomy*, pp. 442–55; J. A. S. Grenville, *Lord Salisbury and Foreign Policy* (London, 1964), pp. 370–89; S. F. Wells, Jnr., 'British Strategic With-

drawal from the Western Hemisphere, 1904–1906', *Canadian Historical Review*, xlix (1968), pp. 335–56.

13. Bourne, *Britain and the Balance of Power in North America*, p. 382.

14. ibid., p. 410.

15. Public Record Office, Cabinet papers, 37/58/87, Selborne memorandum 'Balance of Naval Power in the Far East', 4 September 1901. Naval aspects of the Anglo-Japanese Alliance are covered in Marder, *Anatomy*, pp. 427–34; Grenville, *Lord Salisbury and Foreign Policy Anatomy*, pp. 390–420; Monger, *The End of Isolation: British Foreign Policy*, pp. 46–66; L. K. Young, *British Policy in China 1895–1902* (Oxford, 1970), pp. 295–318; I. H. Nish, *The Anglo-Japanese Alliance* (London, 1966), pp. 174–7, 213–15.

16. M. Beloff, *Imperial Sunset*, i, p. 87.

17. Germany's naval policy and the Anglo-German naval race have been the subject of numerous studies. See especially, Marder, *Anatomy*, pp. 456–514; *Dreadnought to Scapa Flow*, i, *passim*; Steinberg, *Yesterday's Deterrent;* Berghahn, *Der Tirpitz-Plan*; Kennedy, 'Maritime Strategieprobleme'; Kennedy, 'Tirpitz, England and the Second Navy Law of 1900: A Strategical Critique', *Militärgeschichtliche Mitteilungen*, 1970, no. 2; Kennedy, 'The Development of German Naval Operations Plans against England, 1896–1914', *English Historical Review*, lxxxix, no. CCCL (January 1974), pp. 48–76.

18. Quoted in Monger, *The End of Isolation*, p. 82.

19. Fisher's impact upon the navy has been well surveyed in Marder, *Anatomy*, pp. 483–546, and *Dreadnought to Scapa Flow*, i, pp. 14–207; but by far the best way to appreciate his character is to read his fascinating correspondence in Marder's edited volumes, *Fear God and Dread Nought*. See also the fine new biography by R. F. Mackay, *Fisher of Kilverstone* (Oxford, 1973).

20. Marder, *Dreadnought to Scapa Flow*, i, pp. 42–3. The North Sea concentration grew even greater in the years following. (The arguments of R. F. Mackay, 'The Admiralty, the German Navy, and the Redistribution of the British Fleet, 1904–1905', *Mariner's Mirror*, 56 (1970), pp. 341–6, that the redistribution still had the Franco-Russian threat in mind as much as the German one is valid only if one takes the story up to the spring of 1905.)

21. Dr Berghahn's impressive book fully illustrates the long-term technical, financial and political embarrassment caused to the German programme by the introduction of the *Dreadnought*: see *Der Tirpitz-Plan*, pp. 419 ff.

22. Public Record Office, Cabinet papers, 37/84/77, Foreign Office memo, 25 October 1906; 37/89/73, Colonial Office memo, 19 July 1907; 37/89/74, Foreign Office memo, 24 July 1907; Public Record Office, Colonial Office records, 537/348, paper 5520 Secret 'Distribution of the Navy'; Marder, *Dreadnought to Scapa Flow*, i, pp. 53–4.

23. 'A Statement of Admiralty Policy', 1905 (Cd. 2791), p. 6.

24. Preston and Major, *Send a Gunboat!*, p. 161.

25. Public Record Office, Admiralty records, 116/900B (War Orders for Home and Foreign Stations and Fleets 1900–1906), Battenberg memo of 7 January 1905. (The date of this memo throws doubt upon the arguments of Mackay mentioned in note 20.)

26. D. C. Gordon, 'The Admiralty and Dominion Navies, 1902–1914', *Journal of Modern History*, xxxiii, no. 4 (December 1961), pp. 407–22.

27. Marder, *Dreadnought to Scapa Flow*, i, pp. 233–9; P. Lowe, 'The British Empire

and the Anglo-Japanese Alliance 1911–1915', *History*, liv (1969), pp. 212–15; and especially I. H. Nish, *Alliance in Decline: A Study in Anglo-Japanese Relations 1908–23* (London, 1972), pp. 1–98.

28. Cited in Beloff, *Imperial Sunset*, p. 153.

29. This controversy is well covered in Marder, *Anatomy*, pp. 119–231, 266–73, 393–416.

30. This section is based upon Marder, *Dreadnought to Scapa Flow*, i, pp. 272–310; P. G. Halpern, *The Mediterranean Naval Situation 1908–1914* (Cambridge, Mass., 1971), pp. 1–110; S. R. Williamson, *The Politics of Grand Strategy, Britain and France prepare for War, 1904–1914* (Cambridge, Mass., 1969), pp. 227–99; H. I. Lee, 'Mediterranean Strategy and Anglo-French Relations 1908–1912', *Mariner's Mirror*, 57 (1971), pp. 267–85.

31. Lee, 'Mediterranean Strategy and Anglo-French Relations', p. 277.

32. Marder, *Dreadnought to Scapa Flow*, i, p. 294.

33. Cited in Williamson, *Politics of Grand Strategy*, p. 278. Left-wing dislike of a continental commitment is covered in A. J. A. Morris, *Radicalism Against War* (London, 1972).

34. The domestic situation has been well surveyed in G. H. Dangerfield's *The Strange Death of Liberal England* (London, 1935); one does not have to be a supporter of his particular interpretation of the decline of Liberalism to accept that the political discontents were greater than at any time in the preceding seventy years.

35. Marder, *Dreadnought to Scapa Flow*, i, p. 289.

36. R. Langhorne, 'The Naval Question in Anglo-German Relations, 1912–1914', *Historical Journal*, xiv, no. 2 (1971), pp. 359–70.

37. B. H. Liddell Hart, *The British Way in Warfare* (London, 1932), pp. 7–41.

38. Taylor, *Struggle for Mastery in Europe*, pp. xix–xxvi; F. Fischer, *Germany's Aims in the First World War* (London, 1972), pp. 3–49.

39. M. Howard, *The Continental Commitment* (London, 1972), pp. 9–10.

40. This section has been based chiefly upon the works of Howard, Marder, Williamson and Monger cited above. Also important is N. Summerton, *British Military Preparations for a War against Germany*, 2 vols., (Ph.D. thesis, London, 1969).

41. Cited in Marder, *Dreadnought to Scapa Flow*, i, p. 429. See also the important quotation in Lord Hankey, *The Supreme Command 1914–1918*, 2 vols. (London, 1961), i, pp. 128–9.

42. See generally, Barnett, *Britain and her Army*, pp. 272–370; and G. Ritter, *The Sword and the Sceptre*, ii, *The European Powers and the Wilhelminian Empire 1890–1914* (London, 1972), pp. 7–136, 193–226.

43. Haus-, Hof-, und Staatsarchiv, Vienna, P. A. III/153, Szögyeny to Goluchowski, no. 2B of 16 January 1900, reporting a conversation with the Kaiser, who expressed doubts about Britain's future.

44. Williamson, *Politics of Grand Strategy*, p. 20.

45. Cited in Beloff, *Imperial Sunset*, i. p. 73.

46. This transformation is covered in N. d'Ombrain, *War Machinery and High Politics. Defence Administration in Peacetime Britain 1902–1914* (Oxford, 1973); J. Gooch, *The Plans of War: The General Staff and British Military Strategy c. 1900–1914* (London, 1974); P. Haggie, 'The Royal Navy and War Planning in the Fisher Era', *Journal of Contemporary History*, 8, no. 3 (July 1973), pp. 113–32, as well as the studies by Marder and Summerton cited above.

47. Summerton, *British Military Preparations for a War against Germany*, pp. 34–49, 59, 220–97, 320–41, 451–71, 622–8.

48. Cited in Howard, *The Continental Commitment 1914–1918*, p. 46; see also Williamson, *Politics of Grand Strategy*, pp. 108–12.

49. Hankey, *Supreme Command*, i, p. 82; see also N. J. d'Ombrain, 'The Imperial General Staff and the Military Policy of a "Continental Strategy" during the 1911 International Crisis', *Military Affairs*, xxxiv, no. 3 (October, 1970), pp. 88–93.

50. Ritter, *The Sword and the Sceptre*, ii, p. 56.

51. Williamson, *Politics of Ground Strategy*, p. vii.

Chapter Nine: Stalemate and Strain (1914–18)

1. It had misgivings about sending all six divisions out of the country at once, though: see Williamson, *Politics of Grand Strategy*, pp. 364–7.

2. ibid., p. 367.

3. R. Blake, *The Conservative Party from Peel to Churchill* (London, 1970), pp. 195–7.

4. Marder, *Dreadnought to Scapa Flow*, i, p. 431.

5. A. T. Mahan, *Retrospect and Prospect: Studies in International Relations Naval and Political* (London, 1902), pp. 165–7.

6. The general analysis of the naval war which follows is based upon Marder, *Dreadnought to Scapa Flow*, ii–v; J. S. Corbett and H. Newbolt, *History of the Great War: Naval Operations*, 5 vols. (London, 1920–31); and my own articles in the part-works magazine *History of the First World War* (London, 1969 f), ii, no. 7; iv, no. 14; vi, nos. 3 and 12.

7. Marder, *Dreadnought to Scapa Flow*, ii, p. 4.

8. Kennedy, 'German Naval Operations Plans against England', pp. 74–6.

9. Moon, *The Invasion of the United Kingdom*, p. 711.

10. ibid., pp. 503–15.

11. G. Bennett, *Naval Battles of the First World War* (London, 1968), p. 246.

12. Marder, *Dreadnought to Scapa Flow*, iii, p. 206.

13. Bundesarchiv-Militarärchiv, Freiburg, Diederichs papers, F255/12, Hoffmann to Diederichs, 5 June 1916.

14. Quoted in K. Assmann, *Deutsche Seestrategie in zwei Weltkriege* (Heidelberg, 1957), p. 30. Heeringen was at that time Chief of Admiralty Staff and as such technically responsible for the operations plans against England.

15. It is best covered in Marder, *Dreadnought to Scapa Flow*, iv, *passim*, and v, pp. 77–120; Corbett and Newbolt, *passim*; A. Spindler, *Der Krieg zur See, 1914–1918: Der Handelskrieg mit U-Booten*, 5 vols. (Berlin, 1932–66); C. E. Fayle, *History of the Great War: Seaborne Trade*, 3 vols. (London, 1920–24).

16. Marder, *Dreadnought to Scapa Flow*, v, pp. 132–4.

17. ibid., pp. 175–87.

18. The economic statistics in this paragraph come from W. Baumgart, *Deutschland im Zeitalter des Imperialismus (1890–1914)* (Frankfurt, 1972), pp. 79–81; D. K. Fieldhouse, *The Colonial Empires* (London, 1966), pp. 370–71; M. Balfour, *The Kaiser and his Times* (New York, 1972 edn), pp. 437–47.

19. Cited in Marder, *Dreadnought to Scapa Flow*, i, p. 365.

20. ibid., ii, p. 123.

21. Balfour, *The Kaiser and His Times*, pp. 442–6.

22. W. K. Hancock and M. M. Gowing, *British War Economy* (London, 1949), p. 20.

23. Richmond, *National Policy and Naval Strength*, p. 71. The earlier quotation is taken from p. 142.

24. Howard, *The Continental Commitment*, pp. 68–70.

25. Richmond, *National Policy and Naval Strength*, p. 77. For the blockade, see M. Parmalee, *Blockade and Sea Power* (London, n.d., 1925?); M. C. Siney, *The Allied Blockade of Germany, 1914–1916* (Ann Arbor, Michigan, 1957); A. C. Bell, *A History of the Blockade of Germany and of the Countries Associated with Her* . . . (London, 1961); L. L. Guichard, *The Naval Blockade, 1914–1918* (London, 1930); M. W. W. P. Consett, *The Triumph of Unarmed Forces (1914–1918)* (London, 1928).

26. Cited in Marder, *Dreadnought to Scapa Flow*, i, p. 391; see also Mackay, *Fisher of Kilverstone*, p. 456. For a fresh examination of why the 'conjunct advocates' failed, see D. M. Schurman, 'Historians and Britain's Imperial Strategic Stance in 1914', in J. E. Flint and G. Williams (eds.), *Perspectives of Empire* (London, 1973), pp. 172–88.

27. Marder, *Dreadnought to Scapa Flow*, ii, p. 175; see also Hankey, *The Supreme Command*, i, pp. 244–50, *et. seq.*

28. Sir Sydney Fremantle, *My Naval Career, 1880–1928* (London, 1949), pp. 245–6.

29. Quoted in Howard, *The Continental Commitment*, p. 65.

30. P. Guinn, *British Strategy and Politics 1914–1918* (Oxford, 1965), p. 283.

31. The following is taken from: Sayers, *A History of Economic Change in England 1880–1939*, pp. 47 ff; Mathias, *First Industrial Nation*, pp. 431 ff, 463; A. Marwick, *Britain in the Century of Total War: War, Peace and Social Change 1900–1967* (Harmondsworth, Middlesex, 1970), pp. 62–84; W. Arthur Lewis, *Economic Survey 1919–1939* (London, 1949), pp. 74–89; S. Pollard, *The Development of the British Economy 1914–1967* (London, 1969 edn), pp. 49–92; A. S. Milward. *The Economic Effects of the World Wars on Britain* (London, 1970); Barnett, *Collapse of British Power*, pp. 424–8.

32. Barnett, *Collapse of British Power*, p. 426.

33. Halpern, *The Mediterranean Naval Situation*, pp. 358, 364, 367.

34. Lowe, 'The British Empire and the Anglo-Japanese Alliance 1911–1915', p. 225.

35. What follows is based upon Lowe, loc. cit.; Nish, *Alliance in Decline*, *passim*; D. Dignan, 'New Perspectives on British Far Eastern Policy, 1913–1919', *University of Queensland* Papers, 1, no. 5.

36. Marder, *Dreadnought to Scapa Flow*, iv, pp. 43–4.

37. Dignan, 'New Perspectives on British Far Eastern Policy, 1913–1919', pp. 271–4.

38. The Anglo-American naval rivalry of these years has been covered by a number of fine recent studies, the best of these being: Marder, *Dreadnought to Scapa Flow*, v, pp. 224 ff; Beloff, *Imperial Sunset*, i, pp. 229 ff; Barnett, *Collapse of British Power*, pp. 251 ff; S. W. Roskill, *Naval Policy between the Wars*, i, *The Period of Anglo-American Antagonism 1919–1929* (London, 1968), introduction and chaps. I–VIII; W. R. Braisted, *The United States Navy in the Pacific, 1909–1922* (Austin, Texas, 1971), pp. 153–208, 289 ff; M. G. Fry, 'The Imperial War Cabinet, The United States and the Freedom of the Seas', *The Royal United Services Institution Journal*, cx. no. 640 (November 1965), pp. 353–62.

39. Marder, *Dreadnought to Scapa Flow*, v, p. 225; and Braisted, *The United States Navy in the Pacific, 1909–1922*, pp. 409–40.

40. ibid., pp. 437, 440.

41. Beloff, *Imperial Sunset*, i, p. 360.

42. Liddell Hart, *The British Way in Warfare*, p. 41.

43. ibid.

44. Mahan, *Retrospect and Prospect*, p. 169.

Chapter Ten: The Years of Decay (1919–39)

1. R. Higham, *Armed Forces in Peacetime. Britain, 1918–1940, a case study* (London, 1962), p. 135; Roskill, *Naval Policy between the Wars*, i, p. 71.

2. Hobsbawm, *Industry and Empire*, p. 207.

3. What follows is based upon Hobsbawm, *Industry and Empire*, pp. 207–24; S. Pollard, *The Development of the British Economy 1914–1967*, pp. 42–241; W. Arthur Lewis, *Economic Survey 1919–1939*; V. Anthony, *Britain's Overseas Trade* (London, 1967), pp. 17–38; R. S. Sayers, *A History of Economic Change in England 1880–1939*, pp. 47 ff; B. W. E. Alford, *Depression and Recovery? British Growth 1918–1939* (London, 1972); D. H. Aldcroft, *The Inter-War Economy: Britain, 1919–1939* (London, 1970); A. J. Youngson, *Britain's Economic Growth 1920–1966* (London, 1963), pp. 9–140; A. E. Kahn, *Great Britain in the World Economy* (New York, 1946), *passim*; Barnett, *Collapse of British Power*, pp. 476–94.

4. Lewis, *Economic Survey 1919–1939*, pp. 78–9.

5. Pollard, *The Development of the British Economy*, p. 201.

6. Mahan, *The Influence of Sea Power upon History*, pp. 59–82.

7. Mackinder, *Democratic Ideals and Reality*, p. 23.

8. Pollard, *The Development of the British Economy*, p. 203. (The increasing insurance contributions hardly offset this vast rise.)

9. Higham, *Armed Forces in Peacetime*, pp. 326–7.

10. Barnett, *Collapse of British Power*, pp. 237 ff; M. Swartz, *The Union of Democratic Control in British Politics during the First World War*, (Oxford, 1971); A. J. P. Taylor, *The Trouble Makers* (London, 1954), cap. VI; P. M. Kennedy, 'The Decline of Nationalistic History in the West', *Journal of Contemporary History*, 8, no. 1, pp. 91–2.

11. Cited in Howard, *The Continental Commitment*, pp. 78–9.

12. Higham, *Armed Forces in Peacetime*, pp. 326–7.

13. See, *inter alia*, Roskill, *Naval Policy between the Wars*, i, pp. 204–33, 269–355; W. R. Louis, *British Strategy in the Far East 1919–1939* (Oxford, 1971), pp. 1–108; Braisted, *The U.S. Navy in the Pacific*, pp. 465–688; Beloff, *Imperial Sunset*, i. pp. 318 ff; Dignan, 'New Perspectives on British Far Eastern Policy', pp. 271–4; B. Schofield, *British Sea Power* (London, 1967), pp. 72–101; Barnett, *Collapse of British Power*, pp. 263–74; Nish, *Alliance in Decline*, pp. 305 ff; M. Tate, *The United States and Armaments* (New York, 1948), pp. 121–40; I. Klein, 'Whitehall, Washington, and the Anglo-Japanese Alliance, 1919–1921', *Pacific Historical Review*, 41 (1972), pp. 460–83; J. K. McDonald, 'Lloyd George and the Search for a Postwar Naval Policy, 1919', in A. J. P. Taylor (ed.), *Lloyd George: Twelve Essays* (London, 1971), *passim*.

14. Cited in J. Dülffer, *Weimar, Hitler und die Marine* (Düsseldorf, 1973), p. 211.

15. Beloff, *Imperial Sunset*, i, p. 342.

16. Howard, *The Continental Commitment*, p. 79.

17. Higham, *Armed Forces in Peacetime*, pp. 123–4; Roskill, *Naval Policy between the Wars*, i, pp. 230–3.

18. Cited in Louis, *British Strategy in the Far East 1919–1939*, pp. 52–3.

19. Tate, *The United States and Armaments*, p. 121; Braisted, *The U.S. Navy in the Pacific*, pp. 670–73; D. W. Knox, *The Eclipse of American Naval Power* (New York, 1922).

20. See, in general, W. N. Medlicott, *British Foreign Policy since Versailles 1919–1963* (London, revised edn, 1968), pp. 53–81.

21. Schofield, *British Sea Power*, pp. 102–8; Roskill, *Naval Policy between the Wars*, i, pp. 331 ff.

22. Higham, *Armed Forces in Peacetime*, p. 130. (My stress.)

23. E. Bradford, *The Mighty Hood* (London, 1959), pp. 64–88. If this seems a cynical remark it should be noticed that a description of the world tour forms the greater part of the narrative of the *Hood*'s inter-war years in Bradford's biography.

24. Mackinder, *Democratic Ideals and Reality*, p. 170.

25. Chamberlain was surely offering here a re-wording of Bismarck's famous declaration that the Balkans were not worth the bones of a Pomeranian Grenadier. This prophecy was proven horribly wrong in 1914; Chamberlain's in 1939. History occasionally does repeat itself.

26. A. J. P. Taylor, *The Origins of the Second World War* (Harmondsworth, Middlesex, 1969 edn), pp. 45–8.

27. This section is based upon Marder, *Dreadnought to Scapa Flow*, iv, pp. 3–24, and v, pp. 223–4; Howard, *The Continental Commitment*, pp. 80–85; Higham, *Armed Forces in Peacetime*, pp. 147–63; Roskill, *Naval Policy between the Wars*, i, pp. 234–68. And see generally, R. Higham, *Air Power. A Concise History* (London, 1972).

28. Cited in Howard, *The Continental Commitment*, p. 81.

29. Cited in P. Padfield, *The Battleship Era* (London, 1972), pp. 252–8.

30. R. Higham, *The Military Intellectuals in Britain 1918–1939* (New Brunswick, New Jersey, 1966), pp. 165–6.

31. Quoted in Louis, *British Strategy in the Far East*, p. 102. See also, Schofield, *British Sea Power*, pp. 105–6.

32. Howard, *The Continental Commitment*, pp. 80–85, 94, 108.

33. On British policy during the Manchurian crisis, see C. Thorne, *The Limits of Foreign Policy* (London, 1972), *passim*, but especially pp. 66–71, 266–8; Barnett, *Collapse of British Power*, pp. 298–305; Louis, *British Strategy in the Far East*, pp. 171–205; F. S. Northedge, *The Troubled Giant: Britain among the Great Powers 1916–1939* (London, 1966), pp. 348–67.

34. Barnett, *Collapse of British Power*, pp. 296–7.

35. For the following, see Barnett, ibid., pp. 342 ff; Howard, *The Continental Commitment*, pp. 96 ff; M. M. Postan, *British War Production* (London, 1952), pp. 9–52; Higham, *Armed Forces in Peacetime*, pp. 191–242.

36. Higham, *Armed Forces in Peacetime*, p. 218.

37. Cited in Howard, *The Continental Commitment*, p. 98.

38. Higham, *Armed Forces in Peacetime*, pp. 326–7. The 1937 and 1938 figures include the issues under the Defence Loan Act of 1937.

39. ibid., pp. 191–201; Barnett, *Collapse of British Power*, pp. 476–7; Postan, *British War Production*, pp. 2–4, 23–7.

40. See Roskill, *Naval Policy between the Wars*, i, pp. 234–68, 356–99, 467–97, 517–43; Higham, *Armed Forces in Peacetime*, pp. 226–72; Schofield, *British Sea Power*, pp. 145–62.

41. See the powerful criticisms in Barnett, *Collapse of British Power*, and in M. Gilbert and R. Gott, *The Appeasers* (London, 1963).

42. Higham, *Armed Forces in Peacetime*, pp. 220–21; Dülffer, op. cit., 279–354; Schofield, *British Sea Power*, pp. 128–9.

43. A. J. Marder, 'The Royal Navy and the Ethiopian Crisis of 1935–36', *American Historical Review*, lxxv, no. 5 (June 1970), p. 1355.

44. ibid., *passim*: Barnett, *Collapse of British Power*, pp. 350–82.

45. H. Pelling, *Britain and the Second World War* (London, 1970), pp. 22–3; Howard, *The Continental Commitment*, pp. 118–20.

46. S. Woodburn Kirby, *The War Against Japan*, 5 vols. (London, 1957–69), i, p. 17.

47. ibid., pp. 19–20 (my stress); S. W. Roskill, *The War at Sea*, 3 vols. (London, 1954–61), i, pp. 41–2; J. R. M. Butler, *Grand Strategy*, ii (London, 1957), p. 13.

48. Postan, *British War Production*, pp. 12, 23–7, 58–9.

49. ibid., p. 24.

50. Figures from Roskill, *The War at Sea*, i, pp. 50–61, Apps. D–H; Kirby, *The War against Japan*, i, App. 5.

51. A. Toynbee and V. M. Toynbee (eds.) *Survey of International Affairs 1939–1946: The Eve of War, 1939* (London, 1958), p. 608.

52. B. Collier, *The Defence of the United Kingdom* (London, 1957), p. 78.

53. Northedge, *The Troubled Giant: Britain among the Great Powers 1916–1939*, p. 625.

54. Quoted in K. Feiling, *The Life of Neville Chamberlain* (London, 1957), p. 314.

55. Howard, *The Continental Commitment*, pp. 112–33; Barnett, *Collapse of British Power*, pp. 438–575; Butler, *Grand Strategy*, ii, pp. 9–17.

56. ibid., pp. 10–11.

57. A. S. Milward, *The German Economy at War* (London, 1965), pp. 26–7.

58. Howard, *The Continental Commitment*, pp. 134–7; Barnett, *Collapse of British Power*, pp. 12–14, 564.

Chapter Eleven: The Illusory Victory (1939–45)

1. These paragraphs upon the navy's performance in the 1939–45 war are a summary of S. W. Roskill, *The War at Sea*, 3 vols.; Roskill, *The Navy At War 1939–1945* (London, 1960); J. Creswell, *Sea Warfare 1939–1945. A Short History* (London, 1950).

2. G. Bennett, *Naval Battles of the First World War*, p. 311.

3. There is now a superb account of Churchill's period as First Lord by A. J. Marder, *Winston is Back: Churchill at the Admiralty 1939–1940* (The English Historical Review, Supplement 5, London, 1972). See also P. Gretton, *Winston Churchill, and the Royal Navy* (New York, 1969), pp. 252–306; and Roskill, *The War at Sea*, *passim*.

4. See Carl-Axel Gemzell, *Raeder, Hitler und Skandanavien. Der Kampf für einen maritimen Operationsplan* (Lund, 1965), for a fascinating account of the development of this strategy. The British could, and did, fall back to the line Greenland–Iceland–Scotland, but this was much more difficult to patrol.

5. W. S. Churchill, *The Second World War*, 12 vols. (paperback edn, London, 1964), vi, p. 210.

6. A further fifty of the grand total of 785 U-boats sunk were destroyed by surface craft and aircraft together. See Roskill, *The Navy at War*, p. 448.

7. Marder, *Winston is Back*, p. 55.
8. T. K. Derry, *The Campaign in Norway* (London, 1952), pp. 234–5.
9. Roskill, *The Navy at War*, p. 162.
10. Postan, *British War Production*, p. 289.
11. Cited in Marder, *Winston is Back*, p. 19.
12. Feiling, *Life of Neville Chamberlain*, p. 426; Hancock and Gowing, *British War Economy*, p. 72.
13. This section upon the German war economy is based upon: Milward, *The German Economy at War*; W. N. Medlicott, *The Economic Blockade*, 2 vols. (London, 1952–9); R. Wagenführ, *Die deutsche Industrie im Kriege 1939–1945* (Berlin, 2nd edn, 1963); Berenice A. Carroll, *Design for Total War. Arms and Economics in the Third Reich* (The Hague, 1968); Burton H. Klein, *Germany's Economic Preparations for War* (Cambridge, Mass., 1959).
14. Medlicott, *The Economic Blockade*, i, p. 43.
15. See Marder, *Winston is Back*, pp. 31–3.
16. Carroll, *Design for Total War. Arms and Economics in the Third Reich*, p. 104.
17. Klein, *Germany's Economic Preparations for War*, pp. 96–103, 206–25; Postan, *British War Production*, apps. 2 and 4. It is worth pointing out that the British figures included many more heavy bombers, but this does not modify the overall picture of a vast increase in German productivity between the third and fifth years of the war.
18. Klein, *Germany's Economic Preparations for War*, p. 211.
19. H. U. Faulkner, *American Economic History* (New York, 1960 edn), p. 701; A Russell Buchanan, *The United States and World War II*, 2 vols. (New York, 1964), i. p. 140.
20. Milward, *The German Economy at War*, p. 115. The effects of the bombing campaign are carefully analysed in his study. See also Klein, *Germany's Economic Preparations for War*, pp. 225 ff; Medlicott, *The Economic Blockade*, ii, pp. 394–5; C. K. Webster and N. Frankland, *The Strategic Air Offensive Against Germany 1939–1945*, 4 vols. (London, 1961); B. H. Liddell Hart, *History of the Second World War* (London, 1970), pp. 589–612.
21. Medlicott, *The Economic Blockade*, pp. 631, 640.
22. Liddell Hart, *History of the Second World War*, p. 547.
23. J. Terraine, 'History and the "Indirect Approach" ', *Journal of the Royal United Services Institute for Defence Studies*, cxvi, no. 662 (June 1971), pp. 44–9.
24. M. Howard, *Grand Strategy, iv* (London, 1972), p. 3. The raw materials' shortages are described in Postan, *British War Production*, pp. 211–17.
25. ibid., p. 244.
26. Wagenführ, *Die deutsche Industrie im Kriege 1939–1945*, p. 87. It could also be expressed by another figure: whereas German armament expenditure equalled 150 per cent of the combined Anglo-American–Russian expenditure in 1935–7, it was down to 25 per cent of it by 1942 (Wagenführ, p. 86).
27. Klein, *Germany's Economic Preparations for War*, pp. 96–103.
28. Cited in H. G. Nicholas, *Britain and the United States* (London, 1963), p. 32.
29. Hancock and Gowing, *British War Economy*, p. 374. The figures preceding were taken from Klein, pp. 96–103; Postan, *British War Production*, pp. 231–47; A. J. P. Taylor, *English History 1914–1945* (Oxford, 1965), pp. 565–6.
30. Hancock and Gowing, loc. cit.

31. Postan, *British War Production*, pp. 245–6.

32. Cited in Barnett, *Collapse of British Power*, p. 564.

33. Ibid., pp. 13–14.

34. Hancock and Gowing, *British War Economy*, p. 522.

35. Taylor, *English History 1914–1945*, pp. 513–14; Hancock and Gowing, *British War Economy*, pp. 106–20, 224–47, 359–404; Pelling, *Britain and the Second World War*, pp. 116–19; H. Duncan Hall, *North American Supply* (London, 1955); Pollard, *The Development of the British Economy*, pp. 330–39; Milward, *The Economic Effects of the World Wars on Britain*, pp. 47–52; and especially R. S. Sayers, *Financial Policy 1939–1945* (London, 1956), pp. 363–486.

36. Barnett, *Collapse of British Power*, p. 592.

37. G. Kolko, *The Politics of War: Allied Diplomacy and the World Crisis of 1943–1945* (London, 1969), pp. 242–313 and *passim*. Kolko's 'New Left' interpretation of American policy is a very controversial one and it is hard to believe that Washington was so single-minded and cunning in all respects; but his analysis of Anglo-American relations during the war is based upon a wealth of fresh sources which it is difficult to disregard altogether, and it is generally confirmed by less contentious accounts, e.g. G. Smith, *American Diplomacy during the Second World War 1941–1945* (New York, 1965).

38. See Pelling, *Britain and the Second World War*, p. 273.

39. The above has been taken from ibid., pp. 275–8; Kolko, *The Politics of War*, p. 490; R. N. Gardner, *Sterling-Dollar Diplomacy* (Oxford, 1956).

40. The official history by M. Gowing, *Britain and Atomic Energy 1939–1945* (London, 1964), is the most valuable source on this topic.

41. P. Kennedy, *Pacific Onslaught* (New York and London, 1972), p. 53. See also Pelling, *Britain and the Second World War*, pp. 275 ff; Mansergh, *The Commonwealth Experience*, pp. 269–94.

42. Howard, *The Continental Commitment*, pp. 142–3.

43. Allied policy with regard to the future of Europe has been covered in Kolko, *The Politics of War*, *passim*; F. P. King, *The New Internationalism. Allied Policy and the European Peace 1939–1945* (Newton Abbot, 1973); and H. Feis, *Churchill–Roosevelt–Stalin. The War they Waged and the Peace they Sought* (Princeton, 1957).

44. Hancock and Gowing, *British War Economy*, p. 555.

45. Cited in M. Matloff, *Strategic Planning for Coalition Warfare 1943–1944* (Washington, D.C., 1959), pp. 523–4.

46. There are brief but tantalizing hints of such an argument in Barnett, *Collapse of British Power*, pp. 570–75, 586–90; but they remain hints and are not developed far enough to show the full reasoning behind them.

Chapter Twelve: The End of the Road: British Sea Power in the Post-war World

1. Moving into the field of contemporary foreign and defence policies is a risky proposition for a historian attempting to draw some general conclusions whilst international affairs remain in such a state of flux; but this chapter was greatly assisted by the existence of several first-class studies: C. J. Bartlett, *The Long Retreat. A Short History of British Defence Policy, 1945–1970* (London, 1972); P. Darby, *British Defence Policy East of Suez 1947–1968* (London, 1973); A. J. Pierre, *Nuclear Politics. The*

British Experience with an Independent Strategic Force 1939–1970 (London, 1972). See also the thoughtful essay by L. W. Martin, 'British Defence Policy: The Long Recessional', *Adelphi Papers*, no. 61 (November 1969).

2. See F. S. Northedge, *British Foreign Policy. The Process of Readjustment 1945–1961* (London, 1962), for a useful survey of post-1945 policy.

3. Bartlett, *The Long Retreat*, pp. 1–77.

4. Pelling, *Britain and the Second World War*, p. 285.

5. R. E. Robinson and J. Gallagher, with A. Denny, *Africa and the Victorians. The Official Mind of Imperialism* (London, 1961), p. 11.

6. Cited in Darby, *British Defence Policy East of Suez*, p. 1.

7. ibid., p. 15.

8. Mansergh, *The Commonwealth Experience*, pp. 294 ff, covers the history of the Commonwealth after 1945.

9. Northedge, *British Foreign Policy . . . 1945–1961*, pp. 132 ff. For Anglo-American relations, see M. Beloff, 'The Special Relationship: An Anglo-American Myth', in M. Gilbert (ed.), *A Century of Conflict, 1850–1950* (London, 1966).

10. Pelling, *Britain and the Second World War*, p. 292.

11. On this development, see Bartlett, *The Long Retreat*, pp. 39–41, 190–92; W. P. Snyder, *The Politics of British Defense Policy, 1945–1962* (Columbus, Ohio, 1964); and the blast against it by R. A. Clarkson, 'The Naval Heresy', *Royal United Services Institution Journal*, cx, no. 640 (November 1965), p. 319.

12. Schurman, *The Education of a Navy*, pp. 156, 170, 181–82.

13. See the discussion upon this in J. L. Moulton, *Defence in a Changing World* (London, 1964).

14. Pierre, *Nuclear Politics*, p. 344.

15. A. Gwynne Jones (Lord Chalfont), 'Training and Doctrine in the British Army since 1945' in M. Howard (ed.), *The Theory and Practice of War* (London, 1965), pp. 320–21.

16. For example, Cd. 4891, *Statement on the Defence Estimates* (1972). For a more general discussion of the West's maritime problems, see L. W. Martin, *The Sea in Modern Strategy* (London, 1967).

17. Snyder, *The Politics of British Defence Policy*, p. 24; T. Ropp, *War in the Modern World* (London, 1962) edn, p. 401.

18. See especially Pierre's study.

19. ibid., pp. 322–3.

20. *The Military Balance 1973–1974* (International Institute for Strategic Studies, London, 1973), pp. 69–73.

21. Bartlett, *The Long Retreat*, p. 179.

22. See the foreword to *Jane's Fighting Ships 1972–1973* (London, 1972).

23. Pierre, *Nuclear Politics*, pp. 294–6, 324–5, 328–9.

24. For the figures, see *The Military Balance 1973–1974*, pp. 87–95.

25. On this generally, see R. W. Herrick, *Soviet Naval Strategy* (Annapolis, 1968); W. F. Bringles, 'The Challenge Posed by the Soviet Navy', *Journal of the Royal United Services Institute for Defence Studies*, 118, no. 2 (June 1973), pp. 11–16; L. L. Whetton, 'The Mediterranean Threat', *Survival*, xii, no. 8 (August 1970), pp. 252–8.

26. *Jane's Fighting Ships 1972–1973*, p. 76.

27. These comparative statistics have been drawn from Roskill, *The War at Sea*, I and iii, part 2; and *Jane's Fighting Ships 1973–1974* (London, 1973).

28. P. Cohen, 'The Erosion of Surface Naval Power', *Survival*, xiii, no. 4 (April 1971), pp. 127–33.

29. There is now a fine summary by G. Jukes, 'The Indian Ocean in Soviet Naval Policy', *Adelphi Papers*, no. 87 (May 1972). See also the foreword to *Jane's Fighting Ships 1972–1973*.

30. See especially P. Darby's definitive study.

31. *Jane's Fighting Ships 1972–1973*, pp. 76–7.

32. ibid.

33. Schofield, *British Sea Power*, p. 237. See also Clarkson, 'The Naval Heresy', *passim*.

34. Thorne, *The Limits of Foreign Policy*, p. 395, footnote 4.

35. See above, pp. 312–18. For the British economy after 1945, see Murphy, *A History of the British Economy 1086–1970*, pp. 777 ff; Pollard, *The Development of the British Economy*, pp. 356 ff; Hobsbawm, *Industry and Empire*, pp. 249–72.

36. Hancock and Gowing, *British War Economy*, p. 546.

37. Kolko, *The Politics of War*, p. 313.

38. *The British Economy. Key Statistics 1900–1966* (London, n.d., ?1967), table N; and the various tables in D. H. Aldcroft and P. Fearns (eds), *Economic Growth in Twentieth-century Britain* (London, 1969); and S. Hays, *National Income and Expenditure in Britain and the OECD Countries* (London, 1971).

39. *The Times*, 5 December, 1973.

40. C. M. Cipolla (ed.), *The Economic Decline of Empires* (London, 1970), pp. 1, 9–13.

41. Mitchell and Deane, *Abstract of British Historical Statistics*, p. 398.

42. *National Income and Expenditure 1973* (Central Statistical Office, London, 1973), table 49. See also Snyder, *The Politics of British Defence Policy*, pp. 191–6.

43. Mahan, *The Influence of Sea Power upon History*, p. 67.

44. Figures from *Jane's Fighting Ships 1972–1973*. See also Darby, *British Defence Policy East of Suez*, pp. 249–50.

45. *The Military Balance 1973–1974*, p. 76.

46. The section on 'Economy (The British)' in the Index of Bartlett's *The Long Retreat*, gives an indication of this. See also C. Mayhew, *Britain's Role Tomorrow* (London, 1967), chap. 4, 'Peace-keeping and the Pound'.

47. *Jane's Fighting Ships 1973–1974*, p. 76.

48. *The Military Balance 1973–1974*, p. 79.

49. ibid., p. 74; and *Jane's Fighting Ships 1972–1973*, p. 81.

50. H. Kahn, *The Emerging Japanese Superstate* (London, 1971), pp. 101–2. See also his predictions in H. Kahn and A. J. Wiener, *The Year 2000* (London and New York, 1967), especially pp. 29–31.

51. Among the more careful probings about the future of British foreign and defence policy are Pierre, *Nuclear Politics*, pp. 325–42; Martin, 'British Defence Policy'; N. Frankland, 'Britain's Changing Strategic Position' *International Affairs*, xxxiii, (October 1957); and M. Beloff, *The Future of British Foreign Policy* (London, 1969).

Epilogue

1. Cited in Mahan, *The Influence of Sea Power upon History*, p. 327.

2. ibid., pp. 29–82.

3. Cited in Richmond, *Statesmen and Sea Power*, p. 109.

Select Bibliography

(For reasons of space, this bibliography has been limited to works actually cited in the References and no attempt has been made here to compile an exhaustive list of printed sources dealing with British naval, strategic and economic history.)

Albion, R. G., *Forests and Sea Power. The Timber Problem of the Royal Navy 1652–1862* (Hamden, Conn., 1965 edn).

Aldcroft, D. H. (ed.), *The Development of British Industry and Foreign Competition 1875–1914* (London, 1968).

Aldcroft, D. H., *The Inter-War Economy: Britain, 1919–1939* (London, 1970).

Aldcroft, D. H., and Fearns, P. (eds.), *Economic Growth in Twentieth-century Britain* (London, 1969).

Alford, B. W. E., *Depression and Recovery? British Economic Growth 1918–1939* (London, 1972).

Anderson, M. S., 'European Diplomatic Relations, 1763–1790', *The New Cambridge Modern History*, viii, *The American and French Revolutions 1763–93*, edited by A. Goodwin (Cambridge, 1965).

Andrew, C., *Théophile Delcassé and the Making of the Entente Cordiale* (London, 1968).

Andrews, K. R., *Drake's Voyages* (London, 1970 edn).

Andrews, K. R., *Elizabethan Privateering. English Privateering during the Spanish War 1585–1603* (Cambridge, 1964).

Anstey, R. T., 'Capitalism and Slavery: A Critique', *Economic History Review*, 2nd series, xxi, no. 2 (August 1968).

Anthony, V., *Britain's Overseas Trade* (London, 1972).

Ashton, R., 'Revenue Farming under the Early Stuarts', *Economic History Review*, 2nd series, viii, no. 3 (April 1956).

Ashton, R., 'The Parliamentary Agitation for Free Trade in the Opening Year of the Reign of James I', *Past and Present*, no. 38 (December 1967).

Ashton, T. S., *Economic Fluctuations in England 1700–1800* (Oxford, 1959).

Ashworth, W., *An Economic History of England, 1870–1939* (London, 1972 edn).

Assmann, K., *Deutsche Seestrategie im zwei Weltkriege* (Heidelberg, 1957).

Bach, J., 'The Royal Navy in the Pacific Islands', *Journal of Pacific History*, iii, (1968).

Baker, N., *Government and Contractors. The British Treasury and War Supplies 1775–1783* (London, 1971).

Balfour, M., *The Kaiser and His Times* (New York, 1972 edn).

Barnett, C., *Britain and Her Army 1509–1970: A Military, Political and Social Survey* (London, 1970).

Barnett, C., *The Collapse of British Power* (London and New York, 1972).
Barraclough, G., *An Introduction to Contemporary History* (Harmondsworth, Middlesex, 1967).
Bartlett, C. J., *Great Britain and Sea Power 1815–1853* (Oxford, 1963).
Bartlett, C. J., 'The Mid-Victorian Reappraisal of Naval Policy', in K. Bourne and D. C. Watt (eds.), *Studies in International History* (London, 1967).
Bartlett, C. J. (ed.), *Britain Pre-eminent. Studies of British World Influence in the Nineteenth Century* (London, 1969).
Bartlett, C. J., *The Long Retreat. A Short History of British Defence Policy, 1945–1970* (London, 1972).
Baumgart, W., *Deutschland im Zeitalter des Imperialismus (1890–1914)* (Frankfurt, 1972).
Bell, A. C., *A History of the Blockade of Germany and of the Countries Associated with Her . . .* (London, 1961).
Beloff, M., 'The Special Relationship: An Anglo-American Myth', in M. Gilbert (ed.), *A Century of Conflict, 1850–1950* (London, 1966).
Beloff, M., *The Future of British Foreign Policy* (London, 1969).
Beloff, M., *Imperial Sunset*, i, *Britain's Liberal Empire, 1897–1921* (London, 1969).
Bennett, G., *Naval Battles of the First World War* (London, 1968).
Berghahn, V. R., *Der Tirpitz-Plan* (Düsseldorf, 1972).
Blake, R., *The Conservative Party from Peel to Churchill* (London, 1970).
Bond, B. (ed.), *Victorian Military Campaigns* (London, 1967).
Bourne, K., *Britain and the Balance of Power in North America 1815–1908* (London, 1967).
Boxer, C. R., *The Dutch Seaborne Empire, 1600–1800* (London, 1965).
Bradford, E., *The Mighty Hood* (London, 1959).
Braisted, W. R., *The United States Navy in the Pacific, 1909–1922* (Austin, Texas, 1971).
Brassey's Naval Annual (London, 1898).
Bringles, W. F., 'The Challenge Posed by the Soviet Navy', *Journal of the Royal United Services Institute for Defence Studies*, 118, no. 2 (June 1973).
British Economy, The Key Statistics 1900–1966 (London, n.d., ?1967).
Brodie, B., *A Guide to Naval Strategy* (New York and Washington and London, 1965 edn).
Bromley, J. S., 'The French Privateering War, 1702–1713', in H. E. Bell and R. S. Ollard (eds.), *Historical Essays 1600–1750, presented to David Ogg* (London, 1963).
Brunn, G., *Europe and the French Imperium 1799–1814* (New York and London, 1938).
Brunn, G., 'The Balance of Power during the Wars, 1793–1814', in *The New Cambridge Modern History*, ix, *War and Peace in an Age of Upheaval 1793–1830*, edited by C. W. Crawley (Cambridge, 1965).
Brunschwig, H., 'Anglophobia and French African Policy', in P. Gifford and W. R. Louis (eds.), *France and Britain in Africa: Imperial Rivalry and Colonial Rule* (New Haven and London, 1971).
Buchanan, A. Russell, *The United States and World War II*, 2 vols. (New York, 1964).
Butler, J. R. M., *Grand Strategy*, ii (London, 1957).
Callender, G., *The Naval Side of British History* (London, 1924).
Cambridge History of the British Empire, The, i, edited by J. H. Rose, A. P. Newton and E. A. Benians (Cambridge, 1929).

Carrington, C. E., *The British Overseas*, part i (Cambridge, 1968 edn).

Carroll, Berenice A., *Design for Total War. Arms and Economics in the Third Reich* (The Hague, 1968).

Cd. 2791, 'A Statement of Admiralty Policy', 1905.

Cd. 4891, 'Statement on the Defence Estimates', 1972.

Chambers, J. D., *The Workshop of the World. British Economic History from 1820 to 1880* (Oxford, 1968 edn).

Churchill, W. S., *The Second World War*, 12 vols. (paperback edn, London, 1964).

Cipolla, C. M., *Guns and Sail in the Early Phase of European Expansion* (London, 1965).

Cipolla, C. M. (ed.), *The Economic Decline of Empires* (London, 1970).

Clapham, J. H., 'Loans and Subsidies in Time of War, 1793–1914', *The Economic Journal*, xxvii (1917).

Clarke, G. N., 'War Trade and Trade War, 1701–1713', *Economic History Review*, i, no. 2 (January 1928).

Clarke, G. N., 'The Character of the Nine Years War, 1688–97', *Cambridge Historical Journal*, xi, no. 2 (1954).

Clarke, G. N., *The Dutch Alliance and the War against French Trade 1688–1697* (New York, 1971 edn).

Clarke, I. F., *Voices Prophesying War 1793–1984* (London, 1970 edn).

Clarke, J. J., 'Merchant Marine and the Navy: A Note on the Mahan Hypothesis', *Royal United Services Institution Journal*, cxii, no. 646 (May 1967).

Clarkson, R. A., 'The Naval Heresy', *Royal United Services Institution Journal*, cx, no. 640 (November 1965).

Clowes, Sir Laird W., *The Royal Navy, A History*. 7 vols. (London, 1897–1903).

Cohen, P., 'The Erosion of Surface Naval Power', *Survival*, xiii, no. 4 (April 1971).

Collier, B., *The Defence of the United Kingdom* (London, 1957).

Consett, M. W. W. P., *The Triumph of Unarmed Forces (1914–1918)* (London, 1928).

Corbett, J. S., *England in the Seven Years War. A Study in Combined Strategy*, 2 vols. (London, 1918).

Corbett, J. S. and Newbolt H., *History of the Great War: Naval Operations*, 5 vols. (London, 1920–31).

Creswell, J., *Sea Warfare 1939–1945. A Short History* (London, 1950).

Creswell, J., *British Admirals of the Eighteenth Century. Tactics in Battle* (London, 1972).

Crouzet, F., *L'Économie Britannique et le Blocus Continental (1806–1813)*, 2 vols. (Paris, 1958).

Crouzet, F., 'Wars, Blockade and Economic Change in Europe, 1792–1815', *Journal of Economic History*, 24, no. 4 (1964).

Cunningham, A., *British Credit in the Last Napoleonic War* (Cambridge, 1910).

Curtis, E. E., *The Organization of the British Army in the American Revolution* (Menston, Yorkshire, 1972 reprint).

Dangerfield, G. H., *The Strange Death of Liberal England* (London, 1935).

Darby, P., *British Defence Policy East of Suez 1947–1968* (London, 1973).

Davies, K. G., *The Royal African Company* (London, 1957).

Davis, R., 'English Foreign Trade, 1660–1700', *Economic History Review*, 2nd series, vii, no. 2 (December 1954).

Davis, R., 'English Foreign Trade, 1700–1774', *Economic History Review*, 2nd series, xv, no. 2 (December 1962).

Davis, R., *The Rise of the English Shipping Industry in the Seventeenth and Eighteenth Centuries* (Newton Abbot, 1972 edn).

Davis, R., *The Rise of the Atlantic Economies* (London, 1973).

Davis, R., *English Overseas Trade 1500–1700* (London, 1973).

Dehio, L., *The Precarious Balance* (London, 1963).

Derry, T. K., *The Campaign in Norway* (London, 1952).

Dickson, P. G. M., *The Financial Revolution in England. A Study in the Development of Public Credit 1688–1756* (London, 1967).

Dignan, D., 'New Perspectives on British Far Eastern Policy 1913–1919', *University of Queensland Papers*, i, no. 5.

D'Ombrain, N. J., 'The Imperial General Staff and the Military Policy of a "Continental Strategy" during the 1911 International Crisis', *Military Affairs*, xxxiv, no. 3 (October 1970).

D'Ombrain, N. J., *War Machinery and High Politics. Defence Administration in Peacetime Britain 1902–1914* (Oxford, 1973).

Dülffer, J., *Weimar, Hitler und die Marine* (Düsseldorf, 1973).

Ehrman, J., *The Navy in the War of William III 1689–1697* (Cambridge, 1953).

Ehrman, J., *The Younger Pitt. The Years of Acclaim* (London, 1969).

Eldon, C. W., *England's Subsidy Policy towards the Continent during the Seven Years War* (Philadelphia, 1938).

Farnall, J. E., 'The Navigation Act of 1651, the First Dutch War, and the London Mercantile Community', *Economic History Review*, 2nd series, xvi, no. 3 (April 1964).

Farnie, D. A., 'The Commercial Empire of the Atlantic, 1607–1783', *Economic History Review*, 2nd series, xv, no. 2 (December 1962).

Faulkner, H. U., *American Economic History* (New York, 1960 edn).

Fayle, C. E., *History of the Great War: Seaborne Trade*, 3 vols. (London, 1920–24).

Fayle, C. E., 'Economic Pressure in the War of 1739–48', *Journal of the Royal United Services Institute*, 68 (1923).

Feiling, K., *The Life of Neville Chamberlain* (London, 1957).

Feis, H., *Churchill – Roosevelt – Stalin. The War they Waged and the Peace they Sought* (Princeton, 1957).

Fielden, K. 'The Rise and Fall of Free Trade', in C. J. Bartlett (ed.), *Britain Preeminent. Studies of British World Influence in the Nineteenth Century* (London, 1969).

Fieldhouse, D. K., *The Colonial Empires* (London, 1966).

Fischer, F., *Germany's Aims in the First World War* (London, 1967).

Fisher, H. A. L., *A History of Europe*, 2 vols. (London, 1960 edn.).

Fox, G., *British Admirals and Chinese Pirates, 1832–1869* (London, 1940).

Frankland, N., 'Britain's Changing Strategic Position', *International Affairs*, xxxiii (October 1957).

Fremantle, Sir Sydney, *My Naval Career 1880–1928* (London, 1949).

Fry, M. G., 'The Imperial War Cabinet, the United States, and the Freedom of the Seas', *The Royal United Services Institution Journal*, cx, no. 640 (November 1965).

Gallagher, J. and Robinson, R., 'The Imperialism of Free Trade', *Economic History Review*, 2nd series, vi, no. 1 (August 1953).

Gardner, R. N., *Sterling – Dollar Diplomacy* (Oxford, 1956).

Gemzell, Carl-Axel, *Raeder, Hitler und Skandanavien. Der Kampf für einen maritimen Operationsplan* (Lund, 1965).

Geyl, P., *The Netherlands in the Seventeenth Century*, 2 vols. (London, 1961–4).

Gilbert, M. and Gott, R., *The Appeasers* (London, 1963).
Gipson, L. H., *The British Empire Before the American Revolution*, 14 vols. (New York, 1936–68).
Glover, M., *The Peninsular War 1807–1814* (London, 1974).
Gooch, J., *The Plans of War: The General Staff and British Military Strategy, c. 1900–1914* (London, 1974).
Gordon, D. C., 'The Admiralty and Dominion Navies, 1902–1914', *Journal of Modern History*, xxxiii, no. 4 (December 1961).
Gordon, D. C., *The Dominion Partnership in Imperial Defence 1870–1914* (Baltimore, 1965).
Gough, B., *The Royal Navy and the North-West Coast of America 1810–1914* (Vancouver, 1971).
Gowing, M., *Britain and Atomic Energy 1939–1945* (London, 1964).
Graham, G. S., 'Considerations on the War of American Independence', *Bulletin of the Institute of Historical Research*, xxii (1949).
Graham, G. S., *Empire of the North Atlantic* (Toronto, 1950).
Graham, G. S., *The Politics of Naval Supremacy* (Cambridge, 1965).
Graham, G. S., *Britain in the Indian Ocean. A Study of Maritime Enterprise 1810–1850* (Oxford, 1967).
Graham, G. S., *Tides of Empire* (Montreal and London, 1972).
Graham, G. S. and Humphreys, R. A. (eds.), *The Navy and South America 1807–1823* (Navy Records Society; London, 1962).
Grenville, J. A. S., *Lord Salisbury and Foreign Policy* (London, 1964).
Gretton, P., *Winston Churchill and the Royal Navy* (New York, 1969).
Guichard, L. L., *The Naval Blockade, 1914–1918* (London, 1930).
Guinn, P., *British Strategy and Politics 1914 to 1918* (Oxford, 1965).
Haggie, P., 'The Royal Navy and War Planning in the Fisher Era', *Journal of Contemporary History*, 8, no. 3 (July 1973).
Hall, H. Duncan, *North American Supply* (London, 1955).
Halpern, P. G., *The Mediterranean Naval Situation 1908–1914* (Cambridge, Mass., 1971).
Hancock, W. K. and Gowing, M. M., *British War Economy* (London, 1949).
Hankey, Lord, *The Supreme Command 1914–1918*, 2 vols. (London, 1961).
Hargreaves, E. L., *The National Debt* (London, 1966 reprint).
Harlow, V. T., *The Founding of the Second British Empire, 1763–1793*, 2 vols. (London, 1952–64).
Harper, L. A., *The English Navigation Laws* (New York, 1964 edn).
Hays, S., *National Income and Expenditure in Britain and the OECD Countries* (London, 1971).
Heckscher, E. F., *The Continental System. An Economic Interpretation* (Oxford, 1922).
Hellenier, K. F., *The Imperial Loans. A Study in Financial and Diplomatic History* (Oxford, 1965).
Herrick, R. W., *Soviet Naval Strategy* (Annapolis, 1968).
Higgonnet, P. Louis-René, 'The Origins of the Seven Years War', *Journal of Modern History*, 40, no. 1 (March 1968).
Higham, R., *Armed Forces in Peacetime. Britain 1918–1940, a case study* (London, 1962).
Higham, R., *The Military Intellectuals in Britain 1918–1939* (New Brunswick, New Jersey, 1966).

Higham, R., *Air Power: A Concise History* (London, 1972).

Hill, B. W., 'Oxford, Bolingbroke and the Peace of Utrecht', *Historical Journal*, xvi, no. 2 (1973).

Hill, C., *The Century of Revolution 1603–1714* (London, 1961).

Hill, C., *Reformation to Industrial Revolution* (Harmondsworth, Middlesex, 1969).

Hill, C., *God's Englishman. Oliver Cromwell and the English Revolution* (London, 1970).

Hinton, R. K. W., *The Eastland Trade and the Common Weal in the Seventeenth Century* (Cambridge, 1959).

Hobsbawm, E. J., *Industry and Empire* (Harmondsworth, Middlesex, 1969).

Hope-Jones, A., *Income Tax in the Napoleonic Wars* (Cambridge, 1910).

Horn, D. B., 'The Diplomatic Revolution', *The New Cambridge Modern History*, vii, *The Old Régime 1713–63*, edited by J. O. Lindsay (Cambridge, 1957).

Horn, D. B., *Great Britain and Europe in the Eighteenth Century* (Oxford, 1967).

Horsman, R., *The Causes of the War of 1812* (Philadelphia, 1961).

Horsman, R., *The War of 1812* (London, 1969).

Howard, M., *The Continental Commitment* (London, 1972).

Howard, M., *Grand Strategy*, iv (London, 1972).

Howarth, D., *Sovereign of the Seas. The Story of British Sea Power* (London, 1974).

Hyam, R., 'British Imperial Expansion in the Late Eighteenth Century', *Historical Journal*, x, no. 1 (1967).

Imlah, A. H., *Economic Elements in the 'Pax Britannica'* (Cambridge, Mass., 1958).

Innes, A. D., *The Maritime and Colonial Expansion of England under the Stuarts* (London, 1931).

Jane's Fighting Ships (Annual, various years).

John, A. H., 'War and the English Economy 1700–1763', *Economic History Review*, 2nd series, vii, no. 3 (April 1955).

John, A. H., 'Aspects of English Economic Growth in the First Half of the Eighteenth Century', *Economica*, xxviii (May 1961).

Jones, Gwynne (Lord Chalfont), A., 'Training and Doctrine in the British Army since 1945', in M. Howard (ed.), *The Theory and Practice of War* (London, 1965).

Jones, J. R., *Britain and Europe in the Seventeenth Century* (London, 1966).

Jukes, G., 'The Indian Ocean in Soviet Naval Policy', *Adelphi Papers*, no. 87 (May 1972).

Kahn, A. E., *Great Britain in the World Economy* (New York, 1946).

Kahn, H., *The Emerging Japanese Superstate* (London, 1971).

Kahn, H. and Wiener, A. J., *The Year 2000* (London and New York, 1967).

Kennedy, P. M., 'Tirpitz, England and the Second Navy Law of 1900: A Strategical Critique', *Militärgeschichtliche Mitteilungen*, 1970, no. 2.

Kennedy, P. M., 'Imperial Cable Communications and Strategy, 1870–1914', *English Historical Review*, lxxxvi, no. CCCXLI (October, 1971).

Kennedy, P. M., *Pacific Onslaught* (New York and London, 1972).

Kennedy, P. M., 'Maritime Strategieprobleme der deutsch-englischen Flottenrivalität', in H. Schottelius and W. Deist (eds), *Marine und Marinepolitik im kaiserlichen Deutschland 1871–1914* (Düsseldorf, 1972).

Kennedy, P. M., 'The Decline of Nationalistic History in the West', *Journal of Contemporary History*, 8, no. 1 (January 1973).

Kennedy, P. M., 'The Development of German Naval Operations Plans against England, 1896–1914', *English Historical Review*, lxxxix, no. CCCL (January 1974).

Kennedy, P. M., 'The Battle of the Dogger Bank', ii, no. 7; 'The Channel War', iv, no. 14; 'The Dover Patrol', vi, no. 3; 'The Scandinavian Convoy', vi, no. 12: all in *History of the First World War* (London, 1969 f.).

King, F. P., *The New Internationalism. Allied Policy and the European Peace 1939–1945* (Newton Abbot, 1973).

Kirby, S. Woodburn, *The War against Japan*, 5 vols. (London, 1957–69).

Klein, H. Burton, *Germany's Economic Preparations for War* (Cambridge, Mass., 1959).

Klein, I., 'Whitehall, Washington, and the Anglo-Japanese Alliance, 1919–1921', *Pacific Historical Review*, 41 (1972).

Knight, R. J. B., 'The Administration of the Royal Dockyards in England, 1770–1790', *Bulletin of the Institute of Historical Research*, xlv, no. 111 (May 1972).

Knight, R. J. B., 'The Home Dockyards and the American War of Independence', paper read to the 14th Conference of the International Commission for Maritime History, Greenwich, 12 July 1974.

Knox, D. W., *The Eclipse of American Naval Power* (New York, 1922).

Kolko, G., *The Politics of War. Allied Diplomacy and the World Crisis of 1943–1945* (London, 1969).

Landes, D. S., *The Unbound Prometheus: Technological Change and Industrial Development in Western Europe from 1750 to the Present* (Cambridge, 1969).

Langhorne, R., 'The Naval Question in Anglo-German Relations, 1912–1914', *Historical Journal*, xiv, no. 2 (1971).

Lee, H. I., 'Mediterranean Strategy and Anglo-French Relations 1908–1912', *Mariner's Mirror*, 57 (1971).

Lepsius, J., *et al.* (eds), *Die Grosse Politik der europäischen Kabinette*, 40 vols. (Berlin, 1922–7).

Lewis, M., *The History of the British Navy* (Harmondsworth, Middlesex, 1957).

Lewis, M., 'Navies', *The New Cambridge Modern History*, viii, *The American and French Revolutions 1763–93*, edited by A. Goodwin (Cambridge, 1965).

Lewis, W. Arthur, *Economic Survey 1919–1939* (London, 1949).

Liddell Hart, B. H., *The British Way in Warfare* (London, 1932).

Liddell Hart, B. H., *History of the Second World War* (London, 1970).

Lindsay, J. O., 'International Relations', *The New Cambridge Modern History*, vii, *The Old Régime 1713–63*, edited by J. O. Lindsay (Cambridge, 1957).

Livezey, W. E., *Mahan on Sea Power* (Norman, Oklahoma, 1947).

Lloyd, C., *The Nation and the Navy. A History of Naval Life and Policy* (London, 1961).

Lloyd, C., *The Navy and the Slave Trade* (London, 1969 reprint).

Lodge, Sir Richard, *Great Britain and Prussia in the Eighteenth Century* (New York, 1972 reprint).

Louis, W. R., *British Strategy in the Far East 1919–1939* (Oxford, 1971).

Lowe, P., 'The British Empire and the Anglo-Japanese Alliance 1911–1915', *History*, liv (1969).

Lythe, S. G. E., 'Britain, the Financial Capital of the World', in C. J. Bartlett (ed.), *Britain Pre-eminent. Studies of British World Influence in the Nineteenth Century* (London, 1969).

Mackay, R. F., 'The Admiralty, the German Navy, and the Redistribution of the British Fleet, 1904–1905', *Mariner's Mirror*, 56 (1970).

Mackay, R. F., *Fisher of Kilverstone* (Oxford, 1973).

Mackesy, P., *The War in the Mediterranean 1803–10* (London, 1957).

Macksey, P., *The War for America 1775–1783* (London 1970).

Mackinder, H. J., 'The Geographical Pivot of History', *Geographical Journal*, xxiii, no. 4 (April 1904).

Mackinder, H. J., *Britain and the British Seas* (Oxford, 1925 edn).

Mackinder, H. J., *Democratic Ideals and Reality* (New York, 1962 edn).

Maclachlan, A. D., 'The Road to Peace 1710–1713', in G. Holmes (ed.), *Britain after the Glorious Revolution* (London, 1969).

Mahan, A. T., *The Influence of Sea Power upon the French Revolution and Empire*, 2 vols. (London, 1892).

Mahan, A. T., *The Life of Nelson, the Embodiment of the Sea Power of Great Britain*, 2 vols. (London, 1897).

Mahan, A. T., *Retrospect and Prospect: Studies in International Relations Naval and Political* (London, 1902).

Mahan, A. T., *Sea Power in its Relation to the War of 1812*, 2 vols. (London, 1905).

Mahan, A. T., *The Influence of Sea Power upon History, 1660–1783* (London, 1965 edn).

Mansergh, N., *The Commonwealth Experience* (London, 1969).

Mantoux, P., *The Industrial Revolution in the Eighteenth Century* (London, 1964 edn).

Marcus, C. J., *Quiberon Bay* (London, 1960).

Marcus, C. J., *A Naval History of England*, 2 vols. to date (London, 1961–71).

Marder, A. J. (ed.), *Fear God and Dread Nought: The Correspondence of Admiral of the Fleet Lord Fisher of Kilverstone*, 3 vols. (London, 1952–9).

Marder, A. J., *From the Dreadnought to Scapa Flow*, 5 vols. (London, 1961–70).

Marder, A. J., *The Anatomy of Sea Power: A History of British Naval Policy in the Pre-Dreadnought Era 1880–1905* (Hamden, Conn., 1964 edn).

Marder, A. J., 'The Royal Navy and the Ethiopian Crisis of 1935–36', *American Historical Review*, lxxv, no. 5 (June 1970).

Marder, A. J., *Winston is Back: Churchill at the Admiralty 1939–1940*, *English Historical Review*, Supplement 5 (London, 1972).

Martin, B., 'Aussenhandel und Aussenpolitik Englands unter Cromwell', *Historische Zeitschrift*, 218, Heft 3 (June 1974).

Martin, L. W., *The Sea in Modern Strategy* (London, 1967).

Martin, L. W., 'British Defence Policy: The Long Recessional', *Adelphi Papers*, no. 61 (November 1969).

Marwick, A., *Britain in the Century of Total War: War, Peace and Social Change 1900–1967* (Harmondsworth, Middlesex, 1970).

Marx, K. and Engels, F., 'Manifesto of the Communist Party', *The Essential Left* (London, 1960 edn).

Mathias, P., *The First Industrial Nation. An Economic History of Britain 1700–1914* (London, 1969).

Matloff, M., *Strategic Planning for Coalition Warfare 1943–1944* (Washington, D.C., 1959).

Mattingly, G., *The Defeat of the Spanish Armada* (Harmondsworth, Middlesex, 1959 edn).

Mayhew, C., *Britain's Role Tomorrow* (London, 1967).

McDonald, J. K., 'Lloyd George and the Search for a Postwar Naval Policy, 1919', in A. J. P. Taylor (ed.), *Lloyd George: Twelve Essays* (London, 1971).

Medlicott, W. N., *The Economic Blockade*, 2 vols. (London, 1952–9).

Medlicott, W. N., *British Foreign Policy since Versailles 1919–1963* (London, 1968 edn).
The Military Balance 1973–1974 (International Institute for Strategic Studies, London, 1973).
Millman, R., *British Foreign Policy and the Coming of the Franco-Prussian War* (Oxford, 1965).
Milward, A. S., *The German Economy at War* (London, 1965).
Milward, A. S., *The Economic Effects of the World Wars on Britain* (London, 1970).
Mitchell, B. R. and Deane, P., *Abstract of British Historical Statistics* (Cambridge, 2nd edn, 1967).
Monger, G. W., *The End of Isolation: British Foreign Policy 1900–1907* (London, 1963).
Moon, H. R., *The Invasion of the United Kingdom: Public Controversy and Official Planning 1888–1918*, 2 vols. (Ph.D. thesis, London, 1968).
Mordal, J., *25 Centuries of Sea Warfare* (London, 1970 edn).
Morris, A. J. A., *Radicalism against War* (London, 1972).
Moulton, J. L., *Defence in a Changing World* (London, 1964).
Murphy, B., *A History of the British Economy 1086–1970* (London, 1973).
National Income and Expenditure 1973 (Central Statistical Office; London, 1973).
Naval and Military Record, The (London, various issues).
Needham, J., *Science and Civilization in China,* 5 vols. to date (Cambridge, 1954–71), iv, part 3, *Civil Engineering and Nautics.*
Nicholas, H. G., *Britain and the United States* (London, 1963).
Nish, I. H., *The Anglo-Japanese Alliance* (London, 1966).
Nish, I. H., *Alliance in Decline: A Study in Anglo-Japanese Relations 1908–23* (London, 1972).
Northedge, F. S., *British Foreign Policy. The Process of Readjustment 1945–1961* (London, 1962).
Northedge, F. S., *The Troubled Giant. Britain among the Great Powers 1916–1939* (London, 1966).
Oakeshott, W., *Founded upon the Seas* (Cambridge, 1942).
Oppenheim, M., *A History of the Administration of the Royal Navy . . . 1509–1660* (Hamden, Conn., 1961 edn).
Owen, D., 'Capture at Sea: Modern Conditions and the Ancient Prize Laws', paper given at the United Services Institute on 6 April 1905, printed for private use.
Owen, J. H., *War at Sea under Queen Anne 1702–1708* (Cambridge, 1938).
Padfield, P., *The Battleship Era* (London, 1972).
Padfield, P., *Guns at Sea* (London, 1973).
Panikkar, K. M., *Asia and Western Dominance. A Survey of the Vasco da Gama Epoch of Asian History 1498–1945* (London, 1959 edn).
Pares, R., 'American versus Continental Warfare, 1739–63', *English Historical Review*, li, no. CCIII (July 1936).
Pares, R., *War and Trade in the West Indies 1739–1763* (London, 1963 edn).
Parkinson, C. N., (ed.), *The Trade Winds. A Study of British Overseas Trade during the French Wars 1793–1815* (London, 1964).
Parkinson, C. N., *War in the Eastern Seas 1793–1815* (London, 1954).
Parmalee, M., *Blockade and Sea Power* (London, n.d., ?1925).
Parry, J. H., 'The Caribbean', *The New Cambridge Modern History*, vii, *The Old Régime 1713–63*, edited by J. O. Lindsay (Cambridge, 1957).

Parry, J. H., *The Age of Reconnaissance* (London, 1963).

Parry, J. H., *Trade and Dominion. The European Overseas Empires in the Eighteenth Century* (London, 1971).

Patterson, A. Temple, *The Other Armada. The Franco-Spanish Attempt to Invade Britain in 1779* (Manchester, 1960).

Pelling, H., *Britain and the Second World War* (London, 1970).

Penn, C. D., *The Navy under the Early Stuarts and its Influence on English History* (London, 1970 edn).

Perkins, B., *Prologue to War. England and the United States 1805–1812* (Berkeley/Los Angeles, 1961).

Perkins, B., *The Great Rapprochement. England and the United States 1895–1914* (London, 1969).

Pierre, A. J., *Nuclear Politics. The British Experience with an Independent Strategic Force 1939–1970* (London, 1972).

Pirenne, J., *The Tides of History*, ii, *From the Expansion of Islam to the Treaties of Westphalia* (London, 1963 edn).

Platt, D. C. M., 'Economic Factors in British Policy during the "New Imperialism" ', *Past and Present*, no. 39 (1968).

Plumb, J. H., *The Growth of Political Stability in England 1675–1725* (London, 1967).

Pollard, S., *The Development of the British Economy 1914–1967* (London, 1969 edn).

Postan, M. M., *British War Production* (London, 1952).

Potter, E. B. and Nimitz, C. W. (eds.), *Sea Power. A Naval History* (New Jersey, 1960).

Potter, G. R. (ed.), *The New Cambridge Modern History*, i, *The Renaissance* (Cambridge, 1961).

Powell, J. R., *The Navy in the English Civil War* (London, 1962).

Powley, E. B., *The Naval Side of King William's War* (London, 1972).

Preston, A. and Major, J., *Send a Gunboat! A Study of the Gunboat and its Role in British Policy 1854–1904* (London, 1967).

Purcell, V., 'Asia', *The New Cambridge Modern History*, vii, *The Old Régime 1713–63*, edited by J. O. Lindsay (Cambridge, 1957).

Quinn, D. B., 'James I and the Beginnings of Empire in America', *The Journal of Imperial and Commonwealth History*, ii, no. 2 (January 1974).

Rabb, T. K., *Enterprise and Empire. Merchant and Gentry Investment in the Expansion of England, 1575–1630* (Cambridge, Mass., 1967).

Ramsay, J. F., *Anglo-French Relations 1763–1770* (Berkeley, 1939).

Reynolds, C. G., 'Sea Power in the Twentieth Century', *Royal United Services Institution Journal*, cxi, no. 642 (May 1966).

Richmond, H. W., *The Navy in the War of 1739–1748* (Cambridge, 1920).

Richmond, H. W., *National Policy and Naval Strength and Other Essays* (London, 1928).

Richmond, H. W., *Statesmen and Sea Power* (Oxford, 1946).

Richmond, H. W., *The Navy as an Instrument of Policy 1558–1727* (Cambridge, 1953).

Ritter, G., *The Sword and the Sceptre*, ii, *The European Powers and the Wilhelminian Empire 1890–1914* (London, 1972).

Robinson, R. E. and Gallagher, J., with Denny, A., *Africa and the Victorians. The Official Mind of Imperialism* (London, 1961).

Robson, E., 'The Seven Years War', *The New Cambridge Modern History*, vii, *The Old Régime 1713–63*, edited by J. O. Lindsay (Cambridge, 1957).

Rodger, A. B., *The War of the Second Coalition 1798 to 1801. A Strategic Commentary* (Oxford, 1964).

Roosevelt, T., *The Naval War of 1812* (New York, 1968 reprint).

Ropp, T., *War in the Modern World* (London, 1962 edn).

Rosinski, H., 'The Role of Sea Power in Global Warfare of the Future', *Brassey's Naval Annual* (1947).

Roskill, S. W., *The War at Sea*, 3 vols. (London, 1954–61).

Roskill, S. W., *The Navy at War 1939–1945* (London, 1960).

Roskill, S. W., *The Strategy of Sea Power* (London, 1962).

Roskill, S. W., *Naval Policy between the Wars*, i, *The Period of Anglo-American Antagonism 1919–1929* (London, 1968).

Rowse, A. L., *The England of Elizabeth* (London, 1951).

Rowse, A. L., *The Expansion of Elizabethan England* (London, 1955).

Ryan, A. N., 'The Defence of British Trade with the Baltic, 1808–1813', *English Historical Review*, lxxiv, no. CCXCII (July 1959).

Ryan, A. N., 'William III and the Brest Fleet in the Nine Years War', in R. Hatton and J. S. Bromley (eds.), *William III and Louis XIV. Essays 1680–1720 by and for Mark A. Thomson* (Liverpool, 1968).

Saul, S. B., *Studies in British Overseas Trade 1870–1914* (Liverpool, 1960).

Saville, J. (ed.), *Studies in the British Economy, 1870–1914*, 17, no. 1 (1965), *The Yorkshire Bulletin of Economic and Social Research.*

Savory, R., *His Britannic Majesty's Army in Germany during the Seven Years War* (Oxford, 1966).

Sayers, R. S., *Financial Policy 1939–1945* (London, 1956).

Sayers, R. S., *A History of Economic Change in England 1880–1939* (London, 1967).

Schlenke, M., *England und das Friderizianische Preussen 1740–1763* (Freiburg and Munich, 1963).

Schofield, B., *British Sea Power* (London, 1967).

Schulin, E., *Handelsstaat England. Das politische Interesse der Nation am Aussenhandel vom 16. bis ins frühe 18. Jahrhundert* (Wiesbaden, 1969).

Schumpeter, E. B., 'English Prices and Public Finance, 1660–1822', *Revue of Economic Statistics*, xx (1938).

Schumpeter, E. B., *English Overseas Trade Statistics 1697–1808* (Oxford, 1960).

Schurman, D. M., *The Education of a Navy: The Development of British Naval Strategic Thought 1867–1914* (London, 1965).

Schurman, D. M., 'Historians and Britain's Imperial Strategic Stance in 1914', in J. E. Flint and G. Williams (eds.), *Perspectives of Empire* (London, 1973).

Seeley, J. R., *The Expansion of England* (London, 1884).

Semmel, B., 'The "Philosophical Radicals" and Colonization', *Journal of Economic History*, 21 (1961).

Semmel, B., *The Rise of Free Trade Imperialism* (Oxford, 1970).

Sherrard, O. A., *Lord Chatham. Pitt and the Seven Years War* (London, 1955).

Sherwig, J. M., *Guineas and Gunpowder. British Foreign Aid in the Wars with France, 1793–1815* (Cambridge, Mass., 1969).

Silberling, N. J., 'Financial and Monetary Policy of Great Britain during the Napoleonic Wars', *Quarterly Journal of Economics*, xxxviii (1923–4).

Siney, M. C., *The Allied Blockade of Germany 1914–1916* (Ann Arbor, Michigan, 1957).

Smith, C. T., *An Historical Geography of Western Europe before 1800* (London, 1967).
Smith, G., *American Diplomacy during the Second World War 1941–1945* (New York, 1965).
Snyder, W. P., *The Politics of British Defense Policy, 1945–1962* (Columbus, Ohio, 1964).
Spindler, A., *Der Krieg zur See, 1914–1918: Der Handelskrieg mit U-Booten*, 5 vols. (Berlin, 1932–66).
Sprout, M. T., 'Mahan: Evangelist of Sea Power', in E. M. Earle (ed.), *Makers of Modern Strategy* (Princeton, 1952).
Steinberg, J., *Yesterday's Deterrent: Tirpitz and the Birth of the German Battle Fleet* (London, 1965).
Stone, L., 'Elizabethan Foreign Trade', *Economic History Review*, 2nd series, ii, no. 2 (1949–50).
Summerton, N., *British Military Preparations for a War against Germany*, 2 vols. (Ph.D. thesis, London, 1969).
Swartz, M., *The Union of Democratic Control in British Politics during the First World War* (Oxford, 1971).
Syrett, D., *Shipping and the American War 1775–83* (London, 1970).
Tate, M., *The United States and Armaments* (New York, 1948).
Taylor, A. J. P., *The Struggle for Mastery in Europe, 1848–1918* (Oxford, 1954).
Taylor, A. J. P., *The Trouble Makers* (London, 1957).
Taylor, A. J. P., *English History 1914–1945* (Oxford, 1965).
Taylor, A. J. P., *The Origins of the Second World War* (Harmondsworth, Middlesex, 1969 edn).
Terraine, J., 'History and the "Indirect Approach"', *Journal of the Royal United Services Institute for Defence Studies*, cxvi, no. 662 (June 1971).
Thomson, D., *Europe since Napoleon* (Harmondsworth, Middlesex, 1966).
Thomson, M. A., 'The War of the Austrian Succession', *The New Cambridge Modern History*, vii, *The Old Régime 1713–63*, edited by J. O. Lindsay (Cambridge, 1957).
Thorne, C., *The Limits of Foreign Policy* (London, 1972).
Times, The (various issues).
Toynbee, A., and Toynbee, V. M. (eds.), *Surveyof International Affairs 1939–1946: The Eve of War, 1939* (London, 1958).
Tunstall, B., *The Realities of Naval History* (London, 1936).
Tunstall, B., *William Pitt, Earl of Chatham* (London, 1938).
Turner, L. C. F., 'The Cape of Good Hope and the Anglo-French Conflict, 1797–1806', *Historical Studies. Australia and New Zealand*, 9, no. 36 (May 1961).
Wagenführ, R., *Die deutsche Industrie im Kriege 1939–1945* (Berlin, 2nd edn, 1963).
Webster, C. K., *The Foreign Policy of Castlereagh*, 2 vols. (London, 1963 edn).
Webster, C. K. and Frankland, N., *The Strategic Air Offensive against Germany 1939–1945*, 4 vols. (London, 1961).
Wellenreuther, H., 'Land, Gesellschaft und Wirtschaft in England während des siebenjährigen Krieges', *Historische Zeitschrift*, 218, Heft 3 (June 1974).
Weller, J., *Wellington in the Peninsula* (London, 1962).
Wells, S. F., Jnr., 'British Strategic Withdrawal from the Western Hemisphere, 1904–1906', *Canadian Historical Review*, xlix (1968).
Wernham, R. B., 'Elizabethan War Aims and Strategy', in S. T. Bindoff, J. Hurstfield and C. H. Williams (eds.), *Elizabethan Government and Society* (London, 1961).

Wernham, R. B., *Before the Armada. The Growth of English Foreign Policy 1485–1558* (Cambridge, 1964).

Whetton, L. L., 'The Mediterranean Threat', *Survival*, xii, no. 8 (August 1970).

Williams, B., *Life of William Pitt*, 2 vols. (London, 1915).

Williams, E., *Capitalism and Slavery* (Chapel Hill, 1944).

Williams, G., *The Expansion of Europe in the Eighteenth Century* (London, 1966).

Williams, J. Blow, *British Commercial Policy and Trade Expansion 1750–1850* (Oxford, 1972).

Williamson, J. A., *Maritime Expansion 1485–1558* (Oxford, 1913).

Williamson, J. A., *The Age of Drake* (London, 1938).

Williamson, J. A., *The Ocean in English History* (Oxford, 1941).

Williamson, J. A., *A Short History of British Expansion*, 2 vols. (London, 1945 edn).

Williamson, S. R., *The Politics of Grand Strategy: Britain and France prepare for War, 1904–1914* (Cambridge, Mass., 1969).

Wilson, C., 'The Economic Decline of the Netherlands', *Economic History Review*, ix, no. 2 (May 1939).

Wilson, C., *Profit and Power. A Study of England and the Dutch Wars* (London, 1957).

Wilson, C., *England's Apprenticeship 1603–1763* (London, 1965).

Wilson, C., *Queen Elizabeth and the Revolt of the Netherlands* (London, 1970).

Wolf, J. B., *The Emergence of the Great Powers 1685–1714* (New York, 1950).

Wolf, J. B., *Toward a European Balance of Power 1620–1715* (Chicago, 1970).

Wright, L. B., *Religion and Empire. The Alliance between Piety and Commerce in English Expansion 1558–1625* (New York, 1965 edn).

Young, L. K., *British Policy in China 1895–1902* (Oxford, 1970).

Youngson, A. J., *Britain's Economic Growth 1920–1966* (London, 1963).

Index